INSIDE DREA

BY
Anne Marie Yerks
John Pickett
Blaine Tait
Matthew David
Laura Gutman

New Riders

201 West 103rd Street, Indianapolis, Indiana 46290

Inside Dreamweaver 4

International Standard Book Number: 0-7357-1084-8

Library of Congress Catalog Card Number: 00-110882

Printed in the United States of America

First Printing: May 2001

05 04 03 02 01   7 6 5 4 3 2 1

Interpretation of the printing code: The rightmost double-digit number is the year of the book's printing; the rightmost single-digit number is the number of the book's printing. For example, the printing code 01-1 shows that the first printing of the book occurred in 2001.

Trademarks

Warning and Disclaimer

Publisher
David Dwyer

Associate Publisher
Al Valvano

Executive Editors
Stephanie Wall
Steve Weiss

Product Marketing Manager
Kathy Malmloff

Managing Editor
Sarah Kearns

Acquisitions Editor
Linda Anne Bump

Development Editor
John Rahm

Project Editor
Ginny Munroe

Copy Editors
Keith Cline
Krista Hansing

Technical Editor
Eric Lerner

Cover Designer
Greg Klamt

Compositor
Gina Rexrode

Proofreader
Jessica Ford McCarty

Indexer
Lisa Stumpf

Software Development Specialist
Jay Payne

Contents at a Glance

Table of Contents

Part IV Site Management

About the Authors

Anne-Marie Yerks is an author, instructor, fine artist, and designer who specializes in graphics and interface design with Macromedia software. She has taught HTML and Web design at George Mason University and George Washington University. Currently, she develops Web sites and kiosks for the University of Michigan. She has contributed articles to numerous publications about the Web, and has co-authored two books about the Internet. She is in the process of developing a series of Web animations that will go online in late 2001.

John Pickett is a 20-year-old student with plans on majoring in Computer Science at the University of Utah. He is also co-owner of a small Web firm, Blurred Vision Studios L.L.C. (http://www.bvstudios.com), located in Salt Lake City, Utah. He has been using HTML since he was 15 years old, while only expanding his view to business site creation in the past two years. John began using Dreamweaver during version 2.

Blaine Tait is an instructor at Durham College in Ontario, Canada, teaching a variety of Web-based courses such as HTML, JavaScript, Flash Web Animation, Interface Design for the Web, and of course, Dreamweaver. Blaine also operates his Web design and multimedia company, Omnidirectional Studios, just outside of Toronto. They offer computer-based solutions for business, including print and Web design, and rich media creation (Shockwave and Flash animation, 3D content and animation, digital audio, and e-commerce setup and implementation).

Blaine uses Macromedia Dreamweaver in his day-to-day work with Omni. He also uses a host of other Macromedia software in combination with Dreamweaver, such as Flash, Fireworks, and Freehand, as an end-to-end Web-content creation and maintenance system.

Matthew David has been working with multimedia and Web Technologies for over 6 years. He has contributed to books, such as the *Dreamweaver Bible, Flash 5 Magic,* and *Flash: Visual Insight,* and he regularly contributes to Element K Journals' *Multimedia Development and Design* magazine. He has written over a dozen online courses and is the lead instructor for Allen Interactions. In addition to writing, Matthew is an Intranet consultant.

Laura Gutman has worked as a graphic designer for 13 years and a multimedia developer for 10 years. Before that, she was a violinist, technical writer, law student, and professional academic. She earned her Ph.D. in English from the University of St. Andrews (Scotland). Currently, Laura lives with her dog, parakeets, and hundreds of computer toys in Albuquerque, New Mexico. She keeps busy doing freelance development, design and consulting work on multimedia, and Web projects. She also teaches a range of courses in Web design, multimedia design, and programming at the University of New Mexico and at Caliente Media Center (New Mexico's only authorized Macromedia training facility). You can visit her online at http://www.rocketlaura.com.

About the Technical Editor

Eric Lerner is head of Dreamweaver Technical Support at Macromedia. He has been at Macromedia for 10 months, and meets regularly with the development team for Dreamweaver to help make the product more usable. In addition to this book, Eric also reviewed the Dreamweaver 4 documentation, and several other Dreamweaver resources. When he isn't showing co-workers how to use Dreamweaver or making them laugh, Eric enjoys reading, traveling, and snowboarding poorly.

Dedication

From Anne-Marie Yerks:

This book is dedicated to Liana, Alex, and all Web design students whose imaginations make up the world we click through each day.

From John Pickett:

For the patience and understanding of my love, Maryanne. Thanks for sticking with me through the good and the "not so good."

Acknowledgments

From Anne-Marie: Many people have supported my work on this book. I would especially like to thank my mother, Ann Bailey Glasgow, and my grandmother, Lottie Bailey, for their encouragement. And thanks goes especially to my father, Eldred C. Yerks, who taught me DOS on Mr. Sanyo so many years ago. Thanks also to my cousin Christopher David Bailey for use of his office at Good As Gold Investments, and to my cousins Karen and Amanda, and stepfather Rick Glasgow. I wouldn't be writing this if it weren't for the inspiration of coworkers and friends though the years, such as the George Mason IDO folks (Jacquee, Chris, Ronnie, Randy, Saba) who got me started in this amazing field of work, and the DC Web Women mailing list (may it go forever strong). Thanks goes as well to my friends Heather, Kenneth, Wendi, Amy, Laura, Christy, Barry, Paula, Michelle, Justine, Stacy, Dawn, Emre, Hajer, Yousef, and the rest of the empire. Thanks to Britt Funderburk, Eddie James, Marc Klein, and Eric Harshbarger for your expert advice and well thought-out answers to my interview questions. And, of course, I would like to thank New Riders Publishing, specifically development editor John Rahm, and the co-authors of this book. I think we made a great team.

From John: This book has been such an immense learning opportunity for me. I would like to thank everyone at New Riders. Stephanie Wall, who saw I have something special to offer. Linda Bump and John Rahm for their many hours during the long haul. Thank you for your patience and help during this project's creation. I also want to thank Anne-Marie and Blaine; it was a wonderful experience working with you two. Special thanks go out to Laura Gutman, my hero for writing the object and behavior creation chapter on my behalf. I also want to publicly thank Al Sparber, who I'm sure is glad this book is finally done so I'll stop pestering him. I would like to thank Macromedia for indirectly giving me this opportunity, as well as creating such an excellent and diverse product. Keep up the good work!

I would like to thank my parents, Jeff and Cherie, my financial mainstay during this project, and my little (not really, but younger at least) brother Bart; you keep me entertained constantly. Thanks go out to all my relatives, especially my grandparents; including my late grandfather Doug, who taught me to dream. I would like to thank Mike Charo, my long-time friend and business partner. I also would like to thank Reed Sherman for introducing me to the vast world of Dreamweaver and giving me my first opportunity to shine. Blake Atkin, Robert Angus, Mike Strange, and Paul Strange all deserve big thanks for their friendship, support, and constant advise. Joe, Shane, Zack, Lisa, Aliza; thanks for your friendship and support. For anyone else who feels they deserve a pat on the back, well—*pat, pat*—there ya go.

Lastly, I would like to thank my eternal love, Maryanne, for the constant support and love you give me. My only hopes are that the sacrifices of today will reward us in the years to come. And am I excited for them to come! I know you think I want you to read the entire book, although if you got this far I'm satisfied. Love you!

A Message from New Riders

As the reader of this book, you are our most important critic and commentator. We value your opinion and want to know what we're doing right, what we could do better, in what areas you would like to see us publish, and any other words of wisdom you're willing to pass our way.

As Executive Editor at New Riders, I welcome your comments. You can fax, email, or write me directly to let me know what you did or didn't like about this book—as well as what we can do to make our books better. When you write, please be sure to include this book's title, ISBN, and author, as well as your name and phone or fax number. I will carefully review your comments and share them with the authors and editors who worked on the book.

Please note that I cannot help you with technical problems related to the topic of this book, and that due to the high volume of email I receive, I might not be able to reply to every message. Thanks.

    Email: stephanie.wall@newriders.com

    Mail: Stephanie Wall
             Executive Editor
             New Riders Publishing
             201 West 103rd Street
             Indianapolis, IN 46290 USA

Visit Our Web Site: www.newriders.com

On our Web site, you'll find information about our other books, the authors we partner with, book updates and file downloads, promotions, discussion boards for online interaction with other users and with technology experts, and a calendar of trade shows and other professional events with which we'll be involved. We hope to see you around.

Email Us from Our Web Site

Go to www.newriders.com and click the Contact link if you

- Have comments or questions about this book.
- Want to report errors that you have found in this book.
- Have a book proposal or are interested in writing for New Riders.
- Would like us to send you one of our author kits.

- Are an expert in a computer topic or technology and are interested in being a reviewer or technical editor.

- Want to find a distributor for our titles in your area.

- Are an educator/instructor who wants to preview New Riders books for class-room use. In the body/comments area, include your name, school, department, address, phone number, office days/hours, text currently in use, and enrollment in your department, along with your request for either desk/examination copies or additional information.

Call Us or Fax Us

You can reach us toll-free at (800) 571-5840 + 9 + 3567 (ask for New Riders). If outside the U.S., please call 1-317-581-3500 and ask for New Riders. If you prefer, you can fax us at 1-317-581-4663, Attention: New Riders.

Technical Support for This Book Although we encourage entry-level users to get as much as they can out of our books, keep in mind that our books are written assuming a non-beginner level of user knowledge of the technology. This assumption is reflected in the brevity and shorthand nature of some of the tutorials.

New Riders will continually work to create clearly written, thoroughly tested and reviewed technology books of the highest educational caliber and creative design. We value our customers more than anything—that's why we're in this business—but we cannot guarantee to each of the thousands of you who buy and use our books that we will be able to work individually with you through tutorials or content with which you may have questions. We urge readers who need help in working through exercises or other material in our books—and who need this assistance immediately—to use as many of the resources that our technology and technical communities can provide, especially the many online user groups and list servers available.

Introduction

Congratulations! By picking up this book, you
have opened yourself up to more than just the
24 chapters that follow this introduction. You
also have created an opportunity to improve
your Web site and to raise the level of your Web
development skills by learning Dreamweaver 4.
If you are wondering why you should learn

Dreamweaver, take a look at any number of Web sites that are appearing on the Internet today. You will notice a trend toward user interactivity, often created by the use of Flash animations, DHTML, and JavaScript. You also will see that a lot of the truly useful information available on the Internet is extracted from databases and displayed through the use of Cold Fusion or Active Server Pages.

Neither trend is new. The Internet has been evolving into a user-defined environment since its beginning. Even so, a new trend is springing from the old. Now, more than ever before, the programming tools necessary for a fully realized Web site are available to nonprogrammers. On the flip side of the coin, the design tools needed for a great-looking site are becoming available to nondesigners.

Although there is no replacement for knowledge and talent, certain obstacles can be removed to make the path for both designers and programmers easier to tread. With a copy of Dreamweaver 4, and a copy of this book, programming and design challenges are more easily overcome. Hours that might have been chalked up to trial, error, and frustration can now be enjoyed as your Web site becomes a stellar example of form and function.

Instructors will find this book ideal for teaching students about Web design and development. The exercises, review questions, and summaries provide a solid curriculum for any classroom. This book also is ideal for the nonstudent learning Dreamweaver at home or work.

How to Use This Book

Use this book alongside Dreamweaver 4 as a source of inspiration as well as a learning tool and resource guide. Each chapter in this book provides the core knowledge you need to execute specific tasks. The chapters lead you through an exercise, or series of exercises, illustrating the use of a Dreamweaver function as well as offering background information, review questions, and tips for speeding up the process.

The CD-ROM that accompanies this book contains files that correspond to the chapter exercises. For best results, copy the files to your computer's hard drive before you begin the lessons. This way, you can save the files and view them inside a Web browser.

How This Book Is Organized

This book is divided into seven sections. Each part focuses on a particular aspect of site development or a specific set of Dreamweaver functions. Although you do not have to read the book in chronological order, it is advantageous to read all the chapters in a given section to get a full sense of the topic being covered.

This book is divided into the following seven sections:

- **Part I: Introducing Dreamweaver 4 (Chapters 1–3).** This section examines and illustrates the basic concept of site design and development inside Dreamweaver 4. Most important here is the discussion of the Dreamweaver 4 interface. You should read this section if you are new to Dreamweaver and if you want to make the most of the new features found in version 4.

- **Part II: HTML Creation Fundamentals (Chapters 4–7).** This section focuses on the basics of creating HTML documents inside Dreamweaver. Issues such as formatting text and placing and aligning images are covered. The fundamentals of document path structure are examined and related to linking and navigation. The last chapter in this section covers common Web design issues and offers simple solutions.

- **Part III: Advanced Document Structuring (Chapters 8–12).** After looking at the basics, the next logical step is to move into advanced document structuring. In this section, the mysteries behind layers, tables, timelines, forms, frames, and cascading style sheets are revealed. Detailed exercises alongside important background information will help you conquer these tricky techniques and use them for all their worth.

- **Part IV: Site Management (Chapters 13–16).** Webmasters stop here! This section of the book covers Dreamweaver's extensive supply of site management tools. Even if you are a UNIX or Windows NT whiz, you can bring your workplace to a new level of efficiency by making use of Design Notes, templates, libraries, and the check-in/check-out feature. Included here is an examination of find/replace queries that can help you update your sites within seconds.

- **Part V: Rich Media Usage (Chapters 17–20).** For many years, animation and audio were called the future of the Web. This section assumes that the future is here. This is where you should turn when you are working with Flash, Fireworks, and JavaScript, or other plug-ins to create animations and special effects. If you have never used animation, audio, or JavaScript before, don't worry; the exercises show you how. The advantages and disadvantages of using special media files are explored as well.

- **Part VI: Advanced Site Development (Chapters 21–24).** Dreamweaver is one of the first Web development tools that creates clean, editable programming code. This section examines actions, behaviors, and Dreamweaver extensions. Exercises show you how to assign behaviors to objects, install extensions, and help you sharpen your problem-solving skills. Information about Dreamweaver UltraDev is included here as well. This section is especially useful to anyone interested in establishing an e-commerce Web site.

- **Part VII: Appendixes.** The appendixes at the end of this book discuss keyboard shortcuts, browser compatibility, and what's on the CD-ROM.

What You Should Take Away

As your knowledge of Dreamweaver 4 develops, so should your relationship with this book. The information packed into this volume is the cumulative effort of writers, designers, programmers, editors, and many other professionals. The goal we shared was to provide complete coverage of Dreamweaver 4 and to show readers how Dreamweaver can bring Web site design and development to new heights of efficiency and interactivity.

Our goals are now contingent upon the role this book plays in your success as a Web site designer and developer. As a learning aide, a resource guide, and a source of inspiration, this book can serve as both a launching pad and a home base. We hope you will transform the work we have done into a comfortable pit stop, the place where you return again and again to stock up on fuel as you weave your dreams into virtual reality.

Part I

Introducing
Dreamweaver 4

Chapter 1

What's New in Dreamweaver 4

Maybe your friend told you about it, maybe

you have used it since the first version, or

maybe you have to use it for a class at col-

lege. Regardless of how or why, you have

stumbled upon the most customizable and extensible Web-authoring tool on the market today. The Dreamweaver programming team at Macromedia has been hard at work since the release of Dreamweaver 3 and it shows in this newest version.

From better support for version control software, to further development and support of extensions, to the new capability to look up any HTML, JavaScript, or CSS element, Dreamweaver 4 has got it. Before digging in, take a moment to learn about the changes and brand new features Dreamweaver 4 offers.

This chapter covers the following:

- Dockable panels
- Code
- Design
- Collaborate
- Window management

Dockable Panels

Although dockable panels are not new to Dreamweaver 4, they are definitely worth mentioning. You can consolidate desktop space by placing multiple panels in one window. The dockable panels are Assets, Behaviors, Code Inspector, CSS Styles, Frames, History, HTML Styles, Layers, Reference, and Objects. You can drag the tab of each category from one window to another. The exception to this is when the Objects panel is in its own window. You can dock other panels inside the Objects panel; however, you cannot drag the Objects panel onto another panel's window. Dreamweaver tracks these changes and keeps the same format in future sessions. For more on this, see Chapter 2, "Customizing Dreamweaver."

Code

Dreamweaver has taken its superior code-editing power to the next level with the newest version. From editing non-HTML documents to including a JavaScript Debugger, Dreamweaver has come to the mat ready to butt heads with dedicated text editors that it has previously relied on to make it a complete solution. Today, Dreamweaver stands on its own.

Integrated Text Editor

Previously a clumsy and inefficient tool, the HTML Inspector from previous versions has been reworked to be a powerful editor for raw code. You can access the integrated text editor through both the Code view and the Code Inspector. A new Split view enables you to see your page in design mode while you edit with the text editor.

The integrated text editor auto-indents both HTML and JavaScript and offers a color-coding scheme that helps you to easily visualize what's what in your document. Dreamweaver also will open JavaScript and XML files in the Code view automatically, so you're ready to go. You also can define additional types of files to open in this view through your preferences. While in Code view, you can still access Dreamweaver objects and other menu items. You can read more about this improved feature in Chapter 3, "Dreamweaver and HTML," and Chapter 4, "Working with Text."

Split View

You can view both your design and code simultaneously using the Split view. Have your code on top or bottom while you switch between laying out your content in the Design pane and optimizing your code in the Code pane. This type of functionality was feasible only when using multiple monitors in previous versions. The Split view mode is discussed in detail in Chapter 3.

JavaScript Debugger

The new JavaScript Debugger will certainly relieve many headaches for programmers. You can set breakpoints and see your script execute in real-time step by step in Internet Explorer or Netscape. This is not only a great troubleshooting tool, but also an excellent teaching device. You can see how each browser interprets and deals with various functions of JavaScript. Chapter 23, "Scripting and Markup Languages," covers this tool in greater detail.

Code Reference

All those wasted minutes looking up tag attributes and syntax online or in a bulky reference book are over. Dreamweaver 4 ships with an extensive library of HTML tags, CSS styles, and JavaScript objects easily accessed through its interface. As shown in Figure 1.1, you can automatically call up the information you need on a specific item quickly and easily. Chapter 3 shows you how to do so.

Figure 1.1   The Reference panel.

Customizable Keyboard Shortcuts

Standard in products made by Macromedia today is the Keyboard Shortcuts Editor, shown in Figure 1.2. You can change key combinations at your discretion according to what "makes sense" to you. Dreamweaver ships with several predefined sets of shortcuts; however, you can create and save your own as well. You can learn how to create your own shortcut sets as well as choose among predefined ones, as discussed in Chapter 2.

Note

All references to keyboard shortcuts in this book refer to the Macromedia Standard keyboard shortcut set. If you choose your own shortcuts, or use another set, the references used in this book may be incorrect.

Code Navigation

Dreamweaver 4 enables JavaScript developers to quickly sort through their code using the Code Navigation toolbar icon. This functionality is available while in Code view and enables JavaScript professionals to code more effectively. Chapter 3 discusses this feature in more detail.

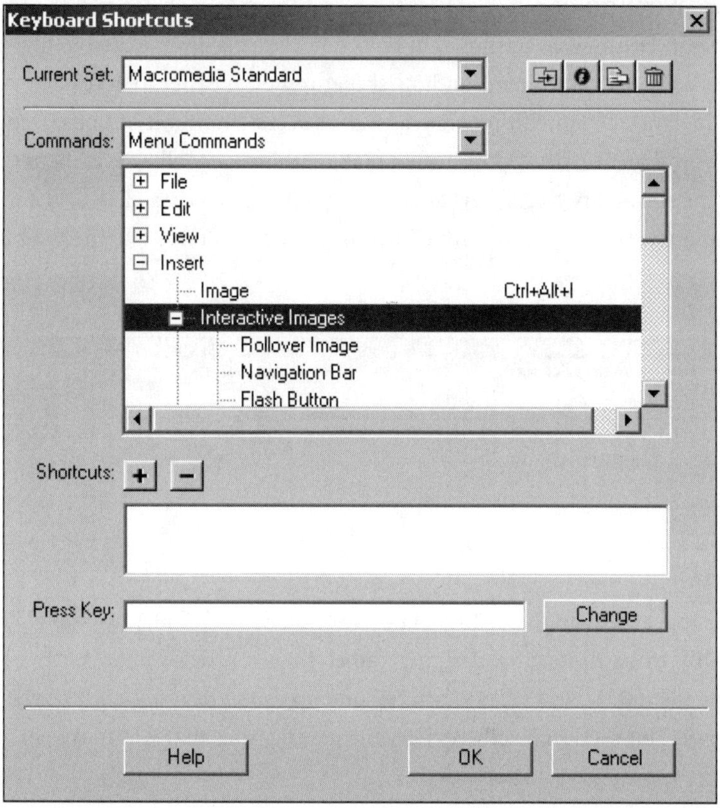

Figure 1.2   Keyboard shortcuts.

Live Syntax Coloring

Dreamweaver 4 enables you to use live syntax coloring. This feature colors your HTML and JavaScript in real-time (as you type). Therefore, developers can know, in a broad sense, what text does on their pages at the glance of a color. It helps organize code in such a way that you do not have to go searching through your text looking for something. Chapter 2 discusses this feature in more detail.

Non-HTML Document Editing

You can use Dreamweaver 4 as a general text editor as well. You can edit your XML, JavaScript, ASP, and other text file types. Additionally, Dreamweaver does not rewrite text in any file type it does not know. Therefore, you can safely edit your ASP documents without Dreamweaver changing your code. Chapter 3 discusses this feature in more detail.

Dreamweaver Toolbar

The toolbar in Dreamweaver, shown in Figure 1.3, has been renovated to make the most commonly accessed menu items and other features even easier to access. You can adjust the page title, the current editing view, as well as access common options. Depending on which view you are in, the options differ, making this new toolbar even better. File management and the ability to preview and debug your pages with a click of the toolbar add to the impressiveness of this revamped feature. Chapter 2 discusses the toolbar in more detail.

Figure 1.3   Dreamweaver's toolbar.

Design

The main appeal of using a WYSIWYG (What You See Is What You Get) HTML editor is the ability to be more of a designer rather than a programmer. With all the code enhancements this newest version offers, sometimes the new design features are left in the shadows. This section briefly reviews the new features that will make your life just a little easier.

Layout View

Accessible from the Objects panel, the Layout view is a new feature that makes creating and managing tables almost as easy as layers. You just click and drag tables and table cells to the dimensions you want and Dreamweaver calculates the most efficient way to create the HTML required for your desired table (and then even creates it).

This brings the learning curve required for successfully manipulating tables down significantly. Because Dreamweaver helps automate the creation and layout of your tables, you willl spend less time pulling your hair out over complex code. Chapter 8, "Layout with Tables," discusses this exciting new feature in more detail.

Macromedia Flash Text and Buttons

You can now utilize the vector-based power of Macromedia's Flash technology coupled with the simplicity of Dreamweaver's interface to create editable, scalable, and neatly printed text.

You can download additional styles from Macromedia Exchange, or be daring and create your own. You learn how to use this vector-based wonder in Chapter 18, "Animation with Flash."

Roundtrip Graphics Editing

Dreamweaver's Roundtrip features offer multiple processes that help edit, optimize, and add images to your Web pages. Combined with the power and extensibility of Fireworks, Dreamweaver's Roundtrip features enable you to edit images on your page in Fireworks with the click of a button. With another click, you can go from Fireworks back to Dreamweaver with your newly edited image. Launch Fireworks automatically and optimize your images in a similar, easy manner. Chapter 4, "Working with Text," and Chapter 6, "Working with Images," discuss the Roundtrip features in more detail.

Common Macromedia User Interface

Macromedia is working hard to consolidate the interfaces of their various products into one consistent style. The hope behind this concept is that once you use and become accustomed to one of their product's interfaces, making the switch to another of theirs will be smooth and easy. Great concept. Excellent implementation.

Collaborate

Have you ever tried working on a large Web site with multiple people? What if two people edit the same file simultaneously? Someone's changes will undoubtedly be overwritten. What if you want to leave a simple note for the next person who edits the file—something they should be wary of, or something that needs to be addressed? Well, Dreamweaver 4 goes beyond its predecessors in collaboration potential. You may take a lot of these features for granted unless you have tried using another editor.

Asset Management

You can now look at nearly all the resources used in your site from one panel: the Assets panel. You can preview and use images, colors, URLs, Flash (as illustrated in Figure 1.4), Shockwave, multimedia files, scripts, and templates. With the Assets panel, you can see the resources being used as well as detailed information relating to them. The Assets panel also enables you to store your most frequently used assets under the Favorites section so that you can quickly and easily access them. Chapter 15, "Workplace Collaboration," discusses the Assets panel in more detail.

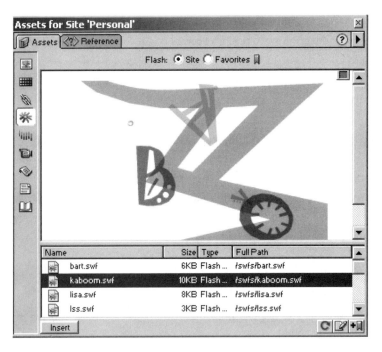

Figure 1.4   The Assets panel.

Visual SourceSafe Integration

Now you can integrate Microsoft's industry-leading Visual SourceSafe with Dreamweaver. SourceSafe is version-control software that large teams utilize to effetively manage and ensure smooth site development. Chapter 15 discusses Visual SourceSafe in more detail.

WebDAV Integration

In addition to Visual SourceSafe integration, Dreamweaver 4 enables you to integrate with any WebDAV-enabled server. This integration gives you better site-management potential. Chapter 15 discusses WebDAV integration in more detail.

Site Reporting

Site Reporting is added to Dreamweaver in its newest version. As seen in Figures 1.5 and 1.6, Site Reporting enables you to create reports that include information such as checked-out files, design notes, combinable nested-font tags, missing alt text, redundant nested tags, removable empty tags, and untitled documents.

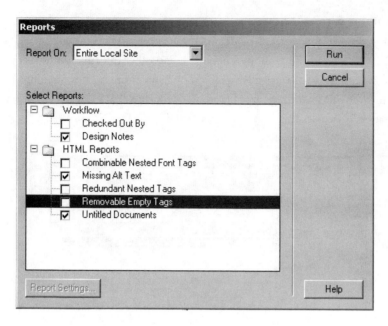

Figure 1.5   Establishing report options.

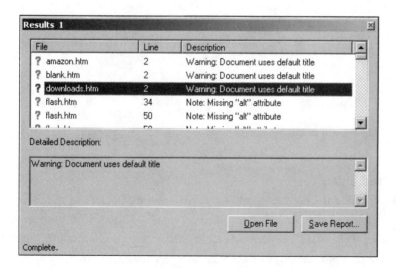

Figure 1.6   Report results.

After the reports are generated, you can save them for later, or open each file and correct the problems immediately. Chapter 14 discusses Site Reporting in more detail.

Configurable Site Window

You can customize the smallest of details in Dreamweaver's Site window. As seen in Figure 1.7, you can set the visibility, alignment, and other information to suit your liking. You also can use your Design Notes to create new columns. These columns can contain custom file information such as file status or file due date. Chapter 13, "Site and File Organization," discusses this feature in more detail.

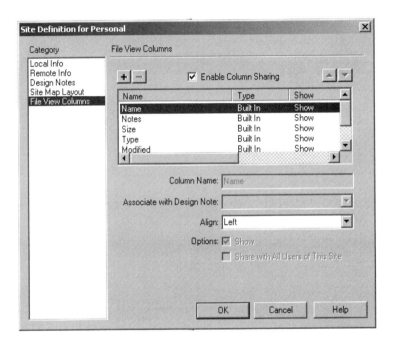

Figure 1.7   Site window.

Integrated Email

Instead of calling the person who has checked out a particular file and asking her to check in, you can now automatically send an email asking questions or giving other instructions. This makes it easier than ever to quickly communicate to other team members with a click of the mouse. Chapter 15 discusses this feature in more detail.

Extension Manager

Part of Macromedia Exchange, the Extension Manager, shown in Figure 1.8, enables you to install, temporarily deactivate, and uninstall objects, behaviors, commands, and many other extensions in Dreamweaver. The Extension Manager also enables you to install extensions into Flash and Dreamweaver UltraDev. Chapter 21 shows you how to use the Extension Manager.

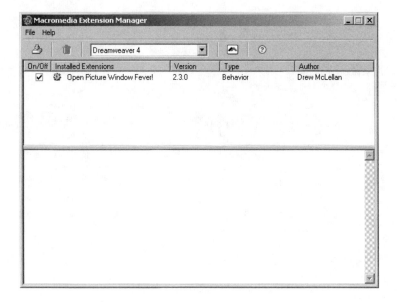

Figure 1.8   The Extension Manager.

Macromedia Exchange

Managed by Macromedia, this Web site works with the Extension Manager to provide access to extensions that can be installed with a click of the mouse. With Macromedia Exchange, you have access to hundreds of objects, behaviors, commands, and other extensions. Figure 1.9 shows some of the DHTML/layers extensions available on the Exchange.

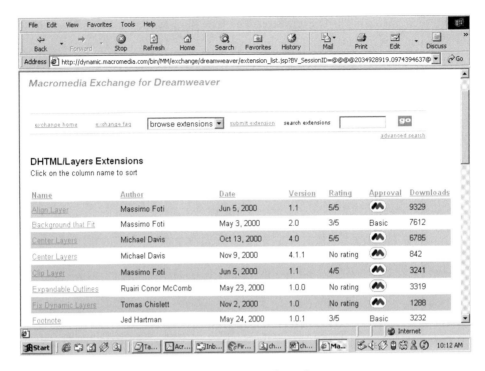

Figure 1.9   DHTML/layers extensions on Macromedia Exchange.

Window Management

Dreamweaver is a multiwindow-based application. It uses separate windows for each new document. This differs from Microsoft Word, for instance, in which each document is created in the same window of the application and you can effectively edit only one document at a time. (Note, however, that Word 2000 opens new windows for each document.)

Dreamweaver uses panels that snap. They will snap to other Dreamweaver panels, windows, or the edges of your screen. As shown in Figure 1.10, you can create a "wall" with your panels, which causes Dreamweaver to open files in a nonintrusive manner.

Dreamweaver opens a new window for each document you open or create, enabling you to position them however you want onscreen. Many times you will have more than one document open at the same time. Dreamweaver has an extremely graceful way of handling this process, while keeping your desktop space fairly clear of clutter.

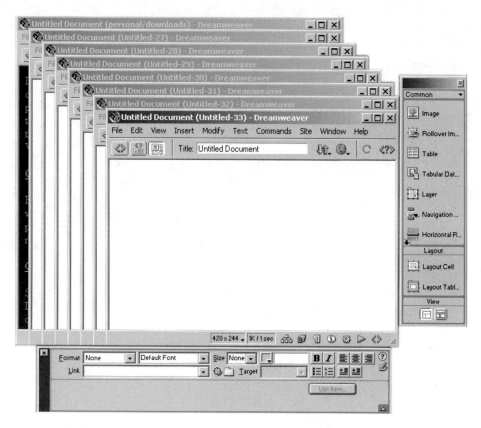

Figure 1.10   New windows being contained by Dreamweaver's panels.

As you can see in Figure 1.10, when opening existing files, or when creating new ones, Dreamweaver creates the initial size such that it does not interfere with your floating panels.

Summary

This chapter has reviewed the changes and new features in Dreamweaver 4. Hopefully, this foreshadowing of the power Dreamweaver provides will help encourage your efforts to become a top-notch Web developer.

Chapter 2

Customizing Dreamweaver

For the most part, applications have an intuitive workflow that is well suited for the majority of users. Sometimes, though, it may become necessary to alter certain behaviors of an application to better fit your practices and to increase productivity.

With Dreamweaver, many processes can be modified to better suit how you work. Instead of arbitrarily altering your work patterns, you can choose to personalize your own copy of Dreamweaver. In this chapter we will cover these ways to customize Dreamweaver:

- Setting preferences
- Viewing palettes and panels
- Choosing a browser for page previews
- Using split views
- Using live syntax coloring
- Creating keyboard shortcuts
- Using the mini-launcher

That said, now is a good time to make the following suggestion: If you are unsure about the principles of any of the features that you will learn to customize in this chapter, try the default settings first. The preferences that are set by default are usually the most intuitive. And for any of the features that you will be learning to use later, it will be easier to refer to help (or this publication) if you have not made any drastic changes to the application.

Two types of preferences exist in Dreamweaver, ones that alter the appearance of the application (eye candy), and those that alter how the application works (functional). This chapter looks at parts of the preferences that alter the functionality and behavior of Dreamweaver.

Preferences Dialog Box

The main area you use to customize Dreamweaver is the Preferences dialog box, which is accessed through the Edit menu; choose Edit/Preferences, or use the keyboard shortcut Ctrl+U (Command+U) Figure 2.1 shows the result of either of these methods.

What you will notice first is that the dialog box is divided into two main columns. The column on the left is titled Category, and the column on the right is initially titled General. The category selected in the left column dictates what content displays in the right column.

The operation of the dialog box should be straightforward enough because it utilizes check boxes, radio buttons, and drop-down menus.

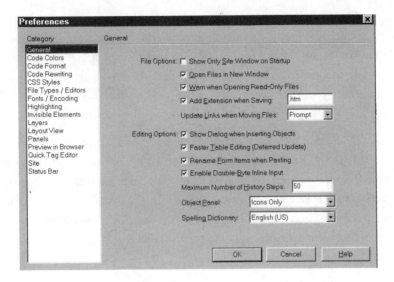

Figure 2.1   The Preferences dialog box.

File Options

By selecting the General option in the Category listing, you are left with two main areas of customization. The first, File Options, enables you to set the way in which Dreamweaver launches, opens, and saves files. Let's break down these choices.

Show Only Site Window on Startup

By default, when the application is first launched, a new document is created titled, named Untitled-1. If you find that you usually have to perform site functions at start-up instead of creating new HTML documents, checking this box will start the program with the Site window of the last site you were working on.

Open Files in New Window

When you are working on an HTML document and you ask Dreamweaver to open another document, it places this file in a new window. If you find that when you open a new file, you no longer need to edit the last one, unchecking this option will enable you to use the same window over and over again.

Warn When Opening Read-Only Files

When this item is checked, Dreamweaver warns you when you are attempting to open or edit a read-only file.

Add Extension When Saving

This option should be pretty obvious to anyone with rudimentary knowledge of the Web. To save you some keystrokes, you can type into this input box the extension that you want your documents to be saved with. .htm is the default that Dreamweaver will tack onto the end of the filename you type when saving a document. If you instead want to use the more modern .html extension, this field enables you to make that distinction.

Incidentally, there is fundamentally little difference between .htm and .html. Older computers had a limit on the number of characters used to name a file. The standard was eight characters for a name, then a period, and then three characters for an extension (namename.ext). On these older systems, asking for a file named namename.ext, would return namename.ext because the information past the third character in the extension was ignored. Because most newer systems exceed this limitation, you can now use .html as a valid extension.

Update Links When Moving Files

This field enables you to select one of three options from a drop-down list. The first option (the default) is Prompt. With Prompt selected, Dreamweaver will always ask you whether to update the links associated with the document you are moving. The second choice, Never, does not allow Dreamweaver to update the links associated. The final option, Always, forces Dreamweaver to automatically alter the associated links without asking first. It is generally recommended that you select Prompt or Always, unless you really know what you're doing.

Editing Options

The next section in the General area of the Preferences panel is titled Editing Options. It has the fields detailed in the next sections.

Show Dialog When Inserting Objects

When you insert certain objects, Dreamweaver will prompt you to input additional information, such as the source file of an image or the formatting information for tables. If you change this setting, you will instead have to manually input this information through the Property Inspector or in the HTML code.

Faster Table Editing (Deferred Update)

To speed table editing, Dreamweaver enables you to make all the changes that you want to a table and waits until you click outside of it to redraw the table. If you want to see real-time changes to your table, you can uncheck this box.

Rename Form Items When Pasting

When duplicating form items inside the same form in an HTML document, it is important to uniquely name those elements, with the exception of like named elements (such as radio buttons). With this option selected, Dreamweaver will automatically rename form elements using a sequential number convention (for example, name becomes name2, name3, and so on) when copying and pasting.

Enable Double-Byte Inline Input

This option enables you to directly insert double-byte input (such as certain foreign-language characters) into the document window. When disabled, a text dialog box appears for you to input or convert the text. However, certain other conditions must be satisfied to do this. On Windows, you need the localized OS and a localized version of Dreamweaver. On Macintosh, you need the appropriate foreign language kit.

Maximum Number of History Steps

Normally when working with Dreamweaver, you have the capability to return to a previous point in the document's history, up to and including 50 previous edits. By entering in a value other than 50 into this field, you can enable Dreamweaver to retain an ever-increasing number of previous states, with no practical software-enforced limit (up to 99,999 previous states). However, there is a practical limit enforced by your hardware. Because history levels are arranged in RAM, the limitation of the number of history steps depends on system memory. If you find that you need a larger number of history states, try increasing this number a bit at a time. If you find that your system starts to slow down or stops responding, reduce the number of steps to the last acceptable value.

Object Panel

The Object Panel field contains a drop-menu enabling you to choose how the Objects panel will appear. The three options are Icons Only, Icons and Text, and Text Only.

Spelling Dictionary

The final field in General Preferences is the Spelling Dictionary drop-down menu. Here you may choose from any spelling dictionary that you have installed. If the language or dialect that you want to use is not found here, you have the option of downloading additional dictionaries online at this address:

```
www.macromedia.com/support/dreamweaver/dictionary.html
```

Code Colors

The next option available in the Category listing is Code Colors. This category enables you to set the colors used in the Live Syntax Coloring feature of Dreamweaver. When you select the category on the left, your screen will look like Figure 2.2.

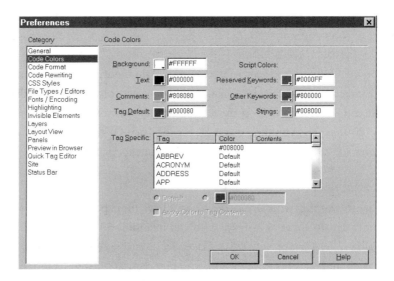

Figure 2.2   The Code Colors options.

You can set code colors in two ways. First, you can set the general color scheme that all elements use when their color is not individually set. Second, you can select specific elements and decide which colors they will be.

Background
This color is applied to the backgrounds of both the Code view and the Code Inspector.

Text
This is the default color of all text in an HTML document, such as `<BODY>` `text color` `</BODY>`. In this case, the two words "text color" would be of the color set for text.

Comments
Whenever HTML comments are used, (`<!—   —>`), the tags and the text contained inside will appear in this color.

Tag Default

All HTML tags will use this color, unless otherwise assigned.

Other color settings available are Reserved Keywords, Other Keywords, and Strings, defining the colors to be used for each.

When you want to be more exact, you can choose to individually assign colors to specific HTML and SCRIPT elements. To do this, you select the element by clicking on its name. This enables the radio buttons underneath the Tag Specific box. By selecting the radio button immediately beside the color palette box, you can change the color specified to whatever you want. Finally, you can also choose to allow this color to override any text that may be contained between the tags.

Code Format

The Code Format preferences (see Figure 2.3) go hand in hand with the previous section because they enable you to further customize how your HTML code is to be laid out and organized.

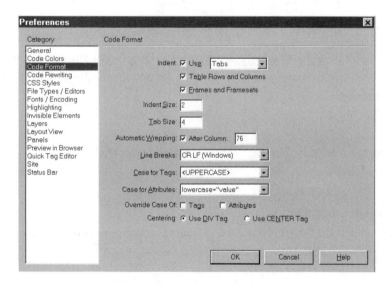

Figure 2.3 The Code Format options.

One of the most important criteria for HTML code to be readable is the use of indents. Because formatting the source code of an HTML document does not have to follow many conventions, HTML code can become almost impossible to read if it is not well organized. By using indentation, you can set up a pleasing visual flow of a document that allows other people to read your source code and interpret what the code is doing. Fortunately, you can set up Dreamweaver to perform this task automatically.

The first section of Code Format is the indent section. It contains three check boxes, a drop-down menu, and two input fields.

Indent

The Indent check box enables Dreamweaver to auto-indent your code according to the other options in the indent section.

Use

The Use menu tells Dreamweaver whether to use spaces or tabs when indenting.

Table Rows and Columns/Frames and Framesets

Here you can enable/disable indenting of table rows and columns, and frames and framesets. This simply tells Dreamweaver whether to auto-indent table and frameset elements to appear easier to read and laid out in a more logical manner.

Indent Size

The Indent Size field sets up the size of the indents. The number you enter here is measured in either tabs or spaces and depends upon the option you chose earlier in the Use drop-down menu.

Tab Size

Finally, the last field is the Tab Size field, which enables you to define in character spaces how large a tab is.

Miscellaneous Formatting

The remainder of the Code Format section is just as straightforward. Let's take a look at its components.

Automatic Wrapping

The Automatic Wrapping check box and the After Column text box determine whether the document will auto-wrap and sets up how many characters are allowed before Dreamweaver will add a hard return to the document. Adding hard returns can be useful when viewing the document source in different applications. Also note that Dreamweaver will insert hard returns only when their presence will not alter the finished Web page.

Line Breaks

Next you can set the format that line breaks will use in your document. Depending on whether the system to which the file is to be sent is UNIX-, Mac-, or Windows-based, the line breaks must be set accordingly.

Case for Tags/Case for Attributes

Case for Tags and Case for Attributes both have the same options, uppercase and lower-case. The option you choose will depend upon your personal preference, which you are used to working with, or any protocol you have set up for your workgroup if multiple people are to use or edit the files.

Override Case of: Tags–Attributes

Next you have two check boxes that enable you to impose the formatting that you set for tags and attributes on all documents that you open, create, or edit. Dreamweaver will do this automatically, so be sure that you want these rules enforced before you select these buttons.

Centering

Finally, you can choose the tag that you want used to center objects. Your choices are the Div tag, which will create the code (`<DIV ALIGN="center">`) or the <CENTER> tag.

Code Rewriting

The next section, which deals with your HTML source code, is the Code Rewriting section (see Figure 2.4). This section tells Dreamweaver how to behave when altering the code.

Rewrite Code

Rewrite Code has three check boxes: Fix Invalidly Nested and Unclosed Tags, Remove Extra Closing Tags, and Warn When Fixing or Removing Tags. The next sections look at these in more detail.

Fix Invalidly Nested and Unclosed Tags

When selected, this check box allows Dreamweaver to actively look at the code, make sure that tags are not overlapping, and make sure that they are properly closed. If it finds problems, it can automatically fix them. An example is that `<H1><I>These tags are invalidly nested</H1></I>` would become `<H1><I>These tags are properly nested</H1></I>`.

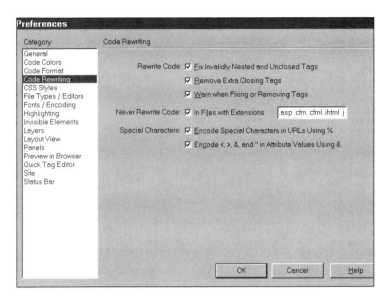

Figure 2.4   The Code Rewriting section.

Remove Extra Closing Tags

If close tags are found and Dreamweaver cannot locate an appropriate opening tag, the close tags are removed.

Warn When Fixing or Removing Tags

When this check box is selected, Dreamweaver will warn you before it performs the last two actions.

Never Rewrite Code: In Files with Extensions

This option enables you to create exceptions to the auto-correcting behaviors that you have been setting up. It's very useful in certain types of files when you do not want to disturb code that falls outside Dreamweaver's auto-editing capabilities.

Special Characters

These settings are best left at their defaults unless you have good reason to change them.

File Types/Editors

Dreamweaver has many strengths, but it is not meant as a standalone application for creating Web sites. Modern Web sites depend on a wide variety of media and sometimes languages and scripts to function. However, Dreamweaver has the capability to direct workflow to the appropriate environments to maintain efficiency.

In the File Types/Editors section of the Preferences panel (see Figure 2.5), you can define how Dreamweaver reacts to different languages, as well as how it deals with graphics, audio, and multimedia files.

Tip

If you are displeased with the way Dreamweaver is rewriting code in your HTML pages, add .htm and .html to the list of file extensions that Dreamweaver should never rewrite.

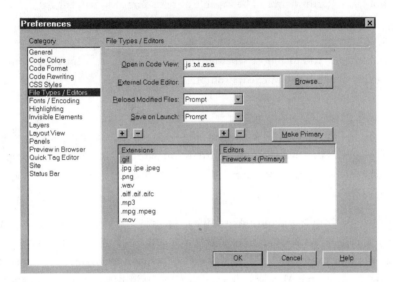

Figure 2.5 The File Types/Editors section.

Open in Code View

The Open in Code View text field enables you to define certain file types (by their extensions) as files in which you need to view just the source code. Placing an extension here and requesting to open that type of file instructs Dreamweaver to open the document window in Code view so that you can enter code directly.

External Code Editor

This field enables you to enter the location of an external editor for making changes to your source code. If you do not know the exact location of the file, you may choose to browse for it. Your version of Dreamweaver probably shipped with HomeSite for the PC or BBEdit for the Mac, and either makes a good candidate for an external editor.

Reload Modified Files

If you alter the code of an open Dreamweaver document in an external application, Dreamweaver must be told what to do when you return to Dreamweaver. This is a drop-down menu that enables you to select one of three choices. Prompt, the default selection, asks the user before reloading the page when it has been altered outside of Dreamweaver. The Always option lets Dreamweaver automatically update the document in the document window, without permission from the user. You would choose the Never setting if you do not want Dreamweaver to be capable of reloading automatically.

Save on Launch

This option enables you to choose whether Dreamweaver will save the file automatically when an external editor is launched; Prompt, Always, or Never are the options available.

Extensions/Editors

At the bottom of the panel, you will find a left and a right pane. By placing an extension in the left pane and then associating that extension with an editor in the right pane, you can set up how Dreamweaver will respond when you choose to edit certain file types with an external editor.

To use this, press the plus (+) button over the left pane. An edit box will appear. Type the name of the extension, (.XXX), and be sure to remember the period that precedes it. You can enter multiple extensions at once to associate with an external editor—just leave a space between each one. Also, you can go back and edit those extensions by selecting them and then clicking on them a second time. To remove them, simply select the extensions that you do not want, and press the minus (–) button.

When you have the extension that you want to add, simply select the extension and hit the + button over the right pane. This enables you to select the application that you want to associate. Be sure to find the executable file (.exe) for the program that you want (choose Browse if you are having trouble remembering the exact location of the file). Choose the file and click Open; you should see the application properly associated with the extension.

Invisible Elements

Because there is so much important code behind the layout of the page, Dreamweaver has a means of informing you where some of these elements are. They are little yellow symbols that will be visible to you in Design view.

The Invisible Elements area of preferences, shown in Figure 2.6, enables you to turn on or off which types of nonvisual elements are marked on the page. Simply use the check box beside the element that you want made visible or invisible in Design view. With the check box toggled on, the marker will be visible; and with the check box toggled off, the marker will not be visible.

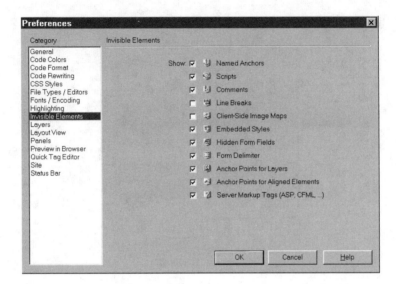

Figure 2.6   The Invisible Elements section.

Layers

With layers you have many different options to consider. Layers have been around for a while now but are still poorly supported by the major browsers. Different tags, attributes, differences between how they are positioned, and even an error in Netscape that causes everything to go haywire if someone simply resizes a window can make working with layers messy. That said, they are useful in certain situations—namely, menus for navigation. With the Layers preferences (see Figure 2.7), you can set up how layers are inserted into your page. You can even have Dreamweaver automatically insert a script to fix Netscape's resizing issues.

Tag

Four different tags can be used to insert a layer. By default, Dreamweaver uses the <DIV> tag. There is no right or wrong tag to use by default, though, because your target browser will determine which tags you will use. Different tags are required in different situations and for different results. However, unless you are creating a site targeted at only one of the major browsers or you are allowing for both through detection scripts, it is probably best to use the <DIV> tag because Internet Explorer and Netscape Navigator both recognize it. You must decide which is right for your everyday situation and choose it here. See Chapter 10, "Using Layers," for further information.

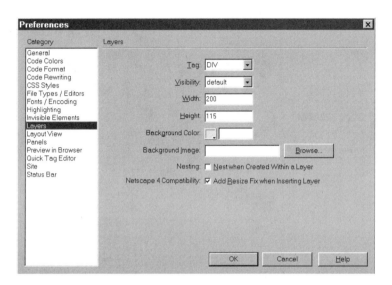

Figure 2.7   The Layers section.

Visibility

This drop-down menu lets you choose the default visibility of a layer when it is inserted into a document. Visibility settings are used for show/hide layer behaviors and time-lines.

Width/Height/Background Color/Background Image

Use these four fields to set the default height, width, background color, and background image of new layers.

Nesting

This check box enables you to choose whether a layer created within the area of a pre-existing layer becomes nested within that layer or sits on top of that layer. If the layer is not nested, its coordinates position it relative to the page, whereas nested layers are positioned relative to the parent layer.

Netscape 4 Compatibility

As mentioned earlier, this is a resize fix for Netscape 4.x and above series browsers. Netscape contains a bug that causes it to lose layers when a user resizes the window containing the document. Dreamweaver can add a JavaScript function to your Web page, which will cause a page to reload whenever the page is resized. By reloading the page, you are making sure that the layer information is intact when the new view is rendered. Be sure that this is absolutely necessary for your pages first, though, because this fix reloads the page and can produce a choppy appearance when this happens.

Panels

One of the key features of Dreamweaver is its use of panels. Just about everything can be accessed from them, and they speed up some of the slower processes (such as hand coding and JavaScripting) of creating Web sites. In the Panels section of Preferences (see Figure 2.8), you can modify how they appear onscreen and how you access them.

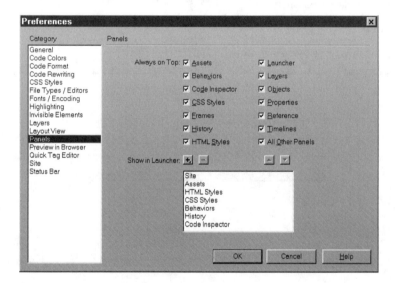

Figure 2.8 The Panels section.

Always on Top

By default, any panels that you open reside in front of the Document/Site windows in Dreamweaver. If you instead want certain panels to be obscured by the Document/Site windows, then deselect their check boxes here.

Show in Launcher

You can think of the launcher in Dreamweaver as a "remote control" for your panels. With it, you can choose control panels that you want to use without having to use the menus or shortcut keys. To select which panels are represented in the launcher, we must add them to the box at the bottom. To add a panel, simply press the + button and select the panel that you want to add. To remove a panel, simply select it and press the – button. Finally to reorder the buttons, select the panel and use the up and down arrow keys. Incidentally, at the bottom-right corner of document windows is an item referred to as the mini-launcher, shown in Figure 2.9. When you make changes to which items are contained in the launcher, the mini-launcher is changed as well.

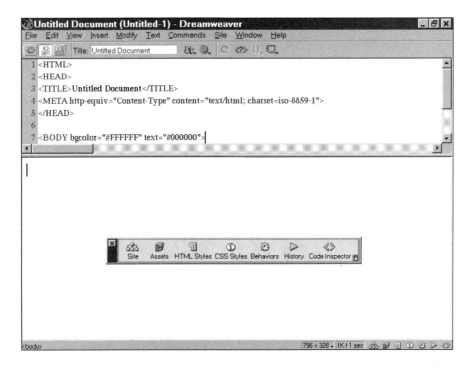

Figure 2.9   The mini-launcher.

Preview in Browser

The Preview in Browser preference (shown in Figure 2.10) determines which browser can be used when you want to preview your Web page or site. Viewing HTML pages in multiple browsers and even cross-platform can be an invaluable tool when developing a Web site. Because Dreamweaver allows for both a primary and a secondary browser to be used, make sure that you at least have a version of Microsoft Internet Explorer and Netscape Navigator to test with. Dreamweaver also allows for pages to be viewed via a local Web. If you want to view the page via a local server, you must be running server software, and this is an option available for the Windows version only. To view active content such as .asp pages properly, you must be running a local server (such as Personal Web Server or IIS).

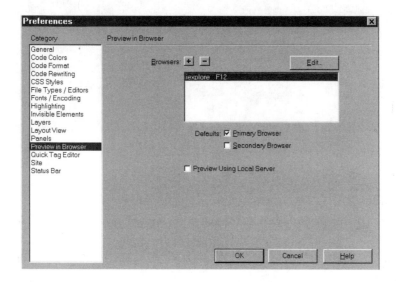

Figure 2.10   The Preview in Browser preferences.

To add a browser, press the + button. You will be prompted to enter a name for the browser, to give the location of the browser's .exe file, and to specify whether it will be used as the primary or secondary browser.

To remove a browser, simply select it and press the – button.

Quick Tag Editor

When using the Quick Tag Editor, shown in Figure 2.11, changes are immediately implemented on your document. If you want to change this, simply deselect the Apply Changes Immediately While Editing check box.

Also while you are working in the Quick Tag Editor, hints are given in the form of a drop-down menu containing attributes and, in certain cases, possible values for attributes for the current tag that you are editing. If you want to turn off these hints, deselect the Enable Tag Hints check box. Finally, you can change how long it takes for the hints to appear by altering the Delay slide bar.

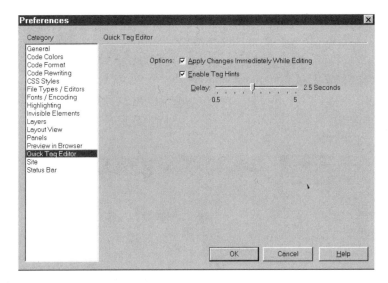

Figure 2.11   The Quick Tag Editor.

Status Bar

The Status Bar preferences refer to the bar at the bottom of the document window (see Figure 2.12). The status bar enables you to perform repetitive tasks quickly, such as selecting a tag for editing, changing window sizes, and even opening and closing panels.

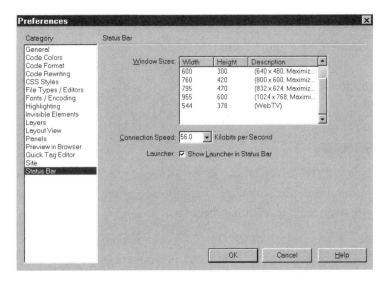

Figure 2.12   The Status Bar preferences.

Window Sizes

The first option you have is the Window Sizes box. Here you can set up the different sizes that your document window can be automatically resized to. Simply click an item to change it, or click a blank area to enter new information. By setting up window sizes approximate to the size of what you expect your end user to have, you can better lay out the site to fit the screen.

Connection Speed

Dreamweaver enables you to know the approximate time that it will take to download your Web page, depending on connection speed. By using the Connection Speed drop-down menu, you can set the speed to which you want your site to be profiled. Simply select the appropriate speed.

Launcher/Show Launcher in Status Bar

This check box enables you to select whether the contents of the launcher are displayed in the status bar. This is referred to as the mini-launcher. Deselecting this option removes the mini-launcher from the status bar.

Summary

This chapter covered the various ways you could customize Dreamweaver including how to set preferences, view palettes and panels, choose browsers for page previews, use split views, use live syntax coloring, create shortcuts, and use mini-launchers.

Chapter 3

Dreamweaver and HTML

By now you should have a basic handle

on how to customize your copy of

Dreamweaver to suit your personal tastes.

You might have started adding a few lines

of text here or a simple table or image map there, just to get the feel of how Dreamweaver works. This chapter discusses the fundamentals of HTML in Dreamweaver. We will go over what makes an HTML document unique, as well as the various ways Dreamweaver allows for creating and editing HTML.

Don't let the chapter title fool you. Although we talk about the bare basics of HTML, we also discuss vital methods for manipulating HTML inside Dreamweaver, which will save you headaches and time in the future if you read over them now. The following list details some of the main things we'll talk about:

- Various head and body attributes and tags
- The difference between logical and physical markup
- How to navigate the three editing modes: Design, Code, and Code and Design
- Dreamweaver's extensive HTML, CSS, and JavaScript reference guide
- How to use the cleanup HTML feature
- How to use external HTML editors in conjunction with Dreamweaver

HTML Basics

When I tell people what I do for a living, they seem amazed. Perhaps some should be, but I think the reactions I typically get are quite exaggerated. The masses seem to think that HTML is a hard-to-comprehend "programming" language that only the computer-savvy are capable of mastering. On the other hand, hard-core programmers accustomed to C or Perl seem to think that HTML is not a *real* programming language at all and that those who think it is are mistaken. So what *is* HTML exactly?

HTML stands for Hypertext Markup Language and is the specification instituted by the World Wide Web Consortium (W3C) outlining how documents should be structured for the Web. Web browser developers use HTML as the basis for how their products will render pages on your screen. A standard must be used for this reason: If each software developer can represent content in its own proprietary way, this would not only make our job a whole lot harder, but it also would produce varied and dissimilar results. Inefficient and bloated code are other side effects of this type of practice.

HTML utilizes elements called *tags* to mark plain text. These tags give special attributes and formatting instructions that browsers interpret and display for the end user to see. Every tag is of this format: <TAG>Here's your content</TAG>. (There are a few exceptions, such as when inserting images that require only the beginning tag.) HTML is not case-sensitive.

You will gain a better understanding of what basic HTML does if you view HTML tags as adjectives. For instance, you might use the words *blue*, *red*, or *yellow* to describe the color of an object, such as a ball. You might also describe a relationship with another object—for example, you might say that something is to the left, to the right, or in the center. Likewise, HTML helps describe the appearance and location of your text, images, and other objects in your Web pages.

In the ideal world, you would be able to draw all your HTML objects in a what-you-see-is-what-you-get (WYSIWYG) editor and get the exact same output when viewed in any browser. Unfortunately, this isn't always the case. Although Dreamweaver does one of the best jobs of writing HTML that is compatible and consistent with as many browsers as possible, sometimes it just can't do it. Other times, you will want to create or edit your own JavaScript code or other code that goes directly into your HTML file. For whatever reason, you can rest assured that one day you will have to edit HTML, and when that day arrives you should already be comfortable with doing the basics. With a tool like Dreamweaver at your side, it couldn't be easier!

<HEAD> Content

An HTML document consists of three regions. The highest is the <HTML> tag, of which every other HTML element is subordinate. The next-highest ordered regions are <HEAD> and <BODY>. <HEAD> information typically defines the Web page as a whole but does not contain anything that will actually display on the page itself. It gives descriptions of what is *inside* the page to Web browsers and search engines. Some tags that go inside the <HEAD> are the title, keywords, a description, the character set to use, and even an automatic refresh attribute. This is also an ideal place to insert most JavaScript that your page may require. Dreamweaver makes it easy for you to add, edit, or delete any <HEAD> tag.

Meta Tags and Other <HEAD> Tags

Meta tags send page information to Web browsers and Web servers. Search engine spiders also parse them. These tags hold information such as the author, keywords, a refresh interval, and the document encoding. Meta tags should be inserted in the <HEAD> area. Because meta tags can be confusing for less experienced users, Dreamweaver makes this task very easy. Before we get into how Dreamweaver controls meta tags, let's review what they look like in HTML:

```
<html>
<head>
<title>Untitled Document</title>
```

```
<meta  name="keywords"  content="these,  are,  keywords,  that,  search,
engine, spiders, will, see">
<meta  name="description"  content="This  tag  provides  a  description  of
the page for search engine spiders.">
<meta http-equiv="refresh" content="60">
<meta  http-equiv="Content-Type"  content="text/html;  charset=iso-8859-
1">
</head>
<body bgcolor="#FFFFFF" text="#000000">
</body>
</html>
```

The previous code is a fairly simple HTML document. There is no "onscreen" content
other than the white background color. (This will be explained in the discussion of the
<body> tag.) The NAME attribute specifies information about the page while the
HTTP-EQUIV attribute specifies HTTP header information. CONTENT is the information the NAME or HTTP-EQUIV attributes describe. Now that we've discussed the
basics of meta tags, we can see how Dreamweaver simplifies the process.

We will be using the Objects panel to insert meta content. The Objects panel can be toggled on and off by clicking Window/Objects (Ctrl+F2). From this panel you can add various kinds of HTML elements, including characters, head, form, frame, invisible and
special elements, and other common HTML elements. It is also possible to add meta tags
and other head elements from the Insert/Head Tags menu.

Tip

Just like most things in Dreamweaver, you can personalize your Objects panel however
you'd like. This topic is discussed in Chapter 21, "Extensions and the Extension Manager,"
and Chapter 22, "Creating Your Own Objects and Behavior."

We will be focusing on the head category of the Objects panel. To switch categories, use
the drop-down menu located at the top of the panel. Clicking on a specific object icon
or dragging that object into the open document will activate a dialog box where you can
input further information so that Dreamweaver can insert meta tags.

Note

If no box appears after clicking an object, you should check your general preferences
and see if Show Dialog When Inserting Objects is checked. If not, you can either check it
or edit your head content by selecting View/Head Content from the menu. This will
enable you to select head elements and edit their content via the Property Inspector. A
second way to view the head content is by selecting Head Content from the View
Options Toolbar icon.

Exercise 3.1   Inserting Various Types of Meta Tags

Meta tags have nearly an unlimited number of options. You can define any type of data to be used as a meta tag; however, it is up to the Web server and the browser to correctly interpret custom tags.

Part I   Inserting Meta Tags

To insert a meta tag, do the following:

1. Click the Meta icon of the Objects panel.
2. Select the Name meta attribute.
3. Enter the value that the attribute should hold—in this case, **copyright**.
4. Enter **Copyright 2000 Blurred Vision Studios L.L.C.** as the content of the value ().
5. The box should look something like what's shown in Figure 3.1. Press OK.

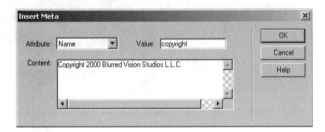

Figure 3.1   The Insert Meta dialog box.

Part II   Inserting a Keyword Meta Tag

This object inserts keywords for search engine spiders to analyze. Some spiders will accept only a certain number of keywords, so it's important to keep this list packed with powerful words that describe the page. You enter words separated by commas into the Keywords text field. To insert a keyword meta tag, follow these steps:

1. Click the Keywords icon of the Objects panel.
2. Enter the keywords **freeware, shareware, programs, download** for your page in the Keywords text box.
3. Your screen should look somewhat similar to Figure 3.2. Press OK.

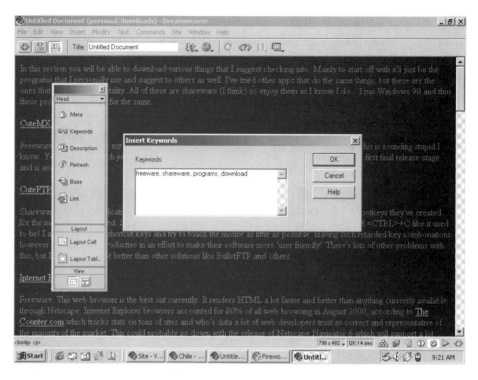

Figure 3.2   The Insert Keywords dialog box.

Part III   Inserting a Description Meta Tag

This object inserts a brief description of what the page is about. Search engines use this content as well in indexing your page. You enter complete sentences describing your page in the Description text field. To insert a description meta tag, do the following:

1. Click the Description icon of the Objects panel.

2. Enter **Download John Pickett's favorite software, including CuteFTP, Internet Explorer, and more!** as the description of your page.

3. Your screen should resemble Figure 3.3 at this point. Now select OK.

Tip

You can learn how to better utilize and manipulate search engines by visiting J.K. Bowman's Spider Food Web site at `www.spider-food.net`.

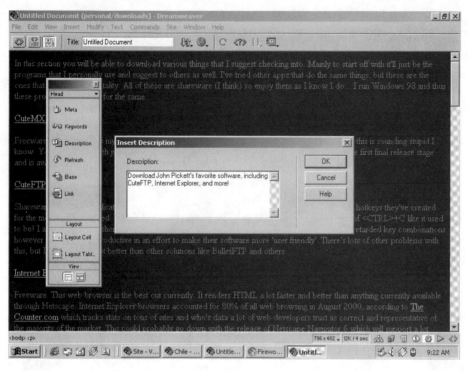

Figure 3.3   The Insert Description dialog box.

Part IV   Inserting a Refresh MetaTag

This meta tag will refresh the Web page at a given interval specified in the Delay text field. The Action selection lets you specify whether the current page should be refreshed or whether a new page should load. If you are creating a news site that is updated every 30 seconds, you might want to automatically refresh the current page every 30 seconds or minute. If you have recently moved your page to a new Web server but still have visitors at the old address, you may specify a timeout of 10 seconds and then load the new address for the user. To make your page automatically refresh or load another URL, do the following:

Note

> You must be careful when selecting the refresh delay. An entry of 0 (zero) will cause the page to reload immediately. This would obviously be an extreme nuisance and drive users away. Likewise, making users sit viewing a message that simply tells them that the site has moved to a new location and that they will be forwarded momentarily is not a good idea either. As a rule, 5- or 10-second timeouts seem to be a good standard to live by.

1. Click the Refresh icon on the Objects panel.

2. Enter 7 as the delay time (in seconds) in the Delay text box.

3. Select what action you want to occur. Selecting Refresh This Document will simply reload the current page after every number of seconds that was specified in the Delay text box.

4. If you selected Go to URL as the action, you must now specify a URL to send the page to after the number of seconds specified in the Delay text box (www.mynewsite.com).

5. Your screen should look similar to Figure 3.4, depending on the options you choose. Press OK.

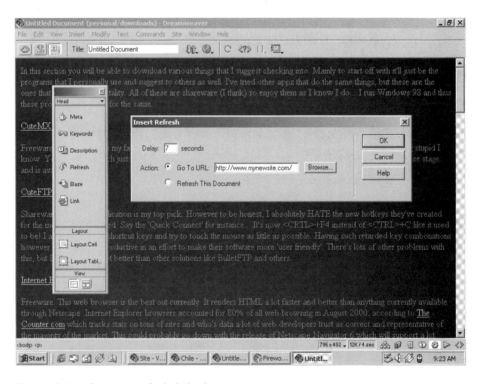

Figure 3.4   The Insert Refresh dialog box.

Part V   Inserting a Base Meta Tag

This tag enables you to change the base directory that document-relative links refer to. You specify the path in the HREF text field and have the option of specifying a target where the linked item should load. This tag can also be used to set the target for all links on your page. If you want every link on your page to open in a new window or the same frame, set it here. This way you don't have to set the target for each individual link.

Insert a base meta tag by doing the following:

1. Click the Base icon on the Objects panel.

2. Enter **http://www.mynewsite.com/old/** as the path that you want to make every link relative to.

3. You can also select a target if you want, although you should just leave it blank for this exercise.

4. You should now have something similar to Figure 3.5. Press OK.

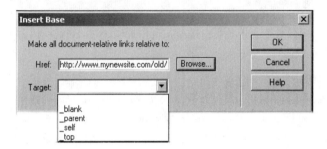

Figure 3.5   You can choose from _blank, _parent, _self, or _top as a target for a base meta tag.

In this exercise, if a document's "real" path was http://www.mynewsite.com/docs/webpage.htm, the new path assigned by the base tag would be http://www.mynewsite.com/old/webpage.htm.

Part IV   Inserting a Link Meta Tag

This tag does not serve the same purpose as a normal link between documents found in the BODY. It serves to define relationships between the document and other external files. Most commonly you will see style sheets linked with this tag. To insert a link meta tag into your page, do the following:

1. Click the Link icon on the Objects panel.

2. Enter the path and filename of the document you want to link. For this exercise, use **styles/textfont.css**.

3. You have the option to enter an ID. This is a special identifier for the linked file. Leave this field blank here. You can also give the linked file a title, which is a short descriptor of the file and can be thought of as having a similar relationship as the document title has with an HTML document. Again, leave this field blank.

4. You can specify a Rel and Rev attribute as well. The Rel attribute specifies the relationship to the linked item. Possible entries include: style sheet, contents, copyright, and index. Enter **stylesheet** to show the relation to a style sheet. Rev specifies the exact opposite relationship and has the same possible entries as the Rel attribute. Leave this field blank.

5. You should now have something similar to Figure 3.6. If so, press OK.

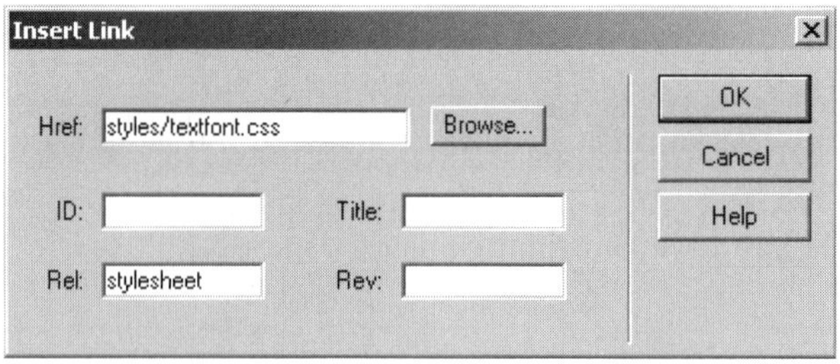

Figure 3.6   Most of the attributes are regularly unnecessary except the Rel attribute.

Inserting Scripts

Integrating various scripts with your Web page is one of the best ways to take user inter-action to the next level. Combined with style sheets, JavaScript and other scripting lan-guages provide the basis of what we call Dynamic HTML, or DHTML. You can see DHTML at work by visiting Microsoft's Web site (www.microsoft.com) and using the top navigation.

Note

Although it is possible to insert scripts in either the HEAD or the BODY, it is consid-ered good technique to include all necessary scripts in the HEAD, so that is discussed here.

As you've come to expect, Dreamweaver offers multiple ways to insert scripts into your HTML. These scripts will most likely be either JavaScript or VBScript, although when using Dreamweaver, JavaScript tends to be more popular.

Tip

Literally hundreds of prewritten scripts are available on the Internet that you can copy and paste into your code. Even better, Dreamweaver uses specially designed scripts called extensions to automate the process. These vigorously defined scripts enable you to set all the actions and properties needed for the script to function in a friendly graphical user interface (GUI). Extensions are covered in great detail in Chapter 21.

Exercise 3.2   Inserting JavaScript or VBScript

Before inserting a script into your HTML, make sure that the Objects panel is active (select Window/Objects or press Ctrl+F2) and that the Invisibles category is selected.

To insert a script, do the following:

1. Position the cursor where you want the script to be inserted in your Web page, and then select Script from the Objects panel. You can access the Script window through Insert/Invisible Tags/Script as well.

2. You must now select what type of script you will be inserting. Options range from generic JavaScript to VBScript. If you don't know what version of JavaScript you are writing, select JavaScript. For this exercise, select JavaScript.

3. You can now enter the scripting into the Content text field. The JavaScript code that you should enter is Macromedia's preload images behavior code found there:

```
<!--
function MM_preloadImages() { //v3.0
   var d=document; if(d.images){ if(!d.MM_p) d.MM_p=new Array();
      var i,j=d.MM_p.length,a=MM_preloadImages.arguments; for(i=0;
      i<a.length; i++)
                  if  (a[i].indexOf("#")!=0){  d.MM_p[j]=new  Image;
d.MM_p[j++].src=a[i];}}
}
//-->
```

4. You should come up with something similar to what is shown in Figure 3.7. Press OK.

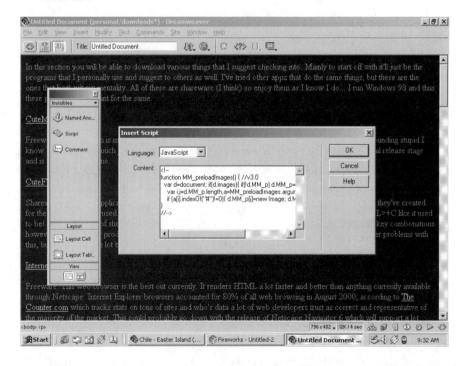

Figure 3.7   Although novice users may use this object to insert JavaScript, you will eventually want to delve into the raw HTML for yourself and do this manually.

To edit a script, make sure that View/Visual Aids/Invisible Elements is checked. Now select the Script icon in your code and view the Property Inspector. You can change the language of the code, select Edit to edit the script manually, or distinguish if the script is either client-side or server-side. You also can link to an external script by entering a file in the Source field or choosing one by selecting the Folder icon next to it.

Some older browsers will not recognize scripts. To circumvent this issue, it is common and strongly suggested to engulf your scripts in comment tags. This will cause the older browsers to bypass the code rather than display it as normal text or return an error. Dreamweaver already does this for its own scripts, but you will have to do it for any scripts that you add manually. The following is an example:

```
<script language="JavaScript">
<!-- This is the start of the comment
function my_function(parameter1,parameter2)
{
all of your script coding goes here
}
//--> this is the end of the comment
</script>
```

Note

> If you want to link to an external script, do not put anything in the Content text field of the script object. After you add the blank script, you can then link it by using the Property Inspector. Likewise, if you have a script in which you've entered content previously and decide to link to a file, be sure to delete the current content of the script.

<BODY> Content

The actual content of a Web page—what the user sees—is contained in the BODY of an HTML document. This includes most everything you encounter while visiting a Web site, including text, images, tables, and so on. Dreamweaver does an excellent job of keeping you focused on the design of a page rather than fiddling with complicated coding. Almost anything that *can* be placed on a Web page can be done so very easily through Dreamweaver's intuitive design interface.

Logical Versus Physical Markup

Something to keep in mind while entering your content is the type of markup that you want to use. Two types exist: logical and physical. Logical markup (or style) defines a relationship to the neighboring tags on a page. Physical markup, on the other hand, is generally specific, regardless of what other kids of tags surround it. An example is the size of your text. Using a logical style, you would use the <BIG> tag. With physical styles, you would specify something to the effect of <FONT SIZE=6>. Which one you use is typically a matter of taste, but sometimes you need to know exactly what the outcome will be before releasing it to the hungry Web surfers that await. Although physical styles can aid you in this endeavor to a degree, utilizing the point or pixel specificity of style sheets will give you more control over the appearance of your elements. Style sheets are discussed in Chapter 12, "Using Cascading Style Sheets."

I've talked with many developers to see whether the majority prefers logical or physical styles. Most prefer physical styles in the absence of style sheets. Some exceptions exist in which logical styles are extremely convenient, however. For instance, the code examples that you see throughout this book could easily be coded in HTML using the <CODE> tag. <CODE> augments multiple characteristics of the text that you enter, making it significantly more efficient to use than a group of physical style tags.

Note

Dreamweaver does not support automatic insertion of all logical style tags. If you choose to use logical tags (or any tag, for that matter) that are not supported in Dreamweaver's interface, you will need to either download an extension that will do it for you (if such an extension exists at the time) or hand-code the tag(s) using the multiple methods that Dreamweaver allows for manual tag placement. Most HTML tags that Dreamweaver won't insert for you automatically either are not widely supported among the popular Web browsers or have become depreciated over time with newer versions of the HTML specification. Editing your raw HTML is discussed in the next section of this chapter.

Which style you prefer is exactly that, a preference. There are advantages as well as disadvantages to using each. These two methods shouldn't be looked at as opposing forces, but rather as separate tools that can be used together to create an effective and efficient Web page.

Commenting Your HTML

Any programmer will tell you of the extreme importance of comments in code. Comments allow responsibility to be shared with many when creating complex programs and routines. Poorly written (or nonexistent) comments will only result in late-night headaches when you need to change something in your code four months later.

The same holds true with HTML. Although perhaps not as vital as the more serious languages, commenting is a valuable asset. Not only can notes of reason and other explanation be included in comments, but hidden information can be conveyed as well. Often a client does not want a small link at the bottom of its pages indicating that a certain company created the page. In this situation, prospective clients visit the site daily and might wonder who created it, but they would never know from the pages. With commenting, you can include a small amount of text at the beginning of the HTML source. This remains hidden from the browser window, but anyone who is really interested can view the source code and easily see who created the page.

Note

> Dreamweaver implements Design Notes, which are very similar to HTML comments but remain at the local level. A single user, or a group of users who are collaborating on a project, can view these notes inside Dreamweaver in an efficiently formatted window. Design Notes are discussed in full in Chapter 15, "Workplace Collaboration."

Exercise 3.3   Inserting and Editing Comments

The previous example may be a farfetched one, but the point is clear. Commenting is a good way to passively advertise, explain techniques used, and present other information that shouldn't be seen in the browser window. You will insert and then edit a comment in this exercise. To insert a comment, make sure that the Objects panel is active (select Window/Objects, or press Ctrl+F2) and that the Invisibles category is selected. Then do the following:

1. Position the cursor where you want the comment to be inserted in your Web page and then select Comment from the list. You can access the Comment window through Insert/Invisible Tags/Comment as well.

2. Enter **This page was designed by Blurred Vision Studios. Check us out at: http://www.bvstudios.com/** as the text you want commented into the Comment text field.

3. You should now have a screen similar to the one in Figure 3.8. Now press OK.

To edit a comment, make sure that View/Visual Aids/Invisible Elements is checked. Then do the following:

1. Select the Comment icon in your page.

2. Now change the bvstudios.com address to level67.net by editing the comment in the Property Inspector. It should then resemble Figure 3.9.

Tip

> Although we have discussed comments in the body, you can insert them in the head area as well. In fact, sometimes (such as when inserting a self-promotion comment) you want the comment as close to the top as possible. Comments are one of the few tags that can even be placed before the opening HTML tag (almost always the first tag in an HTML document). This won't affect the layout or look of the page, but it will allow anyone who views the source to see the comment before anything else.

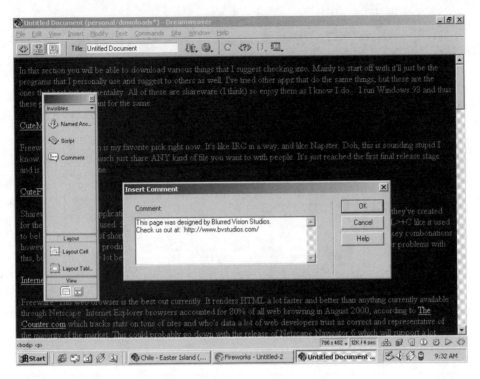

Figure 3.8   Inserting comments not only can give secret credit to yourself, but it also can help you remember why you did something a certain way when you need to edit the page six months later.

Figure 3.9   You can see the current comment content through the Property Inspector.

Page Attributes

When you create a new Web page in Dreamweaver, the default page title is Untitled Document. You likely will not want this to be what your user views when loading the page into a browser, so it should be one of the first things you change. If you are new to creating Web pages, the title is what will be displayed in the upper-left corner of the browser when your pages are viewed. Figure 3.10 illustrates this point. You may also want to change properties such as background color, background image, or the color of your links. You can do all this with the Page Properties dialog box.

Figure 3.10   Notice the page title, AnandTech. This is much more professional than "Untitled Document."

Tip

If you're not quite sure what you want to name your document, you can download and install Paul Madar's AutoTitle Untitled Documents extension, which automatically sets the page title to whatever you name the document .Although this may not be the most flattering title, it certainly is better than the default.You can always go back and change the title at a later time. Downloading, installing, and using extensions are discussed in Chapter 21.

A few ways exist to view the Page Properties dialog box, shown in Figure 3.11. You can either press Ctrl+J (Command+J); select Modify/Page Properties from the menu; or right-click (Ctrl+click) and select Page Properties from the bottom of the pop-up menu in any area of the document window that does not have an object on it. The exception to this rule is that you may right-click text as long as it is outside a table or other object.

Note

The new style of windows keyboards has a special key that acts just like right-clicking. If the cursor is on an "open" space in the document window, you can press this key and use the keyboard arrows to navigate to Page Properties.This key is called the application key and is found directly to the left of the right Ctrl key. Older keyboards may not have this key.

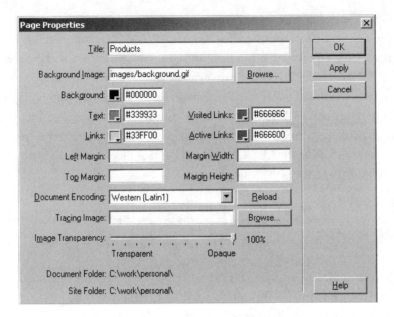

Figure 3.11   You can establish many properties, including the page title.

The following is a list of the various Page Properties attributes:

- **Title.** This is the title of your Web page. When Web browsers parse your HTML document, they place these contents in their title bar. The page title is also used by search engines to display a brief blurb of your page. The title is typically the "linked" text when displayed on a search engine. The HTML format for the title is <TITLE>Your Title Here</TITLE>.

Note

New to Dreamweaver 4, you can modify the page title at any time in the document window. The first way to do this is by making sure that the toolbar is active (choose View/Toolbar) and then changing the title in the toolbar. The other way is by selecting View/Head Content (also accessed by clicking the View Options icon on the toolbar and selecting Head Content) and selecting the Title icon. You can then edit the title in the Property Inspector (choose Window/Properties). This second method can be used to change other <head> content as well.

- **Background Image.** This attribute sets a graphic to be displayed in the background of the screen. These images can be GIF, JPEG, or even PNG images. If the image width and height is less than the content of your <BODY>, the image will be tiled both horizontally *and* vertically.

A brief note is in order here. If you don't want your background image to tile, you can (and must) use cascading style sheets (CSS) to accomplish this nontiling effect. CSS is covered in depth in Chapter 12. The syntax for a background image is <BODY BACKGROUND="image_name.gif">. You will notice that this property is set in the <BODY> tag. Certain *attributes* (such as the page background) must be set in HTML tags and don't use their own tag. These attributes modify or expand on the original function of the parent tag. Likewise, not all page properties are set using the <HEAD> tag, but because they control the main look of the entire page, they are included here:

Tip

You can force your background image to not tile by using cascading style sheets. This is covered fully in Chapter 12.

- **Background.** This attribute sets the background color for the page. Click the color swatch to modify the color used. You can use the eye-dropper tool that appears to select any color currently onscreen. You can also create your own color by choosing the System Color Picker icon. The default color palette contains Web-safe colors that should show up uniformly on most systems.

  To choose from different color palettes, click the drop-down menu located on the right side of the pop-up box, and select from either Color Cubes, Continuous Tone, Windows OS, Mac OS, or Grayscale. Only Color Cubes and Continuous Tone are Web-safe. Selecting Snap to Web Safe, however, will make Dreamweaver automatically select the closest Web-safe color when using the others. These numbers are represented in HTML as hexadecimal and have the syntax <BODY BGCOLOR="#000000">, where #000000 is the hexadecimal representation of the color.

Note

You can also use a number of text color descriptors designated by Netscape in version 1.1 of the Netscape Navigator Web browser. It is recommended that you use hexadecimal, however, because not all browsers support the color descriptors.

- **Text.** This attribute sets the color used for unlinked text on your page. Click the color swatch and apply colors in the same manner as the background color. The syntax for text color is <BODY TEXT="#339933">.

- **Links, Visited Links, Active Links.** Here you can set the color used for text links on your page. The links color is used for all links until a user clicks on them.

The active links color is then briefly used. Finally, the visited links color is used to let users know that they have previously selected a particular link. The syntax for link colors is <body link="#33FF00" vlink="#666666" alink="#666600">. These colors will display only in the browser. All links will always show up as the Links color in the Dreamweaver document window.

- **Left Margin, Top Margin, Margin Width, Margin Height.** Enter pixel values here to adjust the browser default used for page margins. Microsoft uses left and top margins, while Netscape uses margin width and height. Syntax for margins is <BODY LEFTMARGIN="0" TOPMARGIN="0" MARGINWIDTH="0" MAR-GINHEIGHT="0">. Leaving these blank will use the browser default, which is seldom 0. To ensure no margins in your page, you must actively set these numbers to 0.

- **Document Encoding.** This is the character format that you will be using on your page. The default type for most systems is Western (Latin 1). You must reload the character set after you select the new type. The syntax for document encoding is <META HTTP-EQUIV="Content-Type" CONTENT="text/html; Character Set">. More about meta tags is discussed in the next section.

- **Tracing Image, Image Transparency.** You can specify an image to use as a reference or layout guide for your page. The Image Transparency slider adjusts the alpha of this image to differentiate from your content. Using Tracing Images and Layers together can quickly and easily create Web pages. This method is discussed in Chapter 10, "Using Layers." The syntax for these is <BODY TRACINGSRC="image_name.gif" TRACINGOPACITY="100">. These tracing images don't actually appear in a browser; they are just for the designer's reference.

- **Document Folder.** This isn't an adjustable option; it simply reports in what local folder the current document is saved. The area to the right of this property is blank until you save the file. To adjust this, use the Site Files window. Chapter 13, "Site and File Organization," provides more information on file management.

- **Site Folder.** This isn't an adjustable option; it reports what the local Site Folder path is. Again, to adjust this, use the Site Files window. You can learn where to define your Site Folder in Chapter 13.

Editing Your HTML

Dreamweaver allows many ways for modifying your raw HTML from within the program. In fact, there are four main methods of accomplishing this, three of which are directly related to the current page view you're using. You have three "views" to choose from in Dreamweaver: the Design view, the Code and Design view (or Split view), and the Code view. To change your current view, either click the desired view icon on the toolbar or select View/Code, View/Code and Design or View/Design from the menu.

Design View (Quick Tag Editor)

Design view is not only the default view when opening an HTML document, but it is perhaps the most popular view mode as well because it offers the most design workspace for developers. This view is most effective for those who aren't comfortable working with HTML code and also is useful when initially creating or updating a Web page. The view by itself does not allow you to directly edit HTML, but Dreamweaver implements what is called the Quick Tag Editor to assist you in making changes while in this mode.

> **Note**
>
> Although Design view is the default view for HTML documents, other file types have other defaults. For example, JavaScript source files (*.js) open in Code view by default. You can modify these options in the File Types/Editors section of your Preferences. See Chapter 2, "Customizing Dreamweaver," for details on doing this.

> **Note**
>
> You can access the Quick Tag Editor in any of the three views, but it is best suited for discussion in Design view.

To access the Quick Tag Editor, simply select Modify/Quick Tag Editor; press Ctrl+T; or select the Quick Tag Editor icon from the top right corner of the Property Inspector.

The Quick Tag Editor has three edit modes, depending on the current selection of HTML: Insert HTML, Edit Tag, and Wrap Tag modes. Even though Dreamweaver uses its best judgment when deciding which mode to display by default, you can cycle through each mode by pressing Ctrl+T.

> **Tip**
>
> Using the keyboard shortcut Ctrl+T is the only way to cycle through the Quick Tag Editor modes. The other methods used to show the editor don't work because the Quick Tag Editor disappears when it loses focus.

You can position the Quick Tag Editor anywhere you want to by simply clicking and dragging the title bar. This is helpful in certain cases because the Quick Tag Editor typically appears above the current selection or cursor position. The exception to this rule is when opening the editor from the Property Inspector; in this case, it's located next to the Property Inspector. Although this may be perfectly fine for most people, some will be annoyed when the Tag Hints box appears and covers their selection. (You can adjust Tag Hints and other Quick Tag Editor settings under the Quick Tag section of Preferences. This is discussed in Chapter 2.)

Tip

You can toggle between Design view and Code view by pressing Ctrl+Tab. You must already be in one of the two modes to switch the view.

Insert HTML

This mode is the default invoked by calling the Quick Tag Editor when there is no selection made. The window presents you with an open and close bracket. You can enter sole tags, tags with attributes, and content here. When you're done, simply press Enter and the code is inserted into the document. The recently inserted tag and content will be highlighted. If you pause in typing for a moment, the Tag Hints box, shown in Figure 3.12, will appear, offering you possible selections from what you have already typed. When you have finished entering the desired tag and possible content, you do not need to type the closing tag. The Quick Tag Editor will do this for you, again simplifying your task. This mode can be used to insert tags that aren't automatically coded by Dreamweaver, such as the infamous <marquee> tag, which can be found among those listed in the tag hints.

Tip

Clicking on the design area will have the same effect as pressing Enter, except that the code will not be highlighted. To cancel the Quick Tag Editor without having the contents of the Editor take effect, press Esc. Something to keep in mind as well is that, when using Ctrl+T to toggle to the next mode, the code you entered in the previous box will be inserted into your document.

Edit Tag

When a tag is selected and the Quick Tag Editor is invoked, it defaults to this mode. Unlike the other two modes, the Edit Tag mode displays the selected tag along with its current attributes. To edit a tag, simply modify the attributes and content however you want, and press Enter (see Figure 3.13). As with the Insert HTML mode, you may also click on the design area, which will enter your modifications into the HTML.

Figure 3.12

Tag hints can be valuable if you haven't quite mastered the various HTML tags available.

This mode is useful when entering in tag attributes not supported by Dreamweaver. You can enter the main tag along with the majority of the attributes and then quickly add those that Dreamweaver doesn't support through this Quick Tag Editor mode.

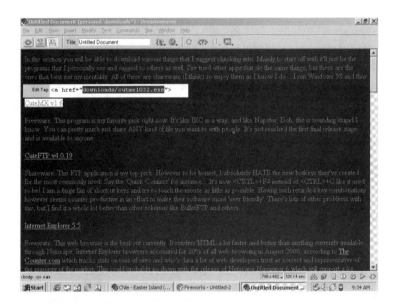

Figure 3.13   Editing a link with the Quick Tag Editor.

Tip

Another way to get the Edit Tag mode of the Quick Tag Editor to appear is to right-click (Option+click) the desired tag in the tag selector at the bottom left of the document window and then select Edit Tag.

Wrap Tag

If your selection contains only unformatted text or objects and you invoke the Quick Tag Editor, the Wrap Tag mode will appear, as in Figure 3.14. The tag that you enter into this box will "wrap" around the selection. For example, if you select the text, "This should be bold… but isn't." and press Ctrl+T, you could apply a bold formatting by simply placing a B between the opening and closing brackets (<B>). When you press Enter, the selection will then be rendered bold.

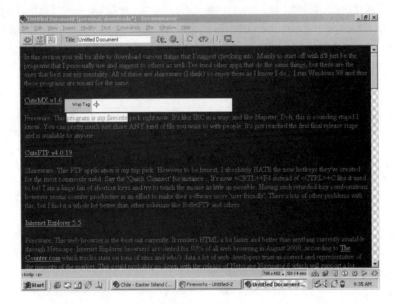

Figure 3.14   What you type here will wrap the current HTML selection.

Note

If your selection contains an opening or closing HTML tag, the Edit Tag mode will appear instead and the parent tag will be selected.

Code View and the Code Inspector

Although it's nice to have the quick, nonintrusive method of inserting and editing HTML that the Quick Tag Editor provides, being able to deal with larger blocks of HTML will help a beginner better understand what's going on in a Web page. It also gives those more accustomed to creating Web pages in Homesite, BBEdit, or other text editors a smoother transition to the WYSIWYG world.

Note

> On a related note, Dreamweaver now includes a JavaScript debugger, which can aid greatly in troubleshooting problem scripts. This feature is discussed in detail in Chapter 19, "JavaScripting with Dreamweaver."

Dreamweaver allows two methods of viewing your HTML source (actually four, if you count the Code and Design view, which is a combination of each view as well as the Quick Tag Editor). The first option is the Code Inspector. This was included in past versions of Dreamweaver. New to Dreamweaver 4, however, is Code view. Both Code view and the Code Inspector give the same interface and functionality; the only difference is that the Code Inspector is a floating window while in Code view and is your main editing interface.

Tip

> A growing number of Web designers have begun using two monitors while designing their Web pages. One monitor would strictly show Design view, while the other would be used to show all the panels and inspectors. The Code Inspector could be placed in this second monitor. This increasingly popular dual-viewing capability is, to a lesser degree, achieved with Dreamweaver's new Code and Design view, discussed in the next section.

To switch to Code view, either click Show Code View from the toolbar or select View/Code from the menu. You can also switch instantly between Design view and Code view by pressing Ctrl+Tab. (Remember that you must be in either Design or Code view initially for Ctrl+Tab to switch between the two views.) To open the Code Inspector, press F10 or select Window/Code Inspector from the menu. You can also use the icon on the minilauncher.

While in Code view (or Code Inspector—these terms can almost be used interchangeably, but a distinction needs to exist for clarification purposes), you can insert images and other HTML elements in the same manner as you would in Design view. Rather than seeing the picture inserted, however, you will see the HTML code for inserting a picture. In Code view, changes made aren't immediately implemented. To make your changes take effect, do one of the following:

- Press F5.
- Press Ctrl+Spacebar.
- Click the refresh icon on your toolbar or your Property Inspector.
- Switch to Design view by either clicking the Show Design View icon on the toolbar or pressing Ctrl+Tab.

The View Options icon on the toolbar gives you an array of popular choices while in Code view. These can also be accessed through View/Code View Options. Each option is outlined in the following list:

- **Word Wrap.** Specifies whether your HTML code should wrap to the next line when it reaches the end of the display. This is solely used as a tool to ease understanding when editing HTML or when viewing the page source from a Web browser. However, it will not affect how your pages are rendered in browsers.

- **Line Numbers.** Lists line numbers in a column on the very left margin of your window (see Figure 3.15). This is useful for debugging problems in your code.

- **Highlight Invalid HTML.** Highlights code that Dreamweaver does not recognize as valid.

- **Syntax Coloring.** Sets the color of HTML elements based on the Code Colors section of your preferences.

- **Auto Indent.** Automatically indents your code based on the Code Format section of your preferences.

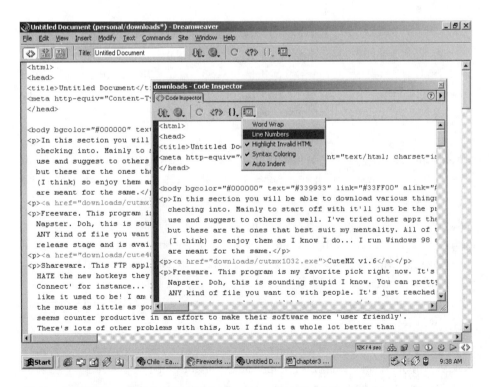

Figure 3.15   Line numbers will soon become your best friend if you do heavy custom JavaScripting.

Another useful facet of this view is Code Navigation. You can navigate between JavaScript functions in your document by using the Code Navigation toolbar icon. This is a fast and effective way for JavaScript professionals to navigate their code.

Code and Design View

The Quick Tag Editor used in Design view is adequate in most instances, but sometimes you'll need to continually edit a block of text or set of tags. To keep invoking the Quick Tag Editor to do this would be very annoying and slow. Similarly, if you are new to the world of HTML tags and have no clue what they actually "do," looking at the source certainly can help you learn how to read and edit raw HTML. Unfortunately, switching back and forth between Design view and Code view is time-consuming and bothersome.

To this end, new to Dreamweaver 4 is the Code and Design view. It allows real-time control over the design and HTML of your page by providing both a WYSIWYG view and the raw HTML code view. To switch to Code and Design view, select View/Code and Design, or click the Show Code and Design Views icon on the toolbar. This will split your workspace into two areas. By default, your HTML code is on the top section, while underneath is your Design view.

You can switch the focus of your cursor between the two views by pressing Ctrl+Tab or selecting View/Switch Views from the menu. You also might want to invert the default layout and have the Design view rather than the code on top. To accomplish this, select View/Design View on Top from the menu, or select Design View on Top from the Options pop-up menu on the toolbar (see Figure 3.16).

You can adjust the ratio of code to Design view space by moving your mouse over the bar separating the two views (the horizontal line directly beneath the scrollbar, if any, for Code view). Your cursor will change pointers to show that it can adjust the height of this window. Simply click and drag until you get the desired proportion.

Although you edit your page in the design portion, Code view automatically updates and jumps to your current editing position. One great thing about this view, especially if you're new or struggling with how HTML is implemented or formatted, is that as you insert pictures, make text bold, or do anything to the document, Code view updates immediately, showing you how the code for each is inserted. This helps you learn how to code raw HTML.

Editing content in the Code view portion isn't quite as instantaneous. You can make changes without them taking effect immediately. You must update the Design view portion in the same manner of updating while in Code view before the changes will show in the design area.

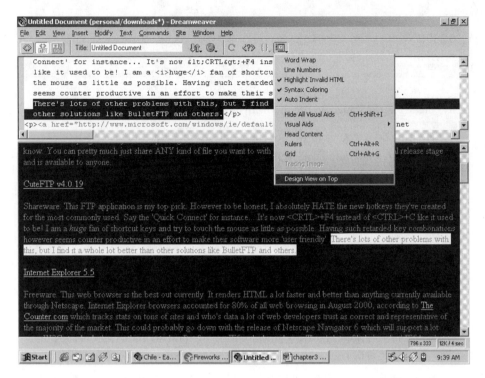

Figure 3.16   Options available when in Split view mode.

Reference Panel

Over time, you will undoubtedly begin to learn some HTML tags, regardless of your past experience. However, memorizing all of them would be extremely difficult. Even if you learned them all, it would be a challenge to know each well enough to define them. Add to that the countless attributes, CSS elements, JavaScript, and other scripting languages that you have the opportunity to use, and you have hundreds, if not thousands, of elements to remember. Most people would probably need a dictionary just to help them sort through all the possibilities.

Dreamweaver agrees. Bundled for free, and integrated completely with Dreamweaver's interface, is an extensive HTML, JavaScript, and CSS dictionary and usage guide. To access it, select Window/Reference, or press Ctrl+Shift+F1. You can control the size of the font displayed by selecting Small, Medium, or Large Font from the drop-down menu located in the upper-right corner of the Reference panel.

Tip

Another way to access the Reference panel is to select the Reference icon located on the toolbar. Doing so automatically displays the description of the tag selected (or cursor position).

To use the Reference panel, do the following:

1. Select the book you want to use. These options include O'Reilly CSS reference, HTML reference, and JavaScript reference. You can make selections by using the pull-down list and using the mouse, or you may use the up and down arrows. Page Up and Page Down are supported in the reference panel as well.

2. Depending on the book selected, you can now select the style attribute, tag, or object you want to find information on.

3. After selecting an element of the book, a general description will be displayed (see Figure 3.17, which shows a description of the <BLINK> tag). This description displays syntax, examples, and a general overview of the function of that particular element. The CSS book provides descriptions only, while the HTML and JavaScript books have expanded information on attributes, properties, and methods. To select an attribute associated with an HTML tag, or to select a property or method of a JavaScript object, use the pull-down menu to the right of the tag or object selector.

The Reference panel is also context-sensitive. This means that if you select a tag in the Code portion of Split view or Code view and then view the Reference panel, it will have automatically selected the entry corresponding to your selection. This feature works only if syntax coloring is turned on.

The upper-right corner of the Reference panel display area specifies whether the current element is compatible with Netscape Navigator and Internet Explorer and, if so, which version first instigated support for it. This area also tells the version of the books' governing structure in which the particular element was introduced (such as CSS 1, HTML 4, or DOM 1). In addition, the CSS book specifies whether the particular style is inherited; the HTML book specifies whether the particular tag requires a closing tag.

Cleaning Up Your HTML

After you've created your Web pages, you've undoubtedly gone back and hacked away at the source code more times than you can count or even used an external editor (discussed in the next section) to get your page *exactly* how you want it to look. So now you're done, right?

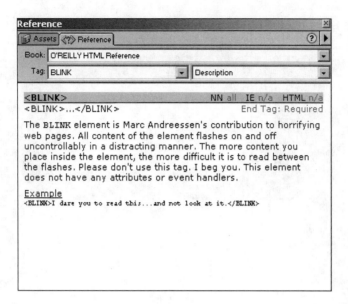

Figure 3.17   The Reference panel shows a description of the element that you select. For example, <BLINK> is one tag that nearly all designers will agree should be used with extreme caution and prejudice.

Well, that depends on how good you are at writing HTML. I won't lie—there's a certain amount of luck involved as well. Most of the time however, you will be stuck with empty tags (tags that have no content between the opening and closing tags), multiple tags (tags that are repeated more than once), and other hard-to-read or noncompliant code.

Dreamweaver makes cleaning up your HTML a very easy process. To clean up your HTML, select Commands/Clean Up HTML from the menu. After selecting what kind of cleanup you want Dreamweaver to perform in the dialog box shown in Figure 3.18, click OK. This may take a little while, depending on the complexity and length of your HTML document.

The following is a list of the options available when cleaning up your HTML:

- **Empty Tags.** This removes tags that have no content between the opening and closing tag. For instance, <i></i> is an empty tag and would be removed, while <i>this needs italics</i> would not be removed.

- **Redundant Nested Tags.** A nested tag is a tag whose parent tag is the same. This includes tag attributes as well. For instance, in <U>this needs to be underlined so people <u>KNOW</u> what I'm trying to say</u>, the u tags around the word "know" would be removed.

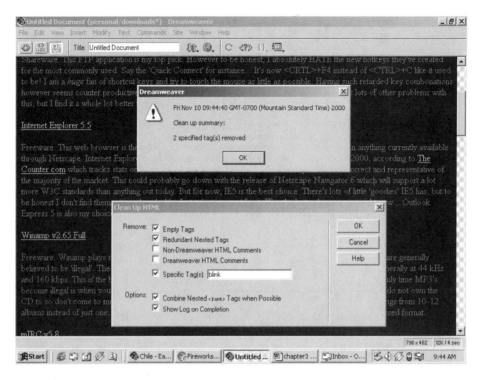

Figure 3.18   Cleaning up your HTML is always a good idea, especially after someone else has had the opportunity to "tweak" your code.

- **Non-Dreamweaver HTML Comments.** This removes comments made in your page that were not issued by Dreamweaver.

- **Dreamweaver HTML Comments.** This removes comments made in your page that were issued by Dreamweaver. This would cause Dreamweaver to stop recognizing the particular document as a template-based page (if it was a template). When updating the template, this page would no longer update. Library items on the page would be affected in the same manner. Likewise, this would affect the Roundtrip capabilities of Dreamweaver. This option uses comments to associate images with their source .png files.

- **Specific Tag(s).** This enables you to remove specific tags, such as <b>, that you might not want in your document. Multiple tags are separated by commas (for example b, blockquote). This removes both the opening and closing instances of the tag.

- **Combine Nested <font> Tags When Possible.** This combines multiple font tags into one tag if each tag contains different attributes (or the same value for like attributes). An example of this is <font color="#339933"><font face="Arial, Helvetica, sans-serif">. This text is dark green in Arial font. </font></FONT> would be combined into the following font tag: <font color="#339933" face="Arial, Helvetica, sans-serif>.

- **Show Logon Completion.** This displays a summary of what Dreamweaver cleaned up after it's finished.

Doing this might not provide much of a visible difference when people view your page online. However, it will allow your page to load more quickly in a browser.

Using External Editors

When you become more comfortable with editing HTML using Code view, or if you've always been a hand-coder in the past and don't want to let go of that control, Dreamweaver enables you to use other programs to edit HTML. Although any program you use is totally separate from Dreamweaver, Dreamweaver does a fairly good job of closely integrating itself with the text editor. It's called Roundtrip HTML.

What Is Roundtrip HTML?

Roundtrip HTML is a process more than anything else—it is the process of opening an external text editor, modifying the document in this separate program, saving the file, and having Dreamweaver automatically keep track of and update any changes made to the file. After you've made your changes in the external editor, Dreamweaver will want to reload the document. Doing so will make Dreamweaver parse the HTML again and rewrite it to reflect your changes, along with your code preferences specified in the Code Rewriting section. One important thing to remember is that Dreamweaver will not rewrite any tag that it does not recognize. It will mark the tag as invalid, but it won't rewrite it. This is useful when editing ColdFusion or Active Server Pages (ASP) in Dreamweaver.

Homesite, BBEdit, TextPad, and Notepad

Homesite is the default external editor bundled with Dreamweaver for Windows. BBEdit is the default for Macintosh versions. To use an external HTML editor, you must set Dreamweaver to recognize it properly:

1. Select Edit/Preferences and go to the File Types/Editors section. You can access your preferences by pressing Ctrl+U as well.

2. Select the Browse button to the right of the External Code Editor box. (If you are using a Macintosh, see the following note.)

3. Navigate to the correct program executable (.exe), and select Open.

Here you can also specify what Dreamweaver should do if it detects that a file has been modified. You can also control whether Dreamweaver should save the file before opening it in the external editor.

Note

The Macintosh version of Dreamweaver is very closely integrated with BBEdit, which is bundled on the Dreamweaver CD. If you want to use an editor other than BBEdit, you must deselect the Enable BBEdit Integration option. BBEdit Integration works very similar to Code view in that it tracks the cursor/selection position and automatically updates both programs to changes made in either interface.

To launch the editor with your current document, select Edit/Edit with Name Of Program. You can also access this by pressing Ctrl+E.

Summary

In this chapter, you've seen how advanced and powerful Dreamweaver is when it comes to manually editing HTML. You learned the basics of HTML and how it is structured, as well as how to navigate and utilize each of the three viewing modes that Dreamweaver offers. We also talked about the Reference panel (which should be any designer's constant companion) as well as how to add the finishing finesse to your pages by cleaning up the HTML code.

Part II

HTML Creation Fundamentals

Chapter 4

Working with Text

No matter what kind of Web page you're

building, the time will come when you will

be working with text inside Dreamweaver.

Either you will be typing your own text or

importing text from other programs, such

as Microsoft Word, or copying and pasting text from the Web. Probably, you will do all three things.

Although dealing with text is not considered to be the most advanced thing a Web developer or designer can do, that doesn't mean it is always easy. Line breaks, fonts, and spacing issues cause frustrations that might make you want to convert everything to 12-point Times New Roman just to be done with it. If you know a few things about text and about how Dreamweaver codes your text behind the scenes, however, you will be able to take advantage of many different styles, colors, and fonts, adding life to your site in a snap.

This chapter covers the following:

- Copying and pasting rext
- Importing text
- Font faces, styles, and sizes
- Text indentation and alignment
- Text color
- HTML styles
- Special characters

On the Web, you will see many different uses of text. Some sites use images for headings and HTML for their body text. A site such as Washingtonpost.com deals with an enormous amount of text every day. The combination of HTML body text and image heads works for them. On their home page, they use mainly HTML text and some image headings (see Figure 4.1). Because they have to cram a large number of links, captions, and blurbs into a very small space, they keep things simple, yet colorful.

In another example, Mindseye.com uses a streaming fonts technique on their site. The results are beautiful (see Figure 4.2).

You can use cascading style sheets (CSS) to achieve a similar look. (Chapter 12, "Using Cascading Style Sheets" discusses CSS in detail.) Throughout this chapter, the merits of using CSS for your text formatting are explained. For now, however, the discussion begins with the basics of copying and pasting text into Dreamweaver 4.

Figure 4.1   The Washingtonpost.com home page.

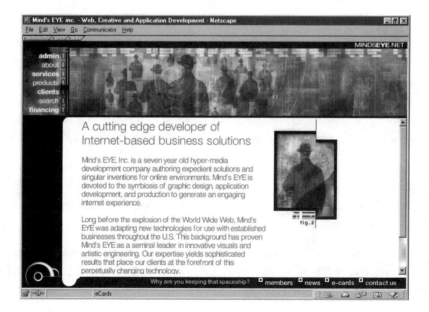

Figure 4.2   Mindseye.com impresses clients with terrific use of type.

Importing Text

This section takes a look at three different situations:

- You want to copy text from the Web browser window (not the HTML code) and paste it into a Dreamweaver document.

- You want to copy text from Dreamweaver and paste it into another program.

- You want to import text from Microsoft Word into a Dreamweaver document to publish on the Web.

Tip

You can spell-check your text inside Dreamweaver. To access the spell checker, pull down Text/Check Spelling from the main menu, or use the keyboard shortcut Shift+F7.

Pasting Text into Dreamweaver

If you copy text from the Web browser window, you have two choices for pasting it from your Clipboard into your Dreamweaver document. Pull down Dreamweaver's Edit menu to see the two options. One is called Paste; the other is called Paste HTML. What's the difference?

Paste inserts your Clipboard contents into your document, retaining the line breaks and, in some cases, the formatting (such as bold letters). If you don't want to inherit another's line breaks (indicated in HTML as <BR>), you have to delete them yourself. To speed up this task, make a selection and use a Find/Replace Query (discussed in Chapter 14, "Site Publishing, Maintenance, and Reporting") to eliminate the unwanted tags. Alternatively, use the Cleanup HTML command, and enter <**BR**> in the box for Specific Tags.

What about the other option? Paste HTML mimics the behavior found in previous versions of Dreamweaver. If you use this option to paste in your text, you will find that all line breaks are removed, leaving you with what looks like an extremely long run-on sentence (see Figure 4.3).

One of the advantages of Paste HTML is that you can give your text a fresh start and use Dreamweaver as your HTML formatting tool, instead of dealing with someone else's idea of how your text should look.

Pasting HTML

Different results will be obtained if you use these two features to paste HTML source code into a Dreamweaver document.

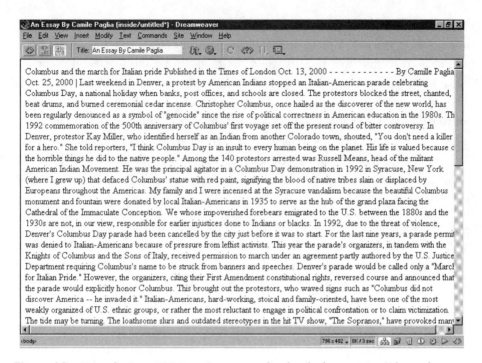

Figure 4.3   Using the Paste HTML option removes line breaks from text copied out of a browser window.

Paste quite literally pastes the source code into your page. In other words, the <BR> tags show up as <BR> rather than as a literal line break.

Paste HTML inserts the physical manifestation of the HTML. Therefore, a <BR> shows up as a literal line break rather than a <BR> tag on the page.

Tip

You can insert your Clipboard text between the <PRE> and </PRE> HTML tags to retain line breaks.

Exporting Text from Dreamweaver

Sometimes you will want to copy text from a Dreamweaver document into another program. In past versions of Dreamweaver, the text you copied would have pasted into another program with HTML tags embedded. In Dreamweaver 4, however, your text pastes into other programs as plain text, *sans* HTML tags. If you want to export the text with the HTML tags, change into Code view (use Ctrl+Tab to toggle Code view and Design view) and select the section you want to copy. If you do it this way, your HTML tags will be included when you paste the text into another program.

Importing Text from Microsoft Word

It happens to every Web designer eventually: Someone sends you a Microsoft Word document, requesting that you "use your magic" to convert this wonderful document into a Web page. Scrolling though the file, you see all that's not wonderful: tables, charts, bulleted lists, and other MS Word formatting that could mean hours of HTML coding for you. It's time to get smart and thank the Macromedia Dreamweaver team for creating the Clean Up Word HTML command. Let's take a look at this command, and explore how you can use it. The example here uses the Mushroom Shrimp Sukiyaki recipe (on your CD, the file is called RECIPE1.DOC). You must open this file inside Microsoft Word to follow along.

To make things quick and easy, copy the text of the recipe onto your Clipboard while in Microsoft Word. Then create a new document in Dreamweaver. From the Edit menu, choose Paste. You then have the text of the recipe inside Dreamweaver, but all formatting such as the text colors and styles are lost. In some cases, this will be what you want. Since print-to-Web conversions are so tricky, you're often better off reformatting the document to fit an electronic environment, especially if it is a smaller document with simple formatting.

You may think it takes too much time to reformat the text inside Dreamweaver, but more than likely, you will save time in the end.

Saving an HTML File from Microsoft Word

If the MS Word document you're dealing with is long and contains elaborate formatting such as tables and charts, you can use the Save As Web Page command in Microsoft Word and open the resulting HTML file in Dreamweaver.

> **Tip**
>
> You can open Word HTML inside Dreamweaver with either the File/Open menu option, or by creating a new document and choosing File/Import/Import Word HTML.

Freshly imported into Dreamweaver, the HTML version of any Word HTML won't look so hot (see Figure 4.4). Take a close look at the code that appears at the top of the screenshot.

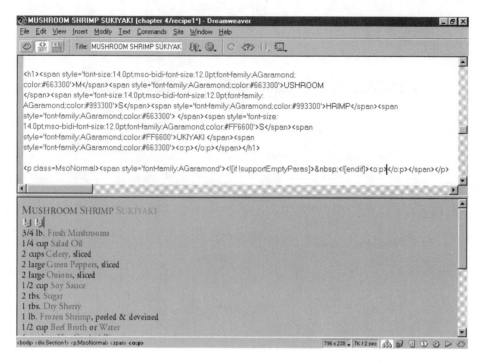

Figure 4.4   Microsoft Word HTML shown in Code view.

The problem with using the Save As Web Page command in Microsoft Word is that Microsoft Word HTML is actually a mix of HTML and XML code. It also includes an abundance of CSS styles and countless <META> tags, which significantly worsen the situation. As you can see, the code in the upper window of Figure 4.4 is a far cry from the plain HTML you would write if coding by hand.

When working with a Microsoft Word HTML file, you have the option of leaving it as is, meaning that you would make no changes to it in Dreamweaver or any other software program. If you do this, the file will usually look presentable in most Web browsers (especially Internet Explorer).

If you need to make changes to the Microsoft Word HTML file in Dreamweaver, however, you should use the Clean Up Word HTML command first to remove extraneous tags. Additionally, using this command removes document-level CSS styles that can extend page-loading time.

To use the Clean Up Word HTML command, open your Word HTML file inside Dreamweaver, and select Commands/Clean Up Word HTML.

Figure 4.5 shows the resulting window. The checked boxes inside this box indicate the Dreamweaver defaults.

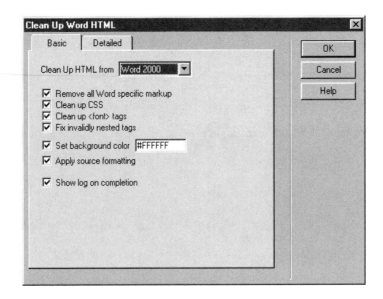

Figure 4.5   The Clean Up Word HTML dialog box.

Inside the box, click the tab marked Detailed to view more about the options. Click OK to accept the defaults and convert the HTML. For more information about the options under the Basic tab, take a look at Table 4.1.

Table 4.1   Basic Tab Options

Option	Description
Remove all Word specific markup	Removes all XML from HTML tags and other Word-specific formatting and other formatting that is specific to Microsoft Word.
Clean up CSS	Removes tags that refer to cascading style sheets, including inline CSS styles (as long as the parent style shares the same style properties). It also removes style attributes beginning with mso, and non-CSS-style descriptions.
	This tag is beneficial because Microsoft Word HTML relies heavily on CSS styles for formatting, most of them being document-level styles that increase page-loading time in the Web browser.
Clean up <font> Tags	Removes the <FONT> HTML tags and converts the default body text to size 2.

Option	Description
Fix invalidly nested tags	Removes invalid <FONT> tags. Invalid <FONT> tags are those found in spots where the <FONT> tag shouldn't be, according to the World Wide Web Consortium (W3C). Specifically, these are the <FONT> tags outside the paragraph and heading (block-level) tags.
Set background color	To use a hexadecimal value to set the background color of your document, enter it into the Text field box. Without a set background color, the document will have a gray background. By default, the background color is white, or #FFFFFF.
Apply source formatting	Applies the source formatting options that you specified in your SOURCEFORMAT.TXT file. This file is located in your Configuration folder. (See Chapter 2, "Customizing Dreamweaver," for more about setting your preferences.)
Show log on completion	Check this box to see a log listing what changes have been made.

You can use the options in the Detailed tab to make even more changes to the conversion.

After you make your selections, click OK. Dreamweaver processes the file and a cleaned-up version of the page appears in the document window.

Tip

> If you find that your HTML code contains unwanted tags even after you clean up, try looking at your HTML Format preferences to make sure you have them set the way you want. Alternatively, you can run a Find/Replace query (covered in Chapter 14) to get rid of even more tags, or run the general Clean Up HTML command.

Tip

> You can download an extension to change the case of Macromedia.com. If this extension is installed, you can easily convert all capital letters to lowercase and vice versa. This is much faster and easier than changing case manually. Go to www.macromedia.com/exchange/ and search extensions for "case."

Formatting Text with the Property Inspector

After you have your text inside a Dreamweaver document and have cleaned up the HTML (if necessary), you can spice up the appearance of the text by formatting the font faces, styles, alignment, and colors. One easy way to accomplish basic text formatting is to select the text and edit the font face, color, and style using the Property Inspector (Ctrl+F3).

Before starting, you should know that the <FONT> tag is used inside your HTML code when you format text with the Property Inspector. This can be something of a disadvantage.

Increasingly, Web designers are turning away from the <FONT> tag in favor of CSS. The reason for this evolution is that CSS offers more font-formatting options and can create better looking text on the Web than what can be obtained through use of the <FONT> tag. In addition, changes in a text style can be made sitewide with one edit to a cascading style sheet.

If you just want to get the job done, and get it done quickly, however, the text-formatting tools on the Property Inspector are available to you. This chapter focuses on formatting text with the Property Inspector. Chapter 12 discusses in more detail how to format text using CSS, and chapters 6 and 8 discuss text effects.

When you work with the <FONT> tag, HTML and browser issues limit your font choices and colors to some degree. With a little creativity, however, you can still offer your users decent-looking text on the Web.

Tip

Know the difference between a soft return and a hard return. This will make working with text in Dreamweaver a little easier. A hard return, indicated by the <P> tag in HTML, is made by pressing the Enter key. The <P> tag is equivalent to a double-space.

A soft return, indicated in HTML by the <BR> tag, is made by holding down the Shift key as you press the Enter key The <BR> tag is equivalent to a single space.

Adding and Removing Fonts

Dreamweaver's default font choices listed in the Property Inspector include ubiquitous sets such as Arial, Times New Roman, Georgia, and Courier. If you want to add a font to the list, select Edit Font List from the Default Font box on the Property Inspector. You then have access to the box shown in Figure 4.6.

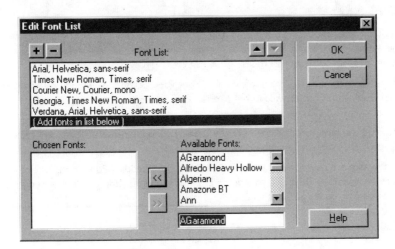

Figure 4.6   The Edit Font List dialog box.

Scrolling through the Available Fonts listing, you will see a listing of the fonts installed on your computer's hard drive. If you want to add a font, be aware that it must also be installed on the end user's system to be visible on any Web pages that you publish. If the user does not have the font installed, the browser defaults to its specified font set.

You can add a font by selecting one from the Available Fonts list and then clicking the box that contains two left-pointing double arrows. You also might need to click the plus sign (+) above the Fonts List to complete the addition The new font will then appear in the Chosen Fonts box and in the Fonts List. If you click OK, the new font will remain in your Default Fonts listing until you remove it.

To remove a font from the list, select it inside the Fonts List, so that it appears in the Chosen Fonts box. Then click the minus sign (–) above the Fonts List to remove the font from your Default Fonts listing.

If you choose Default, your page will be subject to the default font on the viewer's browser, not the default in your browser or in Dreamweaver. If you format text as Default, for example, someone who is viewing your page in a browser with the font Brush Script selected as the default (and some people do this type of thing) will see a much different page from what you are seeing with a more readable default font of Times New Roman or Garamond.

Font Choices

If you think the font choices offered in the Property Inspector are boring, you're not alone. Although we would all like to have more font choices, we are still limited by the browser's capability to display them.

To help this matter along, Microsoft offers a Font Pack of fonts developed especially for screen reading. You can download the pack at `www.microsoft.com/typography/ fontpack/default.htm`.

If you have the pack installed, the specially developed fonts inside the pack will appear when you visit Web sites that specify them.

Also available are new formats such as WEFT (Web Embedding Font Tool), developed in part by Microsoft. With WEFT, your fonts are embedded into the user's browser so that you can use any font you want to use.

Font Faces

Unless you add fonts (as discussed earlier in this chapter), Dreamweaver's Property Inspector offers you the following font-face combinations:

- Arial, Helvetica, sans serif
- Times New Roman, Times, serif
- Courier New, Courier, mono
- Georgia, Times New Roman, Times, serif
- Verdana, Arial, Helvetica, sans serif

When you select type in your document, you can use the pull-down menu on the Property Inspector to choose one of the preceding combinations.

Browsers display the text using the first font in the combination that is installed on the user's system. If you have the combination Times New Roman, Times, and serif selected in the Property Inspector, for instance, the browser shows the first of those that are installed on the user's system. If none of the fonts in the combination are installed, the browser displays the text as specified by the browser preferences.

If none of the fonts in the Dreamweaver default listing of font sets exist on your computer, the font will appear large and ugly onscreen. To work around this, add fonts to the listing using the Edit Font List option in the Font field of the Property Inspector.

Pick whatever you want for your first font (preferably a very readable font). For your second and third font, try to choose one very common Windows font (such as Arial) and one very common Macintosh font (such as Georgia).

Tip

Verdana (sans serif) and Georgia (serif) are both good choices for Web sites. They were developed especially for screen reading by a type designer named Matthew Carter, who was hired by Microsoft to create two very readable screen-based families.

Text Sizes, Styles, and Alignment

Dreamweaver offers you every opportunity to vary the sizes of your type, but what are the differences between +1 and plain-old 1? And what about those heading tags, such as <H1> and <H2>? It is time to take a closer look at those HTML attributes that make all the difference in how a user reads your page.

Headings

Headings provide an easy way to outline your documents. You can use headers of level 1 (<H1>) to indicate major points, headers of level 2 (<H2>) to provide subtopics to those points, and so forth. In HTML, headings are surrounded by an <Hx> tag (with the variable x signifying the heading level).

Figure 4.7 shows the Dreamweaver default heading sizes offered in the Property Inspector's Format menu.

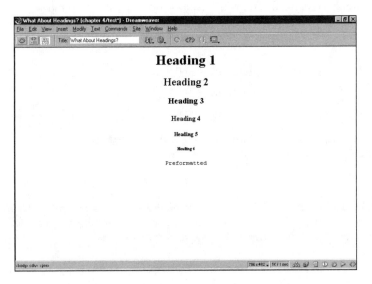

Figure 4.7   The six heading tags and preformatted text inside a Dreamweaver 4 document.

The last option in the list, Preformatted, is a special font style used to allow text formatted in word processors to appear in the browser. The <PRE> tag can prove very handy if you just want to put up a document without coding any HTML.

Font Sizes

You also can use the Property Inspector to specify absolute or relative sizes for your fonts. What's the difference?

Absolute fonts enable you to override the font preferences selected in your user's browser. This way, you have more control over the way your pages look. If you specify a font size of 5, for instance, the font appears in your user's browser as size 5, even if her browser specifies a font size of 6 or 7. The exception is if you specify a font face that the user doesn't have installed on his or her computer. In that case, the browser defaults overrule your specifications.

Relative font sizes are sized in relation to a number specified in the <BASEFONT> HTML tag. If you specify a <BASEFONT> of 5, for example, select Type and use the pull-down menu in the Property Inspector to assign Font Face=+1; your result will be a font size of 6.

If no <BASEFONT> is specified, the relative sizes will usually be relative to size 3, as this is the commonly accepted default size for most browsers. What it boils down to is that the relative font sizes are open to browser interpretation, which can cause unpredictable results.

Also note that Dreamweaver does not display the <BASEFONT> tag in the HTML code; so if you look for it, you will not find it.

When working using the Property Inspector to format text with the <FONT> tag, you might become frustrated at the limited number of font sizes available to you. If so, it is time to learn how to use CSS.

Tip

If you have trouble applying font faces, it could be that you have inadvertently doubled your font tags by applying them too many times. Use the Clean Up HTML command (default settings) from the Commands menu to remove extra tags.

Bold and Italic

You can use the Property Inspector or the Text pull-down menu to style your type as bold or italic. Take a look at Figure 4.8 and identify the bold (B) and italic (I) buttons on the Property Inspector's right side.

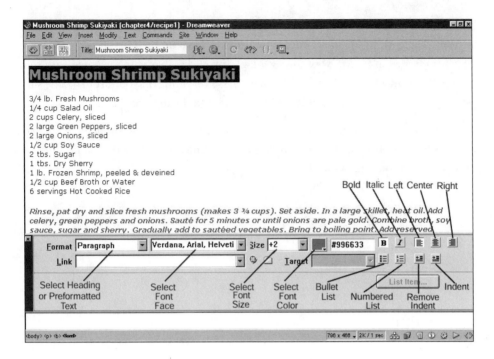

Figure 4.8   The Property Inspector's text-formatting options.

To format text as bold or italic, select the type and click the B or I button in the Property Inspector. This action converts the type to your selected style. If you want to remove the style, select the type and click the B or I button again.

Alignment

The Property Inspector offers three tools for aligning your text to the left, right, or center. Take a look at the Property Inspector in Figure 4.8. The text-alignment tools are to the far right, on the top row, next to the question mark icon.

To align text to the right, left, or center, select it and then click the type-alignment icon you want to use. To remove alignments, select the type again and click the button off.

Making Lists

Numbered and bulleted lists have been around since HTML's beginnings. Commonly, they are used to outline your document's main points and subpoints.

In Dreamweaver, you can use the Property Inspector to make your lists, or pull down the Text menu. Figure 4.8 shows the two icons used to make lists. (They are located below the bold and italic icons.)

In Design view, select your type and click either the bulleted list icon or the numbered list icon. The trick to making a successful list is to separate each list item with a hard return (indicated in HTML with the <P> tag). If your list items are separated with soft returns (the <BR> tag), the list function considers everything on your list to be one single item, and only one bullet point appears adjacent to the topmost list item.

Figure 4.9 shows an example of a properly formatted list and an improperly formatted list. This figure shows the difference between separating list items with a hard return (a <P> tag) and a soft return (a <BR> tag).

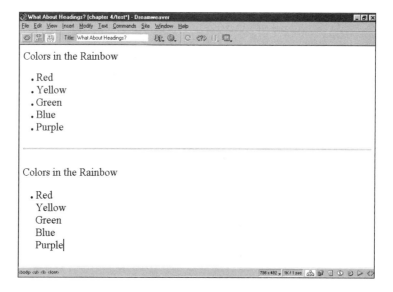

Figure 4.9   A correctly formatted list (top) and an incorrectly formatted list (bottom) inside a Dreamweaver 4 document.

To make a nested list, or a list inside a list, separate the nested list items with hard returns, select them, and press the Indent button on the Property Inspector.

To remove numbered or bulleted list formatting, select the list items. Use the List Item button as a toggle switch to turn the list on and off. It's usually easier to delete items from the list if the toggle switch is off.

Working with lists can be frustrating. You might think that you are doing everything right, but the list isn't formatting properly. The problem here lies with HTML coding. If you click and unclick the icons more than once, you risk doubling your tags inside the HTML code. When this happens, you can solve the problem by pulling down Dreamweaver's Commands menu and selecting Clean Up HTML. This action removes any extra tags and gives you a fresh start.

Indenting Text

Sometimes you want to indent text without adding bullets or list numbers. You can do so by using the indent and outdent icons on the Property Inspector. Figure 4.8 shows these indentation tools. (They are located below the left-align and center-align icons.)

In Design mode, select the text you want to indent and click the indent icon. This moves your text inward. You can click the icon again to move the text in even more. However, doing so involves using multiple <BLOCKQUOTE> tags, which results in sloppy HTML code. A better way to consistently indent text is to use tables. Chapter 8 provides more details about text alignment with tables.

To remove indents, select the text and click the outdent icon. This moves the text back to the left side of your document.

Text Spacing

When spacing text, many people make use of an HTML tag called the non-breaking space, indicated in HTML as . The non-breaking space can be used to provide extra space between lines of type in HTML. In the print-publishing world, this is known as *leading*. HTML does not provide a leading tag, hence the use of non-breaking spaces.

You might find other uses for the non-breaking space. It really does come in handy when you lay out your pages. To insert a non-breaking space into your document, pull down Insert/Non-Breaking Space (Ctrl+Shift+Spacebar).

Be aware that non-breaking spaces are not supported in all browsers.

Text Colors

Colored text can increase the visual impact of your Web pages. For instance, you might want to put your body copy in a color that contrasts against your heads and subheads. You also might want to use other techniques—for example, make colorful headlines, subtle footnotes, or white text that pops out against a black background. Although it's not always easy to make design choices about text color, Dreamweaver helps you to implement those choices after you make them.

In the Property Inspector (you can also use the Text/Color menu option), pull down the text color chip, which is located to the right of the Font Size box (see Figure 4.8). The resulting color palette is where you select your text color. Figure 4.10 shows a black-and-white example.

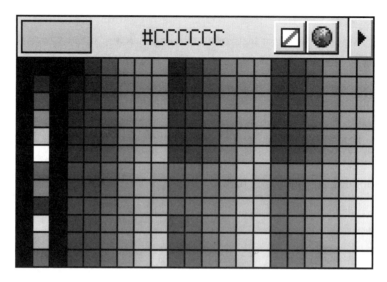

Figure 4.10   The Dreamweaver color palette.

To use the coloring tool, select the type you want to color (from Design mode) and access the coloring menu from the Property Inspector. Pull the cursor across the browser-safe color palette to select the color you want to use and click OK. Dreamweaver 4 gives you a choice among several color palletes including Macintosh- and Windows-specific ones. You can select these by using the context menu in the color palette.

After you choose a color from the Property Inspector, its hexidecimal representation appears in the text field box adjacent to the color chip. This representation consists of a series of letters and numbers preceded by the pound sign (#). In HTML, this representation tells the browser what color to display. Because you're working with Dreamweaver, you don't need to worry about learning exactly how the hexidecimal representation works. If you want to learn more details about Web color, see Chapter 7, "Web Design Issues."

An alternative way to select color is to just type the hexidecimal number you want to use into the color text field box. You can also type in a color name, such as pink or green. Most level-3 or above Web browsers understand common color names. To ensure consistent appearance across browsers, however, use hexidecimal representations of Web-safe color rather than color names.

Tip

When choosing colors, drag the eyedropper off the side of the color palette. Then you can apply the color for anything on your screen just by selecting it with the eyedropper. You can even match colors in Fireworks images. This is a very convenient, yet underutilized, feature of Dreamweaver.

Tip

Use the Modify/Page Properties command to choose a default text color.

To return text to the default color, click the color chip on the Property Inspector to open the color palette. Then click the Strike Through button (also called the eraser) in the upper-right corner to remove the color you no longer want to use.

Text Formatting Made Easier

If formatting text with the Property Inspector is tedious, or if you are working with a large amount of text, it pays to explore options for automating your process.

Cascading style sheets have been mentioned in this chapter several times because they are, increasingly, the preferred way to format text. The amount of control they offer over font faces, styles, and spacing, among other things, cannot be matched by any other method so far.

The list that follows provides more details about CSS and the other ways to format text in Dreamweaver:

- **CSS.** CSS formats text from a remote location such as the head of the document or an external file on the server. If a style is changed during the site design process, all the text that references the CSS style is automatically updated to reflect the changes.

- **HTML tags (such as the <FONT> tag).** This method formats text by using tags immediately surrounding the text that is being formatted (for instance, Bold Words). Although many people find it convenient, quick, and easy, this method of text formatting is discouraged by the W3C.

- **HTML styles.** A user-determined set of specific HTML tags is saved within Dreamweaver to be applied to selected text using the HTML Styles panel (Ctrl+F11). This method enables you to quickly re-apply a set of HTML tags anywhere in your site. If an HTML style is changed or edited, all future uses of that HTML style will reflect the changes, but past instances of that HTML style will not be updated to reflect those changes. HTML styles were developed especially for Dreamweaver.

Because CSSs are the focus of Chapter 12, the following section takes you through the ins and outs of another way (although limited) to add automation to your text formats: HTML styles.

HTML Styles

HTML styles do not have the power of cascading styles sheets, nor do they match the precision of style sheets created in desktop publishing applications such as PageMaker, Quark Xpress, or Microsoft Word; but they can save you the time it would take to reformat heads and subheads across a site or within a document using the Property Inspector.

In Dreamweaver, HTML styles are created by selecting text you have formatted for font face, size, color, style, and alignment and using the add styles icon on the HTML Styles panel to add the styles to the listing. Figure 4.11 shows the HTML Styles panel.

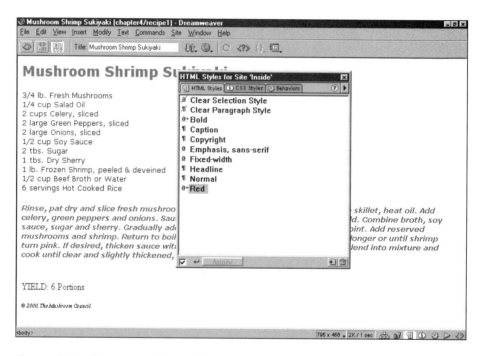

Figure 4.11   The HTML Styles panel.

To access the HTML Styles panel, use one of the following methods:

- Choose Window/HTML Styles (see Figure 4.12).
- In the launcher, click the HTML Styles button.
- In the mini-launcher (bottom of document window), click the yellow paragraph symbol. This is the HTML styles icon.
- Use the keyboard shortcut F11.

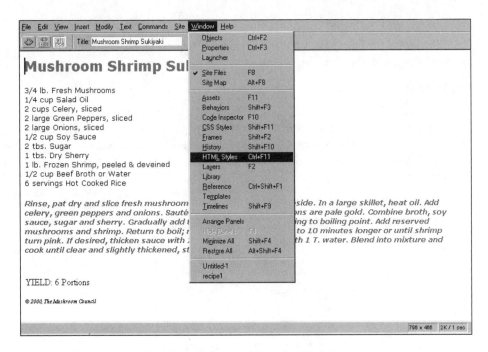

Figure 4.12   Accessing the HTML Styles panel from the Window menu.

Using the HTML Styles Panel

Now it's time to have some fun and actually do something with the knowledge gained in the first part of this chapter, where formatting text with the Property Inspector was covered. Remember the Mushroom Shrimp Sukiyaki recipe? Now you use it to learn about HTML styles. Then you have the opportunity to format another recipe the same way.

Note

It is important for you to understand the difference between a paragraph style and a selection style.

A paragraph style, indicated on the HTML styles panel with a paragraph symbol, applies that style to the entire paragraph, no matter whether any text is selected. In other words, if your cursor is blinking inside a paragraph, and you click a paragraph style in the HTML styles panel, the style will be applied.

A selection style can be applied only if text is selected. A selection style is indicated in the HTML styles panel by a lowercase "a" with a line beneath it.

Exercise 4.1   HTML Styles

Open the file RECIPE1.HTML from the Recipe or Chapter 4 folder on your CD-ROM to follow along with this exercise.

Part I Creating New Styles

1. Inside the document, select the ingredients list, starting with mushrooms and ending with cooked rice. From the HTML styles panel, click the new style icon (located at the bottom of the panel). The Define HTML Style dialog box displays (see Figure 4.13). You are going to define the font face and style used in this list as an HTML style.

Figure 4.13   The Define HTML Style dialog box.

2. In the Define HTML Style dialog box, title the new style **Ingredients**.

3. Click the Selection radio button in the Apply To field. (It will already be chosen as the default.)

4. Click the Add to Existing Style (+) radio button in the When Applying field.

5. Select the font set Verdana, Arial, Helvetica, sans-serif, and choose a font size of 2.

6. Choose a color chip of your choice.

7. Click OK to exit the dialog box.

8. Note that the style Ingredients has been added to the listing in the HTML styles panel. Because the style is a selection style, the lowercase "a" icon has been assigned to it.

Now select the recipe head Mushroom Shrimp Sukiyaki, and create an HTML style called Headline by repeating steps 1–8. This time, use a font size of 5.

Now select the cooking directions and repeat steps 1–8 to create a style called Directions. This time, use a font size of 2.

9. For the last step, select the copyright information at the bottom of the page that reads ©2000, The Mushroom Council and repeat steps 1–8 to create a style called Copyright. For this style, use the Georgia, Times New Roman, Times, serif font set, with a size of 1.

After completing steps 1–9, your HTML Styles panel should list selection styles for Ingredients, Headline, Directions, and Copyright. You use these styles in the next part of this exercise.

Part II Applying HTML Styles

For this part of the exercise, open the file called RECIPE2.HTML from the Chapter 4 or Recipe folder on your CD. You are going to apply the HTML styles from the preceding part of this exercise to sections of this document so that the two recipes will have a consistent look.

1. Select the text Family Night Pizza. Open the HTML Styles panel (Ctrl+F11) and click Headline. This applies the Headline style you created in the first part of this exercise to the selected text.

2. Select the entire ingredients list, starting with Crust and ending with Parmesan Cheese, and click the style called Ingredients in your HTML Styles panel to apply the style to the selected text.

3. Select the pizza cooking directions and click the style called Directions from the HTML Styles panel.

4. At the bottom of the page, select the text ©2001, The Pizza Council and click the Copyright Style from the HTML Styles panel.

After you have finished, the pizza recipe should look similar to the mushroom recipe. Wasn't that easy?

Removing HTML Styles

To remove an HTML style, select the text you want to remove a style from and perform one of the following from the HTML styles palette:

- Select your text and click Clear Selection Style to remove a selection style.

- Insert your cursor into the paragraph you want to change and click Clear Paragraph Style.

Sharing HTML Styles

You can share your HTML styles with other sites or users. To do so, follow these steps:

1. Choose Window/Site Files.

2. From the right pane, open the site root folder, and then open the Library folder.

3. The file called STYLES.XML contains all your HTML styles for the site. Use the site maintenance tools covered in Chapter 14 to upload, download, check in, or check out the styles. This file works like any other file on your site.

Special Characters

When working with text, you will no doubt encounter a need for special characters. *Special characters* are used in a variety of ways, such as to indicate accent marks on words borrowed from other languages (for example, the word resumé). You will also need to use special characters when formatting times, dates, curly quotation marks, or measurements (such as in the recipe exercise).

Your Web pages will look more professional if you take the time to format the special characters. Many people do not take the time to do this because working with special characters can be confusing. Not only do special characters require their own HTML code, they also have a reputation of not showing up in lower-level browsers. Be suspicious of any special character code that contains a number between 127 and 159. These positions are not part of any HTML standard and should not be used for Web publishing.

How to Use Special Characters

Web browsers display special characters only if the HTML they are processing includes the code for the character in the spot where you want it to appear. For example, the special character HTML code for an accented e looks like this:

é

One of the advantages of Dreamweaver over hand-coded HTML is that the special character codes are available to you anytime you need them. This way, you do not have to remember a code for each of the special characters you will use, from the accented e to the copyright symbol to the en dash. To use your special characters resource, follow these steps:

1. In Design mode, choose Window/Objects.

2. On the Objects panel (shown in Figure 4.12), click the arrow in the upper-right corner to pull down the options. Choose Characters.

3. The Objects panel then offers you a series of icons that represent some of the most commonly used special characters. Click the character you want to use and it will appear in your text. If you switch to HTML Code view, you can see the code as it appears in the text.

Alternatively, you can choose Insert/Special Characters from the Dreamweaver main menu.

If the special character you need is not listed, click the Insert Other Character icon, which is also located in the Objects panel, adjacent to the em-dash icon (see Figure 4.14). You also can use the Insert pull-down menu from the main menu bar and select Special Characters/Other.

This option results in a new window from which you can choose a special character (see Figure 4.15). When you click a character icon, it will appear in the text field box at the top of the window. You can also type your own special character code into the box, although it might be easier just to add it to the HTML code yourself.

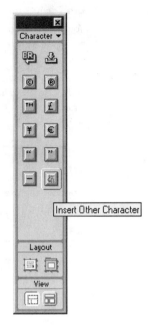

Figure 4.14
Inserting special characters with the Objects panel.

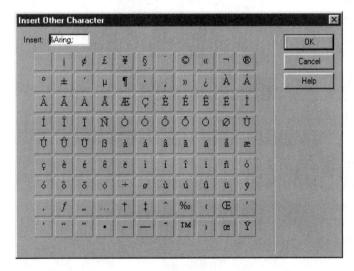

Figure 4.15   The Insert Other Character dialog box.

Em Dashes and En Dashes

You can raise your text to a new level of professionalism by learning what em (—) and en (–) dashes are and then using them correctly.

In print publishing, the em dash is a dash the length of an uppercase "M." It is used to indicate a break in speech, an interruption, or a pause. The en dash is the length of an uppercase "N," and is used in a variety of ways. You can use it to separate times and dates, or after a topic heading.

Consider how an em dash is used in dialogue: "If you interrupt me one more time, I'll—"

To indicate an em dash in HTML, use the following code:

—

Consider the use of an en dash: Hours 12:00 – 5:00 p.m.

To indicate an en dash in HTML, use the following code:

–

Summary

When working with text in Dreamweaver, many options are available. Learning how text is imported and exported from Dreamweaver and other software programs such as Microsoft Word can be a time saver. Even so, it's often advantageous to paste plain text into a Dreamweaver document and format it yourself. Otherwise, you take the risk that unwanted code will litter your document and cause technical problems inside the browser window.

Formatting text for font face, color, style, and alignment can be accomplished using the Dreamweaver Property Inspector. However, many Web designers are turning to cascading style sheets because the W3C is discouraging use of the <FONT> tag. This is in part because cascading style sheets offer much more control over text than what can be achieved by using the <FONT> tag.

If you are working with a small amount of text and have chosen to use the Property Inspector as a formatting tool, HTML styles can speed up the process. By designating formatted text as a style, you can use the style again and again to create a consistent look and feel.

Working with text is challenging, but that challenge can be met by educating yourself about the best ways to work with text and making a decision about what is best for your site.

Chapter 5

Linking and Navigation

This chapter covers the basics of linking

your Web pages together. If you have never

created a link before, you will be happy to

hear that it is very easy. If you have created

links in the past, don't skip this chapter. There is more to linking than just typing in a URL. And if you're working with Dreamweaver, it pays to take the time to learn how links are handled.

Basically, a link gives behind-the-scene instructions on what should appear next on your screen, be it another document in the site you're viewing, or an HTML page on a site in Japan, Denmark, or right in your hometown. These instructions are written in a variety of ways, and they can seem cryptic to someone who has never seen them before.

This chapter also gives you the opportunity to do some exercises that will help you to explore the navigational design tools that Dreamweaver offers. Some new features in Dreamweaver 4 help you build navigation bars and buttons, such as the Insert Navigation Bar option.

This chapter covers the following:

- Types of paths
- Linking text
- Link colors and styles
- Email links
- Named anchors
- Image maps
- Navigational bars
- Jump menus

Path Names

The key to creating links is to understand the relationship between the two files you are linking. This relationship is called the *path*. This chapter briefly explains the concept of path structure. Chapter 13, "Site and File Organization," discusses how Dreamweaver defines sites and handles path structure.

What Is a Path?

Imagine that your boss asks you for a file that is in someone else's office. You must walk down the hall, take the elevator up one floor, open the door to the office where the file is located, and then retrieve the file from the file cabinet. You create a path on this journey. Each time your boss asks for a document from that office, you must repeat the same path. A computer path is not much different.

On your Web site, you offer users the opportunity to request files saved on your Web server. Think of your Web server as the "file cabinet" where you keep the information you want to offer on your Web site. The links might be comprised of images, text, or coordinates on part of a larger image. When the link is clicked, a request is sent to the Web server, asking for a different file from the one currently loaded into the browser.

Understanding path structure means that you know how to make the request work. You have probably experienced (who hasn't?) clicking a link that returned an error page, or nothing at all. This probably happened because the path specified in the code was incorrect, or because the requested file didn't exist. Likewise, if you were instructed to take a file to an office on the 13th floor, but you discovered that there was not a 13th floor, you might return with a similar message, like "Hey, that office doesn't exist!"

Understanding Paths

In Dreamweaver, you have the opportunity to choose how your paths are structured. So, if you don't know the difference between an absolute path and a relative path, sit up and read on.

An *absolute path* is a complete URL. It contains not only the name of the file being requested, but also the name of the Web server where the file is located. It also contains the "http" prefix everyone has come to know and love. Here's an example of an absolute path:

```
http://www.greatsites.com/terrific/wonderful.html
```

When creating links, you can use an absolute URL and the requested document will be retrieved. However, using absolute paths forces the user through the front door of the Web site after clicking each link. This significantly increases the burden on the server and the time it takes to load the page. That is why relative paths are preferable.

There are two types of relative paths: those relative to the document you are linking from (document relative), and those relative to the site root (root relative). This discussion first considers document-relative paths.

Document-Relative Paths

Document-relative paths relate one file to another file. Instead of starting at the site root, the path begins at one file and goes through whichever directories are required to get to the location of the other file. However, both files must be saved in your local root folder before the document-relative path can be established.

Tip

> The best way to deal with document-relative paths is to browse to them in Dreamweaver. Use the file folder icon in the Property Inspector to select the file to which you want to link.

If you want to preview your pages locally inside a browser, you must use document-relative paths. Why? Because most Web browsers have no capacity to understand what local root folder you are using, so the only paths that can be followed are relative to the document currently being viewed. By default, Dreamweaver saves your files with a document-relative path structure.

Note

> If you do not save your file before inserting an image or creating a link, Dreamweaver has no reference for locating the document in which you are working. Therefore, you will get a message prompting you to save the file. If you do not save the file, Dreamweaver creates a link specific to your workstation. This link will not work once you upload your document, so get into the habit of saving your new documents into the proper directory as soon as you create them.

Here's an example of a document-relative path:

```
../poetry/bookshelf.html
```

Imagine the dots to be the "elevator" you would take up or down when retrieving documents from other offices. You cannot use document-relative paths when linking to files on someone else's Web server. Therefore, if you want to link your users to an article on cnn.com or an auction on ebay.com, you have to use an absolute URL (for instance, `http://www.ebay.com`).

Root-Relative Paths

If you are working on a large Web site that uses several servers, or your Web server hosts several different Web sites, you might want to use root-relative paths. You also would use them if you plan on moving files around in your site quite a bit.

Whereas a document-relative path establishes the relationship between two files, a *root-relative path* establishes the relationship between each file and the root of the site. Continuing the office analogy used earlier, it is like establishing the relationship between each of the two offices (the one you exited when you started your journey, and the one you arrived at as your destination) making those two points relative to the lobby of the building.

Root-relative links put a slash in front of the path name, as follows:

`/Poetry/BOOKSHELF.HTML`

In this example, the path leads to the BOOKSHELF.HTML file, located in the Poetry subfolder of the site's root folder. Once again, root-relative links are defined by your server, not by the Web browser. Therefore, if you open a page from your hard drive that uses root-relative links, the links will not work. If you preview the page, Dreamweaver will temporarily convert them into absolute paths. When you click a link, it will not work locally because it is site-root relative. However, it will work on your browser, but you will be able to preview only one page at a time.

Root-relative links are best used for sites where the content is moved around frequently. The advantage root-relative paths have over document-relative links is that paths contained inside your document will still work after you move the file to a new location. So, if you have your company newsletter online, and move the monthly articles to a directory called Archive when the new issue goes online, root-relative links will save you the time it would take to change links to reflect the new path structure.

Path structure can be confusing at times. Fortunately, Dreamweaver makes it easy for you to use absolute, document-relative, and root-relative paths. Your only job is to understand when you need to use which type of path. If you are just beginning to learn how path structure works, take a look at Chapter 13 for more details.

Managing Links

This section covers the basics of creating text links using the Property Inspector and a sample Web site called *The Poetry Bookshelf*. (I will be using document-relative links, except when I am linking outside the site. In that case, I will use absolute links.)

Anatomy of a Link

A URL gets even longer when you look at its HTML code. Take a look at the following example:

`<a href="bookshelf.html">Poetry Bookshelf</a>`

A behind-the-scenes look shows that it is the <A HREF HTML> tag, also called the <A> tag or the <Anchor> tag, that is telling the browser where to take a user who clicks this link.

Like most HTML tags, the <A HREF> tag must be closed. Use an </A> to close the tag when hand-coding HTML.

You can use the <A HREF> tag to link almost any type of file, including the following:

- Text files
- Graphics
- Movies
- Sound files
- Email addresses
- JavaScripts

Dreamweaver offers extensive tools for managing the links on your site. Chapter 14, "Site Publishing, Maintenance, and Reporting," shows you how to change links site-wide and perform other link-management tasks.

Exercise 5.1 Linking Text, Correcting Broken Links, and Using the Point-to-file Icon

The files you need for this sample site are on the accompanying CD-ROM inside the folder labeled Poetry.

Part I   Linking Text with the Property Inspector

In the first part of this exercise, you make text links to the files POETRY1.HTML, POETRY2.HTML, and POETRY3.HTML from the file called BOOKSHELF.HTML. The link text will read as follows:

> Browse Shelf #1
>
> Browse Shelf #2
>
> Browse Shelf #3

Figure 5.1 shows what the page looks like inside the Web browser.

Open the BOOKSHELF.HTML file and use the keyboard shortcut Ctrl+F3 to open your Property Inspector. Click the image that reads Poetry Bookshelf and take a look at the SRC field on the Property Inspector. It will show you the path of the image. The text links you are going to make will have similar path names. However, they will lead the user to another HTML file rather than to an image file.

1. To create the first link to the first file, highlight the text Browse Shelf #1.
2. Click the file folder icon in the Property Inspector; and in the Select File window, click the filename POETRY1.HTML (see Figure 5.2).
3. Make sure the Relative To section is set to Document and click Select. The Link field in the Property Inspector now contains a link to the file called POETRY1.HTML.
4. Link Browse Shelf #2 to the file POETRY2.HTML and Browse Shelf #3 to the file POETRY3.HTML.

Figure 5.1   The file BOOKSHELF.HTML as it appears inside a Web browser.

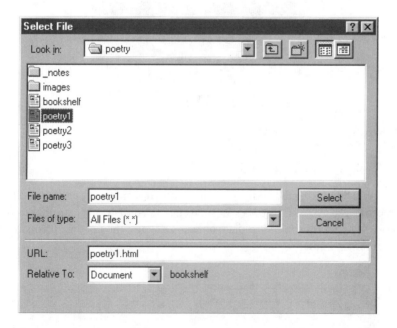

Figure 5.2   Clicking the file folder icon on the Property Inspector to bring up the Select File window.

Note

> If you do not see the Link box, your Property Inspector is probably folded up. To unfold it, click the tiny white arrow (called the expander) in the lower-right corner.

It is a good idea to check your links as you make them. To check the links, choose File/Preview in Browser and choose your browser from the subsequent list. When the page is loaded into the browser, click all three links to make sure they work.

Part II   Correcting a Broken Link

In the file POETRY3.HTML, located in the Poetry folder on your CD-ROM, the link to Home (at the bottom of the page) is broken. If it is clicked inside the browser, an error box appears (see Figure 5.3).

To correct the link, open the file POETRY3.HTML inside Dreamweaver and click your cursor inside the link text. Execute steps 2 and 3 from the first part of this exercise to redirect the link to the file BOOKSHELF.HTML.

Figure 5.3   A broken link alert box.

Part III   Using the Point-toFile Icon

You can create links using the point-to-file icon, which is on the Property Inspector, next to the file folder icon (see Figure 5.4). When using the point-to-file icon, make sure your Site Files window is minimized so that you can see it and the document you are working on at the same time.

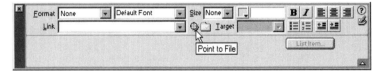

Figure 5.4   Point-to-file icon.

To use the point-to-file icon for link making, follow these steps:

1. In the file BOOKSHELF2.HTML, highlight the text **More Info** in the blurb describing Frank O'Hara's book.

2. With the Sites Files window minimized to a size that enables you to see both windows, click and drag the point-to-file icon to the file called MOREINFO.HTML. This file is located in the Poetry folder along with the other files you are working with in this exercise.

Note that the file you are pointing to will jump to the foreground while you are making your selection.

3. Save the file and preview it inside your browser to make sure it is working.

Removing Links

If you need to remove a link, you can do so using the Property Inspector. Make sure you select the entire text that is linked. If you don't highlight all of it, the sections you don't highlight will stay linked.

To remove a link, follow these steps:

1. Select the link text.

2. Highlight the link path name in the Property Inspector.

3. Press the Delete or Backspace key.

Linking to Other Web Sites

As discussed earlier in this chapter, you must use an absolute path to link to someone else's Web site, or to files on another's Web site. To do this, follow these steps:

1. In your document, select the link text.

2. Click your cursor into the Link box in the Property Inspector.

3. Type the complete URL into the box, including http:// (for example, `http://www.yahoo.com`).

4. Press the Enter key to complete the link.

Link Colors and Underlining

In Dreamweaver, you define link colors via the Page Properties dialog box. To access the box, choose Modify/Page Properties or use the keyboard shortcut Ctrl+J. Figure 5.5 shows the Page Properties dialog box.

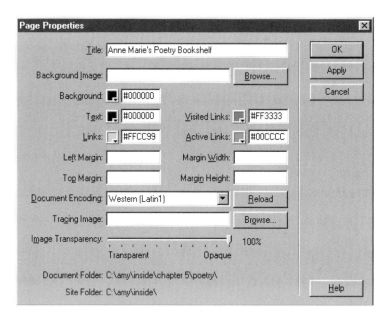

Figure 5.5   The Page Properties dialog box.

In every document, you must define the following colors (unless your document is based on a template). Pull down the Color menu to select browser-safe colors.

- **Links.** This is the link color the user sees when first visiting your site.

- **Active links.** This is the color that lights up when the link is clicked.

- **Visited links.** Links that have already been clicked turn this color after the user returns to the page. This way, users know which links they have already visited.

To define custom colors for links, click the color chip icon next to the Link field in the Page Properties dialog box, and then specify your RGB values in the resulting dialog box. Or, choose a color with the System Color Picker.

Setting Color Schemes

Selecting link, active link, and visited link colors is a challenge. You want to choose colors that show up clearly on a variety of screens. Always be aware that screen brightness varies not only across different platforms (Macintosh screens are usually lighter than PC screens), but also from computer to computer. Therefore, colors that show up fine on your screen might blend into the background on another.

There is no replacement for testing your colors. Look at them on a variety of computers and in a variety of browsers to make sure they are readable. You also can use the built-in color schemes provided with Dreamweaver. To access the color schemes, pull down Commands from the main menu and choose Set Color Scheme. Figure 5.6 shows the resulting dialog box.

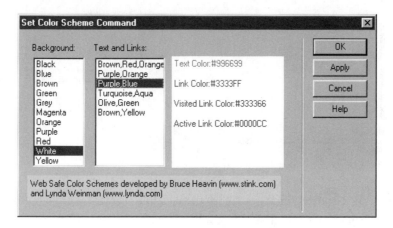

Figure 5.6   The Set Color Scheme Command dialog box.

The color scheme includes colors for the background, links, active links, and visited links. Click a color name in the Background section of the window to see how your link colors will look. Click Apply to use a color scheme in your current document.

Turn Off Link Underlining

In some cases, you will want to override the default link underlining. To turn off link underlining across an entire site, use an external style sheet. (Chapter 12, "Using Cascading Style Sheets," discusses more about external style sheets and cascading styles sheets.) To turn off link underlining for a single Web page, follow the process outlined in the following steps:

1. In Design mode, choose Window/CSS Styles or use the shortcut Shift+F11.

2. Create a new style by clicking the new style icon (it looks like a plus sign over a piece of paper). The icon is located at the bottom of the panel. Or, click the right-pointing arrow at the top of the panel and choose New Style (see Figure 5.7).

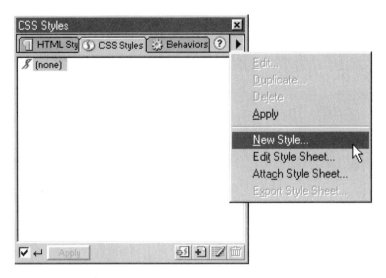

Figure 5.7   Choosing a new style from the CSS panel.

3. Inside the New Style dialog box, click the Redefine HTML Tag radio button. This
    step creates a new HTML style that will remove the underlining from your links
    (see Figure 5.8).

Figure 5.8   Defining the new style.

4. In the pull-down menu box next to Tag, pull down the menu and choose a.

5. Click the radio button next to This Document Only. This way, only the current
    document will be affected by the change.

6. Click OK.

7. In the resulting Type window, click the check box for none in the Decoration
    section (see Figure 5.9). This removes the underline from the link.

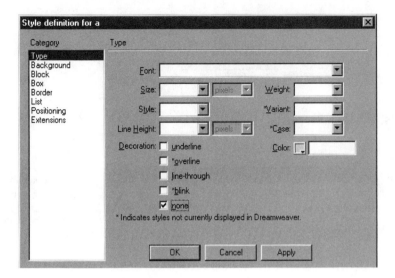

Figure 5.9   Creating a style definition.

The document-level style you just created is inserted into the HTML code for your document.

Email Links

Email links are coded a little bit differently than links to files. An email link will pull up a blank message window. This message window is part of the user's browser. Therefore, if the user doesn't have his browser's mail preferences set up right, the email will not work.

Dreamweaver has an Email Link command. To use it, follow these steps:

1. In the Document window, click your cursor at the spot where you would like to insert an email link. If you want to create an email link from an image, for instance, click the image to select it. Or, select the email link text or image you want to use.

2. Choose Insert/Email Link from the Dreamweaver main menu. Or, use the Objects panel and select Insert Email Link icon from the Common panel.

3. In the resulting Insert Email Link window, type or edit the link text (see Figure 5.10).

4. In the E-Mail field, type the email address to which you want mail to be sent.

5. Click OK.

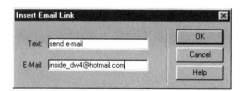

Figure 5.10   The Insert Email Link window.

Email Links with the Property Inspector

Alternatively, you can save a couple of seconds by using the Property Inspector to make your email link. To do so, follow these steps:

1. Select the text or image you want to use for the email link.

2. Click your cursor in the Link field of the Property Inspector and type in the mailto code as shown here:

   ```
   mailto:youraddress@domainname.com
   ```

   Note that there is *not* a space after the colon.

Generating Your Email

You can download a Dreamweaver extension called the E-Mail Generator that will include an automatic subject and body with the email sent from your site. This way, you have an easier way to identify where your email is coming from, and you can include a message so that the sender won't have to write as much.

To locate the extension, go to www.macromedia.com/exchange, and search for "e-mail."

The E-mail Generator icon will appear in the Objects panel under the Common panel after you install it.

Named Anchors

Don't you appreciate it when you visit a Web site where the designers have taken the time to make anchor links? This way, you don't have to scroll up and down to find what you're looking for. When you make a link to a specific place in a document, you are creating what's called a *named anchor link*.

Exercise 5.2   Creating Named Anchor Links

Named anchor links are just a little bit different from regular links. In this exercise, you can practice making them. To work the exercise, open the file called DRUID.HTML.

The file contains month names at the top of the page that need to be linked to the appropriate spot inside the text of the page. Because January is already at the top of the page, start by making an anchor link to February.

1. Scroll down the page to the point at which Druid Star Readings for February begin.

2. From the Insert menu, choose Invisible Tags/Named Anchor (see Figure 5.11). Or, click the Insert Named Anchor button in the Invisibles category of the Object panel.

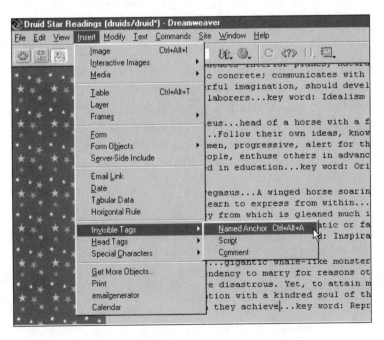

Figure 5.11   Inserting a named anchor link.

3. In the Insert Named Anchor dialog box, type a name for the anchor and click
   OK. (In Figure 5.12, february is used as the anchor name.)

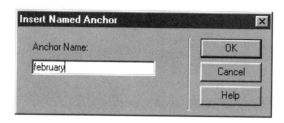

Figure 5.12   Naming the anchor.

Your anchor marker should then appear. If you don't see the anchor marker, choose
View/Visual Aids/Invisible Elements.

Now that you have made the anchor, you need to link to it. Go back up to the top of the
page and select the text that reads February.

Note

When naming your anchors, be careful not to use any spaces in the name. Also
remember that these names are case sensitive. Finally, make sure you are not putting
the anchor itself inside of a layer, because this will fail in certain browsers (such as
Netscape).

1. Click your cursor in the Link field of the Property Inspector. If your Property
   Inspector is not open, use the shortcut Ctrl+F3 to open it.

2. Type **#february** into the Link box. You must put the pound sign in front of all
   your anchor links. If you forget the pound sign, the anchor won't work.

3. Save and preview your page to ensure that the link works. If the link doesn't
   work, check first to make sure that you have spelled it right in the link box. Also,
   note that anchor names are case sensitive.

Note

If you want to link to an anchor in an outside file, you just need to add the anchor
name at the end of the path in the Property Inspector. It would look something like
this:

`otherfile.html#anchor`

To practice making anchors, create anchored links to all the months inside the file
DRUID.HTML.

Anchors with Point to File

You also can use the point-to-file method of linking for anchor links, as follows:

1. First, insert the anchor.

2. Then select the text that you want to link to the anchor.

3. From the Properties Inspector, click the point-to-file icon next to the Link field.

4. Drag the icon to the anchor marker and release it when you see the anchor name appear in the Link field.

Note that you might need to pull the point-to-file icon to the edge of the screen to get the page to scroll up or down.

Linking with Image Maps

Not all links are connected to text or a single image. You also can make links with coordinates. An *image map* is an image that links to many different files. The links are established through the use of coordinates. Each point inside the image is mapped so that it has an X and Y coordinate. Here's an example of what the HTML code for a linked area inside an image map looks like:

```
<area shape="rect" coords="9,181,111,256" href="capricorn.html">
```

The numbers 9,181,111, and 256 create an area inside the image that is then linked to another document. When the user moves a mouse over this area, a hand icon or another icon indicating a link displays. If the area is clicked, an HTTP request is made and a new page is loaded into the current or a new browser window.

You have probably seen sites that show an image map of the United States, and each state is mapped with a link to another HTML document. This is a very common example of the use of image maps.

In Dreamweaver, image maps are created with the Hotspot tool, and the link areas can be made in the shape of a square, rectangle, or polygon. You don't have to retake geometry to make an image map. All you need to do is make a GIF or JPG image, using Fireworks or another imaging program, and place it inside a Dreamweaver document. (For more on placing and inserting images, see Chapter 6, "Working with Images.") Exercise 5.3 takes you through the steps necessary to create an image map inside Dreamweaver.

Exercise 5.3   Creating an Image Map with Hotspots

In this exercise, you use the files in the Astrology folder on your CD-ROM to create an image map with hotspots. Each hotspot will be linked to another HTML document inside the Astrology folder.

1. Open the file called YOURSIGN.HTML from the Astrology folder on your CD-ROM. Note that the file contains an image of the signs of the Zodiac. The area around Aquarius has already been mapped with a hotspot (see Figure 5.13). With the Properties Inspector open, click the hotspot (highlighted in blue), and take a look at the Link field in the Properties Inspector. You should see that the hotspot links to the file AQUARIUS.HTML.

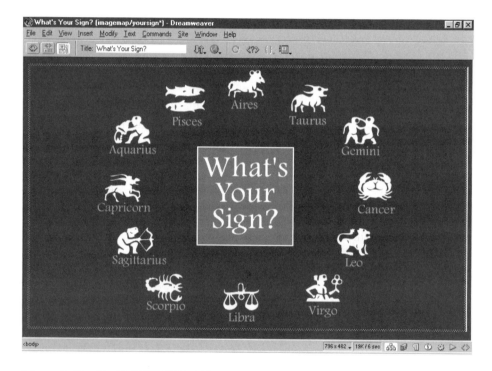

Figure 5.13   The file YOURSIGN.HTML contains an image called YOURSIGN.GIF. This image can be mapped with hotspots.

2. To make a new hotspot, click the YOURSIGN.GIF image. Click the rectangular hotspot tool, located in the lower-left corner (see Figure 5.14).

Use the resulting crossbar tool to draw a square around the first area where you want to create a link.

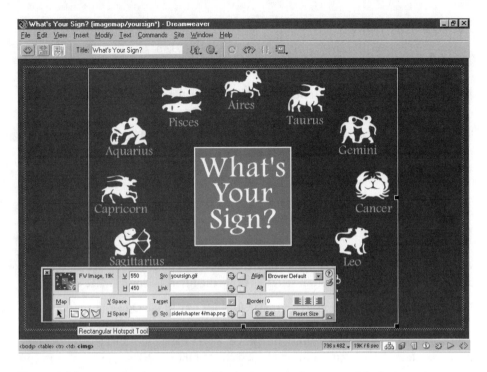

Figure 5.14   Accessing the Hotspot tool in the Properties Inspector while the image is selected.

3. Click the file folder icon on the Properties Inspector to choose the corresponding HTML page for your link. For example, the area for Capricorn should be linked to the HTML document called CAPRICORN.HTML.

4. Create hotspot links for the remaining astrological signs.

5. Save and preview the page to ensure that the image map works.

Removing Hotspots

To remove a hotspot, open the image map document in Design view. Click the blue area that represents the link and press your Delete or Backspace key.

Note

For Fireworks users: You can define hotspot areas as you create your images and save the map to import into Dreamweaver.

Navigation Bars

You can make your site look a bit more complex if you make use of Dreamweaver's Navigation Bar tool.

A navigation bar consists of a series of images that give the user visual cues about where to go next when surfing your page. Sometime a navigation bar contains rollover buttons that light up in a different color when the mouse is held over them. Most of the time, a navigation bar contains a link back to the home page. In the following exercise, you can make a navigation bar in which the links light up when they are rolled over and clicked.

Exercise 5.4   Rollover Navigation Bar

The file NAVIGATE.HTML in your CD-ROM's Astrology folder contains a banner image inside a table. (Note that designing with tables is covered in Chapter 8, "Layout with Tables.") Use this file to make a rollover navigation bar. You can make a navigation bar that contains only two button states by using the Insert Rollover Image command.

In this exercise, you won't specify an image for the Over While Down image. Open the file called NAVIGATE.HTML from the Astrology folder on your CD-ROM and click your cursor underneath the banner image. Or, select the banner image and press the Return key to move your cursor into a blank section of the page. Then, follow these steps:

1. Choose Insert on Dreamweaver's main menu, and then choose Interactive Images/Navigation Bar.

2. In the Insert Navigation Bar dialog box (see Figure 5.15), click your cursor in the Up Image box, and then click Browse. Choose the AIRES_UP.GIF file from the Images folder. This image appears when the page loads.

3. Click your cursor in the Over Image box, and then click Browse. Choose the AIRES_OVER.GIF file from the Images folder. This image appears when a mouse is moved over the image.

4. Click your cursor in Down Image box, and then click Browse. Choose the AIRES_DOWN.GIF file from the Images folder. This image appears after the image has been clicked.

5. Click your cursor in the When Clicked, Go to URL box, and then click Browse. Choose the AIRES.HTML file from the main Astrology directory.

6. Make sure that Preload Images is selected in the Options area.

7. Select Vertically from the Insert menu. Make sure that Use Tables is turned on.

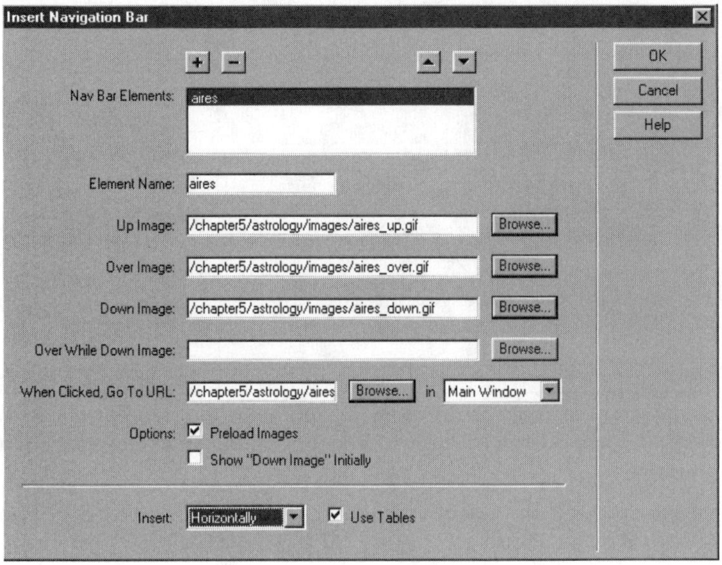

Figure 5.15   Inserting navigation bar images.

You have now added one image to your navigation bar. To add additional images, click the plus sign (+) at the top of the Insert Navigation Bar dialog box and repeat steps 4–7.

After you have added all 12 horoscope signs, click OK.

Save the page and preview it in your browser to see the results. If you made a mistake during the process, you can choose Modify/Navigation Bar.

> **Note**
>
> The Up Image name and Element Name are required when creating a navigation bar. You must fill in these two fields before adding another element.

More About Interactive Navigation Bars

You can use the four button states to create an animation effect for your navigation bars. Try making images for all four states that visually mimic a "real" button that you would press at an ATM machine or some other device.

If you want to make a simple rollover navigation bar with only two states, choose Insert/Interactive Images/Rollover Image from the Dreamweaver main menu (see Figure 5.16).

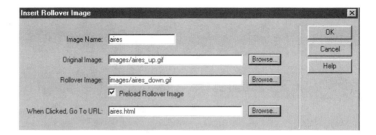

Figure 5.16   The Insert Rollover Image dialog box.

Null Links

Null links enable you to assign behaviors to text or images. You can use null links and behaviors to play sounds when an image is clicked, open pop-up windows, or insert a pop-up message.

To make a null link, select the text or image you want to link, and type a pound sign (**#**) into the Link field on the Properties Inspector. After your null link has been established, open the Behaviors panel by choosing Window/Behaviors or use the shortcut Shift+F3. Pull down the plus sign icon at the top of the panel to view the behaviors you can assign to your anchor. (Your text or image must still be selected to make use of the behaviors.) Chapter 19, "JavaScripting with Dreamweaver," discusses behaviors in more detail.

Jump Menus

One of the most handy navigation tools you can use on your site is a jump menu. More than likely, you have encountered jump menus when surfing the Web. These menus are plain and simple, but they are great space savers and also serve as a "Plan B" in case your users have problems using a more complex navigation system. Figure 5.17 shows a jump menu inside a Web browser.

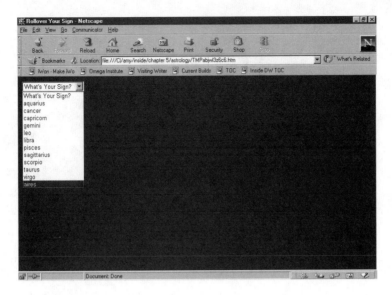

Figure 5.17   A jump menu as it appears in a Web browser.

Exercise 5.5   Creating a Jump Menu

In this exercise, use the HTML files in the Astrology folder on your CD-ROM to make a jump menu that contains a listing of all 12 zodiac signs. To do so, follow these steps:

1. Open the file YOURSIGN.HTML from the Astrology folder on the CD-ROM. Click your cursor in the table row beneath the YOURSIGN.GIF image. This is where you will insert your jump menu.

2. Choose Insert/Form Objects/Jump Menu.

3. Inside the Insert Jump Menu dialog box (see Figure 5.18), click in the text box and type **What's Your Sign?**. This will be a cue for the user to pull down the menu.

4. Click the plus sign (+) at the upper-left side of the dialog box. This adds a new item to the menu.

5. In the Text field, type **Aires**.

6. Next to the When Selected, Go to URL field, click in the box and then click the Browse button to choose the file called AIRES.HTML from the Astrology folder on your CD-ROM.

7. For the field Open URLs In, choose Main Window.

8. In the Menu Name field, type in a short descriptive name, such as **aires**, for the menu item.

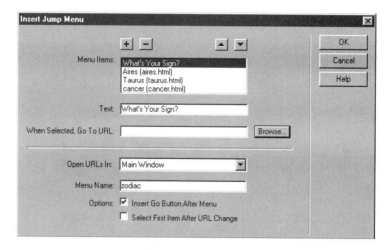

Figure 5.18   The Insert Jump Menu dialog box.

9. Make your selections regarding the check boxes next to Insert Go Button After Menu and Select First Item After URL Change. The first option would place a button reading Go beside your menu. (The Go button is in case you want to go to a menu option but it is already selected.) The second option would place the user's selection at the top of the menu.

10. Add the additional zodiac signs by clicking the plus sign at the top of the dialog box.

11. If you want to move your items around in the listing, use the up and down arrow keys on the right side to do so. Click OK when you have finished.

In your document window, the jump menu will appear in your file with a red dotted line around it. This dotted line indicates that the jump menu is inside of a form tag. Your form objects won't show up in Netscape if they're not inside a form tag. You must save and preview the page inside your Web browser to test the menu.

Editing a Jump Menu

You can make changes to a jump menu after you have created it. To do so, follow these steps:

1. Open the file containing the jump menu in Design view.

2. Open your Behaviors panel by choosing Window/Behaviors or use the shortcut Shift+F3.

3. With the jump menu selected, double-click the onChange event in the Behaviors panel.

4. The Jump Menu dialog box displays. Make your changes and close the box by clicking OK.

To edit the list values, click the jump menu and then press the List Values button in the Property Inspector.

Summary

Linking and navigation is an integral part of creating Web sites. When you are designing a site, give a great deal of thought to the navigation system you're using. You want to provide your users with an easy way to browse through the information on your site.

Also think about your path structure. If you want to preview your HTML pages locally, use a document-relative path structure. If you know that your files are going to be moved around frequently, consider using a site-root, relative-path structure. In both cases, you must use absolute URLs to link to Web sites that exist outside your Web server.

Dreamweaver provides you with many navigation tools. The Properties Inspector helps you link files together quickly and easily. You also can map images with hotspots, build navigation bars that contain rollover images, and make jump menus. In many situations, the best navigation system is one that makes use of a variety of navigation techniques.

Chapter 6

Working with Images

When you work with the Web, you work with images. It doesn't matter if you are a database manager, a Webmaster, or a print designer converting a brochure to HTML.

In the past couple of years, the Web has grown into a virtual work of art. With almost every new Web site published, photographs and illustrations are dusted off, scanned, compressed into GIFs or JPGs, and then uploaded to a Web server that makes them available to the rest of the world.

This chapter covers the following:

- Image file formats
- Placing and aligning images
- Editing images
- Image assets
- Thumbnails and Web photo albums
- Tips for uploading images

Developing your skill in Web imaging requires that you know an image-editing program. After the images have been created, you can then insert, align, and link them inside Dreamweaver. You might use some of the following software programs for making your images:

- Macromedia Fireworks
- Macromedia Freehand
- Adobe Photoshop
- Adobe Illustrator
- Corel Draw
- Microsoft Photopaint
- Paintshop Pro

When laying out a Web page, you usually work with more than just images. You also work with text, images, JavaScripts, animations, and maybe even some other types of data (such as sound files).

Images are an integral part of almost every Web site, but they cannot be used properly unless you have developed some basic skills with alignment using tables. Generally it is not a good idea to place your images inside a document unless they are contained inside a table.

In the exercises that follow, the images are placed into tables and aligned in table cells. Take a look at Chapter 8, "Layout with Tables," if you do not have experience laying out content inside tables.

Imaging File Formats

You might already know about the two image file formats that are widely used on Web sites, GIF and JPEG. In case you don't, here's the information you need to know.

GIFs

The most popular file format for Web images is GIF (Graphical Interchange Format). GIFs are readable by just about every Web browser. (Of course, there are always exceptions; but we won't even go into that area of geekdom here.) Recent versions of image-editing software programs such as Adobe Photoshop and Illustrator, CorelDraw, Microsoft Paint, and others have an option to export your image as a GIF file. Macromedia makes an image-editing program (Fireworks) that works hand-in-hand with Dreamweaver. You might have a copy of Fireworks that came with your Dreamweaver package. (If you haven't used Fireworks, I recommend it.) Fireworks enables you to do a great job optimizing images for the Web, and you can do some of your image editing through the Dreamweaver interface.

No matter which imaging program you use, know that GIFs are best used for line art and other illustrations. (For photographs, use JPEG, covered later in this section.) Areas containing solid color are easily converted into GIF format. With GIFs, you can make choices about the number of colors your image will contain. Just remember, the more colors, the higher the file sizes. Even so, GIFs can be made into much smaller files than JPEGs.

Another advantage of using GIFs is that you can make them transparent. If you scan in a logo that has been printed on a white envelope, for instance, your scan will have a white background. If you save the scan as a GIF, you also save the white background. However, you can remove it with a transparency tool. After an image has been made transparent, you can put it against a colored background without showing any seams.

Transparency is a technique worth learning. Your Web graphics will look much more professional if the white backgrounds are removed. For example, you can create a circular logo image that will appear to be round rather than a circle inside a white square. Go to Web sites such as www.webmonkey.com or www.lynda.com for some good articles about transparency. Alternatively, check the Help files of your imaging software for specific instructions on how to make an image transparent. In Dreamweaver, a transparent image is treated just the same as one that is not transparent. You can, however, use Dreamweaver's color palette to help you create the exact same colors you used in your imaging program for the transparent image's background.

Dithering and Banding

GIFs do have a downside. If you are a designer, you probably love to work with gradients and lots of color variations. Unfortunately, the GIF format is not very friendly to blended color. Unless you save your GIF with a high number of colors, your gradient will show up as nothing but a series of horizontal bands inside the browser (see Figure 6.1). Some Web graphics programs, such as Fireworks, give you an option to "dither" your GIF. If your image contains a gradient, you should use the dithering option so that it will look blended rather than banded.

Figure 6.1   This gradient is banding.

When not dealing with gradients, dithering is something you should avoid. Although it can sometimes provide an interesting effect, it can make your images look amateur. (It also adds significant file size.) The danger in dithering lies with older monitors that display only 256 colors (8-bit color). When your image contains blended color, these monitors have to interpret the colors that lie between the ones they recognize (that is, the colors inside the system palette). When a monitor interprets your colors, they look spotty. This is the dithering effect. Figure 6.2 shows a graphic in which dithering is used to provide a half-tone effect.

JPEGs

Second on the list of Web file formats is JPEG (Joint Photographics Experts Group). JPEGs are the best file format for photographs. If you try to use the JPEG format for line art and other illustrations, your image will look spotty (the spots that show up in JPEG artwork are called artifacts), and you probably won't be happy with it. It also will be unnecessarily large. Like GIFs, you can export JPEGs using one of the Web-imaging software programs listed at the beginning of this chapter.

Photographs usually look great when saved as JPEGs. Many image-editing programs, such as Fireworks, give you the ability to choose the compression level for your photos. A very low number, such as 60, will have a smaller file size than one that is compressed at 90. The higher the number, the better your photograph will look. (I have found that JPEG makes very small files to begin with, so I usually choose a compression level of about 80–90 for maximum quality.) If you and your users are dealing with very slow Internet connections, however, you might want to lower the compression rate or make the image smaller in width and height.

Figure 6.2   The black background and the type in this graphic are dithering, causing a half-tone effect.

If your image is a combination of line art and photography, you might use the GIF file format to avoid artifacts.

PNGs

Another Web image file type is the PNG (Portable Network Graphics) file format. Many Web designers would be very happy if PNGs were viewable in all Web browsers. Unlike GIF or JPEG, PNGs can be saved at many different bit depths. GIF is limited to 8-bit color. JPEGs can be saved at either 8- or 24-bit color. PNGs, on the other hand, can go all the way to 32-bit color. This means you can create gorgeous graphics with beautiful color variations and gradients galore and not worry as much about dithering or banding. Be aware, however, that PNGs are not viewable in all Web browsers. Sometimes a plug-in is required before they can be seen. (A test I did in a classroom one day revealed that only Internet Explorer 4 would display our PNG files. I advise against using PNGs just yet. Make them something to look forward to.)

Note

In Macromedia Fireworks, the default image format is PNG. You must use an "export" command to save your file as a GIF or JPEG.

Marc Klein, Creating the New Frontier

The Web has been a breeding ground for new artists, and Marc Klein is among them. He is the founder of Pixel Industries (www3.pixel-industries.com), a Web design agency in Munich, Germany (see Figures 6.3 and 6.4). He also founded and moderates the Creative Republic listserv, a mailing list for hundreds of new media designers.

The sleek and subtle style of Klein's Web images is brought out all the more with tiny animations that flip, spin, twist, and fade as trancelike techno music creates a rhythm for your online journey. Klein uses arresting phrases to catch a user's eye: "Promenade of Forgotten Dreams," "The Suicide Jumping Tower," and "The Sunflowers of Indian Summer," are titles for his online posters, and have lured many a mouse click. "Content is king," Klein says, "and the written word in combination with expressive image material can evoke a very deep impact."

Klein started out several years ago designing BBSs (bulletin board systems) and icons, but knew that the future would bring more opportunity for new media design. "Netscape Navigator 1.0 at this time was very restricted in what we call today 'Web design.' But for me this was a beginning, some kind of hope and dream that one day a media would exist which offered me total freedom in layout and page design for online media."

Klein makes use of crisp illustrations of the human form and industrial objects. "The GIF image format is still a favorite due to the fact that this file format offers animation methods without the need to install any plug-in. Furthermore, GIF images are very useful and small in file size for creating large background illustrations using eight color schemes or less."

Klein prefers to map out the design process in his own mind before turning to Web design software. "You can create appealing and interesting Web sites by using very simple HTML techniques," he says. "Don't let the software for designing and producing interactive Web sites get you restricted in your own ideas and your own imagination."

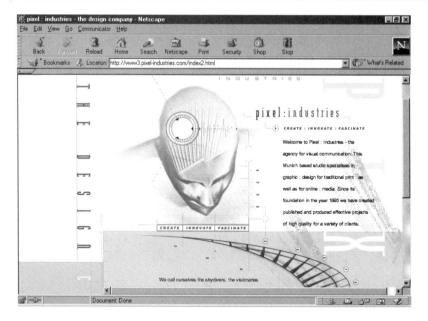

Figure 6.3   The Pixel Industries Web site.

Figure 6.4   Marc Klein's home page at `www.marc-klein.com`.

Designing with Images

Images are more than decorations for your Web site. They should offer users important information about where to locate content and how to navigate. Ideally, they also evoke an emotional response and establish an identity for your site. The process of creating your images and making them look professional should take place before you are laying them out in Dreamweaver. That does not mean, however, that there is no room for creativity after you exit your image-editing program.

Dreamweaver offers you many tools for working with images. Not only do you have the ability to align them exactly where they should be, you also can use the Dreamweaver color palette to match the background color you used in your image-editing program. Your images will become even more useful if you employ Dreamweaver's linking tools, such as hotspots and the rollover navigation bar command. And, if you find that an image needs to be changed, you can use Dreamweaver to launch your image-editing program automatically.

Figure 6.5 shows an image placed inside a Dreamweaver document, in Design view. Below the image is the Property Inspector, which offers information about your image such as its path location, file size, name, and <ALT> tag. If you were to view this image in Code view, you would see that the <IMG SRC> tag is used. In HTML, <IMG SRC> is used to reference an image.

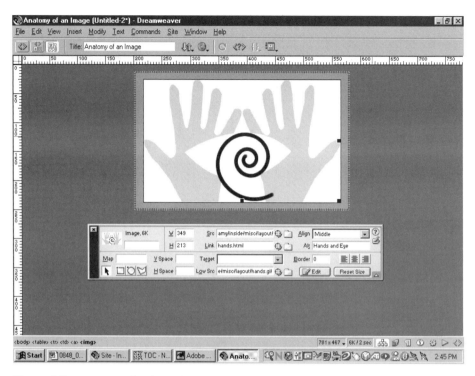

Figure 6.5   Anatomy of an image in Dreamweaver.

What Is an <ALT> Tag?

To assign an <ALT> tag to your image, enter it into the Alt field in the Property Inspector (see Figure 6.5).

As long as you are using the Windows operating system, the <ALT> tag will appear in some browsers as the user holds a mouse over it for longer than a second or two. It also will show up as text in the spot where the image is to appear while the page is loading into the browser.

It is a good idea to use <ALT> tags for your images because they are an aid to visually impaired people who are listening to their Web pages rather than reading them.

You can also download an extension from Macromedia Exchange that will check your HTML documents for accessibility problems. To download the extension, go to Exchange (www.macromedia.com/exchange) and search for "accessibility."

Exercise 6.1   Placing, Aligning, and Spacing Images

This exercise, divided into three parts, shows you the basics of working with images inside Dreamweaver. For all three parts of the exercise, you should be in Design view with the Property Inspector (Ctrl+F3) open.

Part I of the exercise takes you through the steps involved with placing and aligning two images in table cells. Part II leads you through the process of wrapping text around an image (inside a table). Part III shows you how to assign V and H space to an image.

Part I   Placing and Align Two Images in Table Cells

1. Open the IMAGE101.HTML file from the Moire folder on your CD-ROM. In Dreamweaver's Design view, click in the work area and choose Insert/Table.

2. Using the Insert Table dialog box, create a 300-pixel-wide table that has 1 column, 2 rows, and a border of 0. Set Cellpadding and Cellspacing to 0. Click OK when you are finished defining the table size.

3. With the table selected, open the Property Inspector (Ctrl+F3) and choose Center from the Alignment field. This action aligns the table to the center of the page.

4. Now that you have a table to hold the images, click in the top row. Choose Insert/Image, and select the MOIRE.GIF image file from your CD-ROM.

5. After the image has been inserted into the table, click in the bottom table cell and repeat step 4 to insert the image called TITLE.GIF, which is also located in the Moire folder on your CD-ROM.

6. Now that both images have been inserted into the table, they should be aligned inside the table cells. Without selecting the image, click in the top table cell and choose Center from the Horz field on the Property Inspector. Then, choose Top from the Vert field. Do the same alignment for the image in the bottom table cell. When you have finished, both images will be aligned in the center of their table cells.

7. Save the page and preview it inside your browser.

Part II   Wrapping Text Around an Image

1. Open the document WRAPTEXT.HTML from the Moire folder on your CD-ROM.

2. Click in the upper left-hand corner of the document, just before the word Welcome.

3. Choose Insert/Table, and create a table with 1 row and 1 column that is 100 pixels wide. Set the Border, Cell Padding and Cell Spacing to O. Click OK when you are finished to insert the table into the document.

4. With the table still selected, choose Left from the Align field on the Property Inspector. The table should move to the left of the page and the text should move around it. (If the text breaks apart, with one section jumping to the bottom of the page, click in the area where you want to eliminate space and press the Delete or Backspace key.)

5. Click in the table cell and choose Insert/Image. Select the image called MOIRELOGO.GIF from the Moire folder on the CD-ROM. The image then appears inside the table cell.

Part III Assigning V and H Space

After wrapping text around an image, you need to assign some space around the edges of your image so that the text does not hit the sides. Use the V and H text field boxes in the Property Inspector to indicate how many pixels of space you want to place around the sides of your image.

V assigns space vertically. H assigns space horizontally. Although you can assign values for both V and H simultaneously, you cannot assign space to only one side of your image.

To assign V and H spacing to the MOIRELOGO.GIF image, placed in Part II of this exercise, follow these steps:

1. Select the image (not the table) and click in the box marked V Space. Because you do not need to add any vertical spacing to this image, insert 0 into the box.

2. Click in the H Space field and insert 8. This action adds 8 pixels of space horizontally to the image and prevents the image from hitting the text.

3. Save the page and preview it inside your browser. Figure 6.6 shows the final results.

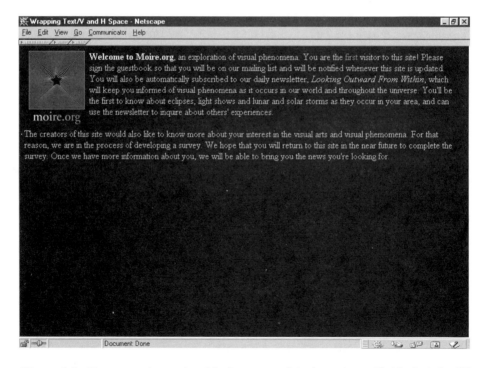

Figure 6.6   Text wrapped around a table. Space around the image is provided by 8 pixels of H space.

With V space and H space, not only can you put space around images, you can also put space around tables.

To remove V or H space, click in the V or H Space field in the Property Inspector and remove the value by pressing the Delete or Backspace key. See Chapter 8 for more information about designing with tables. You can also put space around images using the Cell Padding or Cell Spacing attribute, or by using cascading style sheets.

Linking an Image

After you have inserted an image into your document, you can link the image to another Web site, Web page, a sound or video file, an anchor, or another image. You can also assign a behavior to your image by creating a null link from the image to a behavior (see Exercise 6.3).

Dreamweaver makes it easy for you to link images, but it is still worthwhile to educate yourself on how links are constructed. For more information about the HTML code required to make a link, and about path structure, see Chapter 5, "Linking and Navigation."

Exercise 6.2   Linking an Image

Remember the two files you created in Exercise 6.1? In this exercise, you link them together using the images you placed into the file called IMAGE101.HTML in Part I of the exercise. To get started, open your saved version of IMAGE101.HTML. Make sure that you are in Design view and your Property Inspector (Ctrl+F3) is open.

1. Select the image called MOIRE.GIF, which is located in the center of the top table row.

2. Using the Property Inspector, click in the Link field and click the file folder icon to choose the file called WRAPTEXT.HTML. Alternatively, select the image and drag the point-to-file icon to the file's location in the Site Files window.

3. After the link has been created, the path name will appear in the Link field in the Property Inspector.

4. Repeat steps 1–3, this time using the image called TITLE.GIF, which is located in the center of the bottom table row.

5. Save the file and preview it inside your browser to make sure the links work (see Figure 6.7).

Note

To link your image to an anchor already inside the page, type the anchor name preceded by a pound sign (#) into the Link field in the Property Inspector. Alternatively, use the point-to-file icon to link to the named anchor on your page.

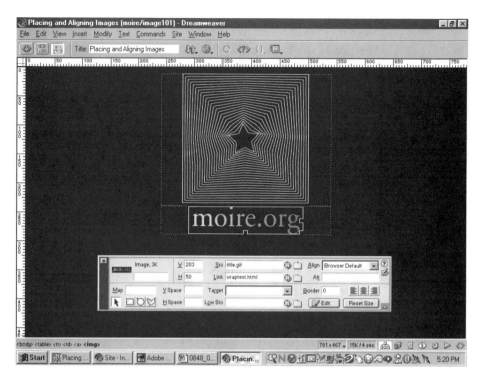

Figure 6.7   The image called TITLE.GIF is linked to the document WRAPTEXT.HTML.

Tip

You can download an extension from Macromedia Exchange that will enable users to print your Web pages by clicking a link. The link can be text or an image. To download the extension, go to www.macromedia.com/exchange and search for "print." Figure 6.7 shows an example.

Image Borders

After you have assigned a link to an image, its edges may become highlighted with a border. This border will be the same color as the <LINK> tag you have established in your document. To remove it, click in the Border field in the Property Inspector. It is located at the far right side. Insert 0 in the field. The border will disappear.

If you want your image link to have a border, use the same Border field in the Property Inspector to specify a size, in pixels. In Figure 6.8, the image has a border of 15 pixels.

Figure 6.8   The gray frame around this image is a border set to 15 pixels.

Assigning a Behavior to an Image

You can assign a behavior to an image by making a null link from the image to one of Dreamweaver's built-in behaviors, found in the Behaviors panel. A null link is a pound sign (#) to which a behavior is attached. JavaScript programmers use the null link technique when writing their code. In Dreamweaver 4, you can make null links without having to write in JavaScript.

Exercise 6.3   Assigning a Behavior to an Image

In the following exercise, you make a null link from an image to a pop-up window behavior. In the end result, a new browser window containing a Shockwave animation will pop up when the user rolls a mouse over the image. This new window will be sized and customized for the purpose it serves. You can complete this exercise with the files found on the accompanying CD-ROM.

1. Open the IMAGE102.HTML file from the CD-ROM. Select the image called MOIRE.GIF, located in the top table cell.

2. Click in the Link field in the Property Inspector. Type a pound sign into the field to indicate the null link (see Figure 6.9).

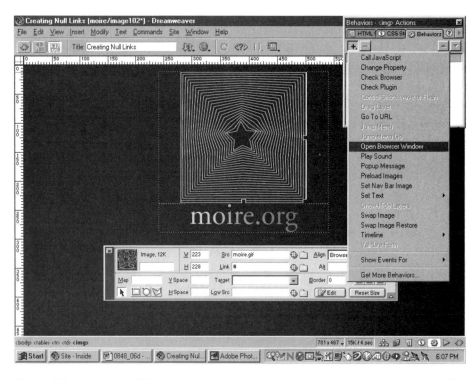

Figure 6.9   The Link field in the Property Inspector contains a pound sign, indicating a null link.

3. Keeping the image selected, access your Behaviors panel by choosing Window/Behaviors. Click the plus sign (+) located at the upper-right corner of the panel.

4. Select the Open Browser Window behavior and enter the specifications shown in Figure 6.10. You are linking to the file called MOVIE.HTML. This file is located in the Moire folder on the CD-ROM. Click OK when you have finished entering the browser size specifications.

5. You should now view the Behaviors panel to make sure the action was assigned. You also need to ensure that the pop-up window you just created will appear when the user clicks the mouse (not when the mouse is held over the image). This requires you to assign the onClick event handler to your action. To do this, select the action inside the Behaviors panel and click the arrow located between the Event and Action areas to access the menu of event handlers. Choose onClick from the listing (see Figure 6.11).

6. Save and preview the image in your Web browser. Roll your cursor over the image to see the behavior work. Figure 6.12 shows a finished version.

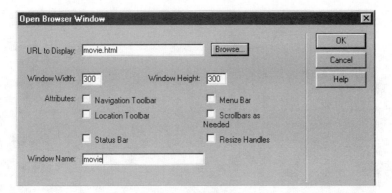

Figure 6.10   Use the Open Browser Window dialog box to specify the size of your pop-up window. You also can establish other attributes, such as scrolling, through this dialog box.

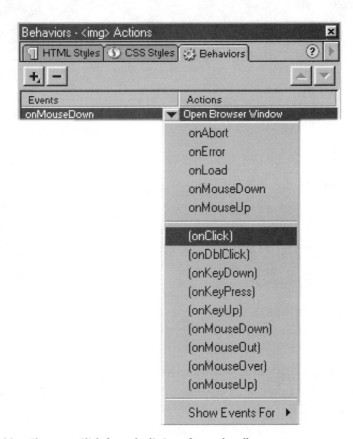

Figure 6.11   Choose onClick from the listing of event handlers.

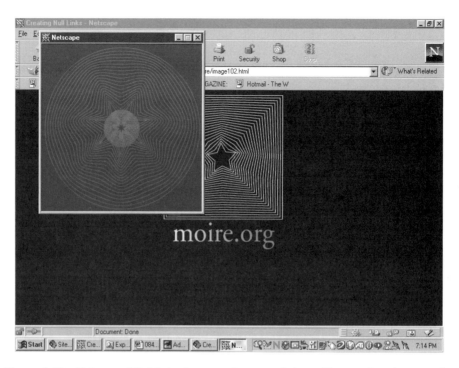

Figure 6.12   Using a null link behavior, a new browser window will open when the user rolls his cursor over the Moire image.

Editing Images

If you need to make changes to an image after inserting it into your Web page, you do not have to remove it and insert it again. Dreamweaver's Property Inspector has two tools you can use for this purpose. One is the Reset Size button, and the other is the Roundtrip Editing button, indicated as Edit on the Property Inspector. Refer to Figure 6.5 to locate them on the Property Inspector.

The Reset Size button returns an image to its original size if you have resized it. Sizing and resizing of images is covered later in this chapter.

Roundtrip Graphics Editing with Fireworks

Dreamweaver 4 has a Roundtrip Graphics Editing feature. This feature has been significantly improved since version 3. Using Roundtrip Graphics Editing, you can edit your images in Macromedia Fireworks via Dreamweaver.

On the Property Inspector, the Edit button will open your image in Macromedia Fireworks and update it with your changes automatically when you return to your Dreamweaver document.

If your image was created and edited in Fireworks, the Fireworks icon appears in the Property Inspector while the image is selected in your open document.

Scanning Images

When scanning images for your Web site, set your scanner software at 72dpi or ppi. There is no need to scan at a higher resolution. The screen resolution is 72dpi; so if your image is the same resolution as the screen, you will not need to resize it.

If you want to make your image bigger than its original size, set your scanner software to scan the image at a higher percentage, such as 150%, but keep your resolution setting at 72dpi.

If you scan your image at a higher resolution, say 300dpi, the monitor must compensate for the high number of pixels. Instead of appearing its true size, the image will be enlarged. When preparing your images for the Web, check their resolution and change it to 72dpi to prevent problems later on.

Tip

If you define hotspots in Fireworks and provide the link information, you can place the resulting image map inside Dreamweaver and use the HTML page you exported from Fireworks to make the map work. Fireworks enables you to zoom in for more precision in drawing hotspots.

Sizing Images

The Dreamweaver Property Inspector provides you with a way to indicate the width and height of your images. The image-size fields are located on the left side of the Property Inspector.

When you insert an image into your Dreamweaver document, the true width and height of the image appears automatically in the Property Inspector's image-size fields. The true width and height is the size the image actually is, as it was created in your image-editing program. In Dreamweaver, the width and height should be measured in pixels. Figure 6.13 shows an example.

You can change the width or height of an image by clicking in either field and changing the numeric value. Keep in mind that it is usually not a good idea to change the size of your images. Although a pixel or two change in width or height won't make a difference, changes of 5 pixels or more will probably cause a loss in image quality (see Figure 6.14).

If you must change image dimensions, it is better to decrease the image size rather than increase it. Increasing image size leads to a great deal of loss in image quality.

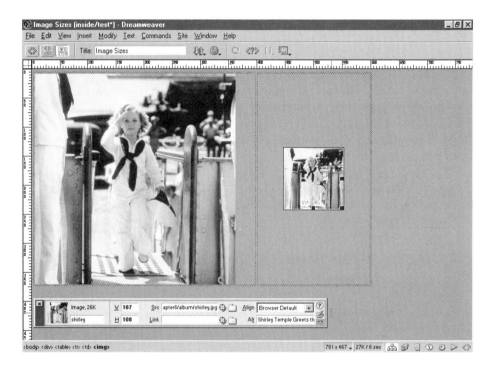

Figure 6.13   The image on the left is its true size. The image on the right has been resized. In the Property Inspector, the height and width of a resized image are shown in bold type.

You can also change the size of your image by clicking and dragging out the resize handles. If you hold down the Shift key while doing this, the image resizes proportionately.

To remove custom sizing, select the image and use the Refresh button on the Property Inspector.

Pixel Spacers

With one type of image, it does not matter whether you make huge adjustments to the width and height values. This type of image is called a *pixel spacer* or *pixel shim*. To make a pixel spacer, make an image in your graphics program that is 1 pixel high and 1 pixel wide. In Figure 6.15, a white pixel shim is used, but you can make them any color you want, including transparent. Be aware that pixel shims occasionally show up as beveled boxes in Netscape for Macintosh, so you probably shouldn't make your spacers extremely large.

Insert the spacer as you would any other image. Then use the Property Inspector to adjust the height and width. Because the image contains only 1 pixel that is only 1 color, no loss of quality occurs when you change the size.

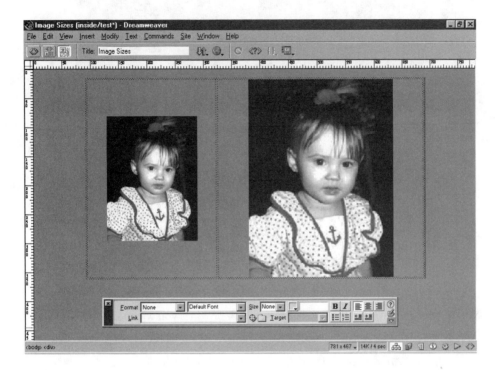

Figure 6.14   The photo on the right has been stretched, causing a loss of image quality.

You can also use colored pixel spacers as background images in table cells. For more information, see Chapter 8. You can also use cascading styles sheets to make rules and adjust spacing. For more information on cascading style sheets in Dreamweaver, see Chapter 12, "Using Cascading Style Sheets."

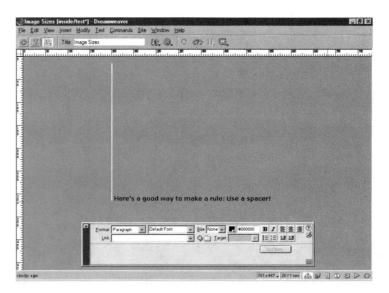

Here's a good way to make a rule: Use a spacer!

Figure 6.15   You can use a pixel spacer to create space or as background colors.

Image Assets

New in Dreamweaver 4 is the Assets panel, which provides you with a convenient way to view all the images you are using in your site. To access the panel, follow these steps:

1. Choose Window/Assets (F11) from the Dreamweaver main menu.

2. Click the Images icon on the left side of the Assets panel.

Figure 6.16 shows the image listing as it appears in my Assets panel. (Every image I have used throughout my site appears in this panel. A notation to the side of the image path name, under the Type field, indicates whether the image is a GIF, JPEG, or PNG.)

Note

> You must have your site cache enabled for the Assets panel to work. Also, be sure you haven't selected the radio button for Favorites; this prevents your images from showing up inside the Assets panel.

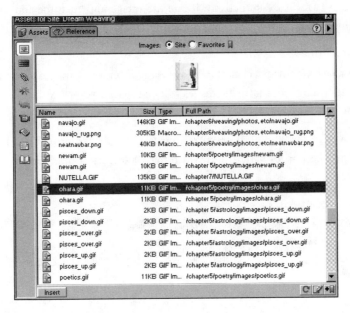

Figure 6.16   An image listing in the Assets panel.

Note

Click the Size column header to arrange the image listing by file size. Alternatively, click the Name column header to arrange the images in alphabetic order by filename.

Placing Images with the Assets Panel

To place an image from the Assets panel, follow these steps:

1. Click in the table cell where you want to place the image.

2. Choose Window/Assets and click the Images icon on the left to open the Images listing.

3. Inside the listing, click the image path name you want to use.

4. Your image will appear in the document.

Favorite Images

As you design, you will probably find that certain images are your favorites and that you use them over and over again. This is likely to happen with the images you use in your navigational system, such as a Home button.

To add an image to the Favorites listing in the Assets panel, locate the image in the listing and right-click (Windows). This action pulls down a window from which you can choose Add to Favorites. Alternatively, locate the image and click the add-to-favorites icon in the lower-right side of the panel and click the OK button in the resulting pop-up message.

To view your favorite images, click the Favorites radio button from the top of the Assets panel's Images listing. Your favorite images will be listed. If you click the Site radio button, your favorite images will once again be mixed in with the site's images.

From the Favorites view, you can organize your favorite images into folders. Figure 6.17 shows my favorite images sorted into two different folders: a Star Signs folder and a Weaving folder.

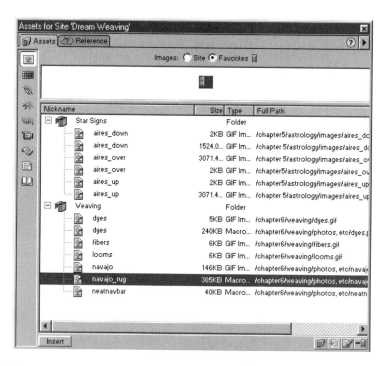

Figure 6.17   Organize your favorite images into folders.

To make a folder for your images, follow these steps:

1. Click the orange accordion file icon at the bottom of the Assets panel. (You should be in the Favorites view of the Assets panel's Images section.)

2. Type in a name for your folder.

3. Select an image or set of images from the Favorites listing and drag them into the appropriate folder.

Image-Listing Options

You can execute other functions for storing and organizing images by right-clicking an image path name in either Favorites or Site view or by using the icons at the bottom of the panel. Figure 6.18 shows a set of options from the right-click pull-down menu. Table 6.1 outlines what each option does and describes its icon.

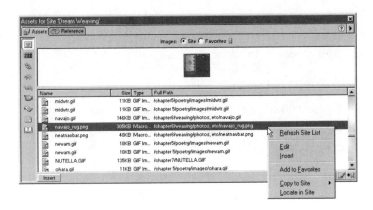

Figure 6.18   The context menu options from the Assets panel, Images view.

Table 6.1   Image-Listing Options

Option	What It Does	Icon
Refresh Site List	This option refreshes the list of available assets based on your site cache. Unused images remain, but images that have been moved outside the site disappear. Similarly, images that have been moved into the site now appear.	Circular arrow
Insert	This option inserts the image.	Insert button
Edit	This option opens the image in Macromedia Fireworks.	Pen and paper
Add to Favorites	This option gives an image Favorite status.	Bookmark with plus sign
Copy to Site	This option copies an image from one site into another site. Choose the site you want to move the image to from the submenu.	
Locate in Site	This option locates a specific image within a site.	

Thumbnails

You might have seen sites that make use of thumbnails, or tiny images only slightly larger than your thumbnail, that are linked to a larger version of the same image. Thumbnails can prove very useful on e-commerce sites, because they enable the user to skim over many different products at once but still offer the opportunity to see desired products at full size.

The e-commerce example is only one of many uses for thumbnails. In Dreamweaver, you can set up thumbnail pages in two different ways. One way is discussed here. The next section discusses the other way to add thumbnails.

To add thumbnail pages, follow these steps:

1. Insert the first of your images for thumbnailing into your document.
2. With the image selected, resize it to your desired thumbnail size by using the Height and Width fields in the Property Inspector.
3. Link the image to itself by using the Link field in the Property Inspector.
4. Repeat steps 1–3 for all the images you want to include in your thumbnail grid.

Note that this process could result in high download time for your page. Even if you resize the images to thumbnails, they will still retain their original file sizes. If you want to reduce the file size of the thumbnail page, use your image-editing program to make thumbnail versions of all your image files and then link them to the larger versions rather than to themselves.

Creating a Web Photo Album

The second way to make thumbnail pages is to use the Dreamweaver command Create Web Photo Album. This command automates the thumbnail-making process so that you don't have to make smaller versions of every image you want to use.

This command works by opening Macromedia Fireworks and batch processing the images you have designated for your Web photo album. The thumbnails are stored in their own folder. Back in Dreamweaver, a series of HTML pages are made for you. These HTML pages will navigate your user through your photo album.

Complete the following exercise using the image files inside the Album folder on the accompanying CD-ROM to make a sample Web photo album.

Exercise 6.4   Creating a Web Photo Album

1. In a new document, pull down the Commands menu and choose Create Web Photo Album.

2. Fill out the fields in the resulting window (see Figure 6.19). Use the image files in the Album folder on the CD-ROM to make the album.

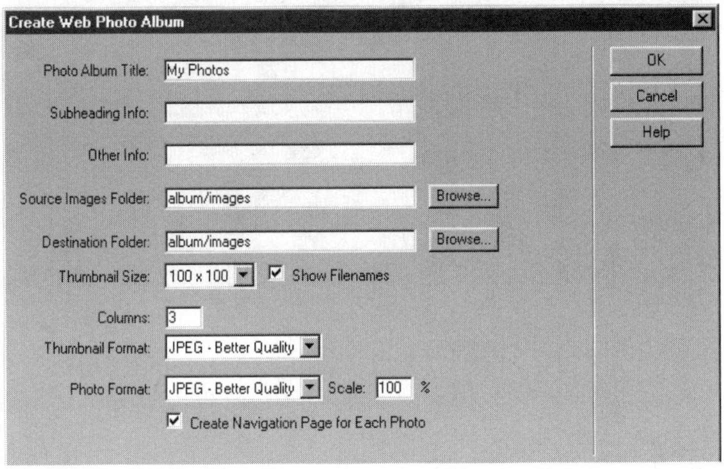

Figure 6.19   The Create Web Photo Album window.

3. Click OK.

4. Dreamweaver opens Fireworks to process your images. After the album has been made, save the file.

5. Preview the file in the browser to make sure it works.

Take a look at the Site Files window to see how Dreamweaver set up your photo album. You can make changes to the page property (F6). (In Figure 6.20, I made my page background black and aligned the images in the center of the table cells—as covered in Chapter 8.)

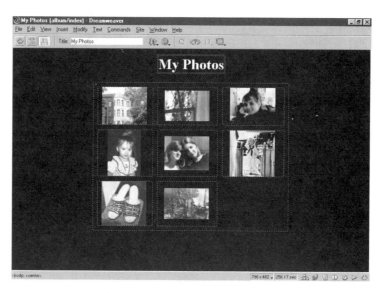

Figure 6.20   The author's photo page.

Tips for Uploading Images

After you have made your images and placed them inside Dreamweaver pages, you need to upload them to a Web server to make them available to others. This is a tiresome task if you have hundreds of images on your site. The following few Dreamweaver tips will make things easier for you:

1. Store your image files in a specific folder, called something like Images. Use sub-folders inside the main folder if you have a large number of images. The Images folder should contain only the images you are using on your site.

   The files you used to make your images, such as Fireworks PNGs and Photoshop files, are better off in their own folder, which you can save on your personal hard drive. Don't upload this folder to the Web server. If you accidentally upload the folder to the server with your Web images, you will be taking up server space unnecessarily.

2. Give your image files simple, uncomplicated names, such as TREE.GIF. Avoid long names and names that have special characters in them. And, above all, make a habit of using lowercase names and extensions for both image and HTML files. This will prevent problems with case-sensitive UNIX systems. If Windows 95 or Windows 2000 tries to give your files uppercase extensions, use a convert-to-lowercase utility to rename the files with lowercase letters. You can get such a utility from a Web site such as www.shareware.com.

3. When working from the Dreamweaver Site Files window to publish your site, upload the HTML pages first. Dreamweaver then asks whether you want to include dependent files. If you click OK, all your image files and the Images folder will be uploaded automatically. This way, you can run out for a cup of coffee while your images are being transferred.

4. *Always* check your newly published site for broken image icons. If you see such an icon, it means that there's a problem with one of your image files. You can use the Dreamweaver Check Links function to locate problems. First, however, check to see whether there is a problem with case sensitivity (see tip number 3).

5. Sometimes we make images, store them in our Web images folder, and never use them in a document. This type of image is called an *orphan*. It is not a part of the network that makes up your Web site. Orphans are often overlooked in the FTP process. To eliminate them, thereby preserving space on your Web server, choose the Orphaned Files functionality located in the Check Links Sitewide command.

Summary

When working with images, your skills with Web layout and design will be tested. You can rise to the challenge by formatting your images correctly in your image-editing program before you use them inside Dreamweaver. Programs such as Macromedia Fireworks prove especially useful for creating low-bandwidth GIF and JPEG images that will download quickly and look great.

Make it a habit to contain your images inside table cells. Free-floating images can cause alignment problems, and they are difficult to control. Images inside table cells are easy to align using the Dreamweaver Property Inspector.

As discussed in this chapter, working in Dreamweaver, you have many opportunities to use your images as something more than decorations. You can link them to other files, assign JavaScript behaviors to them, and create Web photo albums. Stretch your imagination as far as it will go. (Just don't stretch your images with it!)

Chapter 7

Web Design Issues

When you are working with Dreamweaver, you wear a designer's hat even if you don't consider yourself to be an artistic person. I wish I could tell you that Dreamweaver will automatically make your site look great and function well, no matter what you do. I also wish I could tell you that there are a set of rules you can memorize that will keep you from making mistakes in your design— but I would be lying if I told you either of those things. The truth is that the real art of Web site design is the thought you put into your interface, anticipating the mouse-clicks your users will make and addressing the issues that make your site unique from others. Alternatively, you might come to accept that tried-and-true navigation systems are what's best for the information you are offering.

Dreamweaver gives you many different ways to do the same thing, and there are about as many different ways to do different things. The possibilities are truly endless. This chapter takes a look at some Web design issues and gives examples of how you can handle them using Dreamweaver. Take this opportunity to examine your own approach to designing Web sites and learn to use the design tools Dreamweaver provides for all they are worth.

This chapter covers the following:

- Working with color
- Background patterns
- Viewing and editing the grid
- Tracing images
- Screen resolution
- Design strategy
- File sizes

Working with Color

One of the most often used windows, and an important one in dealing with design issues in Dreamweaver, is the Page Properties dialog box, which you can access by choosing Modify/Page Properties (see Figure 7.1). This dialog box is important because it is here where you establish the page title, background color, background image, text color, linking color scheme, and page margins. You also use this window to specify a tracing image (if you're using one). For more information about tracing images, see Chapter 6, "Working with Images." To get started with the Page Properties dialog box, first take a look at how this window enables you to make color choices for your Web site.

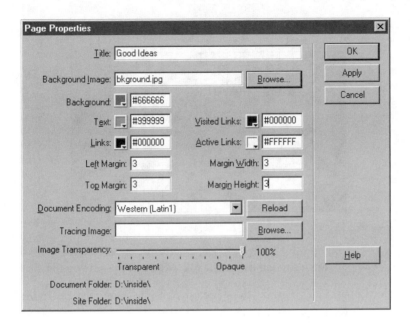

Figure 7.1   The Page Properties dialog box.

Choosing Colors

Dreamweaver makes use of the Web-safe color palette, which helps you to select colors that are less likely to dither on monitors that display only 256 colors. Dithering is a spotty effect that occurs when the computer monitor is not capable of showing a particular color.

From the Page Properties window, you can assign any color in the Web-safe palette to your Text value or any of the link states by pulling down the color chip next to the field name. If you want to change the text color, for instance, pull down the color chip next to Text. Your cursor will become an eyedropper icon, indicating you can select a color. Figure 7.2 shows the color palette.

This color palette is the same in Dreamweaver, Fireworks, and Flash. This way, you can establish a set of color choices and import the resulting graphics into any of the three programs.

As you move the eyedropper icon over the color palette, the hexadecimal representations appear at the top of the palette. Click your desired color to assign it to the field.

In the upper-right corner of the palette are two icons and an arrow.

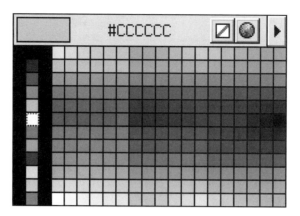

Figure 7.2   The Dreamweaver color palette.

The arrow will pull down a menu listing the following color palette options:

- **Color Cubes.** This will show the standard Web-safe color palette used in Dreamweaver, Fireworks, and Flash.

- **Continuous Tone.** This arranges the colors in the palette according to hue.

- **Windows OS.** This shows the Microsoft Windows system palette. These colors are standard on any computer running Microsoft Windows.

- **Mac OS.** This shows the Macintosh system palette. These colors are standard on any computer running the Macintosh operating system.

- **Grayscale.** This shows only shades of gray.

- **Snap to Web Safe.** Check this option to have Dreamweaver snap Windows and Macintosh systems colors to the Web-safe color palette. This option is selected by default, so do not change it unless you have a good reason. This is used if you select a color from somewhere on your screen using the eyedropper. The nearest Web-safe color will be approximated.

The first icon, a cross-through mark (also called the eraser), returns the color to its default setting when clicked. In other words, clicking this icon is the equivalent of selecting None.

The second icon, a color wheel, opens the Color window, where you can enter in values for Red, Green, and Blue, as well as for Hue, Saturation, and Luminance. Figure 7.3 shows the Color window. Be aware that using the color wheel for color selection is a risk. Custom colors, which are covered later in this chapter, may not display as desired on 16-bit and 8-bit monitors.

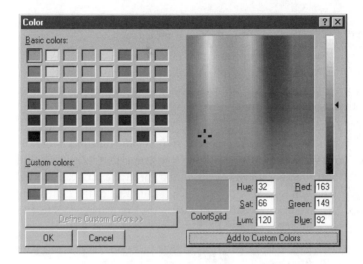

Figure 7.3   The Dreamweaver Color window.

Many designers use the Color window when they are also working in another program. If you have an illustration that was created in Macromedia Freehand, for example, and you want to put it against a matching background in Dreamweaver, you can open the Color window and enter in the RGB values you used in Freehand. The same goes for programs such as Photoshop, Illustrator, Flash, and others.

You also can open both documents and use the Dreamweaver eyedropper to select the color from another Macromedia program. This can be a very useful feature, but sometimes you may not want to take the time to open a program or adjust window sizes so that you can see both programs simultaneously. If you get into the habit of writing down both the hexidecimal and RGB values of your colors as you are working, you will save yourself a great deal of time.

Exercise 7.1   Creating Background and Flash Text Colors

In Exercise 7.1, you adjust the background color of a Dreamweaver document to match the background color of an image called ARTFLOWER.PNG, which is located in the Color folder on your CD-ROM. You also create Flash rollover text and color the text to match the image.

  1. Open the COLORTEST.HTML file from the Color folder on your CD-ROM. This document contains an empty table comprised of two rows and one column. The table has a width of 100% and both rows are set to align contents to the center and top. The background color of this document is set to white (#FFFFFF), the Dreamweaver default.

2. Click your cursor in the top table row. Choose Insert/Image and select the ARTFLOWER.PNG file from the Color folder on your CD-ROM.

3. After you have inserted the image into the document, choose Modify/Page Properties. When the Page Properties dialog box appears, move it to the lower-left corner of your screen. You want to see both the Page Properties dialog box and the image at the same time.

4. Click (*do not* double-click) the square color chip located next to the Background field. When the color palette appears, your cursor transforms into the eyedropper tool. Move the eyedropper out of the Page Properties dialog box until it is located over the light-green background color of the image. The value inside the color palette will read #CCCC99, which is the value of the light-green color (see Figure 7.4). When you see this value, click the eyedropper tool to select it.

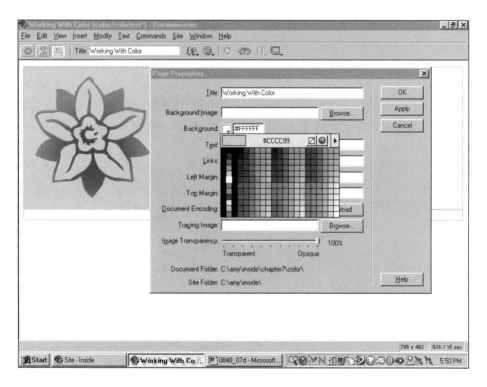

Figure 7.4   Choosing a matching background color using the Page Properties dialog box and the eyedropper tool (not shown).

5. Click the Apply button inside the Page Properties dialog box to ensure that you have selected the color that matches the background image. Click OK when you are ready to exit the Page Properties dialog box.

6. Insert rollover Flash text that reads Welcome below the image. You will choose a
   font from your computer's hard drive in this step, so your Welcome message will
   look a little different from the screen captures that follow. To get started, click
   your cursor in the bottom table row, which is located directly below the image.

7. Choose Insert/Interactive Images/Flash Text to access the Insert Flash Text dialog
   box (see Figure 7.5). Choose a font from the Font pull-down menu and a font
   size of around 30 to 40 points, and then type the word **Welcome** inside the Text
   area (see Figure 7.6).

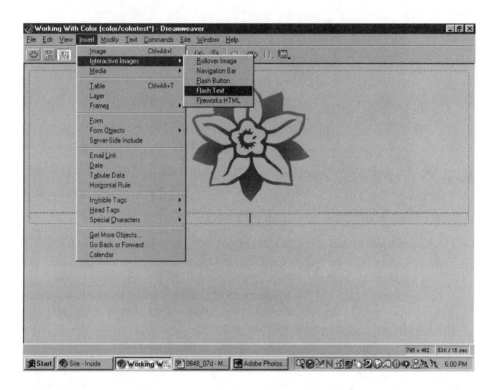

Figure 7.5   Accessing the Insert Flash Text dialog box.

8. Choose the background, text color, and rollover color using the palettes inside
   the Insert Flash Text dialog box. First, click the square color chip adjacent to the
   Background field (located near the bottom of the dialog box). When you see the
   palette, move your cursor/eyedropper out of the dialog box into your document
   until you see the value #CCCC99 appear inside the palette. When you see this
   value, click the eyedropper tool to select it. If you do not select a background
   color for the Flash text, a white background appears by default.

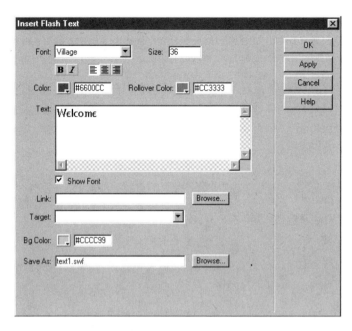

Figure 7.6   The Insert Flash Text dialog box.

9. Now choose a color for the text and the rollover text (the color seen when a user moves a cursor over the area). Click the square color icon next to the Text field inside the Insert Flash Text dialog box (see Figure 7.7). Move your cursor/eyedropper out of the dialog box and over the flower image. Note that as you move your cursor over the flower, the color value inside the palette changes. This change occurs because the flower is made of a color gradient that contains many different colors blended together. Choose a color you want for your text and click the cursor/eyedropper to select it.

10. Repeat step 9 for the Rollover Text field. This is the color a user will see when holding a cursor over the area.

11. Click the Apply button to see how your color and font choices look inside the document. When you are satisfied with them, click OK to exit the Insert Flash Text dialog box.

12. The last step is to test the rollover text to make sure it works. Select the Flash text by clicking it once, and then open the Property Inspector (Ctrl+F3). Click the Play button inside the Property Inspector to activate the Flash text (see Figure 7.8). Then hold your cursor over the text to see what the rollover color looks like. If you want to make changes, select the text and click the Edit button inside the Property Inspector to return to the Insert Flash Text dialog box.

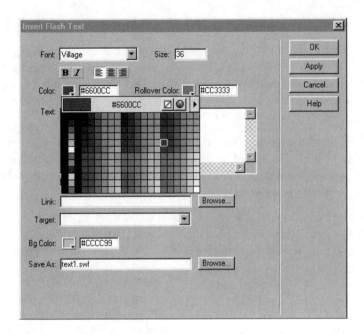

Figure 7.7   Choosing a Flash Text color.

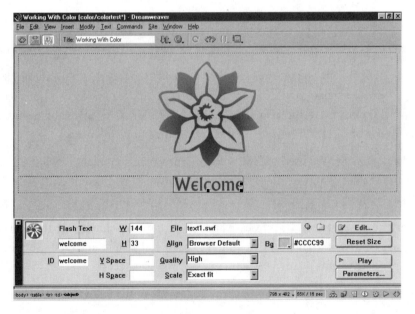

Figure 7.8   The Property Inspector displays options for Flash text. Select the Flash text inside the document to view them.

Note that in Exercise 7.1 you made use of two file types that are not viewable in older Web browsers.

The image called ARTFLOWER is a PNG (Portable Network Graphics) file. Although PNG is the default image type of Macromedia Fireworks, PNGs are not viewable in some Web browsers. For more information about the PNG file type, see Chapter 6.

You also worked with Flash text in this exercise. When you created the text, you also created an SWF (Shockwave Flash) file that was stored on your hard drive. You must upload this file with the other files linked to the COLORTEST.HTML document to enable outside users to view the text. In addition, the browser must contain the Macromedia Shockwave plug-in to play the text.

Although new Web browsers come with a Shockwave plug-in, older browsers require that you download and install the plug-in before any Flash files can be played. For more information about the SWF file type, see Chapter 18, "Animation with Flash."

Custom Colors

Some Web designers are not happy with the limited color choices offered by the Web-safe palette and so use custom colors of their own making. This is a risky decision, but one that is becoming more and more popular as True Color (24- and 32-bit) monitors become more commonplace.

Custom colors display correctly only on monitors that display True Color color. The question that Web designers are now asking is, "How many Web users have True Color?"

A study done by StatMarket (`www.statmarket.com`) showed that only about 38% of today's Web users enjoy the benefits of True Color. Approximately 56% of users are somewhat limited by 16-bit color (also called High Color). The only good news here is that only 6% of users still view the Web on 256-color (8-bit) monitors.

Even though many Web users are still without True Color, you might be willing to sacrifice a loss of color quality or already know that your site will be viewed exclusively on 24- or 32-bit monitors. If so, custom colors are ready and waiting for you.

To create custom colors in Dreamweaver, pull down the color chip next to the field name of the item you want to change, access the Web-safe color palette, and then select the custom color palette icon.

From the resulting Color window (Figure 7.3), do one of the following:

- Click in the color wheel to choose a custom color.

  Or

- Enter a value for Red, Green, and Blue into the text field boxes adjacent to the color values.

Sometimes you will need to access the color wheel even if you want to use RGB values that are Web-safe, because Dreamweaver does not list the RGB values in the color palette. If you are working with a set of colors in an image-editing program and want to use the same colors in Dreamweaver, write down the values you are using in the imaging program and use the custom color feature to get the same color in Dreamweaver. If, on the other hand, you are creating your images in Fireworks, Freehand, or Flash, you can click the Dreamweaver eyedropper tool in a colored area of your Fireworks document to apply the identical color to the selected area of your Dreamweaver file.

Color Assets

New in Dreamweaver 4 is a Color Assets panel, which you can use to help you remember and reuse color values. To access the panel, follow these steps:

1. Choose Window/Assets (F11) from the Dreamweaver main menu.

2. Click the color palette icon on the left side of the Assets panel.

Figure 7.9 shows the color listing as it appears in my Assets panel. Every color value I have used throughout my site appears in this panel. As long as you have a site cache in your site definition, a notation to the side of the color under the Type field will indicate whether the color is Web-safe.

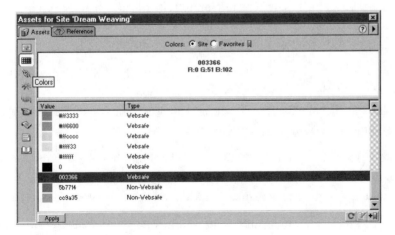

Figure 7.9   Colors listed inside the Assets panel.

Exercise 7.2   Assigning Colors with the Assets Panel

To assign a color from the Assets panel to an element of your Web page, follow these steps:

1. Select the text or other element you want to modify.
2. Choose Window/Assets and click the color palette icon on the left to open the color listing.
3. Inside the listing, click the color chip you want to use and click the Apply button, or drag the color chip from the Assets panel to the selected area.

Your desired color should replace the current color.

Tip

You can play around with colors with less risk by using the Undo keystroke command. This universal command is Ctrl+Z on Windows and Command+Z on the Macintosh. If you assign a color and do not like it, just undo it. (If only real life were that easy!) Dreamweaver enables you to make multiple undos, so you can go back three steps if you need to.

Favorite Colors

As you design, you will probably find that certain colors in the Web-safe palette are your favorites and that you use them over and over again. You might know them so well that you can pick them out of the palette in an instant. You also might have some custom colors for which you have practically memorized the RGB values. To save brain space, store those often-used colors in the Favorites list in the Assets panel's Color listing.

To add a color to Favorites, locate the color in the list and right-click (Windows). This action pulls down a window from which you can choose Add to Favorites. Alternatively, locate the color and click the bookmark icon in the lower-right side of the panel and click the OK button in the resulting pop-up message.

To view your favorite colors, click the Favorite radio button from the top of the Assets panel's Color listing. A list of your favorite colors displays. If you click the Site radio button, your favorite colors display again, mixed in with the site's colors.

From the Favorites view, you can organize your favorite colors into folders. Figure 7.10 shows my favorite colors sorted into two different folders: a Logo Colors folder, and a Background Colors folder.

To make a folder for your colors, follow these steps:

1. Click the accordion file icon at the bottom of the Assets panel. (You should be in the Favorites view of the Assets panel's Color section.)

2. Type in a name for your folder.

3. Select a color or set of colors from the Favorites listing and drag them into the new folder.

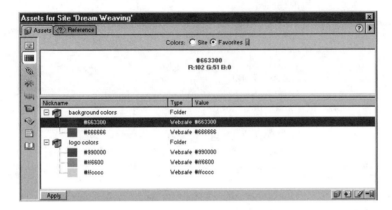

Figure 7.10   Favorite color choices listed in the Assets panel.

Color Listing Options

You can execute other functions for storing and organizing colors by either right-clicking a color in Favorites or Site view, or by using the icons at the bottom of the Assets panel. Figure 7.11 shows a set of options from the right-click pull-down menu. Table 7.1 outlines what each option does and describes its icon.

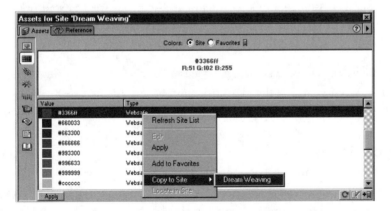

Figure 7.11   You can access Color Listing options through the context menu or the icons in the bottom-right corner of the Assets panel's Color view.

Table 7.1   Color Listing Options

Option	What It Does	Icon
Refresh Site List	This option removes any unused colors from the list and adds in any colors added into the current open document.	Circular arrow
Apply	This option assigns the color to currently selected text or another element in your document.	Apply button
Edit	This option, which is available for favorite colors only, pulls up the Dreamweaver color tool, enabling you to modify the color or change it to a new color. Be aware that changing the color this way will not update all instances of color in your site.	Pen and paper
Add to Favorites	This option gives a color Favorite status.	Bookmark with plus sign
Copy to Site	This option copies a color from one site into another site. Choose the site you want to move the color to from the submenu. Accessed by right-clicking a color in Favorites or Site view.	

Design and Layout

There's a t-shirt sold by a well-respected font house that says "Design Is a Good Idea." I think this phrase sums up what we are all trying to achieve with our Web sites: one good idea after another. After all, wouldn't you love it if someone went to your site, took one look, and said, "What a good idea!" about your navigation bars, or your background patterns, or your use of photographs or artwork? I know I would.

Fortunately, we can all come up with good ideas. The challenge is to bring the good idea to life in a Web page before the idea turns sour. One of the first steps you can take to bring your ideas to life is to make use of Dreamweaver's design tools.

Background Patterns

Many designers opt to use background images rather than a solid color. Choose Modify/Page Properties and click the file folder icon next to the Background Image field to select a file to use for your background image.

For best results, study tiling methods and create a background pattern that does not have seams or repeat itself onscreen (unless that's what you want). Figure 7.12 shows a background pattern as it looks in the image-editing program. Figure 7.13 shows how it looks tiled inside a Dreamweaver document. You also can prevent tiling of background images. One way to do so is to use cascading style sheets, discussed in Chapter 12, "Using Cascading Style Sheets."

Figure 7.12   This is the background image as it looks in Adobe Photoshop.

Grids

To help you with the layout of your images, tables, and other objects, you can turn on Dreamweaver's grid by choosing View/Grid/Show Grid. Figure 7.14 shows a sample grid in Standard view. This grid can be a great design tool. However, the grid does not enable you to obtain pixel-specific positioning that will be rendered consistently by all browsers.

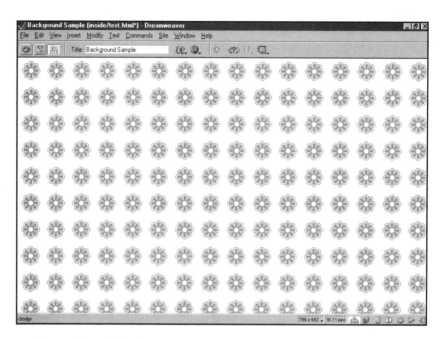

Figure 7.13   This is the background image tiled inside a Dreamweaver document.

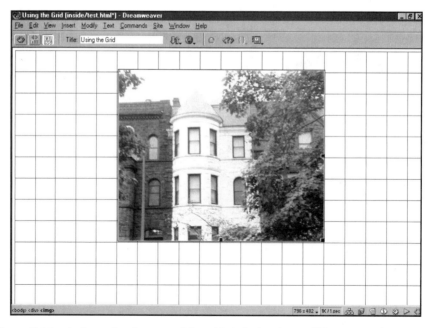

Figure 7.14   A photo placed on top of the grid. Only the photo will be seen inside a Web browser.

To view or edit the grid, choose View/Grid/Edit Grid. The Grid Settings dialog box displays (see Figure 7.15).

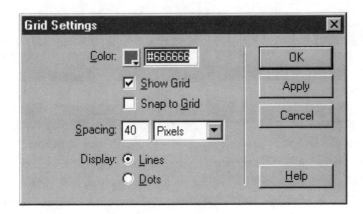

Figure 7.15   The Grid Settings dialog box.

Show Grid

From the Grid Settings dialog box, click the check box adjacent to Show Grid to turn the grid on or off. You do not have to pull up this window to view the grid; you also can execute the keystroke Ctrl+Alt+G, or select it from the View/Grid menu.

Edit Grid

You also can make changes to the grid style and spacing through the Grid Settings dialog box (refer back to Figure 7.15). In this dialog box, you can choose a color for the grid and adjust the spacing of pixels, centimeters, or inches. You also can specify a style of lines or dots for the grid.

Snap to Grid

If you select Snap to Grid from the Grid Settings dialog box or from the View/Grid menu, the items you place on your Web page will automatically align to the grid. You must have the grid turned on for the Snap feature to work.

Grid snapping can prove useful if you really want to align according to the grid marks. If you want to create a less static, more spontaneous layout, grid snapping can be annoying. You will find yourself fighting against the magnetic quality of the grid. Note that you also can manipulate grid snaps with the keystroke Ctrl+Alt+Shift+G. Always be aware that the grid is for use in Dreamweaver only. The alignment of your published

Web page will be determined by the width of the tables used and how various Web browsers read them. In other words, don't let the grid give you a false sense of security.

Note

> If you are looking to make guides like in an image-editing program or a layout program like Quark Xpress, you are out of luck. Dreamweaver doesn't make guides. You might want to use tables or tracing images as a replacement for guides. For more information about tables, see Chapter 8, "Layout with Tables."

Tracing Images

Dreamweaver enables you to place a tracing image beneath your work area. This tracing image can serve as a guide for you when laying out and designing a site. For example, a client might request you to make a Web site of a print brochure (and no electronic files for the brochure are available). You could scan the brochure and use it as a tracing image when building a Web site. The tracing image will not be included with the HTML for your site; therefore, it will not show up when you preview your page.

Tracing images also prove useful in collaborative work environments. A designer can create an image file that shows how a page layout should look. Someone else can then use this image file as a tracing image as the page is being created in Dreamweaver. Always be aware that tracing images, such as the grid, do not show up inside a Web browser.

Figure 7.16 shows a tracing image being used in Layout view with a couple of table cells drawn on top. For more about designing with tables, see Chapter 8.

To place a tracing image, follow these steps:

1. Inside your document window, choose Modify/Page Properties.
2. Click the file folder icon next to the tracing image to choose the image you want to use.
3. Select the opacity for the tracing image—from 0 (completely invisible) to 100% (completely opaque). A good opacity level to start out with is 50%.
4. Click Apply to see what the image looks like inside your document.
5. Click OK when you are satisfied with the opacity level.

Figure 7.16   The Nutella.com site being used as a tracing image in Layout view.

Alternatively, you can place a tracing image and adjust it by choosing View/Tracing Image/Load from the Dreamweaver main menu. The resulting submenu gives you the following four options (see Figure 7.17):

- **Show.** Turns the tracing image on or off.
- **Align.** Moves the tracing image into alignment with the X and Y coordinates of the upper-left corner of the currently selected object.
- **Adjust.** Enables you to choose coordinates for the X and Y position of your tracing image.
- **Reset.** Returns the tracing image to its default position (at the left side of the screen).

Page Margins and Margin Sizes

Page margins are set by choosing Modify/Page Properties (or using the shortcut Ctrl+J). Inside the Page Properties dialog box, type a number, in pixels, for the left and top margins. You also can assign margin width and height in pixels. If you leave the page margin settings blank, certain browsers default to 1- or 2-pixel margins. To turn them off, be sure to input 0 into the box. Also, different browsers support different margin attributes, so be sure to put a 0 in all four boxes to ensure no margins.

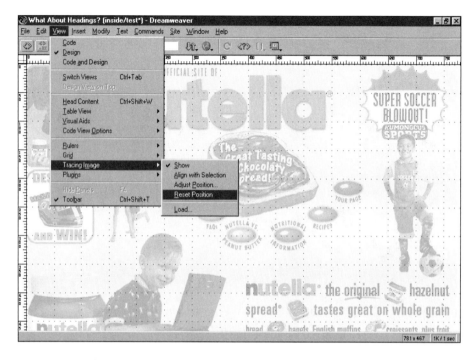

Figure 7.17   Accessing tracing image options.

Experimenting with the margin settings can lead to some new and interesting effects. You can set the margins to 0 to bleed an image into the browser scrollbars. Or, you can use a very high margin setting to push an image or other Web page element into a specific spot.

Rulers

You can turn on the Dreamweaver ruler, which runs along the top and left side of your document, by choosing View/Rulers/Show, or with the shortcut Ctrl+Alt+R.

Figure 7.18 shows the View/Rulers submenu. From this menu, you can choose a setting of pixels, inches, or centimeters for your ruler.

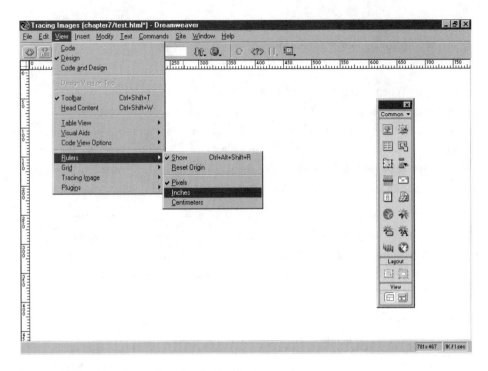

Figure 7.18   Accessing options for the Dreamweaver ruler.

By default, the ruler's origins (the 0,0 coordinate) are set for the upper-left corner of the window. To change the origins, click and drag the corner of the ruler (the white box with two crisscrossing lines) and drag the ruler positioning to your desired point.

To reset the ruler origins to 0, choose View/Rulers/Reset Origin from the Dreamweaver main menu, or double-click the upper-left corner, where the two rulers intersect.

Web Design: The Big Picture

Web design might be your career choice, a hobby, or a chore. Whatever it is to you, understand that there is more to Web design than color palettes, grids, and rulers. The sections that follow examine two important Web design issues: screen resolution and file sizes.

Screen Resolution

Screen resolution is a frequent cause of confusion. You might be letting your good Web site ideas go to waste because you don't know how to scan and adjust the size of your images so that they fit into browser windows.

A first step toward ending this confusion is to know that images made for the computer screens should always be 72dpi (dots per inch) by the time you are importing them into Dreamweaver.

Another tip: When making your Web graphics, measure in pixels, not in inches. The computer is measuring in pixels, so you should too. And unless you know differently, understand that some of your users will not be able to see images or page layouts more than 600 pixels wide. Even if you have a nice big 21-inch monitor, consider the person who doesn't. Also consider that the same site will look a bit different from browser to browser, especially when you cross platforms from PC to Macintosh, or vice versa.

When creating your site, also keep in mind that each user has a predetermined screen resolution already set on his or her computer. For example, my screen resolution is set to 800×600. This means I can see 800 pixels in a horizontal direction and 600 pixels in a vertical direction. If my resolution were set to 640×480, I would be able to see 640 pixels horizontally and 480 pixels vertically.

All Web designers are challenged to come up with designs that can handle the change in viewing area width and height. Here are two common problems:

- Your Web site is too wide to fit into the user's browser, which prompts the browser to add a scrollbar to the bottom of the browser window.

- Your Web site is too narrow for the user's browser, leaving a ribbon of white space on the right.

Although no concrete solutions remedy these problems, you do have options. The first option is to warn the user ahead of time, via a splash screen, that the site he is about to visit is designed for a particular resolution. To take this option a step further, you can add a JavaScript to the first page of your site that will detect the user's resolution, allowing users with the "right" resolution to pass through without receiving a message.

Tip

You can download an extension from Macromedia Exchange that will provide you with an easy way to detect a user's screen resolution and redirect the user to the appropriate set of pages.

To download the extension, go to www.macromedia.com/exchange and search for "resolution." After you have installed the extension, you can pull up a window and specify a resolution-redirect script for three different screen resolutions.

Design Strategy

One way to ensure that your Web site elements use all available screen space is to design your site with percentage-based tables. This technique is sometimes called a "liquid layout." This way, the elements in your site slide out to meet the walls of the browser, automatically resizing themselves to fit into the user's window. See Chapter 8 for more information about creating percentage-based tables with Dreamweaver (it's easy!). The disadvantage of percentage-based designing is that you cannot use that system for your images. Images are a set size and cannot be stretched out or condensed unless you are willing to sacrifice their quality.

The third and last option in this list is to just make a choice from the onset of design as to how many pixels wide your site will be. In Figure 7.19, you see that the designers at Oxygen.com decided on a set width of about 600 pixels for their site, even though users with wide monitors will see extra white space on the right side.

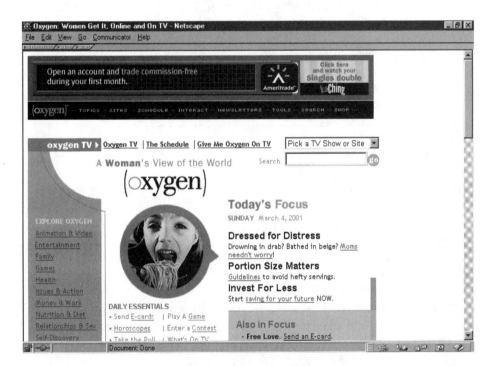

Figure 7.19   Oxygen.com's design makes use of color blocks and white space to minimize the presence of extra space on the right side of the screen.

There are advantages to using a set-width design. For one, you can always use the extra space on the side to insert elements that are not crucial to the message of your site. For example, you could insert an extra set of text links, a couple of square advertisements, a jump menu, or a small survey form for an online poll. Some users will see these additional elements; others will not.

Dreamweaver includes a Window Size menu, located in the lower-right corner of the screen, to help you resolve this issue (see Figure 7.20). To locate the menu, look to the left of the mini-launcher (the series of colored icons in the lower-right corner of the screen). The Window Resize menu is indicated by the currently selected pixel dimensions (such as 760 × 420). Pull down the menu to access a list of screen dimensions.

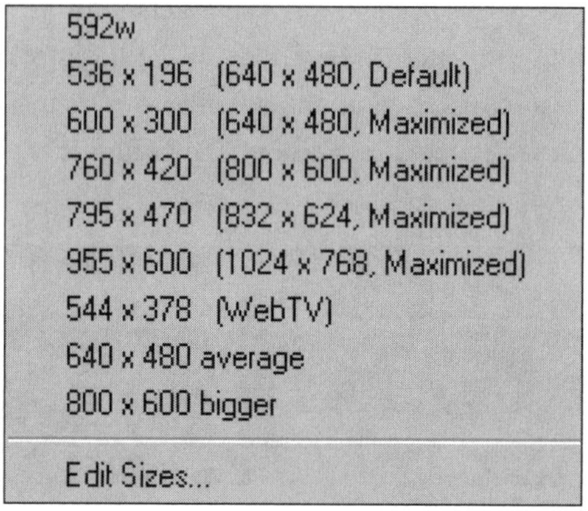

Figure 7.20   The Window Resize menu.

When you select a dimension, your open Dreamweaver document resizes to the dimensions you selected, enabling you to get an idea of what your document will look like at various screen sizes. You can add a new set of dimensions by choosing the Edit Sizes option from the list.

Bandwidth and File Sizes

There's always that one person who will be sure to let you know that your site is too slow! No one likes to hear about how slow his sites are, which is why most Web designers agonize over file size. Some designers follow a rule of thumb: If your page hasn't loaded in 8 seconds, the user will not wait for it to do so.

Sometimes you might be tempted to make your users wait. Wouldn't they rather see a big, pretty picture that takes a few seconds to load than a tiny, blurry picture that loads in a half second? Maybe, but maybe not.

It is up to you how long you will make your users play the waiting game. Consider where your users will be when they are looking at your site. If you know that 75% of them will be enjoying the company's T1 line as they surf, relax a little and boost your image quality.

If even half of your users could be at home on their modems, however, you better make those images small. Otherwise, get ready for the complaints to come in.

Speeding up download time means that you must make every effort to minimize the amount of data contained inside your Dreamweaver files. Large or incorrectly formatted images can cause a Web browser to grind to a virtual stop, and large quantities of text can cause the same problem. Other culprits include audio files, plug-ins, and banner advertisements located on already overloaded outside servers.

Keeping Track of File Sizes

Dreamweaver offers you a few tools to use in your battle against the waiting game. First, you can view the size of each file in your site under the Size heading in the Site Files window (F8). Figure 7.21 shows an example.

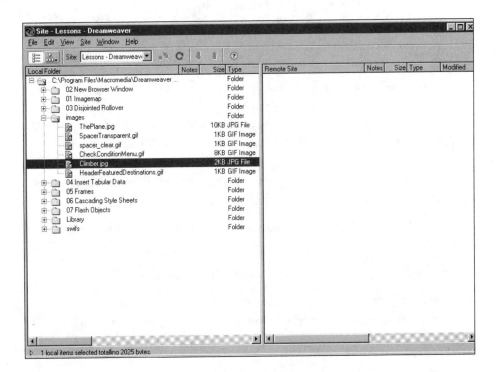

Figure 7.21   Viewing a file size from the Site Files window.

To determine the file size of an image in Dreamweaver, select it and note the file size as it appears in the Property Inspector (see Figure 7.22).

Figure 7.22   Select your image and look at the Property Inspector to view its file size.

To get a sense of how long a currently open file will take to download at a particular speed, use the file size and download speed indicator in the Dreamweaver status bar, adjacent to the mini-launcher and directly to the left of the Window Resize menu. This indicator, marked with a ratio of file size to speed of download, (example: 36K/10 seconds), can be changed to reflect a download speed of your choosing.

To change the download speed reflected in the indicator, choose Edit/Preferences/Status Bar (see Figure 7.23). Use the pull-down menu to assign a new speed.

The following guidelines enable you to minimize download time:

- Break up large amounts of text. Give users the ability to flip through material, moving from page to page at their whim. Text-heavy pages take up valuable seconds.

- Use a graphics-editing program such as Fireworks for your images. The tools that programs such as Fireworks provide for exporting GIFs and JPEGs can't be beat. Adobe Photoshop now includes these tools as well. Learn them and use them.

- Get into the habit of making your images as small as possible. You do not have a lot of space to work with anyway, so use what you have for maximum impact.

- Explore imaging techniques such as posterization, bitmapping, and transparency. These techniques can make your images look more interesting, yet conserve precious bandwidth.

- Try to use the same navigation bar throughout the site. This way, the user has to download it only one time. In Dreamweaver, stash your navigation bar in the library for easy access. See Chapter 16, "Templates and Libraries," for more detail about using the library. You also can reduce download time by using framesets and server-side includes.

- Use thumbnail images to link to large, detailed photographs. For more about making thumbnails, see Chapter 6.

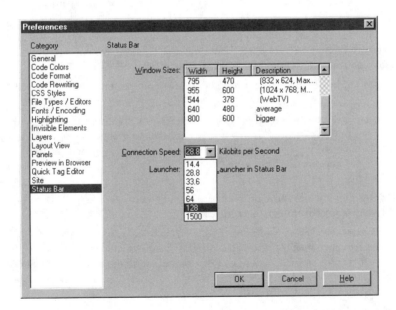

Figure 7.23   Setting a download speed for the status bar indicator from the Preferences dialog box.

Britt Funderburk, Designing for the Web

Britt Funderburk, Design Director at Oxygen Media, Inc., agreed to share a few Web design secrets for this chapter (see Figures 7.24–7.26). Back when Britt and I were friends in college, he was making airbrushed greeting cards and silk-screening quirky T-shirts. Now he's making design decisions for trendy New York multimedia companies. Way to go, Britt!

How did you get started in Web design, and what are you doing now?

Like many graphic designers, I sort of fell into it. I had been designing kiosk and CD-ROM interfaces when the Internet started to take off, so I was already prepared for the transition to interactivity. I started working with the Web at the Discovery Channel Online, which was a terrific experience. Since then I've worked on various projects of different scale on- and offline. I'm working currently with Oxygen Media, the new cable TV and Internet company.

Do you use a grid to help you design Web pages?

I don't use a particular kind of grid, per se. Well-considered information architecture is essential for successful Web sites. Designers need to think less about what their site is going to look like and more about what it is supposed to do. If you can define the purpose of the Web site, the best layout will become more obvious.

Do you think it is important to use only Web-safe colors, or is it okay to use custom colors (now that many monitors can understand them)?

At heart I'm a minimalist, and I've always enjoyed the challenge of working within difficult constraints. But it's really about your audience. If you hope to reach a significant number of people who may not have the latest equipment or browser versions, you should probably consider their limitations and design accordingly.

What's most important to consider when designing a navigational system?

Navigation needs to be clear and consistent. One mistake designers often make is to create completely unique navigation systems for each new Web site they design, instead of leveraging proven systems. This may not be the best approach. By giving your users a nonstandard navigational system, you are requiring them to learn something new before they can really use your site. If someone doesn't "get" your site quickly, he will be gone fast.

When designing a site, how do you deal with browser window widths that might vary from computer to computer?

Although many sites are now being designed for 800 × 600 resolution, 600 × 400 remains the most compatible resolution. Many sites use a "liquid layout" to address the problem of monitor variability. These layouts are designed to fit the smaller dimensions and to expand proportionally to fit larger dimensions as well. This kind of design always feels right regardless of monitor size.

What techniques do you use to control spacing on Web sites?

Back in the old days, we used to use 1-pixel invisible spacers to hold things in place. Now we have cascading style sheets, which enable us to position elements more precisely. But there are still platform and browser inconsistencies that don't allow for the kind of typographic precision that designers want.

What advice would you give to someone just starting out in Web design?

An airplane is not a bicycle, and a Web site is not a television set. In other words, because Web sites are interactive software applications, they require completely different considerations than a poster, or a book. Clear and consistent navigation is essential to the experience. Study and learn from the most popular sites. What makes these sites work? What is it about them that makes them useful? Use the techniques that work on these sites to inform your own designs. Improve on their techniques if you can, but always try to keep it simple.

Figure 7.24   Britt Funderburk, Design Director for Oxygen Media, Inc.

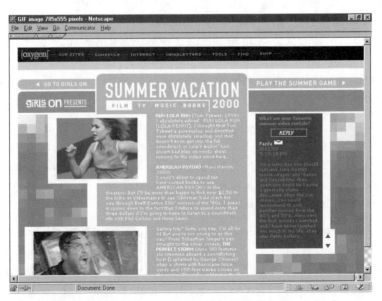

Figure 7.25   A Web layout for Oxygen Media. Designed by Britt Funderburk.

Figure 7.26   This Web layout by Britt Funderburk makes use of horizontal scrolling.

Summary

Web design is a new field. Web designers are challenged by new issues such as dithering, file sizes, and browser window widths. Fortunately, Web designers enjoy the flexibility of their medium. If a color doesn't look right after a site is published, for example, it can easily be changed. This would not be the case with a paper version containing the same information.

The fundamentals of Web design can be learned by reading books and researching the Web for educational sites and online courses. These fundamentals can be put into play using Dreamweaver. Dreamweaver 4 includes tools such as the web-safe palette, color wheel, grid, tracing images, and Window Resize menu to help you work your way through both common and less-common problems.

As browsers that support cascading style sheets and other new formatting tags become more popular, Web designers must keep on top to ensure that their sites are designed to take advantage of the latest Web design techniques. One way to do this is by educating yourself about each Dreamweaver menu and what it offers. Then build your skills using the Dreamweaver tools. Your sites will look better, load faster, and bring you compliments rather than complaints.

This chapter covered design issues, such as how to work with colors. It also covered design and layout issues, including background patterns, tracing images, margins, and rulers. Finally, this chapter discussed design strategies. Hopefully, you have a better understanding of the strategies to employ, and the answers to the questions posed in this chapter will aid you in building a site that meets your goals.

Part III

Advanced Document Structuring

Chapter 8

Layout with Tables

Your life as a Web designer and developer
will be much easier if you know how to lay
out Web pages with tables. Back in HTML's
beginnings, tables were intended to be,
well, tables. They were used to present

statistics or other data in an orderly fashion. In fact, many of the tools used to construct Web sites were created by the scientific community as a way to exchange scientific data. Tables are certainly in that category.

When non-scientific Web designers came along to create fun and interesting sites that had nothing to do with microbes or constellations or weather formations, they saw tables as a handy tool for keeping illustrations, photographs, and text in place. This way, a Web page could look as good as a page from a magazine. Almost. For all their good qualities, tables still lack the level of precision you will find inside Adobe PageMaker or Quark Xpress. For this type of precision on the Web, you need to use cascading style sheets (CSS). Because they are not yet widely supported, however, it's worth your time to learn how to design with tables. You can find more information about CSS in Chapter 12, Using Cascading Style Sheets.

For an example of complex tables, take a look at the HTML source code behind some of the more popular Web sites, such as www.cnn.com. Notice that every chunk of information is contained within a table cell. The small tables are nested inside larger ones, and all the little nested tables are really just sitting inside one big table, like a set of Russian dolls.

It can be hard to keep track of all those tables, which is why many Web designers use high-quality, multifunctional editors such as Dreamweaver. In this chapter, you learn about the many tools Dreamweaver offers for table design.

This chapter covers the following:

- Inserting tables
- Inserting and aligning data
- Table alignment and borders
- Formatting tables
- Coloring tables and borders
- Image slicing with fireworks
- Layout view

Inserting Tables

This section discusses page layout with tables using the Insert Table dialog box. Be sure to also read the Layout View section at the end of this chapter to learn about the new, alternative way to design with tables inside Dreamweaver.

To insert a table, choose Insert/Table from the Dreamweaver main menu. Alternatively, click the table icon in the Objects panel.

Figure 8.1 shows the Insert Table dialog box. Fill out the fields inside the box, described in the following list, to make a table:

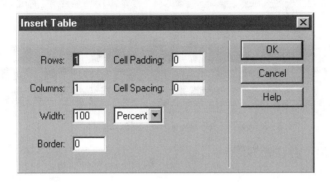

Figure 8.1   The Insert Table Dialog Box.

- **Rows.** This setting indicates the number of rows inside the table.
- **Column.** Here you can indicate how many columns you will have in your table.
- **Width.** This determines the width of the table. Pull down the window to the right of the field name to choose between a pixel value and a percentage value.
- **Border.** With this setting, you can set the size, in pixels, of the border surrounding the table. Insert 0 for no border. Note that borders do not look the same in all browsers. Whereas Netscape might make a fat, beveled border, Internet Explorer might make a skinny, shaded border. Look at your site in a variety of browsers to see how the borders look.
- **Cell Padding.** Use a value, in pixels, to indicate the amount of space separating the edges of the table cell from its contents (see Figure 8.2).
- **Cell Spacing.** Use a value, in pixels, to indicate the amount of space between the table cells (see Figure 8.2).

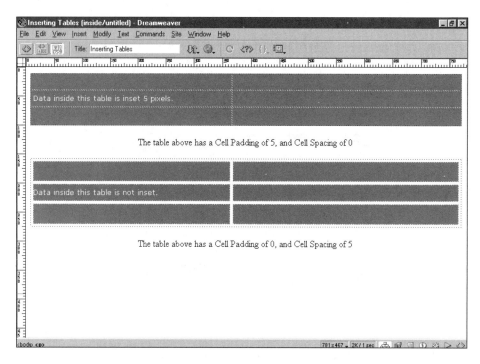

Figure 8.2   Cell Padding and Cell Spacing affect the placement of table cell contents.

Pixels or Percentages?

It helps to have some clear goals for your site by the time you are laying out your Web page. For example, you need to make a decision between pixels and percentages.

If you want to set a specific width for a table, say, 500 pixels, use the pixel value. If you want a liquid table that stretches to fit a variety of browser windows and monitor sizes, however, consider using a percentage-based table. Figure 8.3 shows a percentage-based table and a pixel-based table. Keep in mind that a percentage-based table doesn't have to be set to 100%. You can use whatever percentage width or height you want to use. If you want to fill only 80% of the browser screen, for instance, select the table and type the 80% value into the Width field in the Property Inspector. Likewise for 20%, 50%, or any percentage you choose.

Understanding when and how to use table percentages and pixel widths can be tricky. First you must understand the advantages of both methods.

Percentage-based tables are great because

- You can use them to take advantage of the extra space on big monitors.

- You can designate a specific amount of space for more fluid elements, such as columns of text that don't have to be a set size.

- You do not have to be concerned about setting widths for table cells (so less work for you).

- It is less likely that an element in your page will not show up from browser to browser, because the browser will adjust the sizing based on its own system.

Pixel-based tables are great because

- You can designate a certain area of the browser window to be a set width, and feel confident that it will look pretty much the same in all browsers.

- You can create a cell that is the exact width and height of the image you put inside it, thereby preventing image stretch-outs.

- You can prevent unwanted areas of white space and prevent elements from disappearing off the screen by controlling the width of the table cell serving as a container.

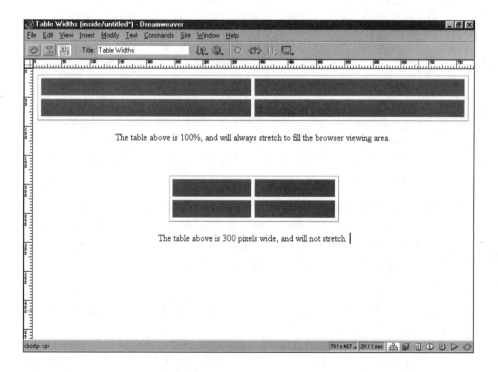

Figure 8.3   A percentage-based table and a pixel-based table as they appear inside Dreamweaver 4.

Sometimes the best solution is to combine percentage- and pixel-based tables, using one or the other depending on what you're trying to do. You might use a 100% table to hold the entire contents of your HTML document, for example; but put individual elements, such as areas of images and text, into smaller tables, each set to a desired pixel width.

Table Tips

To adjust the sizing of an already existing table, you can select a table by clicking the outside edge. (It's tricky, but keep trying.)

However, a superior technique for selecting tables is to use the Tab Selector in the lower-left corner of the screen. With your cursor positioned inside the table, you want to select and click the <TABLE> tag. When the table is selected, a black line surrounds it. Use the Height and Width fields in the Property Inspector (Ctrl+F3) to make changes to the table.

To restore a table cell to its original size after you have deleted or changed the data inside, click your cursor outside the table. This is necessary to refresh the table. Sometimes, if a table is very large, you must use the Dreamweaver scrollbar to find an area outside the table to click your cursor.

Another tip: Select a table and press the right or left arrow key on your keyboard to position your cursor *outside* a table. The cursor will appear as a flashing line the same height as the table it's adjacent to (even if it's very long). Any content you add after doing this will not be inside the table. Press the Return key if you want to move your cursor below the table.

Inserting Data

To insert data such as an image, a Flash movie, or other media into a table cell, click in the cell and choose an option from the Insert menu or the Objects panel. To insert text, copy it to your Clipboard, and paste it inside the cell; or just type it directly into the cell. To move from cell to cell, use the Tab key.

Use the Horz and Vert fields on the Property Inspector (Ctrl+F3) to align the data inside the cell to the right, left, center, top, bottom, or baseline of the individual table cell in which it resides. This is the preferred way to align data inside a cell. Avoid using the Align attribute also found on the Property Inspector if you can.

Make a habit of aligning your data immediately after inserting it. Doing so will prevent problems later on. If you don't align the data, the default alignment will sometimes cause a problem with your design.

To move the data from one table cell to another, select it and drag it to the new location. The table cell lights up when you are able to paste inside it.

Tip

> If your tables are not lining up right when you preview your page in the Web browser, try this:
>
> Cut (not copy) the entire contents of your page, tables and all, to your Clipboard. Then, with the blank page in front of you, insert a new table that contains one row and one column. Select this table and align it to the left. Click in the cell and use the Property Inspector to align the data (not yet pasted in) to the left horizontally and to the top vertically. Assign your desired width to the table in pixels or percentages. Now, paste your Clipboard into the new table.
>
> This table serves as a container for your page's contents. Because you aligned it to the left, all the contents of your page align to the left. You also can use a center or right alignment if you want.

Table Alignment and Borders

After you have inserted your tables, you need to align them. You learned earlier in this chapter how to align data inside a table cell, but here you learn how to align the tables themselves.

The key to success here is understanding exactly what you want to do with your layout. You might want to draw out a sketch before beginning. You also could use the Tracing Image feature available under the Modify/Page Properties menu.

To align a table, select it by clicking the edge or using the Tag Selector (located in the lower-left corner of the screen). When you see the black selection border on the table, you will know that the table is selected. Then use the Property Inspector to choose an option from the Align field. If you align your table to the left or right, the contents of the page that are not inside the table will flow around it.

Table Borders

If you desire, you can assign a value, in pixels, for the border of your table. The table borders act similarly to the image borders covered in Chapter 6, "Working with Images."

You can use table border to emphasize the data inside each cell, for a contrasting effect against a background image, or for many other reasons. Figure 8.4 shows the table border of 4 pixels. (Note that I also colored the border black, and resized the table cells to align with the gradient in my image in the left column.)

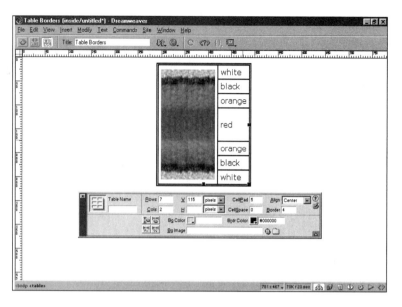

Figure 8.4   This table has a border of 4.

Exercise 8.1   Wrapping Text Around an Image

A common issue in Web design is how to wrap text around an image. This is a space-saving technique that looks very professional, as long as it is done right! In this exercise, use the file called SITEOFDAY.HTML from the Wrapping folder on your CD-ROM. The steps taken to wrap the text inside the file around the image called WYESONG.GIF (also in the Wrapping folder) will teach you how to set table percentages and widths, as well as align a table and cell contents using the Property Inspector. A version of the file (with the table borders set to 1) is shown in Figure 8.5.

1. With the file SITEOFDAY.HTML open inside Dreamweaver, click inside the table cell and select the table by clicking the <TABLE> tag from the Tag Selector in the lower-left corner of the screen. When the table is selected, a black border appears around it.

2. Open the Property Inspector (Ctrl+F3) and change the value in the W (width) field from 100% to 75%. Make sure the Width field setting indicates a percentage mark (%) rather than pixels. After you have changed the percentage value from 100% to 75%, the table will shrink to fill only 75% of your screen.

3. With the table still selected, locate the Align field on the Property Inspector, pull down its menu, and choose Center. The table will move to the center of the screen.

4. Now that the table is aligned, it's time to insert another smaller table inside the text area to hold the accompanying image. First, click inside the existing table, directly to the left of the word "site" in the phrase "site of the day," at the very top of the text area.

5. Choose Insert/Table. Inside the Insert Table dialog box, create a table with one row, one column, with a pixel width (not percentage width) of 220. The fields for Border, Cell Padding, and Cell Spacing should be set to 0. Click OK to insert the table into the document.

6. The table will appear above the text. Correct this by selecting the new table and choosing Left from the Align field on the Property Inspector. This allows the text to move up around the table.

7. Now insert the image into the new pixel-based table you just created. Click in the small table's cell and choose Insert/Image. Locate the image file called WYESONG.GIF and click Select to place it inside your document.

8. If the text doesn't flow around the image, click in front of the purple wyesong.com heading and press the Delete or Backspace key. This action eliminates any space that is pushing the text away from the table. Insert a soft return (Shift+Enter) to move the text down a line.

9. Align the image inside its table cell. To do this, select the image by clicking it once. Then press the right-arrow key to position your cursor inside the cell. Using the Property Inspector, choose a Center alignment from the Horz field, and a Top alignment from the Vert field. The image will move to the center of the table cell.

10. Save the file and preview it inside your Web browser. If the extra 20 pixels of space does not provide an inset area of white space around the image, go back to the file and assign the image an H space value of 5 using the Property Inspector.

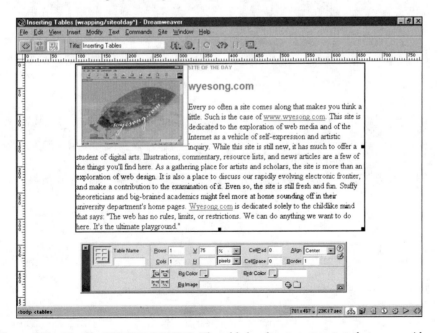

Figure 8.5   The file SITEOFDAY.HTML. The table borders are set to 1 so that you can identify the smaller table inside the larger (selected) table.

Formatting Tables

Dreamweaver's interface makes table editing a simple process. Changing table dimensions when hand-coding can be frustrating because you cannot see the tables change sizes as you work on them. You can adjust the sizes, colors, positioning, border widths, and background images of your tables. (I almost always use the Property Inspector to work with tables, because nearly everything you need is available to you in a single window.)

Spanning Table Cells

Working with tables inside Dreamweaver in Standard view requires that you know how to manipulate your tables' row and column spans. (In Layout mode, you do not have to make adjustments for spanning.)

The Colspan and Rowspan attributes enable you to stretch single table cells across one or more rows or columns (see Figure 8.6).

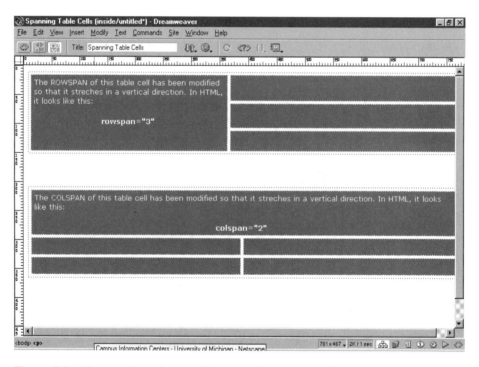

Figure 8.6   The top table makes use of Rowspan. The bottom table makes use of Colspan.

The Colspan and Rowspan attributes prove especially useful when you are creating a table that will contain a combination of images and text. The Web page illustrated in

Exercise 8.2 makes use of Colspan and Rowspan by arranging a long banner image and several small navigational images together inside a table.

To create a row span, follow these steps:

1. Click in the topmost table cell in the area you want to span.

2. Choose Modify/Table/Increase Row Span (see Figure 8.7).

3. Repeat steps 1–2 for the number of rows you want to span. Alternatively, use the keyboard shortcut Ctrl+Y to repeat the steps automatically.

Tip

Row and column spanning can be executed by selecting all the cells simultaneously and pressing the M key. Alternatively, you can highlight the desired cells and click the Merge Cells button on the Property Inspector.

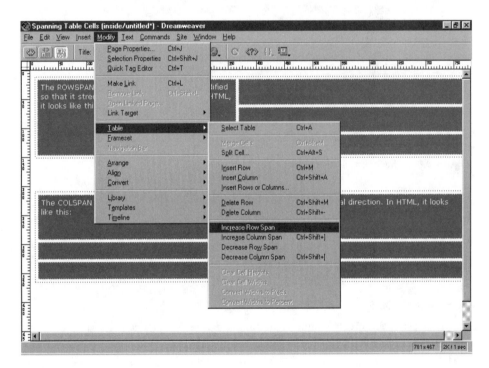

Figure 8.7   Creating a row span inside Dreamweaver 4.

To create a column span, follow these steps:

1. Click in the table cell to the left of the area you want to span.

2. Choose Modify/Table/Increase Column Span or use the keyboard shortcut Shift+Ctrl+].

3. Repeat steps 1–2 for the number of rows you want to span. Alternatively, use the keyboard shortcut Ctrl+Y to repeat the steps automatically.

To remove column or row spanning, choose Modify/Table/Decrease Row Span (or Column Span). You must repeat this procedure for each cell.

Splitting and Merging Cells

Another way to make quick adjustments to cell spans is to use the Split Cell function. This divides a cell into the number of rows or columns you enter into the dialog box (see Figure 8.8).

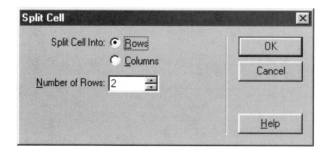

Figure 8.8   The Split Cell dialog box.

You can access the Split Cell dialog box by clicking the Split Cell icon on the Property Inspector, or by choosing Modify/Table/Split Cell. The keyboard shortcut is Ctrl+Alt+S.

The Merge Cells icon is located to the left of the Split Cell icon. It merges two table cells into one.

Exercise 8.2   Designing with Tables

In this exercise, you create a table containing a banner image and a set of navigational images (see Figure 8.9). Open the file WEAVING.HTML from the CD-ROM to get started.

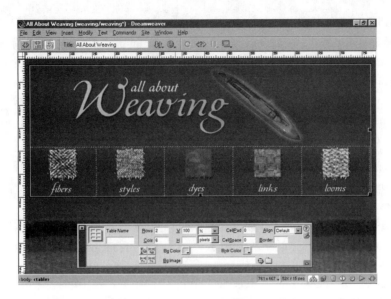

Figure 8.9   The file WEAVING.HTML as it appears inside Dreamweaver.

1. Choose Insert/Table to open the Insert Table dialog box. Create a table with 2 rows and 6 columns. Set the table width to 100%. The fields for Border, Cell Padding, and Cell Spacing should be set to 0.

2. Click in the table cell to the far left. Choose Modify/Table/Increase Column Span.

3. Repeat the spanning procedure five times by executing the keystroke Ctrl+Y. Alternatively, select all 6 columns and press the M key, or use the Merge Cells button on the Property Inspector.

4. With your cursor inside the top row, choose Insert/Image and choose the image file HOME_BANNER.GIF from the Weaving folder on the CD-ROM.

5. Deselect the image by clicking inside the cell, to the right. In the Property Inspector (Ctrl+F3), align the image inside the cell. Select a Horz alignment of Center and a Vert alignment of Top.

6. In the table's second row, click in the column on the far left. Choose Insert/Image and choose the image file FIBERS.GIF from the Weaving folder on the CD-ROM.

7. Deselect the image by clicking inside the cell, to the right. In the Property Inspector, align the image inside the cell. Select a Horz alignment of Center and a Vert alignment of Top.

8. To move to the next column, press your keyboard's right-arrow key. Repeat the Insert/Image procedure to insert the file called STYLES.GIF. Repeat step 7 to align the image inside its cell.

9. Repeat the steps as needed to insert and align the remaining three images: DYES.GIF, LINKS.GIF, and LOOMS.GIF.

10. Save the file and preview it inside your Web browser.

Nested Tables

Most Web sites that use tables effectively do so by using nested tables. *Nested tables* are tables inside of tables inside of tables, ad infinitum. To make a nested table, click in the table cell where you want to add a table and repeat the Insert Table procedure covered earlier in this section. There is really no limit to the number of nested tables you can insert inside a single table cell. However, elaborate nesting strategies can increase the amount of time it takes the tables to load in the browser.

In Exercise 8.3, you create a nested table design. To keep all cells visible, a border of 1 will be assigned to each table until the exercise is completed.

Exercise 8.3   Creating Nested Tables

1. From the Weaving folder on the CD-ROM, open the file called STYLES.HTML.
2. Choose Insert/Table (Ctrl+Alt+T) to access the Insert Table dialog box. Give this table 1 row, 2 columns, and set the width to 100%. Enter a value of 1 into the Border field. (You will change this later.) Click OK.
3. Click in the left cell. Choose Insert/Image from the Dreamweaver main menu (or click the Image icon on the objects palette). Choose the image file called NAVAJO.GIF from the Weaving folder on the CD-ROM. Deselect the image by clicking inside the cell, to the right of the image (or use the right-arrow key). Use the Horz and Vert fields on the Property Inspector to align the image to the left horizontally and top vertically.
4. Move your mouse over the line that separates the two cells and drag to the left until the table cell hugs the image (approximately 28% in width).
5. Move in the right cell. Even though there is nothing in the cell, use the Horz and Vert fields on the Property Inspector to align the cell contents to the left horizontally and top vertically. This ensures that the data you are about to insert into the cell will have the proper alignment. Your cursor should be blinking in the upper-left corner of the right table cell before you go on to the next step.
6. Choose Insert/Table from the main menu (or click the Table icon in the Objects panel). Create a table with 3 rows and 1 column. The Width value should be 450 pixels (not percentages), and the Border should be set to 1. The values for Cell Padding and Cell Spacing should be set to 0.
7. Click in the top of the new nested table. Choose Insert/Image and select the file STYLES_HEAD.GIF from the Weaving folder.
8. Open the file BLURB.TXT from the Weaving folder on the CD-ROM. Select the text, copy it to your Clipboard, and close the file.
9. Click in the second row of the nested table. Choose Edit/Paste HTML.

10. Click in the third row of the nested table. Choose Insert/Image from the main menu and retrieve the image called HOME_OFF.GIF. Using the Property Inspector, link the image to the file WEAVING.GIF, located in the Weaving folder on the CD-ROM.

11. Use your left-arrow key to move your cursor adjacent to the image (still inside the cell). In the Property Inspector, choose an alignment of Right for the Horz field and Top for the Vert field.

12. Select the nested table and use the Property Inspector to assign a Cell Spacing of 5. Set the Border to 0.

13. Select the outer table and use the Property Inspector to set its border to 0 as well.

Save the page and preview it inside your browser.

Figure 8.10 shows the finished page.

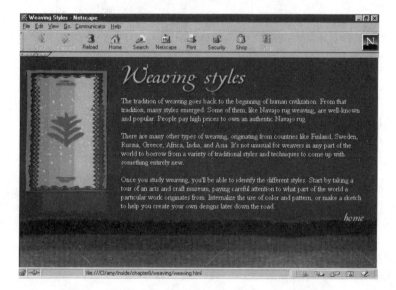

Figure 8.10   The file STYLES.HTML as it appears inside the Web browser.

Modifying Tables

When you are designing with tables in Standard view, you can use the pull-down menu found under Modify/Table to adjust cell spans or to add and delete rows. Figure 8.7 shows the menu.

Inserting Rows and Columns

The Modify/Table submenu enables you to add rows or columns to a table, but it's a little tricky. What you need to know is that you *must* choose the Modify/Table/Insert Rows or Columns submenu to insert more than one row or column to an existing table.

If you select the Insert Row or Insert Column option, only one row or table will be inserted. By default, Dreamweaver places the new row above your cursor location. If this is not what you want, use the Insert Rows or Columns dialog box (see Figure 8.11). This way, you can choose whether you want the row or column to appear above or below your selection point.

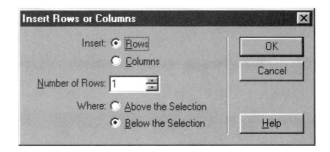

Figure 8.11   The Insert Rows or Columns dialog box.

Tip

Use the keyboard shortcut Ctrl+M to insert a row, and Ctrl+Shift+M to delete a row. To select more than one table cell at a time, drag your cursor over the cells. Each one lights up with a black or colored border when selected. If you select the entire table this way, a screen displays to show the selected area.

Deleting Rows and Columns

To delete rows or columns, click in the first cell to be deleted and choose Modify Table/Delete Row or Delete Column. (Be ready to undo this action with Ctrl+Z in case the result isn't what you want.) To delete multiple rows or columns, highlight them with the cursor and press the Delete key.

Clearing Cell Heights and Widths

Sometimes your tables will not work the way you want them to. This happens to everyone. Problems with misalignment are often caused because table widths or heights are not set correctly. Keep in mind that the combined widths and heights of the table cells must always add up to the total width and total height of the table. Failure to do so results in misalignment and inconsistent results in browsers.

Always remember that Dreamweaver divides your cell widths and heights into percentages as you are working with a table and inserting data into it. To view the pixel or percentage size of a particular cell, click in the cell (don't select the cell content) and look at the Height and Width fields on the Property Inspector.

Also be aware that if you move the dotted lines or border separating the table cells up and down or back and forth, you are setting a pixel or percentage size for that cell. To remove the sizes, use the Width and Height fields in the Property Inspector to change or erase the numeric values.

You also can use the Clear Cell Widths or Clear Cell Heights function found in the Modify/Table submenu (see Figure 8.7). Alternatively, use the Clear Cell Widths and Clear Cell Heights icons (see Figure 8.12) on the Property Inspector to accomplish this task. Remember to select the table before you try to clear the cells.

Converting Pixels and Percentages

Maybe you tried working with percentage-based tables and you didn't like it (or vice versa). All is not lost if you select your table and convert from pixels to percentages or percentages to pixels.

You can use the Modify/Table submenu or the Pixels and Percentages icons on the Property Inspector to make these changes (see Figure 8.12).

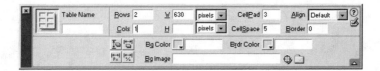

Figure 8.12   The Clear Cell and Pixels and Percentages icons are located on the Property Inspector.

Coloring Tables, Table Cells, and Borders

The visual impact of your tables can be increased if you make use of table cell colors and background images. In Dreamweaver, you can assign a Web-safe or custom color to individual table cells or to an entire table. If your table has a border of at least 1, you can color the border of the table cell. Be aware that border colors for tables and table cells are not supported by all browsers.

If you want to make a background pattern for a table or an individual cell, you can do that as well. Be aware, however, that images used as background for table cells will tile (create multiple copies of themselves) to fill up the area of the cell. Sometimes this is a desired effect; sometimes it's not.

Both the background coloring tools and the Background Image functions for table cells are inside the Property Inspector. Select the table or click inside a cell to see the color chips for Bg Color (background color), and Brdr Color (border color). The Bg Image (background image) field enables you to browse for a background image to assign to a table cell.

Figure 8.13 shows a table in which I colored cells, borders, and used a background image for the entire table. Note that the background image becomes more prominent in Figure 8.14, when the Cell Spacing is changed from 0 to 5.

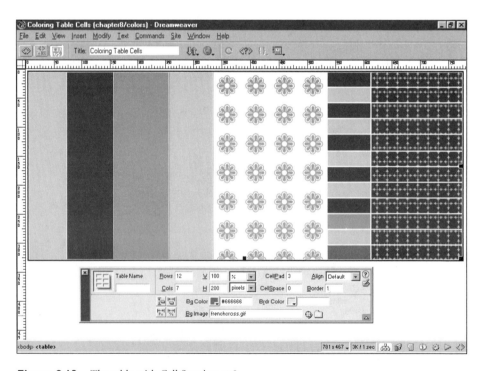

Figure 8.13   The table with Cell Spacing at 0.

To color a table cell, follow these steps:

1. Click in the cell you want to color.

2. Choose a color chip from the Bg field in the Property Inspector. Alternatively, create a custom color with the color palette.

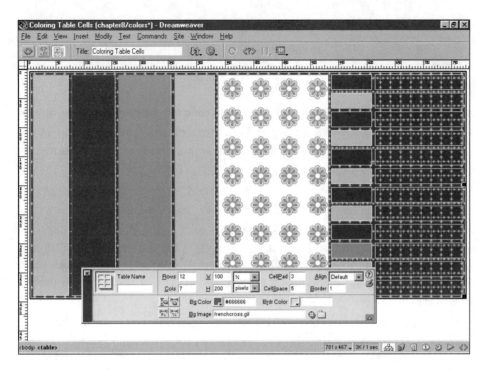

Figure 8.14   The background image and border colors are more prominent when the Cell Spacing is set to 5.

To color a table, follow these steps:

1. Select the table.

2. Choose a color chip from the Bg field in the Property Inspector. Alternatively, create a custom color with the color palette.

For background images, use the preceding procedure with the Bg Image field. Instead of choosing a color chip, use the Browse feature to select a background image for the table cell. You also can use the point-to-file technique by clicking and dragging the point-to-file icon. For more about linking and navigation with point-to-file, see Chapter 5, "Linking and Navigation."

To color a table or table cell border, repeat the procedure, using the Brdr field in the Property Inspector.

To remove table or table cell colors, click in the color fields on the Property Inspector and erase the hexadecimal representation. You also can open the color palette and choose the button for none, which is a square with a diagonal red line through it.

Uses of Colors and Background Images in Tables

Using color and background images in tables and their cells can make your tables look more professional, and it can sometimes help you solve some common Web design problems.

If you have a Flash movie you want to drop into a table cell, for example, giving the cell a white background and a Cell Spacing of 5 can provide a nice frame. Alternatively, use an animated GIF of scrolling lines as a table cell background and put a transparent image on top of it for a sophisticated multimedia effect.

Exercise 8.4   Making Use of Table Cell Background Colors and Images

In this exercise, use the file called BACKGROUNDS.HTML from the Calendar folder on the CD-ROM. Using this file and three images—CELTIC.GIF, MOON.GIF, and CLOVER.GIF (also in the Calendar folder on the CD-ROM)—you assign colors and three background images to the already existing table cells inside the HTML document. Figure 8.15 shows a finished version of this exercise.

1. The file called BACKGROUNDS.HTML contains a table that is already set up as a calendar for March 2001. Your first step is to click in the blank area of the table cells that holds the March 2001 image. (Do not select the image or the nested table that holds it.)

2. Open the Property Inspector (Ctrl+F3) and click the file folder icon next to the Bg field. Select the file called CELTIC.GIF as the background image for the top-row table cell. The Celtic pattern should tile inside the top row of the calendar.

3. Color the table cells that hold the calendar dates. The first date row is located below the row that contains the week names (Mon, Tues, Wed, and so on). To highlight the cells in the first date row, hold your mouse over the far-left side of the row and drag so that each date cell lights up with a black border. When all seven date cells in the row are selected, choose the Bg color chip icon from the Property Inspector and select the lightest gray color from the palette using the eyedropper tool. (The color's hexidecimal representation is #CCCCCC.)

4. Repeat step 3 for the remaining six date rows.

5. Mark the dates March 8 and March 17 with special icons. Click in the table cell under the numeral 8 that contains the words "Full Moon."

6. On the Property Inspector, click the file folder icon next to the Bg field. Select the file called MOON.GIF as the background image for the top-row table cell. The moon image will appear inside the cell.

7. Repeat step 6 for the cell beneath the numeral 17, which already contains the phrase "Luck O' the Irish." This time, choose the image file CLOVER.GIF. The clover image will appear inside the cell.

8. Save the file and preview it inside your Web browser (see Figure 8.15).

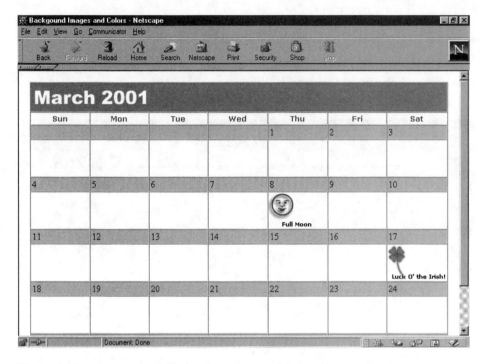

Figure 8.15   The completed file BACKGROUNDS. HTML as it appears in Netscape 4.

When working with table cell images and background colors, it is especially important to view the final results in a variety of browsers. Very often you will find there are difference in how the background images, border colors, and background colors look.

Sometimes using a background image inside a table cell is one of the only ways to accomplish a particular Web design task. In Exercise 8.4, the moon and clover images were used inside table cells as background images to avoid the alignment problems that could have developed if you had tried to do the same sort of thing with nested tables. Be aware, however, that every time you use a background image inside a table cell, you take the risk that tiling could occur when you don't want it to.

Sliced Images and Tables

Many of the most beautiful and complex Web sites make use of image slices and tables. An *image slice* is a portion of a larger image, like a puzzle piece. When image slices are arranged in the same table, and the Cell Spacing and Cell Padding are set to 0, the layout design is seamless and no one can tell that you are actually using a set of chopped-up images.

Image Slicing with Fireworks

Fireworks includes a variety of tools for making image slices and for exporting the slices as a table you can view in Dreamweaver. Figure 8.16 shows a navigation bar sliced in Fireworks with the Image Slicing tool.

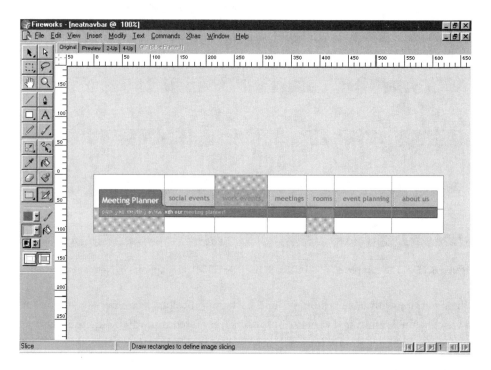

Figure 8.16   This image is being sliced inside Macromedia Fireworks. The screened areas show the slices.

After you have sliced your image, you can name and export each slice individually and build the table in Dreamweaver on your own. Alternatively, you can save the HTML for the table directly from Fireworks.

In Figure 8.17, the Fireworks HTML that contains the table for the image slices is open. (I selected the table and assigned a border of 1, just to take a look at the table with the images inside it. When I set the border back to 0, the images blend together seamlessly [see Figure 8.18].)

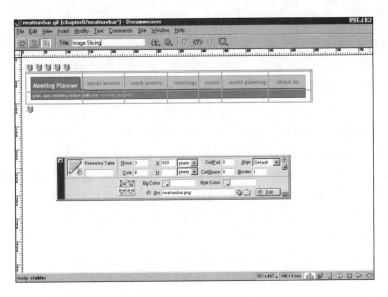

Figure 8.17   The table with a border of 1.

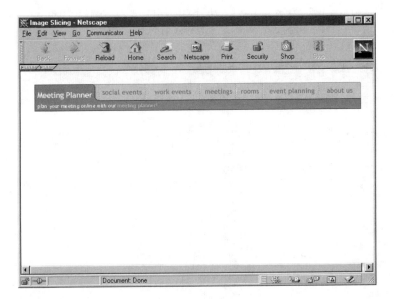

Figure 8.18   When the border is set back to 0, the table is seamless, even inside the Web browser.

When your images are sliced and placed seamlessly into a table, select a specific slice and use the Link field on the Property Inspector to link it to another file. You also can give each slice its own name and <ALT> tag in the Property Inspector. In addition, you can link certain parts of slices using an image map. Chapter 5 provides more details about creating image maps with hotspots.

To combine a Fireworks table into an already existing table, select and copy the entire contents of the Fireworks table from its HTML page. (Ctrl+A selects everything.) Then either make a new table for the image-sliced table or click where you want to place it. Paste the Clipboard contents into the table cell and align it accordingly.

Layout View

New in Dreamweaver 4 is a Layout view that offers you a more fluid, spontaneous way to work with tables. In Layout view, you can draw your table and table cells where you want them to appear (although tables will always snap back to the top-left corner of the page). This method of table design works well with a tracing image. Chapter 7, "Web Design Issues," covers tracing images.

When working with tables in Layout view, you can drag and resize your table cells as needed. You also can make percentage-based table design a bit easier, using the Autostretch Columns function.

To switch from Standard view to Layout view, click the layout view icon at the bottom of the Objects panel. The layout view icon is shown in Figure 8.19.

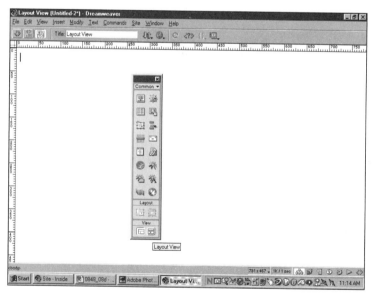

Figure 8.19   Accessing Layout view from the Objects panel.

When in Layout view, take another look at the bottom of the Objects panel in Figure 8.19. There are two icons directly above the View icons. These icons are marked Layout.

To draw a table, click the icon on the right. To draw a table cell (the table will be made for you), click the icon on the left.

Figure 8.20 shows a blank table with one cell as it was created in Layout view. The size of the column is indicated in a slim green line at the top of the table. Click the table size to access the following menu choices (see Figure 8.20):

- **Make Column Autostretch.** This option forces the column to stretch out when there is extra browser window space available. (Use this option with caution, because it can cause data in your table to be surrounded with extra space you may not want.) For design purposes, you can have only one column set to autostretch at a time.

- **Add Spacer Image.** This option inserts a pixel shim for spacing your table elements. Dreamweaver will ask you to specify what spacer image you want to use. Alternatively, you can command Dreamweaver to make a spacer image for you. These spacers, also called shims, prevent browsers from changing the dimensions of your tables.

- **Remove All Spacer Images.** This option automatically deletes all the spacer images in the table.

- **Clear Cell Heights.** This option clears all the cell height specifications. Use this option if you have unintentionally adjusted the cell heights of the table and are having problems with misalignment.

- **Make Cell Widths Consistent**. This option sets all cell widths to a consistent width. Creating consistent cell widths allows the table to resize more efficiently inside the browser. Of course, this option is useful only if you want the widths to be the same size. If you have already established specific cell widths, do not use this feature.

Drawing Table Cells

When working in Design view, it's a good idea to have a clear idea of what you want to accomplish. You need to know from the beginning if you want your columns to autostretch or not, and you should know what width your images and other elements are. This way, you prevent spacing problems.

Tip

Use autostretch for columns that will contain only text. If you use it for images, the column will be able to shrink only until it fits around the image, whereas text columns are infinitely resizable depending on window size.

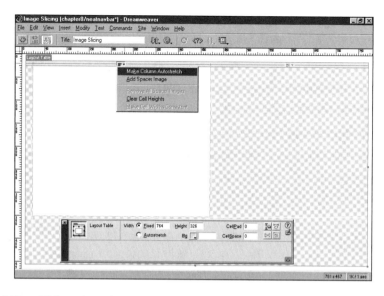

Figure 8.20   Click a column header to access the list of options.

In Figure 8.21, I'm using Design view with a tracing image to build a table that looks similar to a print brochure used by the U.S. Environmental Protection Agency. You can use the same technique to convert your home or office print materials to Web pages.

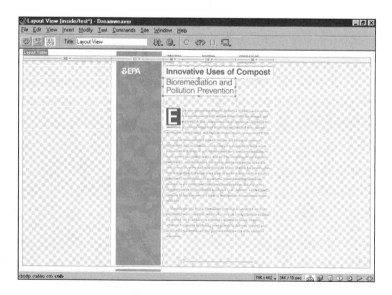

Figure 8.21   Using a tracing image in Design view.

Tracing images can be specified through the Modify/Page Properties dialog box. If your tracing image makes a tiling pattern (it shouldn't), add some white space around it in your image-editing program.

Note that you must reselect the draw table cell icon from the Objects panel each time you want to draw a new cell. Also note that you cannot draw cells on top of one another.

Editing Tables in Design View

If you have tables created in a previous version of Dreamweaver, or another Web design program, you can edit them in Design view. Just open the page containing the table and switch from Standard view to Layout view by clicking the layout view icon in the Objects panel.

Tip

> For print-to-Web conversions, you can make a tracing image of your print document by saving it as a PDF file. Open the PDF file in Adobe Acrobat or your Web browser and size it to fit the window. Take a screen shot (Alt+Print Screen) and open the screen shot in your image-editing program and save it as a GIF or JPG.

HTML Calendars

You make an HTML calendar for your Web site with a calendar extension found on Macromedia Exchange. No table-making time is needed! To download the extension, go to www.macromedia.com/exchange and search for "calendar."

After you have downloaded and installed the extension, click the calendar icon in the "goodies" panel of the Objects panel. The pop-up window shown in Figure 8.22 displays. Enter your choices and click OK. For an example of how the calendar can look, see Exercise 8.4.

Converting Databases and Spreadsheets into Web Pages

Do you have a database or spreadsheet file you want to convert to a Web page? If the data is tab delimited, you can use Dreamweaver to make a table for you with all your columns and data cells intact. If the data is not tab delimited, you can save it that way, usually from a drop-down menu in your spreadsheet or database software program.

Choose Insert/Tabular Data and click the Browse button to choose your tab-delimited data TXT file. Fill out the other options in the dialog box and click OK when you are finished (see Figure 8.23).

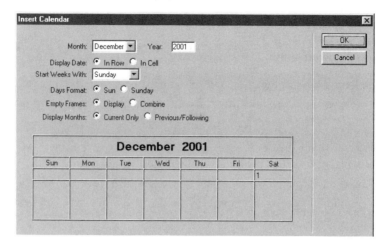

Figure 8.22   The Insert Calendar dialog box.

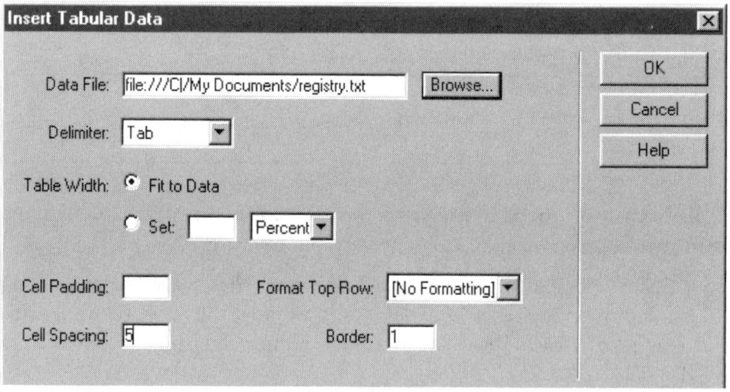

Figure 8.23   The Insert Tabular Data dialog box.

Dreamweaver sorts the data into a table, which will show up in the currently open document.

Summary

To build successful Web sites, you need to develop skill in creating and modifying tables. Although tables were not originally intended to be a Web layout tool, that is what they have become. Because they are relatively easy to make compatible with all Web browsers, tables are holding ground as the number-one way to control the space on your Web site. Although they may be overtaken by cascading style sheets in the near future, it's still worth your time to learn how to design with tables.

Even so, every browser reads tables a bit differently. This is especially true when it comes to table cell background images, borders, and colors. When working with these elements, make sure you view your site in a variety of browsers.

Image slicing and assembly inside a table is another popular Web design technique. You can design a Web page inside Fireworks or another Web-friendly imaging program and slice the final version into GIF files. In Dreamweaver, the slices can be reassembled into a pixel-based table. With Cell Padding, Cell Spacing, and Border set to 0, the image slices should blend seamlessly.

Experiment with the various uses of tables covered in this chapter and with the Dreamweaver design modes to discover how tables can benefit your site.

Chapter 9

Layout with Frames

Framesets are an often-overlooked for-
matting tool when creating a Web site.
With framesets, you can organize multiple
HTML documents into one view (see
Figures 9.1 and 9.2). The power that this
gives the designer should not be ignored.

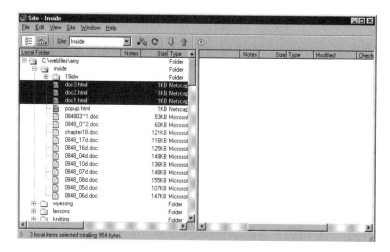

Figure 9.1   Three individual HTML documents.

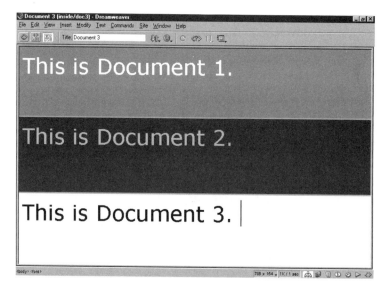

Figure 9.2   The same three documents contained by a frameset.

Typical Web sites often contain elements that are to be repeated throughout (such as navigational features, titles, and logos). You can create these elements once through the use of frames and reuse them across an entire site.

In addition to alleviating repetitious work in a site, the frameset's main advantage is that the elements within it continue to behave as individual HTML documents. Therefore, you can give one frame the capability to scroll, whereas the rest stay static. As well, you can change the HTML document displayed in one frame (or multiple frames) without disrupting or reloading the rest of the frames. This means that you need to load static elements only one time and that these elements always stay in view as you navigate through different content. This in turn enables the user to load only the new data and not the data that is to remain static.

This chapter discusses what constitutes a frameset and shows how you can use Dreamweaver to implement these powerful formatting tools.

This chapter covers the following:

- Frameset basics
- Creating frames
- Sizing and formatting frames
- Targeting frames

Frames and Framesets

To create a layout using frames, you utilize two very different components: the frameset, and the individual frames. When referring to the frameset, it is important to distinguish between two key elements. First is the frameset document, which is made up of HTML code. Second is the HTML code inside of that document, which defines the placement and dimensions of the frames. It is important to realize that the frameset document's purpose is not to contain content. Instead, it is an HTML document that includes the locations of other HTML documents to be displayed in the frames that it encompasses. These documents that the frameset refers to are responsible for the actual content.

The Frameset Document

The frameset is an HTML document that describes how a Web page is to be divided and subdivided into frames. The frames themselves are actually separate HTML documents, laid out according to the <FRAMESET> tags when the frameset document is loaded.

The purpose of a frameset is to divide the page into a series of columns and rows. The <FRAMESET> tag establishes these divisions. Consider the following example:

```
<HTML>
  <HEAD>
      <TITLE>Sample Frameset</TITLE>
  </HEAD>
  <FRAMESET cols="30%,70%">
```

This frameset sets up two columns (because of the two delineated values). The first one is 30% of the width of the entire document. The second takes up the remaining 70%. Alternatively in this example, you could use the rows attribute rather than the cols attribute and create a row using 30% of the height of the document and a second row taking up the remaining 70%. A combination of the two attributes (cols and rows) is also acceptable (see Figure 9.3).

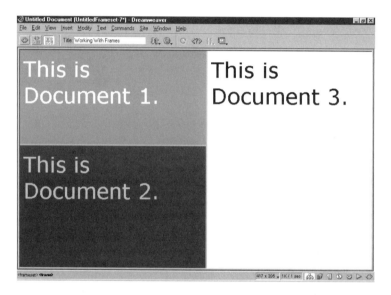

Figure 9.3   Frameset consisting of columns and rows.

Now is a good time to define the values that you assign to the cols and rows attributes. As shown in the preceding example, you can define the dimensions of the frames in terms of percentages of the document window. You also can define a ratio of dimensions (for instance, 2, 2, 4, 2). This value sets up 4 frames, with 20%, 20%, 40%, and 20%, respectively. Both the percentage and ratio method enable you to resize the frames to whatever browser dimensions are available. If, on the other hand, you want to define the exact dimensions of a frame, you can enter in the pixel values (for instance, cols="355, 135"). This obviously divides the document into one column that is 355 pixels wide and a second column that is 135 pixels wide. Finally, a combination of defined and resizable dimensions exists by using a relative in the attribute value. If you were to use cols="500, ", the first column would be 500 pixels wide and the second would be whatever space is left over. If you were to use rows="2, *", the first row would be 2 times greater in height than the second.

Nesting Frame and Frameset Tags

Nested inside of the <FRAMESET> tags are the <FRAME> tags. These tags refer to the Web page to be loaded into a particular frame. The <FRAME> tags are the only tags inside of a <FRAMESET>, except for the nesting of a second set of <FRAMESET> tags. Does all this sound confusing? Compare the source code for a frameset, as shown here, to the resulting frameset in Figure 9.4:

```
<FRAMESET rows="10%,90%" cols="*">
    <FRAME name="topFrame" src="top.html">
      <FRAMESET cols="10%,90%">
            <FRAME name="leftFrame" src="left.html">
            <FRAME name="mainFrame" src="main.html">
</FRAMESET>
</FRAMESET>
```

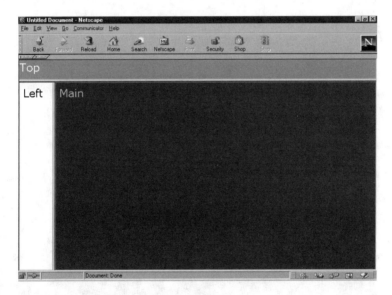

Figure 9.4   Frameset created with the code listed here.

Using Frames in Dreamweaver

This section introduces you to some of the basic tools used in Dreamweaver when creating framesets. These tools include the Objects panel, Frames Inspector, and the Property Inspector.

Frameset and Frame Creation

Dreamweaver usually provides a few different ways to accomplish something, including creating frames. Dreamweaver gives you the following three ways to create a frameset:

- The Frameset menu
- The Frame Borders visual aid
- Click and drag borders

From the Modify/Frameset menu, you can select the way you want to split the current frame (see Figure 9.5). You can then split each subsequent frame to get the desired frame layout. This method is very intuitive if you are familiar with using the menu to alter your documents. If you prefer to work visually, you should probably consider the other two methods.

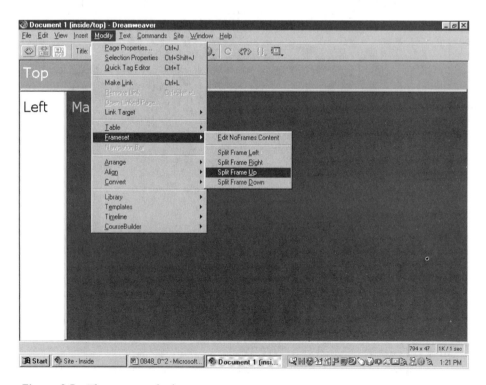

Figure 9.5   The menu method.

You can create a frameset from scratch, using only your mouse if you enable the Frame Borders visual aid from the View menu (see Figure 9.6). With this option selected, a thickened border displays around your document.

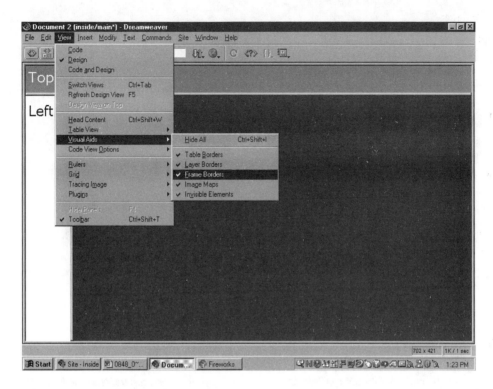

Figure 9.6   View frame borders.

To create a horizontally split frameset, just hover over the thick border at the top of the document until your cursor becomes a vertical arrow set. Then just click and drag the border into your document and let go. Your document will split horizontally. To split the document vertically, repeat this process using the side borders and wait for the horizontal arrow set. You also can select a corner of the border and drag it into the document to create a four-frame document. When splitting frames, if you want the new split to occur only in one frame rather than the whole document, press Alt while clicking the frame to first select it, and then drag to split (keep the Alt key pressed while doing this). This action creates a nested frameset (see Figure 9.7).

Selecting Frames

When creating frames in Dreamweaver, keep a few simple things in mind. A frameset consists of multiple documents. Therefore when you want to alter the frameset, you must have the frameset document selected. To select the frameset, just click the frame borders inside of the document window. Another way to select a frameset is to use the Frames Inspector (Window/Frames). With the Frames Inspector, you will see a scale representation of your frameset, with the names of your frames inside. By just clicking one of the frames, or borders, you can select frameset elements.

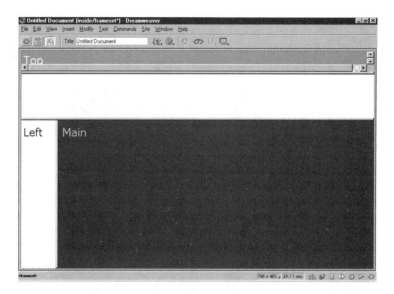

Figure 9.7   A nested frameset has been created in the top frame.

Selected Framesets

You can easily tell whether you have your frameset selected. In Design view, if your frameset is selected, a dotted highlight displays around all your frame borders. With the Frames Inspector, if your frame/frameset is selected, a thick black highlight displays around the borders. If you want to alter only an individual frame, you must press and hold Alt while clicking inside of that frame. Remember that if you want to split an individual frame, you are actually just nesting a second set of <FRAMESET> tags in your existing frameset. When you have your frame properly selected, the dotted highlight displays around the frame.

Finally, you can choose from predefined framesets in the Frames section of the Objects panel. To get there, just locate and click the drop-down menu at the top of the Objects panel (labeled Common by default), and select Frames. Then select the frame you want to split and select the button that visually describes what you want to do.

Using any of the previously described methods, you can quickly create a multiframe frameset. However, using the second method seems to be more intuitive for those who are used to using graphics programs, because it mirrors the creation of guides in most applications.

Saving Frames

Saving the documents belonging to your frameset can be almost as confusing as framesets themselves. To understand this process, it is important to review the structure of a frameset. A frameset is an HTML document that locates other documents (frames) and arranges them in the browser window. The frames are just HTML documents. Therefore, to save exactly what you see when you have completed a frameset, you obviously have to save more than one document. You have to keep just two things in mind when saving a frameset: which save feature you want to use, and which document Dreamweaver is asking you to save.

If you have created a new frameset, as well as the content for those frames, Save All (File/Save All) is the option you want. When this option is selected, any documents in the current window are saved. You also are prompted to name any unnamed documents. Keep in mind the order in which Dreamweaver will save the current frameset. The first document Dreamweaver will attempt to save is the frameset document itself. Second, Dreamweaver will ask you to save the frame at the bottom right of the frameset. From here Dreamweaver works its way through the frameset from right to left moving up a row at a time until all the frames are saved.

If you have created a new frameset, but want to save only the frameset document, just use Save Frameset (File/Save Frameset). This action prompts you to name the frameset if you have not previously named it, or just update the saved version with any changes you may have made.

Linking Frames to the Frameset

If you already have some or all the content prepared, and are only creating a frameset, just use the Property Inspector to have the frames linked to the frameset. First, select the frame into which you want to place the saved document. Then, in the Property Inspector, locate the source (SRC) text field and either type in the address of the file or click the blue folder to browse for the file. After you have done this, the new file appears in the selected frame.

Resizing Frames

The easiest way to resize a frame is with the mouse (click and drag). However, this produces absolute pixel-based dimensions for your frameset, which isn't always the best method when designing for different screen resolutions. Sometimes, therefore, you will probably opt for dynamically sized frames.

Begin by creating a frameset like the one shown in Figure 9.8.

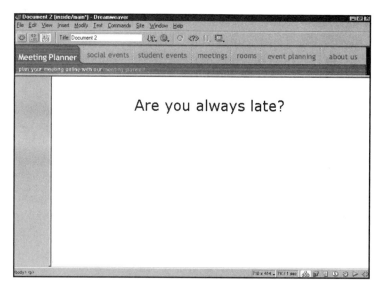

Figure 9.8   A simple frameset.

Now select the entire frameset by selecting the frameset border. This action changes your Property Inspector to the Frameset options (see Figure 9.9). (You also can select the entire frameset border in the Frames panel.)

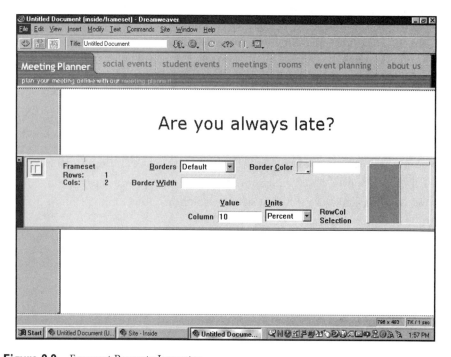

Figure 9.9   Frameset Property Inspector.

Take note of two elements in the inspector. First, at the far right is a representation of your current frameset. Second, at the bottom, is a numeric value followed by a drop-down. These two fields are labeled Value and Units, respectively. To resize your frames from here, first select whether to change the rows or cols. You select which one by using the small representation discussed earlier. Selecting a single cell will select the row or column that contains that cell. Clicking that same cell again will switch the selection from the row to the column and so on (see Figures 9.10 and 9.11).

Tip

When creating a frameset with a navigational frame (a frame to contain your buttons) and a content frame, it is usually best if you allow the content frame to resize, while the navigational frame's size remains absolute. In other words, set the important dimension (width in a left- and right-frame scenario) to an absolute (pixel) value for the navigational frame (left frame) and set the content's important dimension to a relative value. That way, when the user resizes his window, or if his browser is set to a different size than yours, you can be sure that he will be able to see the full navigational frame and that the content will resize when necessary.

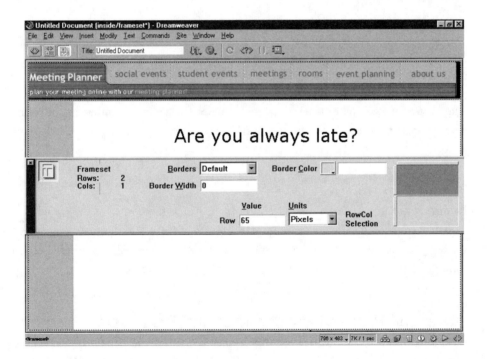

Figure 9.10   Frameset row selected.

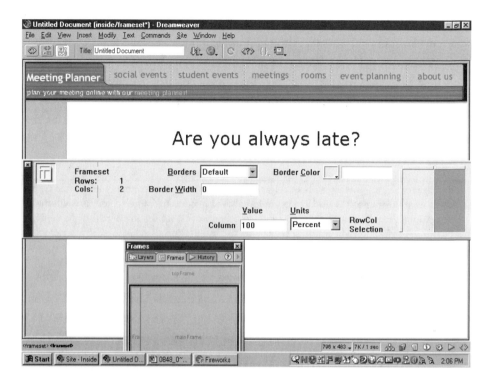

Figure 9.11   Frameset column selected.

After you have the right element selected, you can enter in a number in the Value field. Then from the unit drop-down, you select the type of unit you want to use. It's that simple.

Removing Frames

Removing a frame from a frameset is simple. Just drag the border of the frame into its parent frame. If it is the top-level frame, drag its border to the edge of the document window. For this to work, however, frame borders must be set to Visible. Otherwise, you cannot delete frames.

Advanced Properties of Frames and Framesets

So far this discussion has focused only on the creation of framesets, not on the advanced visual and functional options you have with them. Depending on <FRAMESET> and <FRAME> attributes, you can change how both the frameset displays and how the frame content displays.

Frameset Attributes

Framesets usually stand out because of their borders. However, you can change the appearance of these borders, and even make them disappear.

You can change the width of the borders in your frameset in pixels by entering a number in the Border Width field of the Property Inspector. If you want to remove the appearance of borders completely, just set the Border Width to 0 in the Frameset Property Inspector.

Finally, if you want to, you also can change the color and method used to draw your borders. To change the color, either type in a Web-safe color into the Border Color field or click the box to the immediate left of that field to choose the color from a palette. To change from 3D borders to plain borders, select Yes or No from the borders drop-down. Selecting Default leaves the choice up to the browser.

Frame Attributes

By selecting a frame, you can change the attributes of its tag in the Property Inspector.

> **Note**
>
> A Frames panel is also available for selecting individual frames. Just select Frames from the Window menu, or press SHIFT+F2. One of the benefits of the Frames panel is that it gives a size-accurate view of all the frames in the current document. Just selecting one of the frames in this panel makes that frame selected in the document window (see Figure 9.12).

Some of the attributes offered in the Property Inspector when an individual frame is selected are Name, Scroll, Borders, Border Color, Resize, Margin Width, and Margin Height. Following is a brief description of what these attributes perform and how to set them.

Name

Not to be confused with the filename of the document, the name is one of the most overlooked, but most useful attributes of the <FRAME> tag. First, identifying each frame with a unique and descriptive name enables you to target that specific frame later. Without this name, the frame cannot be targeted by links, which in turn means you have very few options as far as changing content in the frame goes. Second, naming a frame allows easy referencing when it comes to making your frameset active via scripting (see Chapter 19, "JavaScripting with Dreamweaver"). It is a good rule of thumb to never leave a frame unnamed.

Figure 9.12   The Frames panel.

Just a few rules apply when naming frames, but they are very important to remember.

- Never use a reserved name for a frame name. The reserved names are: _blank, _parent, _self, and _top. These are described in more detail later in this chapter in the section titled "Reserved Targets."

- Do not use special characters such as periods, commas, quotation marks, and so on.

- The name should be one contiguous word, without spaces.

Also keep in mind when naming your frames that the name is case sensitive; you must use the exact case whenever you need to reference it.

Scroll

Scroll enables you to set whether each individual frame can scroll. This feature proves particularly useful if you want to fit more information than the size of your frame can handle. The Scroll setting has four preset options available through the drop-down:

- **Yes.** With this selected, your frame will always have a scrollbar, regardless of whether the content fits the frame. Unless you have a specific reason in mind for this option, it is best not to choose it.

- **No.** This option disables scrollbars for this frame, and any content that does not fit in the frame will not be viewable by the client/user. This option is good if you can depend on the content to be an exact size and if you have the frame's dimensions set to an absolute value, which allows for the content. Because of the arbitrary nature of this setting, you should be positive that your end user is viewing your page in at least the same or higher resolution than the resolution of the computer that you are using to develop the site.

- **Auto.** This option enables/disables scrollbars based on the size of the content. This option proves useful if your contents' size is unpredictable in other browsers or if you are not sure about your end users' screen/browser configurations.

- **Default.** This option leaves the use of scrollbars entirely up to the browser.

Borders and Border Color

You can set the type of border and the border color, independent of the entire frameset. By entering values here, you attempt to override the <FRAMESET> tags settings. Attempt is the appropriate word; because if you do not have each border independent of the other, as in a multiframeset document, any that are attached will share their type and color attributes.

Frame Resize

When a frameset is drawn, by default the user has the ability to resize frames by just click-dragging the frame borders.

This is usually not what designers have in mind; therefore you need to use an attribute to stop this default behavior. In Dreamweaver, you just have to click the No Resize check box in the Property Inspector. This action disables the user's ability to drag and resize this frame in the browser. (You may still resize it in Dreamweaver.) Note that this behavior is frame to frame, so you need to repeat this for every frame that you do not want to be resizable.

Margin Width and Height

By default, all documents in your frameset have an offset. That is, they have a buffer around each of their borders where no content can be placed. To turn off this buffer and use the entire frame, use the Margin attributes, and set them to 0. By so doing, you can lay out content right up to the frame borders.

Targeting Frames

When you create a hyperlink in a document, you can choose the frame into which the new document is to be loaded. This gives you the ability to dynamically change elements in your frameset, without reloading the entire document. This ability is called *targeting*.

One of the most popular uses for this is seen in a frameset designed to navigate content. You start by creating a frame, which contains links to various documents, and have those links target other frames in your frameset to contain those documents.

When deciding on a target for a link, you have two options: choose from a list of reserved targets, or target a frame by its name. The following sections discuss these options in detail.

Reserved Targets

A frameset has the following four reserved targets, as mentioned earlier in this chapter:

- **_blank.** This target opens the link in a new browser window, leaving the original window intact.

- **_parent.** This target opens the link in the frameset in which the current frame resides. This one is a bit tricky, because you have to consider how your current frame is nested in the context of the entire document window. If your current frame belongs to the top-level frameset, which is to say that it is not nested, _parent behaves like _top.

- **_self.** This target opens the link inside the frame from which it is called. This is the default setting when the target is not specified.

- **_top.** This target replaces the entire document window.

To use targeting, just create a link inside one of your frames; and in the Property Inspector, choose the name of the target you want your link to point to from the Target drop-down list. All available frame names appear in this drop-down list, including the names of the individual frames contained in the frameset.

Named Frames

As you learned earlier in this chapter, when you create a frameset it is important to name your frames. This section tells you why.

When you want to target a link to a specific frame, you need to call that frame by name. The process of targeting a specific frame is identical to that of using reserved targets, except you choose the name of the frame from the Target drop-down list.

You also may type the information in manually; just remember that the name is case sensitive and that the target will fail to work if typed incorrectly. By utilizing a scripting language such as JavaScript, you may have more than one document load into more than one targeted frame, with a single user action (click). In Dreamweaver, The Goto URL behavior is one such script. Refer to Chapter 19 for more on JavaScript and using behaviors.

The <NOFRAMES> Tag

As with most advanced HTML use, the issue of outdated browsers often arises, and framesets are not an exception. Instead of having to redirect a user to a different HTML page, however, you can use the <NOFRAMES> tag to define what the visitor sees if her browser is frame incapable.

Dreamweaver automatically inserts the <NOFRAMES> tag pair immediately after the code defining your frameset. Inside these tags, you can insert <BODY> tags to create an alternative layout.

To edit the <NOFRAMES> content of your Web page, choose Modify/Frameset/Edit NoFrames Content. The document window changes to reflect the content inside of the <NOFRAMES> tags.

You can treat this window as you would any other document window, and lay out the page. After you have finished, just select Modify/Frameset/Edit NoFrames Content again to return to the frameset.

Summary

With framesets, you can organize multiple HTML documents into one view. Again, the power that this gives designers should not be ignored. This chapter discussed framesets—the basics, creating frames, sizing and formatting frames, and target frames. Hopefully, you now understand the power you have as a designer to use framesets.

C h a p t e r   1 0

Using Layers

If you take the time to learn how layers

work in Dreamweaver, it won't be long

before you realize the tremendous potential

they have to increase the interactivity and

overall appearance of your site. Before your

imagination sweeps you away, however, read this chapter thoroughly. You should have a solid knowledge of what layers are, how they work, and what their technical issues are before you begin using them.

This chapter covers the following:

- Creating layers
- Sizing layers
- Positioning layers
- Setting layer properties
- Nested layers
- Layer preferences
- Converting layers
- Putting layers into motion

About Layers

In the world of computer graphics, the term *layers* is usually defined as the technique of piling images and text objects on top of one another to create a collage effect, or to give illustrations and photographs a sense of depth. After the layered image has been exported out of the software program, it is usually flattened to reduce file size. The original layered document is hidden away on the designer's hard drive, to be pulled up again only if changes need to be made.

If this is how you think of layers, open your mind to a new meaning for the term. In Dreamweaver, layers, which are categorized as a DHTML (Dynamic Hypertext Markup Language) technique, can serve many different purposes besides visual design. They can solve technical issues, be used as a layout tool or an animation method, and more.

First be aware that only version 4 and above browsers will display layers. Older browsers that do not support layers will not display them; either the user will be presented with an error message, or the page will display with missing or misaligned elements. Although Dreamweaver gives you the option to convert your layers to tables so that the page can be viewed in older browsers; this is not a satisfactory solution if you have used overlapping layers or another technique that cannot be re-created in tables.

Layers Versus Tables

For all their disadvantages, layers can provide interesting effects such as show-hide behaviors and timeline animations. And, unlike tables, layers can be positioned anywhere on the page. (Tables snap to the top left by default.)

Show-hide behaviors, animations, and special positioning are more difficult to achieve if you are laying out your page in tables. However, tables are supported by virtually all Web browsers and can be a powerful formatting tool in the hands of a knowledgeable Web designer.

If the design you have in mind can be accomplished using tables, use tables instead and enjoy the peace of mind that comes with knowing that they are supported by almost all Web browsers. If you want to experiment with layers, or if you are working on a design that requires them, however, Dreamweaver offers you the ability to create, edit, and manipulate layers, and you won't have to write a single line of code.

Should Layers Overlap?

In graphics software, layers are placed on top of each other (hence the term *layers*). When working with DHTML layers, however, you should be extra careful when creating layer overlaps. A document containing layers is only as sturdy as the browser from which it is viewed; and if that browser doesn't completely understand or support the tags used to create layers, much could go awry. This is especially true when layers overlap.

If you do use overlapping layers, take the following precautions:

- Test the overlaps in a wide variety of Web browsers on both Macintosh and PC platforms.
- Keep the number of overlapping layers to a minimum. More than 10 and you're asking for trouble.
- Place standard elements inside the layers, such as text, GIF or JPG images, or tables. Try to avoid elements that require plug-ins, or that are not widely supported (such as PNG images).
- If you put tables inside overlapping layers, make sure each item inside the table cells are aligned in a specific horizontal and vertical direction (such as left, top). Using the default setting for table-cell alignment might cause your layers to fall out of place.

Now that you are aware of the risks you're taking when using layers as a design tool, it is time to move on and talk about what you can do with them if you are willing to take that risk.

Note

After you have mastered the use of layers, take things a step further by animating the items inside your layers. Refer to Chapter 17, "Animation with Timelines," for some exercises on animating layers on timelines.

Layer Basics

To effectively work with layers, you must know the basics: how to draw them and organize them in the Layers panel, how to insert content, and how to position them on the page. That's what this section covers. At the end of the section, you will complete an exercise that includes all the above-mentioned basics.

Drawing Layers

You can draw a layer on top of existing content that is not inside a layer, or make a page that consists entirely of several different layers. There is no limit to the number of layers you can make. You should, however, keep the total number of layers to a minimum, especially if any of them overlap. Pages with an extremely high number of layers can take a while to render in a browser, and can be a drain on system resources when working in Dreamweaver. Of course, some people use 50–100 layers on a single page with success. Be aware that these people are the exception to the rule.

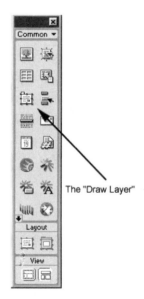

The "Draw Layer"

Figure 10.1
The Draw Layer icon.

When drawing layers, you should be in Standard view, not in Layout view. In Standard view, you have access to the Draw Layer icon in the Object panel's Common panel (see Figure 10.1). If you cannot select the Draw Layer button, you should switch out of Layout view.

When you are in Standard view, you can draw a layer on your page. To do so, use the Draw Layer icon shown in Figure 10.1 or choose Insert/Layer. You should use the Draw Layer icon so that you can control the height and width of your layer as you draw it. Choosing the Insert/Layer menu option gives you a layer with a default width and height.

Tip

You can change the default height and width of your layer, as well as change other default settings that pertain to your layers by choosing Edit/Preferences/Layers.

Your layer will look like a box with smaller boxes (these are the resizing handles) around the edge if it is selected, or a plain beveled box if it is not selected. Choose Window/Layers or use the keyboard shortcut F2 to see the layer you have just drawn listed in the Layers panel. Figure 10.2 shows two layers, with the selected layer highlighted in the Layers panel.

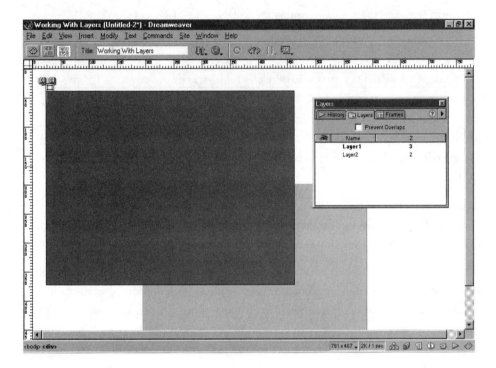

Figure 10.2   The makings of a layered document.

It's a good idea to name each layer so that you can easily identify them in the Layers panel. Just double-click the layer in the Layers panel and type the new name into the text field area after Dreamweaver highlights it. You also can select the layer by the pound sign (#), and rename it in the Property Inspector.

Deleting Layers

If you want to delete a layer, select it in the Layers panel and press the Delete or Backspace key. Shift-click to select multiple layers and delete them all at once. You also can delete them from the page by selecting them and pressing Delete or Backspace.

HTML Code and Layers

By default, Dreamweaver creates layers with the <DIV> tag. You cannot see the <DIV> tag unless you are in Code view (F10). The following is an example of what HTML code for a basic layer would look like. The code is located inside the <BODY> tag:

```
<div id="Layer1" style="position:absolute; width:200px;
height:115px">Layer contents are here.</div>
```

Other HTML tags used in layer creation are <SPAN>, <ILAYER>, and <LAYER>. You can use either <DIV> or <SPAN> for layers to be viewed in Netscape or Internet Explorer 4 and above. The <ILAYER> and <LAYER> tags will produce layers that are viewable only in Netscape 4.x.

To change the default tag, choose Edit/Preferences/Layers and pull down the Tag menu.

Inserting Content into Layers

Although there is often a good reason to make invisible layers, this discussion assumes that you do indeed want to put something in your layers, and that you want them to be visible to your users.

Inserting content into a layer is simple. Click in the layer, and choose an item from the Insert menu. Alternatively, you can paste text or other media from your Clipboard into the layer. You also can drag things off the Assets panel.

Sometimes the most difficult part of inserting content into a layer is selecting the layer. If you have more than one layer on your page, it is easy to get confused as to the placement of the layers. For that reason, get into the habit of using the Layers panel (see Figure 10.3). When you select the layer name from the Layers panel, the layer itself is automatically selected for you and will come to the forefront of the document.

Other ways to select a layer include clicking the layer's HTML marker, clicking the layer's border, and clicking the layer's selection handle.

Figure 10.3   Use the Layers panel to select layers.

Tip

Check the Prevent Overlaps box on the Layers panel (F2) to prevent your layers from overlapping inside the document.

Note

You can select more than one layer at a time. To do so, Shift-click the layer names inside the Layers panel. Alternatively, Shift-click the layers themselves. The last layer you select will be highlighted in black. The other layers will be highlighted in white. This feature proves useful if you want to set many layers to the same dimensions, or the same position.

Sizing Layers

After you have created your layer and inserted content, take the time to size the layer. If you have an image inserted into a layer, for instance, you can size a layer so that it exactly matches the pixel width and height of the image contained inside.

In Figure 10.4, two overlapping layers have been positioned in the center of the page. The bottom layer is a bit larger than the one that sits on top, providing a "frame" for the image. Both layers and the page itself have been given a background color.

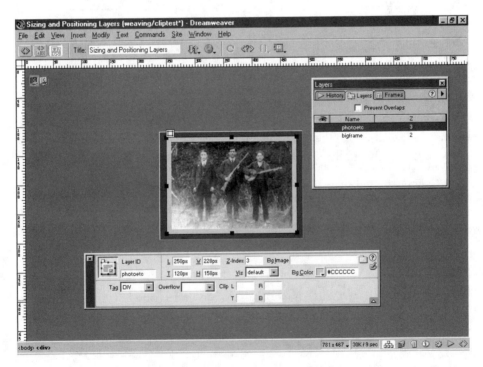

Figure 10.4   Two overlapping layers can create a framing effect. Make sure to test overlaps such as this one in a wide variety of browsers.

To precisely size a layer, you should use the Property Inspector (Ctrl+F3). When you select the layer you want to size, the Property Inspector will offer a set of options. (These options are covered in detail later in this chapter.) In Figure 10.4, the layer containing the photo is 228 pixels in width by 158 pixels in height, as shown in the Property Inspector.

To size a layer with the Property Inspector, follow these steps:

1. Select the layer you want to size by clicking its name in the Layers panel.

2. With the Property Inspector open (Ctrl+F3), enter your desired size, in pixels, into the W (width) and H (height) fields.

3. Dreamweaver will resize the layer. Click in the background area (not inside a layer) to return the newly resized area back to its position in the layer order.

You can also size a layer by dragging its handles outward or inward. You might want to do this to approximate a size for the layer, and then make precise pixel adjustments using the H (height) and W (width) fields in the Property Inspector.

Tip

> You can adjust the size of a layer one pixel at a time. To do so, select the layer, and then hold down the Ctrl key as you press your keyboard's arrow keys in the direction you want to expand or contract.

Sizing Multiple Layers

If you want more than one layer in your document to be the same width, height, or both, you can do so easily. Select the layers you want to resize by Shift-clicking the layers themselves, or their names in the Layers panel. Then, do one of the following:

- Choose Modify/Align/Make Same Width or Make Same Height (see Figure 10.5).
- Enter a W (width) or H (height) pixel value into the Property Inspector, Multiple Layers section (see Figure 10.5).

Positioning Layers

When working with layers, it is important that you understand how to position them within your document. The position of layers inside a document is determined by X and Y coordinates, which you can view and edit using the Property Inspector.

Moving Layers

To position a layer, you can first pick it up and move it to an approximate location on your screen. To move a layer, select the layer by its selection handle (located in the upper-left corner of the layer) and drag the layer to its new location. Release the mouse to secure the layer in its new position.

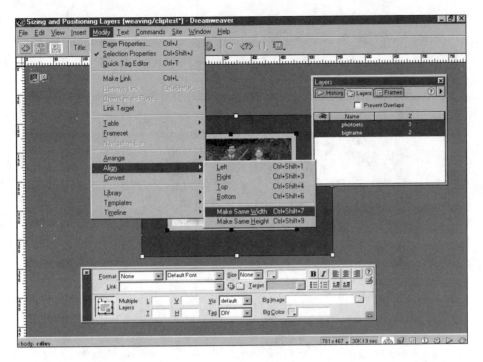

Figure 10.5   When you select multiple layers, the Property Inspector offers you options for sizing them. You can also use the Modify menu to resize the layers.

You can also select the layer and move it pixel by pixel by pressing the arrow keys on your keyboard. Alternatively, position the layer by entering numbers for the L and T fields in the Property Inspector.

Tip

You can align multiple layers by selecting them, choosing Modify/Align, and then choosing an alignment option. The layers will align to the position of the last layer you selected. Be aware that any nested or "child" layers will move as well.

Layer Positioning with the Property Inspector

For precise positioning of a layer, use the Property Inspector. The fields L (left) and T (top) will be available to you when a layer is selected. Use these fields to enter values, in coordinates, of where in the document you want to position the layer. These coordinates are relative to the top-left corner of the page.

If you want a layer to "bleed" into the top and left side of the browser window, for instance, set both coordinates to 0. Add one for each pixel to the right and/or toward the bottom you want to move the layer. If you want, you can even position your layer with negative coordinates, in which case part of the layer will be off the viewable page.

In Figure 10.6, a layer containing the California Redwoods image is set to bleed out of the left and top of the document. In Figure 10.7, the layer has been moved 240 pixels down from the top so that it is positioned at the bottom of the document.

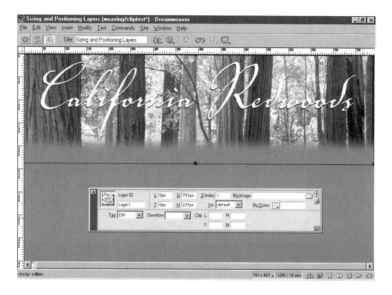

Figure 10.6   This layer bleeds out the top of the screen. Its coordinates are 0,0.

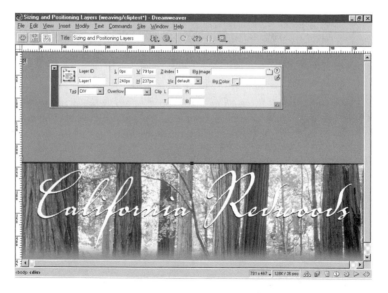

Figure 10.7   The layer has been repositioned to coordinates 0,240.

If you want to avoid working with coordinates, you might consider using the grid. If you enable the Snap to Grid option, your layer will snap to the nearest grid position when you drag and release it. To view the grid, choose View/Grid/Show Grid. Enable snapping by choosing View/Grid/Snap to Grid. Be aware that the grid will not appear inside the Web browser. For more information about editing and working with the grid, see Chapter 7, "Web Design Issues."

Exercise 10.1   Creating and Positioning Layers

In this exercise, you create a document that contains two overlapping layers. This document is part of the Weaving Web site that was begun in Chapter 8, "Layout with Tables."

You might remember from earlier in the chapter the risks of overlapping layers. In this exercise, the risk of overlapping layers is avoided. Because only two layers will overlap, the risk is much lower than it would be if you were working with many layers.

To get started, open the blank file called DYES.HTML from the Weaving folder in the accompanying CD-ROM.

1. Using the Objects panel (Ctrl+F2), click the Draw Layer icon and draw a layer on the page. Don't worry about the width and height of the layer yet.
2. Open the Layers panel (F2) and double-click layer1 in the listing. Rename the layer **colorwheel**.
3. Click inside the layer. Choose Insert/Image and choose the wheel image from the Weaving folder on the CD-ROM.
4. Select the layer by clicking its border, or by selecting it from the Layers panel. Using the Property Inspector (Ctrl+F3), give the layer a W (width) and H (height) of 642 pixels (a perfect square). Note that 642 × 642 is also the size of the image.
5. With the layer still selected, position it on the page using the Property Inspector. Give it an L (left) value of 70, and a T (top) value of 0.
6. Click outside the layer boundaries so that the layer is no longer selected.
7. Using the Draw Layer icon from the Objects panel, draw another layer on the page. Don't worry about its position right now.
8. Using the Layers panel, rename the layer you just created to **swatches**.
9. Click inside the swatches layer. Choose Insert/Table and fill out the Insert Table dialog box (see Figure 10.8). Note that although it is okay, and even good design, to put a table inside a layer, it is *not* possible to put a layer inside a table. The layer will sit on top of the table, and the page will not render correctly in any browser.

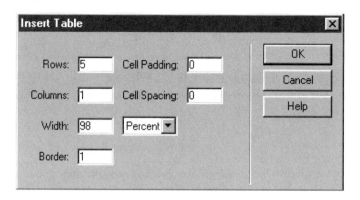

Figure 10.8   Give your table these attributes.

10. Select the table cells in the table by dragging across the table. Using the Property Inspector, give the cell contents a Horz alignment of Left, and a Vert alignment of Top. If you have trouble selecting the table's cells all at once, you can align them individually by clicking inside each table cell.

11. The Weaving folder on the CD-ROM contains a set of five images to insert into the table. Starting with the top row, insert one image into each row, using the following order:

    a. DYEHEAD.GIF

    b. RED.GIF

    c. GREEN.GIF

    d. BLUE.GIF

    e. YELLOW.GIF

Take a look at the table in Figure 10.9 if you want to see how the table should look.

12. After you have all the images in the correct table cell, use the Property Inspector to give the table a border of 0. Align the table to the left.

13. Now it's time to size the swatches layer. Select it by clicking its name in the Layers panel, or by clicking its border. Using the W and H fields on the Property Inspector, give the layer a width of 312 pixels and a height of 411 pixels.

14. With the layer still selected, position it in the document, using the L and T fields on the Property Inspector. Use the coordinate 15 for the L field and 0 for the T field.

15. Save the file and images to your hard drive if you want to view it inside your Web browser.

This exercise created a simple HTML document that contained two layers. The first layer contained a single image, the second, overlapping layer contained a table and five images.

Figure 10.9 shows the final document as it looks in Dreamweaver 4. Figure 10.10 shows the layers as they appear in Netscape 4. No difference here, and that's a good thing! Once again, a document such as this that contains overlapping layers should be tested for accuracy in a wide variety of Web browsers on both PC and Macintosh platforms.

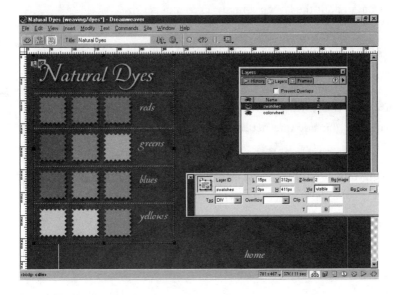

Figure 10.9   The layered page inside Dreamweaver 4.

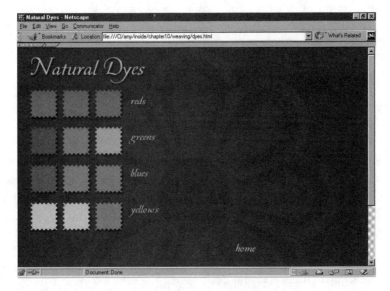

Figure 10.10   The layered page inside Netscape Navigator 4.

Setting Layer Properties

So far you have used the Property Inspector to size and position layers, but there is much more that you can do. Using the Property Inspector, you can set the visibility of a layer, rearrange its stacking order, give it a background color or image, clip it, and give instructions on what to do if the layer's contents exceed its set size.

<DIV> and <SPAN> Layer Properties

More than likely, you will be using the <DIV> and <SPAN> tags for your layers, so that they will work in both Netscape and Internet Explorer 4 and above. Remember that the <LAYER> and <ILAYER> tags are only for layers to be viewed in Netscape 4.x, not for layers to be viewed inside Internet Explorer.

Let's take a detailed look at the layer options for the <DIV> and <SPAN> tags. Refer back to Figure 10.3 if you want to see what the Property Inspector looks like when a <DIV> or <SPAN> layer is selected.

Layer ID

The *layer ID* is the name of the layer. You can use this ID if you are writing a script to manipulate layers. If you change the layer ID in the Property Inspector, it will also change in the Layers panel.

L and T

These fields determine the left (L) and top (T) coordinates of the selected layer. These numbers describe the location of the top-left corner of your layer, relative to the top-left corner of the page.

W and H

Use these fields to set a width and height of the selected layer.

Z-Index

A layer's Z-Index is the order in which it is stacked against other layers inside the same document. The layer with the highest Z-Index will be the topmost layer. The layer with the lowest Z-Index (you can even use negative numbers for Z-Indexing) will be the layer farthest to the back. If you change a layer's Z-Index in the Property Inspector, the change will also be indicated in the Layers panel.

You should use the Layers panel to rearrange the stacking order of layers. To move a layer in front of or behind other layers, follow these steps:

1. In the Layers panel, select the name of the layer that is to be assigned a new position in the stacking order.

2. Click and drag the layer name to the desired position in the layer listing.

3. Release the mouse when a darkened line appears.

You also can accomplish this task by clicking once in the layer's field for Z-Index in the Layers panel, and then typing in a number.

VIS

Use this field to change the visibility of a layer. In Dreamweaver, new layers are assigned a VIS of default. *Most* browsers understand this to mean that the layer should be visible. If this is not something you're willing to risk, select the layer and use the Property Inspector to change the VIS field to Visible. To hide layers, choose Hidden. This attribute is used most often with show-hide layer behaviors.

In the Layers panel, a layer that has a VIS attribute of Inherit will not have an open-eye icon next to it. Change the attribute to Visible to see the icon. If you then change the attribute to Hidden, a closed-eye icon will appear.

When using nested layers, the Inherit attribute can be used to indicate that a child layer should have the same visibility as its parent. For more about parent/child layers, see the section later in this chapter called "Nested Layers."

BG Image and BG Color

Just like tables, layers can be given background colors and images. Use these fields to assign a background color and image for your layer. If you don't want to use background colors or images, just leave these fields blank. If you select multiple layers, you can give them all the same background color or image simultaneously by using these fields in the Property Inspector.

Any background image you assign to a layer or multiple layers will be tiled. If you want to use a single image as a background, make a layer and insert the image into the layer, as you did in Exercise 10.1. Alternatively, if you're working with a larger background image, you could make the layer the same size as the image, so there isn't a need to tile.

Tag

The Tag field determines the type of layer you are creating. Use <DIV> or <SPAN> to make a layer that will work in both Netscape and Internet Explorer 4 and above.

Overflow

If you insert contents into a layer that are larger than the set width or height of the layer, the Overflow option determines what happens to the excess. This setting becomes important because different browsers render layer contents in different sizes. It is possible that you won't use this Overflow setting in one browser, but will need to use it in the other, on the exact same page.

- **Visible.** This choice increases the layer size so that all the layer's contents can be seen. The layer expands to the right and toward the bottom. Note that this setting sometimes causes the contents of one layer to expand over the contents of another layer. Use this setting with caution, and also lay out your pages with lots of distance between layers if possible.

- **Hidden.** Content that doesn't fit into the layer's set size will be hidden from view.

- **Scroll.** In browsers that support layer scrollbars, this option provides them, no matter whether the layer's contents are larger than the set size.

- **Auto.** Scrollbars will appear only if the layer's contents are larger than its set size (again, assuming the browser supports these scrollbars).

Clip

If you want to show only a section of a layer's contents, and hide the rest from view, use the Clip option.

Working in pixels, clip out layer contents by specifying values that represent the amount of distance from the layer's boundaries. Note that T (top) and L (left) values must be relative to the layer, not to the page.

This attribute is very seldom of any use. The only time it can be useful is when working with timelines, because it enables you to create a fade-in or fade-out effect by increasing the Clip value over a number of frames.

Note

You might be tempted to use the <LAYER> and <ILAYER> (Netscape layers) tags because of the features they offer, such as the ability to display another HTML document within a layer.

If so, you should know that the <LAYER> tag and <ILAYER> tag are not used often because they are not supported by Netscape 6.

More About Layers

After you learn to draw and position your layers, take things a step further by exploring the other tools Dreamweaver gives you for layer manipulation. This section covers nesting layers, setting layer preferences, stacking order, and changing layer visibility. You also learn how you can convert layers to tables, and vice versa.

Nested Layers

A nested layer works the same as a nested table: It is just a layer inside another (parent) layer. A nested layer moves with the parent layer and can be set to inherit the parent's visibility attribute.

You should be aware that nested layers will not appear as designed in many browsers. Among other things, certain versions of Netscape will not render anything on your page after the first set of nested layers.

In the Layers panel, nested layers are listed beneath their parent layer (see Figure 10.11). If you want to nest a layer that is not already assigned to a parent, you can do so using the Layers panel.

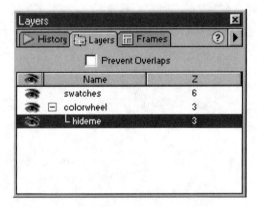

Figure 10.11   The layer named hideme is nested inside the layer named colorwheel.

With the Layers panel open (F2), select a layer from the listing, hold down the Ctrl key, and drag it to the layer you want to assign as its parent. Release the mouse when a box appears around the layer name.

You can also create a nested layer by clicking inside an existing layer and choosing Insert/Layer, or by dragging the Layer icon from the Objects panel into the parent layer. If these techniques don't work, check Edit/Preferences/Layers to make sure your Nested Layer option is turned on.

Tip

> You can draw a nested layer even if the Nested Layer option is disabled if you hold down the Alt key as you draw the layer.

Layer Preferences

If you have a specific use for layers, and you make the same type of layer over and over again, it might be advantageous to set the layer preferences to match your needs. This way, you won't have to adjust your layer every time you make it.

To change layer preferences, choose Edit/Preferences and choose Layer from the list on the left side of the Preferences dialog box. Figure 10.12 shows the window that displays layer preferences, and Table 10.1 details the available options.

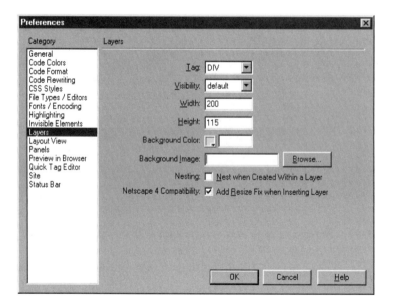

Figure 10.12   Setting layer preferences.

Table 10.1   Layer Preferences

Option	Function
Tag	This option controls the default HTML tag that specifies the type of layer you're making. <DIV> and <SPAN> are the best choices because they will work for both Netscape and Internet Explorer 4 and above. <LAYER> and <ILAYER> work only in Netscape 4.x.
Visibility	Establishes whether your layers are, by default, visible or hidden, or default or inherit.
Width and Height	Use this option to set up a default width and height of the layers you make with the Insert/Layer option.
Background Color	Use the color picker to choose a desired default background color for your layers.
Background Image	Click the Browse button to assign an image file to serve as the default background image for your layers.
Nesting	Enable this option to make a layer drawn within the boundaries of an existing layer a nested layer. This option can always be disabled by holding down the Alt key as you draw the layer.
Netscape 4 Compatibility	This option corrects a problem with layer positioning in Netscape 4 and above browsers by inserting a JavaScript into the head of your document. When this JavaScript is present, your page reloads every time the browser window is adjusted. This reloading is necessary so that the layers will be put back into the position you intended.

Converting Layers to Tables

If you have a layered document that doesn't contain nested layers, and doesn't have layers overlapping each other, you can convert the layers to tables. This way, you can offer a version of your document to people who are using older browsers that do not support layers. Alternatively, you can convert a table-based page to layered page. Note that this process of converting can create complex code that is difficult for the browser to render quickly. If you want to lay out your page freely, you might consider working in Layout view instead.

Both conversion options are available if you select the table or layer you want to convert, choose Modify/Convert, and then specify whether you want to convert layers to tables, or vice versa. Figures 10.13 and 10.14 show the resulting dialog boxes.

Remember to save a backup page in case you don't like the result! Alternatively, press Ctrl+Z to undo.

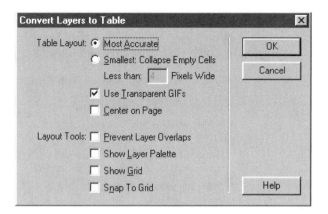

Figure 10.13   The Layers-to-Tables dialog box.

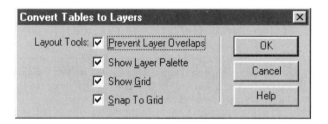

Figure 10.14   The Tables-to-Layers dialog box.

Putting Layers into Motion

When you know how to use layers, you don't have to be a programmer to create animations, scrolling text, or drag-and-drop objects.

When working with layers as a design tool, be aware that browsers read them differently, and that you cannot expect across-the-board results.

You can put layers to use and explore their creative potential in many different situations. If you work on an intranet site and know for sure that everyone who views the site is using Internet Explorer 4 or above, for instance, there is a much lower chance that layers will cause technical problems for you. Another situation in which layers could be used creatively is if you are designing a kiosk that will be running on only a few computers and you can determine what browser will be used.

When you know exactly what browsers will be used to view your layers, you have more control and can take advantage of the possibilities they offer.

Exercise 10.2   Working with the Layers Panel

In this exercise, you work with a variation of the file you created in Exercise 10.1. The purpose of this exercise is to take your work with layers a step further, giving you some practice working with the Layers panel and moving layers within a document. In the end, you will have a layered DHTML document (although it will still have the .HTML or .HTM extension) that will enable users to pick up objects and move them around onscreen.

To get started, open the SWATCHES.HTML file from the Dragdrop folder on the CD-ROM.

1. Open the Behaviors panel (Shift+F3) and the Layers panel (F2). Take a look at all the layers listed. Each color swatch has its own layer, 60 pixels high by 60 pixels wide. Figure 10.15 shows the document with the Layers panel open. Practice picking up the layers and moving them around. Click a layer once to select it, and then grab the layer handle in the layer's upper-right corner and move it (fast).

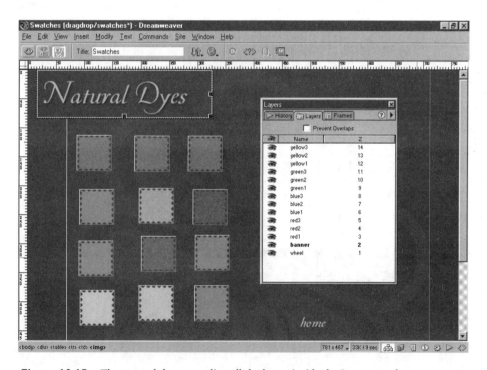

Figure 10.15   The opened document lists all the layers inside the Layers panel.

2. Your job in this exercise is to assign each color swatch layer a Drag Layer behavior. To start, select the layer called red1 from the Layers panel.

3. With the layer still selected, click the red color swatch image inside the layer. When the image is selected, pull down the plus sign (+) icon on the upper-left side of the Behaviors panel and choose the Drag Layer behavior. Note that you *must* have the image selected, not just the layer, to access the Drag Layer behavior.

4. Use Figures 10.16 and 10.17 or the instructions here to fill out the options inside the Drag Layer dialog box. Make sure you choose the layer called red1 for the layer to be dragged (or the name of the layer you want to drag for subsequent behavior assignments).

   a. Choose layer to be dragged from the pull-down menu in the Basic tab.

   b. Choose Unconstrained from the Basic tab.

   c. Choose Entire Layer from the Drag Handle field in the Advanced tab.

   d. Check Bring Layer to Front, Then Leave on Top from the Advanced tab.

   e. Click OK.

With the layer still selected, look at the Behaviors panel to make sure the action was assigned (see Figure 10.18).

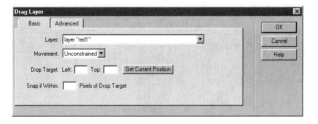

Figure 10.16   The Drag Layer window, Basic tab.

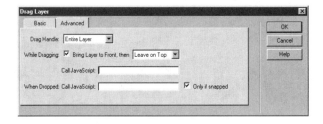

Figure 10.17   The Drag Layer window, Advanced tab.

Figure 10.18   The Behaviors panel with an action assigned to a layer.

5. Repeat steps 2, 3, and 4 for the rest of the color swatches. Note that you will have to change the layer name in the Drag Layer dialog box each time, so check the Layer panel each time you select a layer to confirm which layer you are on.

6. After you have assigned the behavior to each swatch, save the results and the image files to your hard drive and view the results in the browser window. You should be able to pick up each swatch individually and move it around onscreen. (In Netscape 4, I had to click and drag twice.) Figure 10.19 shows what the file looks like in Netscape 4.

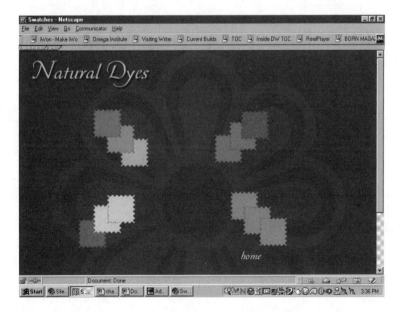

Figure 10.19   In the end, users can create color combinations by dragging the swatches around on screen.

In this exercise, you learned how to create drag-and-drop behaviors for layers. This is just the beginning of what you can do once you know how to assign behaviors to layers. For example, you could expand on this exercise by playing sounds when the user drags the image. You could also use the Drag Layer behavior to snap images into a specific point on the screen. Good luck in whatever you do!

CourseBuilder Extension

Drag-and-drop games can be both fun and educational, a fact not ignored by Macromedia when they created the CourseBuilder extension for Dreamweaver 4 and Dreamweaver UltraDev 4.

With the CourseBuilder extension, a dialog box is used to customize an online learning environment (see Figure 10.20). Projects suited for CourseBuilder might include online exams, surveys, games, and puzzles. After the interface has been created, you insert the needed content, save the files, and publish them to the Web.

The CourseBuilder extension is free if you own a copy of Dreamweaver 4 or Dreamweaver UltraDev 4. You can download it at Macromedia Exchange for Dreamweaver (www.macromedia.com/exchange/Dreamweaver).

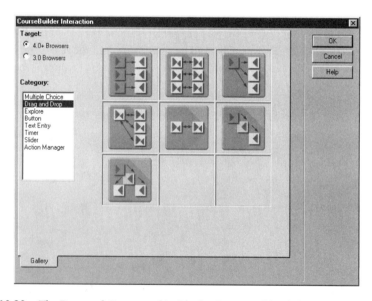

Figure 10.20   The Drag-and-Drop panel inside the CourseBuilder dialog box.

Summary

This chapter discussed ways in which you can create and use layers for sites viewed in 4.x and above Web browsers. The challenge with layers is learning to size them, insert content, and position them on the page. After you have learned the basics, you can go on to more advanced techniques such as creating drag-and-drop objects and animation with timelines. Again, keep in mind that you should preview pages with layers often, and in a wide range of browsers.

Whenever you are working with layers, it is a good idea to surf the Web to see what extensions are available for Dreamweaver and layers.

Chapter 11

Forms

Forms are a necessary evil of modern life. Sometimes it seems as if our entire existence revolves around them. When we enter this world, there is a form to be filled out; when we leave it, there is another.

Unfortunately, the Web offers no escape. But these are not the standard, boring forms that you are accustomed to. These are interactive, enabling your end user to send you feedback, sign up for services, or even navigate your site. These forms can actually make life easier. These are good forms.

In this chapter we will be covering these forms-related topics:

- The form tag and its attributes
- The input tag and its attributes
- Form creation in Dreamweaver with the Objects panel

HTML Forms

By using forms on the Internet, you enable the client to become involved. By filling out a form and submitting it, an end user can sign up for more information, critique a site, or even make purchases. Also by utilizing certain elements from the HTML form, you can design pages with extended functionality. But let's start simple, with an analysis of the HTML code behind a form.

Background

A form asks for specific information from the user, by either listing options or requiring text entry. When the form is completed, the information is sent (submitted) to the server, where a small script sorts and organizes the contents of the form and forwards the results to a database. Typically, a confirmation is then displayed on the user's computer.

For instance, a user might be prompted to enter his name, email address, and phone number into three text fields and then to press Submit. Upon submitting the form, the client computer sends the form's information as a string of information to the server. In this case it might resemble the following:

```
name=Blaine%20Tait&email=rblainet@home.com&phone=9057062895
```

When the script receives this string, it can append this information to a database. It might create this data as comma-delimited information:

```
firstname=Blaine,
lastname=Tait,
email=rblainet@home.com,
phone=9057062895,
```

Finally, the script can return a confirmation page to indicate that the data has been received or to thank the user for taking the time to fill out the form.

Form Elements

The HTML code for form creation is not very complex and is easily learned. It is necessary to at least be familiar with this code to fully utilize and understand the power of forms.

Forms begin and end with the <FORM> ... </FORM> tag pair. Secondly, you nest <INPUT> and <SELECT> tags to add the actual form elements. Now is also a good time to note that a form may have multiple input elements. Here is the basic structure:

```
<FORM>
        <INPUT>
        <INPUT>
        <INPUT>
</FORM>
```

Tip

Form tags can be nested inside other HTML tags. Conversely, other HTML tags may be nested inside a form. However, the tag sets may not overlap, and a form may not be nested within another form.

Now let's go back and fill in the attributes. The <FORM> tag has seven possible attributes. The ones that you will use have to do with the functionality that you want your form to have. By setting attributes to certain values, you can determine exactly how this form will behave when the client interacts with it. You can name it, decide where and how it will send its data, and even determine which object to send the result to (Frame or Window). The <FORM> tag attributes are as follows:

- NAME=""
- ACTION=""
- METHOD=""
- TARGET=""
- ENCTYPE=""
- ACCEPT=""
- ACCEPT-CHARSET=""

Here is an example of a <FORM> tag using hypothetical attribute values:

```
<FORM  NAME="clientinfo"  ACTION="http://www.me.com/cgi-bin/mailform.pl"
METHOD="Post" Target="_blank" ENCTYPE="multipart/form-data">
```

Tip

> When naming forms and, later, form elements, keep a few things in mind. First, do not use spaces or special characters. Second, the name should not use any reserved words (reserved words, are used by scripting languages and can confuse a script interpreter if one is used to name an object). Finally, because you are creating objects that can be recognized by scripting languages (such as JavaScript), it is usually a good idea to name the objects intuitively, to offer little confusion later if you plan to refer to the object in a script. (See Chapter 19, "JavaScripting with Dreamweaver," for more on JavaScript.)

The ACTION attribute sets the destination of the form to an address containing a Perl language CGI named mailform. Common gateway interfaces (CGIs) are scripts used to process the information sent by forms, and they are usually placed in a directory named cgi-bin or cgi_bin. For more on Perl and CGI, see Chapter 23, "Scripting and Markup Languages."

METHOD can be set to Get or Post. With the Get method, the form information is sent to the URL specified by the ACTION attribute, but there is a character limit when this method is used. Also, because this is not a secure method, if this form's purpose is related to e-commerce or contains otherwise sensitive information, the Post method should be used. The Post method sends the form information as input, with no practical character limit. It is also pertinent to point out that Get is the default method with most browsers and is also the most supported format. Which method you use will depend greatly on the CGI or Web-based application that you are using to process the form.

The TARGET attribute is used to point to the frame or window in which the form's returned document is to be loaded. You can choose to use one of four predefined targets, or the identifier (name), for the frame or window you desire. The four predefined targets are as follows:

- **_blank.** Places the result in a new window that appears in front of the current browser window
- **_parent.** Targets the frameset that the current document is residing in
- **_self.** Replaces current document
- **_top.** Replaces the entire contents of the current window, including all framesets

By not specifying a target, _self is assumed.

Note

See also Chapter 9, "Layout with Frames," for more information on naming and targeting frames. For more information on creating and naming windows, see Chapter 19.

The ENCTYPE attribute value determines the file type and format that is to be submitted. The proper format for Get and Post submissions is set by default; however, some advanced usages of forms require that this value be defined.

Form Objects: Objects Panel

Up until this point in the chapter, we have been focusing on the code necessary for a form to be created—and it is very important to have at least a fundamental knowledge of this. However, this book is about authoring Web pages with Dreamweaver, not hand-coding HTML. So let's see how Dreamweaver creates forms.

Exercise 11.1   Creating Forms

1. Open a new document, making sure you are using Code and Design view. Select the Form section of the Objects panel, and press the Insert Form button (see Figure 11.1).

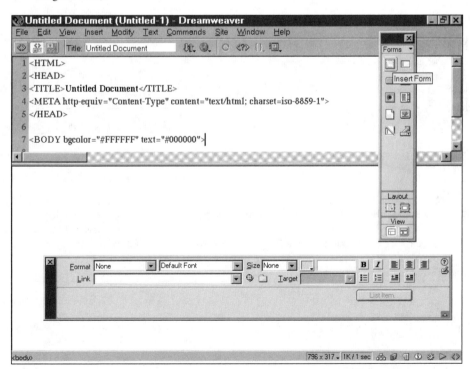

Figure 11.1   The Forms section of the Object panel, and the Insert Form button.

After you press the Insert Form button, the form is placed into the document, represented by a red dashed outline in the design portion of the current view. If you do not see this dashed line, you will need to turn on Visual Aids in your View menu/toolbar. The Property Inspector changes to reflect the options available for the form tag. They are the NAME attribute, the METHOD attribute, and the ACTION attribute (see Figure 11.2).

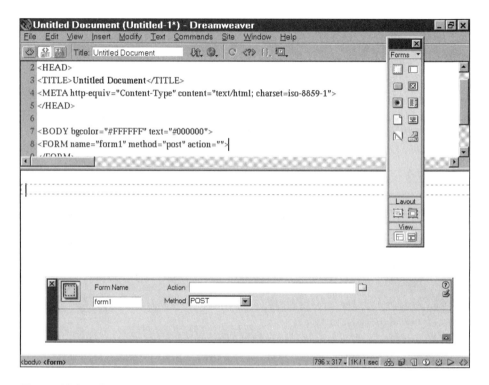

Figure 11.2   The Property Inspector for the form tag.

Quick Tag Editor

To fill in the other available attributes of the form tag, you need to use the Quick Tag Editor. Figures 11.3 and 11.4 show the process. First select the <FORM> tag, and then click the Quick Tag Editor button in the Property Inspector. In the Tag Editor window that appears, fill in the attribute and value, and press the Enter key. Your changes have now been inserted into the <FORM> tag.

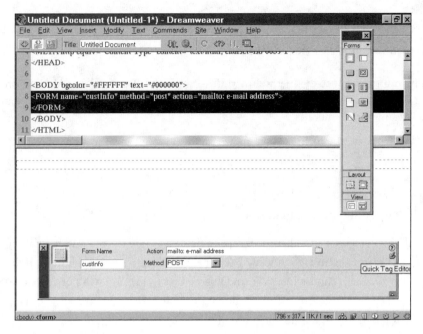

Figure 11.3   <FORM> has been selected.

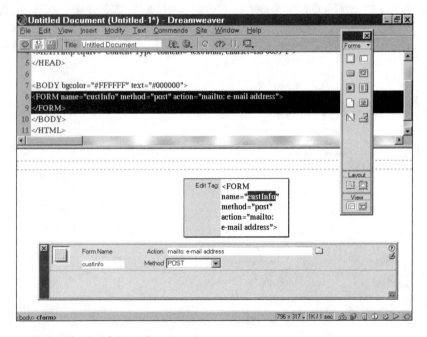

Figure 11.4   The Quick Tag Editor in action.

2. Click in the text box immediately below the words Form Name in the Property Inspector, and give the form a name. Type **custInfo** and press Enter.

3. Next, give your form an ACTION attribute. For the purpose of this exercise, you'll use a dummy URL. Click the ACTION text box, and enter **../cgi-bin/ mailform.pl.** Press the Enter key.

Finally, you need to set the method of your form. Select Post from the Method drop-down box in the Property Inspector. Figure 11.4 also shows an example of the source code Dreamweaver generates.

Now that you have the form tags set up, we can begin to fill in your input objects.

Input Objects: Text Fields

Let's start with the most common type of input object, the text field.

1. Begin by making sure that the insertion point is inside the red outline that represents your form in Design view. Then select the Insert Text Field button in the Object panel, (choose Insert/Form Objects/Text Field). You will notice that a text box is placed inside your form and that the code reflects this as well. Also notice that the Input tag has no corresponding closing tag (See Figure 11.5).

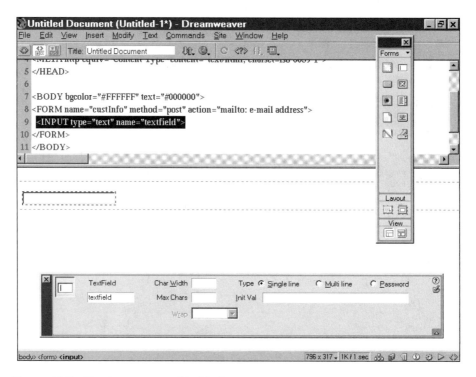

Figure 11.5   New input tag nested inside form tags.

2. From here, you use the Property Inspector to name your input tag. As with all named objects, it is a good idea to use a name that correlates to the object's use. For this text box, you will be obtaining the user's first name, so use the name fName. To name the input object, click in the box directly under the words Text Field, type the name, and press Enter.

Now you will set the size and maximum length of the text box. The size is the width in characters of our text box. To set this, enter the appropriate amount in the Char Width box. The maximum length is the maximum amount of characters that this text box will allow. If this number exceeds the size attribute, the text will scroll in the box created. To set the maximum amount of characters, enter the amount in the Max Chars field.

Next, you will set an initial value to be displayed in the box until the user enters his information. To do this, simply type in the text that we want in the Init Val field (first name), and press Enter. Now you should see something similar to Figure 11.6.

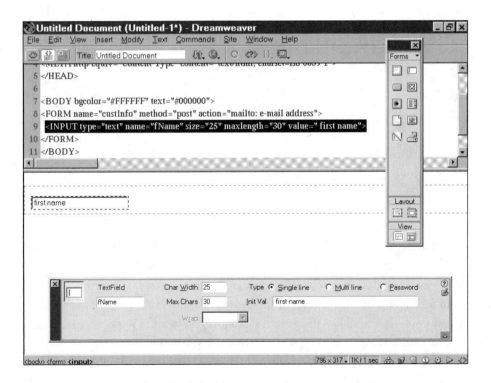

Figure 11.6 Form with one input object.

3. Finally, follow the steps outlined previously to create a text field for the last name (lName) and email address, (eMail). Then, place some text beside each field to further clarify to the user what you want supplied in each text box. To do this, simply place the insertion point beside one of the fields and type a description. Notice how the text is inserted in the code (see Figure 11.7).

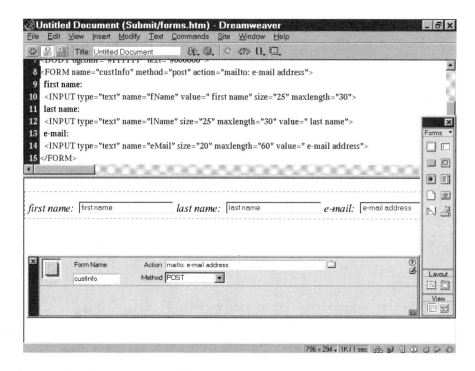

Figure 11.7   Placing text inside a form.

Password Text Boxes

A slight variation on the single-line text field is the password text field. The normal behavior of a text field is to echo what is entered into it onscreen. However, situations arise in which this is not the desired effect. Instead, you can set the INPUT type attribute to password to replace all keystrokes with a default character. On Windows systems, the character used is the asterisk (*); on Macs, the dot (.) is used instead. It is important to understand, though, that the password type in no way encrypts the input that it receives, and it offers only visual protection for sensitive information.

To use the password type, create a single-line text field, make sure that the text field is selected, and choose Password from the Property Inspector. Then, follow these steps:

1. Add a password field to your form. Start by placing the insert point just after our last text box, and again choose the Insert Text Field button from the Objects panel.

2. Now choose Password as the Type in the Property Inspector. Name the box Password.

3. Place the text **type in desired password** beside the new box, to describe what the required input is for this field.

4. Finally, place the word **password** in the initial value field. Finish off this section of the form with a horizontal rule. See Figure 11.8.

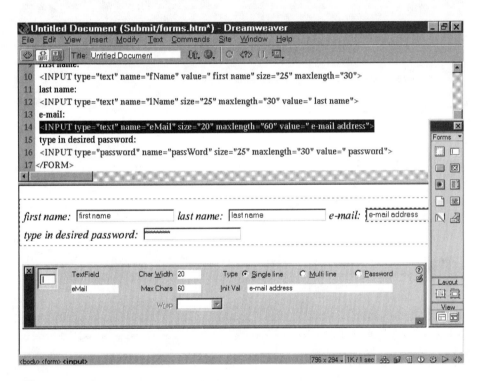

Figure 11.8   Form with a password field.

Multiline Text Boxes

A multiline text field enables for longer and more detailed user input. Visually, it has horizontal and vertical scrollbars and has multiple lines viewable at once (see Figure 11.9). To change a single-line text box to a multiline text box, select the text field and choose Multiline as the type from the Property Inspector. Also take note that multiline text boxes are not INPUT types but are instead a special form tag named <TEXTAREA>.

By default, multiline text boxes do not wrap the text that the user enters into them. To enable wrapping of text, Dreamweaver gives you four options:

- **Default**. Does not insert the WRAP attribute (browser default).

- **Off**. Prevents wrapping.

- **Virtual**. Wraps on the user's display, but is submitted without WRAP.

- **Physical**. Wraps on the user's display and also sends the information to the server wrapped. Utilizes hard returns to accomplish the wrap.

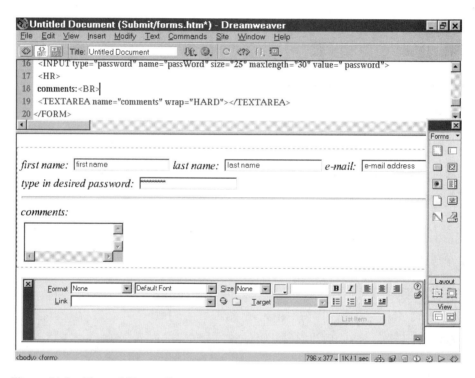

Figure 11.9   The multiline text box.

Virtual and Physical are not supported values for the WRAP attribute in all browsers. If cross-browser compatibility is an issue with your document and you want to have the text wrap, consider having the value of the WRAP attribute equal to hard. This forces the text to wrap both on the user's screen and in the data that is sent when the form is submitted. It has the most compatibility, working with Internet Explorer 4 and above as well as Netscape Navigator 2 and above. Note, however, that to set WRAP equal to hard, you will need to use the Quick Tag Editor.

Try inserting a multiline text box just after the horizontal rule. Set its name to Comments, and set its WRAP attribute to hard using the Quick Tag Editor. Finish it off with some descriptive text. Figure 11.9 shows the multiline text box added to the form.

Check Boxes

A more structured approach to gathering information is to allow a user to select options from a list. With check boxes, the user is free to select (or check) any combination of the choices that you offer. Figure 11.10 illustrates what check boxes look like.

Now let's insert some check boxes in a form. To create check boxes, place the insertion point inside the form area, and select Insert Check Box from the Objects panel. In the Property Inspector, assign a name, and a value to the check box. Do this using the Check Box Name and Checked Value fields, respectively. When the form is submitted, the name and value are returned as name=value.

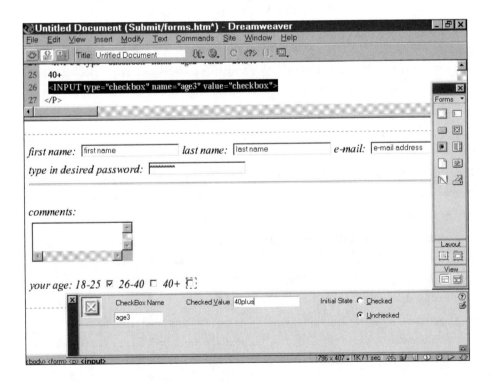

Figure 11.10   Check boxes.

Radio Buttons

Along the same lines as the check box is the radio button. How the radio button differs is that the user is allowed to select one (and only one) item from a group of buttons. Figure 11.11 illustrates what radio buttons look like.

There are some important things to consider when inserting radio buttons. First, radio buttons allow for only one item to be selected in a group. Second, they are grouped by the NAME attribute (to group radio buttons, give them all the same name). Finally, the value attribute is used to identify the individual radio buttons in a group. When the form is submitted, the common name of all the radio buttons in a group is sent along with the value of the radio button that is selected. The following code gives an example:

```
<FORM>
   <INPUT TYPE="radio" NAME="rbset_one" value="option1">
   <INPUT TYPE="radio" NAME="rbset_one" value="option2">
   <INPUT TYPE="radio" NAME="rbset_one" value="option3">
   <INPUT TYPE="radio" NAME="rbset_two" value="option1">
   <INPUT TYPE="radio" NAME="rbset_two" value="option1">
   <INPUT TYPE="radio" NAME="rbset_two" value="option1">
</FORM>
```

In this code there are two groups of radio buttons. The first is `rbset_one`, and the second set is `rbset_two`. Only one of the three buttons in each set can be selected at once. Therefore, if option2 is selected out of the first set and option3 is selected out of the second set, the form would send this:

```
rbset_one=option2
rbset_two=option3
```

Let's insert some radio buttons into your form. The first set will be used to find out the connection speed of the end user, and the second will be used for the operating system that the person is using.

1. Start by pressing Insert Radio Button in the Objects panel. Press the same button three more times. You should now see four radio buttons lined up horizontally. Place your insertion point between the first and second buttons, and type **56k**. Look at Figure 11.11, and fill in the rest of the text.

2. Select each button individually, and rename it to conspeed. To rename a radio button, select it and enter the new name under the words RadioButton in the Property Inspector.

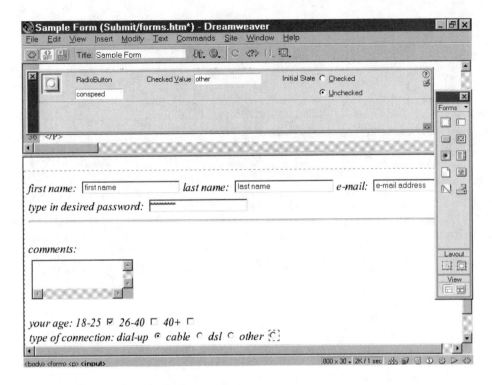

Figure 11.11   One set of radio buttons.

3. Next change the Checked Value text to what you want returned if that particular radio button is selected. In the case of this set, the values will be Dial-up, Cable, DSL, and Other.

4. You can choose to have a particular option selected by default until the user alters that choice. This is accomplished by setting Initial State to either Checked or Unchecked in the Property Inspector. Be careful to set only one button per set to checked.

5. Start a new line, and insert three new radio buttons. These buttons will be named os. Their values will be Windows, Mac, and Other, respectively.

6. Finally, fill in the text around these buttons according to Figure 11.12.

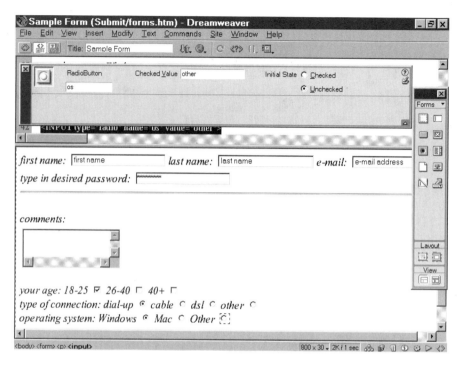

Figure 11.12   The finished radio buttons.

Drop-Down Menus

The drop-down menu provides a means for the user to select an option from a list of multiple items, while taking up very little space onscreen. In addition to reducing the area needed to list the options, the drop-down list is very intuitive because it is a simple element that the user has invariably come across before. Figure 11.13 shows an example of a drop-down menu.

The drop-down menu is made up of two sets of tag pairs. The first set of tags is the <SELECT></SELECT> tag pair. The second set is the <OPTION></OPTION> pair. The following example shows how these tags are nested.

```
<FORM>
  <SELECT>
        <OPTION VALUE="value_1"> label_1 </OPTION>
        <OPTION VALUE="value_2"> label_2 </OPTION>
        <OPTION VALUE="value_3"> label_3 </OPTION>
  </SELECT>
<FORM>
```

It is important to remember that you need to name elements whenever possible. Start by naming the <SELECT> tag. Next, label the <OPTION> tag. This is done between the <OPTION> and </OPTION> tags. Finally, assign a value to the <OPTION> tag.

When the form is submitted, the name that was assigned to the <SELECT> tag, along with the value of the OPTION that was selected, is sent to the server as name=value. The label is the text that appears as the item in the drop-down list.

Exercise 11.2   Inserting Drop-Down Menus into Forms

Now let's use a drop-down menu in your form.

1. To insert a drop-down menu, place the insertion point inside the form area where you want the drop-down to go. You'll want to place it at the end of your current form.

2. Then select the Insert List/Menu button from the Objects panel. This creates the <SELECT></SELECT> tag pair.

3. Use the Property Inspector to name the <SELECT> tag and to choose Menu from the Type choices. Name your drop-down list browserSelect. To enter the label and value information for your drop-down menu, press the List Values button in the Property Inspector. Remember, the label is what the user sees, and the value is the actual data that the form relates to that label. This brings up a window into which you can add labels and values. To enter this information, type in the label of the first <OPTION> tag, press tab, and then type in the value that you want to set this item to. To create a second <OPTION> tag set, press Tab again, enter the label for this <OPTION> tag, press Tab, and type in the value you want, and so on. The first label will be Internet Explorer, and its value will be iE, followed by Netscape Navigator and nN, and finally Other and other. When you are finished creating <OPTION> tag sets, press the OK button.

4. Now that you have set up the drop-down list items, you can choose the option that is initially selected from the Property Inspector: Internet Explorer. Finally, you should insert some descriptive text just before your drop-down menu to inform the client exactly what it is choosing. See Figure 11.13 for the finished drop-down menu.

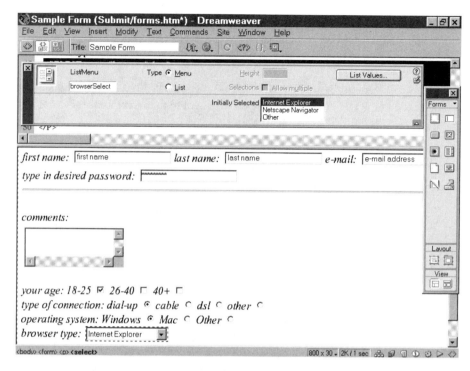

Figure 11.13   Drop-down menu inserted in the form.

Scrolling Lists

A scrolling list is much like a drop-down menu, with a few subtle differences. Instead of having a list drop down, the scrolling list uses scrollbars to display the options. As many or as few of the options can be displayed at once. When you construct the scrolling list, you can enable the list to allow the user to make multiple selections. Figure 11.14 shows the differences between drop-down menus and scrolling lists.

Exercise 11.3   Creating a Scrolling List

To create a scrolling list, follow the same initial steps as when creating a drop-down menu.

1. First select Insert List/Menu from the Objects panel. In the Property Inspector, choose List as the type.

2. Next, press the List Values button, and fill in the information in the dialog box that displays. Press OK, and you will be brought back to the Property Inspector.

3. Finally, choose the height of your scrolling list (number of lines) and specify whether to allow multiple selections.

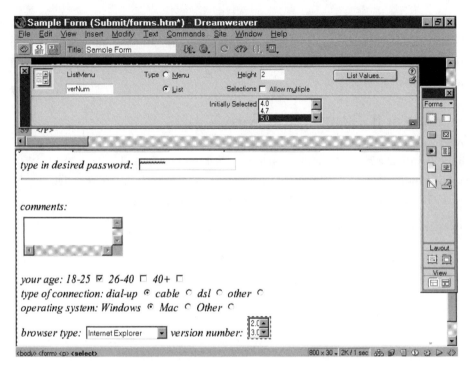

Figure 11.14   A drop-down menu and a scrolling list.

After the drop-down list, set up a scrolling list box named verNum, and insert the following labels and values:

> 2.0 and 2
>
> 3.0 and 3
>
> 4.0 and 4
>
> 4.6 and 4.6
>
> 5.0 and 5
>
> 5.5 and 5.5

Hidden Input Field

The hidden input field is used when you need to pass information from the form to the server that has not been entered by the user or that we don't want the user to see.

The hidden field behaves like other types of <INPUT> tags and is placed into the document much the same way that the text type input is inserted. Select an insertion point and press the Insert Hidden Field button in the Objects panel. The Properties Inspector then prompts you for a new name and value for this hidden field. In Display view, a little yellow marker is placed to represent the item.

File Input Field

The file input field is a means for receiving a file along with the user's submission. Its use is no longer popular due in large part to the more powerful means available through modern email applications.

Sending and Clearing the Form

After you have created a form, you must take one more step to make it useful. You need buttons to make it go. Typically, you'll use a Submit button and a Reset button. The Submit button sends the form information (data) to the location specified by the ACTION attribute of the <FORM> tag. The Reset button clears the form.

To insert a button into your form, follow these steps:

1. Select a suitable insertion point, and click Insert Button from the Objects panel.

2. Choose which type of button this is by selecting either Submit Form or Reset Form from the Action area of the Property Inspector. Name the button and assign it a label (what will be written inside the button).

3. Now, to finalize your form, go ahead and enter a Submit button and a Reset button. See Figure 11.15 for an illustration of form buttons.

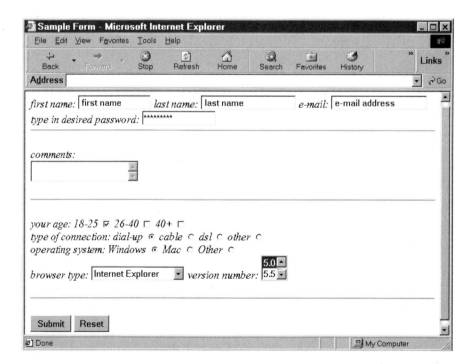

Figure 11.15   The Submit and Reset buttons.

See Chapter 19 for a more advanced look at form usage, including client-side verification, jump menus, and more.

Summary

This chapter discussed forms—the form tag and its attributes, the input tag and its attributes, and how to create forms in Dreamweaver.

Using Cascading Style Sheets

You may have heard the terms *style sheet*,

CSS, *layers*, and others before, but do you

really know what they mean? They are all

descriptions or elements of cascading style

sheets (CSS), a progressing standard brought about by the World Wide Web Consortium (www.w3c.org), the de facto organization for Internet standards.

Where HTML ends, CSS begins—at least, as far as layout and style is concerned. As browser versions continue to rise and developers become more daring, CSS will undoubtedly become an everyday term and will be used in virtually any Web page. Knowing this, it might be a good idea to get a grasp on this exciting technology. Let's start by discussing what CSS *really* is. The following is a list of some of the main things we'll talk about:

- The cascading nature of style sheets
- How to use one style sheet across an entire site
- The difference between HTML styles and CSS
- What all the styles that Dreamweaver allows to be set through its GUI do

Why Use Style Sheets?

In any form of media or visual art, two components dictate how the end result will appear to an audience, whether online or in print: content and style. When referring to online publishing, *content* is the meat of your Web page; it is typically the reason your audience is viewing your Web page in the first place. *Style*, on the other hand, is the finesse, the garnish and other decorative touches that make the dish look appetizing.

Traditional HTML attempts to assist in the styling of your pages, although the current implementation is rather imprecise and limited. This is where cascading style sheets, a W3C proposal for standardizing advanced style attributes for use in Web pages, comes into play. With style sheets, you can not only apply a style to a single element or even page, but you also can use one style throughout your entire site, updating it in one file and having those changes take effect in any page that utilizes that style. Style sheets really break down into two distinct advantages over trying to use HTML:

- **Style.** They enable you to do things that HTML simply can't, such as use layers and other dynamic effects.
- **Workflow.** They enable you to update pages that use CSS throughout your site quickly and easily.

Like food, how much style you add depends heavily on two factors that should be lightly brushed upon. The first factor includes time and money. The budget and the time con-straints given for a site's completion will necessitate including or excluding a certain degree of style from the pages (similar to the differences between a fast food restaurant and a fancy one). The second factor is your audience. Just like a stereotyped trucker might order a 72-oz. steak, the stereotypical 120-pound teenage girl will most likely prefer a good chef's salad any day. Always analyze your target audience to approach the most effective balance of content and style for each application.

Style sheets consist of one or more *rules* that are located either in the individual document or as a separate file that is linked to by the document. A rule contains two main elements: the *selector* and the *declaration*. The declaration is further defined as containing a *property* and a *value*. This is a possible CSS rule:

```
h3 { text-decoration: underline }
```

In this example, h3 is the selector; it is what ties the style sheet to an HTML document. In this case, we are defining a style for the <Heading 3> HTML element. `text-decoration: underline` is the declaration, the definition of how you want the <h3> tag to be affected. To break it down further, `text-decoration` is the property portion or the declaration, with `underline` as the value. This rule will apply underlining to text wrapped in an <h3> tag. You will notice that the other attributes of the <h3> tag are still visible—that is, CSS doesn't remove default styling; it simply extends it. That doesn't mean, however, that you cannot completely redefine the <h3> tag using CSS. Read on to find out exactly how that works.

Grouping Styles

As you just saw, you can change a property of a tag fairly simply. However, I said you could completely redefine a tag as well. Or, how about effectively changing a tag's entire attribute set? This brings us to another feature of CSS. Style sheet rules can contain multiple declarations. Extending the previous example, you could add a color and size property similar to the one shown here:

```
h3 { text-decoration: underline; color: blue; font-size: 14pt }
```

You can group not only declarations, but selectors as well. Instead of separating them by semicolons, however, use commas to group multiple selectors. For example, you could use the following CSS definition to make <Header 3> (<h3>) and <Bold> (<b>) contain the same attributes:

```
h3, b { text-decoration: underline; color: blue; font-size: 14pt }
```

Style Inheritance

Another characteristic of CSS is its capability to span multiple HTML tags through inheritance. For the most part, HTML tags located inside your CSS selector will inherit the declarations of the style encompassing it. For instance, if you set your <h3> tags similar to how they were set up earlier in this chapter, most tags located inside all <h3> tags on your page will inherit the same characteristics.

```
<h3>Welcome to my <em>NEW</em> web page</h3>
```

In this example, the text NEW would inherit the underline, blue coloring, and 14-point font size that the <h3> style exhibits. It would also be affected by the <em> tags that surround it, putting emphasis (italics) on the word.

This inheritance works on a parent/child relationship as well. One of the most useful effects you'll obtain through this property is the capability to establish page-wide attributes with a single style. You can do this by defining a body selector like the following:

```
body { font-family: Arial, Helvetica, sans-serif; font-size: 12pt }
```

This will make every tag in your HTML document (that is capable of having those properties) inherit those properties by default. As you might assume, this isn't an effect that's set in stone; it can be changed on a case-by-case basis inside the document. This is discussed in the next section.

They Aren't Called Cascading for Nothing!

So far we've focused solely on the *style* and *sheets* portion of CSS. However, the element of CSS that is possibly the most crucial—and, at least equal, in importance—is the *cascading* part. As the word implies, *cascading* describes how local styles take precedence over page-level styles, which, in turn, take precedence over global styles.

Perhaps you have an external style sheet that defines all text (one way to do this would be to redefine the <body> tag) as having black Arial text, with a font size of 12 point. This would affect all elements of your HTML document that allow for any of those three properties. This is a good way to establish and maintain a *general* layout and style for your page. However, you might decide that your photo captions should be italicized in an 8-point font size and that you'll use the <h1> tag to mark up the captions. To do this, you would create a second style in which you redefine the <h1> tag. The "most local" style overrides a higher-level style in CSS. This enables you to simply apply your caption style to your captions and have them look the way you want even though they fall under the global style rule.

Putting Styles in Your Pages

Before you learn how to insert and manipulate CSS in Dreamweaver, it's important to understand the three methods of applying styles to an HTML document. These are discussed from methods with the most control to the method with the least control (meaning that a more local method overrides its rules).

Style Attribute

The most local method is to use the style attribute in the specific HTML tag that you want to apply the style to. This method takes precedence over any other style applied. Look at the code here to see how the style attribute is typically used:

```
<div id="Layer1" style="position:absolute; width:358px;height:378px; z-index:1; left: 160px; top: 225px"></div>
```

This code defines a DHTML element known as a layer. These dynamic and powerful elements of HTML are discussed more in Chapter 10, "Using Layers." As you can see, the layer has a location on the Web page that is defined by CSS. Because layers are likely to have different positions, the CSS rules are defined inside each individual layer tag.

Internal Styles

The middle-level style is defined inside the page, but not inside the individual tags. This enables you to define a page style without making a completely separate file. One of the biggest advantages in doing this comes when redefining entire HTML tags, as discussed previously. Although you can add a style rule anywhere in your document, it has become standard programming practice to include them in the head of your document. This is a typical internal style definition:

```
<head>
<meta blah blah…>
<head>
<style type="text/css">
<!--
.background { background-color: #0066FF; background-image: url(bg.gif);
background-repeat: no-repeat }
p { font-family: Arial, Helvetica, sans-serif; font-size: 12pt }
-->

</style>
</head>
</head>
```

Dissecting this code, you first notice that an internal style sheet is contained in a style tag with the `type` attribute set to `text/css`. The next thing that you notice, although you might not understand it, is that the actual definition is enclosed in HTML comments.

This is so that older browsers that don't understand CSS won't display the CSS rules on the screen. As the HTML is parsed, however, the CSS rules will still take effect in browsers that support CSS.

External Styles

The final method is to use external style sheets. These styles are ideal for defining a general style guide for an entire site or company. Changing one rule will affect as many pages as are linked to that file. This is one of the reasons why CSS is so powerful.

External style sheets are applied to a document by creating a link to them. You can do this in one of two ways. The first way is by using the import method. An example of this is shown here:

```
<style type="text/css">
@import "stylesheet.css";
</style>
```

The alternative is to use the link method, as shown here:

```
<link rel="stylesheet" href="stylesheet.css">
```

The link method is placed outside any style tag in your document, although still in the header area. This method is also typically accepted as the standard way of linking to your style sheets, and it is the default method that Dreamweaver uses. This is mainly because the link method is supported in more browsers. The contents of the .css file are of the exact same format as those of any other style sheet. A sample style sheet definition is shown here:

```
.background { background-color: #0066FF; background-image: url(bg.gif);
background-repeat: no-repeat }
p { font-family: Arial, Helvetica, sans-serif; font-size: 12pt }
```

HTML Versus CSS

Chapter 4, "Working with Text," presented what are called HTML styles. If you can use plain HTML in a way similar to CSS, why would you ever use CSS? At least five characteristics of CSS differentiate themselves from HTML styles:

Advantages:

- Greater precision and extensity
- Global nature
- More editing-friendly nature

Disadvantages:

- Is less compatible in browsers
- Could be confusing at first

Dreamweaver 4 allows for at least 65 precise attributes to be established through its CSS Style Definition dialog box. The actual number of attributes allowable is limited only by browser compatibility and the CSS specification, which is much newer than HTML and was created with design and style as a primary motivation. CSS also exhibits and defines a global nature. You can create a single style sheet and apply those rules to every page in your site. Because of this global nature, CSS tends to be easily editable—changing a single file will affect many documents. HTML styles do not exhibit any sort of friendliness toward editing them. After they are applied, HTML styles cannot be edited without manually editing the selection like regular HTML on a tag-by-tag and page-by-page basis.

One disadvantage of CSS is the lack of compatibility, or at least partial compatibility, of the CSS specification in today's Web browsers. Version 3.0 and lower browsers don't support them at all. Version 4.0 browsers support CSS to varying degrees, although not completely, by any means. Version 5.0 and higher browsers are finally beginning to offer extensive support for CSS.

Because HTML styles simply use multiple plain old HTML tags to give the appearance of style, browsers will need to support only HTML well, not CSS. Given that HTML was the language that browsers were created upon, it seems logical that HTML support should be more extensive than CSS. Another disadvantage is the difference in coding structure of CSS. Although CSS is relatively simplistic in nature, it may be confusing at first. However, the rewards of learning to effectively code CSS by hand makes the learning curve involved worthwhile. Another advantage of CSS is that the style sheets enable you to access many properties that HTML won't, such as link overlining.

Exercise 12.1 Comparing HTML Styles and CSS

In this exercise, you learn the primary differences between HTML styles and CSS. This exercise is geared to give you a general understanding of the usefulness and need for CSS. You will use the files located in the Chapter 12 folder on the accompanying CD.

1. Copy the files from the Chapter 12 folder onto your hard drive.
2. Open index.htm located in the Exercise 1 folder inside Dreamweaver. Next, open the HTML Styles panel by pressing Ctrl+F11.

   You should see a style titled Legal Info. If not, click the New Style button and create an HTML style similar to what is shown in Figure 12.1.

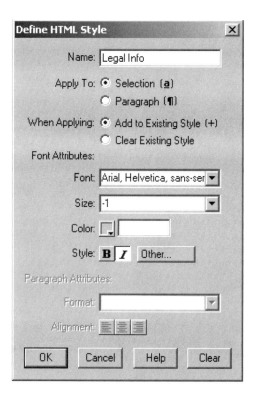

Figure 12.1   If the HTML style doesn't show up automatically, you must create it by yourself.

3. Go to the bottom of the page and select the Legal Info style. This starts with "Call us at" and ends with "webmaster@panam-tours.com."

4. Apply the HTML style Legal Info to this selection by simply clicking on the style name. You also might need to click the Apply button at the bottom of the panel, depending on the way you have set up Dreamweaver. You should end up with something similar to what's shown in Figure 12.2.

5. Now attempt to "unapply" the HTML style *without* using the Undo feature. The only way to do this is to manually remove each style from the selection. Even if you apply one of the HTML styles intended to get rid of the style, you will mess up the bolding in place or even remove the entire centering effect. This is where the difference between HTML styles and CSS is readily apparent.

   Close this file without saving it. If you saved it already, recopy and overwrite the index.htm file from the CD. You will now apply a CSS style similar to the HTML style that you just applied; the only difference is that you will be able to remove it as easily as you apply it.

6. Open the original copy of the index.htm file from the Exercise 1 folder off the CD's Chapter 12 folder. Then open the CSS Styles panel by pressing Shift+F11.

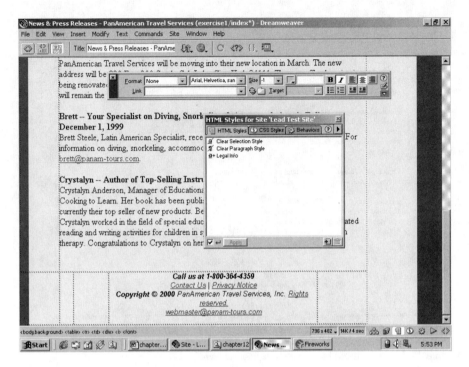

Figure 12.2   If everything went well, the HTML style will look like this.

7. You will notice two styles similar to that in Figure 12.3: background and Legal Info. The background style contains the style that makes the background non-repetitive. You don't need to worry about this style; you'll focus on the Legal Info style.

8. Select the same Legal Info text that you selected in step 2, and then apply the Legal Info CSS style by simply clicking on the name. You might need to also click Apply (found at the bottom of the CSS Styles panel), depending on your Dreamweaver setup.

9. The selected text should become a new style. If you look at the HTML source to see what tags were added, you will see two <span> tags similar to those in Figure 12.4.

10. Now try to unapply the style. To do this, simply select the text again and then click None from the CSS Styles panel. An easy way to select the text affected by the style is to click in the middle of the text and then click the <span.legalinfo> tag selector button at the bottom of your document window.

   Applying the style to the selection might have required two different <span> tags. If this is the case and not all of your text was selected, just use the same method described previously and remove the style again.

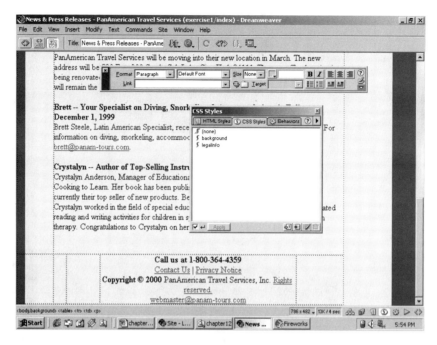

Figure 12.3   You should have two styles in your page.

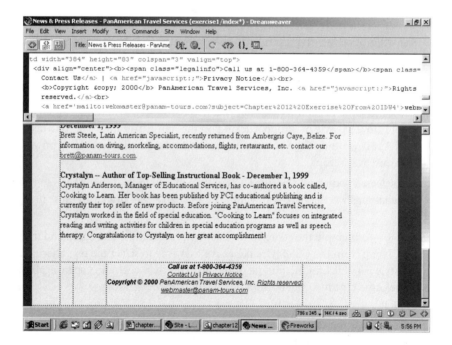

Figure 12.4   A <span> tag enables you to easily apply a style to a selection of text.

Hopefully you now realize the difference between HTML styles and CSS, as well as the important role that CSS can play in making Web developers' lives a whole lot easier.

Creating and Using Style Sheets

Now that you have a basic understanding of what CSS is and when it should be used, you can see how Dreamweaver implements it. You should become familiar with these windows: CSS Styles panel, New Style and Edit Style Sheet dialog boxes, and the Style Definition window. By using these various tools, you will be able to do the following:

- Create new styles
- Apply existing styles to your Web page
- Edit existing styles
- Link to existing styles
- Remove styles from your Web page

We'll discuss the CSS Styles panel first to get a basic feel for the CSS controls that Dreamweaver provides.

The CSS Styles Panel

The CSS Styles panel, shown in Figure 12.5, is where you begin your style creation, application, and maintenance. To access this panel, select Window/CSS Styles from the menu, or press Shift+F11 on your keyboard. If you already have styles embedded in your page, they will be listed in this window. When you create or attach a style to your page, they will be listed here as well.

To apply a style listed in this panel, select the block of text or HTML tag to which you want to apply the style. Then simply click the style that you want to apply to your selection. If the styles can be previewed in Dreamweaver's document window, you will notice the selection change appropriately. Otherwise, you will have to preview the page in a compatible Web browser to see the effects.

By default, styles are automatically applied to your selection. If you want to manually click to apply styles, simply uncheck the box next to the Apply button on the CSS Styles panel. You then must click the Apply button before the selected style goes into effect.

Along the bottom-right side of the panel, you will notice a series of four icons: Attach Style Sheet, New Style, Edit Style Sheet, and Delete Style.

Figure 12.5   The CSS Styles panel.

There is also one more option regarding style sheets: the Export CSS Style option. You can access this command by selecting File/Export/Export CSS Styles from the menu or by clicking the right-arrow icon in the upper-right corner of the CSS Styles panel and then selecting Export Style Sheet from the menu that appears. This enables you to convert existing internal styles into an external style sheet, which can then be applied to other pages.

Creating New Styles

Selecting the New Style button on the CSS Styles panel or New from the Edit Style Sheet dialog box brings up the New Style dialog box, shown in Figure 12.6. Here you can define three important properties for your style sheet: a name, a type, and where the style should be defined. The style name is particularly important because it will be referenced *inside* your pages. You should also remember to follow typical naming guidelines.

The first thing you need to decide is the type of style that you want to create. Options include creating a custom style (class), redefining an existing HTML tag, or using the CSS Selector. The CSS Selector option might be a bit confusing because we haven't discussed it yet; it will be discussed later in this section. The three types of styles are described in the following list:

- **Make Custom Style (class).** Creating a class style enables you to format any selection of text, regardless of the surrounding HTML tags that control that text.

- **Redefine HTML Tag.** This option enables you to redefine the attributes that normal HTML tags exhibit.

- **Use CSS Selector.** This option enables you to establish attributes for specific states of the <A> tag (the tag used to create links).

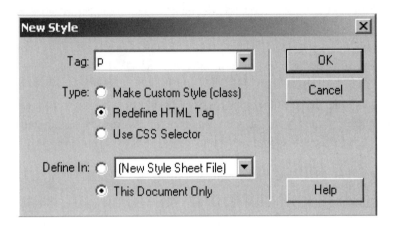

Figure 12.6   Define what type of style you want here.

Next, you should think about where you want to define this style. If you will be using it in this document, you should select This Document Only from the Define In radio buttons. However, if you think that you might be using this style definition extensively in your site, it might serve you well to create an external style sheet file. In short, selecting This Document Only will cause the style to take effect in only *that* document. Creating or adding to an external style sheet (.css file) enables you to use that style in multiple pages on your site. You can even use it on multiple sites because you need to be able to read from that file only from the Web server.

After you have established where the style should be defined and have selected the type of style to create, you need to specify the name, tag, or selector (depending on the type selected) of your CSS style. Here are a few guidelines to remember when entering this information:

- A class name must start with a period followed by a letter. The rest of the name can be a combination of letters and numbers. Additionally, if you forget to enter a period to begin the class name, Dreamweaver will automatically insert one for you.

- The HTML tag that you select must be valid. You can select it by typing one into the text area (without brackets) or by selecting one from the pull-down list. Be careful when selecting an HTML tag to redefine because it can ultimately have wide and serious repercussions in your site.

- A CSS Selector can be any valid selector, such as #webStyle. A drop-down list contains the four most common selectors: a:active, a:hover, a:link, and a:visited. These selectors describe different states that the HTML tag <a> can assume (depending on the user input). Using these selectors, you can redefine how your Web page links look and behave.

After you have defined the basics of your CSS style, click OK. If you have elected to define the style in a new external style sheet, a box will appear allowing you to save the style to a directory of your choice. Otherwise, the Style Definition window will appear. You can set your style properties from this window. For more information on the types of styles and what they do, see the upcoming section "Styles and Attributes."

Editing Styles

Editing an existing style is extremely easy. First, click the Edit Style Sheet button from the CSS Styles panel. This brings up the Edit Style Sheet dialog box, shown in Figure 12.7. From here, select the style that you want to edit from the list and then click Edit. You edit styles in the same manner that you create them from within the Style Definition window. The only difference is that the style's current settings are already filled in their respective areas. Also, with redefined tags, you must select the Edit button to the right to edit their properties.

Linking to Style Sheets

When dealing with large sites, it is usually helpful to create a master style sheet that every page can link to and receive basic formatting options. Each department then can have its own styles defined in the local document that further refine the company's master style sheet.

Two options exist when linking to external style sheets. You can either import the style or link to it. Importing a style simply takes the style definition and places it in your document. The style then is contained and can be edited inside your document. If you import a style, changes to the external copy will *not* take effect in the local copy unless you manually update it or reimport the style.

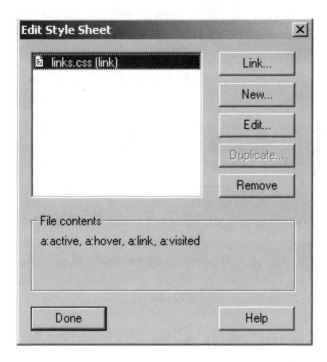

Figure 12.7   The Edit Style Sheet window.

To link to an external style, simply select the Attach Style Sheet button from the CSS Styles panel. You can then browse to the style sheet file. The imported style sheet then is accessible for applying styles in your document.

An alternative method for linking to external styles is through the Edit Style Sheet dialog box. Selecting Link makes the Link External Style Sheet dialog appear. You can either import or link to an external style sheet from this dialog box.

Removing a Style Sheet

With all this talk about how powerful and easy CSS is, it almost seems crazy to think about removing a style from your pages. However, it does happen. Whether you need to completely remove all the style sheets on your site or just want to temporarily disable a style, you will most likely need to do it at least once.

The less damaging method is to simply unapply the style. This keeps any link between the document and an external style sheet intact and also keeps any locally defined styles in your page header. To begin, select the element or range of text to which the style is applied. Next, select None from the CSS Styles panel. This removes any styles that were in effect.

The second method is to completely remove a style from the document. Whether it's an external or internal style doesn't matter; any reference to it in your page header will be removed. However, if you are using classes, the references to the class inside your page remain. To remove these, you must select the text or element in question and then choose the None option in the CSS panel, as described previously. The best way to permanently remove a style is by selecting the Edit Style Sheet button from the CSS Styles panel. Simply select the style to be removed and click Remove. You can also accomplish this by selecting the style in the CSS Styles panel and selecting the Delete Style button. I prefer the first method simply because the style isn't temporarily applied to whatever element I had selected in my document, although this is a purely personal preference.

Exercise 12.2   Creating an External Style Sheet to Remove Underlining from Your Links

In this exercise, you use CSS rules to remove underlining from all the links in your page. This is a very common request and desire that Web designers have, and it is a good place to gain a basic grasp of how powerful CSS styles truly are. You will use the files located in the Chapter 12 folder on the accompanying CD.

1. Copy the files from the Chapter 12 folder onto your hard drive. Open index.htm, located in the Exercise 2 folder inside Dreamweaver.

2. Open the CSS Styles panel by pressing Shift+F11. Next, click the Attach Style Sheet button. This opens the Select Style Sheet File dialog box. Browse to the file plainlinks.css (contained in the same folder as index.htm) and then select it. See Figure 12.8.

3. This automatically links to the style, as shown in Figure 12.9. This particular style redefined the <a> HTML tag. Preview the page in your favorite browser, and test the links. You will notice that the effects occur only on the index.htm page.

4. Go ahead and link to that style sheet from *every* page. After you have done that, preview the index.htm page to see that all the links have no underlining.

5. You will now edit the style sheet plainlinks.css to show an "overline" rather than an underline. To do this, make sure that the CSS Styles panel is open, and then click the Edit Style Sheet button. A screen similar to that shown in Figure 12.10 should appear.

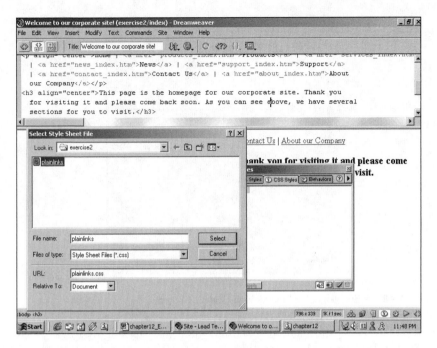

Figure 12.8   You should highlight this file and then click Select to attach it to your current document.

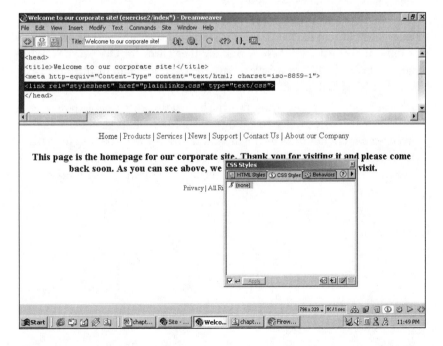

Figure 12.9   Notice the code linking to the external style sheet, as well as the effect it had on the page.

Figure 12.10   Editing the plainlinks.css style sheet.

6. Double-clicking the plainlinks.css (link) label opens a list of the styles contained in that file. Because the only defined style is for the <a> tag, that is all that will appear. Double-click again on the <a> label to open the Style Definition for <a> in the plainlinks.css dialog window.

7. Notice that the only property set is the Decoration attribute, which is set to None. You will want to change this property to display an overline on the link. To do this, simply uncheck the None box and then check the Overline box. When you're done, click OK. Click Save to save the style sheet and then Done to exit the Edit Style Sheet dialog box.

8. Finally, preview the page in your favorite browser (use Internet Explorer or Netscape 6 to ensure proper operation). You also should have noticed that Dreamweaver did not preview the modifications. If you go back to the Style Definition, you will notice that it is marked as a property not previewed in Dreamweaver's document window. See Figure 12.11 for the final product.

Figure 12.11   Your final masterpiece. Don't be afraid to try other combinations for your links.

Styles and Attributes

After you have established the name and type of the style sheet (as well as where it should be defined), or after you have selected to edit a current style, the Style Definition dialog box for that style appears. From here, you can establish what styles you want to define as well as their attributes.

The Style Definition dialog box consists of eight categories (or groups) of styles that you can define. These categories are grouped only to organize styles into similar sections. You can still use styles from multiple categories in one CSS definition. The eight categories are listed here:

- Type
- Background
- Block
- Box
- Border

- List

- Positioning

- Extensions

To move between categories, simply click the category name on the left side of the dialog box. The box will dynamically change to display that category's styles. Also note that styles marked with an * are not previewed in Dreamweaver's document window. To see their effects, you must preview the page in a Web browser. Let's now look at each category and its styles in more detail.

Type Styles

Type styles, shown in Figure 12.12, affect the appearance of your text. One of the most commonly used effects implemented in today's pages from the type category is fixed font size. This is especially effective when designing with layers. Table 12.1 lists the type styles and gives a description of each.

Note

Note that items with an * indicate incomplete, spotty, or buggy support in today's popular Web browsers.

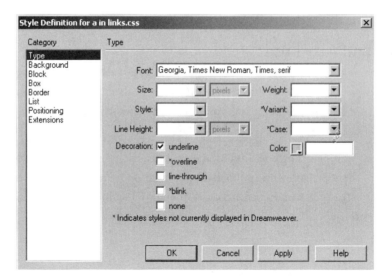

Figure 12.12   Type styles.

Table 12.1   Type Styles

Style	Meaning
Font	Establishes a series of fonts to be used. The first font will attempt to render the page. If the user doesn't have the font, the next one listed will be attempted, and so on. You can also create your own custom list from here.
Size	Specifies the font size as either a precise numerical value or a text descriptor. If a number is entered, you must also specify the unit that the number represents by using the pull-down menu directly to the right. Many designers prefer to use pixels as their unit of measurement because they appear more consistent from browser to browser than the other units of measure.
Weight	Sets the weight of the font. This can be a text descriptor or a number. Experiment with various settings to find out which is best for you. You will find that normal text is around 400 weight, while bold is around 700.
Style	Sets the font as normal, italics, or oblique.
Variant	Toggles between normal or small-caps. With small-caps, all text is displayed uppercase, but the capital letters are still slightly bigger than normal letters.*
Line Height	Sets the line height for your text. You must specify a number and its units. This is the space between lines in your document (typically a few pixels). You can increase or decrease this spacing as desired.*
Case	Makes all your text either uppercase, lowercase, or capitalized.
Decoration	Enables you to establish properties such as an underline, over-line, line-through (strike-through), or blink effect. Be cautious if you decide to use the blink effect; many developers and Web surfers alike deem this extremely irritating. The options in this section enable you to remove the underlines from your links, which many designers desire.
Color	Enables you to establish a font color for your text.

Background Styles

The background styles, shown in Figure 12.13, are dedicated solely to the background of your documents as well as elements in your documents. Originally, page backgrounds were automatically tiled both horizontally and vertically. This tended to limit site creativity while adding to the irritation level experienced when accessing many sites. Thankfully, CSS allows greater control of the background element of your pages. Table 12.2 describes each style and their settings.

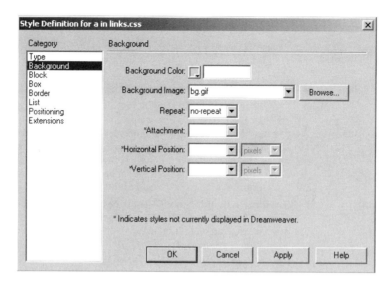

Figure 12.13   Background styles.

Table 12.2   Background Styles

Style	Meaning
Background Color	Enables you to specify a background color through CSS.
Background Image	Enables you to specify a background image through CSS.
Repeat	Affects whether your background image is tiled and, if so, how it is tiled. Four possible settings exist: No Repeat, Repeat, Repeat-x, and Repeat-y. The No Repeat setting forces your image to display once and not repeat at all. Repeat acts like the default method of tiling background images, repeating the image both down and across your page. Repeat-x tiles the image only from left to right across the screen, while Repeat-y tiles the image only down the page.
Attachment	Enables you to either let the background scroll with the page or remain fixed, separate of any scrolling.
Horizontal Position	Enables you to establish positioning of your background image (on the horizontal axis) relative to the top-left of the HTML element to which the style is attached.
Vertical Position	Enables you to establish positioning of your background image (on the vertical axis) relative to the top-left of the HTML element to which the style is attached.

Block Styles

These styles, shown in Figure 12.14, affect blocks of text. These formatting styles offer line- and letter-spacing options, as well as text indenting, something that normal HTML simply will not do. Table 12.3 gives descriptions of each block style.

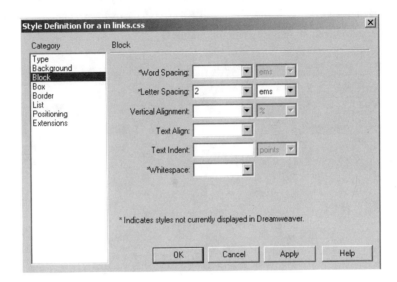

Figure 12.14   Block styles.

Table 12.3   Block Styles

Style	Meaning
Word Spacing	Enables you to establish the spacing used between words. The default unit is ems, which is expressed by using a positive or negative value to describe the amount of spacing.*
Letter Spacing	Enables you to establish the spacing used between individual letters. The default unit is ems, which is expressed by using a positive or negative value to describe the amount of spacing.*
Vertical Alignment	Establishes the vertical alignment of the style. You can use a text descriptor that is listed or enter a numerical value of your own.
Text Align	Defines text alignment as either left, right, center, or justified.
Text Indent	Establishes a value used to indent the first line of text to which the style is attached.
Whitespace	Determines how to handle spaces and tabs. The Pre setting preserves whitespace similar to the <pre> HTML tag. Nowrap wraps text when a tag is inserted.

Box Styles

If you are familiar with table padding, margins, and other settings, the box styles, shown in Figure 12.15, will seem fairly straightforward. They enable you to establish settings for various elements of your page, and they are primarily used with images. You also might notice the double asterisk, noting that those styles affect only certain elements in your document. For instance, both the Float and Clear styles can be previewed only when applied to images. Each style is described in Table 12.4.

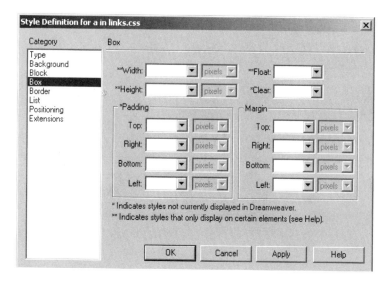

Figure 12.15   Box styles.

Table 12.4   Box Styles

Style	Meaning
Width	Establishes the width of the element to which the style is applied.
Height	Establishes the height of the element to which the style is applied.
Float	Moves the element to the left or right side of the page. Any text that encounters the element will be wrapped around it.
Clear	Typically is used in conjunction with the Float style. This prevents an element from being displayed on the same horizontal plane as a floating element. Both the Float and the Clear style should typically be set to the same value. In addition to Left, Right, and None, the value Both will work, representing both left and right attributes.
Padding	Enables you to set the distance between an element and the border or margins. You can establish different values for the top, right, bottom, and left regions of the element.
Margin	Establishes the margins used between an element's border and other elements on the page. You can define top, right, bottom, and left regions of the element's border.

Border Styles

Border styles, shown in Figure 12.16, enable you to establish and display borders around various elements such as images or text. This is very useful for placing paragraphs of text inside a box. The various border styles are described in detail in Table 12.5.

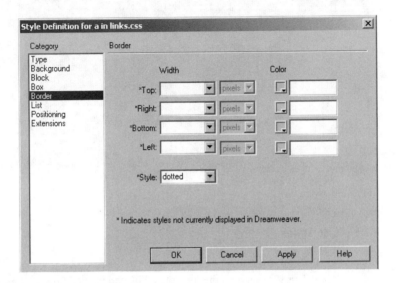

Figure 12.16   Border styles.

Both the Width and Color attributes for each side of the border (top, right, bottom, and left) can be established independent of each other, but we will discuss them only once to avoid repetition.

Table 12.5   Border Styles

Style	Meaning
Width	Sets the width of the border based on a text descriptor.
Color	Sets the color for the side's border.*
Style	Establishes the style of all four sides of the border. Choices include dotted, dashed, solid, double, groove, ridge, inset, and outset borders.

List Styles

This group of styles, shown in Figure 12.17, affects your HTML lists. You can use a custom graphic in place of the default bullets. You can also change the way your lists behave when wrapping text. In Table 12.6, each style is described fully.

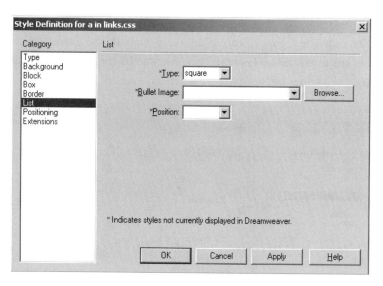

Figure 12.17   List styles.

Table 12.6   List Styles

Style	Meaning
Type	This style specifies the type of list bullet to be used. You can choose among discs, circles, squares, decimals, lowercase Roman bullets, uppercase Roman bullets, and upper- or lowercase alphabetical bullets.
Bullet Image	If you want to use a custom bullet image that's different than the ones listed previously, you can specify an image filename to use instead.
Position	This style affects the way text is wrapped onto the next line in your lists. By default, text will appear indented with your list. You can change this to wrap back to the page margin by selecting Outside.

Positioning Styles

The positioning styles shown in Figure 12.18 offer greater design control and flexibility for compatible browsers. These are also the basis on which layers were created. With the positioning styles, you can specify exact locations for your elements to be positioned. You can also specify whether the location should be absolute (relative to the entire page) or relative to another element. Each style is described in greater detail in Table 12.7.

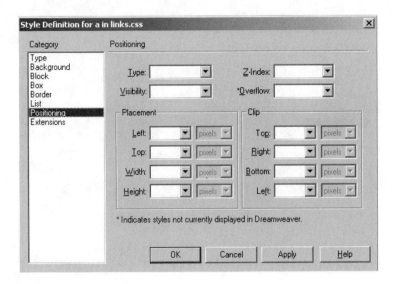

Figure 12.18   Positioning styles.

Table 12.7   Positioning Styles

Style	Meaning
Type	Specifies whether the element's position is absolute or relative to another element. The last choice, Static, offers no positioning of the element.
Visibility	Sets the visibility of an element. The Inherit choice assumes the visibility of the element's parent tag.
Z-Index	Establishes a bottom-to-top ordering of your elements. A higher number makes that element closer to the "top" of your document.
Overflow	Dictates how an element is handled when that same element exceeds its defined width and height. Choices include Visible, in which the dimensions are ignored; Hidden, in which the contents are cut off; and Scroll, in which scrollbars are placed in the element to allow the user to scroll to view the entire element.
Placement	Establishes the whereabouts onscreen for the element with the Left and Top attributes. It also describes the width and height of the element through those respective attributes.
Clip	Defines what part of the element is visible through the Top, Right, Bottom, and Left attributes.

Extensions Styles

The styles listed in the Extensions category and shown in Figure 12.19, such as the Filter style, are those that are extremely new and sometimes radical in nature. It is also important to note that these styles are specific to Internet Explorer only. The styles are described in Table 12.8.

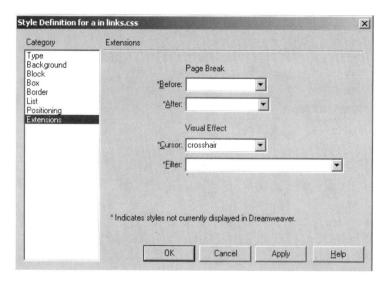

Figure 12.19   Extensions styles.

Table 12.8   Extensions Styles

Style	Meaning
Page Break	Enables you to define page breaks for when your pages are printed by a user. You can establish page breaks before or after the element.
Cursor	Enables you to temporarily change the user's cursor when viewing your page. Choices include Hand, Crosshair, Text, Wait, Default, Help, the eight directional resize icons, and Auto. Some users may be annoyed if you change their cursor, so use this style with caution.
Filter	Enables you to dynamically filter your content when it's rendered on a user's screen. These are similar in nature to Photoshop's filters. I suggest playing with these filters—some of them are rather amazing. You can visit the Web site www.msdn.microsoft.com/workshop/author/filter/reference/reference.asp for more information on these effects.

Summary

This chapter was about CSS, ranging from a discussion of what style sheets really are and how they impact design capabilities to specific styles and their attributes. You also learned how to use and define CSS using Dreamweaver, and you learned the differences between HTML styles and CSS.

Part IV

Site Management

Chapter 13

Site and File Organization

By now you've no doubt created a couple of

pretty nice Web pages and have probably

even linked them to other equally nice

pages you've done. You're probably feeling

pretty good about yourself and your abilities now, like you've actually started to get the hang of this thing. Think again.

Creating the initial pages is just the beginning of a successful Web site. More likely than not, you'll be continually updating, changing, and otherwise modifying your master-pieces to keep them current and up-to-date. Granted, this task doesn't appear very tedious on the surface, but imagine having hundreds or even thousands of pages in your site that you're responsible for. That can get very messy really quickly. So, it's a good idea to understand a couple things before actually creating a rather complex site.

Things like directory structure, addressing methods, and the way your site is set up in Dreamweaver are all things you should take into consideration before starting on a major site. Although Dreamweaver aids you extensively with common and even advanced site management, thorough site planning is still essential to the success of your site. We'll discuss each of these items and more in this chapter. The following is a list of some of the main things we'll talk about:

- How to define your target audience
- Design, layout, and navigation basics
- Ways to organize files and directories
- How to create a site definition in Dreamweaver
- Various addressing methods
- How to create new files

Planning Your Site

Planning is one of the most important things you'll do when creating a high-quality site. Proper site planning will save you more time than you can imagine. From determining your target audience to sitting down and creating a sketch of how you want your site to look, planning is key with Web site development. Resolving these issues before building your entire 150-page site provides obvious benefits.

What Do You Want to Do Today?

The question isn't about just what you want to do today, but also what you want to do a month from now—maybe even a year from now. Defining what you want out of your site before you even start building it will keep your mind focused and your head clear of distractions. You've probably seen some examples of a poorly defined Web site. Many "personal" Web sites that you run across tend to present a chaotic and cluttered message.

Sit down right now and decide what you want out of your site. Whether it's to provide the most up-to-date national news and weather or to provide the latest and greatest in the world of computer video cards, your site needs to have purpose before it has structure.

In writing your site goal (or goals), try to be as specific as possible. Saying that your site will "be the biggest and best site about electronics" is not very specific. On the other hand, saying your site will "provide detailed instruction on the planting and care of the picea pungens (blue spruce tree)" might not be a very good one, either. A balance must be met somewhere in between. A better goal might be to provide a site that will "provide updated news, weather, sports, dining, and other happenings of Salt Lake City, Utah." This goal has a specific region that it applies to (residents of Utah—specifically, Salt Lake City), yet it retains a broad enough range so that you can expand and account for other possibilities in your initial design.

You might want to have a multitiered goal as well. Instead of trying to swallow a whole vision in one gulp, you might decide to break it up into smaller projects, each adding to the previous ones. These are considerations that you should account for in your goal as well as the rest of the planning process.

Who's Going to See It, and How Will They Be Looking at It?

Closely related to your site goals is your target audience. These two steps are sometimes even interchangeable. Occasionally you might know of a specific lifestyle or group of people you want to attract, and *then* you figure out what you want to create for them. Either way, you will need to figure out who you want to visit your site. It would be awfully difficult to create a site for every man, woman, and child. Opinions, priorities, and lifestyles vary with characteristics such as gender, race, nationality, wealth, age, occupation, and others.

Determining who is best suited to visiting your site will help you figure out how to promote your site, as well as determine what type of advertising (if any) you want to have. Additionally, recognizing your target audience will help you create meta tags that effectively drive traffic to your site. (Meta tags are discussed in Chapter 3, "Dreamweaver and HTML.") Something to consider as well is how flexible your goals are in regard to the target audience. Maybe with a few easy modifications to your goal, you can double the number of visitors you get.

Another important factor to consider after you've determined who will come to your site is how they'll be coming. Whether you're creating a site for a company intranet or a financial advice site, knowing how your visitors will get to your site is very important. For instance, many companies use a uniform operating system and browser. In such cases, you might decide to include browser-specific features. Maybe you're creating a Web site offering real estate in Florida. Your target audience might not keep up-to-date on the newest hardware and software, so keeping compatibility for older browser versions and slower hardware might be paramount.

With this, you might opt for a multiversion site. Although this might involve more work, it can offer a few distinct advantages. Users with slower systems won't have to watch choppy Flash intros, while visitors with screaming systems and DSL connections can enjoy every last ounce of it. An increasing number of wireless Web browsers are becoming available as well. Whether they're PDAs or cellular phones, these stripped-down versions of Web browsers will certainly gain momentum in the near future. These are all things that you should consider while determining your target audience.

What Are They Going to See?

After determining the purpose of your site and the target audience, you should begin to develop possible structuring schemes for the site. At the top of the list should be considerations such as the overall design and layout, as well as how you will allow the visitor to navigate through your site. The following sections discuss these in detail.

Design and Layout

This is the part where your creative juices have to flow. Creating a very basic idea or sketch of how you want the site to look and feel will save you a lot of time in the long run. Likewise, creating a detailed plan now will save you a lot of time and grief later. This will help you make logical decisions on where content should be placed or where the navigation items will be best utilized. During this time, you'll also be able to view the site in your mind as a single object, not a collection of various pages. If you create the look and feel before you start adding content, you will create a much-needed consistency throughout your site. If visitors are easily confused by the way your site looks, chances are good that they won't hang around long enough to see if it has valuable content.

Navigation

The navigational method that you use will be one of the most scrutinized aspects of your site. Whether vocally or subconsciously, each user will rate and remember how easy it was to go from page to page. If the interface that you provide is intuitive, simple, and well organized, you can bet that visitors will stick around a while longer.

Your own casual Web browsing will help make you aware of many important design issues when choosing a navigation structure for your site. Undoubtedly at times you become frustrated by poorly formatted content or a hard-to-understand navigation bar. Likewise, you've probably run across some sites that simply amaze you with their simplicity and intuitiveness. In the future, make a mental (or physical) note of such sites for reference when you try to determine what made them so easy to navigate. After all, what good is your content if your visitors can't find it?

Other Considerations

You should consider a few other things when designing a site. The importance of these issues varies from site to site, but to some degree or another all will definitely be factors in how the site functions and appears.

The two most potentially restricting aspects of creating a Web site are money and time. Money will strongly influence the type of technology used, as well as the detail and originality put into the site, and it will possibly dictate how the initial content will be presented to the end user.

Certain technologies such as Flash animations, ASP or other database-driven applications, and custom-written Perl or CGI scripts tend to cost more than basic HTML. Using these features will add to the overhead of your site cost. Designers charge not just for the time used to pump out content, but also for the time it takes to create a unique and catchy design for the site. Basic designs or template-based sites obviously cost less than custom-designed ones.

An example of a site that conforms to tradition and uses a general layout is Cookie Central (www.cookiecentral.com). A more complex design that was created site-specific is PanAmerican Travel Services (www.panamtours.com). Both are fairly clean and simple, but PanAmerican's site is appealing yet original (see Figure 13.1). Also remember that a simple or general design doesn't mean that the site is bad. Most portal sites, such as Yahoo!, have a fairly simple and basic layout, and, though it's basic, the design is extremely popular and effective.

Time is another important consideration—and often a constraint as well—to assess. If you're approached by a company that needs a site completed in two weeks, the length of time allowed for site design will be significantly less than if the same company could wait two months. You might opt for a premade, template-based site for a temporary solution and then create an original site as a second phase. Then again, what if the budget doesn't allow for that type of double site creation? You will find that the timeframe for completion and available finances generally conflict. It's your responsibility to find the happy medium between time and budget constraints.

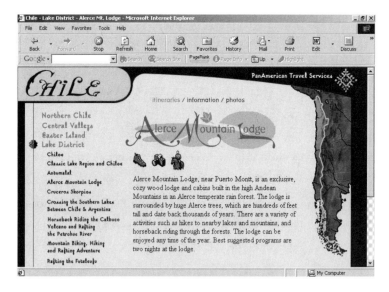

Figure 13.1   PanAmerican Travel Services offers a clean interface while maintaining ease of navigation.

Organizing Files

So now, after all this planning you're itching to start cranking out page after page of your upcoming masterpiece. That's fine, but where are you going to put these files? You have already figured out how the site should be structured visually; now it's time to think about how you should physically create the directories and files that you'll need.

When you create a site with Dreamweaver, you start by creating a local version of the site on your hard drive. In fact, this is how you should always start a site. First define the local root folder within Dreamweaver, and then create the site itself. Dreamweaver is not designed to maintain local sites that aren't on your local machine or mapped network drive, so you must have a local copy. This is called a local site, and it should have the exact same file and directory hierarchy as the public or remote site will. Keeping them the same will make it easier for you and others to understand. In fact, doing this will prevent major problems with future site maintenance. It will also allow you to utilize some of Dreamweaver's site management features, such as tracking links and the synchronize command.

Note

> You can also store your local copy on a floppy disk (if there's enough space), a Zip disk, or some other form of rewritable storage medium besides your hard drive. The only possible problem with using removable media is the tendency that it will become corrupted. If you insist on using this method of local site storage, it's strongly recommended that you back up your data on another medium as well.

Files

Identify the rough number and type of files that you will use in each logical section of the site. You can then begin to determine how they should be organized and separated into subdirectories for easy navigation from the back end. You want to create logical sections, which means that you want to group files together that logically belong in the same directories. Usually this will be very intuitive and shouldn't take much time.

As an example, the National Basketball Association's Web site (`www.nba.com/teamindex.html`) divides each team page into its own directory. This makes perfect sense. If you need to change information for the Miami Heat, you know that every file specifically relating to that team is in the Heat subdirectory.

While you think this process through, keep in mind that browsers keep a copy of every graphic they download. This is called the browser cache, and if you plan ahead, you can utilize this feature to help your pages load faster. By using the same background image source or reusing the navigation bar images as much as possible, the browser will have to download them only once. On additional page views in the same session (sometimes future sessions as well), the browser will load the cached files instead of downloading them again from your server. This typically means faster load times and less bandwidth usage on both the server and the client side, both of which are very good things.

Directories

After you have categorized the logical grouping of your files, you should think about how to further define differences. You will probably want to keep all your images and media files in a place separate from your HTML documents. You might also further divide your media content, such as your .swf or .dcr files. Whether you need to do this depends largely on the size of the site in question. This will let you quickly navigate to the correct file while linking to them in your HTML. If you need to edit or replace an image, you'll know exactly where it's located and can avoid wading through a mess of file types.

This is the basic reason computers use a hierarchy of directories to organize data. You can group a broad subject into a directory and then make additional groupings that are more specific. These specific directories are children of the main directory and are called sub-directories. Figure 13.2 shows a potential site directory structure.

Figure 13.2   One of many ways to organize the files in your site.

Write down on a piece of paper possible directory combinations for your project. You might think that this point seems trivial to the success of your site, but I guarantee that you will save an incredible amount of time by following these simple procedures. After you have managed your site for a while, understanding directories and hierarchies will become much more natural and intuitive. As a result, you'll greatly reduce the time needed for this portion of site development.

Before we talk about how to set up your site information in Dreamweaver, I want to emphasize one more point. If you have all the images and other media type content of your site finished before you begin writing the actual HTML, you will find that the document creation process (the process of putting your design and layout into HTML format) will flow much more smoothly. Likewise, creating a basic "shell" or blank document to act as a placeholder for the final version is advantageous. This enables you to establish any intrasite links at any time, without having to create a new document. When you're working as a team of designers, this might be difficult, but it is highly recommended that, when possible, you create all your images and pages before starting the HTML.

Defining Your Site

Now that you've determined the organization, design, and layout of your site, you can configure Dreamweaver for your site and allow it to help you manage the creation process and future updates. Hoping to organize more than two or three Web pages without the help of Dreamweaver is almost ludicrous.

To set up your site options in Dreamweaver, select Site/New Site from the menu. You can also add a site by selecting New from the Site/Define Sites menu. You can also get to this dialog box by selecting the drop-down menu that lists all your sites in the Site window and choosing Define Sites. The Define Sites dialog box enables you to modify and delete any of your existing defined sites as well.

Local Info

The Local Info area of the Site Definition dialog box (see Figure 13.3) enables you to set options and rules that apply to the local part of your site—that is, the files that are stored locally on your hard drive:

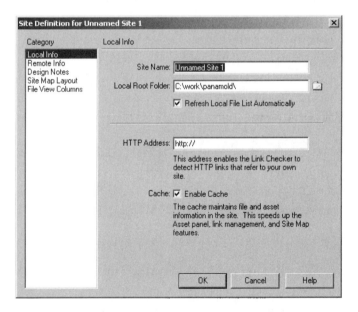

Figure 13.3   Site Definition dialog box window.

- **Site Name**. This enables you to specify the name that you want Dreamweaver to associate with your site. This is displayed in the Define Sites dialog box as well as the menu bar at the top of Dreamweaver's windows. However, this name will never be displayed outside Dreamweaver; it is strictly an internal reference for you.

- **Local Root Folder**. This sets the local directory on your computer (hard drive, floppy, zip drive, and so on) that will be used as the root for your site. You can click the folder icon to graphically navigate to a directory or manually enter a path in the textbox. Note that all files related to your site should be contained somewhere inside this folder or in folders inside it.

- **Refresh Local File List Automatically**. Selecting this option automatically refreshes the local file list every time files are copied to your local site. If you choose to not have it refresh automatically, you can manually refresh the local file list by selecting View/Refresh Local (press Shift+F5) on Windows, or Site/Site Files View/Refresh Local on Macintosh.

- **HTTP Address**. Specifying the URL of your site allows Dreamweaver to correctly verify absolute URLs inside your site. A valid entry would be `http://www.bvstudios.com`.

- **Cache**. Dreamweaver automatically keeps track of certain file and asset information regarding your site. It caches and updates things such as link changes that are necessary when making changes through the Site window. This is a great tool that frees you from keeping track of links that need to be updated if you decide that a file should be located somewhere else. Enabling the cache speeds up this process significantly on small to medium-size sites. On larger sites, enabling this actually slows the process.

Addressing the Local Info section of the Site Definition dialog box is all that is *required* to define a site in Dreamweaver. Typically, however, you want to define the rest of your site (or as much of it as possible) at the beginning. Doing this means that you have one less item on your mental "to do" list.

Remote Info

The Remote Info section of your site preferences defines the information that Dreamweaver needs to accurately publish your pages to a server when they're ready for online viewing (see Figure 13.4). The only option available when you first view the Remote Info section is the Access menu. Options here are None, FTP, Local/Network, SourceSafe database, and WebDAV. What you select here dictates the remaining options. Selecting None offers no options and restricts you from publishing your site via Dreamweaver. You also cannot utilize some of the advanced site management features in

Dreamweaver if you don't establish a remote connection. The remaining options are discussed in the following sections.

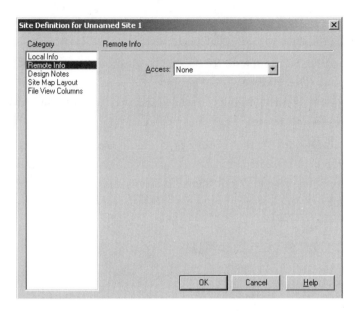

Figure 13.4   The Remote Info section of your site definition.

FTP

FTP stands for File Transfer Protocol and is easily the most widely used method for uploading Web pages to a server. You almost certainly will use this method when creating other organizations' Web pages (see Figure 13.5). Similar to HTTP (the protocol used to transfer Web pages over the Internet), FTP calls for a client and server application. In this instance, Dreamweaver acts as the FTP client, while software on the remote server acts as the FTP server. The following list describes the options needed to use FTP as your remote site connection:

- **FTP Host**. This lets you specify the address for the remote host of your Web server. An example would be `ftp.remotehost.com`. If you don't know this information, contact your network administrator.

- **Host Directory**. This specifies the directory on the server where your site root is located. A directory on the server and a folder on your local computer are synonymous. A lot of servers have the site root set as `public_html/`, although you should check with your hosting company or network administrator if you're unsure.

- **Login**. This is the username of your account.

- **Password**. This is the password used to authenticate your account and gain access to the FTP server. You can select whether Dreamweaver should save your password. If you tell Dreamweaver not to save your password, you will be prompted for it when you connect to the remote site.

- **Use Passive FTP**. Some firewalls require you to use this setting. This enables the client software (Dreamweaver) to set up the FTP session rather than having the FTP server do it. If you're unsure what this should be, leave it unchecked and ask your network administrator.

- **Use Firewall**. Dictates whether Dreamweaver should use the firewall preferences to connect to the FTP server. See Chapter 2, "Customizing Dreamweaver," for more information on setting your firewall preferences, or ask your network administrator.

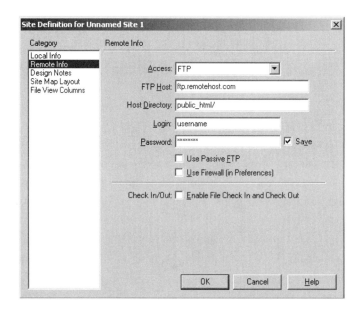

Figure 13.5   Filling out FTP information for your remote site.

Local/Network

A Local/Network connection should be used when the Web server you will be publishing your pages on is located on the same network as you are. Often this option will be used when developing a company intranet site or if you are providing the design and hosting for a site. You must set two options to use Local/Network as your remote site setting: Remote Folder and Refresh Remote File List Automatically (see Figure 13.6).

The Remote Folder setting enables you to set the folder on your LAN to use for the remote site. See your operating system documentation to find out how to map network drives. Selecting the Refresh Remote File List Automatically setting automatically refreshes the local file list every time files are added or deleted. To manually do this, select View/Refresh Remote in the Site window on Windows, or Site/Site Files View/Refresh Remote on Macintosh.

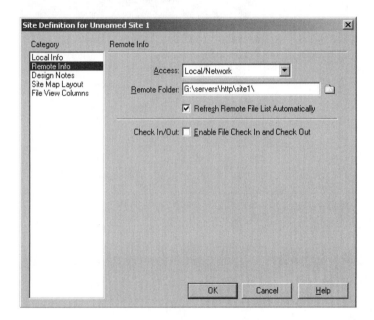

Figure 13.6   Filling out Local/Network information for your remote site.

Check In/Out

By selecting the Enable File Check In and Check Out box, Dreamweaver marks files "in use" as such on the server (see Figure 13.7). This means that other team members can't change the same file you're currently working with. This prevents two people from editing the same file simultaneously, which would result in the loss of one of the members' changes.

Selecting Check Out Files When Opening causes Dreamweaver to automatically check out the file when opening it, marking it as "in use" on the server. Next you should enter the checkout name you want to use when checking out files. This identifies you to other team members, so if you need to edit a file immediately or simply want to confer with whoever is currently making changes, you know whom to contact. Similarly, the email address that you enter gives team members the ability to easily contact you directly from Dreamweaver's interface.

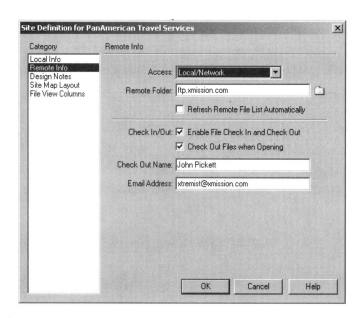

Figure 13.7   Filling out Check In/Out information.

The file Check In/Out system is discussed in great detail in Chapter 15, "Workplace Collaboration."

SourceSafe and WebDAV

If you use Visual SourceSafe or a WebDAV-enabled server to assist in managing your site, select this option (see Figure 13.8). Click Settings for further options regarding each selection (see Figure 13.9). To learn more about Visual SourceSafe and WebDAV, and how they work in Dreamweaver, see Chapter 15.

Design Notes

The Design Notes section of your site definition enables you to decide how you will deal with keeping small notes regarding individual documents (see Figure 13.10). You can clean up your Design Notes by selecting Clean Up from this section. Additionally, you can choose to upload your Design Notes to share with other team members. To learn more about Design Notes, see Chapter 15.

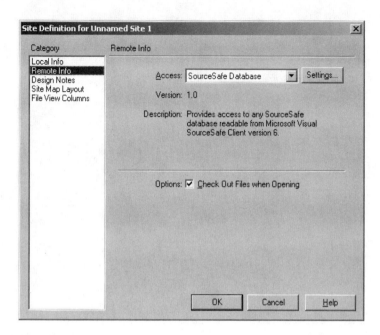

Figure 13.8   Visual SourceSafe integration.

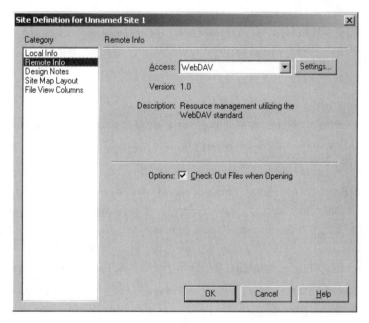

Figure 13.9   WebDAV integration.

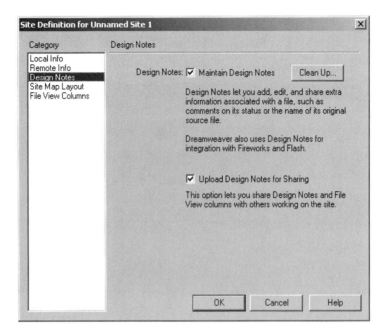

Figure 13.10   The Design Notes section of your site definition.

Note

Design Notes are also used for integration between Dreamweaver and other Macromedia products, such as Flash and Fireworks.

Site Map Layout

This section of the Site Definition dialog box controls how the Site Map view appears (see Figure 13.11). This view is discussed later in the chapter. The following options are available:

- **Home Page**. This sets the HTML document used to reference the root of your site. Use the folder icon to visually select this file, or manually type the path into the text box. You can also set a home page by right-clicking a file in the Site window and selecting Set as Home Page. This document is the page the user first sees when typing in your URL. Typically this will be index.htm or index.html.

- **Number of Columns**. Use this number to specify how many pages to show per row in Site Map view.

- **Column Width**. This is a pixel value telling how wide each of the columns should be.

- **Icon Labels**. Selects what the visual description for each page will be. Selecting filenames returns the actual filenames, such as index.htm or contact.htm. Selecting page titles returns the value of the <title> HTML tag instead.

- **Display Files Marked as Hidden**. This determines whether hidden files should be viewed in Site Map view.

- **Display Dependent Files**. This determines whether files that the HTML document is dependent on should be shown. A dependent file is a file loaded by the HTML code when viewed in a browser. For instance, all the images that you use in your Web pages are dependent files. Without them, your page will not function or display properly.

Tip

The possible filenames for your home page greatly depend on your taste as well as the configuration of your Web server. Some servers allow for home.htm(l) or default.htm(l) to be used as default home pages. If you're unsure what to use, contact your system administrator or hosting company. A server can be configured to use multiple filenames for home pages as well.

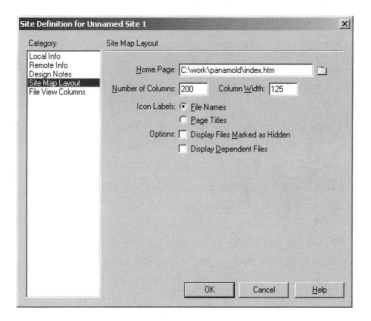

Figure 13.11 The Site Map Layout section of your site definition.

File View Columns

The capability to use your Design Notes to create custom column headings in the File View is new to Dreamweaver 4 (see Figure 13.12). Not only is this a great tool for personal use, but it also can be implemented in a team scenario for maximum productivity. This feature is discussed in detail in Chapter 15. You might notice that some of the options we will discuss are grayed out and unchangeable. This is because they can affect only user-created columns. Each option is outlined in the following list:

- **Enable Column Sharing**. Checking this box grants other team members access to your custom columns. This is a global option, and deselecting it shadows out the Share with All Users of This Site option. In essence, this is an all-or-nothing option, whereas the Share with All Users of This Site option is column-specific.

- **Column Name**. This is the caption used to describe the column. The Dreamweaver default names cannot be changed. You can change only columns that you have manually created.

- **Associate with Design Note**. This tells what part of the Design Notes you want to associate with the particular column. You can enter your own reference or choose from the pre-existing ones (Assigned, Due, Priority, and Status) using the drop-down list.

- **Align**. This dictates the alignment of the content placed in the column.

- **Show**. This enables you to determine whether to show or hide the column. This is helpful in keeping your window clean while retaining the capability to view information that is needed at various times of site development.

- **Share with All Users of This Site**. This specifies whether this column should be shared with other team members working on the site. Selecting this creates and displays the column on the remote site as well. This is a great collaboration tool. This box is shadowed out if either Enable Column Sharing is deselected or the current column selection is a Dreamweaver default.

You can use the + and – buttons to add and delete columns, respectively. You can also change the order in which columns appear with the up and down buttons on the right side. The columns appear left to right beginning at the top of the list.

Note

> You cannot delete a Dreamweaver default column. If you don't want to see it, however, you may deselect the Show option. This hides the column from your view, giving it the appearance that it has been deleted.

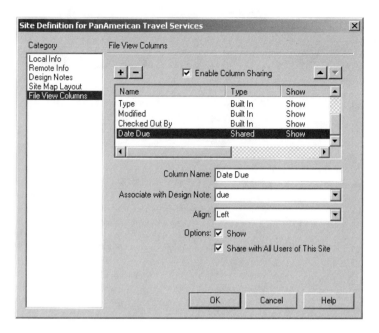

Figure 13.12   The File View Columns section of your site definition.

Exercise 13.1   Defining a Site

For this project, you will simply create a new site definition and create a basic directory structure for future additions. You will use this site definition in future projects, so don't delete it when you're done.

1. Open the Define Sites dialog box (Site/Define Sites) and click New. (See Figure 13.13.)

2. Name the site Corporate (for internal Dreamweaver reference only), set the Local Root folder to C:\work\corporate\, and set the HTTP address to `http://www.corporatesite.com`.

3. Next set up the Remote Info section. Set your remote folder to C:\httpserver\ corporate\. Remember, there is *no* HTTP/Web server actually running in reference to this directory; it's only for practice purposes. If you have access to FTP that you can view via the Internet and with a Web browser, you might consider publishing to it instead. Leave the File Check In/Out system disabled for this exercise.

4. Click OK. Your Site window should now look similar to Figure 13.14.

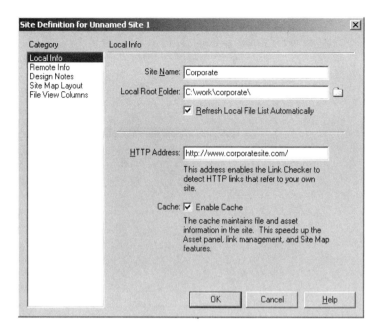

Figure 13.13   Creating your site definition.

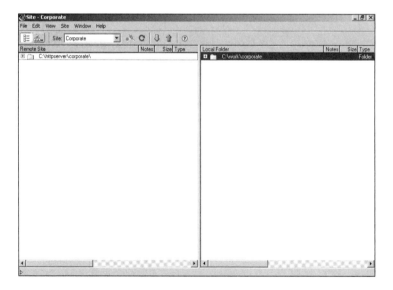

Figure 13.14   The Site window after finishing the site definition.

5. Create seven folders in your local site root: About, Contact, Images, News, Products, Services, and Support. To create these folders, simply right-click the

root folder (C:\work\corporate\) and select New Folder from the context menu that appears. You can do this by selecting File/New Folder from the menu or by pressing Ctrl+Alt+Shift+N in the Site window while the local root folder is highlighted.

Understanding Addressing Methods

Now that you have set up your site in Dreamweaver, you're almost ready to actually start creating some pages. One final topic should be discussed before delving into coding your pages: Understanding the way addressing works in HTML. Nearly everything in your HTML will contain a link. Every image, multimedia file, links to other pages in your site, and links to other sites all contain an address, a path to get from one file to another.

For instance, when a Web browser parses an HTML document, it will undoubtedly come across an <IMG> tag, which calls for the browser to render an image on the screen. The browser looks at the address of the image and makes another request to the Web server for the file indicated. All linking is done in a similar fashion.

Understanding the differences between the various addressing methods will save you a tremendous amount of time in the future. There is no perfect addressing method, but each way offers distinct advantages and disadvantages. Hopefully after reading this section, you will understand when to best utilize each. To learn the specifics of the various methods for linking your content, see Chapter 5, "Linking and Navigation."

Note

In my experience visiting and participating in newsgroups and other forums that discuss Dreamweaver, HTML, and other Web design issues, it is very common for "newbies" to become confused with the difference between absolute and relative addresses, as well as how to use each in Dreamweaver. I encourage you to pay close attention to this section so that you'll understand exactly what is going on in your HTML when you choose to use a particular method.

Absolute Paths

This addressing scheme offers you the capability to link to any Web server that is publicly available, even if the document linking to it is located on another server. Absolute paths are longer than relative paths because they must contain the protocol (HTTP) as well as the server name (www.servername.com).

One distinct disadvantage of using an absolute path comes into play if you change the server name or the name or location of a parent directory. In this case, you would have to update the reference in your HTML document to reflect the changes made. This can be an extremely tedious task and can waste a lot of time.

Note

> If you decide (or are required) to use absolute paths in your HTML document, Dreamweaver's Find and Replace feature will assist you in expediting this process. By identifying unique strings of text in your absolute paths, you can update them all at once. For more on using Find and Replace, see Chapter 14, "Site Publishing, Maintenance, and Reporting."

Relative Paths

Relative paths are much more malleable than absolute paths. Rather than specifying an exact, finite path, relative paths show a relationship with either a document or site root.

Two types of relative paths exist: document-relative and root-relative. Document-relative paths specify a location in relation to the current *document*; being more precise, they specify a relation to the *directory of the document*. Root-relative paths, on the other hand, specify a location in relation to the *site root*. To clarify further, we will refer to root-relative paths as site root-relative paths.

One of the benefits of using document-relative paths is the space that you can save in your HTML code. The space saved might seem trivial with only one link, but it will certainly mean a larger return in the long run.

Document-relative paths offer a solid, all-around approach to linking elements of your HTML document (see Figure 13.15). This is because document-relative paths look at only the same directory in which the file is in currently; it doesn't matter what's above. The exception is when using ../ to move up directories. Fortunately, Dreamweaver tracks filename changes in its interface and prompts you to update the links accordingly. Dreamweaver actually changes the links for you.

Tip

> Use the Browse button whenever possible to link your files. Doing this lets Dreamweaver do the work involved with creating the various types of links. This will save you valuable time and headaches because Dreamweaver—not you—will insert and manage all the hard-to-remember code.

Root-relative paths are very similar to document-relative paths. As the name implies, site root-relative paths are determined in relation to the site root rather than specifying a relation from the current document-relative paths. They are also represented slightly differently. Site root-relative paths begin with a forward slash (/). This is how you can quickly and easily tell what type of relative path is being used (see Figure 13.16).

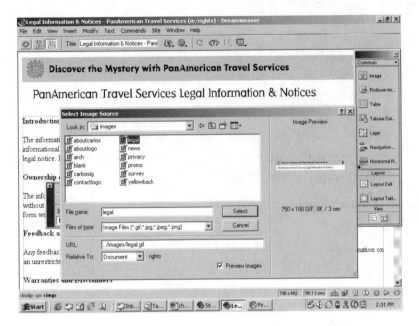

Figure 13.15   An example of a document-relative path.

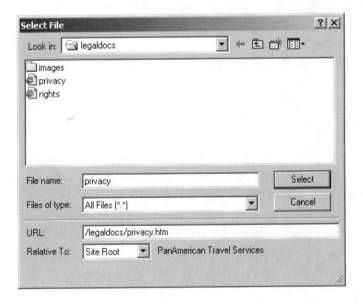

Figure 13.16   An example of a site root-relative path.

Probably the best explanation of when to use site root-relative paths rather than document-relative paths comes from designer Alan Ames of Debbie Does Design (debbiedoesdesign.com):

The only obvious one I know of is made moot by Dreamweaver's link management features ... If you have a large site organized by logical folders, figuring out relative paths can be a real pain involving convoluted tree sketches on scratch paper (when writing HTML by hand), whereas it's fairly easy to remember the root-relative paths.

It also makes for fewer broken links when segments (folders) of the site get moved around. One site-management tip I've heard said to use document-relative links within a folder and site root-relative links when linking to pages in other folders.

In the same conversation, Stefan Walter of Cobion, Inc. (www.cobion.com), had this to say:

Root-relative links are also important if you use server-side includes (SSI). An example is when you have the same menu in different sections of your site that are located in various subdirectories. There you have to use root-relative links if you want to have just one include file for the menu and the links working on every page.

In addition to this excellent advice, you should remember that site root-relative links won't work correctly when previewed locally. This is because the browser can calculate document-relative relationships, but it has no notion of the site root defined in your site definition. If you want to preview your work locally when using site root-relative links, you need to install an HTTP server such as the Personal Web Server locally.

File Creation

You now have a pretty solid grip on how to plan your site design, organize your files into logically arranged directories, and set up your site both locally and remotely in Dreamweaver. You've also gained a better understanding of the three methods for addressing in HTML. Now it's time to learn how to use Dreamweaver to create your files. Although you have previously learned how to use Dreamweaver to make a couple pages here and there, now you'll see how to create multiple files at once, preview your work, and see how to send them to the remote server for live viewing.

Creating New Files

You can create new files in Dreamweaver in a few ways. The quickest and easiest way is to select File/New from the document window or File/New Window (both of which can be accessed with the keyboard shortcut Ctrl+N). This opens a new window where you can create various types of text files, although they will primarily be your HTML documents.

An alternative way to create a new file is to select File/New File from the Site Window menu. This creates the file in a different way than the other method: It creates the file and gives you the opportunity to name it immediately. You can then open it by either double-clicking the filename or pressing Enter after you select the file. This is very useful for creating many files in one swift swoop and then linking and populating them with content later.

Note

You can also use your mouse to right-click the directory in the local side of the Site window in which you want to create the file. You can then select New File from the pop-up menu that appears. You can create directories in the same manner.

By default, each document in Dreamweaver is opened in a new window. You can change this setting in your preferences; see Chapter 2, "Customizing Dreamweaver," for more information on doing this. There is no limit set in Dreamweaver on how many windows can be open simultaneously. However, there is a limit on the amount of system memory (RAM) you have. Keep in mind, however, that if you open 30 windows, your system will slow down significantly. I typically try to keep the number of open windows down to three to five.

When you have multiple windows open, you can change among them by either selecting their taskbar icon or using the Alt+Tab feature in Windows, or by selecting the specific window on Macintosh systems. You can also select the files from a list located at the bottom of the Window menu of Dreamweaver on both operating systems.

Opening Existing Files

As always, there's more than one way to open files in Dreamweaver. The first and perhaps most popular method is to select File/Open from the menu. Pressing Ctrl+O accesses this dialog as well. You can then use the Open dialog box to navigate to the file that you want to edit and click Open.

An alternative method (and the way I typically prefer) is through the Site window. You can double-click a file or press Enter while it is selected. I generally create all my files before putting content in any of them, so navigating through my site in the Site window seems faster than the Open dialog box. If you choose this method, you also might want to set your preferences to only open the Site window when Dreamweaver loads. See Chapter 2 for more information on doing this.

When Dreamweaver opens a file, it always applies a syntax check on the code. It rewrites any code that it recognizes as invalid. You can tell Dreamweaver what kind of code to rewrite, and you can set certain file extension that it should never rewrite in the Code Rewriting section of your preferences. This is covered further in Chapter 2.

Previewing Your Work

In the era of word processors, you can almost always see what you're going to end up with as you create it. This is not always the case with HTML because various browsers provide varying degrees of support for Web standards. Ultimately, the appearance of your page will be determined by the way in which the Web browser interprets your code. As such, it is important to see how the changes that you make will actually affect the page. Dreamweaver's Preview in Browser function enables you to do this extremely easily.

Before you can preview your page in a browser, you must specify this in Dreamweaver's preferences. You can modify the browsers to use in previewing by selecting File/Preview in Browser/Edit Browser List from the menu or by viewing the Preview in Browser section of your preferences. You can also access this list by clicking the Preview/Debug in Browser button (shaped like a globe) on the toolbar and selecting Edit Browser List. You can then add or delete a browser by using the + and – buttons. You can also set your primary and secondary browser (which enable you to access them via keyboard shortcuts). For further instruction on setting up browsers to preview your work, see Chapter 2.

Note

It is *always* a good idea to preview your pages frequently in a variety of browsers. Doing this reduces the chance that you'll waste time later tracking down inconsistencies in your pages across various browsers and operating systems.

One great feature in Dreamweaver is that you can adjust your primary and secondary browsers at any time. This means that you can focus on one browser at a time when previewing for compatibility. When you finish with the primary or secondary browser, you can go into your options again and set another browser as the primary one. This enables you to access this feature by simply pressing F12 instead of navigating through the menu. You can access your secondary browser by typing Ctrl+F12.

After you have designated your browsers, you simply choose File/Preview in Browser/Browser Description to use a particular browser for previewing your document. Doing this opens the browser and displays a temporarily saved version of your page. Dreamweaver does not use the file of the document you're editing for previewing it in a browser. Instead, it saves your file as a temporary file in the directory in which your document resides. New to Dreamweaver 4, these files are marked hidden so that you normally won't even see them. Dreamweaver deletes these temporary files when it exits. Also note that because you are using a different file than the one you are actually editing, previewing further changes to the file in Dreamweaver requires you to go through the File/Preview in Browser menu rather than simply refreshing the page in the browser window.

The main objective of previewing your work periodically is to ensure compatibility between browser vendors and versions. Another factor to consider is the browser platform. If possible, preview your pages on other operating systems occasionally to make sure that you get the results you're expecting. It is always better to spend late nights making your pages look good locally rather than having the whole world tell you of your goof. A major culprit of this is Netscape on Macintosh systems. It renders text noticeably smaller and tends to be the bane of many designers' existence.

Saving Files

All the hard work and good intentions in the world won't amount to anything if you have nothing to show for yourself in the end. This is the basic reason you should save—and save frequently—when working with your HTML documents. Anyone who has experienced one of many types of data loss events will testify to its importance.

It's also a good idea to save your files in Dreamweaver before you start creating links or inserting media, or Dreamweaver will insert a reference to the file on your hard drive rather than an HTTP reference. This is one of the reasons you should always create your files before doing anything with them. The easiest way to do this is through the Site window and by selecting the File/New File or New Directory menu option.

To save your work for the first time in Dreamweaver, select File/Save from the menu, or press Ctrl+S. This brings up the Save As dialog box. You can navigate to a certain directory and enter the filename that you want for your document in this box. Make sure that the location that you ultimately choose resides inside your local root folder. You also might decide to save your file as something other than an HTML document. Use the Save As Type drop-down list to select a different file type.

After you have initially saved the file, you can save your changes to the same file (over-writing the currently saved copy) by selecting File/Save from the menu or pressing Ctrl+S on Windows (or Cmd+S on Macintosh). These file saves occur automatically, transparent to you, and without any input requirements. An easy way to tell whether your document needs to be saved is to see if there is an asterisk (*) located next to the filename of your document in the title bar of the document window. If there is and you save your file, the asterisk will disappear and you will know Dreamweaver has success-fully saved your latest version.

Note

Sometimes you might want to save the same document as two different files. You don't have to copy and paste the HTML code into a new document and then save it. Instead, you can select File/Save As from the menu. This enables you to save a copy of the cur-rent file with a different name. Be sure to remember that after you do this, the docu-ment to which you return will be this new copy of the original document. If you want to return to the original copy, you must open it as discussed in the previous section. As with normal saving, make sure that you save the document somewhere inside the Local Root folder; otherwise, your links could become corrupted.

Backing Up Your Data

Power failure, fire, lightning, hardware failure, or, worse yet, personal negligence can cause all your hard work to be lost. It is extremely important to consider backing up your data on a regular basis. It also might be wise to invest in an uninterruptible power supply (UPS) so that if a natural disaster or other power failure occurs, your computer can remain active long enough to save your work and shut down.

You can back up your data in many ways: to floppies, Zip disks, CDs, tapes, and even off-site via the Internet. I personally keep my working copy on my hard drive. I then have an automated backup run every morning at 4:00 a.m. that saves my important documents and work files. This is saved to an Iomega Zip drive. I change disks regularly as well. After a project is completed, I burn a final copy of all site files, as well as any source files rele-vant to the site, on a CD-ROM and place it in a fire-resistant safe. Finally, I regularly back up my work data offsite via my Internet connection.

Tip

Many online services offer an easy and well-integrated backup option for your work. One such place is @Backup (www.backup.com). For a small annual fee, the company ensures that your data is safe, with multiple copies of your data on its systems at multi-ple locations. Another possible solution is the Auto Backup Extension available on the Dreamweaver Exchange. This is a useful tool available for free to assist with your data backup endeavors.

You might think this is overkill, but just because your company is small does not mean that the importance of your data is small. A small investment now will save you money, time, and peace of mind in the future.

Closing Files

When you are finished editing your files, closing them is a cinch. Simply select File/Close from the menu, or press Ctrl+W (Cmd+W on a Macintosh). If any changes have occurred that have not been saved yet, Dreamweaver will prompt you to see if you want to save them. Selecting Yes saves the changes, selecting No discards the changes, and selecting Cancel returns you to the file that you were editing without saving or closing it.

Uploading Files

After you've gone through the whole process of creating, editing, and previewing your pages locally, it's time to send them off to be scrutinized by the rest of the world. Cross your fingers and send your hard work to the wonderful World Wide Web (or intranet, or whatever else you have).

Generally there are two ways to go about uploading your pages. You can upload a few at a time as you finish them, or you can wait until you are completely finished with all the pages and upload them all at once. Which method is best is really a personal preference, although there are a few considerations to think about when deciding which to do:

- If your project is a facelift for a currently running site, it is probably best to make the change swiftly when all the pages and content are complete.

- If your project is a completely new, previously unaccessed site, you can upload the site in chunks. Either keep the URL to only a select few until the site is complete, or distribute the address and accommodate an "under construction" theme. When using an "under construction" theme, however, remember to finish each area as soon as possible; otherwise, visitors will lose interest because of the lack (or incompleteness) of content.

- It is advised that you upload and "play around" with Web servers that you don't have experience with. You might notice discrepancies that servers you have previously used have not exhibited.

- Some Web servers are case-sensitive, while others are not. Typically UNIX-based servers are, while Windows-based servers are not. You should generally use lowercase letters for your entire filenames to ensure compatibility on any server. This removes the issue of case-sensitivity completely. I also think that using uppercase letters in a filename causes a cold or harsh look when viewed in the browser address bar.

After you have decided when and how you want to upload your files, you can start uploading them. You can do this a number of ways in Dreamweaver. The easiest way to upload the entire site is to select the root folder in the local site pane of the Site window. Then click the Put File(s) button on the toolbar. Dreamweaver asks if you are sure that you want to put the entire site online. Selecting Yes starts the upload process; selecting No cancels it. You can also accomplish this by right-clicking the root folder and selecting Put from the pop-up menu.

Note

Be sure to connect yourself to the Internet or LAN before initiating the uploading or downloading process.

You can transfer one file at a time by selecting it and pressing the Put button. Dreamweaver asks if you want it to include all dependent files as well. These include the images and other objects contained in the HTML document. At this point, you can also tell Dreamweaver not to ask you this again and to always apply the choice you make this time to all future Put operations.

To put more than one file at a time, hold down Ctrl while selecting each file that you want to upload. You can select a range of files by selecting the first file in the local site pane that you want to upload, holding down Shift, and then selecting the last file in the group. This selects all the files between your starting and ending files, including the starting and ending files.

To make your uploading process even easier, Dreamweaver automatically creates any directories on the server that might be needed. This enables you to select a file three folders deep and initiate a Put without manually creating each of the folders. If the folders don't currently exist, Dreamweaver will create them on the server.

Tip

Although Dreamweaver's FTP client (one of the most popular methods of connecting and managing files between your local and remote servers) has improved dramatically from previous versions, many people still like to use their own FTP client, such as CuteFTP (www.cuteftp.com) for Windows, or Fetch (www.fetchsoftworks.com) for Macintosh systems. If you decide to use one of these separate applications, you should remember that they will not upload dependent files—you will have to do this manually. You also must create directories manually. Because of this, you must be extremely careful to maintain the same directory structure on the local and remote side, or you risk having your links fail. Additionally, you will be unable to synchronize your site with a third-party FTP client. If you are new to FTP or file management, you should stick with the built-in FTP capabilities that Dreamweaver provides.

Exercise 13.2   Populating Your Site with Files and Linking Them

For this exercise, you will simply create the files needed for a basic site and then link them. You will use the site definition that you created in Exercise 13.1, so if you haven't done that yet, do it now. Completed example files can be found on the CD-ROM inside the Chapter 13 directory. You will need these files in future exercises, so don't delete them.

1. Create files in each of the directories that you made in Exercise 13.1 with the same filenames. Do this by right-clicking the folder and then selecting New File from the context menu that appears. You can also create new files by selecting New/New File from the menu or by pressing Ctrl+Shift+N in the Site window. This creates a file called untitled.htm and makes its filename editable.

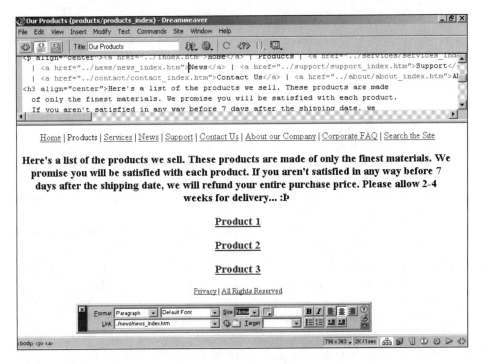

Figure 13.17   The directory and file structure after all folders and files are created.

2. Go through each HTML document and create a basic text-based navigation at the top of the screen; then insert some dummy text (see Figure 13.17). Be sure to use document-relative links so that they will work when you preview them. Remove the link for the current page's text on the navigation line. This helps the visitor identify the current page in an effortless manner. Figure 13.18 shows an example of what your page should look like.

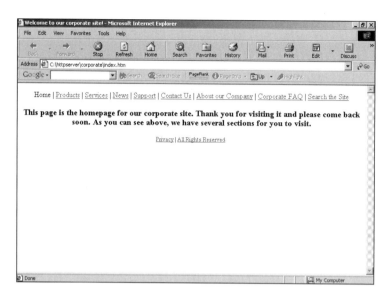

Figure 13.18   The main index page of your corporate site.

3. Go ahead and preview your page. Do this by simply pressing F12.

4. After you have previewed and tested your work, upload your site for public view-ing. Your site isn't going to really be "public," but the practice is still the same. To upload your files, just select the Local Site root folder (C:\work\corporate\) and then press the Put File(s) button. You can also put the files on the remote server by right-clicking the root folder and selecting Put from the context menu or selecting Site/Put (Ctrl+Shift+U) from the menu. Dreamweaver will warn you that you are about to put the entire local site on the remote site.

5. Open your browser of choice, such as Internet Explorer. Press Ctrl+O to get the Open dialog box to appear, or select File/Open from the menu. The specific method to open files varies from browser to browser, although it shouldn't be very hard to figure it out, regardless of the browser you prefer to use.

6. Browse to the index file for your newly uploaded site, and open it. If all has gone well, your page and all its links will function properly.

Summary

The primary focus of this chapter has been determining how your site should be represented, including taking into account everything from file and directory organizational techniques and guidelines to previewing your work on various browsers. You learned how to plan your site layout and navigation, and you also got a step-by-step guide to setting up your site in Dreamweaver. At this point, you also should understand the three methods of referencing files with HTML, as well as what type of situation each is best suited for.

Chapter 14

Site Publishing, Maintenance, and Reporting

Now that you've created your site and possibly even fiddled with uploading and downloading it a few times, you should be aware of some features in Dreamweaver that enable you to easily update and maintain your site. We will also discuss creating site reports that summarize site issues that you might need to resolve. At the end of this chapter, you will know how to use the Site Map, as well as how to search and replace text and HTML source in files and folders contained in your site. The following is a list of some of the main things we'll talk about:

- Exploring the Site window
- Handling basic link management through the Site Map
- Creating an image of a linked hierarchical view of your site
- Easily checking and fixing broken, external, and orphaned links
- Keeping your local and remote sites synchronized
- Executing find-and-replace searches, including the use of regular expressions
- Creating various site reports

The Site Window

The Site window is where you manage your site. You can create, delete, and even link files within the Site window. This window is also very useful for moving files because it allows a visual representation of the process and enables you to update other links in your site to reflect the changes. There are two views to choose from: Site Files and Site Map. The Site Map view contains two subviews: Map Only, and Map and Files. You can access the Site window in several ways:

- Select Site/Site Files.
- Select Site/Open Site/Your Site.
- Press F8.
- Select the Site button from the launcher or mini-launcher.

Of the two views, probably the most popular view of Web designers, myself included, is the Site Files view. This view enables you to use a familiar and simple interface to manage your files. You can quickly compare the layout and structure of both your local site and your remote site because they are both displayed simultaneously. The Site Files view is the default view; however, if you have inadvertently changed the view, you can change back to the Site Files view by pressing F8 or selecting the Site Files button on the left side of the Site Window toolbar.

The Site Files view displays two main window panes. By default, the local files are listed on the right, and remote files are listed on the left side. Although this is the default, you can change it in the Site section of your Preferences. See Chapter 2, "Customizing Dreamweaver," for information on how to do this. The following section explains each button and function involved with the Site window. Refer to Figure 14.1 to see where the buttons are placed.

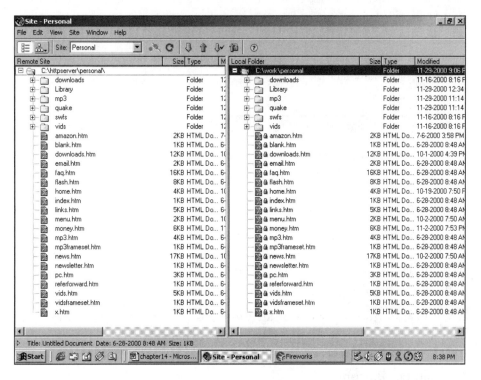

Figure 14.1   The remote site is listed on the left, and the local site is on the right.

Connect/Disconnect Button

The Connect/Disconnect button enables you to connect and disconnect from the remote FTP server. This option is also available if you use a source control system such as SourceSafe or WebDAV. If you publish to a server located locally on your computer or your network, this button will be grayed out and you will automatically be connected to the local server. This button will also be grayed out if you have not specified a remote FTP server in your site definition.

Select the Connect button to connect to the FTP server located in the Remote Info section of your site definition. When you connect, a green light appears in the lower-left portion of the Connect button icon. This lets you know that you're connected to the remote server and changes the button's function to Disconnect. Pressing the button in this state disconnects you from the remote server.

If you are having problems connecting to your remote server (or perhaps if you just want to know what Dreamweaver is really doing when you press that button), you can view the FTP log by selecting Window/Site Log (or Site/Site FTP Log, on Macintosh systems). This provides a real-time client/server log of your FTP requests and responses. This also shows you how Dreamweaver creates directories, uploads and downloads files, and uses many other FTP commands.

Tip

Macromedia maintains a TechNote that lists FTP commands and shows you how to interpret a FTP log. The address for this resource is www.macromedia.com/support/dreamweaver/ts/documents/ftp_errors.htm.

Refresh Button

If you're connected to the remote server, the Refresh button will refresh both local and remote file listings; otherwise, it will refresh only the local listing. You also can refresh the file listing by pressing F5. It should be noted that refreshing simply gets an updated list of the files. It doesn't transfer files or provide any type of synchronization.

If you want to refresh only one of the two listings, select View/Refresh Local (press Shift+F5) or View/Refresh Remote (press Alt+F5) accordingly.

Get and Put Buttons

You will find yourself pressing the Get and Put buttons many times through your Web site design experience. These buttons are the basis for sending the site files to your server and getting files from your server to your local computer for editing.

The Get File(s) button downloads the selected file(s) from the remote site to your local site, overwriting any current copy of the file. Dreamweaver prompts you to ensure that you are aware that doing this will replace your current local copy. Dreamweaver always gets the file(s) from the remote server, regardless of the currently active pane. It also downloads only files that are selected in the active pane. This option is shaded out if you have not specified a remote server in your site definition.

NOTE

When you select to either Get or Put files, the Dependent Files dialog box appears, asking if it should include all files linked to inside the HTML documents. These files include images and other media content. Select Yes or No accordingly. You may also tell Dreamweaver whether it should ask you this in the future. If you decide to have Dreamweaver not ask you in the future, you might decide later that you'd like it to. You can turn on this prompt again by going to the Site section of your Preferences and checking Prompt on Get or Put. If you decide to leave this feature hidden, you may force Dreamweaver to ask you on a one-time basis by holding Alt while selecting the Get or Put buttons.

If Enable File Check In and Check Out is turned on, the files that you download using the Get button will be read-only. To gain full read/write access, you must check out the files. This means that the file can be checked out by other team members, but you still can view it. The following actions perform the same function as the Get button:

- Selecting Site/Get.
- Using the keyboard shortcut Ctrl+Shift+D, or Command+Shift+D on a Macintosh system.
- Right-clicking on the file in the Site Files window and choosing Get.
- Dragging the desired selected files from the remote site window pane to the local site pane. Be careful when doing this to ensure that you are dragging the files into the proper directory. Otherwise, you will break your document relative links. This is more of an issue for Put than Get because Dreamweaver will prompt you to change links when you drag into the wrong local folder.

The Put File(s) button uploads the selected file(s) from your local site to the remote site, overwriting any current copy of the file. You typically use this option when working on a project by yourself and when you are ready to upload site changes. As with the Get File(s) button, files transferred are those selected in the active window pane. This option is also shaded out if you have not specified the remote server in your site definition. The following actions perform the same function as the Put button:

- Selecting Site/Put.
- Using the keyboard shortcut Ctrl+Shift+U, or Command+Shift+U on Macintosh systems.
- Dragging the desired selected files from the local site window pane to the remote site pane.
- Right-clicking on the file in the Site Files window and choosing Put.

- Dragging the desired selected files from the local site window pane to the remote site pane. Be careful when doing this to ensure that you are dragging the files into the proper directory. Otherwise, you will break your document relative links.

Selecting either the Get or the Put button when either no files are selected or the root directory is selected downloads or uploads the entire site. Because this is a fairly extreme event, Dreamweaver notifies you of this and allows you to abort the process. Dreamweaver also automatically attempts to create any needed directories on both the local and the remote site when using the Get and Put buttons.

Check Out and Check In Buttons

When collaborating with others, selecting the Check Out File(s) button utilizes Dreamweaver's Check In/Out system (discussed in detail in the next chapter). The Check Out button downloads the remote site copy of the file(s) and marks them as checked out (or in use) in the remote location. This notifies others on your team that you are currently using the file and that they'll have to wait until you're done with it.

The Check In File(s) button does just the opposite. It uploads the local copy of the file to the remote site and marks it as checked in (or not in use). Other team members can now Get or Check Out this file and make their own changes to it. Checking in a file makes the local version read-only. To edit the file, you must check it out again.

Neither the Check In nor the Check Out buttons are visible if Enable File Check In and Check Out isn't selected in your site definition.

Stop Current Task Button

This button is red and octagonal-shaped (yes, just like those stop signs that you continually ignore, although hopefully you won't treat this one as lightly). It appears only when Dreamweaver does an automated task such as uploading or downloading files, running reports, and performing other similar activities. It's always located in the lower-right corner of whatever window is doing the work. Clicking the red icon causes Dreamweaver to attempt to stop the operation gracefully. I say "attempt" because Dreamweaver does not always stop the action immediately or gracefully. This is due, in some part, to Dreamweaver's extensibility layer. To make it extensible (capable of accepting extensions), some of Dreamweaver's code had to be written in JavaScript. This JavaScript does not tie into the operating system as closely as C code would, so it is occasionally difficult to end a task in Dreamweaver.

Note

Pressing Esc has the same effect as pressing the Stop Task button.

Collapse/Expand Triangle

This triangular icon is located in the lower-left portion of the Site window. When pressed, it changes the two-column view (or Site Map view) into a single-column view of your local site. Pressed again, the icon causes the Site window to restore to its previous layout.

Site Files Button

When selected, the Site Files button formats the Site window into two window panes. By default, the left pane displays the remote site, while the right pane displays the local site. You can adjust which site is displayed on which side in the Site section of your Preferences (see Chapter 2 for more details). The Site Files view is the default view of the Site window. You may also access this function by doing one the following:

- Pressing F8.
- Selecting Window/Site Files.
- Selecting Site/Site Files (from the document window).

Site Map Button

The Site Map button changes the Site window display to show a visual representation of your site. This map is created based on the HTML links in your documents.

Holding down the mouse button when selecting the Site Map button makes a menu appear with the options of Map Only and Map and Files. Selecting Map Only causes the Site Map to fill the entire width of the Site window. Selecting Map and Files causes a small pane on the right (by default) to appear showing the local site, while the Site Map remains in the left pane. When either option is selected, that option becomes the default Site Map view displayed when toggling back to Site Map view from Site Files view. You may also access the Site Map view by doing one of the following:

- Pressing Alt+F8.
- Selecting Window/Site Map.
- Selecting Site/Site Map (from the document window).

Sites Menu

This menu lists all the sites that you have configured in Dreamweaver. You can instantly change to another site by simply selecting it from the list. Clicking the Define Sites text brings up the Define Sites dialog box, where you can add, remove, and edit your site information.

Help Button

This button is located all over the place. Selecting it brings up Dreamweaver's Help system in your default browser. Macromedia has one of the most extensive and complete online help systems I have ever seen. It would greatly behoove you to utilize this superb feature. The button is represented as a white circle with a question mark in the middle. It should also be pointed out that the Help system is context-sensitive in certain instances. If you press the Help button in these context-sensitive dialogues, the Help pages automatically load to information pertaining to what you're currently trying to get help on.

Using the Site Map

The Site Map view is typically a local-only view. Although you can still publish your pages to the remote Web server, you don't have the same sense of control as you do when in the Site Files view. The Site Map view displays your site as a hierarchy of linked files. The topmost file is whatever your home page is. In fact, you won't be able to create a Site Map unless you have defined a home page in your site definition. You can learn how to do this in Chapter 13, "Site and File Organization." Below it are files linked directly from the home page (assuming that the View/Show Dependent Files option is selected). Included as well are email links, external links, and any sort of media embedded in the page. The Site Map continues in this way for every file and link. You can expand or collapse each tree listing with the + and – buttons on the left side of the document icon.

You can access the Site Map from the document window by selecting Site/Site Map or from the Site window by selecting Window/Site Map. Alt+F8 will work in both instances as well. Additionally, if the Site window is already open, you can click the Site Files button on the toolbar. If you press and hold the mouse button for a short time on this button, two further options are listed: Map Only and Map and Files (see Figure 14.2). Selecting Map Only displays the Site Map only; selecting Map and Files displays the Site Map in one side of the window and the local site files in another. By default, the Site Map is on the left.

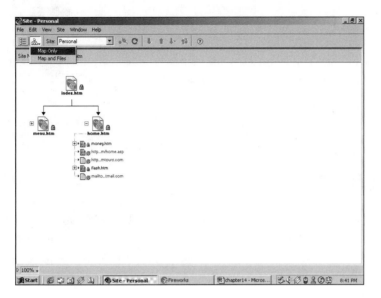

Figure 14.2   You can choose from either Map Only or Map and Files.

If you haven't specified a home page yet, Dreamweaver will prompt you to do so. It uses this page as the root on which the map is built. Defining a home page is discussed in the next section. Certain functions and features in Dreamweaver are local site-specific. The Site Map is such a function—at least, the image representation of the Site Map is local site-specific. You can still do remote site management with the Site Map.

The Site Map uses small icons to give visual clues to a file or links status. A file is typically represented in black. If the link is broken between the file and the file linking to it, it is shown in red. External and special links are represented in blue with a globe icon next to them. Email links are one example of a special link. If the Check In/Check Out system is in use, a green check next to a filename represents a file checked out by you. A red check indicates a file checked out by someone else. Finally, a lock icon indicates that a particular file is "locked" or read-only. This helps prevent accidentally editing files when they're finished.

Note

Be default, the Site Map shows only HTML documents. You can adjust this to show dependent and hidden files. This is discussed in the next section.

Customizing Site Map Layout

As discussed in part of the last chapter, you can customize the look of your Site Map via your site definition. This allows each Site Map to be potentially different without having to adjust the settings each time you switch sites.

To customize your current Site Map, do the following:

1. Select Site/Define Sites from the menu. From the Define Sites dialog box, select the current site and click Edit.

2. Select the Site Map Layout section of your site definition (see Figure 14.3).

3. You can now select the home page for your site. Either type a path in the text field, or use the folder icon to select one. This is the HTML document that Dreamweaver will use as the "root" of your site and will display as the topmost document in your site map. This is analogous to the trunk of a tree, and it provides the base where each branch is generated. In other words, it's typically the index or splash page, the one the user sees first.

4. You can then select the number of columns and the column width for your Site Map display. This number specifies the number of pages to display on each row; the default is 200. You will typically not need to adjust this value because you will rarely have more than 200 pages linked to from your main page.

5. Next you can select whether the Site Map should represent documents by their filenames or their page titles. If you have been diligent in creating effective page titles, this might be a good way to display your site. Displaying your site files by their page titles also gives you an idea of whether the titles are easy to understand. You might be surprised how confusing some page titles can be when you're not looking at the page itself.

6. Finally, you can choose any options that you want to include in your Site Map. The first option enables you to specify whether the site map should show files marked as hidden. When this is checked, hidden files will be shown. When checked, the other option, Display Dependent Files, displays all dependent files (such as images and other files linked in the HTML) in the Site Map. These files are listed in the order in which they are located in the HTML code.

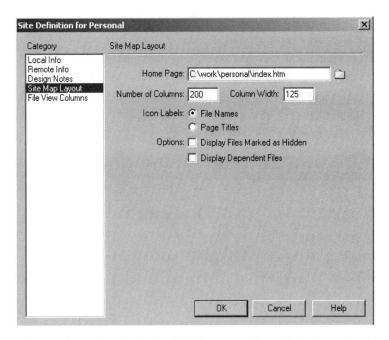

Figure 14.3   Use this section of the site definition to establish settings for the Site Map view.

Adding, Deleting, and Modifying Links

One of the more powerful aspects of using the Site Map is the capability to quickly create new links to documents. This capability enables you to quickly create a functional site with minimal effort on your part. This is handy because you can start linking your pages immediately when placing your content, rather than typing a filename and trying to remember that you had better create that file later.

Creating Links

Would you believe that you can create a link to an existing file in Dreamweaver with *one* click? It's true! Okay, so it's a prolonged click, but that still counts, right? The easiest way to do this is by using the Point to File icon. It appears as a crosshair next to the file icons in the Site Map when you have selected that file. Be sure to view both the Site Map and the files when you do this so that you have something to link to. Click and hold the mouse button on the Site Map button on the toolbar to bring up the list that enables you to view the Site Map and the files simultaneously.

Note

You can create a link without viewing the site files, but the file linked to must already be on the Site Map.

Select the file that you want to use to create the link to another file. The crosshair-shaped Point to File icon appears to the side of the document icon, as shown in Figure 14.4. Using your mouse pointer, click and drag the crosshair to the file that you want to create a link to. When you are hovering over the desired file, you will see an outline around that file, and then you should let go of the mouse button. Dreamweaver creates a link in the originating file. The link is located at the bottom of any other content on the page and has the text of the filename of the linked file.

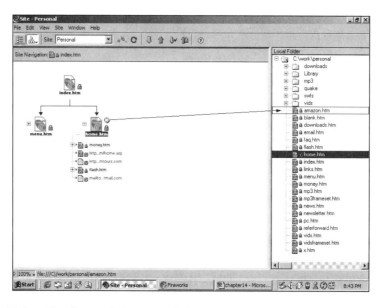

Figure 14.4   Using the crosshair to create links.

You also can use other methods to create links to existing files. You can link to files outside the local site by opening Windows Explorer. You can then drag files from Windows Explorer onto the file that you want to create a link to inside the Site Map. However, you should position the Site window and Windows Explorer so that they don't overlap while doing this.

Another way is to select the file in which you created the link and select Site/Link to Existing File from the Site Window menu. You can also do this with the keyboard shortcut Ctrl+Shift+K. Likewise, right-clicking a file icon in the Site Map and selecting Link to Existing File from the context menu has the same effect. All three ways of invoking this command open the Select HTML File dialog box, where you can navigate to the file to which you want to link. The main advantage that the Link to Existing File command has over using the Point to File icon is that you can easily link to files located somewhere other than your local site. Linking to files outside your local root folder is not advised, however. Instead, strongly consider the option to copy the file into your local root folder if you plan to link to it.

We haven't explicitly described the process, but you can link to a new file in a similar manner. Doing this creates a link in the selected file to a new document. The Link to New File command can be accessed from the Site menu or by right-clicking the selected file. The keyboard shortcut for this command is Ctrl+Shift+N. Doing this brings up the Link to New File dialog box, shown in Figure 14.5, where you can specify the filename, page title, and text for the link created. After you select OK, the file will be created in the same directory as the file it links to.

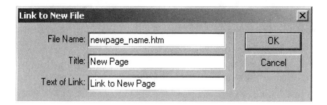

Figure 14.5   The Link to New File dialog box.

Changing Links

Once I was working on a project with a fellow who had done printed media publications for his entire career. This was his first experience publishing on the Internet. After we had finished the site and had made it public, he called me and urgently told me that we had spelled the CFO's name wrong. I calmly explained that this wasn't a problem and that I'd have it fixed within the hour. The urgency to rectify the typo is obvious, but I am still not sure if he realized how simple a task it was. If you're accustomed to doing printed media, publishing on the Web is a whole new ballgame. You can update, fix, and otherwise modify pages on the fly, rather than fixing a master copy, printing completely new material, and redistributing it.

This stands true not only with text within your Web pages, but for filenames as well. And as you've seen countless times before, Dreamweaver 4 helps make this process extremely quick and painless.

To modify the page a link points to from the Site Map, follow these steps:

1. Select the link that you want to modify.
2. Select Site/Change Link from the menu, or use the keyboard shortcut Ctrl+L.

You can also access the Change Link function by right-clicking the link and selecting Change Link from the context menu that appears.

3. This brings up the Select HTML File dialog box. You can now select the new file you want the old link to point to. Click Select when done.

4. After you select the new file, the Update Files dialog box appears, displaying a list of all the files in the site that should be updated.

5. You can immediately select Update to update all the links to this change. If you want to update only certain files, you can select them one at a time by holding the Ctrl button while you click them. After you have selected all the files that you want to update, click Update.

6. If you do not want to update the files, simply click Don't Update.

A similar command in Dreamweaver is the Change Link Sitewide command. To change all the links to a particular file, do the following:

1. Select the file for which you want to change the link.

2. Select Site/Change Link Sitewide.

3. The Change Link Sitewide dialog box appears with the path of the file that you want to change (see Figure 14.6). You also can simply select the Change Link Sitewide command without selecting a file, and then enter the file at this time into the Change All Links To text field.

4. Now select the file or path that you want to update your link references to. This path is input into the Into Links To text field.

5. Click OK. This brings up the Update Files dialog box. The rest of the procedure is essentially the same as that for modifying a single link.

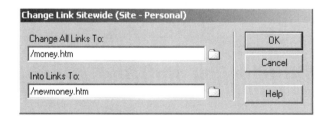

Figure 14.6   The Change Link Sitewide dialog box.

Deleting Links

Sometimes you will want to remove a link between pages. This is accomplished easily from the Site Map. Deleting a link does *not* remove the linked file. It simply removes the link to that file from the selected page. This can be slightly confusing the first couple times, but it gets easier with use. It is also worth noting that when a link is removed from the Site Map, the only way to re-create the link is either by relinking it through the Site Map or by editing the HTML document manually; you cannot "undo" a link deletion from the Site Map.

To remove a link in the Site Map, follow these steps:

1. Select the link that you want to remove.

2. Do one of the following:

    • Press the Delete key.

    • Select Site/Remove Link from the Menu.

    • Use the keyboard shortcut Ctrl+Shift+L.

    • Right-click the link and select Remove Link from the context menu that appears.

Modifying Page Titles

You can modify the page titles quickly from the Site Map as well. To do this, you need to ensure that you are viewing the page titles. Choosing Edit/Show Page Titles or using the keyboard shortcut Ctrl+Shift+T toggles this view.

When viewing the page titles, select a file. Next, click again on the page title text. This makes the title editable, as shown in Figure 14.7. You can do this "slow double-click" somewhat quickly, although doing it *too* quickly opens the file in the document window.

> **Note**
>
> You can also change the page title by selecting the file as previously described and then selecting File/Rename from the menu. Pressing F2 does this as well. F2 is a quick and typically standard method of renaming filenames and page titles via Dreamweaver's Site window.

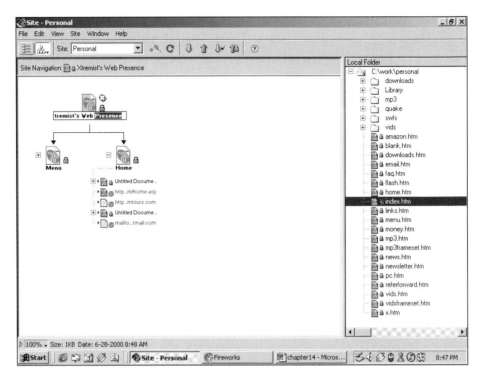

Figure 14.7   Editing page titles from the Site Map view.

Modifying the Site Map Home Page

Before going any further on this subject, I want to clarify that changing the home page used in the Site Map is *not* necessarily the home page of your site. It is simply the page used in the Site Map.

Dreamweaver 4 lets you change the existing home page to either an existing page or a completely new one, including non-HTML files such as an image or an .swf file. Select Site/New Home Page from the menu to create a new home page document. This brings up the New Home Page dialog box. You can enter the filename and page title of your new home page here. After creating this new page, you can re-create your links using the Link to Existing File command as well as the Point to File dragger. This process was discussed in the previous sections of this chapter.

To set an existing page as the new home page in the Site Map, select that file from the local Site window pane (you must be in Map and Files View mode to do this). Then select Site/Set as Home Page from the menu. This re-creates the Site Map with the newly defined home page and its links. You can also select the file in the Site window, right-click, and choose Set as Home Page.

A nice feature in Dreamweaver 4 is the capability to effectively preview the Site Map with a different home page without actually setting a new home page (see Figure 14.8). Do this by selecting View/View as Root from the menu or by using the keyboard shortcut Ctrl+Shift+R. You can also right-click the selected page that you want to preview as the home page to bring up the context menu. From here, select View as Root to change the Site Map layout. This changes the Site Navigation bar located just beneath the Site Window toolbar to show where this page is located in reference to the current home page. You can then click a file icon in the Site Navigation bar to move back up the site until you reach the home page again.

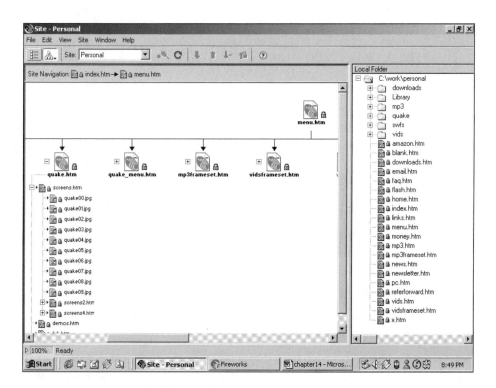

Figure 14.8   Temporarily setting another file as the home page.

Site Map View Options

My grandmother used to be the secretary for a nonprofit organization. One of her responsibilities was to create a monthly report to hand to the president. To do this, I bought and installed Microsoft Word 2000 on her computer. Every month without fail, I received multiple phone calls asking me to come over and stop Word from taking control of her documents. After she was released from the position, I began thinking, "What good do all the bells and whistles do if they are poorly implemented?" Not that I think Word 2000 is a poor program (I use it every day)—simply that just because a program *has* a feature doesn't mean that it should *make* you use it.

Macromedia has realized this while creating Dreamweaver 4. Not only does it include all the bells and whistles you can think of, but it also implements them in the nonintrusive, helpful, and optional manner that many will appreciate. Having said that, the Site Map is no exception. We have discussed already many of the attributes and options involved with the Site Map, but we need to cover a few others as well.

Hidden and Dependent Files

Even as structured and organized as the Site Map is, it can become cluttered from time to time. Dreamweaver 4 has two features that help combat this inevitability. They are the capability to hide a particular file and the capability to show and hide dependent files with a few simple clicks.

By default, all HTML files that are linked in your site are shown in the Site Map. Sometimes you might want to hide a particular file or link to free up viewing space. To set a file as hidden, select the file and then select View/Show/Hide Link from the menu. This link now disappears, as do all files linked in it, from the Site Map. The keyboard shortcut Ctrl+Shift+Y does this as well.

To view the files that you have marked as hidden, simply select View/Show Files Marked as Hidden from the menu. Hidden files are displayed in italics. From here, you can select the file and remove the hidden status of it by selecting Show/Hide Link from the View menu or by pressing Ctrl+Shift+Y while the file is selected.

The second feature, viewing dependent files, is disabled by default. Dependent files include linked images, style sheets that have been linked to, and other media file types. Essentially, any file that is linked to from within the HTML document that isn't HTML is considered a dependent file. Because they're not even files in the first place, email, FTP, and news links are a few of the links that aren't considered dependent files. To view dependent files, select View/Show Dependent Files from the menu.

Using Zoom with Your Site Map

Imagine for a minute that you are the Webmaster for Amazon.com, definitely one of the largest online retailers today. You have thousands of pages to deal with. Now imagine viewing the Site Map in Dreamweaver 4. Scary, huh?

Luckily, Dreamweaver enables you to zoom in or out of your Site Map with relative ease. This enables you to view a larger portion of your site, with the sacrifice of smaller text. The Zoom button is located at the lower-left corner of the Site window (while viewing the Site Map). Selecting it displays the possible zoom percentages: 12%, 25%, 50%, 75%, and 100%, as shown in Figure 14.9.

Saving Your Site Map as an Image

Another "cool" capability of Site Map view is that you can save your Site Map as a bitmap (*.bmp) or ping (*.png) image. Printed out, this offers a constant and readily available visual resource reminding you of the site structure. This can be handy to show to

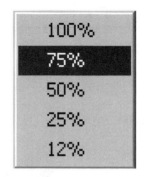

Figure 14.9
You can zoom to 12%, 25%, 50%, 75%, or 100%.

clients, giving them a basic and general feel for how their site will be structured and will look on paper, without having to create complex hand-drawn sketches.

Exercise 14.1   Saving Your Site Map as an Image

To save a copy of your Site Map, follow these steps:

1. Make sure that you're in Site Map view in the Site window with a site selected.
2. Select File/Save Site Map from the Site Window menu while in Site Map view.
3. Navigate to the location where you want to save the image. Then enter a filename to save the image. See Figure 14.10 for an example.

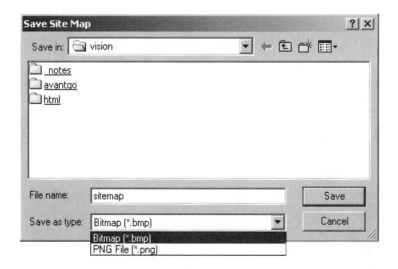

Figure 14.10   Selecting a location to save your Site Map image.

4. From the Save As Type pull-down menu, select the type of file to create. You can create either a .bmp or a .png file.

5. Click Save.

After you have saved the Site Map to a file, you can open and edit it in an image editor. You can also attach the image to an email message or print it. The image dimensions are calculated by Dreamweaver and vary according to the size of the Site Map.

Tip

One of the first things I do after saving a Site Map is open it in Fireworks (www. macromedia.com/software/fireworks/) and export it as a .gif file using Fireworks' image optimization features. This reduces the file size of the image so that I can email it to others easily.

Checking Links

You know the frustration you feel when you're visiting a pretty cool site and you get the famous "404—File not found" error? Yeah, it really takes away from the experience, doesn't it? Don't worry, though, Dreamweaver ensures that you know of every dead link before the rest of the world does.

You can check links one file at a time, check several files or folders at a time, or check the entire site in one massive sweep. The Dreamweaver Check Links function reports three types of possible problems:

- **Broken links**. These are files that have links located internally that don't contain the proper path for the link to work correctly—that is, links to files that are contained in the same site. When a broken link is reported, it means that Dreamweaver could not find the file in the path specified by the link. Sometimes designers use a # symbol as a link to make an object "clickable" but not go anywhere. This is called a null link, and it is used to attach behaviors and events to objects on the page. For example, this would be used when dynamically showing or hiding layers. A better reference now is to replace # with javascript:;. This type of fake link will appear in the external links section. Using a JavaScript fake (or real) link prevents the page from reloading when it's clicked. This can be useful to keep the positioning the same when clicking a link, rather than having the page jump back to the top.

- **External links**. External links are perhaps the most notorious for creating broken images and 404 errors. These are files that are located outside your site. A Web site's Other Resources section has many external links that link to manufacturers' Web sites. External links are displayed so that you are aware of the possible problems associated with them. Note that a link on the external links list does not mean that the link is broken; it simply means that it's beyond the scope of Dreamweaver's file management system.

- **Orphaned files**. These are files that have no incoming links pointing to them. Typically these files are older versions and aren't in use anymore. You can generally safely delete these files. Note, however, that with the extensibility Dreamweaver provides, it is not uncommon to have orphaned files that are really required. Drew McLellan's Open Picture Window Fever! behavior does exactly that. Be careful to make sure that orphaned files aren't necessary before deleting them.

To check the links in a single document, do the following:

1. Save the file before checking its links.
2. Select File/Check Links from the menu, or press Shift+F8. From the Site window, you also can right-click on the file and select Check Links/Selected Files/Folders from the context menu.
3. You can check multiple files and folders in the same manner as discussed previously.

To check the links of your entire site, follow these steps:

1. Save all open documents.
2. Select Site/Check Links Sitewide, or press Ctrl+F8. You also can check the links of the entire site by right-clicking any file or folder and selecting Check Links/Entire Site from the context menu.

After checking your links, the Link Checker dialog box appears (see Figure 14.11). You can select any of the three type of links reported with the pull-down menu at the top. On the left of the box, the file that has the problematic link is displayed. To the right is the specific link that caused the issue. The Orphaned Files section doesn't have a second column because there is no link associated with it.

From here you can either close the Link Checker box or save the list as a tab-delimited text file. This saves all three link types as one file. You can then import the list into a page by using the File/Import/Import Tabular Data option.

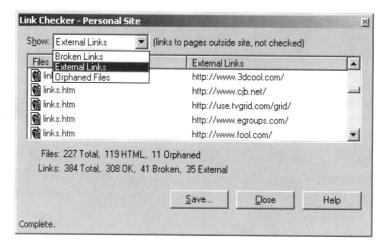

Figure 14.11   After checking the links, you can view all the broken, external, or orphaned links.

Tip

Sometimes I lose track of the Link Checker dialog box. This is because although the box appears in the Site window initially (if you are currently viewing the Site window), it moves to the document window if you switch from the Site window or even click the menu. The only way to get back to the Link Checker box is to switch to the document window. It may even be necessary to open a document if there isn't one currently open.

Fixing Links

Two methods exist for fixing broken and external links (if they actually need fixing). Both are accessed via the Link Checker dialog box (see Figure 14.12). The first way is to double-click the filename of the file with the broken or external link. This opens the file in a document window and highlights the suspect link. If your Property Inspector is active (select Window/Properties, or press Ctrl+F3), the link also is highlighted in the Link or Src section of this inspector. You can then manually type the correct reference or use the folder icon to select a file.

The second method is probably the quickest and easiest, if you know your site well. From the Link Checker dialog box, click once on the link in question (in the right column). This makes the link manually editable. If you're currently troubleshooting the broken links section, a folder icon appears that enables you to easily browse to the correct link. If there are other broken links with the same reference, Dreamweaver asks you if it should update them as well.

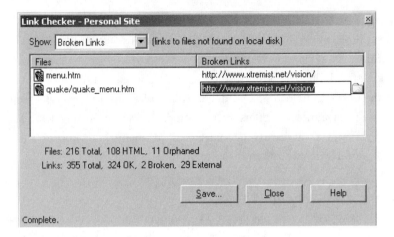

Figure 14.12   Editing a broken link after checking the links.

Note

If you are using the file Check In/Check Out system on your site, Dreamweaver attempts to check out the file so that it can change the link. If it cannot do so, Dreamweaver displays a warning message and leaves the link as broken.

Changing Links

Just how does Dreamweaver update alike broken links after you change just one of them in the Link Checker? Sometimes you may want to change the reference to a particular page in every single document on your site. Dreamweaver offers an extremely straight-forward and easy method for accomplishing this.

To change the link reference of a particular file sitewide, do the following:

1. Select a file in your local site.

2. Select Site/Change Link Sitewide from the menu.

3. Either manually type a link into the Into Links To text box, or use the folder icon to navigate to a new link.

All references to that file will change to reference the new file. The addressing method used for each link remains the same (if the link was site root-relative, it remains so with the changed link). Doing this removes any reference in your site to the selected file, thus making it an orphan. You can delete this file without creating any broken links.

Keeping Your Local and Remote Sites Synchronized

One of the problems Web developers tend to run across after uploading the initial version of their site is that they become confused as to which location has the most current version of each file. The problem is compounded when working as a team. At least if you're the only one uploading and downloading files, you can typically try to keep track yourself. Dreamweaver offers two methods for synchronizing your local and remote sites. First, we will discuss the "old-fashioned" manual method. We will then go over the powerful Synchronize command to do this automatically.

Select Newer Local/Remote Files

You can use the Select Newer Local/Remote commands to manually synchronize your sites. This function compares the modified date on the local machine for each file with the modified date on the remote server for each file. Then it determines which files are located on either site and selects them. To fully synchronize your site, you need to use both functions. To select the newer files on the local site, select Edit/Select Newer Local from the menu. Likewise, to select the new files located on the remote site, select Edit/Select Newer Remote.

Tip

It's important that your sites (both on the remote server and the local machine) maintain accurate time; otherwise, you might inadvertently select older files that Dreamweaver thinks are newer.

After you run one of the commands, all the newer files on that location of the site will become selected in the Site window. If you select the newer local files, pressing the Put button (or pressing Ctrl+Shift+U) uploads them to the remote site. This completes half of the synchronization. The other half occurs by selecting the newer files located on the remote server. After these are selected, you can press the Get button (or press Ctrl+Shift+D) to move those files to your local copy of the site. After doing this, both sites will have the newest versions of each file.

I offer two cautionary statements of advice when using this method to synchronize your site:

- Because Dreamweaver highlights only files that are newer, those that are exactly the same (that is, those that have the same modification date and time) will not be selected. If your site is already synchronized, no files will be selected after running both of these commands. You might think that nothing happened, but it's just that the sites are already up-to-date.

- Because Dreamweaver checks all the files of a site, the Select Newer Remote command could take a long time. This will be the case especially on slower connections to the remote server. Sometimes this might be mistaken as Dreamweaver "freezing."

The Synchronizing Command

The Synchronizing command introduced in Dreamweaver 3 is a much better way of synchronizing your files than the method of manually selecting newer files, discussed in the previous section. You can access the Synchronizing command by selecting Site/Synchronize from your menu. Part of the beauty and power of this command is that you can choose to synchronize as much or as little as you want. This means that you can synchronize just one folder, just one file, or the entire site. You can also choose to remove any file on the remote site that is not located on the local site copy, or vice versa. This is not possible with the previous method.

> **Note**
>
> Remember that the Synchronize command enables you to synchronize a single file, multiple files, or the entire site. If you don't want to process the entire site, you will need to select the files (in the local Site window pane) that you want to synchronize before proceeding.

To synchronize your site using the Synchronize command, follow these steps:

1. After you select the files to synchronize (if not process the entire site), select Site/Synchronize from the menu. This brings up the Synchronize Files dialog box seen in Figure 14.13.

2. From the Synchronize pull-down menu, select to update the entire site or just a group of files.

3. From the Direction pull-down menu, select what you want to do from these options:

   - Put only those files that are newer locally to the remote site. (You will only send files.)

   - Get only those files that are newer remotely to the local site. (You will only receive files.)

   - Synchronize both the local and the remote site with each other. (You will both send and receive files.)

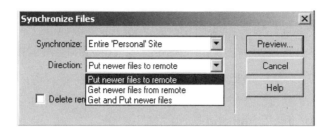

Figure 14.13   Choose to either put, get, or put and get files.

4. If you select Get and Put Newer Files from the Direction menu, go straight to step 5. If you selected one of the other two directions, you can specify one additional option. If you are putting newer files to the remote site, you can select to delete remote files not on the local drive by checking the appropriate box. If you are getting newer files from the remote site, you have the option to delete any local files that aren't on the remote site. To select the delete option, check the box on the lower left. Remember that deleting a file is final and can't be undone. Use this option with great care.

Note

> When synchronizing with the Direction option Get Newer Files from Remote, you can delete files locally that aren't found on the remote server. You should be extremely careful with this option, though. Most designers keep their source files (such as Photoshop *.psd files or Fireworks *.png files) in folders within their local site. However, they typically don't upload these files to the remote site when they publish. Be sure to read the changes proposed in the Synchronize dialog box (after you select Preview from the Synchronize Files dialog box) before actually running the command. Time spent here could save you from spending much more time fixing a hasty decision. If you accidentally delete some local files that you didn't mean to, you still have a chance to salvage them. Rather than being permanently deleted from your hard drive, they are placed in the Recycle Bin (the Trash Can on a Macintosh system). You can restore the files from there, if you want.

5. Press Preview. This processes your files for synchronization and opens the Synchronize dialog box (see Figure 14.14). This is an effective preview of what will happen when you click OK. This box shows you how many files are to be updated, the action that will be taken on that file (get, put, or delete), and the filename of the file.

6. By default, all check boxes are checked in the Action column of this dialog box. Deselecting a check box removes the file from being processed. This enables you to ensure that you know exactly what is happening and lets you change what Dreamweaver does, just in case you know something that it doesn't.

7. Press OK.

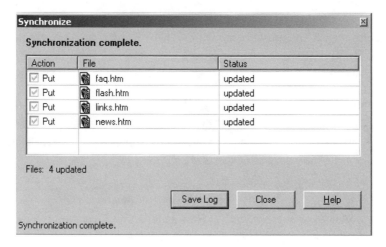

Figure 14.14   After you have completed the synchronization, you will be able to see the actions that Dreamweaver performed.

Dreamweaver shows the progress of the synchronization and, after it's done, enables you to save a text file of the procedure for future reference. You then can import the list into a page by using the File/Import/Import Tabular Data option.

Note

> Even though the Synchronize command is accessed via the Site window, it seems to prefer the document window. If you aren't sure where the synchronize dialog boxes have disappeared to, try switching to (or opening) an HTML document. This most likely will solve the problem.

Find/Replace Queries

Recall the story of the CFO's name being misspelled on a project that I once did (in the "Changing Links" section of this chapter). Imagine if it had been referenced on multiple pages incorrectly. You wouldn't typically think to make names their own library items, so you would need to find every instance of the typo and replace it with the correct spelling. This exact situation brings us to the next topic: performing Search and Replace queries in Dreamweaver.

Occasionally—well, okay, quite frequently—you will want to change a repetitive sentence or phrase in your pages. Although Dreamweaver offers link management, library items, and other features to cut down on the amount of effort needed for hand replacement, it's bound to happen. The Find and Replace dialog box, shown in Figure 14.15, can be as simple and easy to use as the word processor equivalent. Likewise, using regular expressions in your query, it can become as powerful as any other programming tool. There are a few extras because we're dealing with HTML, but if you've used another program's Find and Replace feature, you shouldn't have much trouble adapting to Dreamweaver's interface.

Before we discuss each search method in detail, you will want to know how to invoke the Find and Replace command as well as the commonalities that exist between each search method. To invoke a Find and Replace query, select Edit/Find and Replace from the menu, or use the keyboard shortcut Ctrl+F. Lastly, right-clicking anywhere in your code while in Code view opens a context menu where you can choose Find and Replace as well. This brings up the Find and Replace dialog box in which you will set up your query. Table 14.1 outlines the attributes of a Find and Replace query that are consistent regardless of the type of search performed.

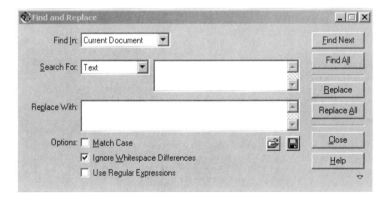

Figure 14.15   Opening the Find and Replace dialog box.

Table 14.1   Find and Replace Attributes

Attribute	Options
Find In	Four options exist here, specifying where to perform the search. Current Document works only if the document window was active before selecting Find and Replace. The name of the document will appear to the right when selected. Entire Local Site searches the whole site. The site name that will be checked is listed to the right. Selected Files in Site searches multiple files for you. Use Ctrl+click to select multiple files in the Site window. Finally, you can also search a folder. When you select this, a text box appears to the right that enables you to manually enter a path. You can also click the folder icon to graphically browse to the folder that you want to search. This searches all files in that folder, including subfolders.

Search For	You have four options to search for. Source Code searches the HTML code. Text searches only text and completely ignores any HTML code. This also ignores code that would separate a text string. For example, "The dog was \<i\>adopted\</i\> by a very nice family." would be "The dog was adopted by a very nice family."
	Text (Advanced) enables you to search for strings either inside or outside certain HTML tags. You can specify the string to be found, as well as whether it has to be (or can't be) found in a particular tag. Finally, Specific Tag allows a detailed search of HTML tags. This is used to add, remove, or change attributes of a particular tag. For example, this feature is very useful when you want to apply a style sheet to a page and need to remove all the \<font\> tags.
Match Case	Checking this causes Dreamweaver to report only instances of the string that exactly match the case of the string provided. In other words, checking this box makes the search case-sensitive.
Ignore Whitespace Differences	This treats all multiple spaces in your HTML as one single space. This option is not allowed if Use Regular Expressions is checked. You can explicitly write with regular expressions to treat multiple spaces as a single space.
Use Regular Expressions	When checked, this enables use of supported regular expressions in your search. The "Using Regular Expressions" section, later in this chapter, explains this feature further.

After you have established your options, you should know the various ways of searching for the string. Dreamweaver 4 provides two methods of searching and two options of searching for each (four total commands):

- **Find Next.** Selecting this starts at the top of the document and scans down it according to the type of search and the search string. If you are searching multiple documents, the search continues to the next document after it has completed the one that it's currently scanning.

  Selecting this button locates the first occurrence of the string. To keep searching, click the Find Next button again. Continue doing this to continue searching to the end of the document(s).

- **Find All.** Selecting this automatically scans the entire document, folder, or site, depending upon which option you choose. A good way of thinking of it is that Dreamweaver automatically presses the Find Next button for you when it finds a match. Don't worry, though—Dreamweaver keeps track of all instances of the string and reports them at the end of the search.

After Dreamweaver is finished scanning, the Find and Replace dialog box expands to list each file and occurrence of the string that it found. From here, you can double-click a file to open it with the Code Inspector active. Dreamweaver then selects that specific occurrence of the matched string.

- **Replace.** Selecting this the first time is exactly the same as pressing Find Next. However, if the Replace button is pressed additional times, it will replace the highlighted string with whatever is in the Replace With text box and then scan for the next occurrence in the file(s).

Tip

If you know that you want to replace a few of the strings you're searching for but not all of them, I have found it a good idea to use the Find All and Replace commands cooperatively. First, you find all the occurrences of the string that you want to replace. Next, double-click each reference in the search results list. This opens the document to that instance for your review.

If it's an instance that you want to replace, make sure that the reference to that occurrence is still selected in the search results list, and click Replace. This lets you replace any number of the string's occurrences.

- **Replace All.** Selecting this opens a cautionary prompt that informs you that doing this is an irreversible action: It cannot be undone. This automatically changes all instances of the string you're searching for with whatever is in the Replace With text box.

I have found that it's a good idea to use the Find All command and then the Replace All command. This at least enables you to skim over the occurrences before taking this action. This gives you the opportunity to pick out any obvious errors in your search pattern and adjust your search before replacing all instances of the string.

Tip

Although you can't undo the Replace All action, you can simply do another Find and Replace with all options the same, except that the Search For and Replace With fields are switched.

Now that we've discussed the similarities of each search type, we can describe the differences in each. The process is generally the same as described previously, but each search type has specific differences that should also be covered.

Searching Source Code and Text

Source code searches enable you to search both the text displayed in the browser and the HTML tags that are in the page. Similarly, text searches simply search the text that will be displayed in the browser.

To search through the source code or text, use one of the methods listed in the previous section to initiate the Find and Replace dialog box. Next, select Source Code or Text from the Search For pull-down menu. In the text box directly to the right, enter the string that you want to search for. If you want to replace instances of that string with another, enter the replacement string in the Replace With text box. Use the methods described previously to search for and replace (if desired) the string(s) entered.

Searching using the Source Code option tells Dreamweaver to scan through the document(s) for the string, whether it's located in regular text *or* an HTML tag. For example, the search string `large tank` would return an occurrence found in the ALT attribute of the <IMG> tag as well as the "Large tank" part of the string `Large tanks` of the second sentence (see Figure 14.16). If the search were looking solely for text, only the second occurrence would have been returned. This is displayed in the following code:

```
<p><img src="sherman_dozer.gif" alt="The Sherman Dozer was a Large Tank">
</p>
<p>The Sherman Dozer was one of the larger tanks used in World War II.
Large tanks like this were built for combat, but this particular model
also served as an engineer bulldozer.</p>
```

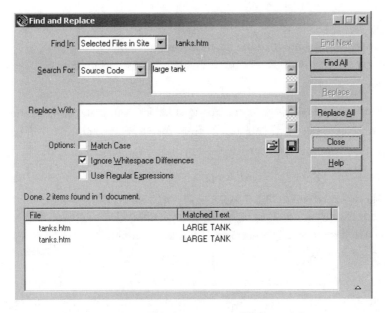

Figure 14.16   Running a normal search for instances of "large tank."

To then replace the instances of "large tank" with the string "small tank," simply type the replacement text in the Replace With text box, as shown in Figure 14.17.

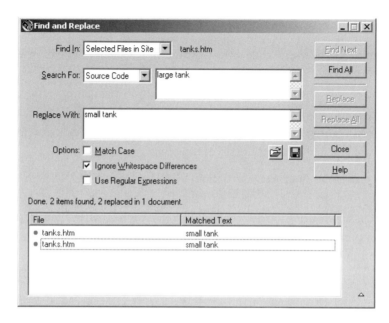

Figure 14.17   Replacing all instances of "large tank" with "small tank."

Advanced Text Searches

Advanced text searches enable you to explicitly search within or outside specific tags (even specifying attributes that the tag must have or cannot have). These are similar to normal text searches with the exception that you cannot specify the tags that you want to include or exclude.

Use one of the methods listed in the previous section to initiate the Find and Replace dialog box. Next, select Text (Advanced) from the Search For pull-down menu. In the text box directly to the right, enter the string that you want to search for.

Notice the + and – buttons just below the Search For area. This is where you get to specify the tag that you want to target. You can choose whether the string should be located inside or outside a tag. You then choose which tag this will affect. If you click the + button, you can further specify other parameters for limiting the search. You can also use this to specify another tag entirely, limiting or expanding your search further.

If you want to replace instances of that string with another, enter the replacement string in the Replace With text box. Use the methods described previously to search and replace (if desired) the string(s) entered.

Specific Tag Searches

Searching for specific tags ignores all text outside HTML tags. This search type is specifically designed to modify attributes of tags. It can do other things as well, such as add, change, and remove tags, or add text before or after the tag. In my experience, most searches for specific tags are done to modify tag attributes.

Use one of the methods listed in the previous section to initiate the Find and Replace dialog box (see Figure 14.18). Next, select Text (Advanced) from the Search For pull-down menu. In the pull-down menu directly to the right, enter the tag that you want to search for. If you want to search for only that tag and you don't care about specific attributes, you can press the – button next to the Attribute field and skip the next paragraph.

Next you will want to create your list of rules for that tag. Do this by selecting an option from the pull-down list directly to the right of the + and – buttons. Options include With Attribute, Without Attribute, Containing, Not Containing, Inside Tag, and Not Inside Tag. You can use the + and – buttons after defining each rule to add or remove rules.

After you have built the list of rules needed for your search, you can begin the search using the methods described previously.

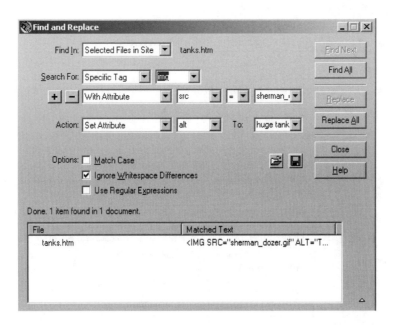

Figure 14.18   Setting up a specific tag replace search is rather complex and takes much forethought.

Using Regular Expressions

Regular expressions are used to test a string against a rigorously defined syntax. When using regular expressions in Dreamweaver 4's Search command, you use regular characters to define a rule, range, or position. For instance, if you are trying to locate all the phone numbers in a Web page but you don't know the actual number, you could use regular expressions to describe the pattern that phone numbers fit. You might also want to find all the email addresses in your source code. Again, you can use regular expressions to do this. You need to be careful and test your expressions rather than assume that you've written them correctly.

Because you use regular characters such as * and ? in regular expressions, you must have an escape character. This effectively disables that instance of the regular expression representation and uses the actual character meaning. This escape character is the backslash (\). For example, to search for the character * and not have it be defined as the beginning of input of a line, you would type *. Similarly, to escape the backslash character, you would type \\.

Table 14.2 lists some of the regular expressions that you can use in Dreamweaver. It's the same one that you'll find in Dreamweaver's documentation (and most any other Dreamweaver book).

Table 14.2   Regular Expressions in Dreamweaver

Expression	Meaning
^ I	Beginning of input of line. ^A matches *A* in "all for one," but not in "one for all."
$ I	End of input of line. $s matches the second *s* in "biscuits" but not the first.
* I	The preceding character zero or more times. om* matches "om" in "mom," "omm" in "mommy," and the *o* in "son."
+ I	The preceding character one or more times. om+ matches "om" in "mom" and "omm" in "mommy," but not the *o* in "son."
? I	The preceding character at most once. (That is, this indicates that the "sen" in "Andersen," and "Sn" in preceding character is optional.) so?e?n matches "son" in "Anderson,""Snack," but nothing in "Soon."
. I	Any single character except newline. r.n matches "Ran" and "run," but not "rain."

x|y |	Either *x* or *y*. `cat¦dog` matches either "cat" or "dog."
{n} |	Exactly *n* occurrences of the preceding `r{2}` matches the two *r*'s in "irre-character. sistible," but not "rounder."
{n,m} |	At least *n* and at most *m* occurrences `0{2,4}` matches the two 0's in of the preceding character. "00EEEE" and the three 0's in "000EEE", but not in "0e0e0e."
[abc] |	Any one of the characters enclosed in the brackets. You can specify a range of characters with a hyphen; for example, `[a-f]` is equivalent to `[abcdef]`. `[rslf]` matches the *r* and *l* in "real," the *f* and *r* in "forever," and the *s* and *f* in "self."
[^abc] |	Any character not enclosed in the brackets. You can specify a range of characters with a hyphen; for example, `[^a-f]` is equivalent to `[^abcdef]`. `[^els]` matches "who" but not "else" in "or else."
\b |	A word boundary (such as a space or carriage return). `\bc` matches the *c* in "cure," but nothing in "juice" or "electronic."
\B |	A nonword boundary. `\Bc` matches the *c* in "juice" or "electronic," but nothing in "cure."
\d |	Any digit character. Equivalent to `[0-9]`. `\d` matches the 2's in "R2D2," but nothing in "Skywalker."
\D |	Any nondigit character. Equivalent to `[^0-9]`. `\D` matches "skywalker" and the *R* and *D* in "R2D2."
\f |	Form feed.
\n |	Line feed.
\r |	Carriage return.
\s |	Any single whitespace character, including a space, tab, form feed, or line feed. `\sone` matches "one" in "is he the one?", but nothing in "someone's there!"
\S |	Any single non-whitespace character. `\Sone` matches "one" in "someone's there!", but nothing in "Is he the one?"
\t |	A tab.
\w |	Any alphanumeric character, including an underscore. Equivalent to `[A-Za-z0-9_]`. `r\w*` matches "running" in "running wildly" and both "ran" and "road" in "He ran down the road."
\W |	Any nonalphanumeric character. Equivalent to `[^A-Za-z0-9_]`. `\W` matches each space and the * in "*certain restrictions may apply."
Ctrl + Enter or Shift + Enter	Return character. Be sure to deselect the Ignore Whitespace Differences option when searching for this, if you're not using regular expressions. Note that this matches a particular character, not the general notion of a line break; for instance, it doesn't match a tag or a <p> tag. Return characters appear as spaces in the document window, not as line breaks.

Exercise 14.2   Performing a Find and Replace Query

For this exercise, use the files located in the Chapter 14 folder on the CD provided with this book.

1. Copy all the files and folders off the Chapter 14 folder of the CD onto your hard drive, and create a site definition for them in Dreamweaver.

2. You will add links to the faq.htm and search.htm pages. They will be placed on the right side of the navigation bar at the top of the page. Look at Figure 14.19 to see that the pages currently don't have the links to these pages.

Figure 14.19   You need to create links to faq.htm and search.htm on the main navigation bar.

3. A casual hint is to do a Find All search first. Then after you've perfected the search string, add the replacement string Open the Find and Replace dialog box.

4. Search the source code of the entire local site for the string "About our Company." Also select the Match Case and Ignore Whitespace options. You should get 15 items found in 15 documents, similar to the results shown in Figure 14.20.

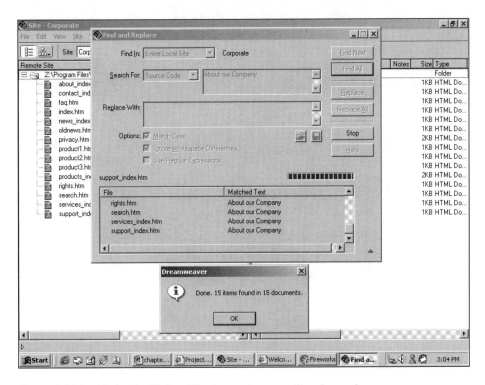

Figure 14.20 Notice the Find and Replace options as well as the result.

5. At this point, you can double-click each instance to see that specific occurrence, but you can now enter the replacement code to add the new links. The code is as follows:

```
About our Company</a> ¦ <a href="faq.htm">FAQ</a> ¦ <a
href="search.htm">Search
```

You must include the string that you've searched for ("About our Company") because whatever you put in the Replace With field will overwrite the original string. When you've entered the code, select Replace All. Figure 14.21 shows your screen when that is done.

6. View the pages again in a Web browser. You should now have links to the FAQ and Search page throughout your site. With one swift action, you have updated 15 pages.

The nice thing about this exercise is that if you mess up, you can just copy the files onto your hard drive again. So don't be afraid to learn how to use this feature even further than we've described here.

Keep this exercise available, though—you will use it in the next two exercises as well.

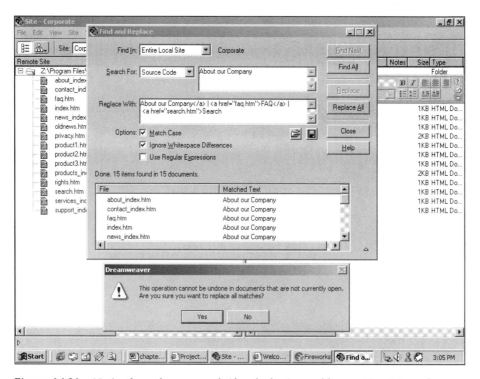

Figure 14.21   Notice the replacement code if you're having problems getting it to work.

Saving and Loading Queries

Occasionally you will find yourself running the same searches repeatedly. Defining all the parameters of a search or a Find and Replace search can be a tedious and complicated task. Luckily, Dreamweaver will let you save and load saved search patterns.

Your queries are stored in the Configuration\Queries subfolder of your Dreamweaver directory. They are XML documents and, as such, can be modified by hand instead of being loaded in Dreamweaver and modifying and overwriting the original query. For most people, it is much safer and easier to leave the XML code to Dreamweaver.

You can save either a search pattern or a find-and-replace pattern. Searches have the file extension .dwq, and Find and Replace searches have the extension .dwr. Don't worry, though; Dreamweaver appends the appropriate extension to the filename so that you won't even need to worry about it.

To save your current query, follow these steps:

1. Click the Save Query button, which has a picture of a floppy disk. See Figure 14.22 to see where this button is located.

2. Type a filename into the File Name text field of the Save Query dialog box. Remember that Dreamweaver will automatically add the extension to your query, so you don't need to add it here.

   It should go without saying, but the filename that you choose here should reflect the intention of the query. This is useful when you have saved multiple queries and want to load one.

3. Finally, click Save. This enables you to load the query at a later time with a few simple clicks.

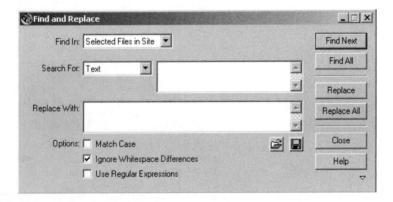

Figure 14.22   Location of the Save Query and Load Query buttons.

To load a saved query, do the following:

1. Click the Load Query button. This button has a picture of a folder. See Figure 14.22 to see where this button is located.

2. The default directory shown is the same as the default directory for when you save a query. If the query file is located elsewhere, you will need to navigate to it.

3. Either double-click or select the file and press Open. This loads your query options into the Find and Replace dialog box.

It's a good idea to double-check the query after it's loaded. It's a good idea to double-check *anything* that will have massive repercussions on your site. If there are changes to be made to your query, you will be able to make them and then replace the original query.

Running Site Reports

Running site reports is a good way to put the finishing touches on your HTML documents. You can get information on combinable nested font tags, missing alt text, redundant nested tags, removable empty tags, and untitled documents. You can also build reports on the status of Design Notes as well as see all the files checked out by a particular team member.

You can run a report on one or many of the report types. Each of the HTML reports is fairly self-explanatory. The two workflow reports—Checked Out By and Design Notes—are a little more complicated. Both the workflow reports and HTML reports are further defined in Table 14.3; their locations are illustrated in Figure 14.23.

Table 14.3   Workflow Reports and HTML Reports

Report	Meaning
Checked Out By	When this is selected or checked, the Report Settings button in the lower-left part of the Reports window is enabled. Click it to bring up a new dialog box where you can enter the name that you want to search for. This search is case-sensitive; however, you do not need to enter the entire string. For example, if you are searching for Jeffrey Stewart, you can simply enter Jeff, Jeffrey, or Stewart.
Design Notes	When this is selected or checked, the Report Settings button in the lower-left part of the Reports window is enabled. Click it to bring up a new dialog box where you can enter the Design Note and Design Note status to search for, as well as the condition that must be met. For example, if you are searching for all Design Notes that have the status of Complete, you would enter Status in the first column and select Contains (selecting Is would also work and would allow only an exact match for the sought status). In the third column, you enter the value you're searching for.
Combinable Nested FONT Tags	These are reports on nested font tags that could be combined. These are font tags nested around the same text, with different attributes. For instance, the following font tags could be combined: <font color="00CCFF"><font size="3">The text that will be displayed</font></font>
Missing Alt Text	This reports any image tag that does not have alternative text defined. This is the text displayed in place of a picture when the visitor has a browser download pictures manually. This option is also used in text-only browsers. This feature is particularly useful when trying to bring sites into compliance for the visually impaired.

Redundant Nested Tags	This option builds a report based on whether a tag is contained within another tag of itself and can be removed. For example, the following code would be reported as a redundant nested tag: \<b\>you will have to explain yourself to \<B\>your parents,\</b\> not me!\</b\>
Removable Empty Tags	These are tags that have no content in them. For example, if the following were in your document, it would be reported: \<table\>\</table\>. Generally these types of things will appear if you do heavy editing of the raw HTML in Code view.
Untitled Documents	This builds a report based on your HTML document(s) page titles. It reports no title and duplicate titles, as well as a title of Untitled Document, the default title that Dreamweaver assigns a document when it's created.

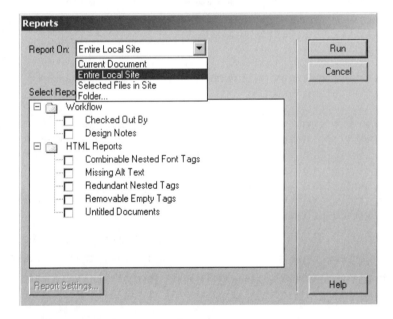

Figure 14.23   You have a lot of reports to choose from.

Tip

The Reports dialog box and results box tend to like the document window more than the Site window. If you ever lose track of them, either switch to an open document or open one and see if you can find them there.

To run a report, follow these steps:

1. Select Site/Reports from the menu. The Reports dialog box appears.

2. Select which documents to process with the Report On pull-down list. You can select to report on the current document (if a document is currently open), the entire local site, selected files (from the Site window), or a specific folder (this searches files in the folder, plus files in any subdirectory of this folder). If you choose the option for a specific folder, you will be able to browse to that folder.

3. You can now select one or more reports to build. Do this by simply clicking on the box to the left of the report name. Reports with checks next to them will be run.

4. Click Run to have Dreamweaver begin running the checked reports.

5. After this is finished, the Results window appears in the document window (see Figure 14.24). The Results window displays the report results. This window has three columns—the first displays the filename in question, the middle displays what line number (if applicable) caused the report to log that file, and the final column displays a short description about why the file was flagged.

Tip

You can sort the results list by clicking a column header. This alphabetically sorts the results for that particular column. If the results are ordered from A to Z in the first column, clicking it again reverses the order (Z to A).

6. You can either open a file to the location of the reported event or save the report for later use (or both).

7. To open a file for edit, double-click the filename. You can also select the filename and then click Open from the results window. This opens the file in Code and Design view (unless you're in Code view, in which case the view remains the same).

8. If you want to save the results for later, you can do so by clicking Save Report. This enables you to save the report as an XML document, which you can format into a Web page, database, or spreadsheet.

9. Close the results window when finished.

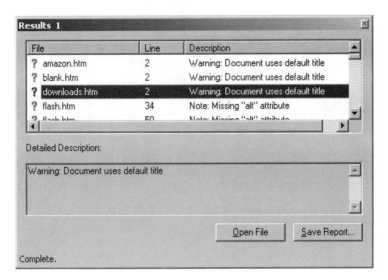

Figure 14.24   A sample result after running a site report.

Reports are great tools that make you aware of attributes in your HTML documents that, while not necessarily erroneous, will make your HTML cleaner and more complete if they're dealt with. A final note on site reports is that they may be run only on your local site.

Exercise 14.3   Running a Site Report

For this exercise, use the files located in the Chapter 14 folder on the CD provided with this book.

1. Copy all the files and folders off the Chapter 14 folder of the CD onto your hard drive, and create a site definition for them in Dreamweaver. If you have done one of the other exercises in this chapter, you can skip this step.

2. Select Site/Reports from the menu to bring up the Reports dialog box shown in Figure 14.25.

3. Run a report on the entire local site that entails all the HTML relative reports: Combinable Nested Font Tags, Missing Alt Text, Redundant Nested Tags, Removable Empty Tags, and Untitled Documents.

   The report should actually not return any results, similar to Figure 14.26. You might go back and remove the titles of certain pages, or otherwise "mess up" the code so that it's still functional but will respond to one of the reports.

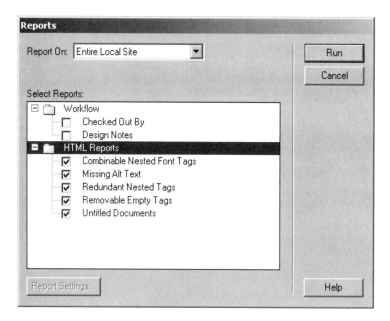

Figure 14.25   Notice the options selected for this report.

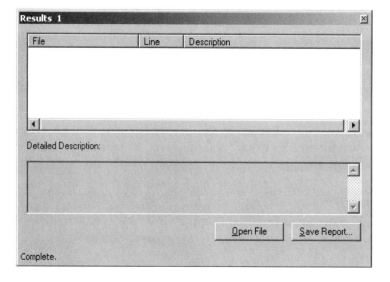

Figure 14.26   If all goes as planned, your results should look similar to this.

Checking Browser Compatibility

It can be very important to check your Web page's compatibility against target browsers. Depending on the type of site you're creating, as well as the audience, certain browsers could be excluded from this check. Today, version 2.0 browsers are not in use very often. Likewise, version 3.0 browsers are losing a lot of ground. A safe rule is to design for version 3.0 and up (again, depending on your target audience). In the near future, you should be safe designing mainly for version 4.0 and above browsers.

Instead of forcing you to install every possible browser on your system and doing an extensive test of your site in each, Dreamweaver checks the compatibility for you. It does this through what are called browser profiles. These are simply text files created that specify what is and isn't supported in a particular browser against which Dreamweaver will compare your pages. Dreamweaver comes with profiles for Netscape Navigator versions 2.0, 3.0, and 4.0, and Internet Explorer versions 2.0, 3.0, 4.0, and 5.0.

Tip

> You can download other profiles from the Macromedia Exchange
> (www.exchange.macromedia.com/). These profiles include a general HTML 4.01 Strict
> DTD and an HTML 4.01 Transitional DTD. These check your pages against standards set
> by the W3C.

Dreamweaver will let you check either a single page or an entire folder. Dreamweaver will not check scripts for browser compatibility. However, Dreamweaver can debug your scripts in those browsers. See Chapter 23, "Scripting and Markup Languages," for information on this feature. To run the Check Target Browsers command on a single file, do the following:

1. Save the current document that you're working on. Dreamweaver will check the last saved document available against its profiles, so make sure that your document is saved.

2. Select File/Check Target Browsers from the menu.

3. This brings up the Check Target Browsers dialog box, shown in Figure 14.27. By default, all browser profiles are selected. You can now select as many or as few as you want. To select more than one profile, hold down the Ctrl key as you click each browser name. To select a range of browsers, select the first browser and then select the last browser name while holding down the Shift key.

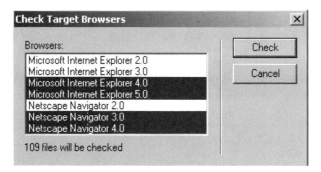

Figure 14.27   Checking the most popular Web browsers is always a good idea before publishing your site.

4. Press Check to begin checking your page.

5. After the check is complete, your primary browser opens and displays a nicely formatted page explaining any possible problems with your page (see Figure 14.28).

6. At this point, you can save your report by selecting File/Save (Save As) from the menu of your browser. It is a good idea to save the report now if you want to keep a copy of it because the report generates only a temporary HTML document.

Note

You can run the Check Target Browsers command only on files or folders located on the local site.

You can also check an entire folder against the browser profiles. Doing this includes all HTML documents in the selected folder, as well as any subfolder. From the Site window, simply select the file(s) or folder(s) that you want to check, and select File/Check Target Browsers from the menu. The remaining process is identical to the one described previously.

Tip

Because you can check an entire folder, selecting the local site root folder and running the Check Target Browsers command checks your entire site.

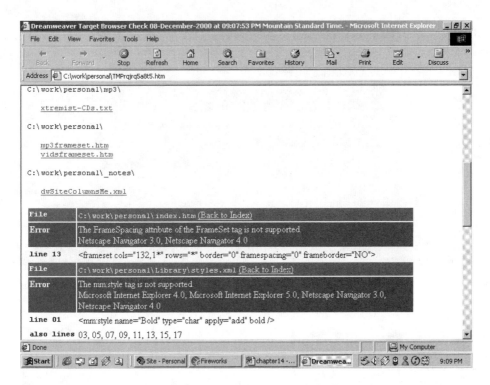

Figure 14.28   Some errors you can live with, but others are vitally important.

Exercise 14.4   Checking the Corporate Site in Target Browsers and Then Synchronizing with the Remote Server

For this exercise, use the files located in the Chapter 14 folder on the CD provided with this book.

1. Copy all the files and folders off the Chapter 14 folder of the accompanying CD onto your hard drive, and create a site definition for them in Dreamweaver. If you have done one of the other exercises in this chapter, you can skip this step.

2. Select the root folder on the local site in the Site window.

3. Select File/Check Target Browsers from the menu. This brings up the Check Target Browsers dialog box, shown in Figure 14.29.

4. Select Internet Explorer 4, Internet Explorer 5, Netscape 3, and Netscape 4 from the list. To select multiple items, hold the Ctrl button while clicking on each list element.

5. Select Check. This performs the Browser Check.

   You might get a few errors returned, similar to those in Figure 14.30. Do not worry about them. If you look carefully, you'll see that they're related to Dreamweaver-specific code and not code that Web surfers will ever see or need.

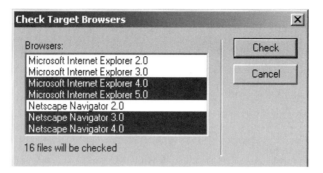

Figure 14.29   Select the four browsers that are selected here.

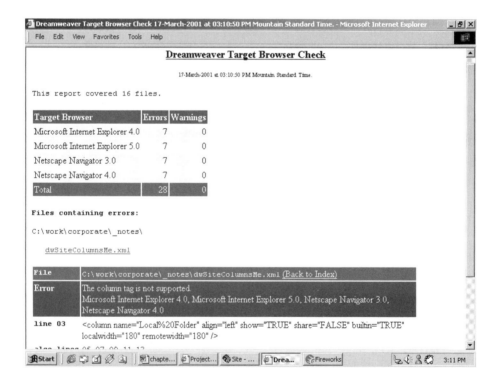

Figure 14.30   Don't worry if you get errors similar to these.

6. Now synchronize your local and remote sites. If you haven't set up a remote site for this exercise or a previous one, do it now. After you've done that, select Edit/Select Newer Local from the menu. This selects all the files that you need to upload to the remote site. You can also use the Synchronize feature if you want, but because this site is extremely small, I suggest using the method already described.

7. Press the Put button. This uploads the selected files to the remote site.

Checking Download Times

Another important consideration is the length of time that it takes for your pages to load. All the flashy graphics and "killer" design in the world won't matter if nobody waits around long enough to see it! Dreamweaver provides a handy download time estimator, located in the lower-right portion of the document window. On the left is the current size of the document. This includes any graphics that are embedded in the page, not just the HTML code. On the right is the estimated time that it would take a visitor to download your page. This time is calculated using the Connection Speed value specified in the Status Bar section of your Preferences. This is covered in further detail in Chapter 2.

Tip

Paul Strange of Level 67 LLC (www.level67.net/), a backend Web development, design, and data availability company, gives the following advice when checking your download times:

"You should tune your site to start displaying information within 8 seconds, no matter what the bandwidth of the user. The entire page should be up in 15 to 20 seconds. Any longer than that, and you start losing viewers."

Those are definitely words to live by.

The type of site you're designing will have a large influence on the data rate you specify. A corporate intranet site would probably allow a faster connection speed, such as 1500Kbps (T1), but a site destined for the Internet would require a speed about 50 times less than that. Figuring on an average 28.8Kbps or 33.6Kbps connection should suffice, in most instances.

Note

The time to download that Dreamweaver calculates is under ideal circumstances. Real download times will vary significantly.

Summary

The main focus of this chapter is to become comfortable with using Dreamweaver's site management tools. We discussed the Site window, including using and configuring the Site Map. We also talked about checking links, keeping your sites up-to-date through the Synchronize feature, and using the Find and Replace command. You learned how to create site reports and how to tackle site-publishing issues such as browser compatibility and page download times.

Chapter 15

Workplace
Collaboration

So far in this unit, we've learned a great

deal about managing, publishing, and

maintaining your site. This chapter focuses

on working with others effectively to

build, publish, and maintain a site.

You will be exposed to new features in Dreamweaver, such as site assets and source-control software integration, including the Visual SourceSafe and WebDAV integration. You will also learn how Design Notes can be set up to efficiently communicate between coauthors without immediate interaction. We will also discuss Dreamweaver's file Check In/Check Out system, which offers a degree of built-in access control. The following is a list of some of the main things we'll talk about:

- How to understand and use site assets

- How to check files in and out

- Source and version control integration

- How to effectively utilize and manipulate Design Notes

- How to run and understand site reports

Note

It will serve you well to understand the concepts discussed in the previous two chapters; their topics are the basis upon which this chapter builds.

Site Assets

New to Dreamweaver 4, the Assets panel keeps track of and enables you to easily update or insert certain elements used in the site, such as images, colors, media files (Flash, Shockwave, and so on), and scripts. This is particularly helpful if you plan to reuse one of these items on many pages throughout your site. The Assets panel, shown in Figure 15.1, organizes items by the *type* of element rather than by the hierarchical directory structure used in the site window. The Assets panel uses your site cache, so it quite literally contains all the elements in each of the categories that follow.

Note

Other types of "assets" exist in a site; however, only the files described in the bulleted list are displayed in the Assets panel.

- **Images.** These are image files such as gif, jpeg, or png contained in your site. (For information on handling and using images, see Chapter 6, "Working with Images.") These are image files that are in your site, regardless of whether they are currently linked to in a document.

- **Colors.** These are all the colors used in your site, including background colors as well as text and link colors.

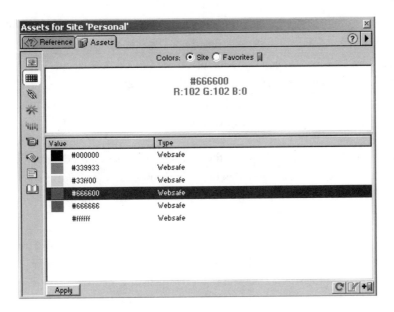

Figure 15.1   The Assets panel.

- **URLs.** These are external URLs found linked to by documents in your site. These include HTTP, HTTPS, FTP, JavaScript, local file, email, and gopher links. (See Chapter 5, "Linking and Navigation," for more information on links and linking in your documents.)

- **Flash movies.** These are Flash movies found in your site. Only the swf files are listed here, not the fla source files or the .swt template files. (Chapter 18, "Animation with Flash," has more information on Flash usage.)

- **Shockwave movies.** These are Shockwave movies found in your site. (Chapter 20, "Inserting Media Objects," explains what these are in detail.)

- **QuickTime and MPEG movies.** These are movies in either Apple QuickTime or MPEG format. (Chapter 20 explains these media types in detail.)

- **Scripts.** These are JavaScript and VBScript files found in your site. Only independent script files are listed. JavaScript located in your pages is ignored. (Chapter 19, "JavaScripting with Dreamweaver," talks more about scripts, specifically JavaScript.)

- **Templates.** These are as frustrating as they are valuable to many users. When used correctly, templates provide an easy way to build and edit similar pages quickly and easily. Before relying too heavily on template-based design, be sure to spend time learning them inside and out. (Templates are discussed in the next chapter.)

- **Library.** Libraries are similar to templates in that you only change one instance to update many. These are typically small content elements that are used on many pages throughout a site. (Libraries are discussed in the next chapter.) This was the Library Palette in Dreamweaver 3.

The Templates and Library sections of the Assets panel behave a bit differently than the rest of them. These items are covered in depth in the next chapter. To move between sections in the Assets panel, simply click the appropriate button, found on the left side of the panel.

To open the Assets panel, click Window/Assets or press F11. The Assets panel uses the site cache to build the asset listing. Each time you run Dreamweaver and open the Assets panel, it must parse the site cache again to create the listing. As such, make sure that you have defined a site with site caching enabled. You can learn how to do this Chapter 13, "Site File and Organization."

The Assets panel is divided into two main subsections: Site and Favorites. To switch between the Site and Favorites sections, simply click the appropriate button at the top of the panel. The Site section lists *all* the assets in the entire site. This is also the default view of the Assets panel. As the name implies, the Favorites section is a custom-built listing of your favorite assets. This helps organize and reduce the clutter that the Site section will run into with larger, more complex sites. These views are available for all assets except for Templates and Library elements. If the assets for your site are not showing up, do the following:

1. Make sure that Site Cache is enabled in your site definition.
2. Make sure that Site is selected from the radio button, not Favorites.

Note

The Favorites section begins completely empty. You must build it up as you go. This can be a slow and tedious process, but it can result in large pay-offs in the end, depending on the structure of your site. Favorite assets are discussed further in the upcoming section "Your Favorite Assets."

You undoubtedly will want to refresh the Assets panel at some point. This is done every time you quit and restart Dreamweaver. However, if you exported an image from

Fireworks into the local site while Dreamweaver was running, you would need to refresh the Assets panel for the new image to appear in the listing.

If you have used Dreamweaver 4's site window to delete a file or remove the last instance of another asset (such as a URL or color), you must refresh the Asset panel listing. To do this, first ensure that you are viewing the site listing. Next, simply access the context menu by right-clicking an asset listed in the Asset panel, and select Refresh Site List from the menu. Another way to access this menu is by clicking the arrow pointing right, located in the upper-right corner of the Assets panel, and selecting Refresh Site List from that menu. The final (and easiest) way to do this is by clicking the Refresh Site List button located at the lower-left corner of the Assets panel.

If you have deleted a file outside Dreamweaver by using a program such as Windows Explorer or Finder, you must refresh the entire site cache as well as the assets listing. Using the same process described previously to access the context menu, or by using the arrow button in the upper-right corner, select Re-create Site List. Likewise, you can press Ctrl+Click for the Refresh Site List button in the lower-right corner of the Assets panel. Again, make sure that you're viewing the site assets rather than your Favorites when you want to do this.

You can preview your assets as well using the Assets panel. This helps keep track of various images and other assets fairly easy. To preview an asset, simply select it from the listing, as shown in Figure 15.2.

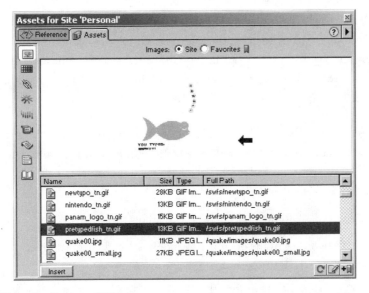

Figure 15.2   Previewing a GIF image.

Inserting Assets

The easiest way to insert an asset into your page is to drag the asset into the document while in Design view. Using the Insert button found in the lower-left corner of the Assets panel is another easy way to do this. Certain assets have extra capabilities. For instance, URLs can be applied to images, not just a selection of text. Templates are applied to the entire page.

Follow these steps to insert an asset:

1. Make sure that the Assets panel is currently in view. Clicking Window/Assets from the menu or pressing F11 toggles the Assets panel on and off.

2. Select either the site or Favorite Assets, and then select the asset category that you want to insert into the document (see Figure 15.3). Remember that every asset in the Favorites listing is also in the site listing, although commonly used assets should be moved to the Favorites listing (if you set it up this way yourself).

    There are no favorites for templates and library items. Also note that templates are not "inserted" into the page but are applied to an entire page. Applying a template is discussed later.

3. In the document window's Design view, position the cursor where you want the asset to be inserted. If you use the drag-and-drop method described later, this step is not necessary. Remember that even though you can "drag and drop" an asset into your page, it will not be placed in the exact spot where you drop it; it will simply be inserted in line with the current HTML on the page. To achieve absolute positioning when inserting an asset, place it in either a layer or a table.

4. When you are ready to insert the asset, select it from the panel and click Insert, as shown in Figure 15.3. You can also do this by right-clicking the asset to bring up the context menu or by using the arrow icon in the upper-right corner of the panel (see Figure 15.4).

Another way to insert an asset is by using a drag-and-drop method. In this manner, you click and drag the asset from the Assets panel onto your page where you want it inserted. If you are inserting a script and want it placed in the head content, make sure that View, Head Content is checked.

To apply a color or a URL to a selection of text, follow these steps:

1. In the Design view of the document window, select the text (or image, in the case of a URL) to which you want to apply the asset.

2. Select either the Colors or the URLs section of the Assets panel. Now select the asset that you want to apply to the selection.

3. Select Apply or right-click the asset to bring up the context menu, and then select
   Apply from the menu (see Figure 15.5). You can also click and drag the asset
   from the panel onto the selection.

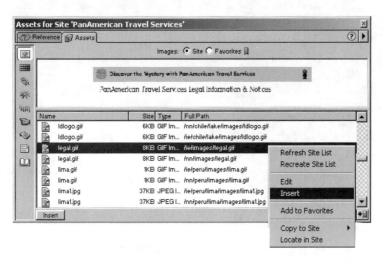

Figure 15.3   Selecting the asset to insert.

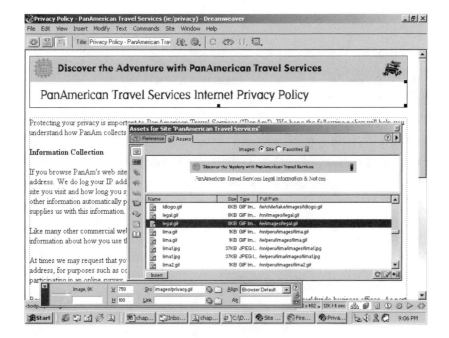

Figure 15.4   Selecting the asset with the context menu. Yup, it's that easy!

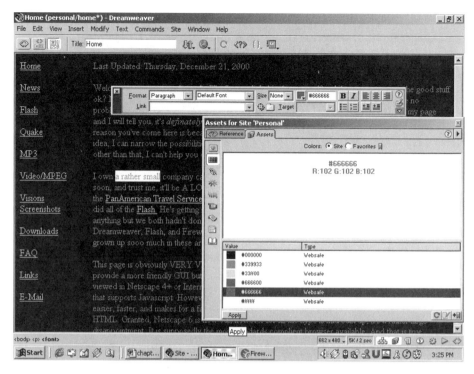

Figure 15.5   Applying a color asset to a selection of text.

To apply a template to the entire page, follow these steps:

1. Select the Template section of the Assets panel. Now select the template that you want to apply to the page.

2. Simply click Apply or drag and drop the template asset listing into the document window. This will apply the template to the entire page. You can learn more about templates in Chapter 16, "Templates and Libraries." Note: If you already have content on the page, you will be asked which editable region you would like to move the content into. Unfortunately, all the content must go in the same editable region initially, although it can be moved into other regions after the template has been applied.

Customizing the Assets Panel

You can customize the Assets panel in many ways. You can use the Favorite Assets feature to keep a separate list of the assets that you use most. If you have a company logo that you use on multiple pages, you can add the logo image to your Favorites listing and then you won't need to wade through all the images that you use only once or twice to get to the one that you use all the time. Favorites are so handy that they've been given their own section in this book. Read "Your Favorite Assets," later in this chapter, for more information about them.

Another method is to change the listing order of the assets. By default, the assets are listed in ascending alphabetical order (from A to Z) by name or value. You can change the order of the listing by clicking the column heading that you want to sort by. This sorts the assets ascending alphabetically by that column's attribute. Clicking a column header a second time sorts the listing alphabetically still, only in descending order (from Z to A). If you sort a column of numbers, such as file size, the ordering will be sorted numerically rather than alphabetically, from smallest to largest (ascending) initially.

You can also change the width of the columns in the Assets panel, as shown in Figure 15.6. To do this, simply hold your mouse pointer directly over the divider line that separates two columns. You will notice that the pointer changes to a double-headed arrow column with a left and right arrow extending from it. You can now click and drag the column to any width that you want. This typically holds true for most windows that use columns.

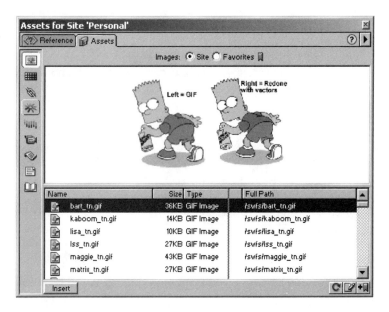

Figure 15.6   Resizing the Type column.

Using Assets Throughout Your Sites

Now that you have a better understanding of how to use the Assets panel, we should discuss the portability of those assets listed there You can copy assets and share them among various sites, or you can find a particular asset in the current site for easy uploading or downloading.

Note

> The Assets panel reflects the assets for the site that houses the document currently in focus. If your site window is set to display the files from site A, but you're currently working on a document from site B, the Assets panel will reflect the assets for site B.

We should also mention that the Assets panel is a document window panel, not a site window. This means that the assets that it displays belong to the currently active document, not to the current site in the site window. This may be a bit confusing at first, but it will become second nature over time.

To copy an asset from one site to another, follow these steps:

1. Select the asset(s) that you want to copy to another site. You can copy entire folders of assets in your Favorites listing.

2. Right-click to bring up the context menu. You can also access this menu by clicking the right arrow button located in the upper-right corner of the panel.

3. Select Copy to Site from this menu, as shown in Figure 15.7. A submenu will appear with a list of the possible sites to copy the asset(s) to. Choose one of these sites to copy the asset(s) to.

The selected asset(s) is copied into the specified site and placed in folders that correspond to their locations in the current site. Any folders that don't already exist are created automatically. It's also important to note that assets copied in this fashion are automatically added to the other sites' Favorite Assets listing.

If you would just like to find where a certain asset or group of assets is located in the local site, follow these steps:

1. In the Assets panel, select the asset or assets that you want to locate.

2. Right-click to bring up the context menu. You can also access this menu by clicking the right arrow button located in the upper-right corner of the panel.

3. Choose Locate in Site from this menu, as shown in Figure 15.8. The site window will appear, and the assets you searched for will be highlighted, as Figure 15.9 shows.

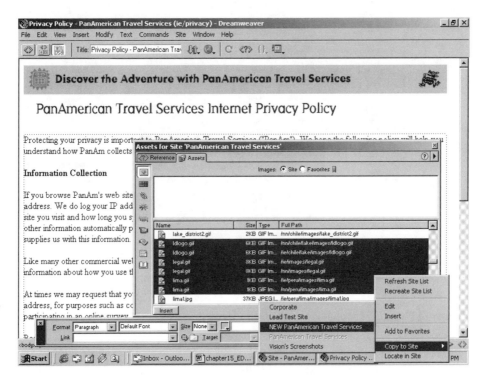

Figure 15.7   Copying site assets to the new site. Notice that you can't copy an asset to the site that it is already contained in.

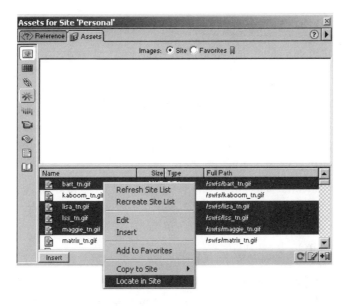

Figure 15.8   Searching for the location of a selection of images in the local site.

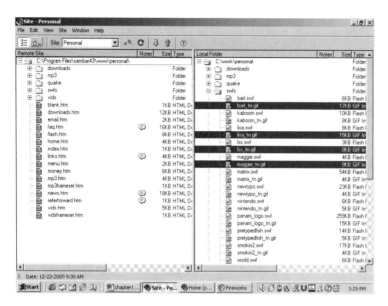

Figure 15.9   The corresponding result of your location search.

The Locate in Site option is not available with colors and URLs. This is because these two asset types do not have files associated with them; they are simply strings of text inside files.

Editing Your Assets

The Assets panel provides an easy way to edit assets as well. This can come in handy when you want to edit multiple pictures but don't want to wade through the complex directory structure of the Site window.

To edit an asset through the Assets panel, do one of the following:

- The easiest and quickest way to edit an asset is to double-click the asset name. This launches the default editor (as specified in your preferences—see Chapter 2, "Customizing Dreamweaver," for more details).

- The other method is to simply select the asset and then click the Edit button found in the lower-right corner of the panel. You can also access the Edit command by right-clicking the asset. This makes the context menu appear. Simply select Edit from this menu.

The type of asset that you want to edit dictates what happens next. With assets such as images and Flash movies, an external application is launched and the file is opened inside that program. In this case, simply edit the asset and then export it again to your local site folder, overwriting the older version.

Colors and URLs will not launch a separate application. In fact, you can edit these types of assets only if they are in your Favorites section. Editing a color brings up a swatch box, shown in Figure 15.10, where you can pick and choose a new color. Editing URLs brings up an Edit URL box, shown in Figure 15.11, where you can change the URL as well as the nickname that the Assets panel uses to describe the URL. Library items and templates will be opened for editing directly in the document window.

Note

> A crucial distinction should be made here regarding the difference between an asset and a library item. If you edit a color from your Favorite Assets list, that color will affect only future uses, not elements that it has already affected. In short, updating or changing a favorite color will not update or change the instances of that color in any of your pages. Library items, on the other hand, will update every instance of themselves. Be aware of these important differences when planning your library items.

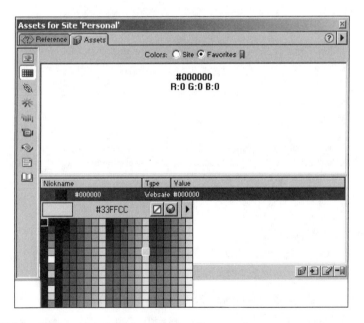

Figure 15.10   Editing a favorite color with the color swatch.

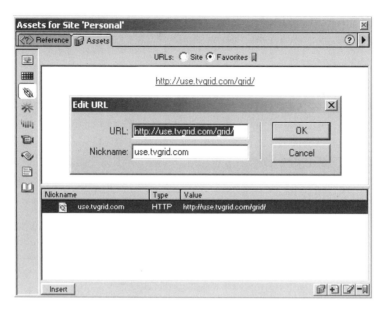

Figure 15.11   Editing a favorite URL.

Tip

If you are editing a color, you can escape the color swatch without choosing a new color by pressing the Esc key.

Note

If nothing happens after you double-click an asset to edit it or use the Edit button, be sure to check the File Types/Editors section of your preferences to see if there's an application associated with that type of file.

Your Favorite Assets

Favorite assets are those that you hand-pick that Dreamweaver *flags* and puts in a special category. All your Favorite assets can be found *somewhere* in the Site Assets listing.

Typically, as your site becomes larger, the number of assets in your site will increase as well. When you begin handling, say, a 30-page site, you might have 50 or 60 different images, if not more! As you can imagine, this would make the site listing rather cumbersome and slow. This is what makes Favorites so nice. You can add only those assets that you use the most. Suddenly your 50-image list is reduced to a dozen or so of the most common images used in your documents.

The value of Favorite assets varies from person to person, but the previous example is not uncommon. This section shows you how to organize and use Favorite-specific features.

Adding to and Removing from Your Favorite Assets

You can add a site asset to your Favorite assets by doing one of the following:

- Select the asset(s) that you want to add, and choose Add to Favorites from the context menu, as shown in Figure 15.12. You can access the context menu by clicking the right arrow button on the upper-right corner of the panel. You can also bring up this menu by right-clicking on the asset(s).

- In the site window, select the asset(s) that you want to add. Then right-click to access the context menu and select Add to Favorites (see Figure 15.12). Any asset that is not recognized or displayed by the Assets panel will be skipped.

- In Design view of the document window, select the asset(s) (or object) that you want to add. Right-click the object(s) to access the context menu. Select Add to [Asset Description Here]. You can add only assets that are valid groups in the Assets panel. Also note that when adding text to your Favorites, Add to Color Favorites will appear if the text does not contain a link; otherwise, Add to URL Favorites will appear.

The results are shown in Figure 15.13.

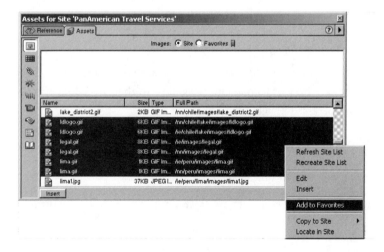

Figure 15.12   Adding six images to your Favorite Assets list.

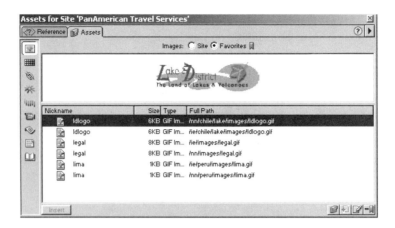

Figure 15.13   Your new favorite images.

To remove an asset from your Favorites list, follow these steps:

1. Select the asset(s) that you want to remove from your Favorites list.

2. Click the Remove from Favorites button. You can also right-click the asset and select Remove from Favorites from the context menu that appears. Or, you can also select the asset in the Favorites list and hit the Delete key. You can remove entire Favorites folders as well, which removes all the folder's contents along with it.

Assets that you remove from the Favorites list are not actually deleted in any way; they're simply removed from your Favorite Assets list.

Grouping Your Favorite Assets

To reduce clutter even further, you can group your assets in folders. This enables you to keep images that are part of your main navigation in their own folder, while keeping other commonly accessed images in another.

Creating Favorite folders and placing assets inside them does not change the location of the actual file in the directory structure of your site that the asset's icon represents; it simply offers an easy way to further organize your assets.

To create a Favorites folder and place assets inside it, simply do the following:

1. Access your Favorites listing, if you have not done so already. Do this by viewing the Assets panel and then selecting the Favorites radio button at the top of the panel.

2. Click the New Favorites Folder button located at the lower-right corner of the panel. You may also select the New Favorites folder from the context menu of an asset. Access this menu by right-clicking the asset.

3. Finally, name the folder and drag the desired assets into the folder (see Figure 15.14).

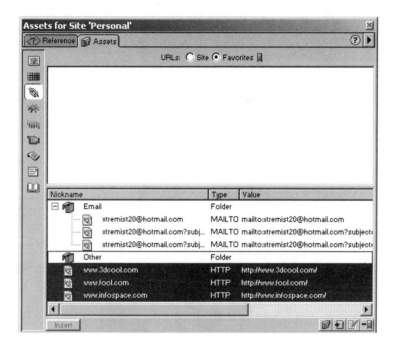

Figure 15.14 Using "virtual" folders to organize your favorite assets.

Creating New Assets

You can also create new color, URL, template, and library assets from the Assets panel. You must be viewing your Favorites to create new colors and URLs. Because the Template and Library sections don't have "favorites," it doesn't matter which section you're viewing before selecting either of these sections.

To create a new color, make sure that the Favorites listing is currently being viewed, and select the Colors section. Click the New Color button in the lower-right corner of the panel. Bringing up the context menu, either by right-clicking in the list or by selecting the right arrow button in the upper-right corner of the panel, and selecting New Color will have the same effect. This brings up a color swatch, where you can pick out your new color. After you have selected a color, you can give it a nickname.

To create a new URL, make sure that the Favorites listing is currently being viewed, and select the URLs section. Click the New URL button in the lower-right corner of the panel. Bringing up the context menu, either by right-clicking in the list or by selecting the right arrow button at the upper-right corner of the panel, and selecting New URL will have the same effect. This brings up the Add URL dialog box, where you can define both the nickname and the URL path for this new asset.

Note

> Notice that any colors or URLs you create in the Favorite Assets listing won't appear in the site listing until they've actually been used in the site.

To create a new template, select the Templates section. Click the New Template button in the lower-right corner of the panel. Bringing up the context menu, either by right-clicking in the list or by selecting the right arrow button in the upper-right corner of the panel, and selecting New Template will have the same effect. This creates a new *.dwt file and then enables you to set a nickname for it. After you have done this, you will need to edit the template and set your editable and noneditable regions.

To create a new library item, select the Library section. Click the New Library Item button in the lower-right corner of the panel. Bringing up the context menu, either by right-clicking in the list or by selecting the right arrow button at the upper-right corner of the panel, and selecting New Library Item will have the same effect. This creates a new *.lbi file and then enables you to set a nickname for it. After you have done this, you will need to edit the library item as usual.

Note

> Templates and library items are discussed in greater detail in the next chapter.

Using Check In/Check Out

When you first start creating Web pages, you probably will be the sole person responsible for them. However, often it will be necessary to collaborate with others in a combined effort to maximize your output. Perhaps one individual is creating the design, another is handling programming such as JavaScript, and a third is in charge of the regular HTML creation. It would be devastating if two people were working on the same file simultaneously. This would cause someone's modifications to be overwritten, losing any work done. Luckily, Dreamweaver offers its own way of allowing you to keep track of files, see who has checked them out, and contact them if you need immediate access to a file.

Note

> Obviously, if you are the sole person working on a site, you will most likely not need to use this feature. However, when working with others, it prevents you from overwriting each other's work.

Checking out a file from the server lets others know that you're currently using it, and Dreamweaver won't let them edit the file (at least, not very easily). This ensures that there is only one version of the file and prevents people from overwriting changes that others make. When a file is checked out, Dreamweaver places a check mark next to the filename in the your Site window. As Figure 15.15 shows, a red check indicates a file checked out by someone other than yourself, while a green check indicates a file that you have checked out. The name of the person who has checked out that file is also displayed in the Site window. Also, if the person provided an email address, you can click on the name in the Site window to send an email directly to that user.

Figure 15.15   Checked-out files are marked with a green check mark, whereas checked-in files have a lock icon next to their names.

Checking in a file causes Dreamweaver to make the local version read-only. This prohibits you from making changes to a file without "permission" to edit it. A checked-in file can be checked out by anyone working on the site. However, Dreamweaver does not make the remote version read-only when a file is checked out, as you may think it should. You should be careful and remember this, especially if you use other applications (such as an FTP client) with your site. You will be able to overwrite these files very easily.

Tip

> When using applications other than Dreamweaver to maintain your site, there is an easy way to see if a file is currently checked out. Dreamweaver places a .lck file right next to the checked-out file. For instance, if you have checked out the file about.htm, Dreamweaver would create an about.htm.lck file to notify you that you should not over-write this file because it's currently checked out and being worked on. Typically, both of these files will be located directly next to each other in a directory listing. However, these .lck files are not visible from within Dreamweaver. You can view them in another FTP program or Telnet window (UNIX). You can also view them on Windows in Windows Explorer, if your preferences are set to show hidden files.

So when is the Check In/Check Out feature ideally used? It is most often utilized in a workgroup environment where multiple people are working as a team on a particular site and plan to work on the same specific files or documents. It should (or could, at least) be used anytime there is more than one computer accessing the files and changing them. This could even be a small office/home office (SOHO) environment in which you are the only person changing the site but may do so from any number of workstations. It is also conceivable that you might take some work on the road with you via a note-book computer and want to make sure that you or someone else doesn't inadvertently modify files from your work or home workstation.

Note

> If you need to take work on the road somewhere, be sure to check out any files that you might need to edit while you're away. You will probably not have access to the remote server while you're gone. This is especially true when the remote site is located on a LAN server. In the worst-case scenario, you can make the files editable (Dreamweaver gives this option when you try to edit them) and use a different FTP client to check them in.

Configuring the Check In/Check Out Feature

The Check In/Check Out system cannot be used until you have established remote site information in your site definition. This is because when you check out a file, you are doing so from the remote site (which everyone on the project has access to) rather that just on your local site folder. Setting up your remote site is discussed in Chapter 13.

To set up your file Check In/Check Out options, follow these steps:

1. Select Site/Define Sites from the menu, select the site that you want to modify, and then click Edit.

2. Select the Remote Info section of your site definition. Either FTP or local/network should be the access method used to enable file check in/check out on your site.

3. Check the Enable File Check In and Check Out box. This will cause additional entry boxes to appear below. These options, shown in Figure 15.16, are listed here:

   - **Check Out Files When Opening.** Selecting this option automatically checks out files when you open them by double-clicking them in the local side of the site window. If you open a file by the Open item of the File menu, you will be prompted to check out the file or open it as read-only, even if this option is selected.

   - **Check Out Name.** The name to use that is displayed in the site window when you check out a file. This should be either your name, if you access files from only one computer, or perhaps a location, such as John-Home or John-Office. This will help you and others know who has checked out the file and where that person might be.

   - **Email Address.** Enter your email address into this area. This will cause your name to become a blue hyperlink in the site window when you check out a file. By clicking this link, other team members can email you regarding the file. Their default email application will open with your email in the To field and the file in question as well as the site that the file is from in the Subject line. It is highly suggested that you utilize this feature of the Check In/Check Out system.

4. After you have selected your options, click OK.

Checking Files In and Out

You can use either the Site window or the document window to check files in and out. Additionally, if you are editing a document and decide to discard the changes you've made, you can effectively "undo" the Check Out function. Each of the ways you can check in or out files is discussed in Exercise 15.1.

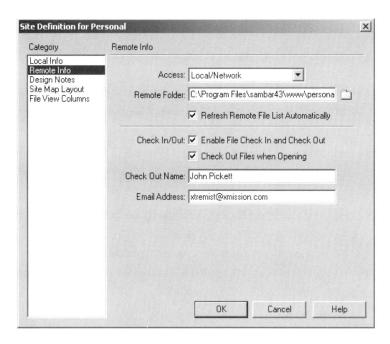

Figure 15.16   Setting up your contact information for the Check In/Check Out feature.

Exercise 15.1   Check Files In and Out

In this exercise, you check a few files in and out to become accustomed to the process. This exercise is divided into two subsections: checking a file out and checking a file in.

Part I Check Files In and Out

1. Make sure that the site you want to check files out of is the active site. The Check In/Check Out system must be in use and defined in the site definition as well. How to do this was discussed earlier in the chapter.

2. Select the file(s) that you want to check out in the site window (see Figure 15.17). Then select Site/Check Out, or press Ctrl+Alt+Shift+D. You can also check out files by clicking the Check Out File(s) button on the site window toolbar or by selecting Check Out from the context menu (right-click one of the files that you want to check out to bring up this menu).

3. If you want to check out the dependent files associated with each file, click Yes from the Dependent Files prompt; otherwise, select No.

When a file is checked out, other project teammates will be unable to edit the file(s) when using Dreamweaver. Other applications such as an FTP client or other HTML editors still can change, delete, and otherwise modify these files, however, so be careful when using other applications when the Check In/Check Out system is in use on a site.

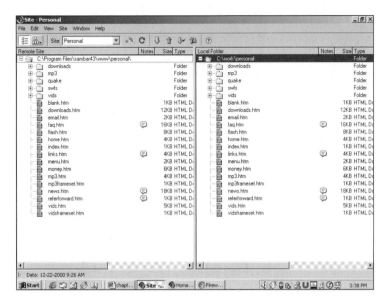

Figure 15.17   Checking out a few files to work on.

Part II Checking Files In and Our

This is the second half of the first exercise. You will now check in the files that you had previously checked out.

1. Make sure that the site you want to check files *in to* is the active site.

2. In the site window, select the file(s) that you want to check in. These must be files that you have checked out, not files that other people have checked out. Next, select Site/Check In, or press Ctrl+Alt+Shift+U. You can also check files in by clicking the Check In button on the site window toolbar or by selecting Check In from the context menu (right-click one of the files that you want to check out to bring up this menu).

3. If you want to check *in* the dependent files associated with each file, click Yes from the dependent files prompt; otherwise, select No.

Checking in files is something that many Dreamweaver users have a hard time remembering to do. They tend to simply use the Put command instead. Although this will still update the remote copy of the file, it will *not* check in the file and remove the checked-out status. You might forget to do so as well and get the occasional email from coworkers wondering what's taking you so long with a file that you were finished with two days ago.

To "undo" a file checkout, select the file(s) that you want to discard any changes to, and select Site/Undo Check Out from the menu. This is different from just checking the file back in because the version of the file returned to the server is exactly the same as the one you originally checked out. You can also right-click on the file(s) in the Site window and select Undo Check Out from the context menu that appears. Choosing this action will close the files, discarding any changes made, and revert to the version that existed before you checked out the file. It will also set your local copy to read-only and allow other teammates to check out the file.

If you check in the currently active document this way, it will be saved (according to your preferences—see Chapter 2) and then checked in to the remote server. If you check out a currently active document this way, the copy on the remote server overwrites it, and any changes you had made that don't exist in the remote version are lost.

Source and Version Control Features

Newly added in Dreamweaver 4 is support for source and version control systems such as Microsoft Visual SourceSafe- and WebDAV-enabled software. If you don't know what either of these applications do, an easy description is that they're "professional" Check In/Check Out systems. They offer greater protection from overwriting files without permission, especially in a larger work environment. Typically, a small office wouldn't *need* to use one of these systems; the systems are much more common in larger corporations.

Both Visual SourceSafe and WebDAV integration can be enabled through the Remote Info section of your Site Definition (Site/Define Sites), under the Access method. After you have set up these options, you can use normal Dreamweaver file maintenance commands, such as the Check In/Check Out feature.

Note

> A few basic differences between Visual SourceSafe and WebDAV could be important when deciding on the right solution for you. VSS is distributed by Microsoft and, as such, is a for-sale solution. It also maintains a database of file information and status for its control mechanism. WebDAV, on the other hand, is a freely distributed "open standard" that runs on top of an existing Web server.

Visual SourceSafe Integration

If you opt for a Visual SourceSafe solution rather than a WebDAV-enabled product, you will need to have a few key elements installed or ready to install. Visual SourceSafe is extremely easy to set up if you are using a Windows-based system to connect to the

SourceSafe database. All you need is the Microsoft Visual SourceSafe 6.0 client. If you will be using a Macintosh-based system, the process is a little more complicated. You will need two pieces of software installed: ToolServer and MetroWerks ToolServer Tool. You can visit the following URL to find out exactly where to download these two utilities: `www.macromedia.com/support/dreamweaver/ts/documents/vss_on_mac.htm`.

Because MetroWerks's solution is compatible with only 5.0 Visual SourceSafe (VSS) databases, it is wise to run your VSS server in 5.0-compatible mode.

Exercise 15.2   Setting Up Visual SourceSafe Integration for Your Site

This exercise will show you how to quickly set up Visual SourceSafe for your site.

1. Access the Remote Info section of the target sites' definition. For information on how to do this, review the section "Defining Your Site," in Chapter 13.

2. Choose SourceSafe Database from the pull-down menu as your remote access method.

3. Click Settings, which appears next to the access pull-down menu. This opens the Open SourceSafe Database dialog box.

4. In the Database Path box, browse to or enter the path of the SourceSafe database that you want to use. This will be a srcsafe.ini file and will be used to initialize SourceSafe.

5. In the project box, enter the SourceSafe project that you want to use as the root of the remote site. Note: This field must contain a $/, but anything else is optional.

6. Enter your username and password into the remaining fields. You can also choose to save your password or require you to enter it each time you connect to the database. Select OK.

7. Choose the Check Out Files When Opening option in the check box if you want Dreamweaver to check out the files from the SourceSafe database when double-clicking them in the site window. Select OK to save these changes.

   You can now connect and disconnect from the SourceSafe database and use normal Dreamweaver file control commands such as Get, Put, Check In, Check Out, and Refresh.

If you are unsure of any of these settings, contact your system or network administrator for assistance. You may also consult the Microsoft Visual SourceSafe documentation, if needed.

WebDAV Integration

WebDAV is a pretty "cool" feature, if you ask me. It can be integrated into HTTP servers such as Apache (`www.apache.org`) and Microsoft's Internet Information Server (IIS).

Short for World Wide Web Distributed Authoring and Versioning, WebDAV is a protocol rather than an application. It defines additional HTTP methods and headers, and is an extension to the HTTP/1.1 protocol.

To setup WebDAV integration for your site, follow these steps:

1. Access the Remote Info section of the target sites' site definition. For information on how to do this, review the section "Defining Your Site," in Chapter 13.

2. Choose WebDAV from the pull-down menu as your remote access method.

3. Click Settings, which appears next to the Access pull-down menu. This opens the WebDAV Connection dialog box.

4. In the URL box, enter the full URL of the site to which you want to connect. This includes the protocol used (http://) as well as the directory, if not simply the domain root. Important tip: HTTP requests are usually routed by the server to port 80. If you want to use a port other than 80 to connect to the WebDAV server (which I recommend), you just append `:PortNumber` to the end of the URL— for example, `http://webdav.org:81` as opposed to `HTTP://Webdav.org`.

5. Enter the username and password used to access the server in their respective areas. This is the password used for the remote server authentication. Additionally, you can choose to save your password for future sessions so that you don't have to enter it again.

6. Enter a valid email address in the Email textbox. This is used on the WebDAV-enabled server to identify who is using a particular file, and it offers contact information accessible via the site window. After you have finished setting up these options, click OK.

7. Mark the Check Out Files When Opening option in the check box if you want Dreamweaver to check out the files from the WebDAV server when double-clicking them in the site window. Select OK to save these changes.

   You can now connect and disconnect from the WebDAV server and use normal Dreamweaver file control commands such as Get, Put, Check In, Check Out, and Refresh.

If you are unsure of any of these settings, contact your system or network administrator for assistance. You may also consult the WebDAV servers' documentation if needed (and it will probably be needed). You can also go to `www.webdav.org` for help.

Utilizing Design Notes

Design Notes enable you to leave notes for coworkers that are associated with specific files. This means that you can track changes to documents, map their progress and history, or update and change a document's completion status. These are only a few possibilities that Design Notes provide. In a single-person project, they can assist you by easily keeping track of what stage a document or image is currently at, as well as maintain any notes to help you remember where you were at on your project.

Design Notes could potentially store any type of information on a file you can think of. We will focus our discussion on saving file information such as file status and other general information, using Design Notes to customize the columns in the File view. Finally, we show how Design Notes are integrated and used in conjunction with Fireworks 4.

General Usage

Design Notes are extremely versatile. They can be created for documents and images. Other objects, such as Flash movies, applets, and other types of media, can have Design Notes assigned to them as well. Before you begin using Design Notes, you should know how to set up basic Design Notes capability in your site. To enable Design Notes, do the following:

1. Access the site definition through the Site/Define Sites menu option (after you select the site in the Define Sites dialog box, click Edit).

2. Go to the Design Notes category of your site definition.

3. Make sure that the Maintain Design Notes option is selected, as shown in Figure 15.18. This is the very basic item that you must have checked to use any type of Design Notes capability on the site.

4. If you also want your coworkers to be able to view your Design Notes (recommended) and want to share your Design Notes with others (in a collaborative environment), select Upload Design Notes for Sharing. This is typically a good idea if many designers are working on the same document. You can view the status of a document or image quickly and easily, as well as see what needs to be done still. An advantage of not uploading Design Notes is that file transfers will tend to be quicker, especially when using a slow connection. If you don't need to upload them, it's just a waste of bandwidth.

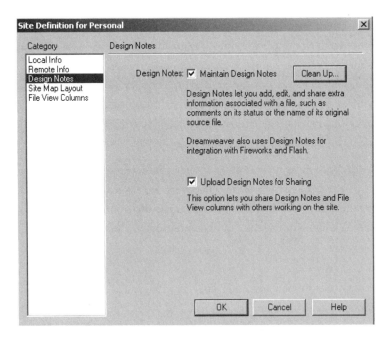

Figure 15.18   The Design Notes section of your site definition.

Although not specifically related to setting up Design Notes access on your site, the Clean Up command in the Design Notes section of your site definition will let you delete all Design Notes that aren't associated with a file (see Figure 15.19). This simply helps keep things tidy.

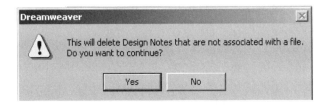

Figure 15.19   Delete existing Design Notes if you choose not to utilize them.

After you have enabled Design Notes on your site, you can add Design Notes to an HTML (or other) document, or other object by following these steps:

1. Selecting File/Design Notes from the menu. Selecting Design Notes from the context menu (right-clicking the file) will also create a Design Note.

    If the file check in and out system is in use, you will need to check out the file before creating (or changing, for that matter) a Design Note for it.

2. This brings up the Design Notes window. You can access two tabs.

3. The initial tab, labeled Basic Info (shown in Figure 15.20), shows the filename, the location of the file, a pull-down menu for the file status, and a place for general comments and notes about the file. You can also click the small calendar button in the upper-right corner of the Notes textbox to automatically insert the current date. Finally, if you want the Design Note to be displayed every time the file is opened for editing, check the Show When File Is Opened option.

4. The All Info tab of this window, shown in Figure 15.21, displays all the Design Notes for the file (including the status and notes that Design Notes edited through the Basic Info tab). From this tab, you can make a new Design Note by entering a name and value pair in the appropriate fields. Then simply click the + button to add it. Similarly, the – button will remove the Design Note currently selected in the Info textbox.

5. When finished, click OK.

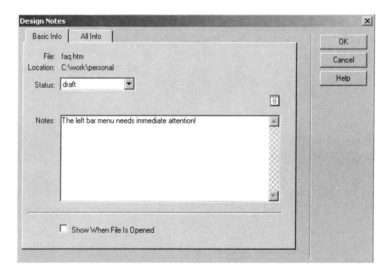

Figure 15.20   On the Basic Info tab, setting the Design Note status to Draft and the Design Note notes to "The left bar menu needs immediate attention!"

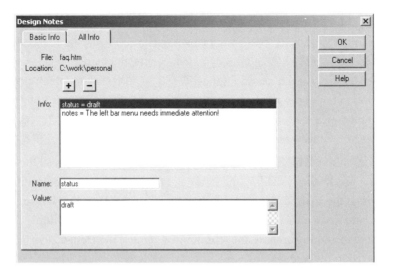

Figure 15.21   The All Info view of Figure 15.20's Design Notes.

Tip

If Design Notes are unfamiliar to you, or if you're having trouble with references to name and value associations, you might consider using the Basic Info tab to set a file status and then checking the All Info tab to see the correlation between the two values and how Dreamweaver 4 assigns them.

Exercise 15.3   Assigning the Status Design Note a Value

We should discuss one more thing to complete our discussion of the basics of Design Notes: how to assign the status Design Note a value other than any of the predefined values you can initially choose from. Learning this will also help you understand how Design Notes work and how to create your own custom Design Notes.

1. Access the Design Notes for the file that you want to change the status of, as described previously. Now click the All Info tab to display all the Design Notes currently in use.

2. Next, type **status** in the Name field, and enter the description (or value) of the status that you want to create in the Value field, as shown in Figure 15.22

3. Finally, click the + button to save the Design Note. Doing this overwrites any current Design Note with the name status of the one you just created. You can now go back to the Basic Info tab and see your new status in the Status pull-down menu.

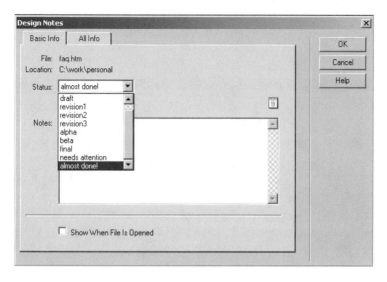

Figure 15.22   Creating a new value for the status Design Note.

Creating custom Design Notes is the basis on which the next section is built. You will now see how you can customize your File View columns using Design Notes to display nearly any type of information about your file.

Customizing the File View Columns with Design Notes

Macromedia has taken the idea behind Dreamweaver 4's extensions and packed some of the same features into Design Notes. One way in which Design Notes *extend* Dreamweaver 4 is the capability to completely customize the File View columns in your Site window. For instance, you might decide that you want to have a column that shows the due date for each file. More realistically, you might have four dates by which you must complete 25% of the site. You could create a column that tells which folders belong to which group (25%, 50%, 75%, and 100%), as well as a column that specifies the due date (October 1, October 15, November 1, and November 15). There are many other examples in which this new feature would come in handy, but let's use this example and see how to set this up. (See Figure 15.23 for the finished product.)

1. Make sure that Design Notes are enabled, and then access the File View Columns section of your site definition. The easiest way to do this is by selecting View/File View Columns from the menu. Other ways of accessing your site definition are discussed in the previous section.

2. The most noticeable option is Enable Column Sharing. You can select this option to allow others to use the same column configuration as yours. This is effective if

you have set up perfect File View columns for a particular project and other team members want to use them as well.

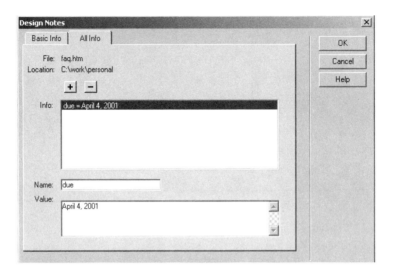

Figure 15.23   Creating a new Design Note called Due with the value April 4, 2001.

3. Here you will find a list of column names (captions), column types, and the current visibility state of that column. Selecting an item from this list changes the values of the fields below this table. This is how you can edit the column's attributes. These attributes are described here:

- **Column Name.** This is the name used in the File view as a "caption" for the column. This is the identifying string of text that you will see.

- **Associate with Design Note.** This field is where the personalization begins. Here you select the Design Note (due, status, percent, and so on) that you want to display in the column.

- **Align.** This is the alignment for the name (caption) of the column. Options include left, right, and center.

- **Show.** Check this to show the column; uncheck it to hide the column.

- **Share with All Users of This Site.** This further specifies limitations for the Enable Column Sharing option. You do not need to share every personalized column with others. To share this column with others, make sure that this option is checked. This option is not available with the built-in columns because anyone using Dreamweaver has access to these columns already. Furthermore, these columns can be hidden but cannot be disabled, so they will always be shared.

4. You can now add a personalized column by clicking the + button. This creates an untitled column. Name the column and establish the other options as described previously. ˙

5. To remove a column from the list, select the column in the site definition box and click the – button. You cannot delete built-in columns, but you can hide them.

Note

You can hide any column except the Name column. This is the very minimum that you must have visible to be able to function effectively when using Dreamweaver.

6. Lastly, you can change the listing order of the columns by selecting a column and then using the Move Up and Move Down buttons found on the right side of the column listing to arrange them in any order you want. The top-most column in this list will become the leftmost column in the Site window; likewise, the bottom-most column listed will be the rightmost column in the Site window.

For my purposes, I created a column that I called Due Date and associated it with the design note Due. This is only half of the process, however. We must now go through the site and create the Due Design Note for any file, folder, or object that we want to have display a due date. I just select certain folders because most of the content within a folder is typically due around the same time. After these Design Notes are established, you will see that the site window now lists a column called Due Date that lists the dates that certain folders are due.

You can also edit the Design Note values associated with custom columns directly from the site window. To do this, select the line that contains the Design Note that you want to edit. Next, click once in the column whose Design Note you want to change (in my example, this is the space under the column Due Date). This makes the field editable, as shown in Figure 15.24. You can add, change, or delete a Design Note very quickly this way.

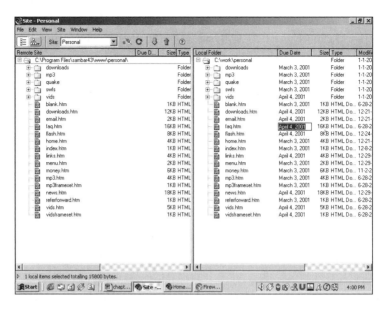

Figure 15.24   Editing a Design Note from the site window.

Using Design Notes in Fireworks

Dreamweaver enables you to launch external editors and edit images used on your pages directly from the document window. This process is discussed in detail in Chapter 6. When you create or open an image in Fireworks 4 and then export it, Fireworks creates a Design Note with the original file's path. This enables you to select an image in your Web page and choose to edit that image; Fireworks automatically launches with the source image (not the exported version) and enables you to make any changes required and then automatically re-export it, updating the image used in your Web page. This is an easy way to manage your images directly through Dreamweaver. To find out more about using the Roundtrip feature in Dreamweaver, check out Chapter 6.

For instance, if you have an image called xtremist_logo.png and export it as xtremist_logo.gif, Fireworks will create a file called xtremist_logo.gif.mno and place it in the same directory as the exported image. Along with the absolute file path, any hot spots or rollovers are saved in the Design Note. When you import the image into a Dreamweaver document, the image Design Note is copied as well.

Building Reports About Project Workflow

You learned in Chapter 14, "Site Publishing, Maintenance, and Reporting," that using reports is an easy and powerful way to gather information about a site. We briefly discussed their usefulness in reporting project workflow statistics. The workflow portion of Dreamweaver reports includes information on what files are checked out by a particular individual as well as Design Notes properties. We will now look at each workflow report in greater detail. Before we get started, though, I should point out that workflow reports require a remote connection to be set up in your site definition, and you must have the ability to connect to the remote site. If you are unsure whether you have done this, see the section "Defining Your Site," in Chapter 13.

Reports on Checked-Out Files

Running a report on checked-out files enables you to see who has checked out any file. You can run a general search to see *everyone* who has checked out a file, or you can narrow the search to a particular individual. As with all the other reports, you can search a single document, an entire site, a specific folder, or the currently selected files (files selected in the local site).

This search is case-sensitive, but you do not need to enter the entire string. For example, if you are searching for files checked out by a team member named Jeffrey Stewart, you can simply enter Jeff, Jeffrey, or Stewart. Be sure to remember that if you're searching for "Jeff," multiple individuals may appear—Jeffrey Stewart as well as Jeff Daniels, for instance.

Tip

> The Reports dialog box and Results box tend to like the document window more than the Site window. If you ever lose track of them, either switch to an open document or open one to see if you can find them there.

Exercise 15.4   Checked-Out File Reports

In this exercise, you will run a report to see checked-out files.

1. Select Site/Reports from the menu. The Reports dialog box appears.
2. Select which documents to process with the Report On pull-down list. You can select to report on the current document (if a document is currently open), the entire site, selected files (from the site window), or a specific folder (this searches files in the folder, plus files in any subdirectory of this folder).

3. Now select the check box next to Checked Out By under the Select Reports area, as shown in Figure 15.25. Remember that you can run multiple reports at once, but we are currently discussing a single report. For more on running reports, see the section "Running Site Reports," in Chapter 14.

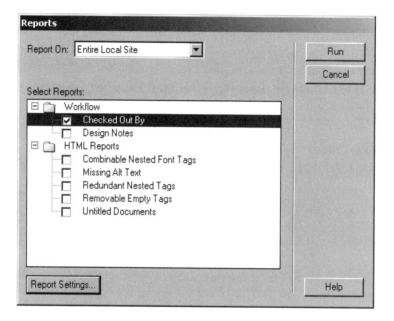

Figure 15.25   Setting up a report on checked-out files.

4. With Checked Out By selected, click the Report Settings button located in the lower-left part of the Reports window.

5. The Checked Out By dialog box now appears. You can enter a string to search for, as in Figure 15.26, or you can leave it blank to search for everyone. When you're done, click OK.

6. If you're ready to run the report, click Run. Dreamweaver runs the report and opens a results box listing files checked out according to your search criteria (see Figure 15.27).

Design Notes Reports

Running a Design Notes report enables you to view Design Note names and values. You can run a general search to see *every* Design Notes attribute, or you can narrow the search to a particular Design Note or multiple notes. As with all the other reports, you can search a single document, an entire site, a specific folder, or the currently selected files (files selected in the local site).

Figure 15.26   Entering the person's name to search for.

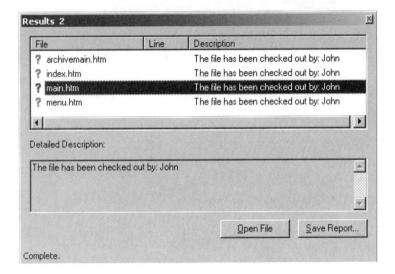

Figure 15.27   You can see that currently John has only four files checked out.

Exercise 15.5   Design Notes Reports

For this exercise, you will run a Design Notes report.

To run a Design Notes report, follow these steps:

1. Select Site/Reports from the menu. The Reports dialog box appears.
2. Select which documents to process with the Report On pull-down list. You can select to report on the current document (if a document is currently open), the entire site, selected files (from the site window), or a specific folder (this searches files in the folder, plus files in any subdirectory of this folder).
3. Now select the check box next to Design Notes under the Select Reports area, as shown in Figure 15.28. Remember that you can run multiple reports at once, but we are currently discussing a single report. For more on running reports, see the section "Running Site Reports," in Chapter 14.

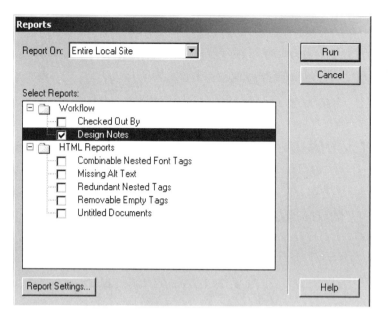

Figure 15.28   Setting up a Design Notes report.

4. With Design Notes selected, click the Report Settings button located in the lower-left part of the Reports window.

5. The Design Notes dialog box now appears. Here you enter name and value pairs and select condition statements to compare. For example, if you are searching for all Design Notes that have the status of Complete, you would enter **Status** in the first column and select Contains (selecting Is would also work and would allow only an exact match for the sought status). In the third column, you enter the value you're searching for—in this case, Complete. (See Figure 15.29.) When you're done, click OK.

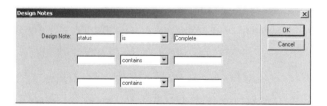

Figure 15.29   Searching for all Design Notes that have a completed status.

6. If you're ready to run the report, click Run. Dreamweaver runs the report and opens a results box listing files checked out according to your search criteria (see Figure 15.30).

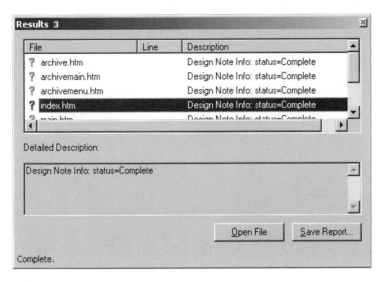

Figure 15.30   You can now see all the files that are completed.

Summary

The focus of this chapter has been using Dreamweaver 4 to effectively collaborate with others on a single project. You learned to use features that can be used in a single-user environment, but emphasis should be placed on their importance in a multiuser environment. You also learned about source and version control systems that Dreamweaver can now utilize. Lastly, you became familiar with the inner details regarding the power of Design Notes and site reports.

Chapter 16

Templates and Libraries

In Dreamweaver, you can use templates
and site libraries to help automate the
process of building and updating sites. As
you'll learn in this chapter, you can create

and then save these elements to designate which parts of a site can be edited. You also can use templates and libraries to make universal changes and create a consistent look and feel throughout the site.

You'll learn about the following functions in this chapter:

- Creating templates
- Using templates
- Attaching and detaching templates
- Using templates with XML
- Creating and using library objects
- Editing library items
- Detaching and deleting library items
- Using JavaScript in library items

About Templates

If you have many similar pages on your Web site, or if you want to maintain a consistent look and feel across your site, then templates can work for you. With templates, you can designate locked and editable regions, making it simple to create uniform pages without changing the design. After the template has been created, it can be made available to other members of a design team.

Even people who have never used Dreamweaver can learn to add information to a template. Templates can be useful when you have content contributors that aren't Web-savvy, whom you do not want to mess up your page. With a template, these individuals can just type their content or insert their graphics into the editable region. The template will protect the rest of your page from them.

I don't recommend using templates if you often have major changes to the layout and design in a site. Templates are best used for lower-level pages that offer simple information. For example, you might use them on e-commerce sites to show each item in an inventory. If you just need an easier way to duplicate a series of objects (such as images in a navigation bar) or some HTML code for a text style, use cascading style sheets or HTML styles. You could also transform your code into a library object. Creating library objects is covered in the second half of this chapter.

What Is a Library?

The second part of this chapter covers the use of Dreamweaver libraries. Read this section even if you aren't interested in using templates because the two offer much different functionality.

You can set up a library to hold elements of a Web site that are used repeatedly. For instance, let's say that you want all lower-level pages in a site to contain a small logo image above a copyright blurb. You could assemble these two elements in a Dreamweaver document, save them together into the library, and use them time and time again by pulling up the site's Library panel and clicking the Insert button.

Fast-forward this scenario a couple of months: Now you have a new logo image, and you want to exchange it with the old one. All that's required is a simple edit to the library item where you stored it the first time, and all the pages that contain the library item can be updated simultaneously. Imagine how your coworkers' jaws will drop when they see how fast you can work (or maybe you can keep that little secret to yourself).

Now that you have a sense of what libraries can do, you're probably interested in templates as well. Let's take a look at how they work.

Creating Templates

Creating templates is relatively simple if you understand what they are and how Dreamweaver uses them.

When you make a template, you are creating a document that will serve as a model for other documents. Think of yourself as an architect developing a blueprint. The template itself should not be published to the Internet; only the pages that are based on the template will be published.

Inside a template, you should insert elements common to the Dreamweaver documents that will be based on your template. For example, you might include a banner, a navigation bar, and a logo image. These elements will be designated as noneditable, or locked, regions. You should also insert areas that will change from page to page, such as the body text. The areas that will change are called editable, or unlocked, regions.

Templates are saved in the Templates folder in your site's local root folder. You do not have to create the Templates folder because Dreamweaver will do this for you automatically. All templates in the folder have the .dwt extension.

It can't be stressed enough that all your templates should *always* be in this folder. Also, you should not include any other (non–.dwt) files in the Templates folder. Dreamweaver has a very difficult job of creating relative links out of many different locations. If the template isn't where it's supposed to be, an error could occur.

You can use an already existing HTML file to make a template, or you can create a template from a blank HTML document. You should be in Design view when you create and use your template. If you are in Code view, the template-related commands will become dimmed.

Exercise 16.1   Creating Templates from Existing HTML Documents

To create a template from an already existing HTML document, do the following:

1. Open the document that you want to transform into a template.
2. Choose File/Save As Template.
3. In the Save As Template dialog box, choose a site from the pop-up window, and then enter a name for the template in the Save As text field box.
4. Click Save.

Note

If the document that you want to save as a template is already attached to another template, you must first detach it before saving it as a new template.

To create a new template, open a blank document and do the following:

1. Choose Window/Templates. Dreamweaver will open the Assets panel with the Templates Category selected.
2. From the Assets panel, click the New icon at the bottom of the panel. The New icon is a small square with a + sign over it.
3. Select the new, untitled template and enter a name for it.

Note

When you create links inside a template, try to use the Folder icon or the Point-to-File feature, both on the Property Inspector.

The reason for this is that when you create a template file based on an existing page, Dreamweaver moves the file into the Templates folder and then makes the necessary modifications to the pathnames to ensure that the links will still work.

You should avoid hand-typing URLs whenever possible because this often results in broken paths in your pages derived from the template. In general, it is always best to let Dreamweaver code the correct path.

Creating Editable Regions

When you have a template, you will need to define editable regions, or the sections that can be changed from page to page. Editable regions appear in colored highlights (the default color is light blue) in the template file, with a descriptive name at the top and additional information about the region enclosed in brackets. The default highlighting color can be changed in the Dreamweaver preferences—see Chapter 2, "Customizing Dreamweaver," for more information.

Figure 16.1 shows a template opened in Dreamweaver with editable regions already marked.

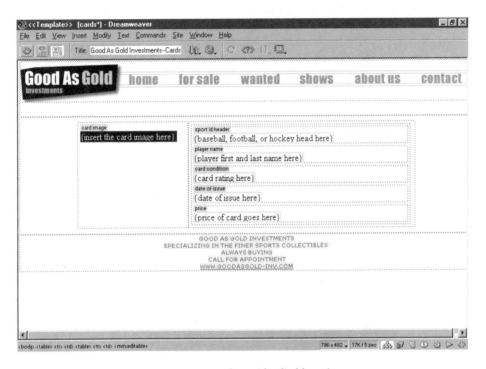

Figure 16.1   A sample Dreamweaver template with editable regions.

The editable regions hold information that can change in each HTML page that is based on the template. This information might be text, images, or other media such as a Flash movie or a Java applet. The areas that are not marked as editable will be locked when you create new files based on the template.

When you create a page based on a template (choose File/New from Template), you can click into the editable regions and add the new data, and then save the page as a separate HTML file. The areas of the file that were not marked as editable regions will remain identical in all pages that were based on the template, and you will not be able to change them in any way.

If you want to make changes to one of the template's noneditable regions, you must open the original template file to do so. As long as you are working inside the template file itself, you can make changes. However, while working in pages that are based on a template, you cannot make changes to areas that are not marked as editable. Bear in mind that any changes made to a noneditable region in a template will be reflected in every page derived from that template across the site.

To define an editable region, do the following:

1. Open your template file.

2. Select the content that you want to define as editable. Choose Modify/Templates/New Editable Region (see Figure 16.2). If you are working in a blank template, just click in the area that you want to define. You can also make a layer, table, or table cell into an editable region.

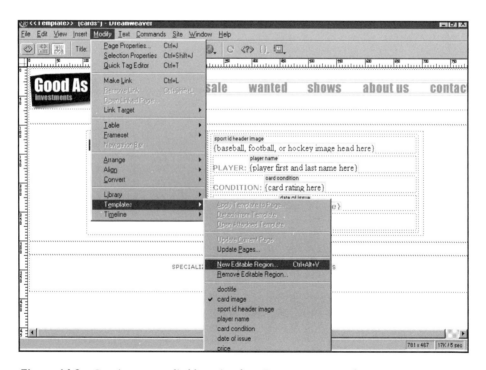

Figure 16.2   Creating a new editable region for a Dreamweaver template.

3. Enter a name for the region in the New Editable Region dialog box. You must give each editable region a unique name. This name will appear in a comment tag in your source code but will not ever appear on the page itself when viewed in a browser.

Note

You can also right-click (Ctrl+click on Macs) the area in which you want to add a new editable region and choose New Editable Region from the context menu. Or, use the keyboard shortcut Ctrl+Alt+V.

Each editable region is listed in the Modify/Templates submenu. A check mark next to a region name means that the area is currently selected. If you are working in a very long or complex page and need to locate an editable region, this window can be very useful: Pull down the menu and select the editable region name, and Dreamweaver will select it in the document.

Note

You can make an editable region in the original template itself, but not in a page derived from the template.

The editable region will then appear with a highlighted rectangle around it. If you want to change the color of the highlight, choose Edit/Preferences/Highlighting to specify the new color with the Dreamweaver color palette.

The name of the new editable region appears in the upper-left corner. If you want to add more information about the area, type it between the brackets ({}) that appear below the region's name. When you save new pages based on the template, the region name and the bracketed information will not show up inside the Web browser.

Tip

If you want to change the name of your editable region, you can select it and use the Tag Editor (Ctrl+T) to change the name inside the HTML code (see Figure 16.3). Note that spaces are indicated with the code %20. You can also right-click or Ctrl+click the area to choose the Tag Editor from the context menu.

When working inside a template, treat the editable regions as if they were objects themselves. Double-click a region's Name tab to select the entire region. You can also delete regions or copy to your Clipboard by double-clicking to select them.

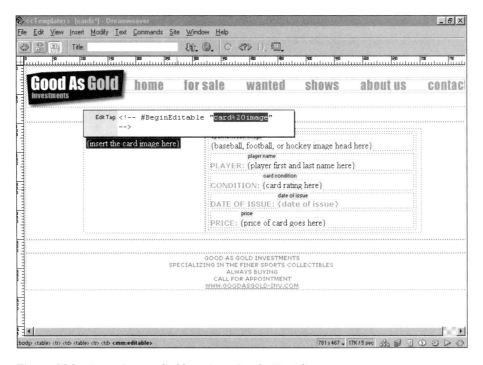

Figure 16.3   Renaming an editable region using the Tag Editor.

Removing Editable Regions

To remove an editable region, do the following:

1. Open the document.

2. Choose Modify/Templates/Remove Editable Region.

3. In the Remove Editable Region dialog box, select the region that you want to remove, and click OK.

Note

The HTML code inside your template file and items based on the template can be viewed in Code view (F10). Dreamweaver marks the regions with the comments #BeginEditable and #EndEditable. You can edit anything between the comments. These comments do not contain proprietary information.

Setting Template Properties

Any changes that you make to the template file also appear in pages that are based on the template. For example, if you open your template file and change the link color to hot pink, all pages that were based on the template will have hot pink links as well. The same is true for other properties such as the page title, margins, and background image.

Choose Modify/Page Properties to specify the link colors, the page title, and the background image when creating the template.

Be aware that the template's page properties cannot be made into an editable region. This means that you must have the same background color, margins, and link colors in every page based on the template. If you want these to vary from the template, you will need to detach the page from the template. Likewise, if you try to change page properties from a file that is attached to a template, the changes will be ignored.

Design Notes

To create Design Notes for an HTML page based on a template, click the filename from the Site Files view and choose File/Design Notes (or pull down the context menu by right-clicking on the filename). You then have access to the Design Notes dialog box, where you can insert information about the file.

Fonts and CSS Styles in Templates

Templates might seem ideal for Web designers who have to pass their carefully constructed interfaces to interns, students, or other beginners who might not take care to format everything correctly. If this is your situation, be aware that you might have difficulty retaining type specifications and other features when you use templates.

When you want to specify specific font faces, sizes, colors, and styles for editable regions of a template, I recommend that you use a placeholder for the text that will be inserted into the region. This placeholder should be formatted as you want it to appear in all pages based on the template, and it should say something generic that will indicate to the template's user that it should be changed (such as Season Headline). Make the placeholder before you make the editable region. Then select it and define the region as editable.

Using the placeholder method will make it easier for you to retain font face, size, style, and color specifications. I've found that font formats made to the bracketed text in the template do not show up in documents based on the template.

Be aware that CSS styles, timelines, JavaScripts, and HEAD section tags will not take effect in documents based on templates. This is because the HEAD section of the document is locked when you attach it to a template. In a document based on a template, the only tag inside the <HEAD> tag that can be changed is the title. However, in Dreamweaver 4, you can add Dreamweaver behaviors to pages based on a template. Dreamweaver will allow these scripts to be inserted but will not allow custom scripts or hand-coding of any kind.

You can still use the template to build your page and then detach it if you absolutely must make edits to the <HEAD> tag.

If you want to use CSS styles, create an external style sheet and link it to the original template. This way, you can go back into the external style sheet and add styles or classes later and then apply them to new pages from the template.

Using Templates

Now that your template is all set up and ready to go, you can begin using it to make HTML pages.

Exercise 16.2   Creating New Files Based on Templates

To create a new file based on a template, do the following:

1. Choose File/New from Template.
2. In the Select Template dialog box (see Figure 16.4), choose a site from the pull-down menu and choose a template from the Templates listing.

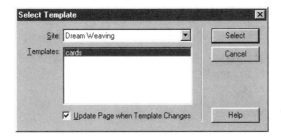

Figure 16.4   The Select Template dialog box.

3. If your want Dreamweaver to make automatic updates to the page when the template changes, click the Update Page When Template Changes box. (The box is selected by default.) Note that if you uncheck this box, Dreamweaver creates a new, detached page from the template, almost like ripping off a sheet from the top of a pad. The entire page is editable and thus not subject to the limitations of templates. At the same time, you don't have to create the foundation for your page because it is already there.
4. Click Select.

In the new document, the entire page contents will be surrounded with a highlighted box, indicating that the page is based on a template. The name of the template appears next to the Template tab in the upper-right corner. Moving your cursor around the page, note that a "no" symbol (a circle with a diagonal slash) appears in locked areas. The symbol disappears when you are in an editable region.

To add or change content in editable regions, select the area by double-clicking its name tab. Or, drag your mouse over the bracketed area and type in the changes.

Make sure that you select the brackets and the content of the brackets and hit the Delete key before you type new information into the editable region or insert an image or media file. Otherwise, the brackets will show up in the Web browser.

After you have added your content, choose File/Save and give your page a name.

Figure 16.5 shows an HTML page that I created based on a template called Cards. Figure 16.6 shows the same page as it appears in the Web browser. Notice that the editable region names do not show up in the browser window.

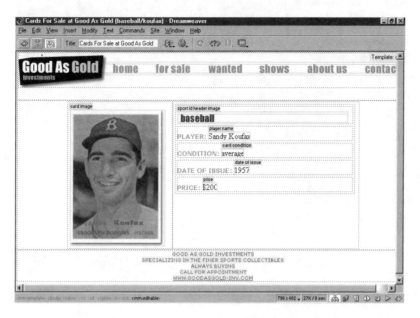

Figure 16.5   The page based on the Cards template inside Dreamweaver 4.

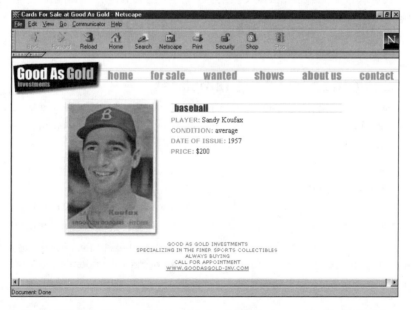

Figure 16.6   Editable and noneditable region marks don't show up inside the Web browser.

From the same template, I made the page shown in Figure 16.7.

Figure 16.7   This page is also based on the template called Cards.

No limit exists as to the number of pages you can attach to a single template. As long as the Update Page When Template Changes box is checked when you create the page (using File/New from Template), then you have to edit only the template itself to make changes in the page properties or the layout and design of noneditable regions.

Attaching and Detaching Templates

The advantage of using templates is that you can make major changes to a large number of pages in a single sweep. This section covers how to attach and detach pages to or from a template.

Attaching a Template

Imagine a situation in which you want to attach your template to a page that you already have created. Maybe you have a new template design that contains the editable region names as your old template design, and you want to update your pages to the new look. Aren't you glad you used templates so that you can do all your updating in a matter of seconds?

Tip

Choose the editable region in which you want all the (orphaned) content on your page to be deposited. Then, after the template is applied, move the items one by one from the (default) editable region to the other editable regions where you actually want them.

To attach a template to an already existing page, do the following. For best results, you should know what template you are going to attach a page to before you add the editable regions.

1. Open the page to which you want to attach the template.

2. Define editable regions using the same editable region names used in the template that you plan to attach. (Remember that you can't apply a template to another template.)

3. Choose Modify/Templates/Apply Template to Page.

4. Choose a site and the template name from the listing. Leave the Update Page When Template Changes box checked if you want Dreamweaver to update the page automatically when you make changes to the template. Click Select.

5. If the Choose Editable Region for Orphaned Content dialog box appears (shown in Figure 16.8), you must choose which editable region the old "orphaned" content should be moved to. Or, click None to delete old content and replace the entire page with the template contents. (Orphaned content is content that will not be included in the new template.)

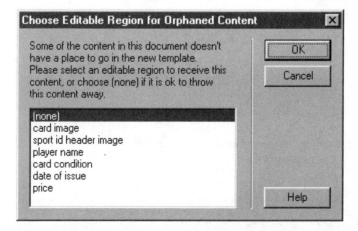

Figure 16.8   Any content in your page that isn't assigned to an editable region in the newly attached template can be moved to a specific editable region. Or, choose None to delete the content.

Detaching a Template

To detach a page from its template, do the following:

1. Open the document.
2. Choose Modify/Templates/Detach from Template.

The page will detach from the template, and all regions will become editable. Additionally, the HTML code and the comment tags defining editable regions are removed.

Updating Pages Based on a Template

When you edit your template, Dreamweaver should give you the opportunity to update all the pages based on the template with the new changes. You can also do the updating manually via the Modify/Templates submenu (see Figure 16.2).

Exercise 16.3   Updating Documents that Share a Template

To update all documents that share a template to reflect the changes you made to the template, do the following:

1. Make the changes to the template and save it.
2. Choose Modify/Template/Update Pages.
3. In the Update Pages dialog box (see Figure 16.9), you can do one of the following (first make sure that the Templates box is checked):
   - Choose Entire Site and choose a site name from the pop-up menu. This updates all pages in the site that are attached to templates.
   - Choose Files That Use, and select a template name from the listing in the pop-up menu. All pages in the current site that are attached to the template will be updated.
4. Click Start to complete the updating process.

To update a currently open document that is attached to a template, choose Modify/Templates/Update Current Page.

Note

If your pages aren't updating when you make changes to the template, you can open the Assets panel and reapply the template by clicking the Apply button. Bear in mind that content you've added to editable regions can be lost this way. Another option is to go into a page that's attached to the template and choose the option for Open Attached Template (Modify/Templates/Open Attached Template). This shows you what template Dreamweaver has the page attached to.

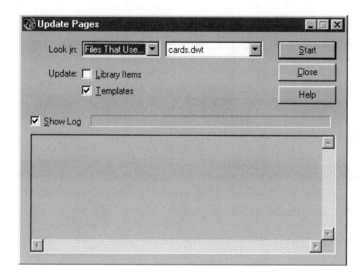

Figure 16.9   The Update Pages dialog box.

Using Templates with XML

The content that you insert into the editable regions in the files based on a template can be exported as Extensible Markup Language (XML) content. Exporting this data as XML data enables you to work with the content outside Dreamweaver. You can also import XML data into a template if the names inside the XML file correspond to the names of your template's editable regions.

When Dreamweaver imports XML data or exports your editable regions as XML data, it pairs the template content (such as text) with the name of the editable region to which it belongs (such as book_review). These are called name/value pairs.

To export editable regions as XML data, do the following:

1. Open the document containing the data that you want to export.
2. Choose File/Export/Export Editable Regions as XML.
3. In the XML dialog box (see Figure 16.10) choose a tag notation (refer to an XML file to determine which one is right for you) and click OK.
4. Name the XML file and save it in the appropriate directory.

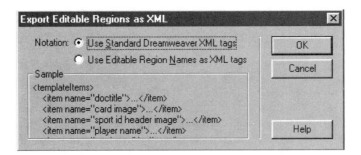

Figure 16.10   The Export Editable Regions as XML dialog box.

To import XML data, do the following:

1. Create or open the template document into which you want to import the XML content.

2. Choose File/Import/Import XML into Template.

3. Select the XML file and click Open.

A new document based on the template specified in the XML file will be created. The contents of each editable region are filled with the data from the XML file.

If your XML data isn't structured exactly right, you might run into trouble. You might want to export a sample XML file from Dreamweaver and then copy your original XML inside it. Save the new file and import it into Dreamweaver.

About Libraries

In this part of the chapter, we'll take a look at site libraries. If you've ever used a desktop publishing application such as QuarkXpress, you might already be familiar with how libraries work. If not, take a look at the section about libraries at the beginning of this chapter, or just keep reading.

When you are working on a site that has many pages, you can make use of a library and save yourself some time. The purpose of the library is to save elements of your site, such as a set of links, into a common area so that you can insert them without having to open up another document.

For example, let's say that you want to put your company's logo, name, address, phone number, and copyright information on every page in the site. Rather than typing in that information over and over again, just do it once and save the logo and text together as a library item. By using a library, you can have Dreamweaver automatically update all pages that contain a particular object. So, if the phone number of your company changes, you can update every single page that contains the phone number all at once—as long as it is part of your library.

The library is always available to you through the Assets panel. I have created library items out of many different combinations of data and updated these items later across an entire Web site in a matter of seconds.

Site libraries differ from templates because they contain individual items rather than entire pages. Also, you can use library items on impulse. No planning ahead is needed if you just want to drop in a collection of data that was saved as a library member.

Creating and Using Library Items

When you create a library item, it is saved in the Library folder of the site in which you are currently working. Remember that all library items within a site are stored in a Library folder, and all library items have the .lbi extension.

Like templates, library items should be kept in this Library folder, and you shouldn't add non–.lbi files to this folder. Dreamweaver needs to make relative links from each library item in a page. To do so, it needs to know exactly where the original library item is stored.

Tip

> If you try to make a library item and Dreamweaver gives you an error message saying the Library folder can't be found, create the folder yourself (use a capital L) and save it into your site. Then try making the item again.

Remember that when you create a library item that contains an image, you shouldn't move the image to another directory after the library has been created. If you do move the image, you'll get a broken image icon when you try to insert the library item into your document.

To create a library item, do the following:

1. In Design view, select the information that you want to save in the library.

2. Choose Window/Library (or click the Library icon on the Assets panel—it looks like an open book).

3. Click the New icon at the bottom of the Assets panel. It looks like a piece of paper with a plus sign on it (see Figure 16.11).

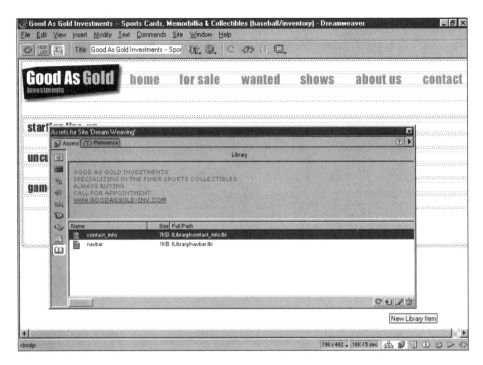

Figure 16.11   The Library panel in Dreamweaver 4.

4. Enter a short name for your object.

The object will now appear in the Library listing in the Assets panel.

To use a library item inside a document, do the following:

1. Click your cursor in the area of your document where you want to insert the Library item.

2. Open the Library section of the Assets panel and select the object from the listing by clicking it once (double-click it to edit it).

3. Click the Insert button in the lower-left corner of the Library listing in the Assets panel, or just drag the library item out onto the page. The library item will appear in the open document in the spot where your cursor is located.

All library members are surrounded by a highlighted box to indicate their association to the library. You change the color or turn it off using Dreamweaver Preferences (Edit/Preferences/Highlighting).

Tip

To drag an instance of a library item onto the page (an already detached version of the library item), you can do a Ctrl+drag to move the item from the library to the page.

Editing Library Items

When you make a change to a library item, all occurrences of the item throughout the site also are changed.

When you double-click an item in the Assets panel's Library listing or click the Open button on the Property Inspector, Dreamweaver opens the item in a new document. This new document is for editing the library item only. This is not a standalone document that you could publish to the Web.

To edit a library item, do the following:

1. Either select the item from the currently open document and click Open from the Property Inspector (see Figure 16.12), or double-click the item's icon from the Assets panel.

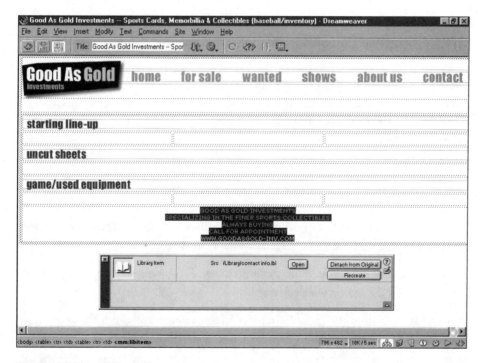

Figure 16.12   Editing a library item in Dreamweaver 4.

2. In the editing window (the background color will be gray), make your changes.

3. Choose File/Save.

4. When the Update Library Items dialog box appears (see Figure 16.13), click the Update button if you want the changes to appear across the site. (If not, you will have to detach the library item.)

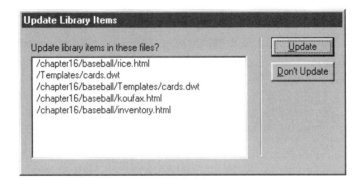

Figure 16.13   The Update Library Items dialog box.

Dreamweaver updates the pages, showing you a log in the Update Pages dialog box. Close the library editing window to return to your document.

Detaching and Deleting Library Items

Sometimes you want to make changes to a library item but not have every occurrence of the item reflect the change. In this case, you can detach a library member so that it stands alone. Be aware, however, that the detached member can no longer be updated automatically.

To detach an item, select it and click the Detach from Original button on the Property Inspector (see Figure 16.12). Alternately, you can select the item and right-click or Ctrl+click and choose the Detach from Original option from the context menu. Or, you can Ctrl+drag the item onto your page from the Library panel.

To delete a library item from your currently open document, select it and press the Delete or Backspace key on your keyboard.

To delete an item from the library, choose Window/Library and select the item's icon from the Library listing in the Assets panel. Click the trashcan icon at the bottom of the panel. Dreamweaver asks if you are sure that you want to delete the item. Remember that if you delete an item, all occurrences of it throughout the site will become detached and can no longer be updated automatically. At the same time, understand that they will not be deleted from the document(s) altogether.

Re-creating Library Items

If a library item appears missing or incomplete in a document, select it and click the Re-create button from the Property Inspector.

You might also use the Re-create button if you have accidentally saved the item into the wrong site.

Copying Library Items

If you have library items that you want to use in sites other than the site in which they were created, you can copy them to another site.

To copy a library item, choose Window/Library and select the item's icon from the listing. Right-click or Ctrl+click the icon to open the context menu. Choose Copy to Site (see Figure 16.14) and then select the site that you want to copy the item into from the submenu.

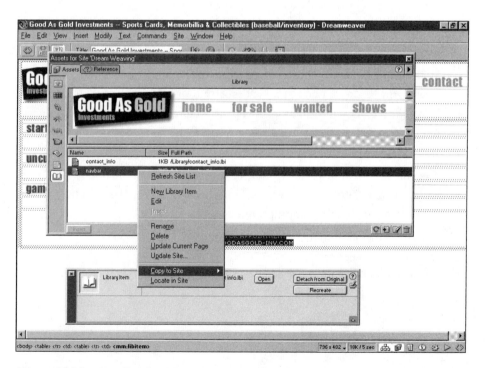

Figure 16.14   Accessing the Copy to Site option from the Library panel in Dreamweaver 4.

Tip

You can also use a library item's context menu to locate the item inside a document.

JavaScript in Library Items

When you create library items that contain Dreamweaver behaviors, only the event handler (onClick, onLoad, or onMouseOver) is copied into the library item file. The JavaScript functions themselves are not copied into the file. When the library item is used inside a document, Dreamweaver then inserts the needed JavaScript functions into the HEAD tag.

Hand-coded JavaScript can be included in a library item is you use Dreamweaver's Call JavaScript behavior when you insert your hand-coded JavaScript. If you do not use this behavior, the hand-coded JavaScript will not be included in the library item.

Because of the way Dreamweaver handles behaviors in library items, you cannot edit behaviors from the library editing window.

To edit the behaviors inside a library item, do the following:

1. Open a document containing the item, detach it from the original, and make any necessary edits to the behaviors.

2. Still working inside the document, re-create the library item by selecting it and clicking the Re-create button on the Property Inspector (see Figure 16.12). Or, delete the old behavior from the Asset panel's Library category and create a new library item with the same name (be sure to use the same spelling and capitalization).

3. To update the item in all the documents that contained the old library item, choose Modify/Library/Update Pages, and choose Files That Use and the name of the library item from the pop-up windows.

4. Make sure that Library Items is selected, and click Start.

Dreamweaver will update the pages and give you a log in the Update Pages window.

Summary

As this chapter discussed, Dreamweaver templates and site libraries can help you automate the processes of building and updating sites. With templates, you can designate elements inside a page or set of pages as editable or noneditable. This helps retain the graphic design and overall appearance of a site, and it makes it easier to make updates sitewide. Templates are created, edited, updated, and applied to pages by using the Templates pane of the Assets panel. They are stored in a folder called Templates, and have the file extension .dwt (for "Dreamweaver template").

A site library is a collection of elements, such as text and images, that can be saved and used again throughout a site. Library items are saved in a folder called Library and have the file extension .lbi (for "library item"). Changes to a single library item occur sitewide unless the item is detached from the original.

Part V

Rich Media Usage

Chapter 17

Animation with Timelines

Do you remember flipbooks? They were
little books that sometimes came as prizes
in bubble gum machines. These tiny books
would reveal a simple animation if you

flipped through the pages very quickly. Upon closer inspection, it became obvious that the animation was actually a series of images, usually cartoon sketches, one to a page. The image on each page was slightly different than the one it followed. Maybe a cartoon character's arm moved up a degree, or a facial expression changed from a smile to a frown. Whatever the difference, the change from page to page caused the animation to look fluid when the pages were flipped.

Flipbooks are a classic example of how animation works—and you can still find them in your local bubble gum machine. But joining them today are a multitude of sophisticated animation software programs such as Macromedia Flash, as well as animation functionality in programs such as Macromedia Director, Fireworks, and Dreamweaver. With animation tools like these under your fingertips, you can join in the transformation of the Web from a still, static environment to one that is bursting alive with motion.

If you want to animate elements of your Web site, first consider where in the site-building process you want to create your animations. For example, if you are creating a banner advertisement that will blink on and off and display a message, your best bet would be to make the banner ad in a Web imaging program such as Macromedia Fireworks. This way, you can have access to the most sophisticated text and drawing tools, yet still have the capability to export the entire animation as a GIF sequence that is easily emailed to prospective clients.

However, if you want to build a knock-your-socks-off Web site with swirling shapes, glowing photographs, digital video clips, scrolling text, and background sounds, you would be best off working with Macromedia Flash. Flash doesn't have the world's best drawing program (although it has improved with the latest version), but it offers you the capability to create complex animations with small file sizes that can be scaled to fit inside any Web browser window.

But say you don't want to go that far. Maybe you're more interested in offering some user interaction using text and static images, and you don't care as much about knocking people's socks off. Or maybe you just want to avoid the use of proprietary plug-ins or Java applets. If so, then dynamic layers using Dreamweaver timelines could be your answer.

This chapter covers the following topics:

- Understanding timelines
- Using the Timelines window
- Creating an animation

- Producing other timeline effects
- Applying animation tips and tricks

The Timelines Inspector

In Dreamweaver—and in DHTML, more generally—timelines are used in conjunction with layers. If the elements that you want to animate are not inside a layer, you will not be able to control them using the Timelines window. (See Chapter 10, "Using Layers," if you are unfamiliar with layers.) You should also be aware that any documents you make that contain timelines should be intended for 4.0 or above browsers. Older browsers don't support the tags that allow timelines and layers to function properly.

Another thing you should know is that timelines can be bandwidth-intensive and should be used sparingly unless you know that your audience will have fast connections and powerful processors (like on an intranet).

When you make timelines in Dreamweaver, you're making use of the Dynamic Hypertext Markup Language (DHTML). DHTML is a combination of HTML, JavaScript, and cascading style sheets (CSS).

With timelines, DHTML enables you to change the properties of layers and images in a series of frames over the period of time specified in the Timelines window. This is done using changing settings for CSS layer positioning over time. Figure 17.1 shows the Timelines Inspector. To access this inspector inside Dreamweaver, choose Window/Timelines, or use the keyboard shortcut Shift+F9.

Understanding the Timelines Inspector

Don't be daunted by the Timelines Inspector. It looks confusing with all those frames and channels, but there is a purpose for everything you see. You might not use all the features provided by the Timelines Inspector, but take the time to learn what they are. Use Figure 17.1 and the definitions provided here to learn your way around.

Playback Head

The playback head is the reddish, rectangular-shaped object that slides along the frame numbers. It shows what frame of the timeline is currently selected in the Timelines window and is displayed on the page.

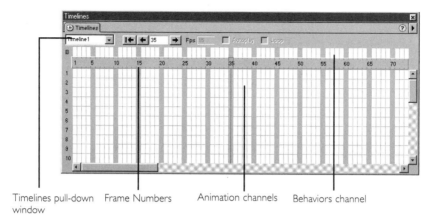

Timelines pull-down   Frame Numbers   Animation channels   Behaviors channel
window

Figure 17.1   The Timelines Inspector is where you create your time sequence and control the
resulting animation.

Timeline Pull-Down Window

Located just below the tab labeled Timeline in the upper-right corner of the Timelines
Inspector, the Timelines pull-down window lists, by number, the timelines contained in
your document. The currently selected timeline appears in the window by default.

Animation Channels

Each animation channel is numbered on the left side of the Timelines window. If your
animation contains frames that show more than one layer on the screen at the same
time, use a separate animation channel for each layer. To add an object to a channel,
select the layer containing the object from the document, and drag it to the frame number in the channel where you want to position it in the timeline.

Animation Bars

The animation bar is the shaded area, beginning and ending with a keyframe (indicated
by a circle), that appears in the animation channel when you add an object. You can add
more than one animation bar to a channel, but you cannot overlap them.

Keyframes

Keyframes are "key" because they indicate when something in the animation, such as the
position of a layer, changes. When you add an object to an animation channel, the beginning and the end of the animation bar contains a keyframe.

You can easily identify keyframes inside a timeline because each one is marked with a small circle. The change between keyframes, such as a movement of a layer from one point to another, is calculated by Dreamweaver. If you want to speed up or slow down an element of your animation, you can insert additional frames between keyframes or adjust the frames per second (FPS) ratio. Remember not to set the FPS too high, though—anything over about 30FPS will not look much faster or clearer. Also, high frame rates consume a great deal of bandwidth and tend to cause errors in certain browsers (especially Internet Explorer for Macintosh).

Behaviors Channel
Marked with a capital *B* on the left side of the Timeline Inspector, the behaviors channel is the spot where you insert behaviors. To insert a behavior, click the frame in the behaviors channel where you want the event or action to occur. Then open the Behaviors panel and click the + sign to access the list of available behaviors.

When you select a behavior, a small, shaded – sign appears in the behaviors channel.

Frame Numbers
The area above the animation channels contains the frame numbers in increments of 5. The very first frame on the left is frame no. 1. The frames then proceed sequentially. Use the text field box labeled FPS (Frame Per Second) located above the behaviors channel to specify an FPS ratio.

For example, setting the FPS to 12 instructs the browser to play 12 frames of the animation for every second. The Dreamweaver default FPS is 15 frames per second, which is a good speed to use when you are learning to animate.

Keep in mind that every frame of your animation will be played after it is loaded into the Web browser. If the Internet connection is not capable of playing the animation at the specified FPS rate, then the rate will be ignored. Again, remember that high frame rates can consume a great deal of bandwidth.

Control Options
To the right of the Timelines window's pop-up menu is a set of controls that you can use to control the viewing of your animation. We'll look at these next.

Rewind
Indicated by a left-pointing arrow and a vertical line, the Rewind button moves the playback head to the first frame in the Timelines window.

Back (Left-Pointing Arrow)

This button moves the animation back one frame. Click and hold down your mouse button to play the timeline backward.

Play (Right-Pointing Arrow)

This button moves the animation forward one frame. Click and hold down your mouse button to play the timeline continuously.

Autoplay

If autoplay is selected, the animation will play automatically as soon as it is loaded into the Web browser. This is accomplished by adding a Play Timeline behavior to an onLoad event in the document's <BODY> tag. Be aware that you must turn autoplay on or off for every timeline in your animation.

Loop

Select the Loop option if you want the timeline to play repeatedly without stopping. Looping is established by adding the Go to Timeline Frame behavior in the behaviors channel after the last frame is played. If you want to specify a certain number of loops, double-click the marker after the last frame to edit the behavior. Be aware that you must set the looping options for every timeline in your animation.

Note

For each timeline that you add, both Autoplay and Loop are set to Dreamweaver defaults. Make sure that you set both options each time you add a timeline to the Timelines window.

Using Flash Movies as Timeline Objects

You can use Flash movies as objects in your DHTML timelines. Here are a few tips to make things go smoothly:

- Remember that you must insert the Flash movie into a layer before you can add it as an object to the Timelines window.

- You must set Autoplay and Loop for the Flash movie using the Dreamweaver Properties Inspector. The Autoplay and Loop options in the Timelines window do not affect the Flash movie; they affect only the layer containing it.

- For best results, don't overlap a layer containing a Flash movie with any other layer. The area in which the Flash movie will play should be dedicated to the movie alone. This is especially true if the Flash object is looping or hidden as the rest of the timeline plays.

Creating an Animation

It's true that there are lots of animation programs to choose from. You might wonder why you should use Dreamweaver to make animations when you could use Flash or Fireworks instead.

One of the advantages of using Dreamweaver timelines is the convenience offered by not having to switch programs as you're working and not having to import files into your document. Again, you also can avoid the use of plug-ins or applets if you use DHTML timelines.

Perhaps the most important thing you can use timelines for is to integrate complex animations and navigational structures into a site. In other words, you can use timelines as a choreographic tool that will "conduct" how and when the various elements of your site will appear and how they will work. This can be particularly useful for creating animated (drop-down) menuing systems, which is one of the most common uses of DHTML timelines today.

Exercise 17.1   Creating Timelines

This three-part advanced exercise covers the basics of animating layers and assigning behaviors to them inside the Timelines window. You'll use the files in the Smoking folder on the accompanying CD to create a faux public service announcement about cigarette smoking. The sequence will scroll a banner image, play a Shockwave movie, and display a closing image followed by a paragraph of text. Thanks to the timeline, these four things will happen automatically when the page is accessed from the server or reloaded inside the browser window.

This exercise is designed for advanced users of Dreamweaver. If you are a beginner, save this exercise until you have completed the rest of the exercises in this book. Or, if you're a risk-taker, go ahead and try it now. But don't say we didn't warn you!

> **Note**
>
> Open the file called showme.html (from the Smoking folder on the accompanying CD) inside your Web browser to see what the exercise should look like when you're finished.

Part I   Creating Timelines With the Timelines Window

To get started, open the file called dontsmoke.html from the Smoking folder on your CD in Dreamweaver. Then follow the steps listed in this exercise:

1. Access the Layers panel by choosing Window/Layers or using the keyboard shortcut F2. The four layers and their content listed inside the panel are already positioned and assigned a visibility attribute (see Figure 17.2). Your job is to use the timeline to orchestrate when they appear.

Figure 17.2   In the file dontsmoke.html, the four layers are already positioned and assigned a visibility attribute.

2. Open the Timelines window by choosing Window/Timelines or by using the keyboard shortcut Shift+F9. Adjust the size of the window, if you need to.

3. In the Layers panel, select the layer named banner. While the layer is still selected, click the arrow key on the upper-right side of the Timelines window to pull down the list of options (see Figure 17.3). Choose Add Object to insert the selected layer into the timeline.

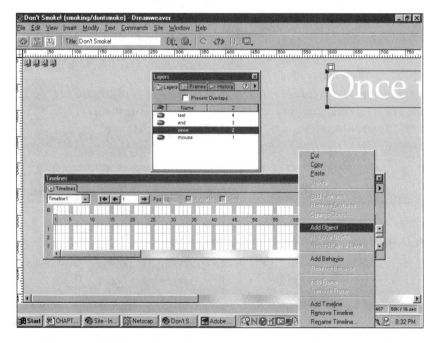

Figure 17.3   Accessing the Timelines window's list of options.

4. Dreamweaver will add the layer named banner into the timeline. An alert message about ways in which layers can be animated will appear. Check Don't Show This Message Again to remove the alert box from your screen.

5. By default, Dreamweaver inserts layers across about 15 frames. However, the Banner layer must span across 55 frames for the end result of this exercise to be successful. To extend the number of frames for the Banner layer, click and drag the last keyframe (indicated in the timeline with a circle) in the Banner sequence until it is located in frame 55 on the Timelines window (see Figure 17.4). The red playback head will move along with you as you stretch out the sequence.

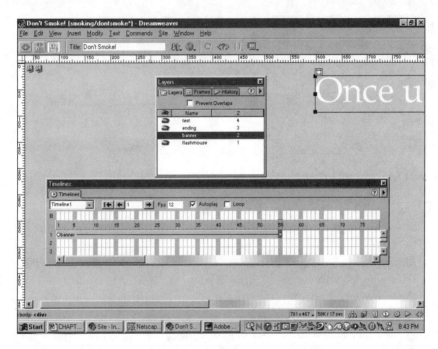

Figure 17.4   Extending the Banner layer's representation in the Timelines window.

6. To make the banner image scroll across the screen, the position of the layer in frame 55 must be changed to the position where the layer and its content (the image) should be when the scrolling is complete. To do this, select frame 55 in the window and open your Property Inspector (Ctrl+F3) to access the layer information.

7. With frame 55 of the Banner layer selected, click your cursor in the L field (indicating the leftmost position of the layer) of the Property Inspector and change the value from 599 to −1171 (see Figure 17.5). Remember that you are changing *only* the position of the layer in frame 55.

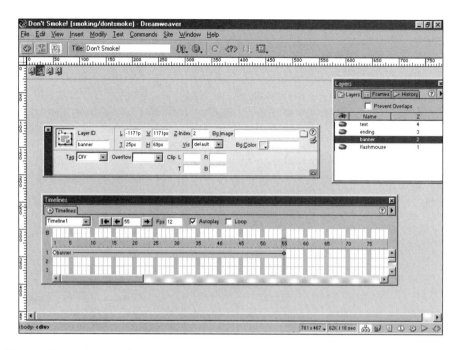

Figure 17.5   Changing the layer position with the Property Inspector.

8. Make sure that the Autoplay check box at the top of the Timelines window is activated. Also make sure that the Loop check box is *not* activated. Set the FPS ratio to 12.

9. Move the red playback head to frame 1. Press and hold the Play button (the right-pointing arrow in the controls area) on the Timelines window, and watch the image scroll horizontally across the screen. Release the Play button to stop scrolling.

10. Preview the file in your browser to ensure that it's working, but keep the file open (you should also save it to your hard drive) to complete the rest of this exercise.

Part II   Adding New Timelines

When working with timelines, be conscious of their length. If your animation is very long, you can break up the sequences by placing different elements in their own timeline. Each timeline is accessed though the Timelines window but can be viewed in its own window.

Because the Loop and Autoplay mechanisms can be different on each timeline, you can use multiple timelines to increase the functionality to your DHTML layers.

In this exercise, the remaining three layers will each be placed on their own timeline. However, they could also be organized into a single timeline with the same final result. We are using different timelines so that you can get the hang of creating new timelines.

To get started, return to the file called dontsmoke.html that you worked on in the first part of this exercise. Then do the following:

1. Create a new timeline by choosing Modify/Timeline/Add Timeline, or by selecting Add Timeline from the Timelines Inspector's Option menu. Your Timelines window should now show Timeline2, with all frames and channels blank.

2. Move the playback head to frame 61 (extend the timeline, if you need to). In the Layers panel, select the layer named Flashmouse. Keeping the layer selected, pull down the Timelines window's Option menu by clicking the right arrow key, and choose Add Object (see Figure 17.3). The layer called Flashmouse should then appear in the timeline at frame 61.

3. Select and drag the last keyframe in the Flashmouse animation bar and move it to frame 119 (see Figure 17.6). Set the FPS ratio to 12. The Loop option should *not* be checked, but the Autoplay option should be checked.

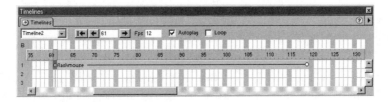

Figure 17.6   The object called Flashmouse should extend from frame 61 to 119. The FPS ratio should be 12.

4. Now that you have added the layer called Flashmouse, move on to the next layer, which is called Ending. First, make a new timeline for this layer by choosing Modify/Timeline/Add Timeline, or by selecting Add Timeline from the Timelines window's Option menu. Your Timelines window should now show Timeline3, with all frames and channels blank.

5. Move the playback head to frame 125 (extend the timeline, if you need to). In the Layers panel, select the layer named Ending. Keeping the layer selected, pull down the Timelines window's Option menu by clicking the right arrow key, and choose Add Object (see Figure 17.3). The layer called Ending should then appear in the timeline at frame 125.

6. Select and drag the last keyframe in the Ending animation bar, and move it to frame 140. Set the FPS ratio to 12. The Loop option should *not* be checked, but the Autoplay option should be checked.

7. Now, there's one more object to add. First, make a new timeline by choosing Modify/Timeline/Add Timeline, or by selecting Add Timeline from the Timelines window's Option menu. Your Timelines window should now show Timeline4, with all frames and channels blank.

8. Move the playback head to frame 145 (extend the timeline, if you need to). In the Layers panel, select the layer named Text. Keeping the layer selected, pull down the Timelines window's option menu by clicking the right arrow key, and choose Add Object. The layer called Text should then appear in the timeline at frame 145.

9. Select and drag the last keyframe in the Text animation bar, and move it back to frame 154. Set the FPS ratio to 12. The Loop option should *not* be checked, but the Autoplay option should be checked.

10.   You have now added all the necessary objects to their timelines. Check to make sure that each timeline has the Autoplay option checked, the Loop option unchecked, and an FPS ratio of 12. The next step, covered in the third part of this exercise, involves assigning behaviors to three of the four animation bars.

Part III   Assigning Behaviors to Timelines

The next part of this exercise takes the animation up a level in sophistication: You will assign behaviors to the timeline objects. In turn, the resulting DHTML code will instruct the objects to behave in a particular way after they are loaded into a Web browser.

In this exercise, you'll set behaviors so that they show and hide objects at a particular time period in the animation. You'll also assign a behavior that will instruct the browser to stop playing the animation on the very last frame.

Return to the file called dontsmoke.html that you were working on in the second part of this exercise.

1. Using the Timelines pop-up window, choose Timeline2 from the listing (see Figure 17.7) and slide the Timelines window's horizontal scrollbar forward so that you can see the animation bar called Flashmouse. Then choose Window/Behaviors, or press Shift+F3 to access the Behaviors panel.

2. In the behaviors channel, marked on the Timelines window with a capital *B*, select frame 61 (the first keyframe in the animation bar), called Flashmouse.

3. Click the + sign on the Behaviors panel and choose Show-Hide layers (see Figure 17.8).

4. In the Show-Hide Layers dialog box, select Flashmouse from the pull-down listing, and then click the button labeled Show (see Figure 17.9). Then click OK to accept the behavior. In the Timelines window's behaviors channel, a horizontal line will appear to indicate that the behavior has been added. If you select the frame in the behaviors channel, you will see the behavior listed in the Behaviors panel.

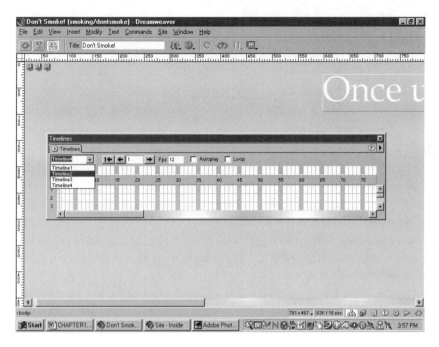

Figure 17.7   Choosing a timeline from the Timelines pop-up window.

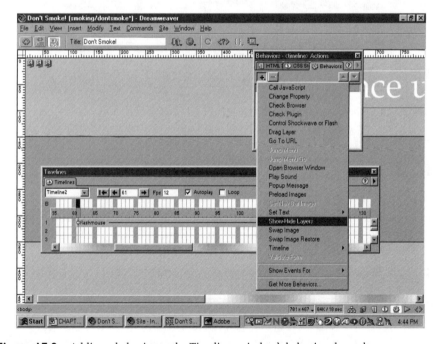

Figure 17.8   Adding a behavior to the Timelines window's behavior channel.

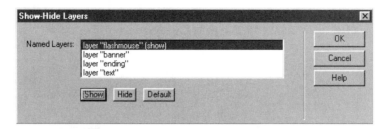

Figure 17.9   The Show-Hide dialog box lists each animation bar by name.

5. Now that you have assigned the Show behavior, you must assign the Hide behavior to the last keyframe in the Flashmouse animation bar. To do this, select frame 119 in the behaviors channel of the Timelines window.

6. To assign a Hide behavior, repeat steps 3 and 4, this time selecting the Hide behavior instead of Show. When you're done, there should be a horizontal line in the behaviors channel above frames 61 and 119.

7. For Timeline3, which contains the animation bar called Ending, repeat steps 2–6, assigning the Show behavior to frame 125 and the Hide behavior to frame 140 (see Figure 17.10).

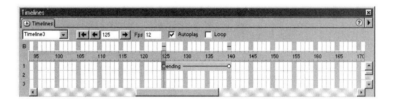

Figure 17.10   The animation bar ending with the Show-Hide behaviors added to the behaviors channel.

Now you're ready to assign the final two behaviors to Timeline4, which contains the animation channel called Text. After this step, you will be able to save the file and view the results in the Web browser.

1. Move to Timeline4 by choosing it from the Timelines pop-up window. Slide the Timelines window's horizontal scrollbar forward so that you can see the animation bar called Text.

2. In the behaviors channel, marked on the Timelines window with a capital *B*, select frame 145. Click the + sign on the Behaviors panel and choose Show-Hide layers (see Figure 17.8).

3. In the Show-Hide Layers dialog box, select Text from the pull-down listing, and then click the button labeled Show (see Figure 17.9). Then click OK to accept the behavior. In the Timelines window's behavior channel, a horizontal line will appear to indicate that the behavior has been added.

4. This time, you'll add a Stop Timeline behavior rather than the Hide behavior. To do this, select frame 154 in the behaviors channel. Click the + sign on the Behaviors panel and choose Timelines/Stop Timeline (see Figure 17.11).

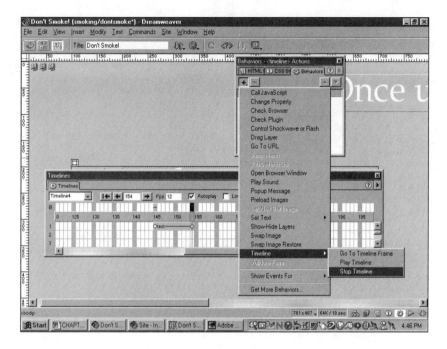

Figure 17.11   Choosing the Stop Timeline option from the Behaviors panel.

5. In the Stop Timeline dialog box (see Figure 17.12), select Timeline4 from the pull-down listing and click OK.

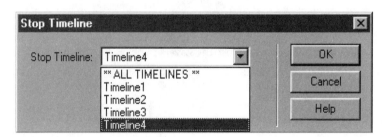

Figure 17.12   The Stop Timeline dialog box.

6. Save the file and view it inside your Web browser. A segment of the finished version is shown in Figure 17.13.

Figure 17.13   A segment of the Don't Smoke timeline as it plays in Netscape 4.0.

Other Timeline Effects

Exercise 17.1 showed a few things you can do with layers and timelines, but that is just the beginning. You can also develop timelines that allow users to control playback and scrolling, or that offer drag-and-drop objects that can be manipulated inside the Web browser.

Each time you want to add a behavior to an animation bar inside the Timelines window, use the behaviors channel and the Behaviors panel, as shown in Exercise 17.1. Or, to add Show-Hide layer behaviors, you can use the Layers panel. Select the desired frame in the Timelines Inspector, add a keyframe, and change the visibility "eye" setting in the Layers panel.

Here's a list of the behaviors you can assign to timeline objects:

- **Drag Layer**. Use the Drag Layer behavior when you want the user to be able to pick up an object inside a layer and move it around inside the browser window.
- **Show-Hide Layers**. This behavior is used to hide or reveal layers at particular frames in a timeline.

- **Play and Stop Timeline**. Use this behavior if you want to allow users to play or stop a timeline. You can set up buttons for the users to control. An example is a frame of text that could be scrolled up or down.

- **Go to Timeline Frame**. This behavior can be used to move the animation forward or backward a specified number of frames. You might use it to create a Web presentation that the user would navigate with buttons.

- **Set Text of Layer**. With this behavior, you can replace the content and formatting of a layer with new content that you specify. Although the content of the layer is changed, other attributes, such as the color, are retained. You can also embed JavaScripts in the text.

Creating an Animation Path

You can create animated text or lock images onto a path by recording the path inside Dreamweaver. This is accomplished by dragging a layer around the screen while the Record Path of Layer option has been activated.

You can use the Record feature in any number of ways. Games or Web screen savers are two examples.

Exercise 17.2   Creating an Animation Path

In this exercise, use the file called ball.gif inside the file called bounce.html to record a path that will show the ball bouncing around the browser window. It's up to you how the ball bounces!

1. With the file bounce.html open inside Dreamweaver, select the layer called Ball from the Layer panel (press F2 or select Window/Layers).

2. Choose Modify/Timeline/Record Path of Layer.

3. Take hold of the layer selection handle (your cursor will be transformed into a crossbar) and drag the layer in a bouncing ball pattern (see Figure 17.14). Release the layer when you are finished.

4. The animation that you created will be represented in the Timelines window (select Window/Timelines or press Shift+F9). Note that a keyframe will be made for each upward or downward motion of the bounce (see Figure 17.15).

Figure 17.14   Dragging the layer called Ball to make an animation path.

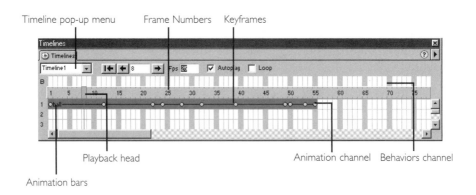

Figure 17.15   A sample "bouncing ball" timeline.

5. Set your FPS ratio to 20, or to a ratio that will play your bouncing ball realistically. Check the Autoplay option in the Timelines window so that the animation will play as soon as it's loaded into the browser window.

6. Save the file and preview it in the browser.

7. If you want to remove the timeline and start again, return to the file and choose Modify/Timeline/Remove Timeline, or choose Remove Timeline from the Timelines window's option menu.

Now that you've gotten a taste of what Dreamweaver DHTML timelines can offer you, aren't you wondering why you would choose to use another animation program?

If you are a burgeoning animator, you can put your brain to work using Dreamweaver timelines. But even if you don't want to create complex cartoons or breathtaking motion, remember that animation can also be the solution for common navigational problems. Slide shows and multiple image rollovers are two examples of animated content that can add interest and functionality to your site.

Animation Tips and Tricks

When you learn the basics of animating with timelines, keep on exploring to see what else you can come up with. Also take a look at some of the DHTML resource sites on the Internet for ideas. One recommendation is www.webmonkey.com. In the meantime, here's a list of tips to follow:

- Smoother motion can be created by extending the animation bar. Pick up the last keyframe and move it to the right to make the animation bar longer. Don't forget to adjust the other elements in your animation accordingly.

- If possible, use GIF images or small JPGs in your timelines. Large files will slow animation and make it appear choppy. Also consider importing in a vector-based Flash animation for a professional effect.

- Use multiple timelines to organize your timeline so that you don't become confused by it. Remember to set Autoplay and Loop options for each timeline.

- Save time by copying and pasting animations. To copy an animation bar, click it one time to select the entire bar, and then choose Copy from the Timelines window's Option menu. Move to the timeline where you want to paste the bar and select a specific frame. Choose Paste from the Timelines window's Option menu to insert the frames.

- Adjust timing in your animation using the FPS ratio. Add blank frames in areas where there should be a pause.

- Don't use too high of an FPS setting. If you need an animation to be shorter, shorten the timeline itself.

Summary

Using Dreamweaver to animate with timelines is accomplished by organizing layers and their contents across a period of time. The Timelines window is used to create animation bars, each containing an object such as text, image, or media file that is to be an element in the final animation.

Dreamweaver behaviors, such as Drag Layer, or the Show-Hide function can be assigned to animation bars to provide user interaction or special effects. To take timelines to their full potential, think of them as a choreographic tool that can make you the director of a show that contains a variety of data types and behind-the-scenes coding.

Dynamic Hypertext Markup Language (DHTML) makes timelines possible. When you create timelines inside Dreamweaver, the necessary DHTML code is written for you and can be seen in Code view. When using timelines, remember that they can be viewed only in 4.0 or above Web browsers. Older browsers do not support the DHTML tags needed to make timelines work properly.

Chapter 18

Animation with Flash

You might have noticed that award-winning Web sites, such as Macromedia's Sites of the Day, usually make use of Flash movies. Although there are many ways to provide animation on the Web, such as with DHTML, animated GIFs, Java, and JavaScript, you would be hard-pressed to find a person who wouldn't be somewhat impressed with the type of animation that Flash can produce.

Whether it's spinning, twirling, twisting, fading, jumping, bouncing, or singing, Flash animation is something spectacular. To make you even more hungry to learn Flash, consider that you can put more power in the punch by intertwining a Flash interface with a dynamic database. This means, among other things, that e-commerce sites can now be beautiful instead of boring. With each new version, Flash has more potential to become a standard for site building.

Those who create entire Web sites in Flash sail around many of the design issues that have stinted Web development for years. For example, Flash movies scale inside the Web browser, eliminating worries about browser window width. Because Flash is a vector-based program, there is less concern about loss of image quality. Although older browsers (under 3.0) usually don't have the Flash Player plug-in preinstalled, it's likely that more people will come to recognize the advantage of Flash sites (and other evolutions of the Web) and will upgrade, if they have not already done so.

The future is looking good for Flash, which is why you'll find new media students in colleges, universities, and technical schools rushing to sign up for Flash classes as soon as they are available. These students understand that Flash is something more than a fad.

In this chapter we'll examine the reasons for this Flash frenzy. We'll also look at these topics:

- How Flash works
- Inserting Flash movies
- Using Flash text
- Inserting Flash buttons

How Flash Works

To understand how Flash works, first be aware that Flash is not a part of Dreamweaver, nor is it part of your Web browser. You must make your movie inside the Flash software program before you can insert it into a Dreamweaver HTML document. It helps to think of Dreamweaver and Flash, both made by Macromedia, as teammates that work together to accomplish a common goal: making a great Web site that looks good and provides tremendous interactivity.

Flash has a history as an animation program that you would use to create cartoons, electronic games, and multimedia presentations. What has separated Flash from other animation programs is that you can export the animations as Shockwave files and play them inside a Web browser.

With each new version, Flash became more adapted to the needs of Web designers and developers. Now it is much more than an animation program. Although you still must understand basic animation programming concepts to use Flash, there is more potential inside the program than what you would need to make a simple animation.

For example, you can send variables from a database into a Flash interface and display the results on the Web with animation. Or, you can develop e-commerce shopping cart applications that will give users an animated interface that can also keep track of how much they're spending and retain their credit card numbers.

The combination of artistic and technical potential has made Flash famous for being the program used for some of the Web's more interesting sites. For example, the Flash developers at Oddcast.com created the interactive Web application shown in Figure 18.1, a moving, speaking "Web-bot" that can be customized at your whim.

Figure 18.1   The Oddcast.com Virtual Host will send shivers down your spine.

Vector Versus Bitmap

One of the terms often flung around when speaking of Flash is vector graphics. If you are one of the poor souls who doesn't understand what this means, read on so that you will no longer be in limbo.

Vector graphics are displayed on your screen or sent to your PostScript printer according to predetermined mathematical equations. Print and Web designers are both big fans of vector graphics because they can be scaled to be very large or very small without a loss of image quality. This applies to both the computer screen and to PostScript printers.

For example, if you want to put your company's logo on a billboard, your print designer wouldn't be able to work with the postcard-sized 72 dpi bitmap that you sent her as camera-ready copy. She would have to re-create the logo as a vector graphic in a program such as Adobe Illustrator or Photoshop, or Macromedia Freehand or Fireworks. The resulting image could be blown up to billboard size, and the edges would be crisp and the color would be true. The next day, she could take the same vector graphic logo and shrink it down to fit into the corner of an envelope and change the color. Again, the edges would be crisp and the color would be true. This is the beauty of vector graphics. An added benefit is that vector graphics have very small file sizes.

Flash is a vector-based program, so any objects that you make with the Flash drawing program are scaled to fit the viewing area. This way, they don't have to be stretched or compressed, and they do not lose quality. The same holds true for any vector shapes that you paste or import into your Flash library. However, it is not possible for a photograph or scanned line art to be treated as a vector graphic. Photographic images, such as JPGs, are bitmapped graphics and cannot be scaled. Other examples of bitmapped graphics (besides BMPs) include TIFs, PICTs, and GIFs.

Computers cannot scale bitmapped graphics without losing image quality because bitmaps are comprised of an arrangement of pixels, and that arrangement cannot be changed. When a bitmapped file is created, its pixel arrangement is as solid as your DNA. Forcing a bitmapped image to fill an area that is smaller or larger than its true size always results in a loss of image quality, and that is true for both screen and print graphics. Bitmapped images also lose quality if they are compressed or if colors are removed (such as in GIF exports).

You can import bitmapped graphics into Flash and use them in your animations. However, know ahead of time that bitmaps can slow the playback of a movie if enough bandwidth is not available, and they increase the file size of the exported Shockwave Flash (.swf) file.

It's not uncommon to use bitmapped graphics in Flash movies, but usually it's a good idea to limit how many of them are used. Otherwise, you could wind up with one slow movie on your hands. Flash gives you some control over this problem by letting you assign an image quality level for the JPGs it exports. The higher the JPG quality, the larger the file size and the more bandwidth it will require.

Identifying Vector Graphics

You can tell the difference between bitmapped and vector graphics with the following procedure.

1. Open the image inside an image-editing program such as Fireworks, or in Flash.

2. Select the image.

3. If movable points appear on the image (see Figure 18.2), it is a vector graphic. You can use the scaling tool to increase or decrease its size without losing quality.

Figure 18.2   A vector image selected in Fireworks can be adjusted by moving the points with the Open Path arrow tool.

4. If no points appear, it might be a bitmapped graphic. Try to ungroup the image to see if points will appear (in Flash, use the keyboard shortcut Ctrl+B). If you cannot get points to appear, you are dealing with a bitmapped image.

Tip

If you paste Fireworks objects into a Flash movie, they will be converted to bitmapped images. To retain vector shapes, use the Copy as Vectors option in Fireworks. Then break them apart in Flash (use Ctrl+B) for editing.

The <OBJECT> and <EMBED> Tags

Because .swf is a proprietary file type, it requires the Macromedia Flash Player to work inside a Web browser. Current versions of Netscape Navigator and Internet Explorer each come with a different version of the Macromedia Flash Player preinstalled.

In Microsoft Internet Explorer, the Macromedia Flash Player is an ActiveX control and must be referred to in HTML with the <OBJECT> tag. In Netscape Navigator, the Player is a plug-in and is referred to with the <EMBED> tag.

This boils down to the fact that both the <OBJECT> and the <EMBED> tags must be used in the HTML for the .swf file to play in Netscape Navigator and Internet Explorer. Here's an example of what HTML code would look like behind the scenes of a Dreamweaver document that contains a Shockwave file:

```
<OBJECT          CLASSID="clsid:D27CDB6E-AE6D-11cf-96B8-444553540000"
WIDTH="100" HEIGHT="100"
CODEBASE="http://active.macromedia.com/flash5/cabs/
swflash.cab#version=5,0,0,0">
<PARAM NAME="MOVIE" VALUE="moviename.swf">
<PARAM NAME="PLAY" VALUE="true">
<PARAM NAME="LOOP" VALUE="true">
<PARAM NAME="QUALITY" VALUE="high">

<EMBED SRC="moviename.swf" WIDTH="100" HEIGHT="100" PLAY="true"
LOOP="true" QUALITY="high"
PLUGINSPAGE="http://www.macromedia.com/shockwave/download/index.cgi?P1
_Prod_Version=ShockwaveFlash">
</EMBED>

</OBJECT>
```

Fortunately, you do not have to know how to code the <OBJECT> and <EMBED> tags. Dreamweaver automatically creates the code for you when a Shockwave file is inserted into a document. However, it's a good idea to have a basic understanding of the <OBJECT> and <EMBED> tags in case you ever need to edit parameters or make other changes.

Do You Know Shockwave?

Working with Flash movies inside Dreamweaver requires that you know at least a little about Flash and the files it produces. This is often an area of confusion. Because quite a few Web designers and developers have never worked with Flash, there are many myths and misconceptions floating around about the appropriate way to export Flash files and how to insert them into HTML documents.

Flash movies inserted inside Dreamweaver HTML documents must be in Shockwave Flash (.swf) format if you want them to play in the browser and if you want to set their parameters. If you create a movie in Flash, it will be saved as an .FLA file and will not play inside most Web browsers unless a version of the movie is transformed into an .swf file with the Export command.

Maybe because it is so catchy, the word *Shockwave* has been a primary source of this confusion. Many people think that Shockwave is a software program, but that is not the case. In fact, Shockwave is a file type. Just as .JPG or .GIF is assigned to an image file that is exported in a particular way from an imaging program, the extension .swf (for Shockwave Flash) is assigned to a file that is exported from Macromedia Flash or

Director (and a few others). The Shockwave file format exports Flash or Director files in a way that allows them to play and look good inside Web browsers.

So, the next time someone asks, "Do you know Shockwave?" please set the record straight.

Flash Generator Templates

Another file type that you should become familiar with is .swt (Flash Generator Template). .swt files enable you to change and replace information inside a Flash movie file. In Dreamweaver, these files are used for Flash button objects. You can use Flash to make buttons and then export them as .swt files and load them into the Dreamweaver Insert Flash Button dialog box.

Your copy of Dreamweaver came with a set of .swt files that have already been loaded for your use into the Insert Flash Button dialog box. These files are located in the Dreamweaver/Configuration/Flash Objects/Flash Buttons and Text folders. Any new buttons that you make in Flash and export as .swt files should also be stored in the same location.

If you're interested in making Flash button templates, take a look at the Flash button tutorial on the Macromedia site. To find it, search the Dreamweaver or Flash Support section at `Macromedia.com` for "Using Button Templates with Dreamweaver."

Tip

Many programs can export .swf files. Flash and Director are just two of them. If you keep your eyes open, you'll be surprised at the number of software programs that have the capability to export a .swf.

Inserting Flash Movies into Dreamweaver Documents

How lucky it is that you decided to learn Dreamweaver—you have an entire set of tools that will make your Flash movies run and look better.

Inserting a Flash movie into a Dreamweaver document couldn't be simpler:

1. Inside a Dreamweaver document, click your cursor in the area where you want the Flash movie to appear. It's a good idea to contain the movie inside a table cell or layer so that you'll have more control over its alignment.

2. Choose Insert/Media/Flash, or click the Flash icon from the Objects panel. See Figure 18.3.

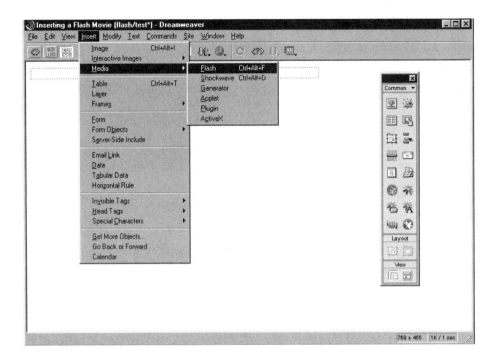

Figure 18.3   Inserting a Flash media object into a Dreamweaver 4.0 document.

3. Select the .swf that you want to insert. The movie will appear inside your document. If it has multiple frames, it will appear as a solid gray box with the Flash icon in the center. See Figure 18.4.

4. Click the Property Inspector to make changes to the Flash Movie Properties or to give the movie a name and ID (see Figure 18.4). To see all properties, click the expander arrow in the lower-right corner.

Setting Flash Movie Properties

The Property Inspector enables you to make changes to the most commonly used settings for Flash movies:

- **Name**. Use this field to assign a name that can be referred to inside a script. The Name field is unlabeled on the Property Inspector. It is located below the Flash icon on the left side. You should not use special characters or space in the name.

- **W and H**. These specify the width and height of the movie in pixels. You can also use the following sizing units: pc (picas), pt (points), in (inches), mm (millimeters), cm (centimeters), or % (for the percentage of the parent object's value). Do not use spaces before the abbreviations—for example: 30%.

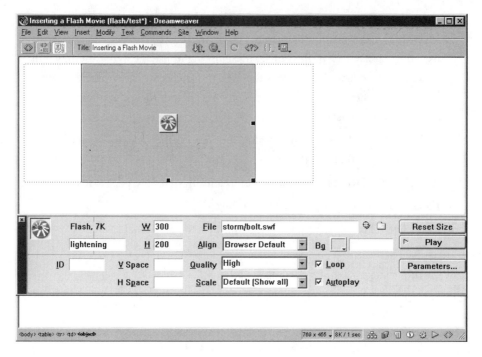

Figure 18.4   Select the Flash object inside your document and open the Property Inspector to make changes to the movie's properties.

- **File**. This field specifies the path to the Flash movie file. Click the folder icon to browse for a file.

- **Align**. Use this field to indicate how the movie should be aligned on the page and inside a Web browser.

- **Bg**. This field specifies a background color for the Flash movie. Use the Dreamweaver color palette to choose a Web-safe color.

- **ID**. Use this field to define the optional ActiveX ID parameter. Most of the time, this parameter is used to pass information between ActiveX controls.

- **V Space and H Space**. Use pixels to specify the amount of whitespace to appear around the Flash movie.

- **Parameters**. Use this field to open the dialog box for entering additional parameters to pass to the movie. This chapter includes a listing of Flash parameters. Be aware that the movie must have been designed in Flash to receive any additional parameters. See your Flash documentation for more details about using parameters.

- **Quality**. Use this field to set the quality parameter for the <OBJECT> and <EMBED> tags that run the movie. The settings relate to the level of antialiasing used during playback of the movie. It's tempting to use the highest setting, but be aware that a faster processor is required to play high-quality movies. See the sidebar, "Parameters for Flash Movies," in this chapter for more information about each quality setting.

- **Scale**. This field determines the scaling amount for the <OBJECT> and <EMBED> tags that run the movie.

- **Autoplay**. This will play the movie automatically when the page loads.

- **Loop**. This will loop the movie indefinitely.

- **Reset Size**. This will refresh the selected movie to its original size.

Exercise 18.1   Inserting and Controlling a Flash Movie

In this exercise you'll use the files in the Storm folder on your CD. With the document called storm.html open in Dreamweaver, you'll insert the Flash movie called lightning.swf and set the movie properties with the Property Inspector. Next, you'll control the playback of the movie by assigning a behavior to hypertext.

A final version of this exercise is in the Storm folder, called storm_done.html. Refer to it if you have trouble completing the exercise. However, save your own final version as storm.html onto your hard drive. Later in the chapter, you'll need it for Exercise 18.2.

1. In Dreamweaver, open the file called storm.html from the Storm folder on your CD. The file contains a table with two rows and one column. Table cell alignment and page properties have already been established for you.

2. To insert the Flash movie, click your cursor in the top table row. Choose Insert/Media/Flash (see Figure 18.5). Use the Browse feature to select the file called lightning.swf from the Storm folder on your CD. The movie will appear as a solid gray box with the Flash logo in the center.

3. Open the Property Inspector (press Shift+F3). Select the Flash Movie by clicking it one time. You should see the Flash movie properties appear in the Property Inspector. Test the movie by clicking the Play button. (If your movie doesn't play, check the Autoplay button.) After you've tested the movie, click the Stop button, which is also located on the Property Inspector when a Flash movie is selected.

4. The next step is to deactivate the Loop and Autoplay options (see Figure 18.6). If these two options are checked on your Properties Inspector Flash settings (as they are by default), uncheck them. Otherwise, the movie will loop (a looped movie will repeat indefinitely). Deactivating Autoplay keeps the movie from playing automatically when loaded into the browser.

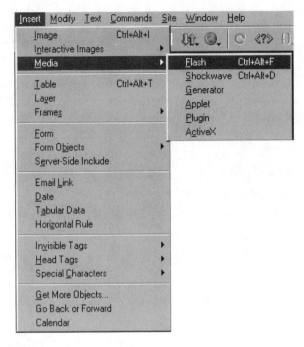

Figure 18.5   Inserting a Flash movie.

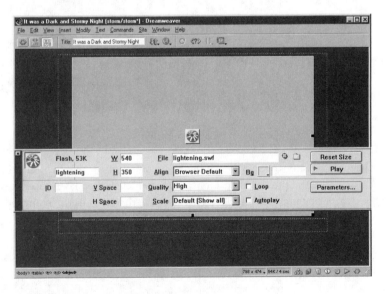

Figure 18.6   Deactivate the Loop and Autoplay features.

5. Select the movie and click the Play button again. This time, only the first frame of the movie will appear. That's because Autoplay is disabled. Click the Stop button before moving on to Step 6.

6. Select the movie and type the name **Lightning** into the Property Inspector's blank Name field, located below the Flash icon (see Figure 18.7). This gives the movie a name, in case you need to refer to it when setting up a timeline or assigning a behavior, which you're going to do next.

7. Now that the movie is inserted, you're going to set up a link so that the user can be the one who plays the movie. To do this, click your cursor into the empty table row below the Flash movie.

8. Type the phrase **How dark and stormy was it?**

9. Highlight the text and type a pound sign (#) into the Link field on the Property Inspector. This is called a null link, and it enables you to assign a behavior to text. Press the Return key to ensure that the link information is coded.

10. With the text still selected, choose Window/Behaviors. Click the plus sign (+) on the Behaviors panel to access the list of behaviors. Choose Control Shockwave or Flash to access the dialog box that you'll use to assign the behavior (see Figure 18.8).

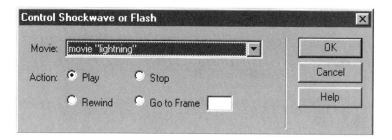

Figure 18.7   The Control Shockwave or Flash dialog box.

11. In the Control Shockwave or Flash dialog box, pull down the menu in the Movie field to choose the movie called Lightning. Then click the Play radio button. This creates a behavior to play the movie. Leave the other options unchecked (but note what they are, in case you want to use them for your own projects). Click OK to exit the dialog box.

12. Select the text again and look at the Behaviors panel. You should see the behavior created in step 11 listed in the box. Select the behavior and pull down the arrow in the center area to access the list of JavaScript event handlers. Choose onClick so that the movie will play when the user clicks the text. If your behavior already says onClick, you can skip this step.

Figure 18.8   Choosing an event handler from the pull-down list in the Behaviors panel.

13. Save the file and view it inside your Web browser to test the movie and behavior.

Note

This exercise makes use of a JavaScript function that controls the Flash movie. Because of this, it's necessary that Java be loaded into the Web browser the first time the movie is played. This takes a few seconds, but it is necessary if you want to give the user control of the movie using the Dreamweaver behavior.

Parameters for Flash Movies

Hand in hand with and embedded inside of the <OBJECT> tags are the <PARAM> tags. These tags, and the attributes with them, set certain parameters on the specific .swf file to be used and information on how it will run.

In Dreamweaver, you normally will not have to set parameters for your Flash movies inside the HTML code. This will already be done for you when you insert the movie using Dreamweaver. However, there might come a time when you will need to code the parameters yourself. Or, you might want to use parameters when creating .swt files. For that reason, we've included this listing of Flash parameters:

- **ALIGN.** Value: L (left), R (right), T (top), B (bottom)

   Template variable: $HA

   This parameter is used to position the movie inside the browser window.

- **BASE.** Value: Base directory or URL

   This parameter enables you to specify a base directory or URL for relative path statements in the movie. Use this if your Flash files are in a different directory than your other files.

- **BGCOLOR**. Value: #RRGGBB (red, green, blue)

  Template variable: $BG

  The background color specified in the Flash movie file (.fla) can be overridden with this parameter. Use the hexadecimal RGB value to specify a new background color.

- **CLASSID**. Value: clsid:D27CDB6E-AE6D-11cf-96B8-444553540000

  This parameter must be entered exactly as shown. It is the identifier for the ActiveX browser control and should be used only with the <OBJECT> tag.

- **CODEBASE**.
  Value:http://www.active.macromedia.com/flash5/cabs/swflash.cab#version=5,0,0,0"

  Enter this value exactly as shown. It is the location of the Flash player ActiveX control, and it will cause the browser to automatically download the control if it is not already installed. Use this parameter only with the <OBJECT> tag.

- **HEIGHT**. Value: pixels (such as 200) or percentages (such as 40%)

  Template variable: $HE

  This parameter specifies the height of the movie in pixels or percentages. You can take advantage of Flash's capability to scale, but you must retain an aspect ratio of 4:3. Some recommended sizes (in pixels) are: 640×480, 320×240, and 240×180.

- **LOOP**. Value: true or false

  Template variable: $LO

  Use the LOOP parameter to specify whether a movie repeats indefinitely or stops at the last frame. By default, the movie will loop.

- **MENU**. Value: true or false

  Template variable: $ME

  Use this parameter to disable the Flash controls menu that is accessed by right-clicking or Ctrl-clicking a Flash movie inside a Web browser. The Flash controls will be replaced with an About Flash option. By default, this parameter's value is true.

- **MOVIE**. Value: moviename.swf

  Template variable: $MO

  This parameter is to be used with the <OBJECT> tag only. It specifies the name of the movie to be loaded.

- **PLAY**. Value: true or false

  Template variable: $PL

  Set the PLAY value to false to prevent the Flash movie from playing automatically when it is loaded into the browser. Set the value to true if you want the movie to play automatically. By default, the value for this parameter is true.

- **PLUGINSPAGE**. Value:http://www.macromedia.com/shockwave/download/index.cgi?P1_Prod_Version=ShockwaveFlash

Use this parameter with the <EMBED> tag only. It is used to locate the Flash player plug-in so that it can be downloaded by the user if it's not already installed.

- **QUALITY**. Values: low, high, autolow, | autohigh, best

  Template variable: $QU

  This parameter determines the level of antialiasing and smoothing to be applied to a Flash movie as it plays inside the Web browser. Antialiased movies usually look better onscreen because they are smooth and crisp. However, they require more bandwidth to play. For this parameter, choose a value based on speed or appearance.

  low eliminates any antialiasing. The Flash movie will not look as good, but it will play faster.

  autolow loads the movie into the browser without antialiasing. As soon as the movie is loaded, antialiasing will be applied only when the movie is receiving enough bandwidth to play at its specified FPS ratio.

  high always applies antialiasing but does not smooth images if they are animated. If images are not animated, smoothing is applied. This is the default value for the QUALITY parameter.

  autohigh begins the playback of a movie with antialiasing applied, but it disables antialiasing if there is not enough bandwidth to sustain the FPS ratio.

  best always provides the best image quality by antialiasing and smoothing bitmapped images, regardless of available bandwidth. No adjustment is made if the movie plays slower than the specified FPS ratio.

- **SRC**. Value: moviename.swf

  Template variable: $MO

  This parameter specifies the name of the movie to be loaded. It should be used only with the <EMBED> tag.

- **SWLIVECONNECT**. This parameter enables you to specify whether a browser should start Java upon loading the Flash movie for the first time. By default, this parameter's value is FALSE. Starting Java takes time, so use this parameter as TRUE only if necessary. An example use of the TRUE value for this parameter is this: When both JavaScript and Flash are on the same page, Java must be running so that the FSCommand will work. However, if you are using JavaScript for a function such a browser detection, or another function unrelated to FSCommand actions, you can use this parameter to prevent Java from running and slowing down the load-in time.

- **SALIGN**. L, R, T, B, TL, TR, BL, BR

  Template variable: $SA

  This alignment parameter specifies where a *scaled* Flash movie will appear inside the browser window. If the movie is not scaled with the SCALE parameter, use the ALIGN parameter to position the movie.

  L, R, T, and B position the move to the left, right, or top or bottom edge of the browser window. The remaining three sides will be cropped if they don't fit.

TL and TR positions the movie to the top left and top right of the browser window and crops the bottom and right or left side.

BL and BR position the movie at the bottom left or bottom right of the browser window. The top and sides will be cropped if they don't fit.

By default, scaled movies are centered inside the browser window. If there is not enough room for the movie, cropping or borders may appear.

- **SCALE**. Value: showall, noborder, exactfit

    Template variable: $SC

    This optional parameter defines how the movie is placed within the browser window when WIDTH and HEIGHT values are percentages.

    The default, showall, makes the movie visible in the specified area without distortion. The original aspect ratio of the movie are maintained. Borders may appear on two sides of the movie.

    noborder scales the movie to fill the specified area, without distortion but possibly with some cropping, while maintaining the original aspect ratio of the movie.

    exactfit makes the entire movie visible in the specified area without trying to preserve the original aspect ratio. Be on the lookout for any distortion that may occur.

- **WIDTH**. Value: pixels or percentages (example: 240px or 300%)

    Template variable: $WI

    This parameter specifies the width of the movie in either pixels or percentage of browser window. If you change the width of the movie to a pixel or percentage value different from what was set in the Flash file, some distortion may occur.

- **WMODE**. Value: Window, Opaque, Transparent

    Template variable: $WM

    This parameter enables you to take advantage of the transparent movie, absolute positioning, and layering capabilities available in Internet Explorer 4.0 and above. Be aware that this tag works only in Windows with the Flash ActiveX control.

    Window plays the movie inside its own rectangular window on a Web page.

    Opaque hides everything behind the movie.

    Transparent reveals the background of the HTML page through all the transparent portions of the movie. Be aware that this may slow down the movie considerably.

    By default, the value is Window.

Using Flash Text

If you want to make a few snazzy-looking headlines in a font other than the Web standards, you might want to use the Flash text feature, which is new in Dreamweaver 4.

To insert Flash text, Choose Insert/Interactive Images/Flash Text, or select Insert Flash Text from the Objects panel.

Before using Flash text, be aware that an .swf file will be created each time you exit the Insert Flash Text dialog box. This .swf file is a Flash movie with one frame.

Also be aware that Flash text is limited to 1,024 characters for each file. Therefore, Flash text is best used for headlines rather than body text.

What you'll probably like about Flash text is that the fonts on your computer's hard drive will be available to you. Your text will be converted to vector shapes, so you won't have to worry about placing the font information on your server. Another big plus is that your Flash text is scalable and can be easily edited in Dreamweaver.

Exercise 18.2   Inserting Flash Text

In this exercise, you'll create a banner with Flash text. Then, you'll link the text to the file you created in Exercise 18.1.

Use the file called banner.html in the Storm folder on your CD. You must save this file to your hard drive (save the entire folder). Otherwise, you'll run into problems when you create the Flash text. A finished version of this exercise is also in the folder, called banner_done.html. Refer to it if you have trouble completing this exercise.

1. Open the file called banner.html. The file contains a table with two rows. In this exercise, you're going to use only the top row. For now, just ignore the bottom row; we'll get to that in Exercise 18.3.

2. Click your cursor in the top row. Choose Insert/Interactive Images/Flash Text. This pulls up the Flash text dialog box. You will use only a few of the fields found in this dialog box (see Figure 18.9).

3. Now you can type the message **It was a dark and stormy night** into the Text area of the Flash Text dialog box. Use the Font and Font Size fields to choose a font and font size for the message. Try to pick a combination that will be large enough to fill up the width of your screen. The font in the example is Arial, 40 points.

4. Pull down the Color chip icon to select white (#FFFFFF) as the text color. Pull down the Rollover Color chip and choose a yellow color.

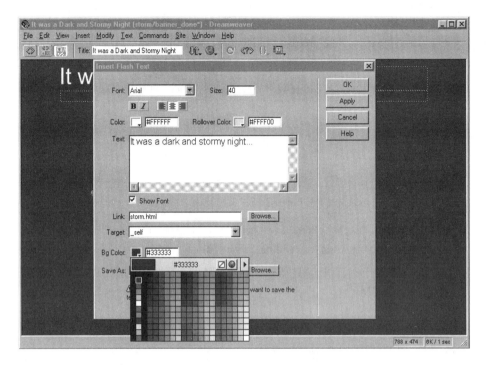

Figure 18.9   Choosing a background color with the eye-dropper tool from the Flash Text
dialog box.

5. Next, you need to give the Flash text a background color. If you skip this step, the
   Flash text will have a default background color of white, which will render your
   white text invisible. Pull down the Bg Color chip and move the eye-dropper out
   of the dialog box so that it hovers over the background color of the open
   Dreamweaver document (see Figure 18.9). When the hexadecimal representation
   reads #333333, click the eye-dropper to assign the color.

6. Click the Browse button next to the Link field, and choose the file called
   storm.html, which you completed in Exercise 18.1. Then, pull down the Target
   menu and choose _self. This determines where the file will open.

7. Take note of the Save As field. After you exit the Insert Flash Text dialog box, an
   .swf (Shockwave Flash) file will be saved to your computer's hard drive. Use this
   field to browse for the area where you want to save your file. You can also rename
   it, if you want.

8. Click Apply to view the text inside the file without closing the dialog box. Make
   any changes that you want to make, and then close the dialog box by clicking
   OK.

9. Your Flash text will appear as an object inside the document. Note that when you
   select the Flash object by clicking it one time, the Property Inspector (Ctrl+F3)

shows you its properties. Don't try to change the width and height of the Flash text using the Property Inspector (doing so could cause a loss of image quality). If you need to edit the text, click the Edit button to return to the Insert Flash Text dialog box. (However, if you do resize the Flash text with the Property Inspector, click the Reset Size button to refresh the image.) See Figure 18.10.

10. With the Flash text still selected, click the Play button on the Property Inspector. This activate the rollover function. Move your mouse over the Flash text to see the rollover color in action. See Figure 18.10.

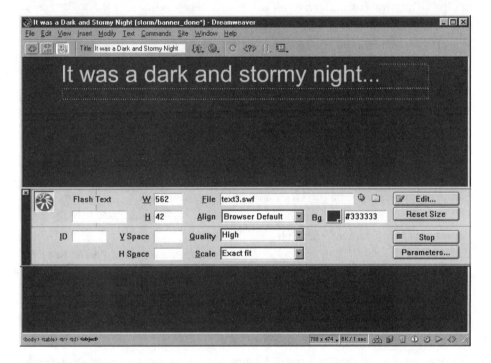

Figure 18.10   Playing the Flash text with the Property Inspector in Dreamweaver.

11. Click the Stop button. Then save the file and preview it inside your Web browser. The text should link to the file called storm.html.

Editing Flash Text

After you've created Flash text, you can make changes to it by selecting the text object and clicking the Edit button in the Property Inspector.

After you edit the Flash text, you might notice a loss of quality in the text object on your screen. For example, the text might look stretched out or squeezed together. Open the Property Inspector (press Shift+F3) and click the Play button to refresh the text size. The distortion will return when you click Stop, but if you save the file and reopen it, the text image will look crisp again.

Using Flash Buttons

Also new in Dreamweaver 4 are Flash buttons, which can be inserted into a document by choosing Insert/Interactive Images/Flash Button, or by clicking Insert Flash Button on the Objects panel (see Figure 18.11).

Dreamweaver comes with a library of Flash buttons already loaded into the Insert Flash Button dialog box. The locations of these files are the Dreamweaver/Configuration/Flash Objects/Flash Buttons and Text folders. Any new buttons that you make in Flash and export as .swt files should also be stored in the same location.

If you're interested in making Flash button templates, take a look at the Flash button tutorial on the Macromedia site. To find it, search the Dreamweaver or Flash Support section at Macromedia.com for "Using Button Templates with Dreamweaver."

Just like Flash text, Flash buttons are .swf files that will be saved on your hard drive. Each time you create a Flash button, another file will be created. You must remember to upload these files along with the HTML document when you publish your site.

The advantage of using Flash buttons as opposed to .JPG or .GIF buttons is that Flash buttons are animated and scalable, and they have very low file sizes.

Figure 18.11
The Insert Flash Button icon on the Objects panel.

Exercise 18.3   Inserting Flash Buttons in Dreamweaver

In this exercise, you'll create a series of Flash buttons inside the Dreamweaver document that you created in Exercise 18.2. The buttons will be linked to the .swf files inside the Storm folder, called rain.swf, bolt.swf, thunder.swf, and wind.swf. These .swf files will each play a sound, and because they are not embedded in an HTML file, they will open a blank browser window. If you want, you can extend this exercise by embedding each sound's .swf file into an HTML document.

1. Open the Dreamweaver document banner.html that you created in Exercise 18.2 from your Storm folder. You'll be inserting the Flash buttons into the nested table located in the bottom table row, beneath the banner. To get started, click your cursor in the cell to the far left.

2. Choose Insert/Interactive Media/Flash Button to access the Insert Flash Button dialog box (see Figure 18.12). Choose a button style (the sample is

Soft-Raspberry) and type **Rain** in the text field. Choose a font face and size (the sample is Verdana, size 12), and link the button to the file rain.swf from the Storm folder.

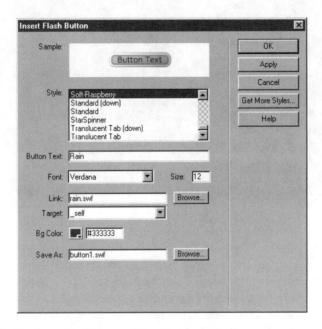

Figure 18.12   The Insert Flash Button dialog box.

3. Choose a background color for the Flash button to match the background of the page (#333333). To do this, click the color chip icon beside the Bg Color field and move the eye-dropper tool out to the background of the Dreamweaver document.

4. Dreamweaver automatically assigns a name for your button. This name appears in the Save As field with the .swf extension. If you want to change the name, you may do so as long as the name has the lowercase .swf extension. Also be aware that the button must remain in the same directory as the .swf file it's linking to.

5. Click the Apply button to see what the button will look like inside the document. When you're satisfied with the way the button looks, click OK to exit the Insert Flash Button dialog box.

6. Repeat steps 2–5 for each of the remaining three buttons: Lightning, Thunder, and Wind, placing each button inside its own table cell. Link the Lightning button to the file called bolt.swf, link the Thunder button to the file called thunder.swf, and link the Wind button to the file called wind.swf. See Figure 18.13.

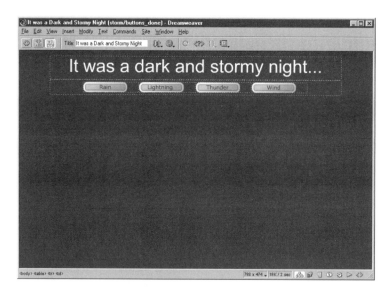

Figure 18.13   The four Flash buttons inside the completed file.

7. Each of the buttons will appear as individual objects inside their table cells. When the Property Inspector is open (press Shift+F3), you can click the Play button to activate the rollover feature. To hear the sounds to which the buttons are linking, save the file to the Storm folder that you saved onto your hard drive, and open the file inside the Web browser.

8. The file buttons_done.html in the Storm folder on your CD contains a finished version of this exercise. Refer to it if you have any trouble completing the steps.

Flash, or Dr. Frankenstein?

"It's not real," warns the stubble-scalped punk rocker who introduces visitors to the Oddcast.com Virtual Host (see Figure 18.14). "It's just a computer-generated fantasy."

Computer eugenics might be a better term to describe the Virtual Host, a Flash project developed by the New York City Web design firm Oddcast.com. The Virtual Host interface consists of an animated human torso centered in a colorful control panel. The Host's gender, hair and eye color, clothing, jewelry, hairstyle, and eyeglasses can be selected by clicking though an array of choices, producing an infinite number of hip urbanites.

"In the Virtual Host's earlier incarnation, as a virtual woman we created named 'K,' we had a lot of people writing love letters. Some of the fans got a little obsessive, which I guess means the illusion worked, but frankly I found it a little frightening," says Chris Dixon, one of the masterminds behind the Virtual Host.

Dixon has been working on the Virtual Host project since its conception. "It started with an experiment we did to see if we could start with a straight-on picture of a face and animate it to look like its talking and looking around," Dixon says. "We kept adding little things to it over time. We finally added good lip synching and the ability for the user to customize it. It really took off when one of our really great designers, James Salanitri, redesigned the look and added the extras that make it fun."

Dixon has been working with Flash since the second version and is optimistic about the program's potential to transform the Web into an animated, interactive environment. "I think with the ubiquity of the plug-in and greater stability and power of future versions, Flash has a very good chance of attracting some hard-core programmers and becoming the standard for all kinds of browser-based software," he says. "With the new live XML socket in Flash 5, for example, people have started using it for experimental, real-time, multiplayer games, and you could even imagine it being used extensively for 'serious' purposes, such as financial sites using it for live stock quotes with graphs."

At Oddcast.com, Dixon and his coworkers use Flash to develop attention-getting, award-winning sites that "look great and have advanced functionality yet still work well on 56K modems," says Dixon. "We have another program that lets users create music videos, and another that lets them interact with an MP3 visualizer." Currently the company is using Flash to create an online Karaoke game.

For programmers who are learning Flash, Dixon has some advice: "I think Flash is a lot of fun and should be approached with a playful spirit. If you can get used to the vector style and programming language, it's a great medium in which to experiment and to work. I would say get a good book and, most of all, study other people's work, especially the source .fla files that you can find on a lot of Flash Web sites like www.flashkit.com."

Figure 18.14   Visit the Virtual Host or play the Beat Sensor at www.oddcast.com.

Summary

This chapter focused on how Flash and Dreamweaver can be integrated to enliven and speed up your site. Flash is becoming more popular because of its capability to scale vector graphics into browser windows of any size. These vector graphics are also very small in file size and don't take a long time to download. Flash movies can also contain bitmapped graphics, which can slow down playback time.

In Dreamweaver, you can insert a Flash movie and set its Properties with the Property Inspector. You can also assign a behavior to a Flash movie that will allow users to control the playback. Other Flash functions in Dreamweaver include the capability to create and edit Flash text and Flash buttons. Although Dreamweaver contains a set of Flash buttons for your use, you can create more buttons in Flash and save them as .swt files and import them into Dreamweaver.

Chapter 19

JavaScripting with Dreamweaver

When most of us think of the average Web

site surfing experience, one of the first

words that comes to mind is *interactive*. As

you know, the Web is made up of many

different technologies. Some of these technologies, such as Flash, allow for animation and sound. Others allow for full-motion video, 360-degree panoramic views, and even online games. But more important than all of these rich media elements combined is the capability to have the client (user) get involved in the presentations that you prepare for the Web. At the core of this interactivity is JavaScript.

On its own, HTML is not a very powerful language for creating involved multimedia content. This is largely because most of the HTML language is devoted to describing elements in a static state. That is, HTML does not offer the capability to change elements over time, and it also doesn't permit clients to do so. JavaScript provides these capabilities. This chapter covers the following topics:

- Basics of JavaScript

- Dreamweaver and JavaScript

- Varieties of script functions

- Where to find JavaScripts

- Inserting a JavaScript

- Editing scripts

JavaScript Basics

Because HTML is a static medium (that is, it is rendered once and does not change), you'll need to rely on other languages to create interactivity and processing. Some of these languages, such as Perl and PHP, run on the Web server, and so they're collectively grouped as server-side technologies. These languages allow for robust programming and functionality, but they all require one thing: They need to receive data from the end user before they can process it. The most obvious drawback is an issue of speed. For the end user to experience any of this interactivity, his computer must send data, wait, receive responses from the Web server, and, in most cases, load another page.

The other set of languages commonly used on the Web are referred to as client-side languages. This means that they are offloaded to the end user's computer to be processed in real time while the page is utilized. This offers a clear advantage over server-side programming because the client can utilize the program without a lag. One thing to realize, however, is that these client-side scripts are not as robust as their server-side counterparts, so, for now, both remain necessary.

For the most part, JavaScript is a client-side technology. In its most common form, it is used in conjunction with HTML code to increase the functionality of an HTML page.

Because of its capability to be placed inline with HTML code, it is a natural for the Web because the program is ready even before the HTML part of the page is. Therefore, if you can see the page, it is already functional.

The basis for JavaScript is what is commonly referred to as object-oriented technology. Consider the two words making up the description: An object, just like a person, place, or thing, is something tangible, something you can have perform an action, or something that can be described. *Oriented* means being centered upon or around. In the case of JavaScript, the objects we are centered on are pieces of a hierarchy whose top is the browser window itself.

This might sound either straightforward to you or a bit overwhelming. Either way, you are right where you need to be to plunge into the heart of JavaScript. Realize that programming for the novice is rough at first, but with your HTML knowledge, you already know more than you think.

Elements

JavaScript is made up of two distinct areas. One is the built-in stuff, such as the programming aspects and the languages syntax. The other half is the stuff you create, such as a user-defined function, (a fancy way to describe a group of instructions that perform a set of tasks) and data that you want to store in memory.

This section examines the pieces, or building blocks, of JavaScript. If you take it slow and try to visualize it as you go, you'll probably grasp it in no time.

Elements: Variables

In their simplest form, *variables* are a means to store information in memory for later use. This can be either *strings* of information (alphanumeric), *numeric* information, or *Boolean* values. A variable is identified with the word *var*. Probably the most confusing to use among newer JavaScript users is string versus numeric variables. Simply put, a string variable relays data, while a numeric variable stores values to be later scrutinized through test or calculation.

To further describe this, let's use a practical example. If you want to remember someone's name and number, you might write it down on a scrap piece of paper. Later you can come back, read what you had written, and choose to write it down in your address book. This is an example of storing a string. It is simply data that you want to read later. This could be written as `var nameAddress = "Joe 555-5555"`.

If you instead write down a number such as 25, you can later use that number to figure out a new value. Let's say that you have 25 apples per box, and you count three boxes of apples total. The apples per box can be expressed as follows:

```
var boxApples = 25
```

The amount of boxes can be expressed as follows:

```
var boxTotal = 3
```

You can use the value stored for apples (25) and multiply with it the value stored for boxes (3) to figure out the grand total:

```
var totApples = boxApples * boxTotal
```

If you asked JavaScript now how much `totApples` equals, it would return 75. This is obviously numeric.

When creating a variable, you simply state this:

```
var nameofvariable = value
```

Here, `var` states that you are declaring a variable, `nameofvariable` is the distinct name that you assign to the variable, and `value` is the information that you want to be stored and associated with that variable.

If you want the information to be a string—that is, you do not want the information to be interpreted—you encapsulate the value in quotation marks:

```
var name = "Blaine"
```

If the information is numerical and you will use it later for computation, you simply write the value without quotation marks:

```
var total = 8
```

Finally, if the information is a true or false value, you simply state `true` or `false`, again without quotation marks:

```
var customer = true
```

To wrap up, if you want to simply retain information, you place quotes around it so that it will not be interpreted. If you want the information to be used to calculate or to state whether a condition is true or false, do not use quotes.

Elements: Objects and Properties

JavaScript is an object-oriented language, which means that it refers to elements called objects to perform its tasks. For the purpose of the analogy, it is practical to consider these objects three-dimensionally, or as if they are physical things. An example might be a box or a balloon.

Furthermore, these objects can be described and differentiated through the use of properties. Considering the previous example, you might state `box.color = "blue"`, where `box` is the object, `color` is the property of the box, and `blue` is the value of the property.

Elements: Methods

To assign a behavior to an object, you use methods. A *method* is an action that the object is to perform (it is important to realize that it is the object and not the user to which these actions belong). To further the analogy, you could say:

```
box.enclose()
```

Here, `box` is the object and `enclose` is the method. You will also note the parentheses after the method. Inside these parentheses you can place an argument. An *argument* is a message that is to be passed to the object. An example might be this:

```
box.enclose("stapler")
```

Realize, however, that not all methods require arguments.

Elements: Functions

Functions enable you to write a statement (or several statements) and use them by stating their name. Take a look at an example:

```
function Package(){
box.enclose("stapler")
};
```

Later when you call this function, `box.enclose(stapler)` will execute. This is particularly useful because you do not have to rewrite this statement each time you want to use it. Also note that the statement is enclosed inside braces ({}). Any statements that you place between these braces will also execute.

Finally, if you want this function to instead facilitate a variety of situations, you can use it along with a variable:

```
var itemname = "stapler"
Function Package(itemname){
box.enclose(itemname)
};
```

By creating the variable named `itemname`, whatever you equate it to will be passed to the function and to the `enclose` method.

Elements: Event Handlers

Event handlers facilitate the interaction between the user and the script that you create. For instance, when a user moves the mouse over a certain graphic and clicks, you can use an event handler to trigger a function:

```
onclick = "Package()"
```

Here, `onclick` is the event handler and `"Package"` is the function to be performed.

Dreamweaver and JavaScript

In Dreamweaver, you have access to prebuilt JavaScripts, through the Behaviors Panel. The Behaviors Panel offers a simple menu-based means of inserting JavaScript into your HTML document (see Figure 19.1).

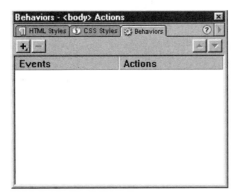

Figure 19.1   The Behaviors panel.

Some of the scripts that you have available through this panel include Form Validation, Browser and Plug-in Detection, Jump Menu Creation, and Pop-up Messages.

To access these and other scripts, simply click the plus symbol (+) drop-down menu (see Figure 19.2).

If you require more scripts (behaviors), selecting Get More Behaviors enables you to access a full array of scripts from the Macromedia Exchange site (www.macromedia.com). Selecting this automatically launches your browser and directs it to the Macromedia site.

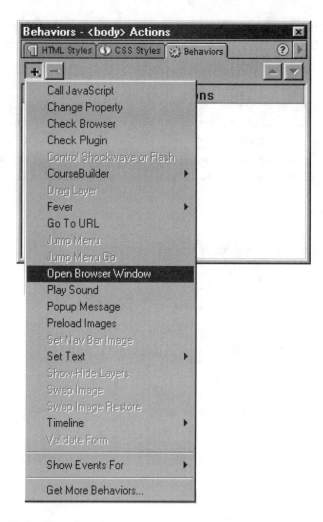

Figure 19.2   The + drop-down menu.

Inserting Behaviors

Inserting these behaviors into your site couldn't be easier. To insert a script, you simply select an appropriate object in your document, (a form, image, or something similar) or an insertion point. Then you pull down the + drop-down menu and select the appropriate behavior. If more information is required for the script, a dialog box will appear prompting you for it.

Exercise 19.1   Pop-up Message Behavior

Now let's insert a behavior as an example. You will insert a pop-up message script that will show a pop-up box with text and an OK button to close it.

1. Open a new document, and place the insertion point at the start of it.

2. Next, select Pop-up Message from the + pull-down menu. After you select the Pop-up Message item, you are prompted to type the text that you want to insert into the box that will be created.

3. Type **Welcome to our site**. When you are finished typing the message, simply select OK. Dreamweaver inserts the appropriate script and event handler to trigger it.

4. Choose File/Preview In Browser/Browser to see the result (see Figure 19.3).

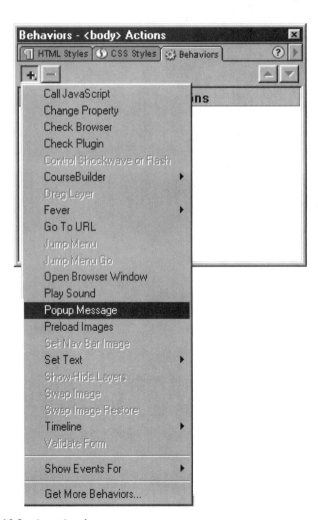

Figure 19.3   Inserting the pop-up message.

As the name suggests, the onLoad event handler should execute the function when the page is first entered. The pop-up message box is actually an alert box, as seen in Figure 19.4.

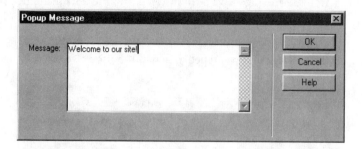

Figure 19.4   Pop-up Message dialog box.

At this point, take note of the Behaviors panel. You will now see that there is an item appearing to reflect your newly inserted script (see Figure 19.5).

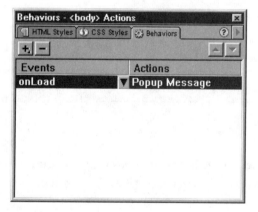

Figure 19.5   The Behaviors panel with the new behavior.

First, you will see that the new item is broken down into two columns. The first one is under the Events column. Any event handlers associated with the script appear intuitively under events. Event handlers are elements that detect user-driven actions. If you want to alter the associated event, simply move your mouse over the event and click the drop-down arrow for the event; then select a new one.

Try the onUnload event, and your pop-up should appear when the user attempts to leave that page. The second column is labeled Actions. This is where the main body of the script is contained.

Now that the script and message have been inserted into the document, test your page by selecting File/Preview in Browser (or press F12) (see Figure 19.6). You should see a blank document appear in your browser and a small message box appear in the center of the screen with the message that you typed and an OK button to close it.

Figure 19.6   Preview in Browser.

Now close the browser, and go back to the document in Dreamweaver. Open your Code Inspector, or select View/Code and Design (if you are not in that view already), and look at the code that Dreamweaver has inserted (see Figure 19.7).

In the <HEAD> section of the document, you should notice that Dreamweaver has inserted a tag named <SCRIPT>. The attribute LANGUAGE is also auto-inserted into the <SCRIPT> tag, and its value is equal to JavaScript. This is to inform the browser that you will be using a different language than HTML until you close the <SCRIPT> tag and to interpret the language as JavaScript. Although JavaScript is the default scripting language in most browsers, this might change in the future, so continue to declare the language for clarity. Next you have a multiline comment tag (<!--), which you use to stop the browser from interpreting your JavaScript as HTML.

```
popup - Code Inspector                                                    ☒
<>Code Inspector                                                        ?▶

⟨!⟩ ⊙. │ C ⟨?⟩ {}. ▦.
<html>
<head>
<title>Javascript Behaviors</title>
<meta http-equiv="Content-Type" content="text/html; charset=iso-8859-1">
<script language="JavaScript">
<!--
function MM_popupMsg(msg) { //v1.0
   alert(msg);
}
//-->
</script>
</head>

<body bgcolor="#FFFFFF" text="#000000" onLoad="MM_popupMsg('Welcome to our site!')">
</body>
</html>
```

Figure 19.7   Source code.

After these two lines of code have been entered, Dreamweaver starts right into the script. Your pop-up message box is made up of a function called MM_popupMsg. Take note that the argument in the `alert` method is set to (msg). Because it is not a string, and because you have not created a variable named msg, you can assume that this will appear later in the script or in the HTML document.

Finally, the comment tag is closed (//-->), and the <SCRIPT> tag is also closed. This is a completed script.

So far you have a script, but on its own it won't execute. You need to have another bit of code to trigger it.

Now if you look at the <BODY> tag, you will see an event handler (see Figure 19.8). After the BGCOLOR attribute and the TEXT attribute, you have this statement:

```
onLoad = "MM_popupMsg('Welcome to our site')
```

In this statement, `onLoad` is the event handler, `MM_popupMsg` calls the function, and the argument (`'Welcome to our site'`) gets passed to the function and to the `alert` method.

Figure 19.8   Event handler.

Editing Behaviors

Now that you have seen how to insert behaviors, inevitably you will need to either remove or alter them.

Removing behaviors is a simple enough task, facilitated by the minus (–) button in the Behaviors panel. Simply select the behavior that you want to remove and press this button.

Editing the behavior is just as easy and also takes place in the Behaviors panel. Dreamweaver has default event handlers associated with the behaviors, and the event handler is automatically inserted (in this case, onLoad). However, in most situations, you can choose from two or more different types of event handlers.

To choose a different event handler, simply click the arrow to the right of the event and select from the list that drops down. The one thing that can be tricky here is that if you associated the behavior with a particular object on your page, you must be sure to select that object before you will see your behavior.

Exercise 19.2   Changing the Pop-up Message Behavior

To change the behavior of the pop-up message, follow the steps in this exercise:

1. Complete the steps contained in Exercise 19.1.

2. Select onUnload from the Events drop-down list (see Figure 19.9).

3. Double-click the action Pop-up Message in the Actions column. When the text that you previously typed reappears, simply type the message **Thanks For Visiting Us**.

4. Preview the results in a browser.

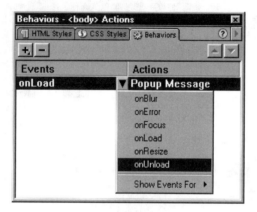

Figure 19.9   Event drop-down list.

Also take note of the last item that appears, Show Events For. By hovering over this item, a second drop-down list appears, enabling you to select from different browser series, such as 3.0 and later browsers (which is selected by default) (see Figure 19.10)

This enables you to be sure that the browsers you are targeting with your site support the event handlers from which you are choosing.

The actions are also editable from the Behaviors panel. By double-clicking an action, the original dialog box that appeared when you inserted the behavior reappears, with all the information that you entered intact (see Figure 19.11).

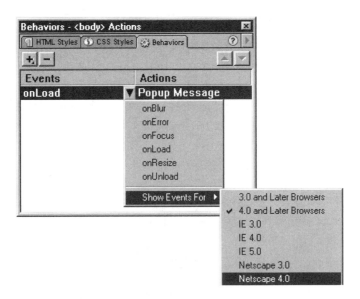

Figure 19.10   Show Events For drop-down list.

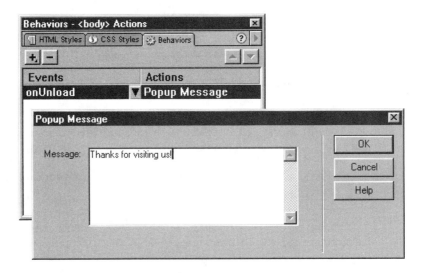

Figure 19.11   Insert Behavior dialog box with information entered.

Now all you need to do is make the changes to the dialog box and click OK when you are satisfied.

Summary

This chapter discussed all the steps necessary to insert, edit, and remove behaviors in your Web page/site. Although they may be more or less complicated in their implementation, all behaviors are utilized in this manner.

Chapter 20

Inserting Media Objects

It's one of the great challenges of Web multimedia to figure out which technology works best for what and how to make everybody play nice. This chapter is about doing just that. You've already seen how Dreamweaver and Flash can be used together to create a media-rich Web experience. Now you're going to learn about Shockwave, QuickTime, RealSystem, Java, and all the various ways you can use them to extend the browser's multimedia capabilities beyond HTML.

These key topics will be discussed in this chapter:

- How browsers handle media content
- How to use Dreamweaver's tools to work with Netscape plug-ins and ActiveX controls
- The most popular plug-in–based media types, including Shockwave, QuickTime, and RealMedia content
- Java applets and how to integrate them into Web pages
- How to insert sound into Web pages
- Plug-in detection

Extending the Browser with Plug-ins and ActiveX

Browsers are essentially HTML decoders. Their job is to translate the markup instructions in an HTML file into a visible, functional screenful of information. By adding JavaScript to your HTML, you can add a certain amount of interactivity to Web pages. But, by themselves, browsers cannot handle the rich variety of media that you might want your pages to contain. They can't display video, they can't manipulate and present sound, and they can't present PDF content or the complex interactivity and animation that games require.

Luckily, browsers are extensible. They can call on external entities to do what they alone can't do. In fact, they do this frequently as you surf the Web, whether you're aware of it or not.

Plug-ins, Helper Applications, and MIME Types

Every time a browser encounters a file, it must determine what kind of file it is and how it should be handled. This is done by examining the file's Multipurpose Internet Mail Extension (MIME) type. The MIME type is part of the information the Web server usually sends along with the file when a Web page is downloaded to a user's computer. It includes a description of the file's category and instructions for what the browser should do with it.

As a backup, in case the Web server does not send the MIME information with the downloaded file, the browser also examines the suffix, or filename extension, of all downloaded files. Some standard MIME types, along with their associated filename extensions, are shown in Figure 20.1.

Some Common MIME Types and Filename Extensions	
MIME Type	Filename Extensions
image/gif	.gif
image/jpeg .jpg	.jpeg
audio/wav	.wav
audio/aif .aif	.aiff
audio/x-midi .mid	.midi
video/mov	.mov
video/avi	.avi
application/zip	.zip
application/x-macbinary	.bin
application/pdf	.pdf
application/x-shockwave-flash	.swf
application/vnd.rn-realmedia	.rm

Figure 20.1   Common MIME types and associated filename extensions.

If the MIME type or filename extension indicates that the file is something the browser can't deal with, it calls on outside help, either a helper application or a plug-in.

A *helper application* is a program that can deal with the file type in question. A helper application can be any program on your computer. Stuffit Expander and WinZip are examples of helper applications. Any time the browser comes across a file with an extension of .zip or a MIME type of application/zip, it will probably attempt to find and launch one of these programs. Any of these programs can also be launched independently of the browser.

A *plug-in*, like a helper application, has functionality that the browser doesn't, but it is not a standalone application. Plug-ins cannot launch and run on their own. Instead, they add functionality to the browser. Plug-ins must reside in the Plug-Ins folder, inside the browser's own application folder. The Flash plug-in, covered in Chapter 18, "Animation with Flash," is an example of this kind of help. When the browser comes across a file with an extension of .swf or a MIME type of application/x-shockwave-flash, it will probably look for and attempt to launch the Flash plug-in (The term "plug-in" is being used here as a generic term for a nonfreestanding browser extension. The two standard browser implementations of plug-ins are Netscape plug-ins and Microsoft ActiveX controls. Both of these are discussed in depth later in this chapter.)

Configuration and Customization

Why do we say that the browser will *probably* respond in a certain way to a certain MIME type? Because each browser must be configured to interpret certain MIME types in certain ways, and any two browsers (even if they're the same version of the same browser on the same platform) might be configured differently. Browsers are already configured when you install them; depending on where you got the browser (promotional or application CD, computer manufacturer install, download from Microsoft or Netscape, and so on), it might be configured differently from other copies of the same browser obtained from somewhere else. And, of course, individual browser users can also customize the configuration.

To examine or customize the configuration of Netscape 4, launch the browser and go to Edit/Preferences. In the Preferences dialog box, select the Navigator/Applications panel. It will look something like Figure 20.2.

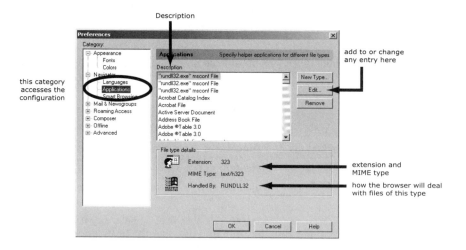

Figure 20.2   The Netscape/Windows Preferences dialog box, showing the Configuration setup. Each MIME type is assigned a helper application, plug-in, or action to be taken if the browser encounters it.

To customize the configuration of Internet Explorer 5, launch the browser and go to Edit/Preferences. In the Preferences dialog box, select the Download/File Helpers panel. That panel and the dialog box for customizing its entries are shown in Figure 20.3.

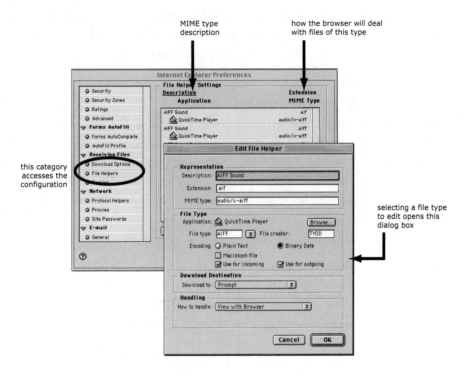

Figure 20.3   The Internet Explorer/Mac Preferences dialog box, and the dialog box for editing a file type entry. Internet Explorer/Windows does not allow changing these preferences.

Potential Configuration Problems

Web authors can't control how browsers will handle given file types; they can only try to predict how their target audience will have their browsers configured and then set pages up to deal gracefully with failure in this regard. (We'll discuss authoring strategies later in this chapter.)

- **Unavailable plug-ins or helpers.** Just because a plug-in or helper application is called for in the configuration setup doesn't mean that it's available on the user's computer. This is the most common problem plaguing Web designers who want a variety of plug-in–based media on their pages.

- **Unknown MIME types.** If a file is downloaded that the browser does not recognize, either by MIME type or filename extension, the user will be asked what to do with the file.

- **Unexpected or inappropriate disposition.** The helper or action specified in the default configuration might not be the one that is expected; it might not even be the best choice, given the particular setup of a user's computer system.

Netscape Plug-ins versus ActiveX Objects

Years ago, to enable Web authors to put media content on HTML pages, Netscape developed the capability to add plug-ins to itself. To support plug-in–based media content, Netscape created the <embed> tag. Although the <embed> tag was never made part of the W3 Consortium's official HTML specification, it was a big hit with users. Internet Explorer adopted the <embed> tag and the plug-in system, and it's now considered a safe, reliable way of inserting media into Web pages. Web pundits still refer to "Netscape plug-ins," but the technology is no longer Netscape-specific.

Meanwhile, Microsoft was developing its own set of technologies to allow applications of all kinds to share information and work together. Object linking and embedding (OLE) and the Component Object Model (COM) eventually developed into ActiveX technology. For Web use, Microsoft built into its browser the capability to understand miniprograms called ActiveX controls, which could control and share information with ActiveX objects placed on a Web page using the <object> tag. ActiveX controls can be written to work with various applications, including Internet Explorer. Microsoft's scripting language, VBScript, can be used to communicate between the ActiveX control and the browser, much as JavaScript (which was developed by Netscape) communicates between plug-ins and the browser.

As a result, there are two ways to insert media content into browsers: as plug-in objects or as ActiveX objects. Whereas both browsers support plug-ins, only IE supports ActiveX; because ActiveX is so tied in with Microsoft's other technologies, it works only in a Windows platform. Because it relies so heavily on ActiveX technology, Internet Explorer does not support plug-in objects nearly as well as Netscape does. In Netscape, you can communicate with plug-in content using JavaScript, but Internet Explorer does not allow JavaScript access to plug-in objects or ActiveX objects; VBScript can be used to communicate with ActiveX objects, but not with plug-in objects. Internet Explorer/Macintosh also does not support ActiveX, which severely limits what you can do to control cross-browser, cross-platform media content.

Also, although most major plug-in developers create ActiveX controls as well as Netscape plug-ins, not all do. Apple, for instance, has not released an ActiveX version of the popular QuickTime plug-in, although QuickTime is supposedly a cross-platform technology.

As Web authors, we tread daily through this minefield. Dreamweaver helps by offering support for both technologies and by taking care of as many details as it can to make pages accessible to as many people as possible. (Of course, even with Dreamweaver you can't ever achieve complete cross-browser, cross-platform compatibility when using plug-in content. It's always a good idea to use media content sparingly, test pages thoroughly in as many browser/platform configurations as possible, and design so that your Web sites will function without the media, if necessary.)

Netscape Plug-ins (the <embed> Tag)

In Dreamweaver, to insert media content using the <embed> tag, you use the Insert Plug-In object. In Dreamweaver 4, this object is part of the Special category of objects. (In previous versions, it was part of the Common category.) It's a generic object that can be used with a variety of plug-in and MIME types. Figure 20.4 shows the object as it appears in the Objects panel, and the Property Inspector that goes with it.

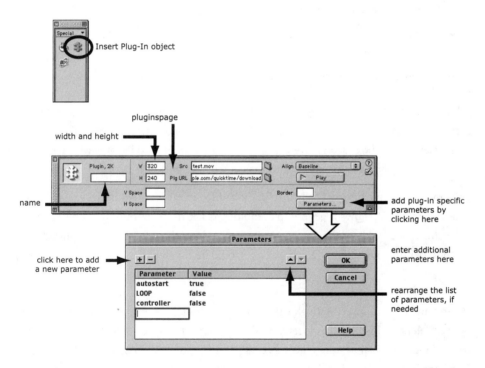

Figure 20.4   The Insert plug-in object, as it appears in the Special Objects panel. Also shown is the Property Inspector for <embed> content, along with the generic Parameters dialog box.

The Property Inspector for elements created with this object includes the following generic parameters that can be used with any media content:

- **Src.** This specifies the URL of the source file for the content. This is required.

- **Pluginspage (Plg URL).** This gives the URL of a site where the required plug-in can be downloaded. If a value is entered in this parameter and the user's browser does not have the appropriate plug-in to handle the source file, the broken plug-in icon will link to this URL. This is optional but recommended.

- **Name.** As with any HTML element, media content must be named if it will be referred to by scripts. This is optional.

- **Width and height.** This specifies the dimensions that the content will take up on the page. These values usually default to 32×32 pixels because Dreamweaver cannot determine the actual dimensions of most plug-in content. This is required by most plug-ins.

- **Vspace and hspace.** This adds whitespace around the content. It is optional.

- **Align.** This determines how the content will align with text when it is placed inline on a page. It is optional.

- **Border.** This adds a border around the content area. It is optional.

Additional parameters associated with specific plug-ins can be added to the <embed> tag by clicking the Parameters button in the Property Inspector, which accesses a Special Parameters dialog box (see Figure 20.4). For each parameter added this way, you must know the parameter's name and what values it will accept.

Dreamweaver won't automatically display embedded media content in the visual editing window; rather, it shows a generic placeholder. Click the Play button in the Property Inspector to see and hear the media. As long as you have the relevant plug-in installed in any browser on your system, Dreamweaver should be capable of displaying any content.

ActiveX Objects (the <object> Tag)

In Dreamweaver, to insert ActiveX media content using the <object> tag, use the Insert ActiveX object. This object is located in the Special category of objects, in the Objects panel. Figure 20.5 shows the object as it appears in the panel, along with the Property Inspector that goes with it. Like the Insert Plug-In object, this is a generic object that can be used with a variety of ActiveX controls.

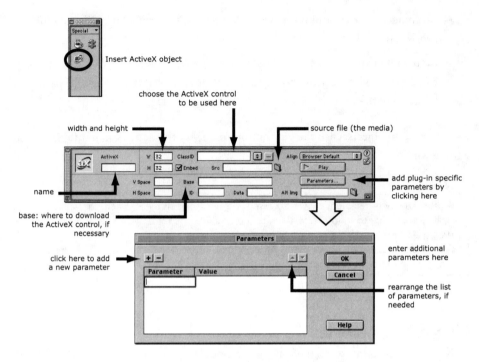

Figure 20.5   The Insert ActiveX object as it appears in the Special Objects panel. Also shown is the Property Inspector for ActiveX content. Sample values for a RealMedia file are shown.

In addition to the parameters listed for plug-in objects, the Property Inspector for ActiveX objects includes the following:

- **Class ID.** This is the name of the ActiveX control to be used to handle the content. The Shockwave, Flash, and RealMedia controls appear on the pop-up list; names of any other controls must be typed in. When a control name has been manually entered, it appears in the pop-up list until it's removed (by clicking the minus [–] button next to the pop-up list).

- **ID.** This is used to refer to the object in scripting. It is optional.

- **Base.** This specifies the URL of a site where the required control can be downloaded. If a value is entered in this parameter and the user's browser does not have the appropriate ActiveX control to handle the source file, the control will be automatically downloaded, if possible. This is optional but recommended.

- **Data.** This specifies the URL of the source file for the content. This parameter is not required by many ActiveX controls (including Flash, Shockwave, and RealPlayer).

- **Alt image.** If the control is not available, any image specified here displays in the browser instead.

- **Embed.** If enabled, this adds an <embed> tag inside the <object> tag, to support Netscape on all platforms and IE on non-Windows platforms. The SRC parameter listed in the Property Inspector is used with this tag.

As with plug-in objects, click the Play button to display the ActiveX object in the visual editing window.

Note

Almost any media element can be accessed without using either <embed> or <object>, by linking directly to it. To create a link to a media file, just set up a text or an image link on a page. Then, in the Property Inspector's Link field, browse to the media file. This is a fairly crude method of getting media on your Web site, however, because it gives no control over parameters or scripting.

Plug-in Technologies

This section looks at several of the most popular plug-in technologies, including Shockwave, QuickTime, and RealMedia. You'll see what kinds of media are included in each, how ActiveX controls and Netscape plug-ins differ, and what parameters and scripting controls each one offers.

Shockwave

Shockwave is a plug-in and related file format that allows content developed with Macromedia Director to be viewed in the browser. Director has long been industry-standard software for developing interactive CD-ROMs. Director movies can contain sound, video, and animation. Director's internal scripting language, Lingo, can create sophisticated interactivity. Using Director Multiuser Server software, Director movies can even be used for multiplayer games, chat rooms, and other Web application tasks. The V12 and PDF Xtras (both developed by Integration Media) for Director can link Director movies to databases and PDF files as well.

For CD-ROM use, Director movies are saved as stand-alone applications called projectors. For Web use, movies are saved in a special "shocked" format, with the .dcr filename extension and application/x-director MIME type. To view this content, users must have the Shockwave plug-in from www.macromedia.com.

Sprite-Based Technology

Director—and, therefore, Shockwave—is sprite-based, meaning that individual presentation elements such as graphics, sounds, and text need to be loaded into memory only once and may be used repeatedly throughout a movie. These elements also are efficiently scripted and animated. Sprite-based technology is memory-efficient and creates efficient files for download.

Streaming

Shockwave is also a streaming technology, which means that movies automatically play as they're downloading, allowing for fairly long, complex presentations to be sent over the Web without users having to wait for them. Like Flash streaming, Shockwave streaming is client-side, which means that no special server setup is required. To learn more about Shockwave, visit `www.macromedia.com/shockzone`.

> **Note**
>
> Flash previously was considered part of the Shockwave technology. The filename extension .swf stood for "Shockwave Flash." Currently, however, Macromedia is marketing Flash as a separate entity from Shockwave. The .swf extension now officially stands for "small Web file."

Figure 20.6
The Objects panel, showing the Insert Shockwave object.

Shockwave Issues

The Shockwave plug-in is cross-browser and cross-platform. It is available as a Netscape plug-in and an ActiveX control. Many corporate Web sites use Shockwave content to provide fun, illustrative, or heavily interactive content to entice users into the site. According to Macromedia, 167 million users worldwide have the Shockwave plug-in installed.

Inserting a Shockwave Object

In Dreamweaver, inserting Shockwave content is done with the Insert Shockwave object (shown in Figure 20.6). This object is located in the Common Objects panel. The object inserts Shockwave content using the <object> tag, with an included <embed> tag.

Note

Previous versions of Dreamweaver allowed Web authors to specify whether the <object> tag, <embed> tag, or both would be used to insert the Shockwave content. Dreamweaver 4 no longer offers this option.

The Property Inspector for Shockwave content is fairly sparse because several basic parameters, such as pluginspage and base, are set automatically by Dreamweaver (see Figure 20.7). Note that width and height are not set automatically; Dreamweaver sets these to a default of 32×32 pixels, regardless of the movie's dimensions. You must find the correct movie dimensions outside Dreamweaver, or use trial-and-error in the browser to set them. If the width and height parameters in the Property Inspector are set smaller than the original movie size, the movie will be cropped; if the dimensions are set larger than the original size, empty space will be added around the edges of the movie.

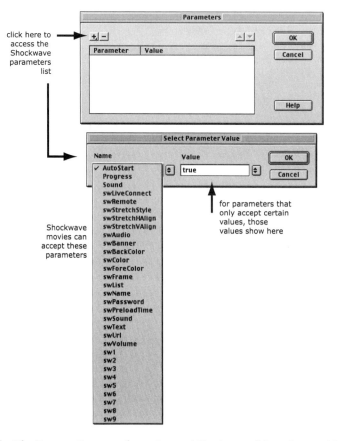

Figure 20.7   The Property Inspector for an inserted Shockwave object, shown with the generic Parameters dialog box and the pop-up list of Shockwave-specific parameters that can be set here.

To access and assign other parameters for the Shockwave movie, click the generic Parameters button in the Inspector's lower-right corner to open the Parameters dialog box. From here, click the + button to get a list of potential parameters that can be set (see Figure 20.7). Most of these parameters tie into Lingo scripting inside the Shockwave movie. See exercise 20.1 for more information on this. Figure 20.8 shows a list of parameters that can be assigned to a Shockwave object and their uses.

Note

> Before beginning any exercises from this chapter, it's a good idea to copy the folder of required media files from the CD-ROM to your hard drive. You'll find the files (wherever they will be stored in the directory). All sample code and screenshots in the exercises will assume that your media files and HTML files are in the same folder.

Exercise 20.1   Inserting a Shockwave Movie

In this exercise, you'll place a Shockwave movie on an HTML page and test its basic properties.

1. Create a new Dreamweaver document and save it.

2. Click the Insert Shockwave object to insert a new Shockwave movie onto the page. In the dialog box that appears, choose sample_movie.dcr.

   If you haven't done so already, copy this file from the CD-ROM onto your hard drive for easier access.

3. Resize the movie to its correct width and height, 640×340.

4. Play the movie in Dreamweaver.

   Click the Play button in the Property Inspector to play the movie; then click the button again to stop the movie so that you can continue working on it.

5. Experiment with resizing the movie and playing it.

   Set the movie's dimensions to smaller than they should be; then play the movie. Set the dimensions to larger than they should be; then play the movie. You'll see how the movie is either cropped or surrounded by empty whitespace, but its contents are never resized.

6. Examine the code. You'll see that the <object> tag has been used to place the movie, with an <embed> tag included.

```
<object classid="clsid:166B1BCA-3F9C-11CF-8075-444553540000"
codebase="http://download.macromedia.com/pub/shockwave/cabs/director/sw.
cab#version=8,0,0,0" width="640" height="340">
    <param name="src" value="sample_movie.dcr">
    <embed src="sample_movie.dcr"
pluginspage="http://www.macromedia.com/shockwave/download/" width="640"
height="340" swliveconnect="true">
    </embed>
</object>
```

Parameter name	Value	Description
name	Any one-word name	Required by the <embed> tag if the movie is to be referred to by scripting.
ID	Any one-word name	Required by the <object> tag if the movie is to be referred to by scripting.
width	Integer (number of pixels)	The horizontal space the movie will be allotted on the page. Dreamweaver cannot determine this automatically. If the width assigned is different from the movie's width, the movie will be cropped or surrounded by empty space.
height	Integer (number of pixels)	The vertical space the movie will be allotted on the page. Dreamweaver cannot determine this automatically. If the height assigned is different from the movie's height, the movie will be cropped or surrounded by empty space.
align	(choose from the pop-up menu)	Determines how the browser will align the movie when text or other page elements are placed next to it (in the same table cell or paragraph, for instance).
bgcolor	(choose from the palette or enter a 6-digit hexadecimal number)	If the width and height values assigned are larger than the movie's dimensions, this color will fill up the rest of the allotted space.
vspace	Integer (number of pixels)	Adds empty white space above and below the movie. Specify a number of pixels.
hspace	Integer (number of pixels)	Adds empty white space to the right and lieft of the movie. Specify a number of pixels.
autostart	True or false	Whether the movie will start playing as soon as it loads.
loop	True or false	Whether the movie will repeat indefinitely, or play only once. This only has effect if the movie's own internal scripting doesn't have its own looping or stopping controls.
sound		
progress		
swLiveConnect swRemote swStretchStyle swStretchHAlign swStretchVAlign swAudio swBanner swBackColor swForeColor swColor swFrame swList swName swPassword swPreloadTime swSound swText swURL swVolume swPreLoadTime sw1 sw2 sw3 sw4 sw5 sw6 sw7 sw8 sw9	Can take any value	These parameters can be used to pass any values to a Shockwave movie. The movie's internal scripting must specifically call the parameter for it to take effect. It's up to the author whether swSound, for instance, passes any information about sound to the movie, or whether it passes completely unrelated information. Internet Explorer requires that passed parameters to Shockwave use these names and these names only. (In Netscape, any parameter name can be used, as long as the Director movie's internal scripting calls on that parameter.)

Figure 20.8   Parameters that a Shockwave movie will accept, with a description of each and suggested values, where applicable.

Passing Parameters to Shockwave

It's possible to pass all sorts of information to a Shockwave movie in the form of parameters entered in the <object> and <embed> tags, as long as the movie knows what to do with the information it's receiving. These parameters include basics such as AUTOPLAY and LOOP, as well as a whole series of parameters that Director authors can tie into the movie's Lingo scripting. Inside Director, these parameters are accessed through the externalParamValue(), externalParamNumber(), and externalParamName() functions. The parameter defined in Dreamweaver must have exactly the same name as the parameter called in the Lingo code.

Exercise 20.2 Creating a Personalized Shockwave Movie

In this exercise, you work with a Shockwave movie that includes a welcome banner. The movie is programmed to expect a parameter called sw1 that specifies the name of a person to be welcomed. Figure 20.9 shows how the call has been set up inside Director. You'll insert the Shockwave movie into a page and add the parameter with an appropriate value.

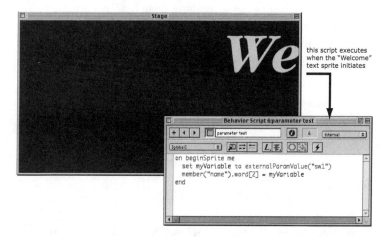

Figure 20.9 The Director interface, showing the sw1 parameter being called. This scripting can be set up and edited only from within Director. The scripting language is Lingo.

1. Create a new file, and save it as welcome.html.

2. Insert the movie welcome.dcr onto the page.

   In the Property Inspector, set the width and height to 640×340.

3. With the movie selected, click the general Parameters button to access the Parameters dialog box.

4. From the Parameters pop-up list, choose sw1:

   It doesn't matter which of the various sw parameters is used for what, as long as the parameter name is on the list and as long as the parameter defined here in Dreamweaver matches the parameter called inside the Shockwave movie.

Note

Netscape allows any named parameter to be passed to a Shockwave movie. Internet Explorer accepts only those that appear on the pop-up list.

5. For the value of the parameter, enter your name.

6. Try out the movie in a browser.

   Does the name you entered come up in the welcome banner? It should. What's the benefit of this? Imagine how easy it can be to quickly customize Shockwave presentations on a Web site, without having to generate new Shockwave movies. Movies can be multipurposed so that the same movie, downloaded once, can serve in several places on the Web site.

Controlling Shockwave with Dreamweaver Behaviors

Although Shockwave movies generally contain their navigation controls internally, they can be also be controlled from the browser with JavaScript (Netscape) or VBScript (MSIE). Dreamweaver offers the Control Shockwave or Flash behavior to start, stop, or send a movie to a particular frame.

Note

These behaviors will not work in Internet Explorer/Mac because IE does not allow JavaScript control of plug-in content. ActiveX/VBScripting also is not available on the Macintosh platform.

Exercise 20.3   Using the Control Shockwave Behavior

This exercise takes you through the steps of applying Dreamweaver's built-in Shockwave control behavior.

1. Open the welcome.html file that you created in the previous exercise.

2. Select and name the Shockwave movie.

As with any other page element, a Shockwave movie must be named before it can be referred to by scripting. Enter a one-word name in the name field of the Property Inspector, as shown in Figure 20.10.

Figure 20.10   Naming a Shockwave movie for scripting.

3. Add the words **play** and **stop** to the page, after the Shockwave movie.

   You need links to click on, to activate the play and stop behavior; the simplest way to create this is with text links.

4. After you've created and formatted the text, link each word to # so that you can attach a behavior to it. Figure 20.11 shows what the screen should look like with these controls in place.

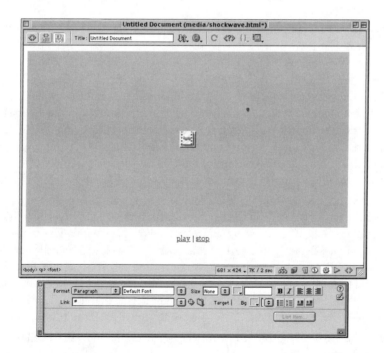

Figure 20.11   Welcome.html with its Shockwave movie and play controls. The Property Inspector shows the link to #.

5. With the Play link selected, go to the Behavior panel and choose Control Shockwave or Flash from the Actions list.

Your named movie should come up automatically in the dialog box that follows; from the action choices, select Play (see Figure 20.12).

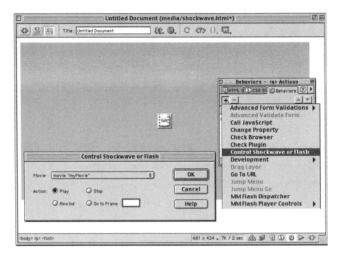

Figure 20.12   The Control Shockwave or Flash behavior in the Actions list, along with the dialog box that the behavior calls up.

6. Repeat the process to add a stop command to the Stop text link.

7. Optional: Set the movie to not play automatically when the page loads in the browser. Do this by clicking the generic Parameters button in the lower-right corner of the Property Inspector to access the Properties dialog box. In this dialog box, click the + button to open the list of Shockwave parameters. (Figure 20.7 shows how to access this list of Shockwave-specific parameters.) From the list, choose the Autoplay parameter; enter a value of false.

Why is this step optional? It seems logical to start with the movie not playing because you're going to all the trouble of inserting a Play button—and it's a little weird, from the user's perspective, to open a Web page with a Play button and a movie that's already playing. But remember, the Play and Stop behaviors won't work in IE/Mac. So, if you turn off Autoplay and rely solely on the Play command to start the movie, users with that browser/platform combination won't ever be able to see the movie play. You might decide that it's better to start with the movie already playing. (It's all part of the joy of Web multimedia.)

8. Test the movie in a browser or two. The behaviors should work in all browsers except Internet Explorer/Mac.

Controlling Shockwave Beyond Dreamweaver

If you're willing to write some of your own JavaScript code, you can control Shockwave movie behavior beyond the built-in Dreamweaver behaviors. Figure 20.13 shows a list of JavaScript commands that Shockwave movies can accept from the browser.

JavaScript Commands a Shockwave Movie Can Accept

Command	Argument	Description
Stop()	—	Stops the movie playing.
Play()	—	Starts the movie playing from the current position.
Autostart()	True or False	Determines whether the movie plays automatically when the browser loads the page.
Rewind()	—	Sets the movie back to frame 1.
GotoFrame(x)	integer	Sends the movie's playback head to a certain frame number.
GotoMovie(location)	Movie URL	Loads another movie in place of the current movie.
GetCurrentFrame()	—	Returns the current frame number.
EvalScript(string)	text string	Sends a text string into a movie to be used by the Lingo on EvalScript handler. (The most powerful of these commands, the EvalScript() command can be used to send almost any information into a Shockwave movie.)

Figure 20.13   JavaScript commands that can be sent to a Shockwave movie. The Arguments column specifies the information that must be included between the parentheses at the end of the command name.

The code for a basic JavaScript function to control a Shockwave movie looks like this (elements that you can customize appear in italics):

```
<script language=""JavaScript"">
function controlShockwave {
var shock;
if (navigator.appName == ""Netscape"") {
    shock = document.mymovie;
  } else {
    shock = mymovie;
  }
shock.Play();
}
</script>
```

Remember, of course, that no JavaScript functions will work in Internet Explorer/Mac.

Shockwave Conclusion

If you're creating Shockwave content, you don't have to use Dreamweaver at all to create your HTML. Director has a Publish feature that will generate an HTML shell for a

Shockwave movie. If your needs are more complex, you can use Macromedia's Aftershock utility, an application capable of generating HTML pages complete with extensive JavaScript functionality. Aftershock can be used with Shockwave and Flash files. When an HTML page has been created with Aftershock, if you open it in Dreamweaver it will look like the page shown in Figure 20.14.

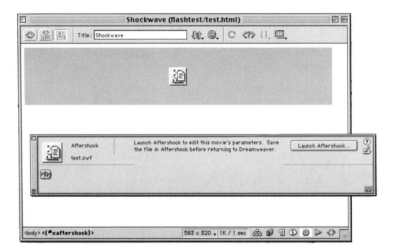

Figure 20.14   An HTML file that was created in Aftershock, as it appears in the Dreamweaver editing window. Note that the Property Inspector does not allow direct editing, but it is set up to launch Aftershock.

QuickTime

Don't be fooled. Just because QuickTime is made by Apple doesn't mean that it's only for Macs. QuickTime is a cross-platform system-level extension and browser plug-in that provides synchronized media and interactivity similar to that found in Shockwave and Flash. QuickTime movies are made of synchronized tracks—video tracks, sound tracks, music tracks, sprite tracks (for interactive and animated elements), 3D tracks (for 3D modeling), VR (virtual reality) tracks, text tracks, and even Flash tracks, each of which can contain an entire Flash movie, interactivity and all.

Note

To learn more about QuickTime, visit www.apple.com/quicktime. Apple has also published the QuickTime Developer Series of books, including an in-depth volume on *QuickTime for the Web.*

Streaming and FastStart

All QuickTime 4 movies are automatically set up to download using FastStart. FastStart embeds all the information that the movie needs to start playing in the first few frames, so the movie can start playing shortly after download has begun. As long as the data rate required by the movie doesn't exceed the modem connection speed, the movie should play smoothly from then on.

The true glory of QuickTime, however, is QuickTime server-side streaming. Unlike the client-side streaming used in Shockwave and Flash, server-side streaming means that data is not actually downloaded to the user's computer but is delivered one frame at a time, similar to a broadcast signal being sent to a TV or a radio. Streaming content can come from a live stream (like a live audio or video broadcast), or it can come from large files stored on a Web server. If you want to take advantage of QuickTime streaming, you'll need to find or set up a Web server with QuickTime streaming server software. (Various versions of the server software are available, including a free Linux version.)

QuickTime Issues

The QuickTime plug-in has long been considered a staple of Web multimedia, ubiquitous and reliable on both Mac and PC platforms in both major browsers. According to a recent Apple announcement, 100 million copies of the QuickTime player and browser plug-in have been distributed and installed worldwide.

Unfortunately, at the time of this writing, Apple has not released an ActiveX control for QuickTime, which limits you when scripting QuickTime content in Internet Explorer. QuickTime works very well with Netscape.

In June 2000, RealNetworks licensed QuickTime for use with RealPlayer, which means that the Real G2 plug-in (and ActiveX control) can also display QuickTime content. Scripting commands intended for use with the QuickTime plug-in may not work as expected, however.

All professional-level audio, video, and animation software is capable of creating QuickTime content. QuickTime authoring programs include Electrifier Pro (Mac only), LiveStage (Mac/PC), and Adobe GoLive (Mac/PC), which includes a pretty nifty little QuickTime authoring miniprogram inside the Web editor. Limited authoring capabilities are also built into QuickTime Pro. Flash can also export interactive presentations as QuickTime movies.

Various free utilities for working with QuickTime—including Plug-In Helper, which is discussed later—are available at `www.developer.apple.com/quicktime/quicktimeintro/tools/`.

Inserting a QuickTime Object

In Dreamweaver, you insert QuickTime content using the Insert Plug-In object described previously. (Don't try to use the Insert ActiveX object because there is currently no ActiveX control for QuickTime.)

Note

> If you're interested in extending your copy of Dreamweaver, a QuickTime object is available from the Macromedia Exchange. This extension adds a special Insert QT object to the Common objects and provides QT objects with a special Property Inspector for easy access to QT parameters.

The Property Inspector for QuickTime content is generic, of course, because you're using a generic plug-in object to insert it. As with Shockwave, width and height are always set to a default value of 32×32 pixels. If the dimensions are set smaller than the original movie size, the movie will be cropped, not scaled; if the dimensions are set larger than the original size, empty space will be added around the edges of the movie.

QuickTime movies accept a wide variety of parameters. To assign any parameter not listed in the Property Inspector, click the Inspector's generic Parameters button to open the Parameters dialog box. From here, type in parameter names and values manually. (Unlike the Parameters dialog box for Shockwave content, this dialog box does not come with a helpful list of parameters to choose from.) Figure 20.15 shows a list of useful parameters that QuickTime movies can accept.

Exercise 20.4   Inserting a QuickTime Movie

In this exercise, you'll insert a QuickTime movie into an HTML page (the movie shows some of the versatility of the format, incorporating MIDI data, vector graphics, and video) and set various parameters to affect its performance.

1. Create a new HTML file. Save it as quicktime1.html.

2. Using the Insert Plug-In object, insert sample.mov.

    If you haven't done so already, copy this file from the CD-ROM onto your hard drive for easier access.

3. With the movie selected, set some basic parameters.

    In the Property Inspector, set the basic parameters as follows:

    width = 416

    height = 326

    pluginspage = http://www.apple.com/quicktime/download

    (The true height of the movie is 310 pixcls, but you're adding 16 pixels for the controller bar that will appear at the bottom of the movie onscreen.)

\<embed\> Parameters for QuickTime Content in HTML

Parameter name	Value	Description
src	URL	The name of the movie to be played.
pluginspage	"http://www.apple.com/ quicktime/download"	Where the browser will try to download the QT plug-in, if needed.
type	"application/x-quicktime"	In case the server doesn't send the MIME type with the downloaded file, this ensures that the browser will know how to display it.
name	any one-word name	Required by the \<embed\> tag if the movie is to referred to by scripting.
width	integer (number of pixels)	The horizontal space the movie will be allotted on the page. Dreamweaver cannot determine this automatically. If the width assigned is different from the movie's width, the movie will be cropped or surrounded by empty space.
height integer	(number of pixels)	The vertical space the movie will be allotted on the page. Dreamweaver cannot determine this automatically. If the height assigned is different from the movie's height, the movie will be cropped or surrounded by empty space. (To resize the movie, see the SCALE paramter, below.)
align	(choose from the popup menu)	Determines how the browser will align the movie when text or other page elements are placed next to it (in the same table cell or paragraph, for instance).
bgcolor	(choose from the palette or enter a 6-digit hexadecimal number)	If the width and height values assigned are larger than the movie's dimensions, this color fill up the rest of the allotted space.
vspace integer	(number of pixels)	Adds empty white space above and below the movie. Specify a number of pixels.
hspace integer	(number of pixels)	Adds empty white space to the right and left of the movie. Specify a number of pixels.
autostart	true or false	Whether the movie will start playing as soon as it loads.
loop	true or false	Whether the movie will repeat indefinitely, or play only once. This only has effect if the movie's own internal scripting doesn't have its own looping or stopping controls.
controller	true, false, qtvr	Whether a controller bar will appear at the bottom of the movie, and what kind of controller bar it will be. By default, the controller includes play, stop, and pause buttons. Use the qtvr controller for QuickTime virtual reality movies. (If the controller is visible, set the height parameter to the movie's height plus 16 pixels. Otherwise, the controller will be cropped.)
scale	"Aspect", "ToFit" or a number	This determines whether the movie will appear at its original size, or enlarged or reduced. "ToFit" will scale the movie to match the width and height parameters; "Aspect" will do the same, but without distorting its aspect ratio. A scale value of larger than 1 will enlarge the movie; smaller than 1 will reduce the size.
volume	integer from 0–100	Determines the volume of any audio in the movie.
kioskmode	true or false	If true, doesn't allow the user to save a copy of the movie.
starttime	a time indicator, specified in hours:minutes:seconds: thirtieths — the movie's beginning is 00:00:00:00	Determines at what point in the movie it should start playing.
endtime	(same as above)	Determines at what point in the movie it should stop playing. The entire movie still has to download, regardless of start and end time settings.
href	absolute or relative URL	If this parameter is present, clicking anywhere on the movie will launch the specified URL.
target	"myself" or the name of a window or frame	If you're loading a new QT movie with the HREF, use "myself" to load it into the same place as the original.
playeveryframe	true or false	Movies may drop frames when playing on slower computers, because the CPU can't keep up with the data rate. If this parameter is set to true, the movie will play all frames, even if it must slow down the frame rate to do so.
qtnextn	A URL specified like this: "\<URL\>" If a target is specified, the value must look like this: "\<URL\> T\<target\>"	Specifies a movie to play after the current movie is finished. Optional target values include \<myself\> (to replace the current movie), \<quicktimeplayer\> (to launch the QuickTime Player application) or any window or frame name. The name of the parameter must end in an integer (represented by n in the column to the left). Like this: qtnext1, qtnext2, etc. Multiple qtnext parameters can be used to play a series of movies. (Note: the URL must be absolute, or relative to the QuickTime movie file, not the HTML file that contains it.)

Figure 20.15   Some useful parameters that can be used with QuickTime content. (This list is not exhaustive.)

Tip

If you have QuickTime installed on your computer, you have the QuickTime player application. To determine the original dimensions of a QT movie, open it in this program and go to Movie/Get Info. In the panel that opens, go to the pop-up menu on the right and choose Size.

4. Try playing the movie. If you have QuickTime on your system, Dreamweaver should be capable of previewing the movie by clicking the Play button in the Property Inspector.

5. Experiment with some other parameters.

In the Property Inspector, click the Parameters button to access the generic Parameters dialog box. Try the following parameters:

- controller = false

  (Preview the movie and you'll see that, without the controller bar, there's no way to start or stop the movie. You'll also have an extra 16 pixels in the movie's height setting.)

- volume = 50

- loop = true

- autoplay = false

  (You'll certainly need the controller back on for this one!)

- scale = ToFit

  (After you've set this parameter, resize the movie so it's really short and squatty. You'll see how the movie resizes to fill the space, even if it means distorting the picture.)

- scale = Aspect

  bgcolor = #FF0000

  (Leave the movie short and squatty, and preview again. The movie won't be distorted anymore, and you'll see the red background color filling in part of your page.)

- href = http://www.newriders.com

  (When this parameter has been set, clicking on the movie in the browser should connect you to the New Riders home page.)

- href = totem.mov

  target = myself

  (As long as the totem.mov file from the CD-ROM is in the same folder as sample.mov, clicking the movie should replace the first movie with the new totem movie.)

- qtnext1 = <totem.mov> T<myself>

(In the browser, let the movie play in its entirety. When it's finished, the totem movie should automatically replace it. Note the unusual syntax for the value entry.)

Exercise 20.5   Using Plug-In Helper to Create a Movie Series

Plug-In Helper is one of several free utilities available from Apple for working with QuickTime movies. With Plug-In Helper, you can embed parameters directly into a QuickTime movie, instead of adding them to the <embed> tag in the HTML. When is this a good thing? If you use HREF or QTNEXT1 to replace one movie with another, you can set separate parameters for each movie.

Plug-In Helper can also embed copy protection into QT movies so that they can't be saved to a user's hard drive from the browser. (Warning: As the QuickTime gurus at Apple will tell you, no method of copy protection is completely hacker-proof. The best that you can hope for is to discourage the average user from "accidentally borrowing" your files.)

In this exercise, you'll create an endless moving picture show, where each movie continues to loop until the user clicks on it, at which point it is replaced by the next movie. (To see the final result you're after, open the pictureshow.html file on the CD-ROM.) You'll be working with three movies that have already had some parameters built into themselves, using Plug-In Helper.

Why do you need Plug-In Helper for this? Just to see, try it first without the utility.

1. Create a new file. Save it as pictureshow_test.html.

2. Using the Insert Plug-In object, place the file nefertiti_plain.mov on the page.

   If you haven't done so already, copy this file from the CD-ROM onto your hard drive for easier access.

   Any movies with "plain" in their names have no embedded parameters.

3. Add the necessary parameters to the movie.

   You want the movie to loop continuously, with no controller to get in the way. And you want the movie to link to another movie if it's clicked. So, add these parameters:

   width = 428

   height = 321

   loop = true

   controller = false

   href = mummy_plain.mov

   target = myself

4. Try out the movie!

   You'll probably find a few problems right away. First, the mummy movie comes in with its controller trying to show. Second, when the mummy is in place, there's no way to load any other movies. That's because no new <embed> parameters loaded when the new movie loaded.

5. Replace nefertiti_plain.mov with nefertiti.mov.

   The new movie has several parameters embedded in it: LOOP, CONTROLLER, HREF, and TARGET were added with Plug-In Helper. Figure 20.16 shows the Plug-In Helper interface and the added parameters for the nefertiti.mov file.

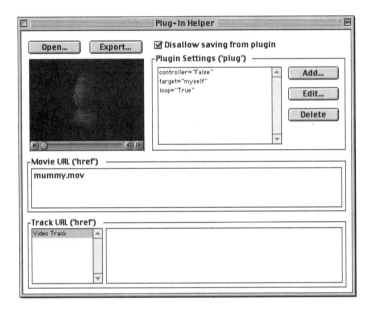

Figure 20.16   The Plug-In Helper interface, showing nefertiti.mov. Note that, instead of adding an HREF parameter, the movie has been assigned a URL. This has the same effect as setting a parameter. The target is still a parameter. (The movie has also been copy-protected.)

6. In the Parameters dialog box in Dreamweaver, remove all parameters.

   If there are parameters in both places, the ones that you enter in Dreamweaver will win. You don't want to confuse the browser.

7. Now try the movie.

   Because of the embedded parameters, all three movies that play should load without controllers and should loop. Each movie should launch a new movie when it's clicked.

Working with QTVR Objects

QuickTime Virtual Reality (QTVR) is a kind of QT movie that includes a virtual reality track. VR tracks contain data, from either cameras or computer-generated from 3D animation software, that lets you interact with scenes and objects in three dimensions, exploring at will.

Two kinds of QTVR movies exist: VR panoramas and VR object movies. A panorama shows the viewer a scene; the viewer can scroll around in the movie, panning, tilting, and zooming, to see a 360° view of everything around him, as if he were standing in place inside the scene looking all around himself. The position where the viewer stands, and everything he sees around him, is called a node. In a multinode panorama (one that includes more than one node), the viewer can click on hotspots to move from node to node. For instance, in one node you might be looking around a living room; clicking the kitchen door takes you to the kitchen node.

An object movie shows an object; the viewer is free to drag the object and view it from any angle.

For the most part, QTVR movies behave just like any other QT movie in the browser. A special set of parameters can be applied to them, however. These parameters are listed in Figure 20.17.

correction	"None" or "Full"	Shows a VR panorama with or without correcting for warping (horizontal and vertical distortion)
fov	an angle	Sets the initial field of view (zoom)
pan	an angle from 0–360	Sets the initial pan angle of a VR movie.
node	integer representing a node ID	Sets the initial node for a multinode VR movie.
til	an angle	Sets the initial up/down tilt in the view of a VR movie.

Figure 20.17   Parameters relevant to QTVR movies.

Working with Streaming QuickTime

A streaming QT movie is a special kind of QT movie delivered by a streaming server using real-time streams. The streaming process uses Real-Time Streaming Protocol (RTSP) instead of Hypertext Transfer Protocol (HTTP). To take advantage of QT streaming, therefore, your Web server must be set up to handle RTSP. A streaming QT delivery can originate from a live broadcast or from files stored on the server or elsewhere.

To prepare a QT movie for streaming, it must be saved in a special streaming format. This can easily be done using Apple's QuickTime Pro software. Then the movie must be placed on the streaming server. The movie must be accessed from your HTML page using an absolute address that includes the RTSP protocol, like this:

```
rtsp://www.domain.com/mymovie.mov
```

Sometimes browsers get confused by this method of addressing and don't know which plug-in to activate to handle the movie. A good way to write the <embed> tag for a streaming movie is like this:

```
<embed src="fake_movie.mov" ...
qtsrc="rtsp://www.domain.com/mymovie.mov">
```

The file fake_movie.mov is a very small placeholder movie that you create; it won't actually play unless the streaming movie can't be found or accessed. The QTSRC parameter specifies the movie that will actually play. In Dreamweaver, you can enter the QTSRC parameter in the generic Parameters dialog box. Figure 20.18 shows the QTSRC parameter and others especially for streaming QT movies.

Parameters for Streaming QuickTime		
parameter	value	description
starttime	a time indicator, specified in hours: minutes:seconds: thirtieths — the movie's beginning is 00:00:00:00	Determines at what point in the movie it should start playing.
endtime	(same as above)	Determines at what point in the movie it should stop playing. Start and end times can be specified for any QT movie, but unless the movie is a streaming movie, the entire file will have to download anyway, so it's not a very efficient parameter to set.
qtsrc	URL	Causes the plug-in to ignore whatever movie is specified in the SRC parameter, and plays another movie instead. Useful to make sure browsers don't try to play QuickTime movies with other plug-ins; and to specify streaming movies.
qtsrcchokespeed	a number, representing bits per second; or "movierate"	Specifies the maximum bandwidth the streaming file can use. For users with very fast connections (like T1 lines), this stops the streaming process from overwhelming the server or hogging all available server bandwidth.

Figure 20.18   QuickTime parameters relevant to streaming movies.

Controlling QuickTime with JavaScript

QuickTime content both is and isn't controllable using JavaScript. QT movies function as JavaScript objects; a wide variety of properties and methods can be applied to them.

Unfortunately, as of this writing, all this control works only in Netscape. Internet Explorer currently has no way to allow JavaScript to communicate with plug-in content that uses the <embed> tag—and, of course, there is no ActiveX control for QuickTime, so it isn't possible to use the <object> tag. Figure 20.19 shows some useful JavaScript commands that can be used with QT, all of which work fine in Netscape.

Enabling JavaScript

Before any QT movie can accept JavaScript commands, you'll have to enable it. In the Parameters dialog box, set the parameter enablejavascript to true.

JavaScript in, JavaScript Out

Although it isn't possible in Internet Explorer to send JavaScript commands to a QT movie, it is possible in both browsers to use QT movies to send JavaScript commands out to the browser. Clicking on a QT movie—or even on a certain spot in a QT movie—can activate just about any JavaScript function you like. There are a couple of ways to do this, as you'll see next.

Using the HREF Parameter

The <embed> tag's HREF parameter can accept a JavaScript statement instead of a URL. The script is activated when the user clicks on the movie. The command can be a complete, simple JavaScript statement, or it can be a call to a function defined in the document head. The only limitation is that the only way to activate the command is to click on the movie itself, so it isn't possible to create multiple external buttons or controls. The syntax looks like this:

```
<embed name="test" src="vaquita.mov" width="320" height="240"
enablejavascript="true" href="javascript:callThisFunction()">
</embed>
```

This method still doesn't do too well in Internet Explorer.

Using Plug-In Helper

A more powerful method that actually works in both browsers is to use Plug-In Helper to embed a movie URL or a track URL inside the movie itself. Using this method, if you have several QT movies linked using the QTNEXTx parameter, each movie can have a separate URL that executes a different JavaScript when clicked. If your QT movie has several video tracks—whether they're sequential or simultaneous—you can use Plug-In Helper to assign a different URL to each track. The movie then behaves like a moving image map, executing a different function depending on where or when a user clicks.

Properties & Methods of QuickTime Objects

Parameter name	Value	Description
src	URL	The name of the movie to be played.
pluginspage	"http://www.apple.com/ quicktime/download"	Where the browser will try to download the QT plug-in, if needed.
type	"application/x-quicktime"	In case the server doesn't send the MIME type with the downloaded file, this ensures that the browser will know how to display it.
name	any one-word name	Required by the <embed> tag if the movie is to be referred to by scripting.
width	integer (number of pixels)	The horizontal space the movie will be allotted on the page. Dreamweaver cannot determine this automatically. If the width assigned is different from the movie's width, the movie will be cropped or surrounded by empty space.
height	integer (number of pixels)	The vertical space the movie will be allotted on the page. Dreamweaver cannot determine this automatically. If the height assigned is different from the movie's height, the movie will be cropped or surrounded by empty space. (To resize the movie, see the SCALE paramter, below.)
align	(choose from the popup menu)	Determines how the browser will align the movie when text or other page elements are placed next to it (in the same table cell or paragraph, for instance).
bgcolor	(choose from the palette or enter a 6-digit hexadecimal number)	If the width and height values assigned are larger than the movie's dimensions, this color will fill up the rest of the allotted space.
vspace	integer (number of pixels)	Adds empty white space above and below the movie. Specify a number of pixels.
hspace	integer (number of pixels)	Adds empty white space to the right and left of the movie. Specify a number of pixels.
autostart	true or false	Whether the movie will start playing as soon as it loads.
loop	true or false	Whether the movie will repeat indefinitely, or play only once. This only has effect if the movie's own internal scripting doesn't have its own looping or stopping controls.
controller	true, false, qtvr	Whether a controller bar will appear at the bottom of the movie, and what kind of controller bar it will be. By default, the controller includes play, stop, and pause buttons. Use the qtvr controller for QuickTime virtual reality movies. (If the controller is visible, set the height parameter to the movie's height plus 16 pixels. Otherwise, the controller will be cropped.)
scale	"Aspect", "ToFit" or a number	This determines whether the movie will appear at its original size, or enlarged or reduced. "ToFit" will scale the movie to match the width and height parameters; "Aspect" will do the same, but without distorting its aspect ratio. A scale value of larger than 1 will enlarge the movie; smaller than 1 will reduce the size.
volume	integer from 0–100	Determines the volume of any audio in the movie.
kioskmode	true or false	If true, doesn't allow the user to save a copy of the movie.
starttime	a time indicator, specified in hours:minutes:seconds: thirtieths — the movie's beginning is 00:00:00:00	Determines at what point in the movie it should start playing.
endtime	(same as above)	Determines at what point in the movie it should stop playing. The entire movie still has to download, regardless of start and end time settings.
href	absolute or relative URL	If this parameter is present, clicking anywhere on the movie will launch the specified URL.
target	"myself" or the name of a window or frame	If you're loading a new QT movie with the HREF, use "myself" to load it into the same place as the original.
playeveryframe	true or false	Movies may drop frames when playing on slower computers, because the CPU can't keep up with the data rate. If this parameter is set to true, the movie will play all frames, even if it must slow down the frame rate to do so.
qtnextn	A URL specified like this: "<URL>" If a target is specified, the value must look like this: "<URL> T<target>"	Specifies a movie to play after the current movie is finished. Optional target values include <myself> (to replace the current movie), <quicktimeplayer> (to launch the QuickTime Player application) or any window or frame name. The name of the parameter must end in an integer (represented by n in the column to the left). Like this: qtnext1, qtnext2, etc. Multiple qtnext parameters can be used to play a series of movies. (Note: the URL must be absolute, or relative to the QuickTime movie file, not the HTML file that contains it.)

Figure 20.19   Properties and methods of a QuickTime movie object in JavaScript. Only Netscape is capable of passing JavaScript commands to QT movies.

Exercise 20.6   Using a QT Movie with Dreamweaver Behaviors

Perhaps you'd love to add JavaScripts to your QT movies, but you don't want to write the scripts yourself. With just a little work in code view, and the help of Plug-In Helper, you can take advantage of Dreamweaver's prewritten behaviors to help. In this exercise, you'll click on a movie to set the text of a layer.

1. Create a new file; save it as qt_layers.html.

2. Draw a layer where you want your movie to sit, and insert totem.mov inside that layer.

   The proper dimensions of the movie are 416×310 (not including the controller bar). Feel free to set any other parameters you want, except HREF. As we'll see here, most plug-in content can function within a layer. Use the Property Inspector to rename the layer Movie.

3. Draw another layer, next to the movie where a caption of descriptive text might sit.

   Name this layer Blurb. Don't let it overlap the movie layer—as plug-in content doesn't work with z-index properties very well.

Tip

> If you use plug-in content in layers, don't try anything fancy with the layers. A layer containing plug-in content will always be in front of other layers, regardless of its z-index. The visibility can be set to hidden only if the movie is not playing. The layer might not animate correctly or be draggable.

4. In the Blurb layer, create a simple text link.

   Dreamweaver won't let you assign behaviors directly to QT movies, so you're going to set up a temporary text link to attach the behavior to. Just type something like **click me** or **test**, and link it to #. (See Figure 20.20.)

5. With the text link selected, go to the Behavior Inspector and choose Set Text/Set Text of Layer from the Actions list.

   This behavior lets you dynamically change the contents of a layer. In the dialog box that comes up, enter the new text that you want the Blurb layer to display when the user clicks on the QT movie. Figure 20.20 shows this happening.

6. Test the page in a browser. If all is working well, passing your mouse over the text link should make the descriptive text that you entered in the behavior appear.

7. In Code view, find the function call that was added to the text link, and copy it.

   The code will probably look something like this (the portion that you should select and copy is highlighted):

```
<p><a href=""#""

onMouseOver="MM_setTextOfLayer(''blurb'','''',''The statue
shown here is a lovely example of bird totems from the
long-dead Karaoke civilization.'')"> test</a>
</p>
```

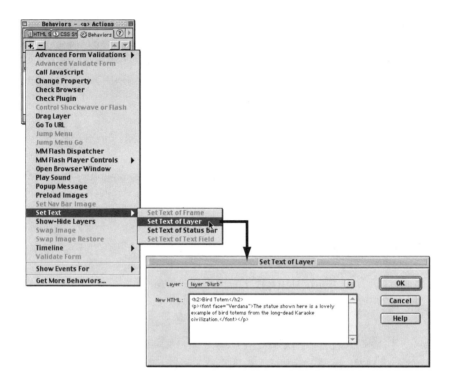

Figure 20.20   Assigning the Set Text of Layer behavior to a temporary text link on the page.

8. In the Visual Editor, select the QT movie and open the generic Parameters dialog box. Enter the code as part of an HREF parameter.

Remember, the code in the HREF value field needs to start with "javascript:", followed by the JavaScript command to execute. For this exercise, the entire code to be entered in the value field should look like this:

```
javascript: MM_setTextOfLayer('blurb','','The statue shown here
is a lovely example of bird totems from the long-dead Karaoke
civilization.'
```

To get this code entered, just type in the first part yourself, and then paste the function call that you copied in the previous step. It'll look pretty crowded in the Parameters dialog box, but it'll work fine.

9. Test the movie.

   In the browser, click on the movie. The text of the Blurb layer should change.

10. Remove the text link—carefully!

    Now that the movie is executing the command, you don't need the text link anymore. But you can't just delete it because then Dreamweaver will delete the entire function from the document head. To delete the text link, go to Code view and manually remove it. Look in the head section; you should still have two functions inside a <script> tag there. Your QT movie command should still work.

Exercise 20.7   Controlling a QT Movie with Track URLs

In this exercise, you'll be working with a QT movie that has two video tracks; each has a URL associated with it that calls a JavaScript function. By defining those functions in the <head> of your HTML document, you can send commands to the movies or use the movies to execute any other JavaScript commands that you want. Of course, you can't alter the function calls without using Plug-In Helper to modify the movie file, so your defined functions will have to be specific. But the results will work in Netscape or Internet Explorer.

The movie you'll be using is called multitrack.mov. Figure 20.21 shows the Plug-In Helper window with the video tracks appearing and the function calls assigned.

Figure 20.21   The Plug-In Helper settings for multitrack.mov. (The multitrack movie itself was stitched together from smaller movies using QuickTime Pro.)

1. Create a new file. Save it in the same folder as multitrack.mov, and call it
   multitrack.html.

2. Using the Insert Plug-In object, place multitrack.mov on the page.

3. Assign the following parameters to the movie:

```
width = 272
height = 372
controller = false
loop = true
enablejavascript = true
```

4. Define two functions in the head section of your document.

   There's no way to do this without a little hand-coding. We'll start by entering
   some function frameworks. The movie tracks are looking for functions called
   FirstFunction() and SecondFunction(), so that's what we'll create.

```
<script language="JavaScript">
function FirstFunction() {
//whatever we put here will happen
//when the top movie is clicked on
}
function SecondFunction() {
//whatever we put here will happen
//when the bottom movie is clicked on
}
</script>
```

5. Try adding something very simple to test it out, such as an alert message.

   Change your code so it looks like this:

```
<script language="JavaScript">
function FirstFunction() {
alert("This is the first function");
}
function SecondFunction() {
alert("This is the second function");
}
</script>
```

   Then test your movie in a browser. Clicking each movie should bring up a different pop-up window with the message you specified. (See Figure 20.22.)

6. Try some more useful scripts!

   If your JavaScript vcoding ability is up to scratch, you can code those two functions to do whatever you want (except control the QT movie itself). If you'd
   rather rely on Dreamweaver behaviors, you'll have to go into Plug-In Helper and
   rewrite the track URLs. All Dreamweaver behaviors pass arguments to functions,
   so you can't set up generic functions like this.

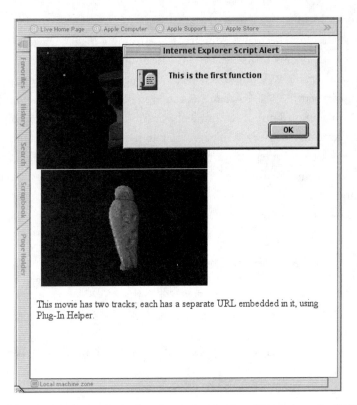

Figure 20.22   Testing the JavaScript function embedded in a QT movie track. Clicking the top movie causes the alert to pop up.

QuickTime Authoring

If you want your QT movies to have fancy internal controls and you want those controls to work in all browsers, your best bet is to do the authoring in QuickTime. QT sprite tracks can be "wired," which means that they can function as interactive elements (that is, buttons).

QuickTime movies can also be embedded in Shockwave movies. As long as the user has the QuickTime system extension on his computer, the browser only needs to access the Shockwave plug-in or ActiveX control to handle the movie. So, the Web author can pass parameters to Shockwave (as in exercise 20.7) and the Director author can write Lingo commands that use those parameters to control the QuickTime movie. This is also useful for ensuring that your pages work in a wider variety of browsers, since the Shockwave offers both Active-X and Plug-In for both platforms.

RealSystems Media

RealNetworks has long been at the forefront of streaming media delivery for the Web. The various components of its RealSystem—RealAudio, RealVideo, RealPix, RealText, and RealFlash—enable Web authors to place a variety of streaming media content on Web pages. Different RealMedia elements can even be combined into multimedia presentations using an offshoot of XML called Synchronized Media Integration Language (SMIL). For streaming delivery, Web pages containing RealMedia content must reside on a Web server with RealServer software. Browsers use the RealPlayer application and the Real G2 plug-in and ActiveX control to handle these media types. According to RealNetworks, more than 170 million users worldwide have RealPlayer and its associated browser utilities installed.

Note

SMIL is not part of the RealSystem technology; it's just a markup language, like HTML. SMIL files can also be read by the QuickTime player and browser plug-in, and by Windows Media Player. To learn more about SMIL, visit the W3C Web site at www.w3c.org.

Figure 20.23 shows the various RealSystem MIME types and their associated filename extensions.

JavaScript Commands a Shockwave Movie Can Accept		
Description	**MIME Type**	**Filename Extensions**
RealAudio	audio/x-realaudio	.ra
RealAudio	audio/vnd.rn-realaudio	.ra
RealVideo	video/vnd.rn-realvideo	.rv
RealPix	image/vnd.rn-realpix	.rp
RealText	text/vnd.rn-realtext	.rt
RealG2 with Flash	image/vnd.rn-realflash	.rf
SMIL document	application/smil .smi	.smil
Ram	audio/x-pn-realaudio	.ram
Embedded Ram	audio/x-pn-realduio-plugin	.rpm

Figure 20.23   Commonly used MIME types and filename extensions for RealSystem media files.

Note

To learn more about RealMedia, visit RealNetworks' Web site at www.realnetworks.com.

RealMedia Issues

The RealSystem technologies are compatible across platforms and browsers. Although it is fairly common for RealMedia clips to open in RealPlayer, it is also possible to embed them in Web pages. A RealG2 plug-in and a RealG2 ActiveX control are both available, for best results, in both browsers.

Streaming

To take advantage of RealSystems streaming, the media must be housed on a RealServer. If you don't require streaming, however, but simply want to take advantage of RealPlayer and its plug-ins, you can use a standard Web server.

Content Creation

RealAudio and RealVideo files can be created in many professional video and audio programs. RealPix files (which present and coordinate a series of still images) can be created using any text editor; the images themselves are standard JPEG, GIF, or PNG files that have been prepared for streaming delivery with JPEGTRAN, a free utility available from RealNetworks. RealText files (used for displaying and animating text) and SMIL files can also be created in any text editor. RealNetworks also has a variety of content creation software available—RealProducer, RealPresenter, and RealSlideShow. Some of these programs even come in free, basic versions, and many are available cross-platform.

RAM Files and RAMGEN

Because of how RealMedia files are set up to work on the server, they require a special metafile called a RAM file (filename extension .ram or .rpm) to work properly. RAMGEN is a utility function of RealServers that dynamically creates this RAM file for you; links to RealMedia files housed on RealServers with RAMGEN must use a special addressing scheme that includes a RAMGEN parameter. If RealMedia files are accessed from computers or servers without RAMGEN (such as regular Web servers), you must create the RAM file manually.

Inserting RealSystems Media Objects

In Dreamweaver, you can insert any RealMedia content using the Insert Plug-In or Insert ActiveX objects. Using the ActiveX object gives you access to any additional scripting control built into the ActiveX control (though, of course, this scripting works only in Internet Explorer/Windows). If you're not planning on scripting the object, the insertion method used doesn't matter.

Exercise 20.8   Inserting a RealAudio Sound Using <embed>

For this exercise, you start by assuming that the RealAudio clip will be housed on a user's local computer or on a standard Web server. Then you'll see how to adapt the process for RealServer use.

1. Find the RealAudio file jazzy1_surestream_32.rm.

    This file is on the CD-ROM. If you haven't already done so, copy it to your hard drive for easier access.

    If you have RealPlayer on your system, you can launch the sound file directly in that program and test it out.

2. Create a RAM file for local access.

    For development purposes, you're going to link to a local copy of the sound file (the one you just found). Because there's no RealServer and no RAMGEN involved, you must create your own RAM file. RAM files can be created in any text editor—or in Dreamweaver, using its Code view.

    In Dreamweaver, create a new file; save it as realmusic.rpm (note the filename extension). Go to Code view and remove the default HTML framework.

3. Enter the URL of the RealAudio file in the RAM file.

    The RAM file should contain one line of code, and that code should be a URL. The URL can be absolute or relative, but it must have a protocol.

    Assuming that you saved your RAM file in the same folder as the music file, the code in the RAM file should look like this:

    ```
    file://jazzy1_surestream_32.rm
    ```

    The "file://" notation is the protocol for referencing a locally stored file. The rest of the line is the relative address linking the RAM file to the sound file. (If you have your sound file stored in a different folder from the RAM file, be sure to include this in your code.)

    When you're done, save the file and close it.

4. Create a new file; save it as realaudio.html.

    This will be the Web page that contains the music clip. For this exercise, leave the page empty except for the clip; in the real world, you'll probably want text and other content on the page as well. There's no problem with this.

5. Using the Insert Plug-In object, insert the RAM file that you just created.

    Note that you aren't inserting the sound file itself. This is important! RealMedia files must refer to either a RAM file or the RAMGEN utility on the RealServer, or they won't function.

6. Set the parameters for the sound file.

    Figure 20.24 shows the parameters accepted by the RealPlayer and Real plug-in. Only SRC, WIDTH, and HEIGHT are required. In this case, you're working with a file that has no visual component, so the width and height refer to the sound control panel that will be inserted into the page.

Parameters for RealSystems Media			
Parameter name	**Value**	**Default**	**Description**
src	URL	[required parameter]	Specifies a source clip.
width	number (percent or pixels)	[required parameter]	Sets the window or control width.
height number	(percent or pixels)	[required parameter]	Sets the window or control height.
maintainaspect	true or false		Preserves the image's aspect ratio if the width and height don't match the original size.
autostart	true or false	false	Determines whether the clip starts playing as soon as the page loads.
backgroundcolor	color name or RGB hex value		Sets the background color for the clip.
loop	true or false		Determines whether the clip loops indefinitely, or plays only once.
numloop	number		Loops the clip a given number of times.
center	true or false		Centers the clip in the window.
console	name, _master or _unique		Links multiple controls.
controls	control name	all	Adds RealPlayer controls to the Web page.
nojava	true or false	false	Prevents the Java virtual machine from starting as the movie loads. (Java is only needed if JavaScript will be used to control the clip.)
region	SMIL region		Ties a clip to an existing SMIL region.
shuffle	true or false	false	Randomizes playback.
nolabels	true or false	false	Suppresses presentation information.
nologo	true or false	false	Suppresses the RealLogo.

Figure 20.24   Parameters accepted by RealPlayer, the Real G2 plug-in, and Real G2 ActiveX control.

You'll see later how to play with the control panel settings. For now, you'll assume a default control setup and set the width and height to 350×100.

7. Try out the page in a browser.

Assuming that you've got RealPlayer and its plug-ins, your browser page should look like the one shown in Figure 20.25. Because you didn't set an AUTOSTART parameter and this parameter defaults to `false` for this plug-in, you'll have to click the Play button in the control panel to get the music to play.

8. Experiment with additional parameters.

Feel free to try any of the parameters that you think you understand from those listed in Figure 20.24—in particular:

- `pluginspage = http://www.realnetworks.com`

  (This parameter appears as Plg URL in the Property Inspector. This parameter is not listed in Figure 20.24 because the Real plug-in doesn't use it, but the browser will use it, if the plug-in isn't on the user's machine.)

- nojava = false

  (If this parameter is not set, Netscape will launch the Java virtual machine as soon as the clip loads, which can make the page seem very slow to download. Java is necessary only if you'll be using JavaScript to control the clip, which you're not.)

- controls = Choose from the list in Figure 20.26.

  The CONTROLS parameter determines which controls will show up in the sound control panel. It accepts a wide range of possible values, all of which are listed in Figure 20.26. Note that, depending on which settings you choose here, you'll probably want to adjust the width and height as well.

Figure 20.25   The realmusic.html file as it appears in the browser, with the default control panel showing at its recommended size.

9. Change the RAM file for an audio clip that's going to be accessed from a standard Web server.

   Remember that he RAM file lists the protocol and relative URL of the sound file to be played. Although it's good to use local addressing (as you've done) while developing a page, before the page can be uploaded to the Web, the RAM file must be changed to show the Web address of the sound file.

To do this, open the RAM file in Dreamweaver and go to Code view. Instead of the file protocol and relative URL, type in an absolute Web address, such as this:

```
http://www.webdomain.com/media/ jazzy1_surestream_32.rm
```

If you want to try this, you can enter a real address here and upload the HTML file, RAM file, and music file onto a Web server and try to access it. There's no way to test it locally because it's an absolute URL.

RealSystems :
Control Parameter Values

Value	Description	Suggested size
all, or default	Displays all controls	375x100
imagewindow	Displays the image window, for video and animation	176x132 or more
controlpanel	play, pause, stop, fast forward and rewind, position slider, volume slider, mute button	350x36
playbutton	play/pause button	44x26
playonlybutton	play button	26x26
pausebutton	pause button	26x26
stopbutton	stop button	26x26
FFCtrl	fast forward control	26x26
RWCtrl	rewind control	26x26
MuteCtrl	mute button	26x26
MuteVolume	mute button and volume slider	26x88
VolumeSlider	volume slider	26x65
PositionSlider	clip position slider	120x26
TACCtrl	clip info field	370x32
HomeCtrl	The Real logo	45x25
InfoVolumePanel	presentation information, along with volume slider and mute button	325x55
InfoPanel	presentation information panel	300x55
StatusBar	status panel (shows informational messages), plus network congestion LED and position field	300x50
StatusField	status panel only	200x30
PositionField	clip's current place in the presentation timeline, and total clip length	90x30

Figure 20.26   Possible values for the CONTROLS parameter for RealSystem media clips. Because different control setups are different sizes, use the recommended width and height values shown here for each setting.

10. Change the HTML file so that it will work with a sound accessed from a RealServer.

Again, if you don't actually have access to a RealServer account, you won't be able to test this. But here's the procedure:

• First, forget the RAM file; it's no longer necessary.

- Second, open the HTML file and select the plug-in content placeholder to access the Property Inspector. For the SRC parameter, you'll need to enter an address something like this:

```
http://realserver.company.com:8080/ramgen/media/
jazzy1_surestream_32.rm?embed
```

You can discuss the details of exactly how this URL should appear with your RealServer administrator.

Exercise 20.9   Inserting a RealMedia SMIL Presentation Using <object>

For the most part, the procedures for working the RealMedia are the same whether you're using <embed> or <object>. However, you should watch out for a few differences. In this exercise, you'll be working with a visual clip that contains RealAudio, RealPix, and SMIL instructions for synchronizing them.

1. Find the realdemo.smil file.

   This file is on the CD-ROM. If you haven't already done so, copy it to your hard drive for easier access. If you have RealPlayer on your system, you can launch the file directly in that program and see what the presentation should look like.

   If you want, you can also open it up in Dreamweaver or in a text editor to see how it's constructed. This SMIL file synchronizes several RealMedia files—slideshowtext.rt, fadein_simple.rp, and jazzy1_surestream_32.rm. All those source files must remain in the same relationship to the SMIL file as specified in the code for the presentation to work.

   You can also open slideshowtext.rt and fadein_simple.rp in a text editor, if you like. You'll see that the RP file calls on several JPEG images. These source images must also remain in the same relationship with the RP file as specified in the code for the presentation to work.

2. Create a RAM file; save it as realdemo.rpm.

   As in the previous exercise, you can create this file in Dreamweaver. In Code view, select and delete the entire HTML framework; then add a protocol and relative link to the SMIL file. Assuming that the RAM file is in the same folder as the SMIL file, the line of code will look like this:

```
file://realdemo.smil
```

   Save the RAM file and close it.

Note

RAM files with an extension of .rpm open their contents in the browser; RAM files with an extension of .ram launch RealPlayer.

3. Create a new file in Dreamweaver; save it as realdemo.html.
4. Create a table in this file to control layout.

Although it's not necessary to place elements in a table, you're going to see how to spread various RealMedia elements across a layout.

Create the table with a width of 256; Cell Padding, Cell Spacing, and a border of 0; three rows; and one column.

When the table is inserted, set the top cell to 256 pixels high and the middle cell to 20 pixels high.

5. Using the Insert ActiveX object, insert the RAM file realdemo.rpm into the top cell of the table.

   Remember that inserting an ActiveX object is a two-step process. After the object is inserted, use the SRC parameter in the Property Inspector to choose the file to insert.

6. In the Property Inspector's ClassID field, choose the Real G2 ActiveX control.

   Real G2 should come up as an option in the pop-up menu, as shown in Figure 20.27. If it's not on that list, you'll have to type it in manually. The listing should look like this:

   ```
   clsid:CFCDAA03-8BE4-11cf-B84B-0020AFBBCCFA
   ```

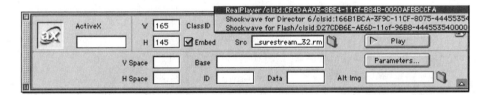

Figure 20.27   The ActiveX Property Inspector, with the Real G2 control showing in the ClassID pop-up menu.

7. Set the basic parameters.

   The dimensions of the presentation (which you could look up in the SMIL file, if you needed to) are 256×256. Set the width and height to match that.

   Set the BASE to http://www.realnetworks.com.

8. Set other parameters, including CONTROLS.

   If you try out your presentation in the browser without setting any more than these parameters, it won't look like much; that's because you haven't told the plug-in to display the image.

   In the generic Parameters dialog box, set the following parameters:

   ```
   controls = imagewindow
   autostart = true
   ```

   Now if you try out the page in a browser, the slideshow should show up and it should play automatically. Figure 20.28 shows how it should look.

Figure 20.28   The realdemo.html file in the browser, with the CONTROLS parameter set to IMAGEWINDOW.

Of course, there's no way to control the presentation because the control panel is no longer showing. You'll address that next.

9. Copy the ActiveX placeholder into the bottom cell of the layout table.

   Here's the problem: You can't add a control panel to the existing media clip because the CONTROLS parameter must be set to either IMAGEWINDOW or one of the control panel settings; it can't be set to both. So, you're going to put the media clip on the page twice—once as an image window and once as a control panel.

   Copy the ActiveX placeholder; then put the cursor in the bottom cell of the layout table, and paste. Resize the new placeholder to 256×26, and set its table cell alignment to Top. Figure 20.29 shows what the page should now look like in Dreamweaver.

10. For the new placeholder, set the CONTROLS parameter to PLAYBUTTON.

   If you try out the page in a browser after doing this, you should see a lovely movie and set of Play/Stop controls, as shown in Figure 20.30. But you'll soon discover that there's a problem: The two aren't connected. As far as the browser knows, there are two independent instances of the movie onscreen. You need to link them.

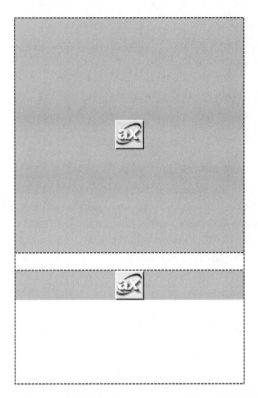

Figure 20.29   The realdemo.html file, with two copies of the RAM file in place.

Figure 20.30   The realdemo.html file as seen in the browser, with the console and image window showing.

11. For each instance of the movie, add a CONSOLE parameter; set it to MAIN.

The CONSOLE parameter enables you to link separate pieces so that the browser knows they're supposed to function as one big console. All elements that share a common console name will be treated as one. It doesn't matter what the name is, as long as it's the same for all the pieces.

It's also a good idea to remove the AUTOSTART parameter from the second clip instance.

Now try out the movie in a browser, and you'll find that the Play and Stop controls actually do play and stop the movie.

You can create as many individual console pieces as you want, to control your Real presentation, spread out over an entire page or grouped together however you like. Just create new placeholders, change the CONTROLS parameters, and make sure that the CONSOLE names all match. Mix and match the controls; it's like playing with blocks!

Tip

Remember, when it comes time to upload the presentation to a Web server or RealServer, you'll need to change the SRC of every single clip instance on the page.

Exercise 20.10   Editing RealText, RealPix, and SMIL Files

As you've seen, many of the elements in RealMedia presentations are text-based. SMIL, RealText, and RealPix are all derivatives of XML and can be edited in any text editor or in Dreamweaver's Code view. (For more information on using Dreamweaver with different markup languages, see Chapter 23, "Scripting and Markup Languages.")

In this exercise, you'll edit the presentation used in the previous exercise. You'll see how simple this can be and how Dreamweaver can help us with it.

1. Find the fadein_simple.rp file. Save it as fadein_simple_2.rp.

This file is in the Fadein folder, with the rest of your RealMedia files.

2. Open fadein_simple_2.rp in Dreamweaver and change the code to add another image to the slideshow.

Does the code look familiar but different? RealPix is a special markup language developed by RealNetworks, based on XML, to control the presentation of images.

Find the code that refers to the images in the slideshow. Make the changes as shown in Figure 20.31, to add an image called peppers.jpg. Note that the code includes time indexes—events are synchronized using these indicators. You'll need to change the time indexes so that the slides all fit within the 70-second duration of the clip. (You don't want to make the clip any longer than it is because the music is only 70 seconds long.)

```
<imfl>
    <head
      timeformat="dd:hh:mm:ss.xyz"
   duration="0:70"
   bitrate="12000"
   preroll"0:10"
   width="256"
   height="256"
   aspect="true"/>

   <!-- Use images no larger than 14k.
   If you use larger images, check this file in
   the RealPix Bandwidth Calculator to make sure it
   will stream. -->

   <!-- Assign handle numbers to images -->

   <image handle="1" name="btfly.jpg"/>
   <image handle="2" name="cows.jpg"/>
   <image handle="3" name="elephant.jpg"/>
   <image handle="4" name="frog.jpg"/>
   <image handle="5" name="hippo.jpg"/>
   <image handle="6" name="peppers.jpg"/>


   <!-- Fade in images -->

   <fill      start="0:00" color="black" />
   <crossfade start="0:01" duration="0:02" target="1" />
   <crossfade start="0:12" duration="0:02" target="2" />
   <crossfade start="0:24" duration="0:02" target="3" />
   <crossfade start="0:36" duration="0:02" target="4" />
   <crossfade start="0:48" duration="0:02" target="5" />
   <crossfade start="0:60" duration="0:02" target="6" />

</imfl>
```

Figure 20.31   The code for fadein_simple_2.rp, with added code for a new image. The code to be added or changed is highlighted.

3. Open slideshowtext.rt and save it as slideshowtext_2.rt. Change the code to add another caption for the slideshow.

   The code for this file is in RealText format, another derivation of XML. RealText language controls the appearance and animation of text.

   Change the code in this file to match that shown in Figure 20.32. Note especially the changed time indexes. The text should appear shortly after its related picture has faded in and should disappear before the picture has faded out. All these time stamps must be coordinated for the presentation to work.

4. Open realdemo.smil and save it as realdemo_2.smil. Change the code so that it refers to the new RT and RP files you just created.

   This is a SMIL file, written in another XML derivation. SMIL is used to put different media elements together, synchronizing where and when they appear relative to one another. SMIL controls screen layout and the presentation timeline. When used to create RealMedia presentations like this, the SMIL file synchronizes RealMedia; SMIL can be used with other kinds of media to create QuickTime movies.

   Change the code in this file to match that shown in Figure 20.33.

```
<window type="generic" duration="70" bgcolor="black" width="256" height="20">

<time begin="2"><center><font color="#FFFFFF">Butterflies</font></center>
<time begin="10"/><clear/>.
<time begin="14"/><clear/><center><font color="#FFFFFF">Cows</font></center>
<time begin="22"/><clear/>.
<time begin="26"/><clear/><center><font color="white">Elephants</font></center>
<time begin="34"/><clear/>.
<time begin="38"/><clear/><center><font color="white">Frogs</font></center>
<time begin="46"/><clear/>.
<time begin="50"/><clear/><center><font color="white">Hippos</font></center>
<time begin="58"/><clear/>.
<time begin="62"/><clear/><center><font color="white">Peppers</font></center>
</window>
```

Figure 20.32   The code for slideshowtext_2.rt, with added code for a new caption. The code
to be added or changed is highlighted.

```
<smil>
<head>
<layout>
<root-layout id="main" width="256" height="256" background-color="black"/>
<region id="r1" width="256" height="256" />
<region id="r2" width="256" height="256" />
<region id="r3" width="256" height="20" left="0" top="236"/>
</layout>
</head>
<body>
<par>
<audio src="jazzy1_surestream_32.rm" region="r1" dur="70"/>
<ref src="fadein/fadein_simple_2.rp" region="r2" dur="70"/>
<textstream src="slideshowtext_2.rt" region="r3" dur="70"/>
</par>
</body>
</smil>
```

Figure 20.33   The code for realdemo_2.smil, with references to the changed RealPix and
RealText files. The code to be changed is highlighted.

5. Create a new RAM file for the new presentation. Save it as realdemo_2.rpm.

    In Dreamweaver, create a new file. In Code view, delete the HTML framework.
    Enter the protocol and relative URL of the SMIL file, like this:

    `file://realdemo_2.smil`

6. Create a new HTML file; save it as realdemo_2.html. Insert the new RAM file.

    Use either Insert Plug-In or Insert ActiveX object. Set the dimensions to
    256×256. Set AUTOPLAY to TRUE.

7. Try it out in a browser. Does it work?

    If you want to try out a revised SMIL file without having to create a RAM file or
    HTML file, you can also open it directly in RealPlayer.

RealSystems Media Summary

If you're going to be working a lot with RealMedia, you might want to extend your copy
of Dreamweaver by installing the Real G2 custom objects. Created by RealNetworks and

available from the Macromedia Dreamweaver Exchange, these objects create a new Real G2 category in the Object panel with a complete set of objects for RealAudio, RealVideo, RealFlash, and so on. The objects will even write RAM files for you. There are also extensive help sections—including detailed instructions on using RealText, RealPix, and SMIL markup languages—at the RealNetworks Web site, `www.realnetworks.com/devzone`.

Extending the Browser with Java

If you're tired of playing the plug-in game, there's another totally different way of extending the browser's capabilities: Java. Java animations are not as smooth as those created in Shockwave or Flash. Java also does not support server-side or client-side streaming, and it isn't as easy to create or work with as any of the plug-in technologies you've been reading about. However, the great thing about Java that makes it sometimes preferable to Shockwave, QuickTime, or whatever is that it doesn't rely on the user having particular browser plug-ins or ActiveX controls installed.

What Is Java?

Java is a platform-independent, object-oriented programming language created by Sun Microsystems. (Despite the similarity in names, Java has no relation to JavaScript.) Although Java can create fully functional free-standing applications, it can also create mini-applications, called *applets*, that run inside a Web browser. Because Java is a complete programming language, similar to C or C++, Java applets can be as powerful and diverse as you like. Java applets are commonly used for everything from online games to animation and special effects, visitor counters, and clocks, calculators, and navigation tools.

How Java Works

To understand what makes Java so well-suited to Web use, you need to know how it's different from other programming languages.

Computers don't "understand" C++ or Java or any other programming language, not directly. Computers understand a numeric language called machine code. After a program is written, in whatever language, it must be compiled, or translated, into machine language. Machine language is platform-specific; this is why your copy of Dreamweaver will run only on a PC or only on a Mac. Programs must be compiled for a certain type of computer, and then they will run only on that type of computer.

Java is different. Java is compiled to run on a fake computer called a virtual machine. The *virtual machine* is actually a program itself, which is compiled to run on a specific platform. On Windows computers, the virtual machine is Microsoft VM; on Macs, it's Mac OS Run-Time for Java (MRJ). When a Java application or applet is run on a virtual machine, the virtual machine translates the code into platform-specific machine code. Thus, the Java applet itself is platform-independent.

Note

To learn more about Java, visit Sun's Web site at www.java.sun.com. To learn more about implementations of the Java virtual machine, visit Microsoft at www.microsoft.com/java, and Apple at www.apple.com/java.

Java Issues

The good news is that Java applets are not only platform-independent, but they're also browser-independent; as soon as a browser encounters an applet on a Web page, it launches the virtual machine and steps out of the way. There are no plug-ins to worry about. The only things needed to run a Java applet are a virtual machine (which most computers already have installed) and a Java-enabled browser (which almost all browsers are).

The bad news is that nothing is perfect. Some virtual machines are slower and buggier than others; it takes time to launch the virtual machine, which can seem like excessive download time to a frustrated user. And because the virtual machine is running through the browser, complex applets that require lots of processing power can (and do) crash browsers.

There can also be security issues around Java. Some so-called "hostile" applets are actually designed to behave like viruses; others can cause damage to a system accidentally. It's the job of the virtual machine to protect the computer system from these dangers, but virtual machines themselves can never be completely hackproof. Consequently, many institutions that deal in sensitive information will set their firewalls not to accept any Java, and individuals may choose to disable Java in their browser preferences.

Java and Media

Java applets can contain images and sounds. All images must be GIF or JPEG files. If a Java applet uses sound, it doesn't matter which plug-in your browser normally uses to handle sound because it's not the browser that's going to be handling the sound, it's the virtual machine. All sounds in Java applets must be AU files (filename extension .au). Java cannot handle video, although it can create animations or "fake video" from a series of still images. Java animations are not as smooth and do not run as quickly as those created in Flash, Shockwave, or QuickTime.

Working with Applets

Working with applets is not like working with Shockwave or QuickTime movies, or any other kind of Web media, because applets are not structured like those elements. Your first encounter with an applet will probably involve the words: "What are all these bits and pieces, and where's the applet?"

Class Files

A basic compiled Java *applet* is a file with the filename extension .class—not .java, which is used for uncompiled source code only.

However, an applet often consists of more than just one file. A complex applet may have several class files, of which only one is the applet itself. The others are supporting players that the applet will call on as it works. With some applets, naming conventions make it clear which is the main file—if the program is called Tabulator and there's a class file called tabulator.class, for instance. But with other applets, it can be a challenge knowing which class file to actually embed in the Web page. (The best applets usually have documentation that spells this out for you.)

Media Files

If an applet uses any media files—images, sounds, movies, and so on—these will also be in separate files, sometimes in separate folders. You must keep the internal folder structure of the applet the way the applet author intended, or the applet won't be capable of finding its media files.

Archive Files

You might come across a Java applet that has been packaged up into one or more archive files. These files will have a filename extension of .jar, .zip, or .cab. With an applet like this, you'll have to refer to the archive file(s) and the main class file in your HTML code. Refer to the applet's documentation to find the name of the class file (because it's inside the archive, and you can't get in there).

Obtaining Java Applets

Where do Java applets come from? Most of them are written by Java programmers. There isn't one standard authoring environment for creating them. This is why every applet is so different from every other applet.

If you want to use Java on your Web site, you can program it yourself, hire someone else to program it, or use one of the many prewritten applets available on the Web and elsewhere. Sun's own applet resource page (`www.java.sun.com/applets`), which has links to other major resource sites as well as a selection of applets to download, is a good place to start looking. Some applets are free, some are shareware, and some are commercial. Some are also better documented than others and allow more customization. Some work better than others.

Java from Director

If you want to create your own Java applets but don't want to become a programmer, you can use Director. Director's Save as Java Xtra lets you author an animation or interactive movie in Director and then tell Director to create and compile the Java code. Many of Director's capabilities don't translate to Java, though, so not all Shockwave movies can be repurposed as Java. Also, Java applets do not run as smoothly or quickly as Shockwave movies, nor do they launch as quickly, nor is Java as stable on multiple platforms as Shockwave. For quality and overall user experience, it's better to use Shockwave. (But, of course, that brings you right back to the "what if they don't have the plug-in?" problem. And the whole reason for using Java is to avoid that problem.)

It's also possible to create a Director movie both as a Shockwave movie and a Java applet, and then use JavaScript in the HTML page to send the user to the version that his browser supports. Macromedia's Aftershock utility (discussed previously) can create this code for you, or you can use Dreamweaver's Check Plug-In behavior to set it up yourself.

Note

The slideshow_java.html file on the CD-ROM shows a Director movie saved as Java and placed on a Web page. The slideshow_shock.html file shows the same Director movie saved as Shockwave and placed on a page.

Java from Flash

You can also create Java applets from Flash movies—again, with multiple limitations.

It works this way: In the Flash application folder, inside the Players subfolder, there's a folder called Flash Player Java Edition. This folder contains a Java applet, with the file Flash.class as its central file; this applet is a Java version of the Flash Player. The applet takes a parameter called `moviename`—if you pass the name of a SWF file, the Java player will play the Flash movie.

Disadvantages? Well, there are plenty. First, the SWF file must be in Flash 2 format, which limits what kind of fancy animation and interactivity it can contain. Second, because the entire player must download to the user's computer, the file size is several hundred kilo-bytes. Even after the player downloads, the user's virtual machine must launch. Finally, the animation won't be quite as smooth or quick as a regular Flash experience that uses the Macromedia plug-in.

The only advantage? It doesn't use a plug-in. (You can see why this method of distribut-ing Flash doesn't get used very often, but it might come in handy sometime—you never know.)

Note

> The flash_java.html file on the CD-ROM shows a Flash animated banner used as part of a Java applet.

Working with Applets in Dreamweaver

Dreamweaver provides several features for working with Java applets, including the Insert Applet object and the Applet Property Inspector. You can use these tools to insert an applet into an existing page, or to examine and alter the sample HTML code that usu-ally comes with commercially available Java applets.

Inserting an Applet

In Dreamweaver, you use the Insert Applet object, found in the Special Objects panel, to place Java applets in a page (see Figure 20.34). The actual process is pretty simple. Click the applet object. In the dialog box that opens, browse to the appropriate CLASS file, and click OK. There! You have an applet. If you look at your code, you'll see that the applet has been inserted using the <applet> tag.

Note

> According to the W3 Consortium's official HTML specifications, you should be using the <object> tag to place Java applets, not the <applet> tag. Not all browsers support the <object> tag for this use, though, so it's still customary to use the <applet> tag.

Figure 20.34 shows the Insert Applet object as well as the Property Inspector for a Java applet. Aside from the standard parameters (WIDTH, HEIGHT, VSPACE, HSPACE, ALIGN, ALT, and NAME), the only two settings available are Code and Base. Code is the name of the class file. Base is the name of the folder, if any, that contains the Java applet files. (It's cus-tomary to store an applet in its own folder so that all the files that comprise it can easily be kept together.) Additional parameters used by specific applets are added with the generic Parameters button.

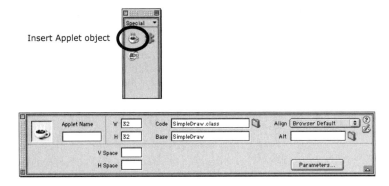

Insert Applet object

Figure 20.34   The Insert Applet object and the Property Inspector for a Java applet. Because every applet is different, this is another generic inspector, with a Parameters button for adding applet-specific parameters.

Exercise 20.11   Inserting a Simple Java Applet

In this exercise, you're going to insert the world's simplest Java applet. It's actually a fairly useless applet called SimpleDraw, used mostly as a teaching exercise for beginning Java programmers, but it will introduce you to the peculiarities of working with applets.

1. Find the SimpleDraw folder and examine its contents.

   This applet is in the SimpleDraw folder, on the accompanying CD-ROM. If you haven't done so already, copy this folder and its contents from the CD-ROM onto your hard drive, for easier access.

   You'll see that the folder contains three class files. Can you tell which of them is the applet? With this applet, the filenames make it obvious: SimpleDraw.class is the applet. The other class files will be called on by SimpleDraw.class as it runs, but these needn't be called specifically in the HTML.

2. Create a new file; save it as simpledraw.html.

   Don't save this file in the SimpleDraw folder itself. Save it one level up, if you want your results to match the ones shown here.

3. Using the Insert Applet object, insert the SimpleDraw applet into your page.

   When the dialog box comes up asking for an applet to insert, choose SimpleDraw.

   When the applet is in place, note that the CODE and BASE properties have been filled in with the name of the class file and the SimpleDraw folder (see Figure 20.34).

4. Set the width and height of the applet.

   Dreamweaver doesn't know the proper width and height, so it has filled in the 32×32 default values.

The only way for you to know the proper dimensions, or even whether the applet needs certain dimensions to function property, is to read the applet documentation or experiment.

For SimpleDraw, there are no specific dimensions required, although the width and height need to be set to at least 150×50.

For now, set the dimensions to 200×200.

5. Try the applet in a browser.

SimpleDraw is simple. There are no other parameters to set.

When you try out the page in a browser, you should see a screen like that shown in Figure 20.35. Click inside the applet area to draw a square or circle of the specified color. You can change the shape or color using the pop-up menus at the top.

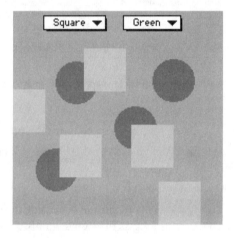

Figure 20.35   SimpleDraw running in a browser.

You should also note that you probably had to wait a few moments for the virtual machine to launch. As the applet runs, the status bar at the bottom of the browser window will say something like "Applet running" or "Applet loaded."

Now that you understand how the applet functions, you can also see why the dimensions are flexible. The larger the applet area is, the more room the user has to draw squares and circles. Is this how all applets work? No—every applet is different.

Exercise 20.12   Inserting an Applet with Multiple Parameters

In the real world, few applets are as simple as SimpleDraw. In this exercise, we'll insert an applet that puts a continually changing series of quotes on the Web page. (This applet is one of several freebies offered at the Sun Java site, www.java.sun.com/openstudio/ guide.html. To see it in action on a Web page, look on the CD-ROM for the quotes_ finished.html file.)

According to the documentation, the applet takes several parameters. Figure 20.36 lists them. Some of these parameters may be optional, and others may be required; the documentation doesn't specify. You'll use them all.

```
bgcolor: The background color of the applet in RGB hexadecimal.
bheight: The border height.
bwidth: The border width.
delay: The delay between frames in milliseconds.
fontname: The name of the font.
fontsize: The size of the font in points.
link: A URL to load if the applet is clicked.
number: The number of quotes.
quoteN: A "|" delimited string where the first item is the quote, the second item
        is the company, the third item is the RGB hexadecimal text color, the
        fourth item is the RGB hexadecimal background color and the last item
        is the length of time in seconds to display the quote. N represents a
        value between 0 and number - 1.
space: The distance in pixels between the quote and the company.
```

Figure 20.36   Parameters for the Sun quotes Java applet, along with descriptions and suggested values.

1. Find and examine the Quote folder, which contains this applet.

   You'll see several class files. Can you tell by their names which one is the applet? (It's a little trickier than it was with SimpleDraw.)

2. Create a new file; save it as quotes.html.

   It's up to you whether you save the file inside or outside the applet folder. The applet will work either way, as long as the CODE and BASE parameters are entered correctly. If you want your exercise to match the examples shown here, save the file outside the folder.

3. Using the Insert Applet object, insert the applet.

   The main class file that you should insert is JavaQuote.class. The codebase option should say Classes or should show the path to the classes file if your page is saved more than one level up from the .class file.

NOTE

Java is case-sensitive! Make sure that all references to files, folders, parameters, and values are in their correct case, or your Java applets won't work.

4. Set the width and height to 300×125.

   The documentation doesn't specify a desired width and height. Experimentation will show you that dimensions aren't crucial for this applet. Just choose values that fit in with the rest of your page, and let all the quoted text show.

5. Set parameters for the applet.

Use the generic Parameters dialog box to enter these parameters. Refer to the parameters list in Figure 20.36, and choose values as you like.

You might find it difficult to see what you're doing when you try to enter the quote parameter because it's fairly long. If you like, you can type the quote first in a text editor such as NotePad or SimpleText, and then paste it into the parameter's value field. You can also work directly in Dreamweaver's code view, of course, if you feel comfortable there.

When you're done, your Parameters dialog box will look something like the one shown in Figure 20.37.

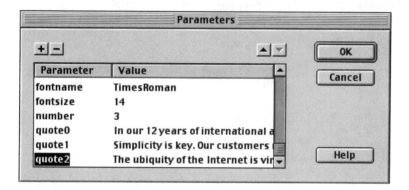

Figure 20.37   The Parameters dialog box, showing entered parameters and values for the Sun quotes Java applet. (Only the last few parameters are visible.)

6. Try it out in a browser.

If everything was entered correctly, your virtual machine should load and show you an ever-changing set of quotes. Back in Dreamweaver, you can experiment with other parameter settings to see how to customize the applet.

Java Conclusion: Using More Complex Applets

With more complex applets, including those that have been packaged in JAR, CAB, or ZIP archives, it's often easier and better not to use the Insert Applet object. Instead, because almost all applets come with sample HTML code showing how they should be inserted on a page, just copy and paste that code into your file, or use the sample page as the basis to create your own file. If you do this, you'll need to make sure that your HTML file is in the same place relative to the applet as the sample source—if the sample file sits in the same folder as the applet, for instance, place your HTML file in the same folder as the applet.

When you're finished your copying and pasting, of course, if you view the page in Dreamweaver's visual editor, you'll be able to select the applet and check the Property Inspector, just as if you'd inserted the applet yourself.

Putting Sound on Web Pages

One very popular use of media in Web pages today is sound. Sound effects, background sounds, voice-overs, demonstration music—you name it, Web authors are doing it. All the different options covered so far in this chapter have handled sound in one way or another. But what's the best way to put sound on the Web? And what should you know about sound to maximize your sound power?

Digital Sound: Terms and Concepts

Before getting into the nitty-gritty of coding sound into Web pages, let's take a look at some basic digital sound terminology. The more you understand how sound works on the computer, the more you'll know what you can and can't do with it on the Web.

Sampled vs. Synthesized sound

Two main kinds of digital sound exist: sampled and synthesized. *Sampled sound* originates in the real (nondigital) world—voices, concerts, recording studios, and common household sounds turned into sound effects—and then is digitized, much as a photograph is scanned into a computer. Just like when a photograph is scanned, the digital sampling process for sounds can collect a lot of data or a little data. The more data is collected, the higher the quality is and the larger the file is. Sampled sound files are notoriously large, often too large for standard modem speeds to handle. Consequently, most Web pages use short, fairly low-quality sounds or rely on sound loops (a short piece of music that plays repeatedly) exclusively.

Synthesized sound is created on the computer and played back using synthetic musical instruments built into the computer. A synthesized sound file does not contain actual soundwave information; instead, it holds instrumental and musical instructions for re-creating the sound on the computer. Synthesized sound files are tiny, especially compared to sampled sounds. A 5-minute piece of synthetic music can be stored in less than 20K. The same piece of music, encoded as sampled sound, would be several megabytes. The only disadvantage to synthesized sounds is that they sound synthetic and generic. If you want to hear the Beatles singing "Yesterday," you need sampled sound; if you don't mind a bunch of synthetic computer instruments playing "Yesterday," you can use synthesized sound.

Standard File Formats

The most common file formats for sampled sound files on the Web are WAV, AIF, AU, and MP3.

- WAV files are native to the Windows operating system. This is probably the most common sound file format on Web pages. Browser plug-ins generally have no trouble with WAVs.

- AIF files are native to the Macintosh operating system. They're less common than WAVs, but they're equally well supported by browser plug-ins.

- AU files are native to the UNIX operating system. They don't compress very well, and they are not found on Web pages as much as they once were. They are the only format usable in Java applets.

- MP3 files are well-known for providing very high-quality sound with amazingly small file sizes. To play an MP3 file, you must have an MP3 player. Many browsers are not configured to handle MP3 files, so they are not commonly found embedded in Web pages. More often, MP3s are downloaded and then played offline.

The standard file format for synthesized sounds is MIDI. MIDI files are well understood by browser plug-ins, and they appear on the Web quite often as background music.

The Plug-in Problem

At the beginning of this chapter, you saw how browsers use MIME types and filename extensions to determine which plug-ins should handle which media types. So far, this chapter has dealt mostly with media types that can be handled by only one plug-in or another—there's only one Shockwave plug-in, for instance, and all .dcr files get handled by that plug-in or not at all.

With sound, things get a lot more complicated. Many plug-ins and helpers can handle any of the sound file formats listed previously. Netscape's LiveAudio plug-in, Windows Media Player, WinAmp, QuickTime, and RealPlayer can all handle sound files. Which one the browser calls on depends on how the browser is configured; as you have seen, there's no standard configuration for browsers.

Does it matter which plug-in handles the sound, as long as it plays properly? Different plug-ins accept different parameters and offer different choices for control, but if you can't target a particular plug-in, you can't take advantage of these. Also, each plug-in has its own kind of sound control window or control panel that it uses to let the user play, stop, rewind, and so on. Some controllers are large, some are small, and some even open in separate little floating windows. If you're designing a Web page around a sound controller, wouldn't it be nice to know how much space to leave for it?

Inserting Sounds

In Dreamweaver, you can insert a sound on a page using the Insert Plug-In or Insert ActiveX object. If you choose to insert as ActiveX, you can do more things to control the sound (although the controls work only in Internet Explorer on the Windows platform). If you don't plan to use any ActiveX features, it doesn't matter which option you choose. The standard insertion method for most Web authors is to use the <embed> tag (the Insert Plug-In object).

> **Note**
>
> If you're interested in extending your copy of Dreamweaver, you might want to try Massimo Foti's custom Audio Embed object, available from the Macromedia Dreamweaver Exchange. This object uses the <object> tag and includes a whole list of ActiveX parameters, giving you an idea of what can be done to control sound in Internet Explorer/Windows.

Exercise 20.13   A Simple HTML Jukebox

In this exercise, you'll create a page that enables the user to sample several looping music tracks. The exercise isn't designed to create a bulletproof page, but it will demonstrate the unpredictability of browser configurations. When you've finished creating the file, try it out on as many different computers as you can, and see how many variations on a theme you can find.

1. Open the file jukebox.html.

   You'll find this file, along with several music files, in the JukeBox folder on the CD-ROM. If you haven't done so already, copy the entire folder to your hard drive so that you can work on it.

   You'll see that the file contains four empty table cells waiting to have sound controls put in them.

2. Using either the Insert Plug-In or the Insert ActiveX object, insert funkyloop1.wav into the first jukebox slot.

3. Set the width and height.

   Here's the tricky part. The placeholder that Dreamweaver gives you will become the sound controller in the browser. But because you don't know which controller is going to show up, how do you determine correct dimensions? You have to make your best guess. Netscape's LiveAudio plug-in creates a control that is 144×60 pixels, so that's a good default value to start from. You might find, though, as you check out the page with different browser configurations, that you prefer different dimensions.

4. Set the optional parameters.

Because you're not targeting a specific plug-in, you can't be entirely sure what parameters will be accepted. Luckily, there's no penalty for assigning a parameter that the plug-in doesn't understand. For this exercise, you'll set the parameters as follows:

```
loop = true
autoplay = false
autostart = false
volume = 50
```

All plug-ins should understand the LOOP parameter. Some plug-ins understand AUTOPLAY, while others use AUTOSTART; you've "overloaded" the parameters by specifying both. Some plug-ins understand VOLUME, and some don't, but there's no harm in assigning it. Assuming that the plug-in understands volume to be a percentage between 0 and 100, your setting of 50 should soften the sound so that it's nice and mellow.

5. Repeat this process for all four jukebox slots, inserting a different music loop in each.

Assign all the previous parameters to each. When you're finished, your page should look like the one shown in Figure 20.38.

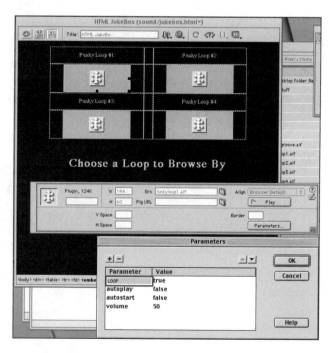

Figure 20.38   The jukebox.html file, with sound files inserted into the appropriate table cells. The placeholders have been sized to 144×60 pixels each. The Property Inspector and Parameters dialog box shows the setup for each sound file.

6. Test the file in a browser.

Can you tell from the sound controls that appear what sound plug-in is being used? Does the control panel fit nicely in your page? How about the sound parameters? Did the sounds autoplay, or not? Do they loop? Did the volume parameter have any effect?

Figure 20.39 shows how the jukebox page looks when the browser calls the QuickTime plug-in to handle the sounds. The QuickTime controller is a little small for the amount of space allocated, but it's not bad.

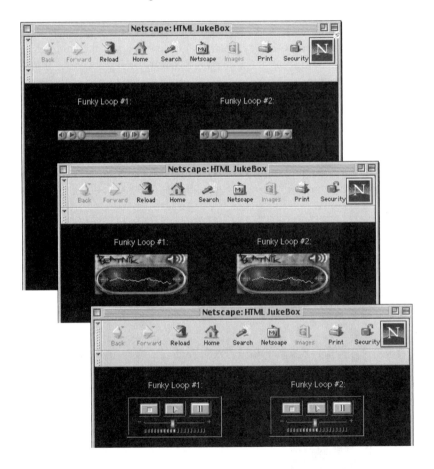

Figure 20.39   The jukebox.html file, as it looks in a browser using the QuickTime, Beatnik, and LiveAudio plug-ins.

Exercise 20.14   Inserting Invisible Background Music

Background music is a sound file that automatically starts playing when the page loads, without drawing too much attention to itself. Because the goal of background music is to be in the background, there's generally no visual indication of its presence on the page (no controller, in other words). So, in this exercise, you'll learn how to make music invisible.

1. Open any of the files from previous exercises (preferably one that doesn't already have sound on it), or create a new file and save it.

2. Place the cursor at the top of the page, before any other content, and insert the acousticgroove.wav sound file.

    You want the background music to start playing as soon as the page starts loading, so you need to place it at the top of the page. Don't worry if the placeholder pushes the other page elements out of alignment; the next step will take care of that.

3. Set the width and height of the placeholder to 2×2.

    You don't want the controller to take up any room, so you make it nice and tiny. Don't set it to less than 2×2, though, because smaller values can crash some browsers.

4. Set the optional parameters.

    In the generic Parameters dialog box, enter these parameters:

    hidden = true

    autoplay = true

    autostart = true

    loop = true

    volume = 25

    The HIDDEN parameter hides the 2×2 sound control panel. Then you can set the sound to start playing automatically and go on playing indefinitely. Of course, this is a little bit dangerous; you've just taken the controller away from the user and then set the music to never stop. You don't want people to go screaming from your site because they hate the music. With a sound loop as short as the one you're inserting, however, if it didn't loop, it wouldn't be much of a background. Some, but not all, plug-ins will accept a numeric value in the LOOP parameter. If you set looping to a number, though, and the plug-in doesn't understand that value, it will default to no looping at all.

5. Try out the page in a browser.

    Does the music play? Is the controller properly invisible? Is the music obnoxious? Too soft? Too loud? At least you don't have to worry about what size the control panel is!

Controlling Sounds

Do you want buttons that make little "click" sounds when they're clicked? Do you want cool graphic sound control panels that fit in with the rest of your page design and that don't change size and appearance based on plug-in configuration? Then you want to control your sounds.

JavaScript and the Play Sound Behavior

For the same reasons that you couldn't reliably use JavaScript to control QuickTime, you can't rely on JavaScript to start and stop sounds from playing. Not all browsers allow JavaScript control over plug-in content.

Dreamweaver's Play Sound behavior is a case in point. It seems simple: Create a button or text link, apply the behavior, choose a sound file to play, and whenever the user clicks the button, the sound should play. The only problem is, in some browsers it works and in some it doesn't. This isn't a problem with the behavior; it's a limitation of the browsers.

Exercise 20.15   Playing a Sound with JavaScript

In this exercise, you'll see the limitations of the Play Sound behavior, and you'll see how you can maximize its effectiveness despite browser limitations.

1. Create a new file. Save it as play_sound.html.
2. Insert the button image clickme.gif.

   If you haven't done so already, copy this file from the CD-ROM onto your hard drive for easier access.

3. Assign a # link to the image so that you can attach a JavaScript to it.
4. Apply the Play Sound behavior to the image.

   You can find the Play Sound behavior in the Actions list of the Behavior panel. Figure 20.40 shows the behavior being assigned. For the sound file to play, choose click.aif.

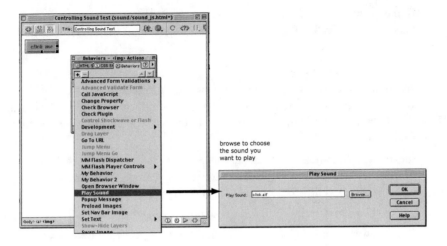

Figure 20.40   Applying the Play Sound behavior to a linked button.

5. Examine your page and the Property Inspector.

You'll probably notice immediately that a new plug-in placeholder appears on the page. That's the sound file. The Play Sound behavior automatically inserts the sound file, using the <embed> tag, and assigns various parameters to it. If you select the sound placeholder and examine the Property Inspector, you'll see these parameters (see Figure 20.41).

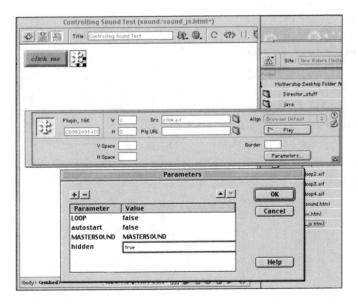

Figure 20.41   The Property Inspector for a sound file inserted using the Play Sound behavior.

Note that the width and height have been set to 0. This is a dangerous setting that can cause problems in some browsers; it's best to set the dimensions to 2×2.

6. Try the page in one or more browsers.

Depending on the browser you're using, how it's configured, and the platform you're working on, you may or may not hear a sound when you click the button. In some browser configurations, a new window will open up with the sound playing in it.

The most you can hope for from this behavior is that it will work in some browsers and not be obnoxious in others. Opening a new window is obnoxious if all you want is a little button-click. Luckily, this is an easily fixed problem.

7. Edit the behavior's script so that it doesn't open a new window.

In Dreamweaver, go to Code view and find the MM_controlsound function in the document's head.

Tip

When you're in Code view, click the double curly brace icon at the top of the document window to get a pop-up list of all functions defined in the document. Choose MM_controlsound from the list, and you'll be taken right to it.

The last line of the function looks like this:

```
else window.location = sndFile;
```

Put two forward slashes in front of it to turn it into a comment, like this:

```
//else window.location = sndFile;
```

Disabling a line of code like this, by making it into a comment, is called commenting it out. It's a little less drastic than deleting the code entirely, in case you decide later that you want it back in.

8. Try the behavior in as many browsers as you can.

No browser should open a new window to play the sound. You should get either a sound or no sound. And that's the best you can hope for, using JavaScript to control an embedded sound.

Putting It All Together

Now that you have all the facts, how do you put everything together into one nice, functional Web page? Let's finish up by looking at some strategic options.

Do the Authoring in the Media Files

If you really want reliable, controllable media, the simplest answer is to avoid browser scripting entirely. Flash, Shockwave, QuickTime movies, RealPlayer SMIL files, Java—all of these offer internal scripting. If you want buttons that make "click" sounds when you click them, make them in Flash. (Unfortunately, Dreamweaver's new Insert Flash Button object doesn't allow for adding sound to the buttons it creates; you'll have to use Flash itself for that.) If you want music with a cool-looking control panel, put the sound and the controls into a Flash, Shockwave, QuickTime, Java, or RealPlayer movie, and insert the whole thing into your Web page. If you want controllable video files, build the controls into a QuickTime file, or put the QuickTime video into Shockwave.

The CD-ROM files include flash_sound.swf, a Flash-based sound control panel; qt_sound.mov, a QuickTime sound control panel; slideshow.dcr, a Shockwave movie that includes controllable video; and click_button.swf, a Flash button complete with sound effects. Check out these files and see how they work in a Web page.

Work Sneaky with Frames

Start thinking outside the box—or inside the frame, anyway. If you're willing to use frames in your Web site, you can do some lovely things to integrate media files into pages without running into any scripting nightmares.

Controlling Background Sounds

You know that you can't reliably use JavaScript to control sounds on a page. But you also know that an autoplaying, looping sound will play only as long as the file containing it is loaded in the browser window. What if you control the sound by loading and unloading different pages?

To see how this works, find the sound_frameset.html file on the CD-ROM and open it, first in a browser and then in Dreamweaver. Figure 20.42 shows the interface as it appears in the browser. Figure 20.43 shows how it breaks down into files and frames.

Figure 20.42   The sound_frameset.html file, as it appears in a browser.

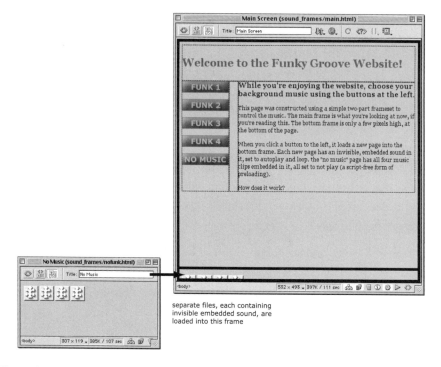

separate files, each containing invisible embedded sound, are loaded into this frame

Figure 20.43   The sound_frameset.html file, as it appears in Dreamweaver, with frame divisions and frame pages showing.

In the browser, it works like this: Click a button, and a background sound loop starts playing. Click another button, and the loop is replaced by another. Click the No Music button, and all the music stops.

In Dreamweaver, you can see that it's constructed like this: The page is a frameset with one big frame covering most of the browser window and one skinny little frame called musicFrame at the bottom. Clicking a button loads new pages into musicFrame. Four of the loaded pages contain nothing but embedded music files, each set to autoplay and loop. The fifth page (the page that's loaded when the frameset first opens) contains all four music files, but each with autoplay set to `false`. This silently preloads the music. (If you're not worried about preloading, you could also leave this fifth page completely empty.) The whole effect works because there's no scripting. You're working *with* the browser limitations instead of *against* them to start and stop the music.

Loading Multiple Movies

Just as you can't use scripting to control sound, you can't control movies, either. But you can use a similar technique to the one just described to create the illusion that you're doing just that.

To see how this effect works, find the movie_frameset.html file on the CD-ROM, and open it. Figure 20.44 shows what you'll see in the browser. Figure 20.45 shows what's going under the hood, so to speak.

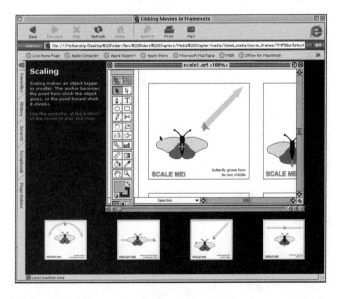

Figure 20.44   The movie_frameset.html file, as it appears in a browser. Clicking a button at the bottom of the screen loads a new movie at the top and changes the text that appears at the left.

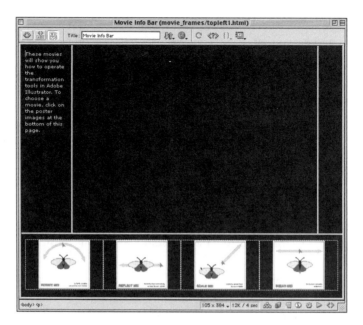

Figure 20.45   The movie_frameset.html file, as it appears in Dreamweaver, diagrammed to show how it was constructed. Three frames are involved; clicking a button in the bottom frame loads a new file into the movie frame and rewrites the text in the top left frame.

In the browser, it works like this: Click a button at the bottom of the screen. A new movie loads and a new bit of descriptive text comes up on the left.

In Dreamweaver, you can see that it's constructed like this: The file contains three frames—infoFrame, movieFrame, and navFrame. Each movie is embedded into its own HTML file, none of which is loaded to begin with. Each button is linked to one of the movie HTML files and loads it into the movieFrame. Each button also has a Dreamweaver behavior attached that rewrites the text in the infoFrame when the button is clicked. (The text could have been changed by loading a new file into the infoFrame, if you want to avoid scripting altogether.)

Dealing with Plug-in Detection

So, you've decided to use content that requires one or more plug-ins or ActiveX controls on your Web site. What do you want to do about those potential site visitors who won't have the proper browser setup?

Strategic Decisions

Do you want to provide alternate content?

Creating non–media-intensive versions of everything you do is time-consuming and makes site maintenance twice as much work. But do you want to leave a portion of your potential audience high and dry, without anything to look at?

If you do provide alternate content, how do you want to direct visitors to it?

Your basic choice is between being visible and being invisible about redirecting users.

Visible redirection means starting your site with a page that asks users, "Do you have the such-and-such plug-in?" Clicking a Yes answer sends the user to the media-intensive pages. Clicking No sends the user to the alternate pages. If users aren't sure whether they have the plug-in, it's a good idea to put some sample plug-in content on the page for them to see: "If you can see this animation/video/hear the music, you have the plug-in." You can also provide a link to where users can download the required plug-in, if you want. Visible redirection annoys some users, who say that they don't like the extra step between them and the Web site, but it is pretty foolproof and easy to set up.

Invisible redirection means detecting plug-ins behind the scenes and automatically sending the user to one set of pages without him realizing that it's even happening. This is an attractive option because it streamlines your Web site from the visitor's point of view. However, it can be tricky to set up, and a lot of things can go wrong with it.

Scripted Detection with the Check Plug-In Behavior

The standard method for invisible plug-in detection is to use a JavaScript that executes when the page loads. That's what Dreamweaver's Check Plug-In behavior does.

You can use this behavior in two ways:

- The behavior can be put in the page that contains the media content. If the plug-in is found, the browser stays on the page; if not, the browser is sent to an alternate page.
- The behavior can be put on an empty, dummy page. In this case, if the plug-in is found, the browser is sent to the page containing the media; if not, the browser is sent to the alternate page.

Figure 20.46 shows the file structure for each of these scenarios.

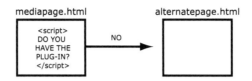

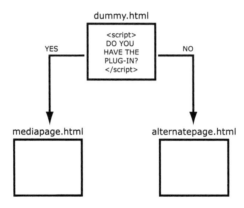

Figure 20.46   Two different ways of setting up files for the Check Plug-In behavior (or any other scripted detection).

The second scenario is more efficient for downloading because it doesn't make visitors without the plug-in wait for a complex page full of media to start loading before they're sent to another page. The first scenario is easier to set up and maintain because there's one less HTML file to keep track of.

To use the Check Plug-In behavior, follow these steps:

1. Start by creating all the files you'll need. You'll need at least the file containing the media and a page of alternate content. You also might want to create a blank, dummy page that will eventually contain only the behavior and nothing else.

2. Open the file into which you want to insert the behavior. This might be the media page, or it might be the dummy page.

3. In the tag selector, click the <body> tag. The behavior needs to be called from this tag.

4. In the Behavior Inspector, choose Check Plug-In from the Actions list. The dialog box that comes up will look like the one shown in Figure 20.47.

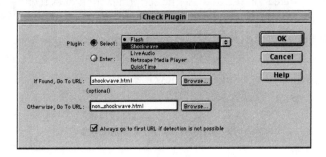

Figure 20.47   The Check Plug-In behavior dialog box, with sample entries in place.

5. From the pop-up menu in the dialog box, choose the appropriate plug-in that you want to test for. The most commonly used plug-ins are available; if your plug-in isn't listed, you'll have to type in its name yourself.

6. In the other fields of the dialog box, enter the names of the files that you created earlier. If you're adding the behavior to the page containing the media, leave out the optional "if found" destination file. If you're adding the behavior to a dummy page, enter the media page as the "if found" destination. Enter the name of the alternate content page as the "if not found" destination.

7. Important! Make sure that the option Go to First Page If Detection Is Impossible is selected. Some versions of Internet Explorer do not allow JavaScript plug-in detection. If this option is *not* selected, users with that browser will always be sent to the alternate content, even if they have the plug-in. (Obviously this is a very distressing experience!)

Limitations of Scripted Detection

If it involves scripting, something can go wrong with it. As noted previously, some browsers don't allow scripted detection. Also, if you're using the Check Plug-In behavior for your scripting, it's important to keep in mind that this script checks for only the presence of a plug-in, not the version. What if your QuickTime content requires the QuickTime 4.1, but the user has only QuickTime 3? The Check Plug-In behavior will direct your users to the QuickTime version of your Web page, but they won't be able to access the content. Those users are high and dry.

If all this makes you nervous, you might want to consider detection methods that don't involve scripting.

Scriptless Detection

This rather sneaky detection method uses no scripting, but it does require that you have access to the authoring capabilities of whatever media format you're using. The method, which is diagrammed in Figure 20.48, will work for any media type that has authoring capabilities (Flash, Shockwave, QuickTime, and RealPlayer). For Exercise 20.16, you'll use Shockwave. When you get the idea of how it works, you should be able to adapt it to whatever media type you need.

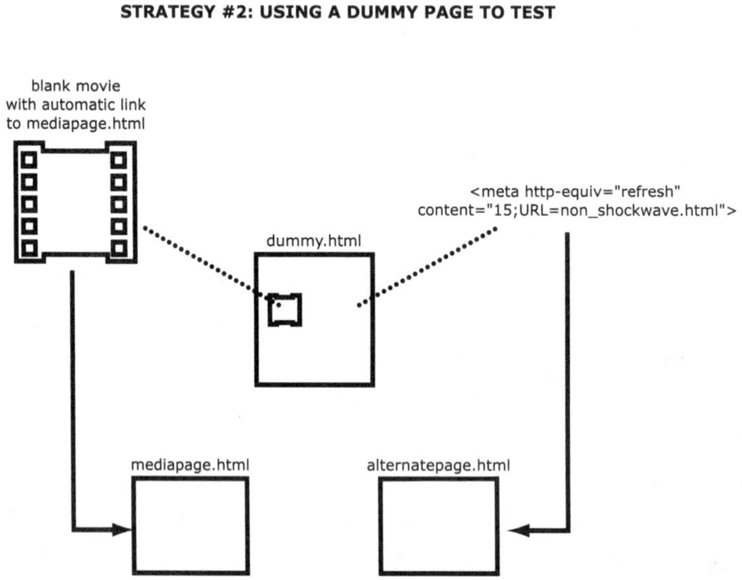

STRATEGY #2: USING A DUMMY PAGE TO TEST

Figure 20.48   Scriptless detection using a dummy media movie and a <meta> refresh tag.

Exercise 20.16   Script-Free Detection of the Shockwave Plug-in

The following steps demonstrate script-free detection of the Shockwave plug-in:

1. Create three HTML files: Call them shockwave.html, non_shockwave.html, and dummy.html.

   Like the scripted detection method covered previously, this method starts by sending the user to a blank, dummy page, where the detection occurs. Depending on the results of detection, the user will be sent to the Shockwave or the non-Shockwave page.

2. In the shockwave.html file, insert the Shockwave file slideshow.dcr.

    The correct dimensions for this movie are 400×400. No other parameters
    need be set.

3. In the non_shockwave.html file, insert the file slideshow.jpg.

    This file is just a JPEG image of the first picture in the slideshow, for purposes
    of this exercise. Obviously, in the real world, you'd want a more functional
    alternative, probably using JavaScript and a series of images.

4. In the dummy.html file, insert the file shocktest.dcr.

    This Shockwave movie consists of one frame only and an empty stage (so don't
    be surprised if it doesn't look like anything if you try to preview it). The single
    frame contains a Lingo statement:

    ```
    on exitFrame

        gotoNetPage shockwave.html

    end
    ```

    This statement means that as soon as this frame of the shocktest movie plays, the
    browser will open shockwave.html. Figure 20.49 shows how the Director file for
    this Shockwave movie was set up.

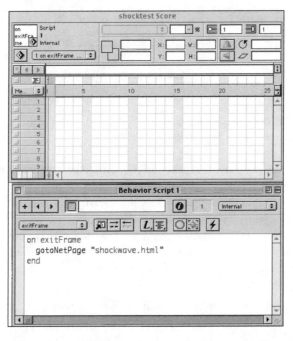

Figure 20.49   Setting up the shocktest.dcr movie in Director. This shows the empty stage
nd the Lingo statement set to play at the end of the first (and only) frame
of the timeline.

What does this do? If the user has the correct Shockwave plug-in, the shocktest.dcr movie will play; if the movie plays, the browser will be redirected to the Shockwave page of the Web site. That takes care of users who have the plug-in.

5. Still in the dummy.html file, insert a <meta> refresh tag.

   Using the Head objects section of the Objects panel, find the Insert Refresh object and click to insert it. This object adds a <meta> tag to the head of the document that automatically loads a new page in the browser window after a set period of time.

   When the Refresh dialog box comes up, set the time limit to 15 seconds. Set the destination page to non_shockwave.html. Figure 20.50 shows the meta refresh tag object and dialog box, as it should appear.

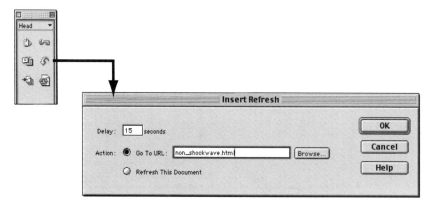

Figure 20.50   Inserting the meta refresh tag into dummy.html in Dreamweaver. The Object dialog box shows the correct entries for redirecting the browser to the non-Shockwave file.

What does this do? Fifteen seconds after loading, the page will automatically redirect itself to the non-Shockwave page of the Web site. The theory is, if the user has the plug-in, then the shocktest movie will play, and this refresh tag won't have a chance to execute because the dummy page won't be loaded anymore when the 15 seconds is up. If the user doesn't have the plug-in, the shocktest movie won't play and the browser won't be redirected, so 15 seconds will eventually go by and the page will be redirected to the non-Shockwave page. It's pretty slick.

6. Open dummy.html in the browser and see what happens.

   If you have the version of the Shockwave plug-in needed to play the movie, you should very quickly be whisked off to view the slideshow. If you don't, you'll soon be looking at a JPEG image.

Scriptless Detection with Other Plug-ins

As you can see, whatever media type you're working with must have a means of calling a new URL into the browser window for this method to work. For Shockwave movies, that means is Director's GoToNetPage Lingo command. Here's how you would accomplish the same thing in other programs:

- **To test for the Flash plug-in**. Use Flash's `GetURL()` ActionScript statement.

- **To test for the QuickTime plug-in**. Using Plug-In Helper, add a parameter of `qtnext1=[URL]`.

Summary

In this chapter, you got a taste of the major different technologies available for adding media content to the Web. Are these the only technologies? No! the Web is worldwide and full of variety. This chapter didn't discuss Beatnik, an alternative plug-in for handling sound, or MetaStream, a plug-in for handling streaming 3D content. It also didn't discuss Windows Media Player or the AVI file format for video. As you read this, more media technologies no doubt are being thought up and implemented. If you want a different media experience for your Web visitors, it's up to you to do the research; then use Dreamweaver's tools, as you've been doing, to put it all together.

Part VI

Advanced Site Development

Chapter 21

Extensions and the Extension Manager

By now you're probably getting fairly good

at using Dreamweaver to create the Web

pages you've always wanted. However,

one element might be lacking: the use of

extensions. Extensions simply add to the functionality of Dreamweaver. Many types of extensions exist, including behaviors, commands, objects, and inspectors.

We will focus primarily on using behaviors in your pages. Among other things, behaviors allow your Web pages to "do" something. Using image rollovers, instituting layer movement, and even dynamically setting the text of a layer or frame can all be accomplished by using behaviors. We will also cover how to install, manage, and remove Extensions by using the Extension Manager. The following is a list of some of the main things we'll talk about:

- What extensions are and how they will enhance your Dreamweaver experience
- How to utilize behaviors
- The most common actions and events
- How to use the Extension Manager to download, install, and manage extensions

What Are Extensions?

Dreamweaver in itself is undoubtedly one of the most powerful and easy-to-use code-editing tools available today. However, we also live in a world in which software and computer hardware advance at an astounding rate. Having realized this, Macromedia designed Dreamweaver to be not only extremely customizable, but also extensible. You're probably familiar with the term *customizable*, but you may not know what *extensible* implies. It is simply meant to show the capability that Dreamweaver has to be "added upon" to extend its default (original) capabilities. One of the ways to extend the built-in capabilities of Dreamweaver is to install and use (what are appropriately called) extensions. Types of extensions include these:

- **Behaviors**. These extensions help add life to your page by enabling the user to interact with or make your page "do" something. Behaviors consist of an event that is triggered by an action. Allowable actions vary from browser to browser. Behaviors are discussed fully in the remainder of this chapter. Creating your own behaviors is also covered in the following chapter.
- **Commands**. Commands can be partially thought of as macros. They are often a method for automating tasks that you may perform often. Commands also provide an easy way of applying an element or formatting scheme across an entire site. Although the process of using a command across the entire site is painless enough, actually creating the command is very difficult.
- **Objects**. These are probably one of the most basic extensions; they are easy to use and to develop. Typically, clicking an object icon inserts that particular object at the current cursor position. With some objects, such as the flash object,

additional input is required. Making your own objects is discussed in the next chapter.

- **Inspectors**. You have heard certain elements in Dreamweaver referred to as inspectors. The Property Inspector and the Code Inspector are apparent examples—they enable you to graphically and easily modify or establish settings or attributes of elements in your page. It is not uncommon for extension developers to design custom inspectors that work together.

How Are Extensions Organized?

It is important to know how extensions in general are organized in relation to their directory structure. Macromedia's Extension Manager effectively automates extension installation, removal, and their "on/off" status, but sometimes you might need or want to get your hands dirty and manually edit your Configuration folder.

As shown in Figure 21.1, all extensions are stored and referenced from the Configuration subfolder of your Dreamweaver 4 installation directory. A typical path on a Windows-based machine might be C:\Program Files\Macromedia\Dreamweaver 4\Configuration\.

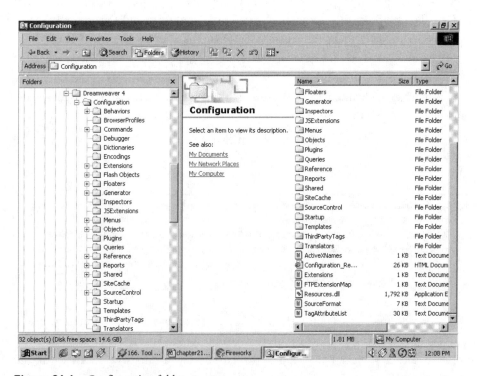

Figure 21.1   Configuration folder structure.

In this directory, you will notice probably 20 or more subdirectories. The ones we will concern ourselves with are the Behaviors and Objects directories. The other directories typically follow a similar organizational scheme and don't need to be discussed in detail.

Note

> Before getting too far into the folder structure, it is *extremely* important to warn you of the possible outcomes of changing your folder contents and moving them around. You could inadvertently ruin your entire configuration when doing this. You should *always* create and maintain a backup of the Configuration folder either on another location on your hard drive or on a floppy disk or other removable media. This will enable you to quickly and painlessly restore your original settings if you accidentally goof up.

Behaviors Folder

The Behaviors folder contains two subfolders: Actions and Events. You typically will not need to edit or otherwise modify files in the Events folder. This folder simply contains the possible events for certain event selections that you might want to limit or expand. It also contains the default event used when applying the events to various HTML elements.

The other folder, Actions, contains an HTML and JavaScript file for each behavior. The HTML file establishes the user interface used to set and edit that behavior's properties. The JavaScript file contains the actual "code" that makes the behavior do what it's supposed to do. Unless you know what you're doing, you probably shouldn't change the contents of the JavaScript file. However, you can modify the contents of the HTML file to create a new user interface (UI). Although this is possible, it would be considered unethical to remove the developers' credit, so it should be discouraged. Likewise, you run a higher risk of botching the code so that it gives either unpredictable or incorrect results.

Note

> Most extension developers spend vast amounts of time perfecting the user interface as well as the code for their extensions. If your intended interface modification is something that everyone would enjoy rather than something that should simply be changed to accommodate your desires, you should consider proposing the changes to the developers themselves. This will allow countless others to enjoy the added effectiveness that your design changes might contribute.

There may be (and, by default, are) subfolders in the Actions directory. Common examples are the Set Text and Timeline directories. Putting similar extensions in these directories creates a submenu that appears when clicking to attach a behavior to your document, as illustrated in Figure 21.2.

Objects Folder

The Objects folder contains many subfolders, including Characters, Common, Forms, Frames, Head, Invisibles, Special, and Tools. Your folder may have more subfolders or fewer subfolders, depending on your configuration. Each subfolder describes the kind of objects contained within it. For example, the default objects in the Common subfolder are E-Mail Link, Fireworks HTML, Flash Button, Flash Text, Flash, Generator, HR, Image, Layer, Navigation Bar, Rollover, Shockwave, SSI, Table, and Tabular Data. All these objects are typically used very often and thus reside in the Common folder. Likewise, objects in the Invisibles folder (such as Anchor, Comment, and Script) are all elements that are invisible to the end user.

The Objects panel is built around these subfolders. As seen in Figure 21.2, the different categories available in this panel are referenced from the directory structure of the \Configuration\Objects folder.

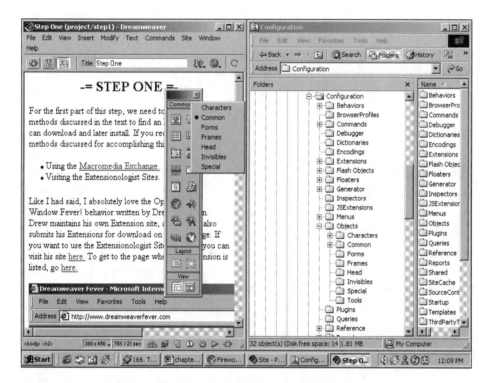

Figure 21.2   The Objects panel parallels the Objects subfolder.

Looking at the contents of these subfolders, you will notice that most objects contain an HTML file as well as a GIF icon file. Some complex objects require user interaction to set their properties and additionally use a JavaScript file as well. In an object, the GIF is simply used as the icon that you click in the Objects panel to activate the specific object. In a basic object, the HTML file contains only the HTML code needed to add the character or other element to your document. More complex objects resemble behaviors in that the HTML file establishes a user interface and uses the JavaScript file to dynamically create the HTML needed to insert the desired object. You will learn how to make your own objects in the next chapter.

Using Behaviors

Behaviors are one of the most important types of extensions. You will find yourself using them constantly in your daily work. Whether you created them yourself or installed them from the Macromedia Exchange, they behave in exactly the same way. Behaviors are composed of two elements: the action and the event.

The action part of the behavior is what the behavior actually "does." If you attach the Go to URL behavior to your page, a description for the action might be that it causes a browser window to load a URL. The events are what must be done to trigger the behavior action. Common events are onClick, onMouseDown, and onMouseOut. Most events are fairly self-explanatory. Common events and actions are shown and described later in this section. Now that you have a handle on what behaviors accomplish, let's look at how to use them in your pages.

The Behaviors Panel

The Behaviors panel, shown in Figure 21.3, is the primary method (and really the only method besides raw HTML editing) for inserting and managing behaviors in your documents. To access this panel, select Window/Behaviors from your menu, or press Shift+F3. Using this panel, you can add, delete, modify, and specify a specific order to your behaviors. Working with behaviors might be a bit confusing at first, but with a few rules, you'll find them easy to use in no time.

Note

It is possible to hide all your active panels. Do this by pressing F4. This button toggles the visibility of all your panels and is extremely useful, especially if you're using a single, small monitor.

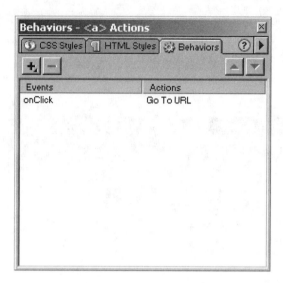

Figure 21.3   The Behaviors panel.

Adding a Behavior

To attach a behavior to your HTML document, make sure that the Behaviors panel is activated and then press the + button. This opens a list of all the behaviors currently installed. You might notice that certain behaviors are dim, while others are in black text, as shown in Figure 21.4. You can apply only behaviors that are in black text.

This is because the Behaviors panel is context-sensitive, and not every behavior can be applied to every HTML tag or element. The attachable behaviors vary from tag to tag and, as such, so does the drop-down menu that you get when clicking the + button. Knowing this, we can define our first rule of using behaviors: The Behaviors panel displays attachable behaviors in black text, according to the current HTML tag selection in your document.

After you have selected the behavior that you want to add from this menu, a dialog box will appear specific to that behavior. In fact, each behavior uses a custom-built user interface. Add to that the existence of hundreds of extensions available from third-party sources, and it's impossible to describe in detail all the possible ways to input information for every behavior. At the end of this section, some common behaviors and their settings are shown.

A lot of behaviors can be applied only to the <A> tag (the tag that, among other things, links pages). Occasionally (and, many times, quite frequently) you will want to attach a behavior that requires a link to a selection of text or image. Unless the selection is already a link, you will need to create what is called a fake (or null) link. This is a link that doesn't go anywhere yet that allows you to attach behaviors that require a link. You can do this by entering **javascript:** in the link field of the Property Inspector. This causes the text or image to become a link, but when you click on it, nothing actually "happens."

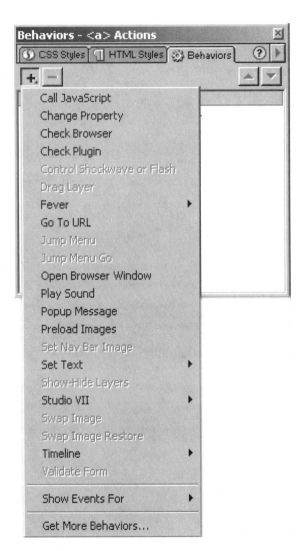

Figure 21.4   Only bolded behaviors can be applied.

After you have set and established the properties for the behavior, click OK on that behavior's configuration dialog box. You will notice that the behavior is now listed in the Behaviors panel, as seen in Figure 21.5. If you select another HTML element, the list will probably clear (unless the element that you select has a behavior attached to it). This leads us to our second rule: The Behaviors panel lists only the behaviors associated with the currently selected HTML element or tag.

The Behaviors panel functions similarly to how the Property Inspector works. They are both context-sensitive and will dynamically update the options that they allow you to choose or edit, depending on the current selection on your page.

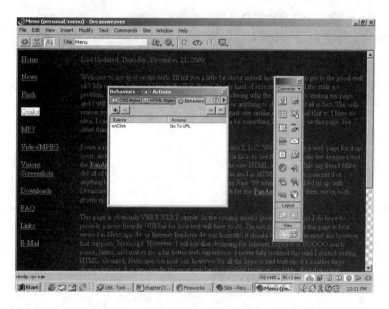

Figure 21.5   Behaviors listed are attached to the selected tag.

The final step in adding a behavior to your page is selecting an event to trigger the behavior. An event is always selected by default, but it might not be the appropriate event for this particular instance. To select a new triggering event, follow these steps:

1. Select the behavior for which you want to set the event in the Behaviors panel.

2. Click the down arrow located on the right side of the Events column. This brings up a menu listing possible events.

3. Select the event that you want to trigger the behavior.

Certain events are compatible only with certain browsers and browser versions. This limits the choices for events. Luckily, Dreamweaver enables you to limit the events listed automatically so that you don't accidentally choose an event that is incompatible with your target browsers. You can set the configuration to show events for by either clicking the + button on the Behaviors panel or clicking the down arrow located on the right side of the events column (while a behavior is selected). Next, select Show Events For from the list. This brings up the submenu shown in Figure 21.6, which enables you to view and change the criteria for listing behavior events. This brings us to our third rule: Events are listed only if they are compatible with the currently selected browser event list. Be sure to select events that cover your audience adequately.

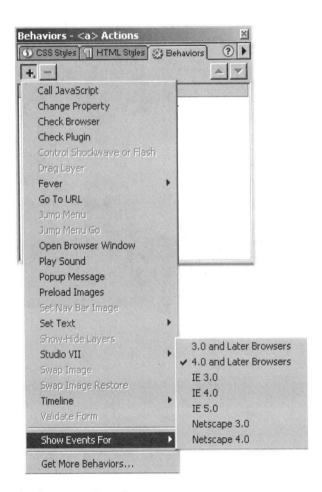

Figure 21.6   The Show Events For submenu.

This feature is useful when designing both intranet sites, in which you typically assume that everyone will be using the same browser (Internet Explorer 5.5, for instance) and sites to be viewed over the Internet, in which you must use the lowest common denominator for your page creation (any 3.0 or higher browser). Keep in mind, however, that choosing 3.0 or higher will significantly limit the available number of events on the list; it's a give-and-take relationship.

A persistent question that will probably exist, at least in the foreseeable future, is, "What is the lowest browser you should develop for use over the Internet?" Similar questions arise regarding screen resolution and color depth. Currently, popular opinion is 3.0 and higher browsers, 256 colors, and 800×600 resolution. I have personally started developing for 4.0 and higher browsers (unless specifically required not to), in an effort to push technology further and faster. The 3.0 or 4.0 design question is almost split down the middle at the moment, and you should be safe developing specifically for 4.0 and higher browsers. TheCounter.com posts global statistics for browsers used from various Web sites. As shown in Figure 21.7, in October 2000, only 6% of traffic recorded (more than 554 million visitors) were browsers other than Internet Explorer 4.0+ or Netscape 4.0+. Although still a large number in itself, the advantages that 4.0 browsers provide strongly outweigh any advantages gained by sticking with 3.0 and higher browsers.

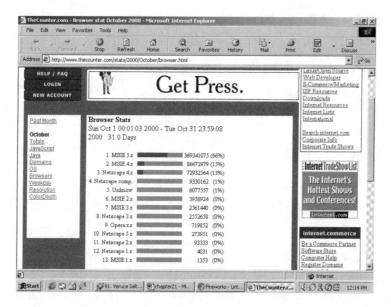

Figure 21.7   Global browser statistics for October 2000.

Tip

Although the suggestions for site development are accurate, for the most part, you still need to evaluate your site demographics. For instance, when designing for an international audience, it is generally good to expect a fair amount of 3.0 browsers and a lower-bandwidth connection. Factors such as these, which you might otherwise forget to consider, should play a large role when determining what HTML elements you use in your pages.

Ordering Behavior Sequence

After adding the behavior to your page, Dreamweaver automatically sorts the list of attached behaviors alphabetically by the Events and then Actions columns. You can further organize your behaviors if you want a certain action to take place before another. This is not a typical scenario because most actions aren't dependent on each other.

To reorder a behavior, follow these steps:

1. Select the behavior that you want to move from the Behaviors panel.

2. Move the behavior either up or down by using the up and down arrow buttons located on the upper-right part of the panel.

3. The order in which behaviors appear in the Behaviors panel is the same order in which they appear in the raw HTML code.

Notice that behaviors must be grouped with like actions in the Behaviors panel. This occurs for a few reasons, the most important and perhaps logical being that only one event may occur at any given time. Even the onClick and onDblClick events occur separately. It would be senseless to organize and mix actions of different events.

Deleting Behaviors

As is true with most things in life, destruction occurs faster than construction. The same holds true for removing behaviors from your pages. You can easily do this with the Behaviors panel.

To remove a behavior from your page, follow these steps:

1. Select the behavior that you want to remove from the Behaviors panel.

2. Click the – button or press the Delete key.

Common Events

As discussed previously, events are what take place to trigger an action. You could also describe them as the *activator*. Various browsers support different events. Luckily, Dreamweaver enables you to customize the list that it displays as possible events according to your target browser(s). The following list covers the common actions in Dreamweaver and states which browsers support them. (Legend: IE3, 4, and 5 = Internet Explorer versions 3.0, 4.0, and 5.0; NN 3 and 4 = Netscape Navigator versions 3.0 and 4.0.)

- **onAbort (NN3, NN4, IE4, IE5)**. Occurs when the user stops the loading of an image object by either clicking a link or pressing the Stop button in the browser.

- **onBlur (NN3, NN4, IE3, IE4, IE5)**. Occurs when the focus is moved from the target window, frame, or form element objects.

- **onChange (NN3, NN4, IE3, IE4, IE5)**. Occurs when the user changes a text field, textarea, or select list element.

- **onClick (NN3, NN4, IE3, IE4, IE5)**. Occurs when the user clicks the form element or link.

- **onDblclick (NN4, IE4, IE5)**. Occurs when the user double-clicks a document, area, or link object.

- **onError (NN3, NN4, IE4, IE5)**. Occurs when the loading of a document or images causes an error.

- **onFocus (NN3, NN4, IE3, IE4, IE5)**. Occurs when the focus is moved to the target window, frame, or form element objects.

- **onHelp (IE4, IE5)**. Occurs when the user clicks the browser Help button or selects Help from the browser menu.

- **onKeyDown (NN4, IE4, IE5)**. Occurs when the user depresses a key on a document, link, or a Textarea object.

- **onKeyPress (NN4, IE4, IE5)**. Occurs when the user presses or holds a key.

- **onKeyUp (NN4, IE4, IE5)**. Occurs when the user releases a key on a document, image, link, or Textarea object.

- **onLoad (NN3, NN4, NN3, IE4, IE5)**. Occurs when the document is completely finished loading in the browser window.

- **onMouseDown (NN4, IE4, IE5)**. Occurs when the user depresses a mouse button on a button, document, or link object.

- **onMouseMove (IE3, IE4, IE5)**. Occurs when the user moves the cursor.

- **onMouseOut (NN3, NN4, IE4, IE5)**. Occurs when the user moves the cursor outside a specific area such as an image or text link.

- **onMouseOver (NN3, NN4, IE3, IE4, IE5)**. Occurs when the user moves the cursor inside a specific area such as an image or text link.

- **onMouseUp (NN4, IE4, IE5)**. Occurs when the user releases a mouse button on a button, document, or link object.

- **onMove (NN4)**. Occurs when the user or a script moves the window or a frame.

- **onreadyStateChange (IE4, IE5)**. Occurs when the ReadyState property changes. This enables you to monitor the state of data retrieval without calling the ReadyState value.

- **onReset (NN3, NN4, IE3, IE4, IE5)**. Occurs when the user resets the form.
- **onResize (NN4, IE4, IE5)**. Occurs when the user or a script resizes the window or a frame.
- **onScroll (IE4, IE5)**. Occurs when a user scrolls either up or down on a page.
- **onSelect (NN3, NN4, IE3, IE4, IE5)**. Occurs when the user selects from a form element's input field.
- **onSubmit (NN3, NN4, IE3, IE4, IE5)**. Occurs when the user submits a form.
- **onUnload (NN3, NN4, IE3, IE4, IE5)**. Occurs when the user exits or reloads a page.

Common Actions

Now that you're at least aware of the possible events that you can use to trigger actions, we'll briefly describe each of the behaviors that come included with Dreamweaver 4:

- **Call JavaScript**. Enables you to execute a specific line or function of JavaScript when the given event occurs.
- **Change Property**. Enables you to change the properties of certain elements on your page, such as layers and forms.
- **Check Browser**. Redirects users with various browsers and browser versions to specific URLs that you specify. Quite frequently, you will add this to the body tag of a very simple page that will work on most any browser with an onLoad event.
- **Check Plug-in**. Enables you to redirect users based on plug-in information. For example, you could direct users with Flash installed to the Flash version of your site and direct those who don't have Flash installed to the HTML version.
- **Control Shockwave or Flash**. Enables you to control Shockwave and Flash elements through regular HTML links.
- **Drag Layer**. Enables you to make your layers draggable. This would be useful when creating an online puzzle. You can specify many attributes, such as whether the layer snaps to a target or whether the layer can be moved only vertically or horizontally.
- **Go to URL**. Enables you to load a URL into the current window or a frame on your page.
- **Jump Menu**. Typically does not require to add this behavior on your own. When you add a jump menu from the forms submenu, Dreamweaver automatically attaches this behavior.

- **Jump Menu Go**. Because a jump menu automatically loads the selected item list, a go button is typically unneeded.

- **Open Browser Window**. Enables you to open a URL in a new browser window with properties such as width, height, and other browser interface elements.

- **Play Sound**. Enables you to play a sound on the target event. You can use this to make a sound play whenever you click a link or roll over an image.

- **Pop-up Message**. Displays a JavaScript alert. The alert contains only an OK button, so it's best used to display information or a state rather than for making choices. You can also use JavaScript functions, properties, or other expressions by enclosing them in braces ({}).

- **Preload Images**. Downloads and caches images used on your page but not downloaded by default. A common example of this is when using rollover images. Preloading them prevents the browser from having to establish a connection and download each rollover image when the user moves the mouse over the image.

- **Set Nav Bar Image**. Turns an image into a Navigation Bar and works in conjunction with the Navigation Bar feature. You can insert a Navigation Bar by selecting Insert/Interactive Images/Navigation Bar from the menu.

- **Set Text of Frame, Layer, Status Bar, or Text Field**. Enables you to dynamically set the text for the respective elements.

- **Show-Hide Layers**. Enables you to show, hide, and restore the original visibility of layers.

- **Swap Image**. Enables you to swap a target image with a second image.

- **Swap Image Restore**. Restores the original image changed with the swap image behavior. This behavior is automatically added when you apply a swap image action.

- **Timeline actions**. Enables you to play and stop a timeline, as well as go to a specific timeline frame.

- **Validate Form**. Enables you to confirm that valid data is entered into your form fields before submitting a form. You can check field by field by attaching it to the onBlur event of a particular form element, or you can check the entire form when the user clicks the Submit button by using the onSubmit event.

Using the Extension Manager

The Extension Manager, shown in Figure 21.8, was introduced during the life of Dreamweaver 3. Coupled with the Macromedia Exchange Web site, it has quickly become the standard for installing and managing extensions. The Extension Manager ships with Dreamweaver 4 and currently supports Extensions for Dreamweaver, Dreamweaver UltraDev, and Flash. In the future, additional products will undoubtedly take advantage of this innovative companion program.

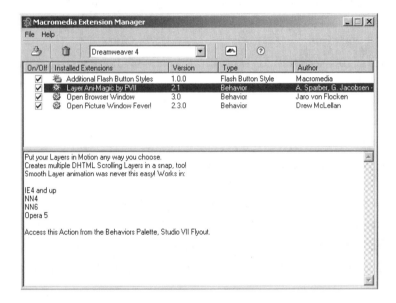

Figure 21.8   The Extension Manager.

Downloading and Installing Extensions

Before the Extension Manager was released, most extensions were packaged as compressed .zip files and were available only on the author's individual Web site. You manually extracted the necessary files into the appropriate directories. Removing an extension or turning it off consisted of deleting or moving the extension files out of the directory.

After the Extension Manager was released and Exchange was active, authors slowly picked up on the new .mxp format for their extensions. Although Exchange has taken the extensions world by storm in the past year, some people still offer extensions for download on their personal Web sites. We will discuss both using Exchange and using a personal site for downloading the extensions you need.

Macromedia Exchange

Macromedia Exchange is by far the most popular method for finding extensions today. You can visit Exchange by pointing your Web browser to `www.macromedia.com/exchange/`. You can also get to Exchange by selecting File/Go To Macromedia Exchange from the Extension Manager's menu. On the home page for the Dreamweaver section of the Exchange, you can find out more about extensions, see featured extensions, or search for a particular extension. Exchange also boasts hundreds of valuable extensions for download in several categories. These categories include accessibility, app servers, browsers, DHTML/layers, fireworks, Flash media, learning, navigation, productivity, rich media, scripting, security, style/format, tables, text, and e-commerce.

Two ways exist by which to effectively search for extensions. The first method is more effective if you know the name of the extension you're looking for or have a pretty good idea what it might be called. If this is the case, you can enter the text string to search for in the text box on the right side of the screen (as shown in Figure 21.9) and then click Go. This searches for extensions in all categories that might fit your search string.

Figure 21.9   Searching for the Open Picture Window Fever! behavior.

Note

You can also click the Advanced Search text link to further refine elements of your search, such as the type of extension, the category you want to search in, or even the rating (scale of 1 to 5) that the extensions have received.

The second method is to browse particular categories one at a time. You can do this by selecting a category from the drop-down list on the Dreamweaver Exchange home page. You will automatically be taken to that categories list of Extensions, such as the one shown in Figure 21.10. From this page, you can download various extensions specifically relating to that area of Web development. Every extension also has its own discussion forum on Exchange, which is found by going to the download page for that extension. This offers a useful facet for getting (or giving) advice on that specific extension.

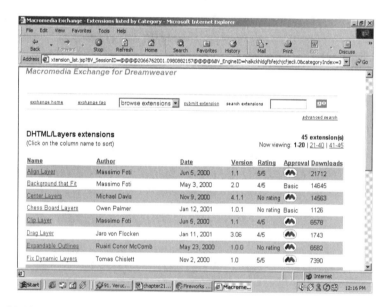

Figure 21.10   The DHTML/Layers category.

Tip

With either method, you can easily sort the table data by clicking the desired column title.

Extensionologist Web Sites

Where the word *extensionologists* originated, I'm not sure. What I do know is that everyone who knows one of these elite few respects and admires their contributions to the

Dreamweaver community. These are the men and women who create the extensions that you use in your everyday life. Helping maintain the feeling of a genuine Dreamweaver *community,* they typically make their offerings available at no charge to the public. Before Exchange was created, you could obtain their extensions only on personal sites. It was not uncommon to have a list of 20 or more sites bookmarked so that you could gather various extensions.

A shortened list of sites still in existence today is provided in Appendix A, "Keyboard Shortcuts." Because of the diverse nature of these sites, I can only offer assurances of their value when searching for extensions. If you can't find what you're looking for on Exchange, these types of sites are an invaluable resource readily available to you.

Installing Extensions

Regardless of where you go for your extensions, you will need to get them installed. Installing them is fairly quick and straightforward. To install a downloaded extension, follow these steps:

1. Make sure the Extension Manager is installed, that you have closed Dreamweaver, and that you have downloaded the extension that you want to install. Now double-click the .mxp file that you want to install.

2. This should bring up the Macromedia Extensions Disclaimer. Read it and click Accept if you want to continue.

3. You will now be notified that the extension has successfully been installed. You will notice it listed with the other extensions.

4. If Dreamweaver is running, restart it so that your recent modifications will take effect

Exercise 21.1   Downloading and Installing a Behavior

After you discover Exchange, you will probably find yourself spending a few afternoons just browsing all the various extensions that are available for download. Eventually, you will want to download a few extensions to test yourself, so that's what this exercise focuses on. You will download and install the JustSo Picture Window Extension by E. Michael Brandt.

1. Open your favorite Web browser and point it to www.macromedia.com/ exchange/dreamweaver/. At this point, you might need to sign into Exchange. If you don't already have a username and password, you can begin the registration process from this page as well.

2. The extension that you're looking for is located in the Productivity section of Exchange. Select Productivity from the Browse Extensions pull-down menu, as shown in Figure 21.11.

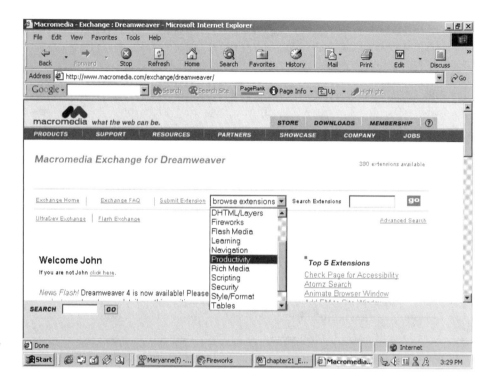

Figure 21.11   Selecting the Productivity category of extensions.

3. At the time of this writing, the JustSo Picture Window Extension was located on the third result set under the Productivity category (Extensions 41–60; shown in Figure 21.12). When you find it, click the extension name. If you can't find it, enter **picture** in the Search Extensions text field and press Go. This alternative method will return only a few extensions, including the JustSo Picture Window Extension.

4. At this point, you are presented with the extension's Web page. To download the .mxp file that the Extension Manager requires to install the Extension, click the appropriate download icon, depending on your operating system (Windows or Macintosh). For ease, save the .mxp file on your desktop.

5. To install the extension, make sure that Dreamweaver is closed. Then double-click (or otherwise run/open) the .mxp file. It will automatically launch the Extension Manager and present you with a Macromedia Extensions Disclaimer (shown in Figure 21.13) to which you must agree to install the extension.

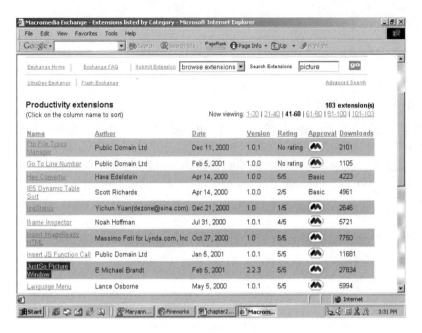

Figure 21.12   If you can't find the highlighted extension, enter the search pattern shown here, and you should get a hit.

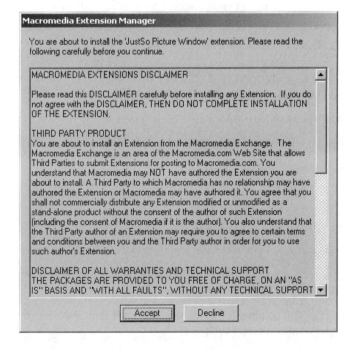

Figure 21.13   Read this disclaimer!

6. Dreamweaver will then notify you if the extension was installed correctly. If it was, you can now quit the Extension Manager, restart Dreamweaver, and start using the extension.

Managing Extensions

After you have installed all the extensions you could ever imagine using, you have the daunting task of maintaining your extensions. Actually, it's not that daunting—in fact, you might never have to do a thing! The quickest way to manage your extensions is by selecting Commands/Manage Extensions from the menu. This opens the Extension Manager.

Sorting Extensions

Sorting your extensions can be useful if you have a long list of them installed on your system. If you want to check for newer versions of extensions, view all extensions by a certain author, or even by the type of extension.

To sort your list of extensions, open the Extension Manager and select Dreamweaver 4 from the application pull-down menu. This lists all the installed extensions in Dreamweaver. Now just click the column title of the category that you want to sort by. Your extensions are now sorted in descending order relative to that category. Clicking the column again reverses the sort order (ascending). Figure 21.14 shows the columns that you can sort by. These categories are listed here as well:

- **On/Off**. Displays whether an extension is currently active.
- **Installed Extensions**. Displays the name of the extension.
- **Version**. Displays the version number of the extension.
- **Type**. Displays the type of extension (Object, Behaviors, Command, and so on).
- **Author**. Displays the author's name.

Turning Extensions On and Off

Occasionally it is helpful to temporarily disable certain extensions. For example, you might want to do this when you have a large number of extensions installed and want to improve Dreamweaver 4's performance. Disabled extensions are repackaged and stored in a subfolder of the Configuration folder.

A check in the On/Off column indicates that the extension is currently enabled. No check indicates that the extension is disabled. You can toggle this check mark by either clicking in the check box or selecting the extension and pressing the Spacebar.

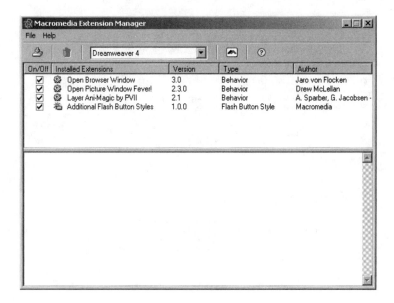

Figure 21.14   Sorting columns by the type of extension.

Submitting Extensions

If you have the desire and knowledge, you can create your own extensions. Whether you share them with the rest of the world is up to you. However, Macromedia has made it extremely easy for you to do so. To begin the process, you must have created an extension and packaged it according to Macromedia's documentation. (The next chapter also discusses creating your own extensions and is an excellent resource during the process.) After you have created, tested, and packaged your extension as an .mxp file, select File/Submit Extension from the Extension Manager menu. This takes you to Exchange. You will need to enter your password again to continue. Note that you will have to re-enter your password even if you normally have it saved for you. Figure 21.15 shows some of the remaining process and is described to you on the site as you go.

I can't emphasize enough how important and crucial extensive testing is to your extension's acceptance. Test your extensions on as many browsers and platforms as possible. After you are confident of your extension's stability, it might be a good idea to post it on Macromedia's news servers under the Dreamweaver section, asking for people to help discover any bugs in your code so that you can submit it for display on the exchange.

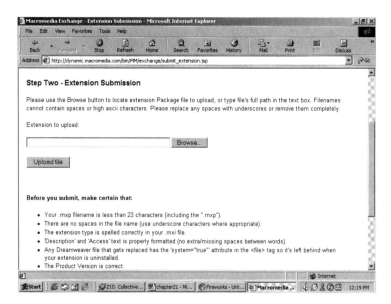

Figure 21.15   Submitting an extension.

Importing Extensions

The Extension Manager also enables you to import extensions from other installations of Dreamweaver. You can also install similar extensions from other Macromedia programs such as Dreamweaver UltraDev or font extensions from any program.

To import extensions into your current Dreamweaver installation, follow these steps:

1. Make sure that Dreamweaver is the selected product in the product pull-down menu in the Extension Manager. Then select File/Import Extensions from the menu.

2. Now select the product to import the extensions from. If the product isn't listed in the pull-down menu, type or use the Browse button to locate the path of the software installation directory. This should be the root directory, not the configuration folder.

3. Select OK.

4. The Import Extensions window shown in Figure 21.16 now appears. Make sure that all the extensions you want to import are selected, and then press the Import button.

5. If you want to change the product you import from, simply click the Product button.

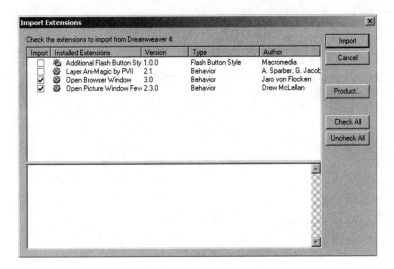

Figure 21.16   Importing extensions.

Uninstalling Extensions

Under certain circumstances, you might need or want to remove an extension from your system. The Extension Manager offers a graceful way to completely remove extensions that it has installed.

To permanently remove an extension from Dreamweaver, follow these steps:

1. Make sure that Dreamweaver 4 is selected in the product pull-down menu in the Extension Manager.

2. Select the extension that you want to remove from the list of extensions.

3. Select File/Remove Extension from the menu. You can also press Ctrl+R, press Delete on your keyboard, or click the Remove Extension icon on the toolbar.

4. Confirm that you want to remove the extension.

Summary

The primary focus of this chapter has been the effective utilization of extensions—specifically, behaviors—in your Web pages. We have discussed the various behaviors that come shipped with Dreamweaver, as well as where to download new ones. We also talked about the Extension Manager. Topics ranging from installing, managing, and removing Extensions were covered. Finally, you also learned what the most common events and behaviors do.

Chapter 22

Creating Your Own Objects and Behaviors

In the previous chapter, you learned how to

take advantage of Dreamweaver extensions

written by other people. Now it's time to

learn to write your own! In this chapter,

you'll get some hands-on experience creating custom objects and behaviors, and you'll learn how to package them up and share them with the rest of the Dreamweaver community. In particular, you'll learn to do the following:

- Create a simple object that inserts the same code into the page every time
- Create a custom object that uses a dialog box to collect user input and insert customized code into the page
- Create an editable, reusable custom behavior
- Troubleshoot and bulletproof objects and behaviors for distribution to others
- Package a behavior or object into an installation file that can be used with Extension Manager
- Submit a packaged extension to the Macromedia Exchange

Before Getting Started

Although writing Dreamweaver extensions isn't just for propeller-heads, it isn't for sissies, either. To work with object and behavior files, you need to be fairly comfortable reading and writing HTML code, and you need at least a basic understanding of JavaScript. In particular, before you tackle this chapter, you should be familiar with the following:

- The basic language structure, syntax requirements, and concepts of JavaScript (expressions, operators, variables, and so on)
- How to work with JavaScript functions
- How to use JavaScript to process data collected by HTML forms

Tip

If you're a JavaScript newbie, or if your skills are rusty, you might want to have a JavaScript reference available as you work. The handiest reference is Dreamweaver's own online JavaScript Reference panel. If you want more in-depth information, the O'Reilly series books on JavaScript (*JavaScript: The Definitive Guide*, *JavaScript Pocket Reference*) are a valuable resource. Danny Goodman's *JavaScript Bible* is also a wonderful reference and teaching resource.

In addition to the standard rules and regulations of JavaScript, Dreamweaver has its own application program interface (API), consisting of predefined objects, functions, and procedures for processing scripts. In the course of this chapter, you'll get a taste of the Dreamweaver API, and you'll be introduced to the parts of the API that you'll need to write basic objects and behaviors. If you want to go beyond this chapter and seriously explore Dreamweaver extensions, the best resource is Macromedia's own manual, *Extending Dreamweaver*. This manual comes in PDF format on the Dreamweaver application CD; it can also be downloaded from the Dreamweaver support page on the Macromedia Web site (www.macromedia.com/support/dreamweaver). I highly recommend printing it out, popping it in a three-ring binder and keeping it next to your pillow—er, your computer—as you work.

So, are you ready to start extending?

Working with Objects

In the last chapter, you learned that objects are created from files stored in Dreamweaver's Configuration/Objects folder. In this section, you'll learn what a well-formed object file looks like, how Dreamweaver processes object files, and how to build your own objects from scratch.

What Are Objects?

An object, in terms of Dreamweaver's API, is an HTML file that contains, or uses JavaScript to construct a string of HTML code to insert into the user's document. That string of code can be anything from this:

```
copyright John Smith, 2000
```

to this:

```
<font face= "Georgia, Times, Times New Roman, serif" size="2">copyright
John Smith, 2000</font>
```

to this:

```
<table width="200" height="200" border="1">
        <tr>
                <td align="center" ><font face= "Georgia, Times, Times New
Roman, serif" size="2">copyright John Smith, 2000</font></td>
        </tr>
        </table>
```

In other words, it's anything that can validly sit in an HTML document. The code gets inserted wherever the user's cursor is when the object is chosen.

What Files, Where

If you look inside the Configuration/Objects folder, you'll see several subfolders, the names of which you should recognize as the categories of objects accessible in the

Objects panel. Open up one of those folders (Common, for instance), and you'll see dozens of files, corresponding to the individual objects in the Common Objects panel. Each object consists of from one to three files, all with the same name but different extensions. These files are listed here:

- **An HTML file** (Table.html, for instance). This is the object file itself, the file that contains or returns the code to be inserted. This is the only file that *must* be present to constitute an object.

- **A JavaScript file** (Table.js, for instance). This file contains JavaScript instructions for constructing the code to be inserted, in the form of one or more JavaScript functions, and is called on from the HTML file. This file is optional: It is entirely legal to contain the JavaScript functions in the head section of the object's HTML file instead of saving it to an external file. As experienced scripters know, it can be easier to keep track of and update JavaScripts if the code is in a separate file, but it isn't necessary.

- **An image file** (Table.gif, for instance). This file contains a 16×16 pixel image that Dreamweaver uses to represent the object in the Objects panel. This file is also optional: If there is no image file, Dreamweaver will supply a generic image icon to represent the object in the panel.

Figure 22.1 shows some typical sets of object files.

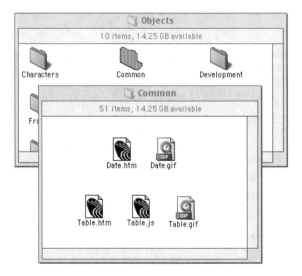

Figure 22.1   The Objects/Common folder, containing the files for the Insert Date object (two files only) and the Insert Table object (three files).

Object files must be stored in one of the folders inside the Configuration/Objects folder. The folder in which they're stored determines what portion of the Objects panel they'll appear in.

Structure of a Simple Object File: No Dialog Box

Some objects use dialog boxes to collect user information, and some don't. Those that don't are (not surprisingly) easier to create. Figure 22.2 shows a simple object file that doesn't call a dialog box.

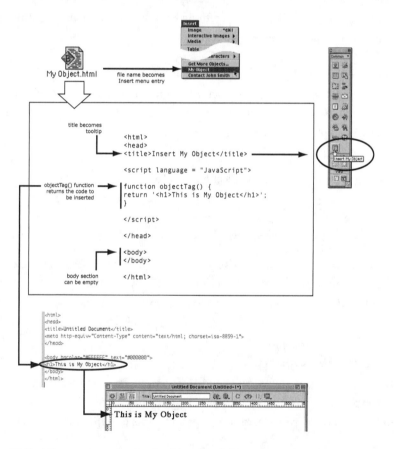

Figure 22.2   The structure of a simple object file, and how it translates into a Dreamweaver object.

The key elements of the file are as follows:

- **Filename.** This becomes the Insert menu entry for the object.

- **Page title**. This becomes the ToolTip that pops up to identify the object in the Objects panel.

- **objectTag() function**. This JavaScript function is the most important element of the object file. The function returns the exact code that you want the object to insert into your document, enclosed in quotes. The objectTag() function is part of the Dreamweaver API, so it doesn't need to be defined. It also doesn't need to be called; Dreamweaver calls it automatically when the object is chosen.

In the example shown in Figure 22.2, the code returned by the objectTag() function is a simple level 1 heading. Notice how everything between the quote marks, in the return statement, becomes part of the user's document.

Structure of a Fancier Object File with a Dialog Box

More sophisticated objects do more than insert pre-established code; they collect user information and use that information to customize the inserted code. Figure 22.3 shows the structure of an object file that creates a dialog box to collect user input and then constructs the code to insert based on that input.

The added element in this kind of object file is HTML Form, which becomes the dialog box for collecting user input and customizing the code. Note that the form as written doesn't include a Submit button. Dreamweaver supplies the OK and Cancel buttons automatically. The form needs to have only the fields for collecting data.

In the example shown in Figure 22.3, the code returned by the objectTag() function is a level 1 heading, but with the content to be determined by the user. Notice how a variable is used in the objectTag() function to collect the form input and pass it along to the return statement.

Making Your Own Objects

Did the previous information seem awfully theoretical? In this section, you'll get some hands-on experience making your own objects. You'll move from simple objects to complex, and along the way you'll learn some tips and tricks for efficient object-handling.

Before Getting Started...

Writing your own objects involves hand coding, for which you'll need a text editor. If you're an experienced scripter, you probably already have a favorite text editor (NotePad, SimpleText, BBEdit, HomeSite, and so on); you can use any text editor to code your Dreamweaver objects. You are also free to use Dreamweaver itself to code your objects;

both Layout view and Code view come in handy. Although it might seem like a dangerous way to proceed, Dreamweaver has no problem editing its own extensions. This is because Dreamweaver accesses only the extension files when it's loading extensions, which happens only when the program launches or when you force it to reload extensions.

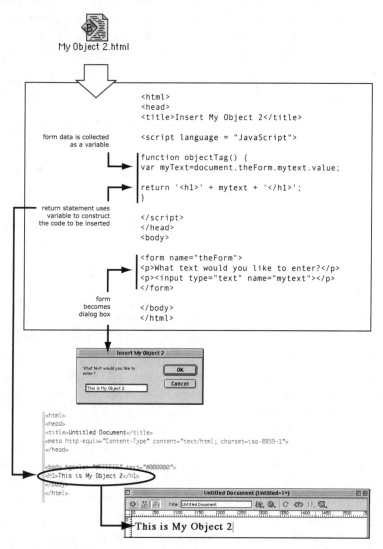

Figure 22.3   The structure of a full-featured object file, and how it translates into a Dreamweaver object.

When you're coding and testing extensions, it's easy for file management to get out of hand. A good strategy is to create a special working folder, stored outside the Dreamweaver application folder. Keep the following items in this folder:

- A backup copy of the Configuration folder. Whether you're adding new extensions or changing existing files, it's courting disaster to work on your only copy of this folder. If things get hopelessly messed up, you can replace your customized Configuration folder with this clean one; it's quicker and easier than reinstalling the whole program.

- A shortcut (PC) or alias (Mac) to Dreamweaver's Configuration folder and any of its subfolders you'll be accessing frequently.

- Test files (you'll be generating several of those in this chapter's exercises).

- Files for packaging extensions.

- Any extensions that you want to keep inactive during your development work.

While you're working on the exercises in this chapter, keep your working folder open, or leave a shortcut or alias to it on your desktop; otherwise, you'll be doing a lot of navigating through your hard drive.

Exercise 22.1   Setting Up Shop

In this exercise, you'll get your working space in order and learn some of the basic extension-developing features available in Dreamweaver. You'll create a custom objects folder where you can store your exercise objects, and you'll get some practice loading and reloading extensions.

1. Make sure Dreamweaver isn't running. If Dreamweaver is open and running on your computer, quit the program. You do this to experiment with how and when Dreamweaver loads extensions.

2. Find and open the Configuration/Objects folder on your hard drive. As you saw previously, every object file must be stored in a folder within the Configuration/Objects folder; every one of those folders correlates to a set of objects in the Objects panel. You can also add new object sets to the panel by adding your own new folders to the Configuration/Objects folder.

3. Create a new folder inside the Configuration/Objects folder. Name it Custom. When you're developing new objects, it's a good strategy to put them in a special folder called Custom or Development, at least until you're sure they're running properly.

4. Launch Dreamweaver. Every time you launch Dreamweaver, the program checks the Configuration folder and loads all extensions inside.

5. Check the Objects panel for a new category called Custom. In the Objects panel, click the triangle that accesses the pop-up Objects menu. There should now be a category called Custom (see Figure 22.4). Of course, if you choose that category, it'll be empty; that's because, so far, the Custom folder that you created is still empty.

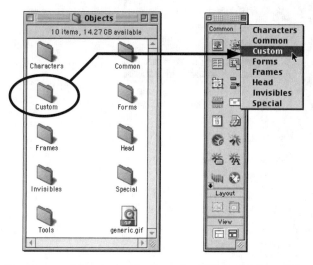

Figure 22.4   New Custom folder in the Configuration/Objects folder, and the resulting Custom category in the Objects panel.

6. Without quitting Dreamweaver, rename the Custom folder as Development. If you're on a PC, minimize Dreamweaver; if you're on a Mac, hide Dreamweaver or send it to the background. On your hard drive, go back to the Configuration/Objects folder and find your Custom folder. Rename it Development.

7. In Dreamweaver, check the Objects panel categories again. Go back to Dreamweaver. Repeat step 5, checking the Objects panel to see what categories of objects you have to choose from. Your new category should still appear as Custom, not Development. This is because Dreamweaver hasn't yet noticed the name change.

8. Force Dreamweaver to reload extensions without quitting and relaunching. Hold down the Ctrl/Opt key and click the pop-up triangle in the Objects panel. The Reload Extensions command should now appear at the bottom of the pop-up menu (see Figure 22.5). Choose that command. Although some extension-related tasks require the program to be relaunched, most updating can be done more quickly this way.

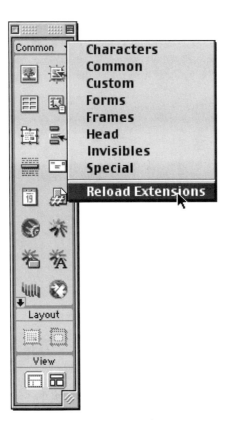

Figure 22.5   Ctrl/Opt-clicking the pop-up triangle in the Objects panel reveals the Reload Extensions command.

9. Check the Objects panel categories again. Now release the Ctrl/Opt key and click the pop-up triangle to access the object categories. Your custom category should now show up as Development.

What does this mean? Dreamweaver doesn't constantly access the object files; rather, it accesses them once as it launches. Any time you change an object file, you must make Dreamweaver notice your changes by either quitting and relaunching the program or Ctrl/Opt-clicking the Objects panel pop-up and choosing Reload Extensions.

Exercise 22.2   Making a Simple Object

The simplest objects are those that don't call up a dialog box for user input and, therefore, always return the same code. The simple object that we'll create in this exercise is a contact information line that links to an email address—just the sort of thing you might want to put at the bottom of all your Web pages.

To create this object, use the text editor of your choice. Save all exercise files in the Development folder that you created in the last exercise.

1. Decide on the exact line of code that you want the object to insert. In this case, this will be a one-line piece of text, formatted however you like, with an email address embedded in it. The result should look like Figure 22.6.

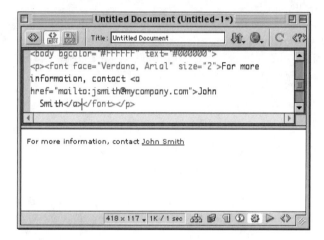

Figure 22.6   The inserted code for the Insert John Smith Contact Info object (shown in Layout and Code view).

If you don't want to type in all this code by hand, remember that you can use Dreamweaver's visual editor to create the final result; then go to the Code Inspector or Code view, and the code will be there, written for you.

2. Create the basic object file, with all structural elements in place. Open your text editor—or, if you prefer to work in Dreamweaver, open the Code Inspector—and enter the basic required code as described previously. You can leave out the details specific to this object, for now. Your code framework should look like this (elements that you'll be replacing later with custom text appear in bold):

```
<html>
<head>
<title>Title Goes Here</title>
<script language="JavaScript">
function objectTag() {
return 'inserted code goes here';
}
</script>
</head>
<body>
</body>
</html>
```

3. Enter a page title into the code. This will become the ToolTip that shows in the Objects panel.

   Most Dreamweaver ToolTips start with Insert (though this is convention only, not a requirement). A logical title for the current file, therefore, might be Insert John Smith Contact Info. The top portion of your code should now look like this:

```
<html>
<head>
<title>Insert John Smith Contact Info</title>
```

4. Insert the desired line of code as the return statement of the objectTag() function. If you have the line of code already typed into your computer, you can just copy and paste it in; otherwise, type it in manually now.

   Note that the entire return statement must be in quotes. They can be single or double quotes; just make sure that they're in balanced pairs.

   Your code should now look like this:

```
<html>
<head>
<title> Insert John Smith Contact Info </title>
<script language="JavaScript">
function objectTag() {
return '<p><font face="Verdana, Arial" size="2">For more informa-
tion,    contact    <a    href="mailto:jsmith@mycompany.com">John
Smith</a></font></p>';
}
</script>
</head>
<body>
</body>
</html>
```

5. Save your file in the Development folder. Call it Contact John Smith.html.

   Remember, object files must be in the proper folder, or they won't be recognized as objects. Make sure that you're saving the file into your Development folder. The extension can be .htm or .html—Dreamweaver accepts either.

The filename will become the menu command that appears in the Insert menu, so it's good practice to name it something descriptive. Unlike browsers and Web servers, Dreamweaver allows spaces in filenames and respects case changes. A filename such as Contact John Smith.html will work fine and will look good in the Insert menu. A filename such as jsmith_contact_info_1.html will also work, but it won't look as nice (or be as understandable) in the menu. Capitalization will also carry through to the menu entry.

6. Test your object!

   If you already have Dreamweaver running, Ctrl/Opt-click the pop-up triangle in the Objects panel to access the Reload Extensions command.

   If you don't have Dreamweaver running, launch it— the extension will be loaded automatically.

   Create a new document, if there isn't one already open.

   Check the Development category of the Objects panel. The new object should be there, represented by a generic object icon. Position the cursor over the icon, and the ToolTip should appear (see Figure 22.7).

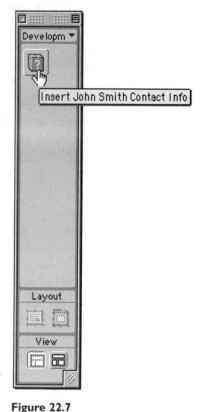

Figure 22.7
The new custom object with a generic icon and ToolTip.

Click on the object. Your desired code should be inserted into the document.

Congratulations! You've made your very first object.

Tip

Don't waste your time making custom icon files for objects while they're still in the development phase. Wait until the object is all polished and perfectly functioning; then dress it up with a custom icon. (See Exercise 22.6 for how to make an icon file.)

Note

If your object doesn't show up in the Objects panel at all, then either you saved it in the wrong place, you didn't append the HTML extension to the filename, or you need to reload Dreamweaver's extensions. Even an invalid object file will show up in the Objects panel if it has a valid name and is stored in a valid location.

If your object shows up but there's something wrong with the code, you'll probably get an error message when Dreamweaver tries to execute the objectTag() function. Dreamweaver's error messages are fairly specific in what went wrong and what needs fixing.

Exercise 22.3 Adding a Dialog Box

Your simple object is fine as far as it goes, but it's not a very flexible or useful object because it always returns the same code, no matter what. What if you want to link the contact information to someone other than good old John Smith? A fully functional object would bring up a dialog box that would ask for user input and then would enter that information into the code. That's the object you'll build next.

1. Open Contact John Smith.html and save it as Contact Info.html. Why reinvent the wheel? Let's build on our previous success by adding a dialog box and tweaking the objectTag() function's return statement to collect user input.

2. Change the page title of the new object file to Insert Contact Info.

   Remember, the page title creates the ToolTip that identifies the object in the Objects panel; right now, the page title of this file is identical to the title of the object that you worked on earlier. This makes it difficult to tell the objects apart in the panel, especially because both objects currently have generic icons.

3. Decide what pieces of the code you want to replace with user input. Check Figure 22.6 to remind yourself what the end product should look like.

   For this object, you'll probably want to ask the user for a contact name (instead of John Smith) and an email address (instead of sending everything to poor John Smith's email).

4. Create an HTML form that will serve as a dialog box to collect this information. To be functional, your form will need two text fields: one to collect the name and another to collect the email address. So, the simplest form you could possibly come up with might look something like the one shown in Figure 22.8.

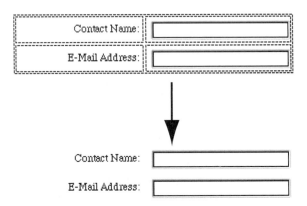

Figure 22.8   The form for the Contact Info object dialog box, as it appears in Dreamweaver's Layout view and as you want it to finally appear.

Open Contact Info.html and build the form in the body section of that file. If you like coding forms by hand, go to it. If you'd rather use a visual editor, open the file in Dreamweaver and use Dreamweaver's visual editor to build it. Figure 22.8 shows how the designed form might appear in Dreamweaver's Layout view.

Note

> If you're building your form in Dreamweaver's visual editor, method and action properties will be automatically added to the <form> tag. Your form doesn't need either of those because the form isn't going to be processed in the standard way. You can safely remove these properties from your code. Dreamweaver will also add background and text color properties to the <body> tag; you should remove these and let Dreamweaver determine the appropriate color scheme for the dialog box.

Your form code should look like this:

```
<form name="theForm">
<table>
        <tr valign="baseline">
                <td align="right" nowrap>Contact Name:</td>
                <td align="left">
                        <input type="text" name="contact" size="30">
                </td>
        </tr>
        <tr valign="baseline">
                <td align="right" nowrap>E-Mail Address:</td>
                <td align="left">
                        <input type="text" name="email" size="30">
                </td>
        </tr>
</table>
</form>
```

5. Add variables to the objectTag() function to collect form data.

   Open the Contact Info.html file in your text editor. The first step in processing user input is to declare two variables to collect the information from the two text fields in the form. These variables will be local to the objectTag() function and thus must be declared inside it.

   Add two local variable declarations to your function, each initialized to the value of one of the form fields. The code of your objectTag() function should now look like this:

```
function objectTag() {
var contact = document.theForm.contact.value;
var email = document.theForm.email.value;
return '<p><font face="Verdana, Arial" size="2">For more informa-
tion,   contact   <a   href="mailto:jsmith@mycompany.com">John
Smith</a></font></p>';
}
```

6. Rewrite the return statement, substituting the two variables for the name and email address. If you're an old coding hand, this will be a piece of cake. If you're a novice at JavaScript, the trickiest bit is balancing the opening and closing quotes

so that you don't end up with any unterminated string literals.

Your objectTag() function should now look like this:

```
function objectTag() {
var contact=document.theForm.contact.value;
var email=document.theForm.email.value;
return '<p><font face="Verdana, Arial, sans-serif" size="2"> For
more information contact <a href="mailto:' + email + '">' + contact
+ '</a></font></p>';
}
```

Note

Why declare variables instead of putting the references to the form directly into the return statement? No reason, except that it keeps the return statement from getting too long and unwieldy. The following code would work just as well:

```
return '<p><font face="Verdana, Arial, sans-serif" size="2"> For more
information contact <a href="mailto:' + document.theForm.email.value
+ '">' + document.theForm.contact.value + '</a></font></p>'
```

Figure 22.9 shows your complete object file code.

```
<html>
<head>
<title>Insert Contact Info</title>
<script language = "JavaScript">
function objectTag() {
var contact=document.theForm.contact.value;
var email=document.theForm.email.value;
return '<p><font face="Verdana, Arial, sans-serif" size="2"> For more information contact <a
href="mailto:' + email + '">' + contact + '</a></font></p>';
}
</script>
</head>
<body onLoad="initializeUI()">

<form name="theForm">
<table>
  <tr valign="baseline">
    <td align="right" nowrap>Contact Name:</td>
    <td align="left">
      <input type="text" name="contact" size="30">
    </td>
  </tr>
  <tr valign="baseline">
    <td align="right" nowrap>E-Mail Address:</td>
    <td align="left">
      <input type="text" name="email" size="30">
    </td>
  </tr>
</table>
</form>
</body>
</html>
```

Figure 22.9   Complete code for the Contact Info.html object file.

7. Test your object. In Dreamweaver, reload extensions and try to insert the new object. You should get a lovely dialog box that looks like the one shown in Figure 22.10.

Figure 22.10   Dialog box for the Contact Info object.

When you fill in your information and click OK, a customized contact information line should appear in your document.

Note

As with the previous exercise, if there's a problem with your code, Dreamweaver should give you a helpful error message. Read the error message, try to guess what it means, and then go back to your code and look for problems. Compare your code to the previous code to see what might be wrong.

The most common things that go wrong in this kind of object file are misnamed variables and form elements; invalid variable declaration and initialization statements; and mismatched single and double quotes in the return statement.

Exercise 22.4   Refining Your Object

In this exercise, you'll see that, while the only required JavaScript function for an object is the objectTag() function, you can add other optional functions. In fact, you can define any function that you like in the head section of the object file. As long as you call the function in the <body> tag, using the onLoad event handler, Dreamweaver will execute the function as soon as the user chooses the object.

The local function that you'll add in this exercise addresses a minor annoyance that you may have noticed in the dialog box that your object calls up. When the dialog box comes up, the insertion point is not in the correct position for you to immediately start entering data. That's not a life-threatening problem, but it's less than slick.

1. Open the Contact Info.html file in your text editor. Because this is not major surgery, you'll work on the same object that you created in the last exercise instead of creating a new object.

2. Add an initializing function to the document head. Somewhere inside the <script> tags in the document's head section, add the following code:

```
function initializeUI()
{
document.theForm.contact.focus();
document.theForm.contact.select();
}
```

What does this function do? The first line officially gives focus to whatever form element is named within it—in this case, the Contact field (your first text field).

The second line selects the text (if any) in whatever form element is named within it—again, in this case, the Contact field.

Note

> This function is used in many of the objects that ship with Dreamweaver. (Macromedia does not prohibit borrowing pieces of code.) Because the function is not part of the API, there's nothing magic about its name. If you'd rather name it something different, feel free to do so.

3. Call the function from the <body> tag. Add the following code to the <body> tag of the object file:

<body onLoad="initializeUI()">

Because this function is not part of Dreamweaver's official object-handling procedure, it must be specifically called.

4. Reload extensions and test the object. Now try it out. Save and close the object file. In Dreamweaver, reload extensions and choose the object from the Objects panel. The insertion point should be primed and ready to enter data into the Contact field of the dialog box.

Exercise 22.5   Creating a Separate JS File

Although it won't affect the functionality of the object, you might decide that separating the JavaScript from the HTML portion of the object makes upkeep easier.

In this exercise, you'll separate the JavaScript and place it in a JS file, using a link inside the main object file (the HTML file) to access it.

1. Make a copy of the object file. Because this is a major change to your object, it's a good idea to make a copy of the original file to work on. You can use the File/Save As command in your text editor, or you can duplicate the file from Windows Explorer or the Macintosh Finder, whichever you prefer. If you keep both your duplicate and your original in the Development folder, you'll need to give each file a different name; if you want it to retain the same filenames, you'll have to move the original file to another folder. (Also, if you keep both files in the Development folder, Dreamweaver will show two generic icons in the Objects panel. If this is the case, you'll need to give each different object file its own unique page title so that the ToolTips that identify them in the Objects panel will be unique.)

2. Open the object file in your text editor or in Dreamweaver, and select the JavaScript in the head section.

As you know if you're an experienced scripter, the JavaScript code that can be copied to an external file is the code that would normally appear in the HTML document's head section—the functions, in other words. So you start by selecting all the code that appears between the opening and closing <script> tags. You should select the bold code shown here:

```
<html>
<head>
<title>Contact Info</title>
<script language="JavaScript">
function objectTag() {
var contact=document.theForm.contact.value;
var email=document.theForm.email.value;
return '<p><font face="Verdana, Arial" size="2">For more informa-
tion,                          contact                          <a
href="mailto:'+email+'">'+contact+'</a></font></p>';
}
</script>
</head>
```

3. Cut the selected code, and paste it into a new text document. Cut that code to the Clipboard (Edit/Cut). If you're working in a text editor, create a new document and paste in the code (Edit/Paste). If you're working in Dreamweaver, create a new document; then open the Code Inspector for that new document, and select all the code in the source editor and delete it. Then paste in the new code.

Note

Dreamweaver automatically supplies the HTML framework for all new documents; if you don't need that framework, it is safe to select the code and delete it.

4. Save the new document as Contact Info.js. The new document, which contains only the JavaScript code from the head of the original object file, must be saved as a text file with the .js extension. It should be stored in the Development folder, and named to match the object file.

Note

Actually, the filename doesn't need to match the object file, and the script file doesn't need to be stored in exactly the same folder as the object file, as long as the correct name and relative URL are given when the two files are linked. However, it is recommended to keep to a naming convention like this because it makes file management much easier.

5. In the object file, change the <script> tags to link to the JS file. The head section of the original HTML object file should now look like this:

```
<head>
<title>Contact Info</title>
<script language="JavaScript">
</script>
</head>
```

Change the opening script tag so that it looks like this:

```
<head>
<title>Contact Info</title>
<script language="JavaScript" src = "Contact Info.js">
</script>
</head>
```

6. Save and close both files. Figures 22.11 and 22.12 show what the complete code should look like in the two files.

Figure 22.11   The complete code for Contact Info.html, substituting the external file reference for the JavaScript.

7. In Dreamweaver, reload extensions and try out the object. If you correctly moved the JavaScript code and correctly entered the link information in the object file, the object should work in exactly the same way it worked before.

Note

If you linked from the object file to the JS file incorrectly, one of two things will happen: If there's a local function, such as initializeUI( ), Dreamweaver will report a JavaScript error when the <body> loads and tries to call that function (see Figure 22.13). If there are no local functions, Dreamweaver won't report an error, but the object will insert some strange code into your page. (The link from the HTML file to the JS file must be a relative address. If both files are in the same folder—which is definitely the safest way to go—the address will simply be the name of the JS file. If you want to store the JS file in another folder, you must enter the correct relative address, including any subfolder or parent folder information.)

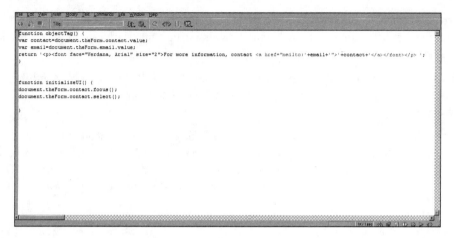

Figure 22.12   The complete code for Contact Info.js.

Figure 22.13   Dreamweaver error message showing the result of incorrect linking between the object file and its external JS file.

If you didn't paste the correct code into the JS file, you'll probably generate a JavaScript syntax error, and Dreamweaver will generate an error message.

Exercise 22.6   Creating an Object Icon Using Fireworks

Professional-looking objects have their own icons. When the development phase of your object is done, the finishing touch is to make an icon file to represent it in the Objects panel.

The requirements for an icon file are as follows:

- The file must be a GIF image file, preferably no larger than 16×16 pixels. (Larger images will work, but they'll be squashed into an 16×16 pixel space in the panel.)

- The file must have exactly the same name as the object file it goes with, but with the GIF extension. For this exercise, therefore, the name must be Contact Info.gif.

- The file must be stored in the same folder as the object file it goes with. For this exercise, the icon file must be stored in the Development folder.

Icon files can have any colors you like, and the icon can look like anything you can imagine. You'll quickly discover, though, that designing icons that clearly communicate what they represent, when there are only 256 pixels to play with, is a real art.

This exercise won't show you how to create a graphic to use as an object icon; that's beyond the scope of this chapter. But you will see how to use an existing graphic as an icon file.

1. Create, adapt, or borrow a 16×16 pixel GIF file containing an icon. If you have access to a good graphics program (such as Macromedia Fireworks) and want to create your own icon, do it. Otherwise, use the Contact Info.gif file on the CD. (If you make your own file, make sure to name it Contact Info.gif.)

> **Tip**
>
> You don't have to create your icons from scratch. You can start with an existing icon and adapt it to your needs. The Contact Info.gif file on the CD was adapted from Macromedia's E-Mail.gif file.

2. Put the icon file in the Development folder. Remember, the icon must be stored in the same folder as the object file.

3. Reload extensions, and take a look at your icon. In Dreamweaver, reload extensions.

4. In the Objects panel, access your Development objects. If all went as planned, you should have a beautiful custom icon in place (see Figure 22.14).

Working Smart with Objects

Congratulations! You now know the foundation skills for making Dreamweaver objects. How can you make objects work for you?

Analyze Your Needs

As you've seen, any piece of HTML code that you repeatedly use in Web pages is a candidate for an object. The best object candidates, though, are pieces of code that you need to customize and then insert—changing the name and email address, specifying a certain URL to link to, and so forth.

Any time you find yourself going through the same steps over and over as you add content to Web pages, ask yourself these questions:

- Is the code I'm inserting similar enough each time that I could create an object from it?

Figure 22.14
The Contact Info object, as it appears in the Objects panel with its new custom icon in place.

- Are there differences in the code each time, or is it exactly the same code? (If the code is exactly the same each time, requiring no customization, it might be more efficient to use a recorded command or even a library item.)

- How many more times do I think I'm likely to need to insert this code? Will my need continue after today, after the current assignment, indefinitely? Creating an object is a time-consuming solution if the need is only very temporary.

- Do I have some extra time right now to devote to making this object? (Never try a new, challenging solution when your deadline is 45 minutes away.)

Depending on your answers, you'll know if it's time to crack open Dreamweaver and fit a new custom object inside.

Expand Your Horizons

When you feel comfortable with the basic object-making framework as presented here, expand yourself. Read through the *Extending Dreamweaver* manual to get ideas of what's possible in the Dreamweaver API. Take a look at some of the objects that come with Dreamweaver, to see how they're structured and what refinements they include.

Working with Behaviors

Ah, behaviors! This is where the glitz comes in, all those neat little prewritten JavaScripts that Dreamweaver allows you to add to your web pages at the click of a button. Believe it or not, basic behaviors are only slightly more complicated than objects to create— though, as always, the more you know about JavaScript, the better (and more spectacular) your results will be.

In this section, you'll learn what a well-formed behavior file looks like, how Dreamweaver processes behavior files, and how to build your own behaviors from scratch.

What Are Behaviors?

A behavior, like an object, is a snippet of code that gets inserted into a Dreamweaver document when the user chooses from the behaviors list. Instead of adding HTML code to the document (also like an object), however, a behavior adds JavaScript code.

Behaviors are constructed the same way objects are: Dreamweaver API procedures and functions enable you to return the exact string of code that you want inserted into your document.

For a variety of reasons, however, behaviors are inherently more complex than objects:

- A behavior inserts two pieces of code—a function (in the document head) and a function call (in the body section, wherever the cursor is when the behavior is chosen).

- Preferably, a behavior should be editable after it has been inserted, by double-clicking it in the Behavior panel. (To edit objects after they've been inserted, you use the Property Inspector. Although it is possible to create a custom Property Inspector, it's not a task for the faint of heart.)

- Preferably, a behavior should specify which event handlers can be used in the function call; it should be inaccessible in the behaviors list (grayed out) if the current selection is inappropriate.

Note

Dreamweaver behaviors always insert JavaScript code into the document in the form of a generic function, defined in the head section, and a customized function call, defined in the body.

What Files, Where

Like objects, each behavior consists of an HTML file (the behavior file), which either contains JavaScript code or is linked to an external JS file. Behavior files are stored in the Configuration/Behaviors/Actions folder. Like the Objects folder, the Actions folder can contain folders inside itself; each folder corresponds to a submenu within the behaviors list. Again like the Objects folder, any new folder added to the Actions folder will result in a new submenu in the behaviors list (see Figure 22.15).

Structure of a Simple Behavior File

Like object files, behavior files have their own required structure, and Dreamweaver has a set procedure for dealing with them. Figure 22.16 shows the framework code of a basic behavior file, containing only the required elements.

The key elements of the file are listed here:

- **Page title.** This becomes the name of the behavior as it appears in the behaviors list.

- **Defined function.** This is the JavaScript function that the behavior will insert in the head section of the user's document. It will be inserted exactly as coded here. This function must have a unique name—no other defined function in the entire Actions folder can use this name.

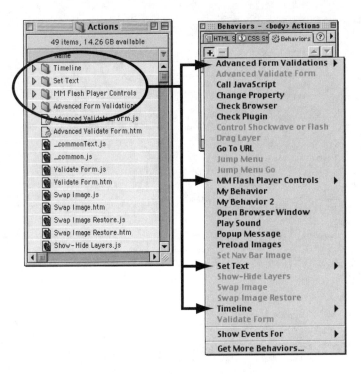

Figure 22.15   The Actions folder, showing its subfolders, and the corresponding submenus in the Behavior panel's behavior list.

- **behaviorFunction() function.** This JavaScript function, part of the Dreamweaver API, must return the name of the function defined previously (without the ending parentheses). This function is called automatically when the behavior is chosen and, therefore, needn't be called in the behavior file.

- **applyBehavior() function.** This function, also part of the Dreamweaver API, must return the exact code of the function call as it will be inserted into the user's document. In a more complex behavior that requires arguments to be passed to the function, those arguments must be included in the return statement. This function is called automatically when the behavior is chosen and, therefore, needn't be called in the behavior file.

- **<body> tag elements.** Any code in the body section of the file will appear in a dialog box when the behavior is chosen. All behaviors automatically call up dialog boxes. If the behavior requires user input, create a form (as with object files). If the behavior requires no user input (as in the example here), some content must be placed in the body, or an empty dialog box will appear.

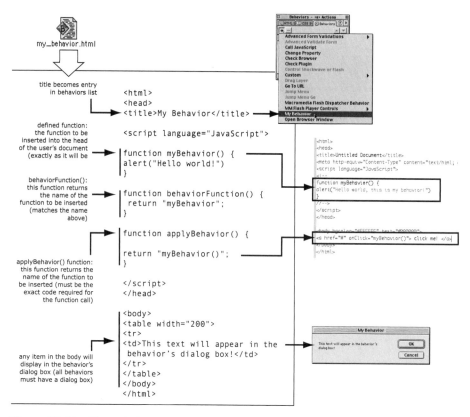

Figure 22.16   The code framework required for a basic behavior file.

In the example shown in Figure 22.16, the function returned is a simple pop-up alert. Notice how the function and function call appear in the user's document, exactly as presented in the code.

Structure of a Fancier Behavior with a Dialog Box and Other Refinements

The behavior shown previously contains all the necessary elements and will work properly. However, it is unusually simple (requiring no user input and passing no arguments from the function call to the function), and it is missing several key enhancements (such as control over the event handler used and features that will allow the behavior to be edited in the future). Figure 22.17 shows the code for a more full-featured behavior, complete with all these (optional) features.

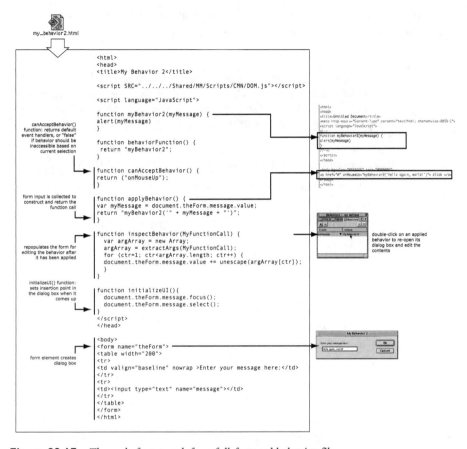

Figure 22.17   The code framework for a full-featured behavior file.

In addition to the elements listed, the key elements in this more full-featured behavior
are as follows:

- **HTML form.** As with object files, the form becomes the dialog box for collecting
  user input. In behavior files, the form is used to collect arguments for the function call to pass to the main function.

- **Link to script.js file.** This link gives you access to several utility functions for
  handling strings; one of these functions, the extractArgs() function, is extremely
  useful in coding the otherwise complex inspectBehavior() function, listed later.

- **canAcceptBehavior() function.** This function, part of the API, returns either
  true, false, or a list of one or more default event handlers. In more advanced files
  than the one shown here, this function can also determine what kind of object
  the user has selected in the document, and whether that object is acceptable for

applying this behavior. If the function returns false, the behavior will appear grayed out in the behaviors list. This function is called automatically.

Note

> Determining when a behavior should be grayed out in the behaviors list requires more in-depth knowledge of the Dreamweaver API and the Dreamweaver document object model (DOM) than is possible in this chapter. Read the *Extending Dreamweaver* manual and examine other behaviors to learn more about this.

- **inspectBehavior(*functionCall*) function**. Also part of the API, this function must be used to collect information from a behavior that has already been applied and to repopulate the behavior's dialog box for editing. This function makes it possible for the user to open the Behavior panel, double-click an existing behavior, and be presented with a dialog box that contains the current settings for that behavior. The function is called automatically. Dreamweaver automatically passes the behavior's function call, as a string, to the function.

- **initializeUI() function**. This function, which is not part of the API, does the same thing in behavior files as it does in object files: It places the cursor in a certain field of the dialog box and selects any contents for easier text entry. This function must be called using the onLoad event handler in the <body> tag.

In the example shown in Figure 22.17, the code returned by the defined function is a pop-up alert message, but with the content to be determined by the user. Notice that the defined function itself remains generic; the input collected by the form is used to add an argument to the function call.

Making Your Own Behaviors

In this section, you'll get some hands-on experience making your own behaviors. It should go without saying that you need to be able to write and understand the code for a particular JavaScript function and function call before you can turn that code into a behavior.

Exercise 22.7   Setting Up Shop

Start by getting your working space in order. As you did with objects previously, you'll create a custom behaviors folder for storing your exercise behaviors, and you'll learn a few of the quirks of reloading extensions when working with behaviors.

1. Make sure that Dreamweaver is running. One of the goals of this exercise is to see how behavior extensions reload.

2. Find and open the Configuration/Behaviors/Actions folder on your hard drive. Minimize or hide Dreamweaver, if necessary, so that you have access to your desktop.

3. Create a custom behaviors folder. In the Actions folder, create a new folder. Call it Development. Leave the folder empty for now.

4. In Dreamweaver, reload extensions. Ctrl/Opt-click the triangle at the top of the Objects panel, and choose Reload Extensions—this is the same procedure you followed when working with objects.

5. In the Behavior panel, access the behaviors list and look for a new submenu. Click the + sign in the inspector to open the behaviors list. A new folder should result in a new submenu appearing in the list.

   Probably, however, you won't see any new Development submenu. Why not? Reloading extensions does not cause Dreamweaver to recognize new or renamed files or folders in the Actions folder; it recognizes only modifications within files. To get Dreamweaver to see the new submenu, you'll have to do it the old-fashioned way: Quit the program and launch again.

6. Quit Dreamweaver and relaunch it. Then look again for the submenu. This time, your submenu should appear. Of course, it will be an empty submenu because the Development folder is empty. But your new behaviors will appear there. Every time you add a new behavior, you must quit and relaunch; when you modify an existing behavior, you can reload extensions without quitting.

Exercise 22.8   Making a Simple Behavior

A simple behavior is one that doesn't require arguments to be passed from the function call to the function and that, therefore, doesn't need a form to collect user input. The simple behavior that you'll create in this exercise is a script that automatically resizes the browser window to a certain size.

Create and edit the exercise files in your favorite text editor or in Dreamweaver's Code Inspector. Save the behavior file into the Development folder created in the previous exercise. Save the test files in your working folder.

1. Create (and test) the JavaScript function and function call that you want the behavior to insert.

   The first step in creating a successful behavior is writing and testing a stable, functional script for the behavior to insert into a user document. This file is where you will do just that—it isn't going to be the behavior file, so save it in your working folder, not the Development folder. Call it resize400_test.html.

   The document head should include a JavaScript function for resizing the window and also should include a function call from within the body. The code should look like this:

```html
<html>
<head>
<title>Testing Resize Script</title>
<script language="JavaScript">
function resizeTo400() {
   window.resizeTo(400,400);
}
</script>
</head>
<body>
<a href="#" onMouseUp=" resizeTo400()"> Click me!</a>
</body>
</html>
```

Tip

> When writing JavaScript functions to be used as behaviors, you don't have to worry about adding the lines of code that will hide the script from older browsers. Dreamweaver will add those lines of code automatically when your behavior is applied.

2. Test your behavior in a browser (or two). Open the test file in a browser and click on the test link. The window should resize.

   If there's a problem, go back to the code and do some troubleshooting until the window resizes. The script needs to work before the behavior that inserts it will work. For best results, of course, try the behavior in several major browsers before declaring it "well-behaved."

3. Create a basic behavior file, with all structural elements in place. Create a new HTML file. This will be the behavior file, so save it in the Development folder in the Actions folder. Call it Resize400.html.

   Start by entering the framework code, as shown in Figure 22.16. Then add your newly devised function and function call in the appropriate places. Your final code should look like this (elements that have been customized from the basic framework are shown in bold):

```html
<html>
<head>
<title>Resize Window to 400</title>
<script language="JavaScript">
function resizeTo400() {
   window.resizeTo(400,400);
}
function behaviorFunction() {
   return "resizeTo400";
}
function applyBehavior() {
   return "resizeTo400()";
}
</script>
</head>
```

```
<body>
<table width="200">
   <tr>
          <td>This behavior will resize the user's browser window to
400 pixels wide and 400 pixels high.</td>
   </tr>
</table>
</body>
</html>
```

4. Relaunch Dreamweaver. If Dreamweaver is currently running, quit the program. Then launch the program again so that the new behavior loads.

5. Create another HTML test file. Call it resize400_behavior_test.html and save it in your working folder. In the new file, create another simple text link (linking to #), just like the first test file. Don't add any JavaScript to this file.

   Your code for the new file should look like this:

```
<html>
<head>
<title>Testing Resize Behavior</title>
</head>
<body>
<a href="#">Click me!</a>
</body>
</html>
```

6. Open the new test file in Dreamweaver and apply your new behavior. When the file is open in Dreamweaver, try to apply your behavior the same way you'd apply any behavior, by selecting the linked text and clicking the + in the Behavior panel. The new behavior should now appear in the behaviors list, under the Development submenu, as shown in Figure 22.18. The dialog box shown in Figure 22.18 should appear when you choose the behavior.

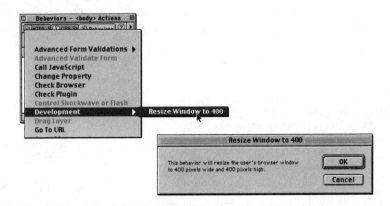

Figure 22.18   The various interface elements for the Resize Window behavior: the behaviors list, with Development submenu and behavior's menu entry, and the resulting dialog box.

If there's a JavaScript syntax error in your behaviors file, Dreamweaver will give you an error message as soon as you click the + in the panel. Examine the message and see if you can fix the code.

If there are no syntax errors, you'll be allowed to choose and apply your behavior. But this doesn't mean that the code got inserted correctly.

1. Examine the file's HTML source code to see if the script got properly inserted. Open Dreamweaver's Code Inspector and take a look at the code. It should look just the same as the code you entered yourself, back in step 1 in Exercise 22.8.

   If it doesn't, you'll need to do some troubleshooting. Look for the differences between the inserted code and the original, hand-entered code. Then examine your behavior file. Find how the two correlate, and adjust the behavior file. Then try the behavior again.

2. Test the inserted behavior in a browser. In a browser, repeat the test that you performed on the original code back in step 3 in Exercise 22.8. The JavaScript should work just as well as the code you entered by hand. You've made a behavior!

Exercise 22.9   Adding Arguments to the Function Call

In this exercise, you'll build on the previous behavior. Instead of inserting a script that always resizes the window to the same dimensions, you'll insert a script that asks the user for a desired width and height and then resizes the window to those dimensions. To accomplish this, you'll need to add a form to the behavior file's body and do some fancier scripting in the applyBehavior() function. As in the previous exercise, you'll start by using your test file to create a working version of the function and the function call that you want to insert.

1. Open resize400_test.html and alter the code so that the function call passes arguments to the function. If you want to keep your original test file safe from harm, make a copy of it to work on for this exercise. Save the copy as resize_test.html.

   When you're done, your code should look something like this:

```
<html>
<head>
<title>Testing Resize Script</title>
<script language="JavaScript">
function resizeBrowserWindow(width,height) {
   window.resizeTo(width,height);
}
</script>
</head>
<body>
<a href="#" onMouseUp="resizeBrowserWindow(400,400)">Click me!</a>
</body>
</html>
```

2. Test the revised script in a browser. As before, make sure that the behavior works in as many browsers as possible before declaring it seaworthy. If it doesn't work, troubleshoot until it does.

3. Save the Resize400.html behavior file as Resize.html, and open that file in your text editor.

4. In the behavior file, change the function to match the revised function developed previously. The <script> tag in the head section of the document should now look like this:

```
<script language="JavaScript">
function resizeBrowserWindow(width,height) {
    window.resizeTo(width,height);
}
function behaviorFunction() {
    return "resizeBrowserWindow";
}
function applyBehavior() {
    return "resizeBrowserWindow()";
}
</script>
```

5. Delete the contents of the behavior file's body section, to make way for the form you'll be creating in the next step.

6. In the body section, design and create a form to collect the required information from the user. Your form will need two text fields: one for width and one for height. Code for the new body section of the behavior file might look like this:

```
<form name="theForm">
<table>
   <tr valign="baseline">
          <td align="left" colspan="2" nowrap> Resize the browser
window to these dimensions:</td>
   </tr>
   <tr valign="baseline">
          <td align="right" nowrap>New width:</td>
          <td align="left">
                 <input type="text" name="width" size="8">
          </td>
   </tr>
   <tr valign="baseline">
          <td align="right" nowrap>New height:</td>
          <td align="left">
                 <input type="text" name="height" size="8">
          </td>
   </tr>
</table>
</form>
```

Remember, you can always design the form in Dreamweaver's visual editor, if you want. The form should end up looking something like the one shown in Figure 22.19.

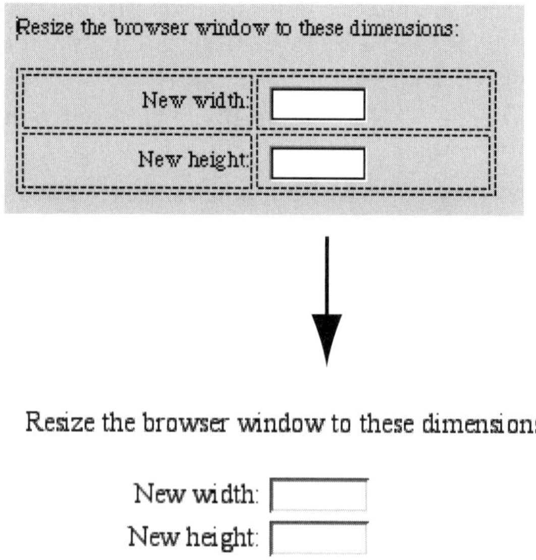

Figure 22.19   The HTML form for the Resize Window behavior dialog box, as it would appear in Dreamweaver's Layout view and as interpreted by a browser.

5. Rewrite the applyBehavior() function to return a function call that uses the form information. Remember, the applyBehavior() function needs to return the function call exactly as it will appear in the user's document.

   This function's return statement will have to construct the code for your desired function call using concatenation. Your code for the applyBehavior() function should look like this:

```
function applyBehavior() {
  var width=document.theForm.width.value;
  var height=document.theForm.height.value;
  return "resizeBrowserWindow(" + width + "," + height + ")";
}
```

6. Reload extensions and try out your new behavior. In Dreamweaver, create another test file with a text link in it. Reload extensions, and try your new behavior. Does it work? Does it insert the proper code? If not, do some troubleshooting.

7. Refine the dialog box with initializeUI(). Any time there's a dialog box, the local function initializeUI() makes sure that the insertion point lands in a handy place.

   In the behavior file, add the function, specifying the width text field as the focus (it's the first field in the dialog box). It should look like this:

```
function initializeUI() {
  document.theForm.width.focus();
  document.theForm.width.select();
}
```

Also remember to call the function in the <body> tag. The call will look like this:

```
<body onLoad="initializeUI()">
```

Exercise 22.10   Adding the canAcceptBehavior() Function

The most powerful use of this function—determining whether a behavior will appear grayed out in the behaviors list—is beyond the scope of this chapter. But you can specify a default event handler to be used with the function call.

1. Duplicate the behavior file, if you want. If you're afraid of goofing up your lovely working behavior file, make a duplicate of it; remember, though, that you'll have to change the name of the defined function and the page title for the duplicate to work properly.

   If you're feeling brave, go ahead and work on the behavior file that you created in the previous exercise.

2. Add the canAcceptBehavior() function to the head of the file, specifying whatever event handler you want the behavior to use.

   This one's pretty simple. Just add the following code somewhere inside the <script> tags in the document's head section:

   ```
   function canAcceptBehavior() {
   return ("onMouseUp");
   }
   ```

3. Test your revised behavior. You know the drill: Make a test file, reload extensions, and apply the behavior. Examine the code inserted by the revised behavior; the function call should now look like this:

   ```
   <a href="#" onMouseUp="resizeBrowserWindow(300,300)"> click me </a>
   ```

Exercise 22.11   Creating a Separate JS File

Before you can add the finishing touches to your behavior, you'll need to separate it into an HTML file and a JS file, like you did with Contact Info object.

1. Make a backup copy of Resize.html, just in case. Store the backup outside the Configuration folder, in your working folder.

2. Move the JavaScript functions into an empty text file. Open Resize.html in your text editor. Select everything between the opening and closing script tags, in the head section.

Cut them to the Clipboard. Then create a new, empty text file and paste them into it. The pasted code should look like this:

```
function resizeBrowserWindow(width,height) {
   window.resizeTo(width,height);
}
function behaviorFunction() {
   return "resizeBrowserWindow";
}

function applyBehavior() {
   var width=document.theForm.width.value;
   var height=document.theForm.height.value;
   return "resizeBrowserWindow(" + width + "," + height + ")";
}

function canAcceptBehavior() {
return ("onMouseUp");
}

function initializeUI() {
   document.theForm.width.focus();
   document.theForm.width.select();
}
```

3. Save the new file into the Development folder. Call it Resize.js. Remember, rec-ommended practice is to name the HTML and JS files identically and to store them in the same folder.

4. In Resize.html, add a link to the JS file. Add the link to the <script> tags where you removed the functions. Your <script> tags should now look like this:

```
<script src = "Resize.js"></script>
```

5. Reload extensions, and try out your new behavior. As long as all your copying, pasting and linking was correct, the behavior should function the same as it did before. (If it doesn't, check your code.)

From now on, when you have function changes, you'll change the JS file. The HTML file needs changing only if you update the form, add another function call to the body tag, or add another script tag (you'll be doing that in the next exercise).

Exercise 22.12   Adding the inspectBehavior() Function

What's the point of this function? Try this: In Dreamweaver, create a test file and apply your behavior. Then take a look at the Behavior panel, where you should see the behavior listed along with its event handler. Double-click the behavior to see and possibly change its parameters.

When the dialog box comes back up, it's empty, as shown in Figure 22.20. Dreamweaver has not retrieved the values that you originally entered into the dialog box, so you have no way of knowing what they are unless you look at the source code.

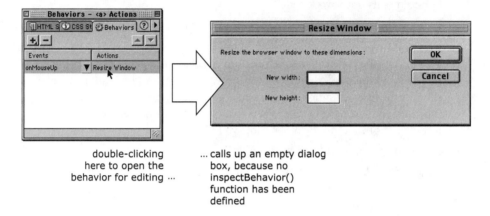

double-clicking
here to open the
behavior for editing ...

... calls up an empty dialog
box, because no
inspectBehavior()
function has been
defined

Figure 22.20   Editing a behavior that has no inspectBehavior() function.

Does this strike you as a real shortcoming? The purpose of this exercise is to fix that problem, by collecting the information from the function call that has been inserted and repopulating the dialog box with that information.

1. Duplicate the behavior files, if you want. Again, if you're afraid of goofing up your existing behavior files, make a backup copy of them, stored in your working folder.

2. In Resize.html, link the behavior file to the string.js file.

   Dreamweaver's Configuration folder contains a bunch of helpful all-purpose JavaScript functions in JS files, ready for you to use in your extension files. You can check them out—they're all in the Configuration/Shared folder. The file that you're going to link to is called string.js—it's in the Shared/MM/Scripts/CMN folder. This file contains several functions for working with strings. It makes the inspectBehavior() function much easier to script.

   To link your behavior file to this JS file, you'll need to add another script tag to the head section of the HTML file, this one containing the relative address of string.js. Your code for the head section of the HTML file should now look like this:

```
<head>
<title>Resize Window</title>
<script src="Resize.js"></script>
<script src="../../../Shared/MM/Scripts/CMN/string.js"></script>
</head>
```

Why did you do this? Because the function you're going to write next (in your JS file) is going to call on several functions from the shared JS file, and these links will allow the two JS files to communicate.

3. In Resize.js, enter the basic framework of the inspectBehavior() function. Start by adding this framework code:

```
function inspectBehavior(resizeFunctionCall) {
}
```

This part of the code collects the function call that the behavior had earlier inserted into the user's document, for inspection. Dreamweaver automatically submits the inserted function call as an argument to the inspectBehavior() function; you just have to enter some sort of argument name, such as resizeFunctionCall (or any other name you like).

4. Extract the arguments from the inserted function call.

Simply by declaring the function, you have collected the inserted function call as a string; now you need to extract the parts of that string that correspond to each argument. This requires some fairly fancy scripting involving substrings—but this is why you linked to the string.js file. That file contains the extractArgs() function, which, when passed a function call, extracts the arguments and returns them as an array. Now all you need to do is pass your collected function call to the extractArgs() function, create an empty array, and feed the return statement from that function into it. The added code looks like this:

```
function inspectBehavior(resizeFunctionCall) {
  var argArray = new Array;
  argArray = extractArgs(resizeFunctionCall);
}
```

5. Use the extracted arguments to repopulate the form (dialog box).

Your new array, argArray, now contains an element for each argument in the function call. In the array, argArray[0] contains the function call itself. The arguments start at argArray[1]; for your behavior, this means that argArray[1] contains the new width of the resized window the behavior is creating, and argArray[2] contains the new height. Because there are only those two arguments in the inserted function call, there are no more elements to the array.

All you need to add now is the code that assigns each array element back into its original form element. For your behavior, the code you need to add looks like this:

```
function inspectBehavior(resizeFunctionCall) {
  var argArray = new Array;
  argArray = extractArgs(resizeFunctionCall);
  document.theForm.width.value = argArray[1];
  document.theForm.height.value = argArray[2];
}
```

That's it! You now have a complete inspectBehavior() function. Your completed code for the behavior should look like that shown in Figures 22.21 and 22.22.

```
Resize Window (Figures/Resize.html) - Dreamweaver
File  Edit  View  Insert  Modify  Text  Commands  Site  Window  Help
<html>
<head>
<title>Resize Window</title>
<script src="Resize.js"></script>
<script src="../../../Shared/MM/Scripts/CMN/string.js"></script>
</head>
<body onLoad="initializeUI()">
<form name="theForm">
  <table>
    <tr valign="baseline">
        <td align="left" colspan="2" nowrap>
        Resize the browser window to these dimensions:
        </td>
    </tr>
    <tr valign="baseline">
      <td align="right" nowrap>New width:</td>
      <td align="left">
        <input type="text" name="width" size="8">
      </td>
</tr>
<tr valign="baseline">
      <td align="right" nowrap>New height:</td>
      <td align="left">
        <input type="text" name="height" size="8">
      </td>
</tr>
</table>
</form>
</body>
</html>
```

Figure 22.21   Complete code for Resize.html, with all links in place.

6. Try out the revised behavior. Reload extensions in Dreamweaver and create another test file. Because the code changes are now being made to an external .js file, you can actually use your old test file. Apply the behavior, adding whatever width and height values you like; then try double-clicking its name in the Behavior panel. If everything is working properly, the dialog box should open up with those values in place (see Figure 22.23).

If you have a syntax error, you'll get an error message.

If you didn't correctly link to the string.js file, Dreamweaver will bring up an error message saying that extractArgs() has not been defined.

If you didn't access the array correctly, the dialog box will open with the wrong values in the wrong places, or with empty text fields, or with "Undefined" showing up in one or more text fields.

If any of these things happen, check and tweak until it works.

```
File Edit View Insert Modify Text Commands Site Window Help

function resizeBrowserWindow(width,height) {
    window.resizeTo(width,height);
}
function behaviorFunction() {
    return "resizeBrowserWindow";
}

function canAcceptBehavior() {
return ("onMouseUp");
}

function applyBehavior() {
    var width=document.theForm.width.value;
    var height=document.theForm.height.value;
    return "resizeBrowserWindow(" + width + "," + height + ")";
}

function inspectBehavior(ResizeFunctionCall) {
  var argArray = new Array;
  argArray = extractArgs(ResizeFunctionCall);
  document.theForm.width.value = argArray[1];
  document.theForm.height.value = argArray[2];
}

function initializeUI() {
  document.theForm.width.focus();
  document.theForm.width.select();
}
```

Figure 22.22   Complete function code for Resize.js, with the inspectBehavior() function in place.

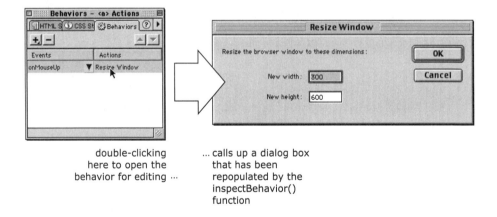

double-clicking   ... calls up a dialog box
here to open the   that has been
behavior for editing ...   repopulated by the
                            inspectBehavior()
                            function

Figure 22.23   Editing a behavior that has a properly defined inspectBehavior() function.

Note

> You have seen that extension files should work the same whether the JavaScript code is embedded in the HTML file or is placed in a separate JS file. One exception to this: In behaviors, when linking to shared files (such as string.js), on some platforms the behavior will not work correctly unless the functions are placed in a separate JS file, as you have done here.

Building Your Own Behaviors

If you've completed all the exercises here, you have the foundation skills to create successful Dreamweaver behaviors. You've also seen that there's a lot more to learn and a lot more that you can do with behaviors. To extend your behavior-making power, check out the *Extending Dreamweaver* manual, examine existing behavior files, and take a closer look at the shared files, such as string.js—these are all valuable resources.

As with objects, though, you should begin by examining your needs. Although it is tempting to create the biggest, baddest behavior on the block—inserting scripts that make browser windows quake and multimedia pour from the computer—it's often the simple, workhorse JavaScript tasks that will give you the most mileage. What JavaScript functionality do you often wish you had quick access to, but don't? Are there existing Dreamweaver behaviors that you wish operated just a little differently? Ask yourself these questions as you work, and you'll soon know what custom behaviors you'll want to add.

Sharing Extensions

If your object or behavior is helpful to you, maybe it will be helpful to others. Of course, the more people you share with, the more your extension will need to be cleaned up, dressed up, and made reliable and understandable. If you're not sure what this means, take a look at the extensions that ship with Dreamweaver. They're well-documented; the code is bulletproofed; they have standardized, well-designed interfaces; and they're nicely packaged. None of this happens by accident.

Do You Want to Share?

First of all, you need to ask yourself whether you really want to share. If an object or behavior is probably going to be useful only to your personal workflow, client requirements, or current assignment; if your code is lacking many of the niceties that other people will expect; and if you don't have time to spare getting things in shape to share, you can stop reading right here, and just continue using your custom-made extensions yourself.

On the other hand, you might work in a group setting where all the Dreamweaver users in your office would benefit from your custom extension. Or, you might be a public-minded soul who thinks that the world-at-large can benefit from your brilliance, and you want to submit your extension to the Macromedia Exchange. If that's you, read on!

Bulletproofing

Bulletproofing means making sure that your extension will work under a variety of conditions without breaking. The more diverse circumstances your extension will be used in, the more bulletproof it should be.

How do you bulletproof? Read on.

Test the Inserted Code

No object or behavior is better than the code it inserts. Make sure that your code is worth inserting. Create sample Web pages using code that was inserted with your custom extension. Does the code work successfully across platforms? Does it work in different browsers? Macromedia recommends making sure that your code works in all the major version 4+ browsers and "fails gracefully" in version 3 browsers.

Test the Insertion Process

If there's not a dialog box with opportunities for user input, then the code should insert the same every time. If there is a dialog box, however, then consider the following:

- What happens if the user leaves all values at their defaults and just clicks OK? Does Dreamweaver crash? Does garbage get inserted into the user's document?

- What happens if the user enters unusual or wrong data in the dialog box?

- What do you want to have happen in either of these circumstances? You can code the extension so that valid code gets entered no matter what, you can cause an alert message, or you can simply make the extension not insert code at all unless the user input meets certain criteria. It's up to you.

Note

> Macromedia recommends that you let the user enter whatever input he desires, as long as it's not going to actually "break" the page—in other words, a result is considered acceptable if the browser will simply ignore the incorrect or nonstandard code rather than generating JavaScript errors, crashing, or exhibiting any other noticeable problems. This is recommended because coding standards evolve—so what's nonsensical code today might be perfectly valid tomorrow—and because users don't like being boxed in by too-rigid requirements for code entry.

A good example of a well-bulletproofed insertion process is Macromedia's own table object. As a learning experience, open Dreamweaver and try using this object with strange dialog box entries. You'll find that the following are true:

- Left to its defaults, the object inserts a valid table based on the last time the object was used.

- Fields that correspond to optional table parameters can be left blank, with the result that the inserted code simply doesn't include those parameters.

- The rows and columns fields, which must have certain values for the table code to function, will not accept invalid entries. Any non-numeric entry, or 0, will be replaced by a 1.

Test the Object/Behavior Itself

You already know that it works on your computer, with your version of Dreamweaver and your operating system. But ask yourself these questions:

- Does it work with older versions of Dreamweaver?

- Does it work on versions of Dreamweaver that are configured differently than yours?

- Does it work on computers that are configured differently than yours?

- Does it work on different platforms?

It may be that some of these things don't matter. If your extension needs to work only in your company, and if you only have PCs running Windows 2000 and Dreamweaver 4, then who cares if it runs correctly on Dreamweaver 2 on a Macintosh or Windows 95? Even though you might not need to fix a certain limitation, though, it's a good idea to be aware of it so that you can share intelligently.

> **Tip**
>
> Macromedia requests that all behaviors submitted to the Exchange include, as part of the defined function, the version of Dreamweaver that they are intended to work with. This information should be added as a comment to the defined function, like this:
>
> ```
> function resizeBrowserWindow(width,height) {   //v3.0
> ```

Exercise 22.13   Testing a Custom Behavior

This exercise uses the previously mentioned testing criteria to improve the Resize Window behavior we created earlier in this chapter. (If you don't have the complete code for this object, you can find it on the accompanying CD-ROM.)

1. Test the inserted code. The inserted code, in this case, is a JavaScript function that resizes the current browser window. How robust is this code?

   According to the O'Reilly online JavaScript reference provided with Dreamweaver, this function should work in Netscape 4+ and in Internet Explorer (see Figure 22.24).

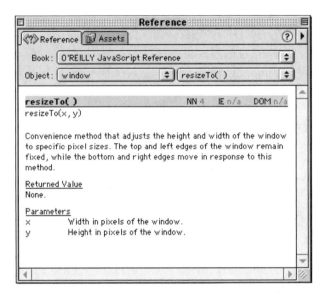

Figure 22.24   Dreamweaver's Reference window showing the O'Reilly information for the resizeTo() function.

If you want to be thorough, test this by actually trying the code in as many different browser/platform configurations as you have access to. For purposes of this exercise, assume that the O'Reilly information is correct.

2. Adjust the behavior accordingly. You can't do anything about the script's failure to work in Netscape 3. But you can ask yourself if it will "fail gracefully" in that browser.

   If you try the script in Netscape 3, you'll see that the browser simply ignores it—no harm, no foul. This qualifies as failing gracefully, so there's no adjustment needed.

   See what happens when the behavior is used with default values. As your behavior is currently written, there are no default values for the width and height arguments. What will happen if the user tries to enter the behavior that way? Try it, and you'll see that the code is inserted incompletely:

```
<a href="#" onMouseUp="resizeBrowserWindow(,)"> click </a>
```

The simplest way to avoid this problem is to put default values into the dialog box. Do this by altering the form code so that it looks like this:

```
<table>
  <tr valign="baseline">
        <td align="right" nowrap>New width:</td>
        <td align="left">
              <input    type="text"    name="width"    size="8"
value="300">
        </td>
  </tr>
  <tr valign="baseline">
        <td align="right" nowrap>New height:</td>
        <td align="left">
              <input    type="text"    name="height"    size="8"
value="300">
        </td>
  </tr>
</table>
```

Do this and then try out the revised behavior. The dialog box should always come up with the default values in place.

4. Try the behavior with invalid input. Try the resize behavior and see what it does if you enter non-numeric data, or zeroes, or empty fields, as shown in Figure 22.25. What happens?

You already know that leaving the fields empty is a dangerous proposition. Entering zeroes is equally dangerous. Entering non-numeric data will generate JavaScript errors in Internet Explorer and is definitely a bad idea. Perhaps you should fix this problem.

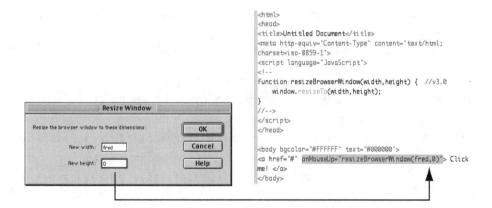

Figure 22.25   Non-numeric data, or zeroes, entered into the Resize Window behavior dialog box, resulting in invalid arguments passed to the function in the user's document.

5. Rewrite the behavior to disallow invalid input. Rewrite the applyBehavior() function so that the form fields are each validated before the function call is inserted. Valid data should be positive integers only; you also might want to consider extremely large numbers invalid. If no valid data is present, make the behavior resort to its default values.

Depending on your scripting style, you may choose to implement this error-checking in any number of ways. Your code may end up looking like this:

```
function applyBehavior() {
var width=document.theForm.width.value;
var height=document.theForm.height.value;
if (width=="" || width<1 || width>2000 || parseInt(width) != width)
{
width=300;
}
if (height=="" || height<1 || height>2000 || parseInt(height) !=
height) {
height=300;
}
return "resizeBrowserWindow(" + width + "," + height + ")";
}
```

6. Try out the revised behavior. What happens now when you try to break the behavior by entering some bizarre data (or nothing at all) in the dialog box? It should default to 300×300, or whatever default width and height you decided on. Your behavior is now bulletproof—or, at least, more bulletproof than it was before.

Design: Testing for Usability

Although you can test for technical errors, the best people to test for design and usability errors are other people—preferably people who have no knowledge of your development process and who are not themselves software developers. Beta testers may indeed find ways to break your extension—in which case, you're back to bulletproofing.

More likely, though, they'll find problems in your design. Is the object or behavior's name self-explanatory, as it appears in menu listings and ToolTips? If it's an object, is its icon communicative and intuitive? If it has a dialog box, is the dialog box attractive and intuitive to use? Does the whole interface blend in well with the Dreamweaver main interface? Is the desired purpose of the extension clear? Does the extension do what users think it's going to do? Is it lacking some key functionality? Do they perceive it as potentially useful?

If the answer to any of these questions is a resounding "No!," you have some redesigning to do.

Tip

> Macromedia offers a set of UI guidelines to help you create intuitive, functional interfaces that blend in well with the rest of the Dreamweaver interface. To see these guidelines, go to the Macromedia Exchange for Dreamweaver page (www.macromedia.com/exchange/dreamweaver) and click the Site Help topic Macromedia Approved Extensions. The code for this chapter has been written to follow these guidelines as much as possible.

Documenting

So, you think you're going to remember what this extension is supposed to accomplish six months from now or a year from now? Probably not. And if you can't remember it, obviously no one else can, either. Always, always, always document what you're doing—for your benefit and everyone else's.

Commenting

Always comment your code. Always. Macromedia recommends it—you know it's the right thing to do. Commenting will help you troubleshoot and update the object or behavior in the future. It also will help others learn from your process. (The examples shown so far in this chapter haven't been commented so that you could better examine the code for learning purposes. In the real world, they would be full of comment lines.)

Online Help

According to Macromedia, every extension should have some sort of online help, accessible from the extension's dialog box. Dreamweaver is configured to make adding help files easy for you.

- **Help in the dialog box.** If your object or behavior is so simple that a sentence or two is all the explanation that anybody will ever need, you can put that in the dialog box. Macromedia recommends that you add a table cell at the bottom of the layout, with the cell background color set to #D3D3D3. (Figure 22.26 shows an example of this.)

- **Help in a help file.** If your extension needs more explanation than a sentence or two, put the information in an HTML file. Store the HTML file in a new, personalized folder in the Configuration/Shared folder. (Figure 22.27 shows an example of this.) Place a Help button in the extension's dialog box, linked to that file.

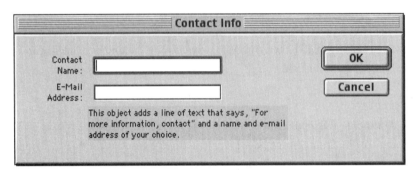

Figure 22.26   The Contact Info object, with a brief help statement added to the bottom. The top view, taken from Dreamweaver layout view, shows the additional table cell used for formatting.

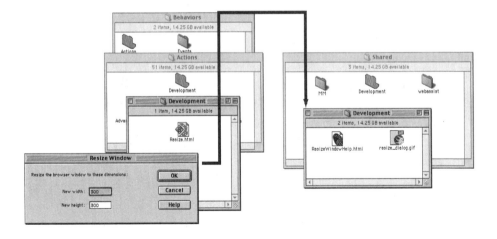

Figure 22.27   The Resize Window behavior dialog box, with a Help button. Clicking the button tells the behavior file to call on a help file (ResizeWindowHelp.html) in a custom folder (Development) in the Configuration/Shared folder.

Exercise 22.14   Adding Online Help to Your Behavior

In this exercise, you'll refine your Resize Window behavior by adding a Help button to the dialog box and linking it to an HTML file in the Shared folder.

1. Create a folder in the Shared folder to store your help documents.

   Using Explorer or the Finder, open the Configuration folder and the Shared folder inside it. Create a new folder in here; call it Development. Figure 22.28 shows how the folder structure should look.

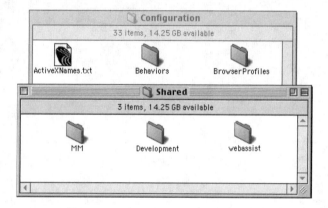

Figure 22.28   The folder structure of the Configuration/Shared folder with the new Development folder created inside.

2. Create the HTML file. Your help page should include information on what the behavior does, every field and what content it can accept, and any other information you think users will find helpful.

   You can create your own HTML file or use the file ResizeWindowHelp.html, located on the CD. Figure 22.29 shows an example of what a typical help file might look like.

   Save the file as ResizeWindowHelp.html in the Configuration/Shared/Development folder.

3. Add the Help button to your behavior's dialog box. Open the behavior file ResizeWindow.js in your text editor. Add this framework code for the function:

```
function displayHelp() {
}
```

   The displayHelp() function is part of the Dreamweaver API; when present, it is called automatically, so you don't need to call it.

   When you've done this, reload extensions and try out your revised behavior. When the dialog box comes up, there should be a Help button in place, like the one shown in Figure 22.27. (Of course, because the function is empty so far, clicking the button won't get you anywhere.)

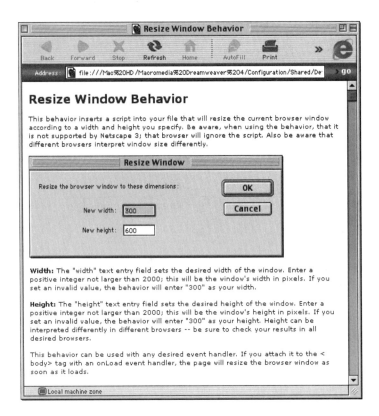

Figure 22.29   The Resize Window behavior's help file, as it will appear when viewed in a browser.

4. Link the Help button to your help file.

The standard thing you do with Help buttons is link them to help files. This is done with a function that is part of the Dreamweaver API, dw.browseDocument(). This function takes an absolute URL as its argument. If your help file is located on the Web—maybe on your own company Web site so that users have to come to you to get the latest and greatest help—just enter an absolute Web address as the argument. In this case, the help function would look like this:

```
function displayHelp() {
dw.browseDocument("http://www.mycompany.com/dwHelpFiles/ResizeWindo
w.html");
}
```

Because your help file is going to end up on the user's hard drive, the code needs to return an absolute pathname to that file. Luckily, the Dreamweaver API function, dw.getConfigurationPath(), returns the absolute address to the Configuration folder. All you have to do after getting that information is figure out the path to the help file relative to this root and concatenate the two together. So, the code you should enter looks like this:

```
function displayHelp() {
var myURL = dw.getConfigurationPath();
myURL += "/Shared/Development/ResizeWindowHelp.html";
   dw.browseDocument(myURL);
}
```

Enter this code. Then, reload extensions and try it out. If the proper help page doesn't load, double-check the code and tweak it until it does. Make sure that you've entered the path from the Configuration folder to your help file exactly—depending on how you've named your files and folders, your path may differ from the one shown here.

Note

The two API functions introduced here are both methods of the Dreamweaver object. Methods of this object can be written as dreamweaver.*functionName*() or dw.*functionName*(). The second choice offers fewer opportunities for typos.

Distributing

How are you going to get your lovely object or behavior into Configuration folders everywhere? Read on for instructions.

Packaging for the Extension Manager

The Extension Manager is becoming the standard method of painless extension installation. Therefore, this is the most accessible way to share your extensions.

Lucky for us, the Extension Manager not only installs extensions, but it also packages them up neatly into special installation files. The process is even relatively painless. The steps are listed here:

1. Put all the required files (help files, HTML files, JS files, and GIF icons) in one folder, outside the Configuration folder.

2. Create an installation file. This is an XML document with the filename extension .mxi that contains all the instructions needed for installation: where the files should be stored, what versions of Dreamweaver and what platforms the extension requires, the author's name, the type of extension, and a description. The formatting required is very exact. The best approach for beginners is to start from the samples included with the Extension Manager. These files include a

blank file (blank.mxi) to use as a template and a sample file (sample.mxi) filled in with information for a simple object.

3. Launch the Extension Manager, and go to File/Package Extension.

See Figure 22.30 for a sample folder containing all the proper files to package the Contact Info file. This last exercise takes you through all the steps to create this folder.

Figure 22.30   The assembled elements of the Contact Info object, all ready for packaging.

Exercise 22.15   Packaging an Extension

In this exercise, you'll pack up the Contact Info object for sharing with the world.

1. Copy all needed files into one folder. Somewhere on your hard drive, outside the Configuration folder, create a new folder. Name it whatever you like and will remember (something like Contact Info Files, maybe).

   Find all the files that make up the behavior, and copy them there. Files that you should include are listed here:

   - Contact Info.html
   - Contact Info.js
   - Contact Info.gif

2. Open the blank.mxi file to use in creating the installation file. Duplicate it and save it in your collection folder as ContactInfo.mxi.

   On your hard drive, find the Extension Manager application folder. Inside that folder, find the Dreamweaver/Samples folder. Inside there, you should see blank.mxi. (Figure 22.31 shows where to find these items.)

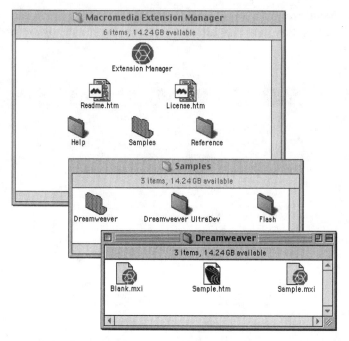

Figure 22.31   The Extension Manager application folder structure, showing sample.mxi and blank.mxi.

After you've made the duplicate file, open it in your text editor.

Tip

You can download a PDF file containing detailed instructions for creating installation files from the Macromedia Web site. Go to the Macromedia Exchange for Dreamweaver page (`www.macromedia.com/exchange/dreamweaver`), and click the Site Help topic Macromedia Approved Extensions.

3. Fill in the blanks with the information for your object. The blank file has all the framework you need. By examining the sample file, you can get an idea how it should be formatted. For your extension, fill in the blanks until your code looks like that shown in Figure 22.32.

A few tips about filling in the code:

- **For the author name.** Enter your name (John Smith, Web Genius has been entered here—there's no law against being fanciful).

- **For the filenames.** Enter the complete path from the Dreamweaver application folder root, as shown. If you want your extension to create any new folders in existing folders, enter them as part of the path (SmithStuff has been entered here to create a new folder within the Objects folder). If the object included any added folders within the Shared folder, they would have been added in the same way.

- **For the version number**. Your extension, like any other piece of software, gets its own version number. Start with 1.0, and increment the number if you later revise the extension.

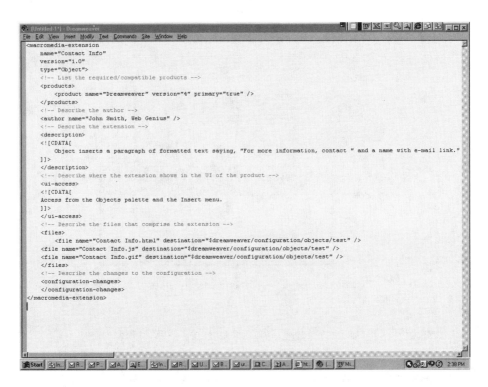

Figure 22.32   The complete code for ContactInfo.mxi. Information that has been added to the framework from blank.mxi is highlighted.

6. Package everything together with the Extension Manager. Launch the Extension Manager. Go to File/Package Extension.

   For the name of your extension, choose something descriptive that obeys the standard naming conventions (no empty spaces, no more than 20 characters, no special characters). Make sure that you leave the .mxp extension in place.

   When you're asked to choose a file, choose ContactInto.mxi.

   If there aren't any problems, the Manager will generate an extension file in the same folder as the .mxi file. If there are problems, you'll get an error report. Most often, these are problems with the .mxi file. If there are, go back to your text editor, fix the reported errors and try again.

   Figure 22.33 shows how this process will look in the Extension Manager.

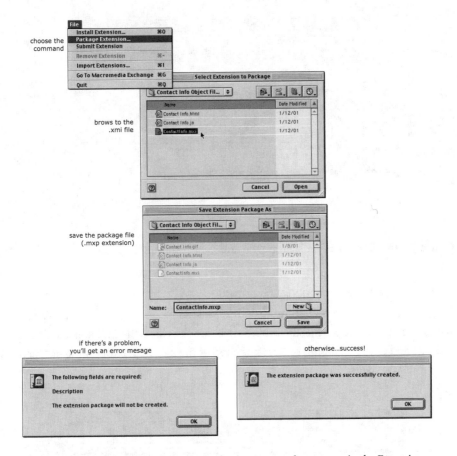

Figure 22.33   The steps through the packaging process, as they appear in the Extension Manager.

7. Use the Extension Manager to install your new extension. Quit Dreamweaver, if it's running. In the Extension Manager, go to File/Install. When the dialog box comes up, browse to ContactInfo.mxp.

   If everything's hunky dory, you should get an alert message telling you that the extension was installed successfully. Your custom extension should also now appear in the Extension Manager window, as shown in Figure 22.34.

8. Launch Dreamweaver and check that everything installed correctly. If all went as smoothly as reported, a new category should appear in the Objects panel, named SmithStuff or whatever you called your custom folder. Your object should be the only thing in that category. Check the ToolTip; try inserting it. Then pat yourself on the back—you did it!

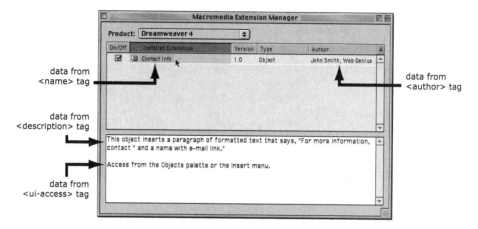

data from
<name> tag

data from
<author> tag

data from
<description> tag

data from
<ui-access> tag

Figure 22.34   The Extension Manager window, showing the installed Contact Info object.

Submitting to the Macromedia Exchange

The ultimate in sharing is submitting your extension file to the Macromedia Exchange. When you have the .mxp file, the procedure is simple: Go to the Macromedia Exchange Web site and click the Submit button at the top of the page. Then follow the instructions to submit (see Figure 22.35).

Figure 22.35   The Macromedia Exchange home page with the Submit button.

When you have submitted an extension, Macromedia engineers will run it through a series of tests. One of three things will happen:

- If it fails, it gets returned to you with comments.
- If it passes the basic tests, it gets put on the Web site as a Basic, or unapproved, extension.
- If it also passes the more comprehensive tests, it becomes a Macromedia Approved Extension.

To learn more about the testing process and how to get your extensions accepted and approved, visit the Web site and click any one of the Site Help FAQ topics. This will take you to an extensive categorized list of questions and answers.

Summary

You already know that Dreamweaver is a terrific Web editing environment. This chapter has shown you how you can make it into a perfectly personalized Web editor for your workflow needs. As much as you've seen, though, you've only touched the surface of all that is possible with extensions. Check out the *Extending Dreamweaver* manual. Visit the Exchange Web site and read the various support files there. If you're really serious, you can join the Extensibility Newsgroup (go to `www.macromedia.com/support/dreamweaver/extend/form/`). Dust off your JavaScript books. And start rewriting history.

Chapter 23

Scripting and Markup Languages

At some point every Web designer gets
curious and will check under the hood to
examine the HTML that Dreamweaver
is generating. At first it looks like

gobbledygook. After time, however, it does make sense. Indeed, many designers often brag that eventually the only way to design Web sites is to get the basic design completed with Dreamweaver and then to hammer and tong the rest out by hand-coding in Notepad.

Dreamweaver is an adept tool. The developers at Macromedia created it under the principle that designers and developers would want to use it. The release of Dreamweaver 4 has allowed the developer fast access to the areas of the site that they need the most: the code.

This chapter covers the following:

- HTML Source Code view
- Color coding
- Line numbers
- Debugging
- XML
- XHTML

The Code Warrior

Are you a code warrior? A *code warrior* is someone who has wondered how a Web page is created and has asked himself, "How was that trick on the page done? Can I do that myself?"

Ask yourself this simple question: Have I ever selected View Source from my Web browser when viewing an interesting Web page? If the answer is yes, you are a code warrior. Your interest has been piqued and your curiosity can take it no longer—you need to know how the code was created.

Dreamweaver provides a solid solution for code warriors. You no longer have to battle the long scripts in Notepad to find out a trick or two. Dreamweaver provides a code viewer right smack dab in its own WYSIWYG tool, as shown in Figure 23.1.

The power for the developer comes from careful use of the code viewer. For the beginner, it is a great tool to use to learn HTML; for the developer, it is a power-horse tool.

Code Viewer

Opening Dreamweaver, a user can locate the Code view from the three buttons in the top-left corner of the program, as shown in Figure 23.2.

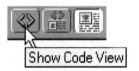

```
   ⟨⟩  ⟨⟩ ⟨⟩    Title: Untitled Document          ⟨⟩ ⟨⟩   C  ⟨?⟩  {}, ⟨⟩,
 3  <title>Untitled Document</title>
 4  <meta http-equiv="Content-Type" content="text/html; charset=iso-8859-1">
 5  <script language="JavaScript">
 6  <!--
 7  function MM_jumpMenu(targ,selObj,restore){ //v3.0
 8    eval(targ+".location='"+selObj.options[selObj.selectedIndex].value+"'");
 9    if (restore) selObj.selectedIndex=0;
10  }
11  //-->
12  </script>
```

Figure 23.1   Dreamweaver's code viewer gives a developer immediate access to the code of a
Web page.

Dreamweaver provides a developer with the following three options to view the code
being written:

- Show Code View
- Show Code and Design View (Split View)
- Show Design View

Each view provides a unique way to work when creating Web pages in Dreamweaver.

Design View

The most common view is the Design view. This is the default view for creating pages in
Dreamweaver. The Design view shows all the objects on the page as they would appear
inside a Web browser. The view is WYSIWYG (What You See Is What You Get), whereby
you can drag and drop elements—such as layers, tables, and images—without having to
ever view a single line of HTML or JavaScript.

Code View

A new view for Dreamweaver 4 is the Code view. Selecting this view
changes the layout of the page from WYSIWYG to code for the page.
Figure 23.3 shows Dreamweaver in just Code view.

Show Code and Design View

You can truly have the best of both worlds. This is demonstrated with
the Show Code and Design View option. In a single window, a developer
can drag and drop objects onto the page and immediately touch up the
code for the object in Code view. Figure 23.4 demonstrates the split-
pane view.

Figure 23.2
Dreamweaver enables a
user to work in Design
view, Code view, or a
mixed environment of the
two.

```
1 <html>
2 <head>
3 <title>Untitled Document</title>
4 <meta http-equiv="Content-Type" content="text/html; charset=iso-8859-1">
5 <link rel="stylesheet" href="mystyle" type="text/css">
6 <style type="text/css">
7 <!--
8 .NewHeadline {   font-size: 18px; font-weight: bolder; color: #333333}
9 -->
10 </style>
11 </head>
12
13 <body bgcolor="#FFFFFF" text="#000000">
14 <object classid="clsid:D27CDB6E-AE6D-11cf-96B8-444553540000" codebase="http://download.m
15 <param name=movie value="text2.swf">
16
17 <param name=quality value=high>
18 <param name="BGCOLOR" value="">
19 <param name="SCALE" value="exactfit">  .
20 <embed src="text2.swf" quality=high pluginspage="http://www.macromedia.com/shockwave/dow
21 </embed>
22 </object>
23 </body>
24 </html>
```

Figure 23.3   The Code view reveals all the HTML code for a page.

```
19 <tr>
20 <td> </td>
21 <td> </td>
22 <td> </td>
23 </tr>
24 </table>
25
26 </body>
27 </html>
28
```

Figure 23.4   Designers can immediately access the code while modifying the design without switching programs.

Exercise 23.1   Showing Code and Design View

The Split view enables designers who are inexperienced with HTML to see what is being developed as they work in WYSIWYG mode. These steps demonstrate how this is done:

1. With Dreamweaver open on a blank page, change the view to Show Code and Design view.

2. Observe in the Code window that, even with a blank page, there is HTML already created. You will see the <HTML>, <TITLE>, <META>, and <HEAD> tags, among others.

3. From the Objects panel insert a table with 3 columns, 3 rows, and a width of 75%.

4. The <TABLE> HTML tags are created in the Code view. The tags are comprised of <TABLE>, <TR>, and <TD> tags. You can modify each of these.

5. Select the <TABLE WIDTH=75%> tag and change it to <TABLE WIDTH=600px>. In the Design View window, the table has now changed width from 75% to 600 pixels.

6. Choose the first <TR> tag and change it to <TR BGCOLOR="#CCFFCC">. This places a light-yellow background to the first row in the table.

The constantly changing Web standards require that a developer be able to access the code to apply the latest feature. This will become even more important with XML and XHTML.

The Code Panel (Option Number 4)

Previous versions of Dreamweaver provided access to the source code only through the use of the Code panel. The *Code panel* is a floating panel and can be docked with other panels while a developer is working on a page. The Code panel is shown docked with the Objects and CSS Styles panels in Figure 23.5.

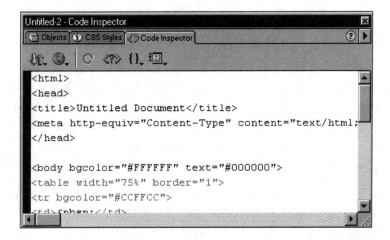

Figure 23.5   The Code panel can be docked with other floating inspectors and panels.

The Code panel provides some unique advantages over the Code view and Code and Design view when docked with other inspectors and panels. All the tools and features of the Code view are available, such as line wrapping and line numbers. As a developer, you can be working in Design view with the Code panel immediately available.

Unfortunately, the advantage of the Code panel is very much its disadvantage. The floating Code panel has the curse of the other panels: It takes up a lot of real-estate space.

Most computer monitors have a finite amount of space available in which to work. Another panel means more room is taken from your design.

For this reason, the Code panel is a silent fourth option. Using the Code and Design View option is a less cluttered alternative to the Code panel.

Visual Aids

The capability to work with source code is a fundamental requirement JavaScript developers or Web programmers demand in a tool. The Code view in Dreamweaver gives them this. To aid speedy development, a number of helpful tools are added to the Code view. From the View menu, select Code View Options to show the following options:

- Word Wrap
- Line Numbers
- Highlight Invalid HTML
- Syntax Coloring
- Auto Indent

Line Numbers and Syntax Coloring are useful options. It can be a real nuisance to count the lines one by one. Having the line numbers along the left side allows even the longest scripts to be scanned quickly.

The Syntax Coloring is a time-saving tool for creating and writing script. Different colors can be associated with different types of code. For instance, normal HTML is presented as dark blue, keyword tags (such as the <OBJECT> tag) are light blue, JavaScript is red, and inline script is green. It is much faster to debug color code script instead of stepping through and reading and understanding the function of every line.

As you can imagine, the colors used to define scripts can be customized. To change any of the colors, just open the Preferences dialog box (from the main menu, Edit/Preferences) and select Code Colors (see Figure 23.6).

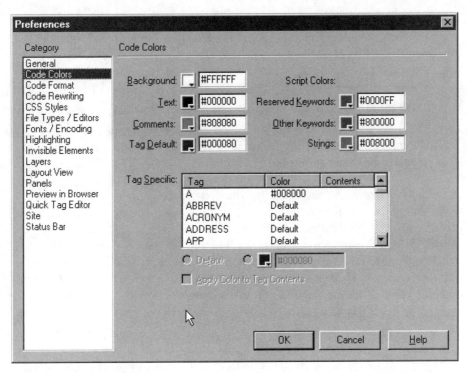

Figure 23.6   Source code colors can be modified.

Exercise 23.2   Modifying the Colors in Code View

These steps show how to change the colors and why doing so may prove beneficial:

1. With Dreamweaver open, change the view to Code view. Open the Web page COLOR_SYNTAX.HTM from the accompanying CD-ROM.

2. Along the left side is a heavy blue margin. The code for the page will be highlighted in the body of the page.

3. Select the syntax color (View/Code View Options/Syntax Coloring).

4. The Web page contains a simple Flash animation. In addition to the animation is additional JavaScript that zooms in the Flash movie. Observe the script. At the top of the document, a tag called <SCRIPT> is highlighted in red. This script opens the beginning of the JavaScript. The closing tag is also red. In between the tags, the JavaScript code is different colors, such as variables on line 8 are blue and the name of the variable (FDK_loaded) is black. Farther down the page, at line 33, begins the script that identifies that a plug-in is being used. The <OBJECT> and <EMBED> tags are Microsoft's and Netscape's tags used to identify plug-ins. For this instance, the <OBJECT> tag is red. Note, however, that the Netscape tag does not have a unique color identifying it. It is blue, the same color as the parameter tags. The next step will demonstrate how to change this.

5. Select Preferences from the Edit menu. The Preferences dialog box displays. Select the Code Color category. From the Tag Specific list scroll through until you reach EMBED.
6. Below the Tag Specific list is a color selector. Choose the color selector and change the color to #009933.
7. Check the Apply Color to Tag Contents option. This forces all the content within the <EMBED> tag to be the green color #009933. Select OK.
8. The color for the <EMBED> tag on lines 39–40 is now green. Experiment with changing the colors of other scripts.

In addition to Syntax Coloring and Line Numbers are the Word Wrap and Auto Indent tools. Both of these tools enhance how the script is viewed. The Word Wrap forces lines of script that go beyond the view of the available screen to be wrapped around. This creates the illusion that the script is on several lines. In actuality, the script is still on one line. Turning the Word Wrap off demonstrates how the script did, in fact, only occupy one line. Figure 23.7 illustrates how a line of code can be wrapped. When you look at the example, observe the line numbers. The line numbers appear to skip lines. This is because the line is wrapped.

```
31 <body bgcolor="#FFFFFF" text="#000000">
32 <p><a href="#" onClick="FDK_zoomFlash('colorsyntax','25')">Zoom</a></p>
33 <p><object classid="clsid:D27CDB6E-AE6D-11cf-96B8-444553540000"
codebase="http://download.macromedia.com/pub/shockwave/cabs/flash/swflash.cab#version=4,0,
0" width="494" height="102" id="colorsyntax" name="colorsyntax">
34 <param name=movie value="color_syntax.swf">
35
36 <param name=quality value=high>
37 <param name="BGCOLOR" value="">
38 <param name="SCALE" value="exactfit">
39 <embed src="color_syntax.swf" quality=high
pluginspage="http://www.macromedia.com/shockwave/download/index.cgi?P1_Prod_Version=Shockw
eFlash" type="application/x-shockwave-flash" scale="exactfit" width="494" height="102"
bgcolor="" name="colorsyntax" swliveconnect="true">
```

Figure 23.7 The Line Wrap tool makes visible code that would be hidden off the right hand edge of the editor in normal view.

Auto Indent will indent sections of the code. Dreamweaver automatically does this when it creates code in Design view. Indented code is much easier to read. If a page that has been either written by a different program or by hand is being edited, the code may not be indented. This can make it harder to read. Applying the Auto Indent makes it easier to read.

Note

When applying the Auto Indent, Dreamweaver does not modify the code. It is adding a visual aid to read the code, the same as Word Wrap and Syntax Coloring. When Auto Indent is turned off, the original structure of the code is restored.

The final visual aid that Code view provides is Highlight Invalid HTML. Simply put, this feature highlights in yellow any HTML that Dreamweaver does not recognize. For example, tags that are not closed correctly are identified with a bright-yellow background.

Maximizing Code

With the ever-expanding Web programming vocabularies (HTML, CSS, JavaScript, and so forth), it can be easy to forget what a specific piece of code does. Is the <B> tag the same as the <STRONG> tag? To help battle this problem, Dreamweaver provides an invaluable tool for code developers: the Reference panel.

You can open the Reference panel with Ctrl+Shift+F1 (Macintosh users use Cmd+Shift+F1), or Windows/Reference. Figure 23.8 shows the Reference panel.

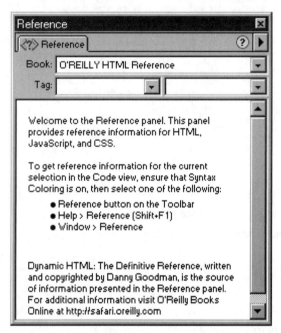

Figure 23.8   The Reference panel is an easy-to-use reference tool.

The Reference panel works only when Code Coloring is enabled. In addition, each query is context sensitive. When working in Code view, select a tag. From the top of the screen, choose the Reference button. The Reference panel then checks to see what type of script it is examining. The panel checks three different types of script: HTML, JavaScript, and cascading style sheets. Each of these references is taken from books published by O'Reilly Press. In Figure 23.9, the Reference panel is providing the information on the

<TD> tag. The lower panel provides a description of the tag, along with examples of how the tag is used. More complicated tags are returned with richer information.

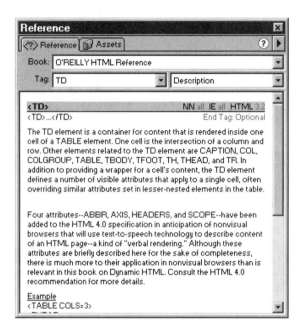

Figure 23.9   The Reference panel.

Exercise 23.3   Using the Reference Panel

The following steps teach you how to use the Reference panel:

1. Open COLOR_SYNTAX.HTM from the CD in Dreamweaver. Change the view to Code view.
2. From line 2, choose <HEAD> and run the Reference panel by selecting the button with the <?> tag. What are your results? The results will identify the <HEAD> tag from the O'Reilly HTML reference.
3. Select the word Function from line 10 and run the Reference panel again. The result shows that the term is JavaScript and provides an explanation of the code.

The Reference panel is a great tool to quickly understand new syntax in code.

Debugging

Mistakes can happen when code is being modified by hand. Everyone makes them, particularly with complex JavaScript. To help minimize mistakes in scripts, Dreamweaver supports a debugging tool that will analyze the script.

Exercise 23.4 Debugging

The debugging tool is run in conjunction with your Web browser. To see it in action, follow these steps:

1. From the accompanying CD-ROM, open DEBUG.HTM in Dreamweaver. Several mistakes have been made in the script of the page.

   Before debugging points, preview the page by selecting F12. There are errors detailing that the scripts did not execute correctly. JavaScript is a black-and-white language; it either works or it does not.

2. Now preview the same page, but press ALT+F12. This initiates the debugger tool.

3. The tool runs and stops at line 8. It reports that the syntax is not correct on this line. As a developer, you can now examine the line to find out what is wrong. Indeed, the first word, VARS, should be read var. Change the word and save the document.

4. Run the debugger again. The debugger should now stop on line 32. If line 32 is not highlighted, choose the Go to Line button. Once again, the line can be examined for any errors. Change the first number 4 to the word for. This corrects the error.

Running the debugger reduces the amount of hunting required to find errors in script.

Facing the XML Future

A new era is dawning. The humble Web browser is undergoing a major change. A new, lean cousin is replacing HTML. The lingua franca of the Web may well become XML, the eXtensible Markup Language.

XML is a lean scripting environment in which the reliance on a browser's support for specific codes is eradicated. No longer does a page need to be developed to work in Netscape's Navigator 3, 4, and 6, and work with the many flavors of Microsoft's Internet Explorer. XML takes the support of standards away from the browser and places it into the hands of the developer. Okay, so how does it do that?

The structure of XML appears very similar to HTML. Pages are formed of tagged content. The tags are used to categorize the content. The tags do not format the content. Cascading style sheets and extensible style sheets (XLS) format tags on the page. The browser, independent of default standards, is forced to present the XML document as defined by the developer.

The following example shows a section of an XML document:

```
<?xml version="1.0"?>
<newsfeed>
<channel cid="about.entertainment.hl"
title="About.com: Entertainment"
date="05/03/2000"
time="11:17 PST">
<headline
href="http://log.isyndicate.com:8880/pscripts/hit/kixbiqvkczawz%2526ijw
cb.mvbmzbiqvumvb.pt%2526pbbx%253a%252f%252fzilqw.ijwcb.kwu%252fmvmzbiq
vumvb%252fzilqw%252ftqjzizg%252femmstg%252fii597355i.pbu%25258nXU%253d1
0_656_B"
date="Thu, May 04, 2000 11:05 AM"
time="11:05 PST">Webcasters of the World Unite</headline>
<headline
href="http://log.isyndicate.com:8880/pscripts/hit/kixbiqvkczawz%2526ijw
cb.mvbmzbiqvumvb.pt%2526pbbx%253a%252f%252femjewzab.ijwcb.kwu%252fmvmz
biqvumvb%252femjewzab%252ftqjzizg%252femmstg%252fii505755i.pbu%25258nXU
%253d10_657_B"
date="Thu, May 04, 2000 11:05 AM"
time="11:05 PST">Elements of Bad Design</headline>
<headline
href="http://log.isyndicate.com:8880/pscripts/hit/kixbiqvkczawz%2526ijw
cb.mvbmzbiqvumvb.pt%2526pbbx%253a%252f%252fktiaaqkbd.ijwcb.kwu%252fmvm
zbiqvumvb%252fktiaaqkbd%252ftqjzizg%252femmstg%252fii505655i.pbu%25258n
XU%253d10_656_B"
date="Wed, May 03, 2000 11:17 AM"
time="11:17 PST">Senator Coleman?</headline>
</channel>
<channel cid="hollywood.news"
title="Hollywood Online: News"
date="05/04/2000"
time="04:03 PST">
<headline
href="http://log.isyndicate.com:8880/pscripts/hit/kixbiqvkczawz%2526pwt
tgewwl.vmea%2526pbbx%253a%252f%252feee.pwttgewwl.kwu%252fvmea%252fbwxab
wzqma%252f50-59-7555%252fpbut%252f6-7.pbut"
date="Thu, May 04, 2000 04:03 PM"
time="04:03 PST">Whatever Happened to Shania Twain?</headline>
<headline
href="http://log.isyndicate.com:8880/pscripts/hit/kixbiqvkczawz%2526pwt
tgewwl.vmea%2526pbbx%253a%252f%252feee.pwttgewwl.kwu%252fvmea%252fbwxab
wzqma%252f50-59-7555%252fpbut%252f6-8.pbut"
date="Thu, May 04, 2000 04:03 PM"
time="04:03 PST">EXTRA: All About the &apos;Disgusting&apos; Rap</head-
line>
<headline
href="http://log.isyndicate.com:8880/pscripts/hit/kixbiqvkczawz%2526pwt
tgewwl.vmea%2526pbbx%253a%252f%252feee.pwttgewwl.kwu%252fvmea%252fbwxab
wzqma%252f50-59-7555%252fpbut%252f6-9.pbut"
date="Thu, May 04, 2000 04:03 PM"
time="04:03  PST">B.O.  FORECAST:   &apos;Gladiator&apos;  Steps  Into
```

```
Ring</headline>
</channel>
</newsfeed>
```

The is a basic XML newsfeed. This document has not been formatted. The formatting will be done by the cascading style sheet in the browser.

XML is made up of the following features:

- Classified content
- Document type definition
- CSS and XLS

XML is the first language that can truly work on different operating systems, Internet devices, and products. A properly formatted XML document will display in a Web browser (such as Netscape 6), a Nokia cell phone (through WML, the Wireless Markup Language), a Motorola pager, or a Palm PDA.

Classifying Content Versus Defining Presentation

The content on an XML page is classified through the use of tags. The structure of a simple XML document is as follows:

```
<?xml version="1.0"?>
<library>
<Book>
<Title>Flash 5 Magic</Title>
<Author>Scott Hamlin and David Emberton</Author>
<Category>Web Publishing </Category>
</Book>
<Book>
<Title>Inside Dreamweaver 4</Title>
<Author>Various</Author>
<Category>Web Publishing </Category>
</Book>
<Book>
<Title>Dreamweaver 4 Magic</Title>
<Author>Al Sparber</Author>
<Category>Web Design</Category>
</Book>
</library>
```

The document declares itself as an XML document with the opening line, <?xml version="1.0"?>. For any XML documents to be properly executed, this opening statement must be added.

The structure of XML appears to be very similar to HTML. The content is structured in a readable format, not machine code. Each section is separated by what appears to be ordinary HTML tags. The reality, however, is that none of the tags are HTML tags. If this document were run through Netscape 4, it would not recognize the document and would not be able to format it.

The power of the document is that is does not format the data. The tags can be managed and modified with scripting by either the server delivering the content or through JavaScript and CSS on the Web browser.

Keeping the content separate allows the document to be delivered to a multitude of programs. The same XML file can be delivered to Internet Explorer and Flash players.

The power of this can be seen with Dreamweaver, specifically how Dreamweaver uses XML within its own program to control features.

Exercise 23.5   XML in Dreamweaver

This exercise shows how XML-formatted documents are part of how Dreamweaver works:

1. From the accompanying CD-ROM, open the Site Import Export extension called MX157851_SITEIMPEXP1_0_3.MXP and install it with the Extension Manager. This extension allows the configuration settings for a site to be exported to an XML file. This file can then be imported by anyone into his or her version of Dreamweaver. This immediately provides them with all the configuration settings for your site without having to manually configure the site.

2. Open Dreamweaver. From the File menu, choose Export/Export Site. From the Export Site dialog box, choose which sites you want to export. Choose the Export button and place the file on your desktop.

3. The exported file is called DWSITES.XML. Double-clicking the file opens it in Dreamweaver. The code will not make much sense viewed in Design view. Change the view to Code view. The page is laid out as an XML document.

4. To use this document, select File/Import/Import Site to import the configuration of the site. Dreamweaver leveraged XML to manage the content.

Note

Microsoft's Internet Explorer 5+ has the best support for XML, with limited support in Internet Explorer 4.01+. Netscape 6 also supports XML.

Customizing Tags

The "extensible" in XML is derived from the flexibility of the language. The preceding example was XML displayed at its most simple form: a declaration and some simple tags. You can easily extend the document. You can add richer information by extending the document. In many ways, it is like categorizing content into different fields in a database table. The following example shows how easily a brand new tag, called <Description>, can be inserted into the file:

```
<?xml version="1.0"?>
<library>
<Book>
<Title>Inside LightWave [6]</Title>
<Author>Dan Ablan</Author>
<Description>Inside LightWave [6] is not just another rehash of the doc
set. Its comprehensive tutorials take you to the completion stages for
several real world projects.
</Description>
<Category>Web Publishing </Category>
</Book>
<Book>
<Title>Harry Potter and the Goblet of Fire</Title>
<Author>J.K. Rowling</Author>
<Description>Harry Potter is now in his fourth year at Hogwarts.
Prepare yourself for his most exciting adventures yet!
</Description>
<Category>Childrens/Adventure</Category>
</Book>
</library>
```

Tags can be added very swiftly in Dreamweaver to comply with XML standards. The Quick Tag Editor, located on the Properties Inspector, can wrap a tag around content on the page (see Figure 23.10).

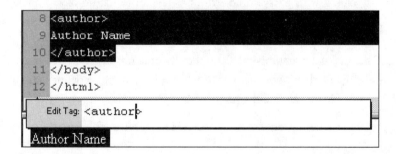

Figure 23.10   The Quick Tag Editor enables you to add HTML tags and custom XML tags with the correct opening and closing tags.

You can find additional information on XML at www.xml.org, www.biztalk.org, and www.w3.org. Each site provides a wealth of information on the latest document type definitions (DTDs), XML vocabularies, and support in third-party products. The XML revolution is coming, and it will be here sooner rather than later.

Transitioning to XHTML 1.0

December 19, 2000 marked the day when HTML made a bold move. Tim Berners-Lee, author of the World Wide Web and Director of the World Wide Web Consortium (www.W3.org), announced his support for XHTML 1.0, the eXtensible Hypertext Markup Language. XHMTL is essentially addressing the needs of many developers: the creation of an HTML standard that is XML based. XHMTL is the first major revision of HTML since 1997.

Making HTML XML-Compliant

To make HTML XML-compliant, and modular, a number of syntactical rules must be followed. The most important rule is the proper management of tags. Browsers have been very loose in their support for Strict HTML. The proper closure of tags (such as the <H1> tag) is not always needed, as with the use of the <p> tag. The following script shows some HTML that will display accurately in any current Web browser:

```
<html>
<body bgcolor="#FFFFFF" text="#000000">
<p><font face="Arial" size="4">The following  text  will  be  displayed
correctly in an HTML Web.
<p>Even though some of the tags are not correctly closed.
```

Strict XHTML would not display this script. To begin with, the <p> and <font> tags are not correctly closed with a </p> and </font>. The strict nature of tag management within XML requires that all tags be correctly closed. In addition, the <font> is not supported in XHTML. Only cascading styles sheets can be used to format the display of XHTML. The final statement missing from this document is the XML declaration at the top of the document identifying the type of XML document being defined and the location of the DTD file to translate the XML tags.

For the preceding code to work correctly as XHMTL, it must look like the following:

```
<?xml version="1.0"?>
<!DOCTYPE html PUBLIC "-//W3C//DTD XHTML 1.0 Strict//EN"
    "http://www.w3.org/TR/xhtml1/DTD/xhtml1-strict.dtd">
<html xmlns="http://www.w3.org/1999/xhtml">
<head>
```

```
<title>XHTML Page</title>
<style type="text/css" xml:space="preserve">
 body {
  background-color: #FFFFFF;
  color: #000000;
 }
 P {
  Font-Family: Arial;
  Font-Size: 14pt;
 }
</style>
</head>
<body>
<p>The following text will be displayed correctly in an XHTML
Web.</p>
</html>
```

Note

> If you are using Dreamweaver, HTML can be made XHMTL-ready by eliminating the use of the <font> tag. Leveraging cascading style sheets to format text will allow for a smooth transition to XHTML.

Several new features are added to the document. The first immediate change is the addition of the XML declaration at the top of the document. The insertion `<?xml version="1.0"?>` declares that the following document is an XML document and should be treated with the rules as used with any XML document.

Following the XML declaration is a <DOCTYPE> that declares which DTD is being used. The document type is `html PUBLIC "-//W3C//DTD XHTML 1.0 Strict//EN"`, the Strict translation of XHTML.

There are three types of XHTML: Strict, Transitional, and Frames. XHTML-Strict is the implementation of XHTML as defined in the complete XHTML 1.0 standard; XHTML-Transitional is a definition of XHTML that allows for HTML 4 tags to be used within the syntax, to allow for a transition from one language to the next; XHTML-Frames is a version of the language that allows for Netscape frames to be used within XHTML-formatted Web pages.

The next line, `http://www.w3.org/TR/xhtml1/DTD/xhtml1-strict.dtd`, directs the browser to download the appropriate DTD file to translate the document.

The XHMTL namespace is defined within the <HTML> tag. This identifies where the namespace is located on the Internet.

Formatting with the <font> and <body> tag is not allowed in XHTML. To replace the tags in the first version of the document is a cascading style sheet. The <body> background color and default text color are identified as white (#FFFFFF) and black (#000000), respectively. The presentation style for the <P> tag is defined as font Arial and size 14pt.

The rest of the document is presented as it would be in HTML, but without the formatting tags.

These are but a few of the changes that must be made to a document for it to be XHTML compliant. Many tags that have been used by HTML designers have been removed. As has already been noted, the <font> tag must be replaced with CSS. The same is true for the <Center> tag. This tag must now be a CSS style. The italics tag, <I>, must be replaced with the equivalent <EM> tag, and the bold tag, <B>, must be replaced with <STRONG>.

Dreamweaver creates code that is immediately ready to be migrated to XHTML. You need to remember just a few rules:

- Do not use the <font> tag. To avoid using the <font> tag, do not modify code with the Text Properties Inspector. Instead, format text with CSS.
- The HMTL tag at the top of the page must be modified in the Code view to the following:

```
<?xml version="1.0"?>
<!DOCTYPE html PUBLIC "-//W3C//DTD XHTML 1.0 Strict//EN"
"http://www.w3.org/TR/xhtml1/DTD/xhtml1-strict.dtd">
<html xmlns="http://www.w3.org/1999/xhtml">
```

- Close all tags that are opened correctly. For instance, any opening <P> must have a closing </P>.

If you follow these three simple rules, there is no reason why any site created in Dreamweaver cannot be immediately migrated from HTML 4 to XHTML.

A complete description of how to make a document XHTML compliant is detailed at the World Wide Web Consortium Group's Web site (www.w3.org/MarkUp). The site contains comprehensive documentation on the new standard, including links to tools that convert HTML 4 pages into XHTML.

The W3C provides a set of tools to prepare Web pages for XHTML. The tools can be located at the W3C HTML Validation Service (http://validator.w3.org) site. One particular tool, HTML Tidy, enables you to convert poorly written HTML documents, such as those generated by Microsoft Word, and make them compliant to XHTML standards.

Contrasting XHTML with HTML 4

HTML 4 bears many similarities to XHTML. Both languages require the use of CSS for formatting and both require the closure of tags for paragraphs. In many ways, XHMTL is just a reformulation of HTML 4 to follow the rules of XML. By reproducing HTML 4 as an XML language, many of the extensions that will be added to XHTML can be done successfully in a modular format.

XHTML 1.0 allows new Internet devices—such as PDAs, game consoles, and interactive TV boxes—to be kept current with the latest Web page standards. All that is needed is a browser that understands XML and DTDs. A designer can still use text-editing tools to develop Web pages.

With the rapidly changing face of the Internet, the inclusion of a modular and extensible language, such as XHTML, is a natural fit.

Facing Browser Compatibility Problems

When working with new and emerging technologies, the designer and programmer will always be faced with the challenging question: Should I use a new feature in the latest browser, knowing that many customers may not have that browser, or should I design for the lowest common browser?

This is a teaser question. A good way to help answer this question is to examine the Web server log files for your site. Each Web server generates text files (logs) that record information about each and every visitor to your site. Some of the information captured includes the type of Web browser used. Programs, such as WebTrends, interpret the data in log files and provide usage graphs.

Microsoft's Internet Explorer currently dominates the browser landscape with over 80% penetration, of which 90% of those users are using Internet Explorer 5.0+. Of the remaining 20%, 15% of users are browsing with Netscape 4+ and the final 5% are using Netscape 1–3, AOL browser, Mozilla, Netscape 6, Opera, and other third-party Web browsers. These numbers come from Nielsen/Netratings (`www.nielsennetrat ings.com`). Therefore, a Web site built for Netscape 4 and Internet Explorer 5 will reach the largest potential audience. Only 5% will not be able to view the pages.

You may ask, "Is it worth developing a site for all browsers?" Your answer lies in determining whether the final 5% carries enough value to merit designing the site for all browsers.

An easier task is designing Web sites for intranets. Many companies have established a standard of a single Web browser for the entire company. Whether this is Netscape 2 or Internet Explorer 6 does not matter. Knowing the program that will be used to present the material in the Web page increases the number of tools a developer can leverage. If the designer knows that Internet Explorer 6 is being used on an entire intranet, for instance, he can embed fonts for page formatting into a cascading style sheet. The designer has absolute certainty that the page using the embedded font will display correctly, unlike an 80% guarantee on the Internet.

When developing for the Internet, a designer must always be aware of which browsers are most commonly used. This year alone, Netscape 6 and MSDN Explorer are being released. Each browser will have a massive impact on how Web pages are designed and built. Knowing what your audience is using enables you to make an educated guess regarding how to build the pages on your site.

Standards change, and Dreamweaver enables you to keep up with them. Dreamweaver enables you to build sites that comply with the emerging standards.

Summary

Code is at the very heart of all Web pages. Dreamweaver provides a great tool set to help you get started. At some point, however, you will need to create or modify code directly. The Code view provides the user not only with the code, but also with tools to easily view and edit the code.

The number of Web "languages" is constantly increasing. Knowing and being able to write code for Web pages is a necessary skill to fully understand the Web pages of tomorrow.

Chapter 24

Database-Driven Web Sites

Web sites are increasingly growing in complexity. Sites that are generated page by page are rapidly becoming replaced by database-driven sites. The benefit of a database-driven site is that the content is dynamically generated by a database, such as Microsoft's Access or IBM's DB2.

Accessing the rich information in a database requires more than just HTML, JavaScript, and cascading style sheets. It requires access to the database through the Web server itself. This is called *server-side scripting* and is a powerful extension to any developer's list of skills.

This chapter examines how to leverage databases through server-side scripting. Macromedia's enhanced version of Dreamweaver, Dreamweaver UltraDev, is used to demonstrate the speed and efficiency of dynamic data-driven sites.

This chapter covers the following:

- What a dynamic database-driven site is
- How databases can be used
- How to use UltraDev and understand its relationship to Dreamweaver
- How to use the test database included on the CD to build a dynamic site
- How to add a new entry to the database and how to update existing entries

Static Versus Dynamic

By design, Dreamweaver enables you to build Web pages. A site is created, and content is added to it. This type of development is often referred to as a *static site*. In contrast, a *dynamic site* contains Web pages that receive their content from a database. The database is maintained outside of the site. As the content in the database changes, the content on the site is forced to change. A good example of a dynamically driven site is Cnet's Web site (www.cnet.com). The news content is updated and maintained through a database. The content presented on the site is dynamically generated from the database. If a new story is released, the moment the database has the story it can be presented on the site through the dynamic pages.

On the surface, dynamic pages look the same as conventional Web pages. Indeed, if you were to look at the source code for a Web page presented on Cnet's site, you would not see anything different from a standard Web page. The difference lies on the servers.

The Web server is an integral part of dynamically generated Web sites. Your understanding of what a Web server is and how you can use it will determine your ability to create dynamic content.

The Web Server

At the core, every Web server has a single task: to deliver Web pages via the HTTP (Hypertext Transfer Protocol) standard. This is what has formed the backbone to the Internet.

Most Web sites were originally developed on the UNIX operating system. To add inter-activity, such as image maps and randomly generated images, a scripting language called Perl was used. Perl quickly became a popular way to create dynamic content for the Internet. The most famous of Perl applications is the online guest book, to which a user can add his or her name and comments about a site.

Perl is good for simple actions, such as random text (which was fine for a site back in 1995). However, today's rapid economy demands data-rich sites that allow for massive interaction. To facilitate this, several new scripting languages have matured over the past five years. Of particular note are Microsoft's Active Server Pages (ASP), Sun's Java Server Pages, and Allaire's Cold Fusion.

Each of these languages has inserted hooks into Web servers that allow for scripting extensions to run. For instance, Microsoft's Active Server Pages wraps tags in and around the HTML. Specific commands in the tags call for the code to be executed on the Web server.

On the CD that accompanies this book, you can find a file called TIME.ASP. This file is developed to run on Microsoft's Internet Information leveraging using Active Server Pages. Figure 24.1 shows the ASP page displaying the time and date.

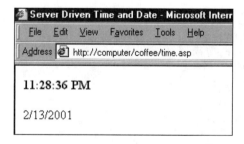

Figure 24.1   The browser displays a page with the time and date.

This simple trick can be created with a JavaScript. In this instance, server-side scripting is used. In this example, the server creates the "time" and "date."

The following code generates this simple page:

```
<%@LANGUAGE="VBSCRIPT"%>
<html>
<head>
<title>Server Driven Time and Date</title>
</head>
<body bgcolor="#FFFFFF" text="#000000">
<p><b><%=time%></b>
</p>
<p><%=date%>
</p>
</body>
</html>
```

The differences in the code are immediately evident. The first line that appears before the <html> tag declares to the Web server that the script that will be executed in this page is VBScript. *VBScript* is a subset of Microsoft's Visual Basic language. Both JavaScript and VBScript are used to write Microsoft's Active Server Pages.

A second change is the command that generates the time and date in the final pages: <%=time%> and <%=date%>.

Both of these commands are unique to Active Server Pages. The use of the opening and closing % informs the Web server that script must be run on the Web server.

Besides Microsoft's Active Server Pages, many other popular scripting languages run through Web servers. Table 24.1 lists the most popular scripting languages used on Web servers, the operating systems these servers can run on, and the type of scripting language that is used.

Table 24.1   The Most Common Web Servers

Web Server	Description	Operating Systems	Scripting Language
Apache	Apache is the most popular Web server in the world. Nearly 50% of all Web sites run on Apache. Apache supports Java Server Pages written in Sun's programming language, Java.	UNIX, Linux, Macintosh, Windows 2000, and Windows NT	Java Server Pages
Microsoft's Internet Information Server	The second most popular Web server is Microsoft's Internet Information Server (IIS).	Windows NT, 2000, and XP	Active Server Pages

Web Server	Description	Operating Systems	Scripting Language
	IIS enables Visual Basic developers to easily build database-driven sites. Consequently, IIS is the most popular intranet server.		
Cold Fusion Server	A very popular application server is Cold Fusion, with its unique and easy-to-use scripting language.	UNIX, Linux, Windows NT, and Windows 2000	Cold Fusion Markup
IBM Websphere	Growing in popularity is IBM's Websphere. Websphere is tied tightly to DB2 databases and Sun's Java Server Pages.	UNIX, Windows NT, and Windows 2000	Java Server Pages

There are other, less-popular scripting languages as well (such as Python, TCL/TK, and PHP).

Databases

The database is the second integral factor (after the Web server) when developing a dynamically driven Web site. Many different types of databases are available. Being able to access a database to retrieve, review, and modify entries is critical for any Web application.

On the CD, you will find a database called COFFEE.MDB. The database was developed with Microsoft's Access 2000. Access is the world's most popular database. It is light and flexible. For small to mid-size applications, it is a good fit. For more robust applications, it is worth investing in an enterprise Database solution (such as Oracle or Sybase).

Table 24.2 outlines the more popular databases together with their ease of use and scalability.

Table 24.2   The Most Popular Databases

Database	Description	Ease of Use	Scalability
Microsoft Access	The world's most popular database can create a rich and useful database in a matter or minutes.	Access is very easy to use. However, its ease of use also lends itself to not scaling very well to large corporate sites that might require millions of entries.	An Access database can allow as many as 50 people to simultaneously access it from a Web page. Any more than that, and the database does not respond very quickly.
Oracle	Larry Ellison saved his company a billion Oracle's dollars two years in a row with Oracle 8i database. As you can imagine, the "i" in the name stands for "i"nternet.	Oracle is not for the faint of heart. The databases can quickly scale to tetrabytes in size (that's nine zeros) and still perform effortlessly. The massive scalability does mean, however, that someone who fully understands the Oracle database environment must create the databases.	Many large-scale sites run on databases. The efficient design of the software delivers amazing results in data-driven Web sites.
Sybase	Sybase is a solid database environment that will work in both UNIX and Microsoft NT/2000 platforms.	Sybase is, as with Oracle, a difficult environment in which to develop. An expert should be consulted for developing Sybase databases.	Mid- to large-scale sites run very well on Sybase.
Microsoft SQL Server	The big brother to Microsoft's Access is Microsoft's SQL Server. SQL Server can manage the scale and size of databases that will always elude Access. SQL, however, can import Access databases. This allows for databases to be designed in Access and then immediately migrated to SQL.	SQL Server is a moderately difficult server to run. If you have any experience with Microsoft's Management Console, SQL will be familiar.	SQL has made many new landmarks in scalability, such as the largest online database (1.2 tetrabytes). And it's fast, too.

All databases manage content in tables of data. Each table is built up of rows of data called fields. A field can have its own set of properties. For instance, a date field may capture only numbers set as a date, or a name field may allow only a certain number of letters to be written. Figure 24.2 illustrates a table from COFFEE.MDB.

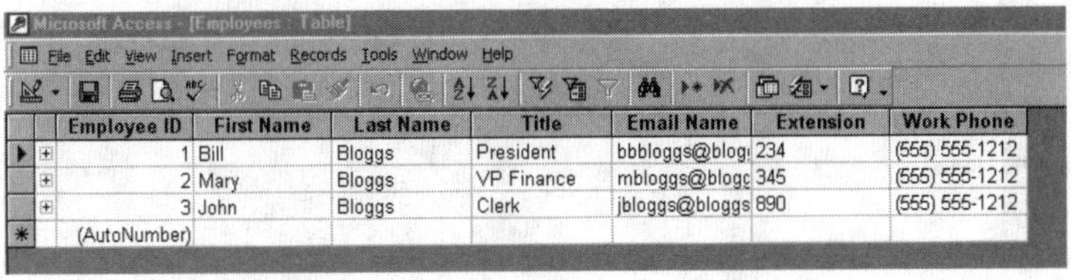

Figure 24.2   The COFFEE.MDB is created from a set of tables and formatted fields.

Knowing which database is being used and the structure of that database is critical for building any Web-based application. Without this knowledge, accurate development is difficult to impossible.

Aligning the Stars–Using UltraDev

The third factor (after the Web server and the database) is the code needed to create a site. The Web server needs the code so that it will know how to present a page. As you can imagine, this can get very complicated. Complicating matters even further are the many different scripting languages: ASP, CFM, and JSP, to name but three.

Until very recently, a designer had to understand how to write a particular language for a given site. The level of difficulty was very high. To the rescue has come Macromedia with Dreamweaver UltraDev. UltraDev is the poster-child example for how Dreamweaver can be extended above and beyond itself. UltraDev has the look and feel of Dreamweaver. The main exception is four new features: Data Bindings, Connections Manager, Server Behaviors, and Application Server Models.

Site Definition

A critical component to the successful creation of a dynamic site is the selection of the correct server model in the Site Definition dialog box. UltraDev includes additional settings for application servers, or servers that execute server-side scripts. Figure 24.3 shows the Site Definition dialog box. It is the same as Dreamweaver's except for one category: Application Server.

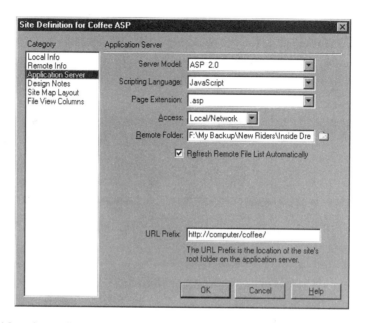

Figure 24.3   The Application Server category defines what type of server scripting technology should be used for the development of the site

The Application Server category requires a number of fields to be completed. The most important is the Server Model field.

In the Server Model field, you have three options:

- ASP 2.0
- Cold Fusion 4.0
- JSP 1.0

The three types refer to the three different scripting languages supported by UltraDev. Unlike other scripting products, UltraDev is not configured for a single scripting environment. The three most popular scripting languages are supported: ASP 2.0 (Microsoft's Active Server Pages 2.0), Cold Fusion 4.0, and JSP 1.0 (Sun's Java Server Pages 1.0).

Knowing what Web server will be used to present the pages is critical when selecting which server model to use. If you choose JSP 1.0, for instance, the code generated will not run on Microsoft's Internet Information Server or Personal Web Server.

The next box asks what scripting language will be used for creating the code. The default for ASP 2.0 is VBScript; however, JavaScript can also be used.

The page extensions are necessary for the server to correctly render the page. For instance, IIS, by default, will translate any ASP code in a Web page with the extension .ASP. The same is true for Cold Fusion and Java Server Pages that use the extensions .CFM and .JSP.

The remaining settings are the same as the Remote Info category.

The Connection Manager is the most important element of a site. It has one single basic function: to connect to databases. The tool is located at Modify/Connections. With this selected, a window that lists all the current connections to databases will open. Figure 24.4 lists Coffee as a database.

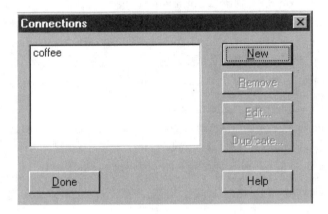

Figure 24.4   The Connections dialog box lists all the databases to which the current site is linked.

When you select the New button, options on how to access a database display. The list of options depends on the application server model chosen in the Site Definition dialog box. For instance, JSP sites will access a database through JDBC connectors, whereas Active Server Pages can use either ODBC, ADO (Active Data Object), OLE DB, or a DSN-less connection. Figure 24.5 shows the settings for the Coffee connection database. The settings are for an ODBC connection to an Access database. The source for the database is located from the Data Source Name drop-down box. If a data source cannot be located, the Define dialog box can be launched to configure a new data source. In this case, the data is in an Access database. The ODBC DSN connection can locate data from a wide range of sources, including the databases in Table 24.2.

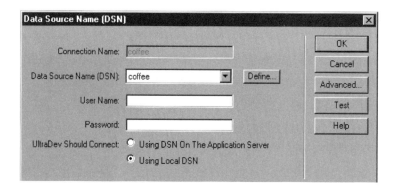

Figure 24.5   The connection to the Access database is through a DSN (ODBC) connection.

When a source has been located, a user ID and password can be added, if necessary. The database included on the CD does not require either a user ID or password. UltraDev also can choose to use the DSN on either the local or remote server. This is important when connecting to data sources that require special connecting software. An example of this is an Oracle database. The Oracle connecting software is almost 80MB in size. It may not be convenient to keep this on a local computer.

The final step in validating a connection is to select the Test button. If the connection can be made, a message box displays stating `Connection was successfully made`. This is the message you want to see. If a failure message appears, contact the database administrator and request assistance in connecting to the data source.

The two final additions are the Data Bindings and Server Behaviors panel.

Data Bindings and Server Behaviors

The Data Bindings panel visually lists all the available fields for a table. Each field can be dragged and dropped onto the page. When viewed through a Web browser across the Web server, the field will show the name of a record on the database (see Figure 24.6).

The Server Behaviors behave similar to conventional behaviors. The Server Behaviors are actions, written in the correct server script, that are executed by the Web server. Figure 24.7 demonstrates how the Server Behaviors can be easily added to code on a page.

In many ways, UltraDev gives the developer the tools necessary to align the stars correctly and build a database-driven Web site without too many problems.

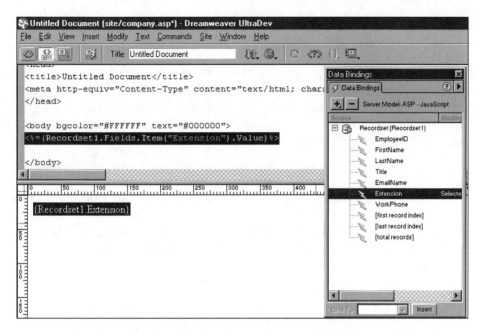

Figure 24.6 The Data Bindings panel provides a view of a table's fields. Each field can be dragged onto the page.

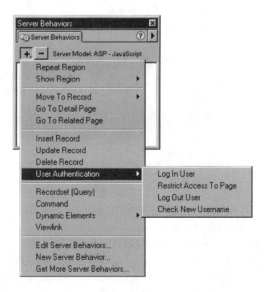

Figure 24.7 Server Behaviors are very similar to conventional behaviors in that they apply interaction to content on the page.

Creating a Dynamically Driven Site

UltraDev makes connecting to databases and creating dynamic sites very intuitive.

Exercise 24.1   Setting Up a Database-Driven Site and Creating the First Dynamic Page

The following exercise takes you through the steps required to create a fully dynamic site. The exercise has been configured for Microsoft's Internet Information Server; however, the steps used to complete the exercise can be easily modified for Java Server Pages or Cold Fusion.

1. To begin with, the server and database must be configured to work with UltraDev. In Internet Information Server or Personal Web Server, create a folder for the Web site. Name the folder Coffee (see Figure 24.8). In that folder, create a subfolder called Database and place the COFFEE.MDB database located on the CD into the folder. If you have trouble creating a folder in IIS, consult your Web server administrator.

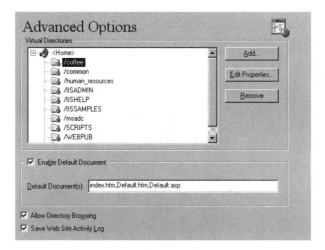

Figure 24.8   Personal Web Server is a lightweight counterpart to Internet Information Server. Small intranet applications run very well on Personal Web Server.

2. The ODBC connector must be configured to create a DSN connection to the Access database on your local computer and the server. Follow the next steps for both the server and your local computer. Both ODBC connectors must point to the same file. This will ensure that the same data is being used. UltraDev requires a local DSN entry on your computer for it to work. This is not needed with connection strings, such as OLE DB connections.

3. From the Windows Start button, select Settings/Control Panel. From the Control panel, open ODBC Data Sources.

4. Select the System DSN tab and choose the New button. From the Create New Data Source window, choose Microsoft Access Driver (*.mdb) and click the Finish button.

5. The ODBC Microsoft Access Setup window will launch. Add Coffee for the Data Source Name. This is the name that UltraDev will use to locate the database. Click the Select button and locate the COFFEE.MDB database. With the database selected, click OK and then click OK a second time to close the ODBC Data Sources window.

6. Open Dreamweaver UltraDev. From Site, configure a new site. The Remote Info must point to the Web server that will run the application server code. For this example, the site must point to Microsoft's Internet Information Server or Personal Web Server (see Figure 24.9).

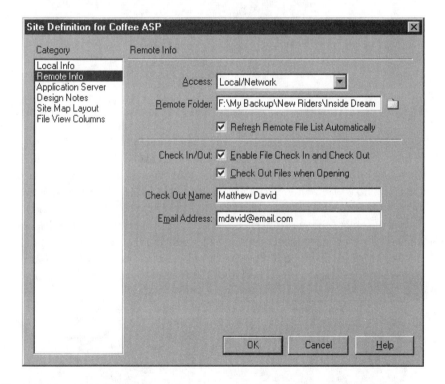

Figure 24.9   The Remote Info points to a networked path directly to the Web server.

7. The application server settings must be configured. The server model must be ASP 2.0, the script language is VBScript, and the page extension is .asp (see Figure 24.10). The URL prefix should be the name of the Web server followed by the directory. UltraDev enables you to view the dynamically driven page by pressing F12 in the editor. This launches the Web browser to view the ASP-driven page. Click OK to save the settings.

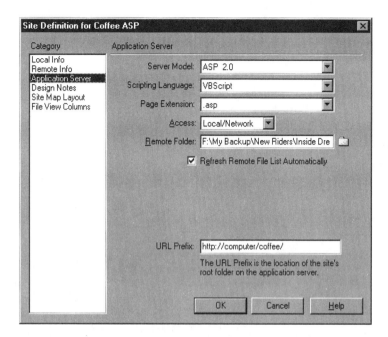

Figure 24.10   The application server settings are configured to create Microsoft Active Server Pages.

8. A connection to the Access database must now be created. In Dreamweaver UltraDev, select Modify and choose Connections to launch the Connections dialog box. Choose New and select Data Source Name (DSN). Name the connection coffee and, from the drop-down menu, choose coffee (see Figure 24.11). This is the link to the Access database. Select the Test button. An alert displays: Connection was made successfully. This tells you that the connection to the database is good. If you do not receive this message and are told that a connection was not made, you must check the ODBC connection to the data source.

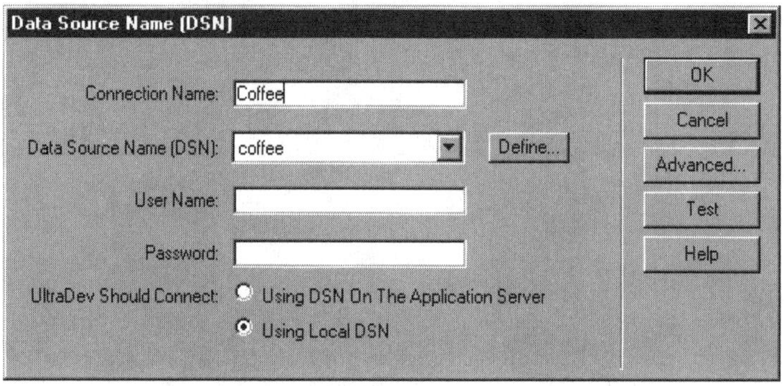

Figure 24.11   The connection points to the Coffee Access database.

9. Open a new page in Dreamweaver UltraDev. Save the page as DYNAMIC_TEST.ASP. This page will be the first page to which database-driven content will be added.

10. Open the Data Bindings panel. The Data Bindings panel will bind the data from the database to the page. Currently, no data is bound. From the plus sign (+), choose Recordset (Query). The Recordset dialog box opens. Name this Recordset1. From the Connection drop-down menu, choose coffee (see Figure 24.12). This links to the connection created earlier.

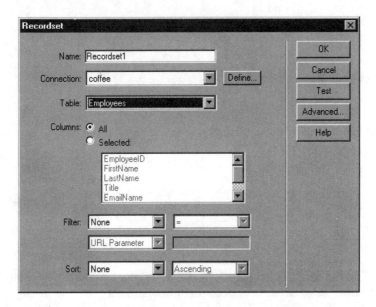

Figure 24.12   The DSN connection created earlier links the Data Bindings panel to the Access database.

11. A list of the available tables in that database should now appear in the Table menu. Choose Employees. The remaining settings will be kept at their defaults. At this point, however, specific records can be fine-tuned. This is important for large databases that will want to share massive amounts of data with the server. Choose the Test button to preview the records in the database (see Figure 24.13). Click the OK button.

12. The Data Bindings panel now displays a database icon that can be expanded to show all the records for a database. Alongside each field entry is a lightning bolt to represent live data. Select the field called FirstName and drag it onto the page. A block of code is placed onto the page, {Recordset1.FirstName} (see Figure 24.14). This code calls the FirstName field located in the connection Recordset1. Press F12 and the latest value to be added to the FirstName field in the

Employees table from the COFFEE.MDB database. This site is now dynamic. If the record is modified in the database the Web page will be automatically updated. Save the page.

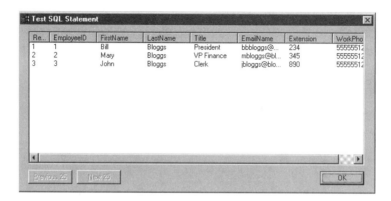

Figure 24.13   Running the Test will preview the first 25 records as defined by the query created.

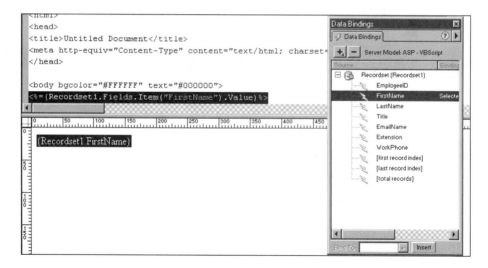

Figure 24.14   Development is much easier when data-bound elements can be dragged and dropped.

Exercise 24.2   Creating a Complete Database-Driven Site

Unfortunately one page does not make a Web site. As a developer, you are going to be asked to create a rich site where a customer can complete new forms, edit current records, and easily view information in the database. UltraDev provides the tools to do this quickly and easily.

1. To create the dynamic site, a number of pages must be created. From Dreamweaver UltraDev, create the following pages:
   - DEFAULT.ASP
   - EMPLOYEE.ASP
   - NEWEMPLOYEE.ASP
   - UPDATEEMPLOYEE.ASP

2. Open DEFAULT.ASP. Set up the Data Bindings panel to access the Coffee connection as outlined in Exercise 24.1. Open the Objects panel and select Live Objects. Select the Master Details object.

3. The Insert Master-Detail Page Set creates all the content on a page that will enable a user to view a list of records in a database and, through hypertext links, view the details for a specific record. From the Master Page fields, delete all the records, except FirstName and LastName, by selecting the name of the record and choosing the minus sign (–).

4. Alongside Detail Page Name, browse for the EMPLOYEE.ASP file. Select EmployeeID from Detail Page Fields and select the minus sign. Click OK.

5. The content for a master page is created. The EMPLOYEE.ASP file opens with new content. Save both files. Preview DEFAULT.ASP. The first name and last name of each person in the Employees table will be listed on the page. Selecting the first name from each listing takes the user to a Details page about that employee.

6. If a new employee joins the company, that person must be entered into the database. To do this, use the Insert Record Insertion Form. Open NEWEMPLOYEE. ASP. From the Live Objects list, and select Insert Record Insertion Form.

7. The object opens. From the Connections list, choose Coffee. From the Insert into Table box, choose Employees.

8. Select the page DEFAULT.ASP for After Inserting Go To. This command redirects the user to a Web page after he has completed the form.

9. From the Form Fields, select EmployeeID and select the minus sign. EmployeeID is automatically filled out by Access. Click OK. Save the page and preview it by pressing F12. The page can be filled out and submitted. On submission, you will be redirected to the home page for the site. Automatically, the entries on the home page have been updated to reflect the new entry just added. All the entries on the home page are listed in the order they have been posted into the database.

10. The final page will allow a record to be updated on the database from a Web browser. Open UPDATEEMPLOYEE.ASP and choose the Insert Record Update Form.

11. The Insert Record Update Form opens. From Connections, choose Coffee. For Tables to Update, choose Employees. From the Form Fields, select EmployeeID and select the minus sign. The EmployeeID field is the key field in the database. Changing this will create a new record instead of modifying an existing record. To prevent this, the EmployeeID field is not even sent to the browser for modification. Click OK and save the file.

12. Before viewing the document in your Web browser, open DEFAULT.ASP. On DEFAULT.ASP is a link that will allow a unique record to be edited. On the right side of the dynamic record field LastName, add the word **edit**. Highlight the entire word. Open Server Behaviors, select the plus sign and choose Go to Detail Page. Click the Browse button on the Go to Details Page dialog box and locate the UPDATEEMPLOYEE.ASP file. Click OK and save the page.

13. The final step is to reopen UPDATEEMPLOYEE.ASP. A server behavior must be added to this page. From Server Behaviors, choose Move to Record – Move to Specific Record. This will allow the correct record to be presented when a user selects the edit link on DEFAULT.ASP.

14. Preview DEFAULT.ASP. Select edit alongside one of the names in the list. The UPDATEEMPLOYEE.ASP page will load all available information on that person. You can make changes. After the changes have been made, click the Update button. The updated information is now sent to the database to modify that specific record.

15. The final result is a Web site on which you can preview a list of employees, view the details on any one employee, add new employees, and modify the data for any existing employees. With UltraDev, you can create a site like this in less than one day.

Summary

Dreamweaver UltraDev demonstrates the sheer power and flexibility of using databases within a Web site. The collection of intuitive tools built in to UltraDev makes it possible for any designer to develop dynamic Web sites. If you know Dreamweaver, Dreamweaver UltraDev is the next logical step.

Part VII

Appendixes

A p p e n d i x   A

Keyboard Shortcuts

Table A.1   Main Menu Commands

Command	Windows	Macintosh
File		
New	Ctrl+N	Command+N
Open	Ctrl+O	Command+O
Open in Frame	Ctrl+Shift+O	Command+Shift+O
Close	Ctrl+W	Command+W
Save	Ctrl+S	Command+S
Save As	Ctrl+Shift+S	Command+Shift+S
Preview in Browser	F12	F12
Debug in Browser	Alt+F12	Option+F12
Check Links	Shift+F8	Shift+F8
Exit	Ctrl+Q	Command+Q
Edit		
Undo	Ctrl+Z	Command+Z
Redo	Ctrl+Y	Command+Y
Cut	Ctrl+X	Command+X
Copy	Ctrl+C	Command+C
Paste	Ctrl+V	Command+V
Copy HTML	Ctrl+Shift+C	Command+Shift+C
Paste HTML	Ctrl+Shift+V	Command+Shift+V
Select All	Ctrl+A	Command+A
Select Parent Tag	Ctrl+Shift+<	Command+Shift+<
Select Child	Ctrl+Shift+>	Command+Shift+>
Find and Replace	Ctrl+F	Command+F
Find Next	F3	F3
Indent Code	Ctrl+]	Command+]
Outdent Code	Ctrl+[	Command+[
Balance Braces	Ctrl+'	Command+'
Toggle Breakpoint	Ctrl+Alt+B	Command+Option+B
Launch External Editor	Ctrl+E	Command+E
Preferences	Ctrl+U	Command+U
View		
Switch Views	Ctrl+Tab	Command+Tab
Head Content	Ctrl+Shift+W	Command+Shift+W
Standard View	Ctrl+Shift+F6	Command+Shift+F6
Layout View	Ctrl+F6	Command+F6
Hide All	Ctrl+Shift+I	Command+Shift+I
Show	Ctrl+Alt+R	Command+Option+R
Show Grid	Ctrl+Alt+G	Command+Option+G

Command	Windows	Macintosh
Snap To Grid	Ctrl+Alt+Shift+G	Command+Option+Shift+G
Play	Ctrl+Alt+P	Command+Option+P
Stop	Ctrl+Alt+X	Command+Option+X
Play All	Ctrl+Alt+Shift+P	Command+Option+Shift+P
Stop All	Ctrl+Alt+Shift+X	Command+Option+Shift+X
Show Panels	F4	F4
Toolbar	Ctrl+Shift+T	Command+Shift+T
Insert		
Image	Ctrl+Alt+I	Command+Option+I
Flash	Ctrl+Alt+F	Command+Option+F
Shockwave	Ctrl+Alt+D	Command+Option+D
Table	Ctrl+Alt+T	Command+Option+T
Named Anchor	Ctrl+Alt+A	Command+Option+A
Line Break	Shift+Return	Shift+Return
Non-Breaking Space	Ctrl+Shift+Space	Command+Shift+Space
Modify		
Page Properties	Ctrl+J	Command+J
Selection Properties	Ctrl+Shift+J	Command+Shift+J
Quick Tag Editor	Ctrl+T	Command+T
Make Link	Ctrl+L	Command+L
Remove Link	Ctrl+Shift+L	Command+Shift+L
Select Table	Ctrl+A	Command+A
Merge Cells	Ctrl+Alt+M	Command+Option+M
Split Cell	Ctrl+Alt+S	Command+Option+S
Insert Row	Ctrl+M	Command+M
Insert Column	Ctrl+Shift+A	Command+Shift+A
Delete Row	Ctrl+Shift+M	Command+Shift+M
Delete Column	Ctrl+Shift+-	Command+Shift+-
Increase Column Span	Ctrl+Shift+]	Command+Shift+]
Decrease Column Span	Ctrl+Shift+[	Command+Shift+[
Left	Ctrl+Shift+1	Command+Shift+1
Right	Ctrl+Shift+3	Command+Shift+3
Top	Ctrl+Shift+4	Command+Shift+4
Bottom	Ctrl+Shift+6	Command+Shift+6
Make Same Width	Ctrl+Shift+7	Command+Shift+7
Make Same Height	Ctrl+Shift+9	Command+Shift+9
Add Object to Library	Ctrl+Shift+B	Command+Shift+B
New Editable Region	Ctrl+Alt+V	Command+Option+V
Add Object to Timeline	Ctrl+Alt+Shift+T	Command+Option+Shift+T

continues ▶

Table A.1   continued

Command	Windows	Macintosh
Add Keyframe	F6	F6
Remove Keyframe	Shift+F6	Shift+F6
Text		
Indent	Ctrl+Alt+]	Command+Option+]
Outdent	Ctrl+Alt+[	Command+Option+[
None	Ctrl+0	Command+0
Paragraph	Ctrl+Shift+P	Command+Shift+P
Heading 1	Ctrl+1	Command+1
Heading 2	Ctrl+2	Command+2
Heading 3	Ctrl+3	Command+3
Heading 4	Ctrl+4	Command+4
Heading 5	Ctrl+5	Command+5
Heading 6	Ctrl+6	Command+6
Left	Ctrl+Alt+Shift+L	Command+Option+Shift+L
Center	Ctrl+Alt+Shift+C	Command+Option+Shift+C
Right	Ctrl+Alt+Shift+R	Command+Option+Shift+R
Bold	Ctrl+B	Command+B
Italic	Ctrl+I	Command+I
Edit Style Sheet	Ctrl+Shift+E	Command+Shift+E
Check Spelling	Shift+F7	Shift+F7
Start Recording	Ctrl+Shift+X	Command+Shift+X
Play Recorded Command	Ctrl+P	Command+P
Site		
Site Files	F8	F8
Site Map	Alt+F8	Option+F8
Get	Ctrl+Shift+D	Command+Shift+D
Check Out	Ctrl+Alt+Shift+D	Command+Option+Shift+D
Put	Ctrl+Shift+U	Command+Shift+U
Check In	Ctrl+Alt+Shift+U	Command+Option+Shift+U
Check Links Sitewide	Ctrl+F8	Command+F8
Window		
Objects	Ctrl+F2	Command+F2
Properties	Ctrl+F3	Command+F3
Site Files	F8	F8
Site Map	Alt+F8	Option+F8
Assets	F11	F11
Behaviors	Shift+F3	Shift+F3
Code Inspector	F10	F10

Command	Windows	Macintosh
CSS Styles	Shift+F11	Shift+F11
Frames	Shift+F2	Shift+F2
History	Shift+F10	Shift+F10
HTML Styles	Ctrl+F11	Command+F11
Layers	F2	F2
Library		
Reference	Ctrl+Shift+F1	Command+Shift+F1
Templates		
Timelines	Shift+F9	Shift+F9
Arrange Panels		
Show Panels	F4	F4
Minimize All	Shift+F4	Shift+F4
Restore All	Alt+Shift+F4	Option+Shift+F4
Help		
Using Dreamweaver	F1	F1
Reference	Shift+F1	Shift+F1
Dreamweaver Support Center	Ctrl+F1	Command+F1

Table A.2   Site Menu Commands

Command	Windows	Macintosh
File		
New Window	Ctrl+N	Command+N
New File	Ctrl+Shift+N	Command+Shift+N
New Folder	Ctrl+Alt+Shift+N	Command+Option+Shift+N
Open	Ctrl+O	Command+O
Open Selection	Ctrl+Alt+Shift+O	Command+Option+Shift+O
Close	Ctrl+W	Command+W
Rename	F2	F2
Delete	Del	Del
Check Links	Shift+F8	Shift+F8
Exit	Ctrl+Q	Command+Q
Edit		
Cut	Ctrl+X	Command+X
Copy	Ctrl+C	Command+C
Paste	Ctrl+V	Command+V
Select All	Ctrl+A	Command+A
Find and Replace	Ctrl+F	Command+F
Preferences	Ctrl+U	Command+U

continues ▶

Table A.2   Site Menu Commands

Command	Windows	Macintosh
View		
Refresh	F5	F5
Refresh Local	Shift+F5	Shift+F5
Refresh Remote	Alt+F5	Option+F5
Show/Hide Link	Ctrl+Shift+Y	Command+Shift+Y
View as Root	Ctrl+Shift+R	Command+Shift+R
Show Page Titles	Ctrl+Shift+T	Command+Shift+T
Site		
Disconnect	Ctrl+Alt+Shift+F5	Command+Option+Shift+F5
Get	Ctrl+Shift+D	Command+Shift+D
Check Out	Ctrl+Alt+Shift+D	Command+Option+Shift+D
Put	Ctrl+Shift+U	Command+Shift+U
Check In	Ctrl+Alt+Shift+U	Command+Option+Shift+U
Check Links Sitewide	Ctrl+F8	Command +F8
Link to New File	Ctrl+Shift+N	Command+Shift+N
Link to Existing File	Ctrl+Shift+K	Command+Shift+K
Change Link	Ctrl+L	Command+L
Remove Link	Ctrl+Shift+L	Command+Shift+L
Window		
Site Files	F8	F8
Site Map	Alt+F8	Option+F8
Assets	F11	F11
Minimize All	Shift+F4	Shift+F4
Restore All	Alt+Shift+F4	Option+Shift+F4
Help		
Using Dreamweaver	F1	F1
Reference	Shift+F1	Shift+F1
Dreamweaver Support Center	Ctrl+F1	Command+F1

Table A.3   Code-Editing Keys

Command	Windows	Macintosh
Select Parent Tag	Ctrl+Shift+<	Command+Shift+<
Balance Braces	Ctrl+'	Command+'
Select All	Ctrl+A	Command+A
Copy	Ctrl+C	Command+C
Find and Replace	Ctrl+F	Command+F
Find Next	F3	F3
Paste	Ctrl+V	Command+V
Cut	Ctrl+X	Command+X
Redo	Ctrl+Y	Command+Y
Undo	Ctrl+Z	Command+Z
Switch To Document	Ctrl+Tab	Command+Tab
Toggle Breakpoint	Ctrl+Alt+B	Command+Option+B
Select line up	Shift+Up	Shift+Up
Select line down	Shift+Down	Shift+Down
Character select left	Shift+Left	Shift+Left
Character select right	Shift+Right	Shift+Right
Move to page up	PgUp	PgUp
Move to page down	PgDn	PgDn
Select to page up	Shift+PgUp	Shift+PgUp
Select to page down	Shift+PgDn	Shift+PgDn
Move word left	Ctrl+Left	Command+Left
Move word right	Ctrl+Right	Command+Right
Select word left	Ctrl+Shift+Left	Command+Shift+Left
Select word right	Ctrl+Shift+Right	Command+Shift+Right
Move to start of line	Home	Home
Move to end of line	End	End
Select to start of line	Shift+Home	Shift+Home
Select to end of line	Shift+End	Shift+End
Move to top of file	Ctrl+Home	Command+Home
Move to end of file	Ctrl+End	Command+End
Select to start of file	Ctrl+Shift+Home	Command+Shift+Home
Select to end of file	Ctrl+Shift+End	Command+Shift+End
Copy2	Ctrl+Ins	Command+Ins
Paste2	Shift+Ins	Shift+Ins
Cut2	Shift+Del	Shift+Del

Table A.4   Document Editing

Command	Windows	Macintosh
Quit Application	Alt+F4	Option+F4
Go to Next Word	Ctrl+Right	Command+ Right
Go to Previous Word	Ctrl+Left	Command+Left
Go to Previous Paragraph	Ctrl+Up	Command+Up
Go to Next Paragraph	Ctrl+Down	Command+Down
Select Until Next Word	Ctrl+Shift+Right	Command+Shift+Right
Select From Previous Word	Ctrl+Shift+Left	Command+Shift+Left
Select From Previous Paragraph	Ctrl+Shift+Up	Command+Shift+Up
Select Until Next Paragraph	Ctrl+Shift+Down	Command+Shift+Down
Close Window	Ctrl+F4	Command+F4
Defer Table Update	Ctrl+Space	Command+Space
New in Same Window	Ctrl+Shift+N	Command+Shift+N
Preview in Primary Browser	F12	F12
Preview in Secondary Browser	Ctrl+F12	Command+F12
Debug in Primary Browser	Alt+F12	Option+F12
Debug in Secondary Browser	Ctrl+Alt+F12	Command+Option+F12
Exit Paragraph	Ctrl+Return	Command+Return

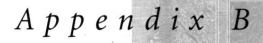

Appendix B

Browser
Compatibility

Wouldn't it be nice if you could just sit down,

create a few layers anywhere on screen, link

to an external style sheet, insert text, images,

and some multimedia, preview it in your

favorite browser, and know it will look exactly like that when viewed on any platform with *any* browser? The answer, of course, is yes. And while standards for creating Web pages this easily continue to strive toward this "ultimate" goal of uniform browser interpretation, anyone holding his breath for that day may never live to see it.

Probably the most frequent discouraging comments I hear when talking to other designers is the inconsistent implementation of HTML (and other more recently created standards such as CSS, XML, JavaScript, or DHTML elements) in even the most popular browsers available. Due to this, designers must spend vast amounts of time (or hire someone else to do it) testing their pages in each of their target browsers just to assure themselves that the pages they publish will look good on Netscape Navigator or Opera, even though they might prefer Microsoft Internet Explorer. After testing these various browsers, you might feel pretty good about your site. Don't get your hopes up too much, however; you now have to do it all over again on other platforms such as Macintosh and possibly Linux.

Tip

A good (and painfully obvious) rule of thumb in browser compatibility is the newer the browser, the more standards supported. If an element works correctly in Internet Explorer 4, you can generally assume it also will work in Internet Explorer 5.5. This holds somewhat true across browser companies (Explorer 4 is comparable in features to Navigator 4); although when crossing browser company lines, you should *not* just assume it will work.

Today's ideal Web page will not just be compatible with most standards, it also will be compatible with most browsers. Your job is to discover (invariably through countless hours troubleshooting) the perfect balance of each. This appendix lists links that will assist in your endeavor to unearth the hidden and often notorious incompatibilities between W3C (www.w3c.org/) standards and how they are implemented (along with proprietary features) in the popular browsers of today.

Note

The World Wide Web Consortium (W3C) is the "official" entity responsible for establishing and guiding online standards. Following is an excerpt from their Web site (www.w3c.org):

The World Wide Web Consortium was created in October 1994 to lead the World Wide Web to its full potential by developing common protocols that promote its evolution and ensure its interoperability. W3C has more than 400 member organizations from around the world and has earned international recognition for its contributions to the growth of the Web.

Webmonkey

`http://hotwired.lycos.com/webmonkey/reference/browser_chart/`

Webmonkey has always been an excellent first stop for Web authors who are either just starting out or who want to learn what's around the corner. Webmonkey also has published a table for browser compatibility that is by far the easiest to read and understand. Operating systems such as Windows, Macintosh, Linux, UNIX, and even NextStep and OS/2 are included. More than 32 different browsers are included, with a total of 63 versions of those browsers. The table includes compatibility information on Java, frames, tables, plug-ins, font size, font color, JavaScript, cascading style sheets (CSS), gif89, DHTML, I-Frames, table color, and XML. Although Webmonkey does not offer extremely detailed information, you will know if you even have a chance of getting certain HTML elements to work in your target browsers by visiting this page. Highly recommended!

Westciv.com

`www.westciv.com.au/style_master/academy/browser_support/`

> The browser compatibility guide was developed to help Web page developers ease the frustration of developing using cascading style sheets. Every different version of Navigator and Explorer, for the Macintosh and for Windows supports style sheets differently. Throw in Opera and WebTV, and we have a recipe for real headaches. It is possible to use style sheets to great effect in Web development, but these differences make it less than straightforward.
>
> If you develop Web pages, and want to use Style Sheets (or want to make using style sheets less of a pain) then this guide is for you.
>
> `www.westciv.com.au/style_master/academy/browser_support/about_the_guide.html`

I couldn't have said it better myself! Seriously though, this guide provides *extreme* depth regarding the CSS implementation of various browsers, including Internet Explorer 4.0x, 5.0x, and 5.5 for Windows; Internet Explorer 4.0x, 4.5x, and 5.0 for Macintosh; Netscape Navigator 4.0x, 4.5, and up for Windows and Macintosh; Netscape 6 (Mozilla M14); Opera 3.61 for Windows; and finally WebTV. If you want to know how your style sheets will react in your target browsers, this site is a must see!

NetMechanic

`www.netmechanic.com/cobrands/click2commerce/compat_check.htm`
NetMechanic's HTML Toolbox Browser Compatibility robot is typically a good gauge to use to quickly determine how affected your visitors will be by certain unsupported HTML elements. There are a few quirks with regard to how the robot processes Web pages, but you learn to read through these quickly. The two obvious faults with this page are the faulty frames support as well as the tendency to mark tags or attributes it is unfamiliar with as bad code, making your rating plummet. Use with discretion.

The Web Standards Project

`www.webstandards.org/`
This site is more like a "news" and action site rather than a compilation of tables and list of features. You can bet that if anything relating to Web standards can be improved upon, these guys will be on the case. Their editorials and public letters to various organizations are entertaining to read, while offering a disgruntled designer's point of view on the subject. If for no other reason, check out this site to see what the new "hot topic" in the Web standards community is.

Netscape Standards Challenge

`http://home.netscape.com/browsers/future/standards.html`
This page describes the compatibility of Web standards between Internet Explorer and Netscape 6. As you can see in the address, the page is published by Netscape and as such, is undoubtedly skewed in their favor. It is a fairly easy-to-read document, however, and will show you in general what the latest and greatest browsers will do, and more importantly, what they won't do.

As a final note on your search for reaching harmonic peace with established standards and support for such in today's Web browsers, consider the following points and remember them while designing your Web pages:

- Use CSS with font sizes set to pixels. This unit of measure renders most consistently across multiple browsers and platforms.
- Use layers sparingly. Do not lay out pages using layers—particularly nested layers. Browsers render layers in various ways depending on version and platform. To avoid this altogether, use tables to lay out your pages.

- Leave some wiggle room. Browsers render fonts, layers, and form elements in different sizes. Leave some space in your layout for elements to expand without overlapping, or significantly changing the look of the page. For example, a page that is packed very tightly with content, and only reviewed in Netscape on Macintosh, will almost definitely look very different in IE on Windows.

- Be careful when using CSS. Always make sure the attribute you are using is supported in both major browser versions. Dreamweaver's online CSS reference will help you determine which browsers support the desired CSS element. You can find the CSS reference in the Reference panel (discussed in Chapter 3, "Dreamweaver and HTML").

- Be sure to specify the margin width, margin height, left margin, and top margin attributes of the <body> tag. This ensures that both browsers will render margins in a similar fashion. (Note that browsers will still offset your pages in various ways, but this minimizes the problem.)

- Most importantly, test your pages in all possible browsers, on all possible platforms, all throughout the development process. Do not expect your layout to just end up looking the same in all browsers. Actively preview and change layout with the expectation that things will shift around a bit.

Appendix C

What's on the CD-ROM

The accompanying CD-ROM is packed with all sorts of exercise files and products to help you work with this book and with Dreamweaver 4. The following sections contain detailed descriptions of the CD's contents.

For more information about the use of this CD, please review the ReadMe.txt file in the root directory. This file includes important disclaimer information, as well as information about installation, system requirements, troubleshooting, and technical support.

System Requirements

This CD-ROM was configured for use on systems running Windows NT Workstation, Windows 95, Windows 98, Windows 2000, and Macintosh.

Loading the CD Files

To load the files from the CD, insert the disc into your CD-ROM drive. If autoplay is enabled on your machine, the CD-ROM setup program starts automatically the first time you insert the disc. You may copy the files to your hard drive, or use them right off the disc.

NOTE: This CD-ROM uses long and mixed-case filenames, requiring the use of a protected mode CD-ROM driver.

Exercise Files

This CD contains all the files you'll need to complete the exercises for *Inside Dreamweaver 4*. These files can be found in the root directory's InsideDW4 folder. Please note, however, that you'll not find any folders for chapters 1, 2, 3, 9, 11, 15, 16, 19, or 21; these chapters contain exercises for which you do not need to access any project files.

Read This Before Opening the Software

By opening the CD package, you agree to be bound by the following agreement:

Index

Symbols

A

B

S

T

The Inside Dreamweaver 4 CD

The CD that accompanies this book contains all the example files provided by the authors to enable you to work through the step-by-step projects using Dreamweaver 4.0.

For a complete list of the CD-ROM contents, please see Appendix C, "What's on the CD-ROM."

Accessing the Project Files from the CD

To load the files from the CD, insert the disc into your CD-ROM drive. If Autoplay is enabled on your computer, the CD-ROM setup program starts automatically the first time you insert the disc. You may copy the files to your hard drive, or use them right off the disc.